What the Critics Say About
ROSE

"Why not [a biography of] Rose Kennedy? If your answer is that there is nothing new to say about her, guess again. Mr. Higham finds something, and uses it to startling dramatic effect . . . a fun read."

—Florence King,
The New York Times Book Review

"A carefully drawn portrait of the Fitzgeralds of Boston, political and brassy."

—Rima L Firrone,
Star-Banner (Ocala, FL)

"The 104 years of [Rose's] life are all here, minutely detailed."

—Gloria Horstman,
Star-News (Pasadena, CA)

"*ROSE* is the first biography to take a detailed look at the life of the matriarch . . . a particularly loving look at Rose."

—Ann Zivotsky,
The Blade-Citizen (Oceanside, CA)

Books by the author

The Duchess of Windsor
Howard Hughes: The Secret Life
Elizabeth and Philip *(with Roy Moseley)*
Merchant of Dreams: Louis B. Mayer, M-G-M and the
   Secret Hollywood
Kate: The Life of Katharine Hepburn
Bette: The Life of Bette Davis
Marlene: The Life of Marlene Dietrich
Princess Merle: The Romantic Life of Merle Oberon
   (with Roy Moseley)
Orson Welles: The Rise and Fall of an American Genius
The Art of the American Film
A Distant Star
Spring and Death
The Earthbound
Noonday Country
The Voyage to Brindisi
Trading with the Enemy: An Exposé of the Nazi-American
   Money Plot 1933–1949
American Swastika
*Rose: The Life and Times of Rose Fitzgerald Kennedy

*Published by POCKET BOOKS

—— THE LIFE AND TIMES OF ——
Rose Fitzgerald Kennedy

ROSE

CHARLES HIGHAM

POCKET BOOKS

New York   London   Toronto   Sydney   Tokyo   Singapore

POCKET BOOKS, a division of Simon & Schuster Inc.
1230 Avenue of the Americas, New York, NY 10020

Copyright © 1995 by Charles Higham

All rights reserved, including the right to reproduce
this book or portions thereof in any form whatsoever.
For information address Pocket Books, 1230 Avenue
of the Americas, New York, NY 10020

ISBN: 0-671-89027-1

First Pocket Books paperback printing March 1996

10 9 8 7 6 5 4 3 2 1

POCKET and colophon are registered trademarks of
Simon & Schuster Inc.

Cover photos courtesy of AP/Wide World

Printed in the U.S.A.

To the Palafox family—
my guardian angels

Author's Note

All thoughts and feelings of Rose Fitzgerald Kennedy, and of other individuals in this book, have not been a matter of conjecture. They are drawn from paraphrased letters, published diary entries, autobiographical books and articles, and interviews on television, on radio, or in the press. Mrs. Kennedy's letters, housed in the collections listed in the bibliography, are numerous, illustrative, and in most cases have not been accessed by other family biographers.

No coward soul is mine,
No trembler in the world's storm-troubled sphere;
   I see Heaven's glories shine.
And faith shines equal, arming me from fear.

—Emily Brontë, "Last Lines"

Contents

xi

Contents

Contents

15
Rose at the White House • *385*

16
A Death in Dallas • *413*

17
Nightmare Train • *442*

18
Twilight and Evening Star • *468*

ROSE

Prologue

On the bleak afternoon of November 22, 1963, on a New England beach strewn with seaweed and spindrift, a tiny woman, heavily wrapped against the wind, walked alone. Her face was worn but unchanging, marked with an immense inner strength. Although a nephew, a daughter and a son joined her one by one, and although she was grateful for their presence, she was, as she had always been, essentially alone, shielded behind a wall she had built to protect herself from the world.

That day, her son, the president of the United States, had been killed, suddenly and brutally, and she asked herself, looking up at the sky, Why? Why had a man of immense talent and promise, with a beautiful wife and two handsome children, one of the two most powerful men on earth, been taken away at the height of his powers? One day, she knew, God would have an answer for her; but now, for the first time in her life, she could only question, and question again. She pulled herself together, fought back the tears. If she fell apart, the whole of her family would fall apart with her. She was its linchpin, its centrifuge. She must go on: the least known, the least discussed, the least written about— but in truth, the most dynamic, single-minded and controlling family figure of all the legendary Kennedys.

Chapter 1

Life in the Slums

❧

Rose Elizabeth Fitzgerald was not born, as she, her family and the world have believed for more than a century, on July 22, 1890. She was born on July 21. Her birthplace was not a house, as biographers have described it, but a humble tenement, made up of six flats, the building, including the land, valued at no more than $6,500. The address, 4 Garden Court Street, has suggested to many a quiet, leafy street in a decent middle-class suburb, but in fact it was one of the dirtiest and most squalid thoroughfares in North America, a last remaining enclave of the Irish, who were being pushed out by Italian immigrants.

Rose's father, John Francis, was the sixth clerk in the Third Division of the Custom House Statistical Department, the fourth of ten sons of an Irish immigrant peddler turned farmer and grocery-store owner. John Francis had started promisingly; he had won a scholarship to the exclusive Boston Latin School. But he had dropped out of Harvard Medical School in 1885, his sophomore year. The reason he gave later was that he could not afford to continue—that he had to support his siblings, who, he lied, were all younger than he. But his father's will shows that he was left approximately $2,000, a one-ninth share of two

3

tenements, at 379-381 and 465-467 Hanover Street, Boston, and land, at 4 Webster Place. That share would be worth at least $75,000 in present-day money, and his brothers all received the same amount and did not need supporting.

The real reason he left was a lack of interest in pursuing a medical career. He had set his heart on politics. Short, stocky, ruddy-cheeked, he was a neighborhood athlete who could run any kid off his feet; he was a firecracker who seldom stopped talking. It was said that if you asked him the time, he would describe in detail the workings of his watch.

His cheerful, toothy charm concealed a single-minded ambition along with a manic drive and antic impatience, and a state of crackling nervous tension that could cause him to explode in sudden displays of anger.

His only recorded eccentricity was his refusal to enjoy tobacco, liquor or even coffee in an age when any up-and-coming young man enjoyed spirits and a good cigar. He got away with this oddity of behavior by stating that he was an athlete in training.

Most people either hated or loved him; there were few in the middle. His confidence could infuriate or attract; his radiant charm could delight or disgust. He was propelled by anger; it gnawed into him that he was prohibited from entry into the world of the Boston upper crust—the tiny universe of the Brahmins who ruled the gray metropolis with elegant regality and self-conscious Anglophilia from their aeries on Beacon Hill or their shuttered retreats in Back Bay. Sheltered behind rich velvet curtains, cosseted by their servants, the Cabots, Lodges and Saltonstalls were bedrock Yankees, deeply anti-Catholic, despising the Irish who had invaded North End long before Rose was born and turned it into a slum. To the Brahmins, the Italians who followed the Irish into the neighborhood were even worse; they regarded the immigrants as infidels, renegade Catholics who might soon unravel the fabric of Bostonian society. John Fitzgerald drank in a loathing of Beacon Hill and Back Bay snobs with his mother's milk.

He was nicknamed Honey Fitz because, as a boy, he had

had a sweet tooth and was always eating candy or smearing molasses or powdered sugar on his bread. Yet, from the start, his political career was scarcely sweet and comforting. After his aborted stay at Harvard, he sniffed politics as a way to money and power; starting at the bottom, he fast-talked his way into a job with North End's ward boss, Matthew Keany, in the scum task of ward heeler, a form of lowlife that flourished at the time.

Ward heelers shanghaied voters for the ballot boxes by promising jobs to those who played ball and blacklisting those who didn't. A man who refused to yield to Fitzgerald's charm and rat-a-tat praise for Keany could find himself jobless, blacklisted and run out of town. The tough young Irishman's job was to pack the meeting halls with Keany supporters, who cheered to brass bands and noise-makers and disposed of hecklers with swift kicks in the pants. Fitzgerald was good for the job. There were few self-questionings in his mind, few shadings, mysteries or guilts in this sharp-toothed pit bull.

The only puzzle he presents is why, of all people in the world, he chose as bride a young Acton, Massachusetts, farm girl named Mary Josephine ("Josie") Hannon.

There were dozens of marriageable girls who were prettier, cleverer, born of the motley collection of Irish-American contractors, saloonkeepers and undertakers who flourished in Boston in those days. Apart from her looks and figure, which were in no way out of the ordinary, Mary Hannon had little to offer a rampant politician on the make. The daughter of a Massachusetts farmer, more at home with chickens and eggs and plows and cows than with political or financial news, working as a humble tailor's assistant, she had none of the sophistication necessary to entertain Fitzgerald's guests, form a network of supporters in the women's clubs, play cards or show any other social skills.

Is it possible that the marriage, the groundwork of which was laid when the couple were childhood sweethearts, resulted from Mary's thinking she was pregnant? Unlikely, given her strict Catholic upbringing, Fitzgerald's fear of scandal and the morality of the time. A more probable interpretation is that, like so many men of forcefulness, virility and hard ambition, the twenty-six-year-old ward heeler was not looking for a woman who might challenge, confront or correct him, but rather for a willing subsidiary —a suitably healthy mother for his children and an undemanding homebody companion.

He was soon to find out that the young woman's demure, shy exterior concealed a stubborn, puritanical and deeply religious character far removed from his own. His life was ruled by expediency, hers by duty, honor and propriety. She believed a wife and mother should be utterly selfless. He lived by the law of the jungle and the street; she lived by the rules of bishop, priest and rosary.

They were married on September 18, 1889, in St. Bernard's Church in historic Concord, Massachusetts, just a short distance from Josie's birthplace in Acton. Within a month, the bride was pregnant, and Honey Fitz had to get a better job in the corrupt world of the customshouse.

Josie's decision to have Rose baptized within two days of her birth tells us all we need to know of her fundamentalism; in those days, it was believed that if a child should die before it was christened, it would be condemned to hell for eternity along with mortal sinners.

At the time of Rose's birth, Benjamin Harrison, a former Civil War general, was president; the Senate was dominated by business monopolists; the White House was an entrepôt of unbridled money and power. Loose talk about the 1890s being a time of American innocence can easily be corrected. From Chief Executive to small-fry politician, Washington society mirrored a nation's cheerful corruption.

Rose's childhood in the rented flat at 4 Garden Court Street was dominated by Italians. In the five years before her birth, the Irish settlers had begun to move out, and the Avellinos from the Avelline province of Central Italy had moved in. The North End was a hellhole, an extension of the worst areas of the country from which they had come. The Boston statistician William De Marco has described Rose's district of birth as Calcutta: the most crowded and filthy 100 acres in North America. Garden Court Street was a mere twenty-four feet wide; its gutters ran with excrement; litter blew about; the one public bathhouse was shared by hundreds. Going to the toilet meant standing in a line at an outhouse in a tenement building's backyard. The only place to empty a chamber pot was into the kitchen sink.

Drunks and prostitutes roamed the streets along with gangs of stiletto-carrying youths. Driven out of Italy by disease, war and military oppression, the settlers were embittered with the Church, which they blamed for failing to help them in their plight. They seldom attended Mass, had little interest in learning to read, write or learn English, and had an open contempt for the police.

As Rose was taken out in her baby carriage, she saw historic houses, like that of Paul Revere, overflowing with abandoned, homeless riffraff; hurdy-gurdy men with pet monkeys grinding away for pennies; fruit sellers and hardware salesmen crying out from their corner carts. The stench of urine mingled with the heavy perfume of ripe fruit, flowers and vegetables.

Above all, she was aware of noise: of Italians shouting from building to building strung with laundry; of urchins skimming stones in the gutters or playing handball; of arguments echoing up through the tenement walls or the narrow staircases; of the cries of sexual pleasure or terminal pain that no one could block out in so public and exposed an environment.

It is easy to see why, later in life, she longed, more than anything, despite her love of parties and travel and the raising of nine children, for solitude.

Fitzgerald wouldn't be in customs for long; he had determined how he might rise in politics. He was in the midst of a pliant and illiterate electorate. The Italian vote was an untapped source for anyone on the make. While others ignored these immigrants, he corralled them into a following. He learned every name of every family, found out when a child was sick, fixed jobs for out-of-work arrivals and learned Italian well enough to be able to communicate with everyone. He knew how to deal with padrones, agents who forced Italians to pay them commissions if they got them jobs; he learned to appease the Black Hand. He promised parks and baths. He joined the immigrants in fetching coal from rat-infested dumps on Southampton Street.

When Rose was two, Fitzgerald, an ardent Democrat, joined the Common Council as representative of Ward Six, which, despite its officious name, was no more than an unauthorized club of ambitious young men who raised money for public facilities to secure support for their political purposes. He turned up on street corners, sometimes with his wife and Rose and her younger sister Agnes, shouting his annoyance at present conditions. The Sicilians grew to love him: he was alive and humorous; he sang popular songs; he was attractive and muscular and proud.

More than her somber, withdrawn mother with her catechisms and her rosary, Fitzgerald was his daughter's idol from the beginning. As she went through teething, Fitzgerald started up an insurance business at 10 Tremont Street, with his brother Henry as partner. Insurance was a path to influence. The humblest immigrant wanted his family taken care of if he fell victim to industrial accidents or to the cholera and malaria that swept through North End year after year. An insurance man could find ways to cover a family cheaply; he could go straight to the top in the community. Bars were often wrecked in fights; a saloon-keeper would need to be insured for that probability. Contractors faced the danger of their men tumbling from ladders or being buried under bricks when walls collapsed; Fitzgerald could save them from ruin in lawsuits.

His web spread wide. Matthew Keany died suddenly, leaving the vacancy of ward boss. Fitzgerald took over. And he didn't stop there: he ran for the state senate.

Expertly blending Italian and Irish elements, he rallied to his cause such rank outsiders as Jews and blacks. Banners and brash speeches landed him a state senate seat for the Third Suffolk District in 1892. It was only a step to Congress. He was elected on November 6, 1894, when Rose was four, after a tough electoral campaign; he was one of only three Catholics in the House.

For Rose, it was painful, even at that early age, to lose a father to Washington. But she didn't yet—not right away. He had contracted tuberculosis; on doctor's orders, he was sent to a sanitarium in Asheville, in the Blue Ridge Mountains of North Carolina.

In the meantime, Rose was subjected to a life of rigid

discipline. Her mother pushed her through the strenuous rituals of a Catholic upbringing: learning the catechism, praying day and night before the Virgin in the living-room shrine, decorating the Virgin's feet with fresh flowers, saying prayers before every meal. A benefit came at last: restored to health, Fitzgerald invited his wife and children (there was a third baby now, a boy named Thomas Acton) to attend President William McKinley's Inauguration in March 1897. Although McKinley was a Republican, Honey Fitz, now in his second term, was his ardent fan. How he squared this enthusiasm with his Boston Democrat friends and supporters must seem mysterious; but, his eye always to the main chance, he sought favors anywhere, even in the Opposition.

The visit to Washington was the biggest event of Rose's childhood; it was influential in giving her a first taste of the excitements of politics. Hating crowds, Josie must have found the events of that chilly spring day well-nigh unendurable. But for Rose they were thrilling.

She had a grandstand seat at the Inaugural parade, a panoply of American power, the troops marching past, brass bands blaring popular military tunes, the crowd cheering hysterically. The Pension Office was too crowded to allow for dancing at the Inaugural Ball, but Rose was dazzled by the silks and satins of the women and by the gold braid, medals or white tie and tails of the men.

The next day, she and Agnes went to a reception in the East Room, where children of Republican and Democratic party leaders were presented. Everyone there must have been on tenterhooks in case Ida McKinley had one of her fits. An epileptic, she would grow rigid in seizures; it was her husband's custom to toss a table napkin over her face at state dinners, so nobody would see her expression.

The Fitzgeralds led the children forward. The president turned to a proud Honey Fitz and said, of Agnes, with a remarkable lack of tact, "I declare this is the prettiest little girl ever to be seen in the White House."

The effect of the statement on Rose can only be imagined. It rankled her for years; it sharpened her ambition to be the most attractive, the best and brightest of children from that moment on.

Next day, Rose was received in the chamber of the House of Representatives. Speaker David G. Henderson embraced her and said to her father, "Where do these children get their good looks from, John?" Fitzgerald knew what he was doing; he gestured toward his wife. "Now I know!" Henderson exclaimed, and the chamber was filled with laughter.

Fitzgerald's introduction of Rose to politics was no idle gesture. His wife would not tolerate constant public exposure, gossip and hullabaloo. An attractive child was both emblem and mascot. A beautiful girl could dazzle in place of a woman who was dowdy, repressed and graceless.

The return to 4 Garden Court affected even the recessive Josie, because she put her foot down and insisted the family move to a country address. The question was where. To leave the North End would be dangerous; congressmen were not supposed to live outside the wards that had stimulated their careers. But she was adamant. She would return to the town where she had been married and where so many of her relatives lived.

The family took the train to Concord in July. Fitzgerald rented a house at 391 Main Street. It was not in the best part of town and stood uncomfortably close to Warner's Pail Factory, the Damon Manufacturing Company and Boston Harness Works, all of which had chimneys that belched smoke and sounded whistles day and night. Trains ran less than a quarter of a mile behind the house, shaking its structure vigorously.

But at least Main Street was lined with elms and had small strips of lawn running up to the porches. A bicycle craze was in full swing, the newfangled velocipedes causing a riot of excitement. The city was ablaze with the sounds of the Concord Artillery Band. The heat was suffocating; sunlight burned the grass dry; flags flew everywhere. It was an exciting place to be—and Fitzgerald received a prize almost immediately. His neighbor, Postmaster Abiel H. Chase, announced that he was about to resign and handed his sinecure over to the new arrival.

Fitzgerald introduced his daughters to the historical literary sites that made Concord famous. It is easy to imagine him, in a straw hat, his face flushed, talking nonstop, taking them to the house where Nathaniel Hawthorne wrote *The House of the Seven Gables;* to Henry Thoreau's Walden Pond, "clear, deep, green"; and to the house where Louisa May Alcott wrote *Little Women.*

An additional treat was a trip to Old Orchard Beach, north of Portland, on the coast of Maine. The Fitzgeralds, who had visited the town before, moved happily into F. G. Staples's Sea Shore House, a grand hotel of creaking wood set on a knoll overlooking the ocean. Everyone loved the palm court orchestra, the dining room cooled by ceiling fans, the spacious, airy suites. Rose joined her parents and sister in walks at Pine Point, rides on the miniature railroad at the pier, and evenings on the veranda when the shore became a fairyland of lights and the fashionable crowd gathered to exchange gossip and laughter in Indian basket chairs.

She returned to Concord in September. Neither flood nor fire nor the murder of a neighbor, Mary Butters, by a madman, could stop the child from marching off to the white clapboard West Concord School (not Public School, as it has been called) each morning, talking incessantly to her sister Agnes about everything under the sun. She studied under the beloved teachers Susie Wood and Edward Loughlin. Like most of her generation, she was influenced by the McGuffey New England Readers, which were compulsory study material for all pupils. William H. McGuffey supplied not only the basis of subject learning but a set of moral principles, which ruled Rose's life. He called for "integrity, industry, temperance, courage, politeness and intellectual virtues." He taught that war was evil, the devil's work; one of his Readers attacked Alexander of Macedon for earning glories through bloodshed. Rose's belief that war was wicked would surface constantly through her life as it would through her future husband's.

Rose was schooled in American optimism; girl or not, she would model herself on the boy who stood on the burning deck, "whence all but he had fled," in "Casabianca," the oft-quoted poem of her generation. Throughout her life, she would face blood and political cannonballs and the death of loved ones with a stoicism McGuffey as well as her priests instilled in her. She would "die rather than disobey God's rules," as McGuffey so irrevocably stated it.

In the Concord classroom, she would read aloud, verse by
verse, accompanied by her fellow pupils, poems that emphasized moral uplift and the necessity for saintly suffering.
She was encouraged to "push open literature's gates," as
McGuffey put it. That included studying British writers, but
the anti-British attitude exemplified by the Readers and
emanating from their Irish-American author does not appear to have influenced her.

Above all, the Readers made her aware of the unique
power of America; she would remain an awestruck patriot
for the rest of her life. As McGuffey put it, and the pupils
learned it by heart, "The United States is the freest, most
enlightened and powerful government [sic] on earth."

America as godhead, education as religion, virtue as a
guide—these were the staples of Rose's existence. As she
grew older, her earlier acquaintance with the home of the
author of *Little Women* was deepened by several visits. She
became engrossed in the pages of that moralistic novel. She
could find a passage to identify with as early as the first page
on which the antic heroine, Jo, says, sadly, "We haven't got
Father, and we shan't have him for some time." The
statement, referring to a parent who was serving in the Civil
War, had great poignancy for Rose. She was suffering from
frequent absences of her own dad, and the heart of her
existence was her mother, who was a more severe version of
the benign Marmee of the novel.

In her life of genteel near-shabbiness, she can only have
responded to Jo's sister Meg's longing for a "lovely house
full of luxurious things," and with nothing but "pleasant
people" in it. She would achieve the first of these shared
ambitions, if not entirely the second. The book's pages
reminded a devoted public that in order to satisfy ambition,
the reader must not stray from the narrow path of family, or
from the intrinsic loyalty desirable in younger siblings.
These lessons Rose took very much to heart.

Obedience, the scorning of idleness, the rejection of self-
pity and sloth were always desirable. Misery was self-
indulgent; happiness was to be earned. Quarrels were discouraged at home or in class. McGuffey used the parallel of
the birds in their nests: if they lived in harmony, why
shouldn't we? God willed fate; submission to fate is manda-

tory. Rose was taught not to question God's decisions. She remained a McGuffeyan.

Nevertheless, despite the emphasis on self-humiliation, Rose proved to be guilty of what she would have been told was the sin of pride. She was seized by manic ambition. She would be top of her class if it killed her. Seeing her sister Agnes munching a sandwich, she snapped irritably, "What's a congressman's daughter doing eating bread and molasses?" She had forgotten that this was her father's favorite food—if one excepted bread and peanut butter. She learned the piano with such expertise that Agnes was quite outdone by her. She sang better than Agnes. She even learned to play a violin, fiddling away until, no doubt, everyone in her household went nearly mad. She wrote notes busily with a quill pen dipped in a china inkwell; she talked incessantly, sang popular hits, and studied under the bedclothes. She was a handful.

In 1899, her father received a serious blow. He belonged to the so-called Board of Strategy, an influence-peddling group of politicians and businessmen who met at regular intervals at the popular Quincy House Hotel. One of the circle was the influential East End ward boss Patrick Kennedy, father of Joe, one of Rose's childhood companions. Subdued and discreet, Kennedy disliked the brash, extroverted Honey Fitz, believing that it was desirable for an up-and-coming political figure to be at least superficially polished and controlled. He felt that Honey Fitz had had more than enough time in Congress. He brought about his defeat by supporting a rival candidate. This was a considerable shock to Josie, Rose and the rest of the family.

Fitzgerald was unfazed. He would become mayor of Boston. In order to achieve this ambition, which he would not be able to do immediately, he had to leave Concord, which lay outside Boston proper, and return to the dreaded North End. We can only imagine his wife and daughters' protests as they had to pack up their belongings and move out of the sprawling, comfortable Concord house and settle by June into another slum, just a stone's throw from 4 Garden Court.

The new address was 8 Unity Street. It was an ugly apartment building with a high wall at the back that cut off the flow of air and loomed over a noisy schoolyard. Into the flat Honey Fitz crammed no less than thirteen people, all of whom showed up in the census of 1900. In addition to himself, Josie and Rose, Agnes and two younger children, Eunice and John, were included, along with Rose's uncles Michael, a policeman; Edward, Joseph and Henry, clerks; and a cousin, Ellen Dayman, acting as housekeeper, and Ellen's daughter Elizabeth, a salesgirl.

This show of family consolidation in the district may have been excessive, but it worked. Forgiven for his exile in Concord, Fitzgerald was again at the center of Italian activity, and he organized for his prospective constituents a spectacular Italian-language show, "The War in Africa," about the Roman general Scipio, at the Artillery Building. He appeared once more on street corners, reminding his audiences of his campaigns for reform. He had established a significant record; appalled by the foul meat supplied to the troops in the suppression of Philippine rebellions, he had taken a rotten steak to the White House and deposited it on the president's desk. He had exploded into the army hospital at Montauk Point, which housed the veterans of the Spanish-American War, had protested against the absence of proper doctors or nurses, and had piled a posse of physicians and RNs onto a midnight train at his own expense and let them loose in the wards at 3:00 A.M. He had carried dying men, stricken with typhoid fever, on stretchers when they had arrived off the ships; he had fulfilled their final wishes and visited their families.

He made the bricks of his reputation with the straws of his promises. Meantime, he saw an opportunity for further self-promotion; for $500 he snapped up a failing magazine, *The Republic,* and rushed from office to office, department store to department store, factory to factory, selling advertising space to his friends in big business. He published an advertisement for a clothing store he had opened himself, with his grinning face greeting the reader next to the picture of a handsome suit. He used the magazine as a platform; he attacked the Brahmins in editorial after editorial, calling for better conditions for the oppressed working class. He built circulation rapidly. Soon, he was making a stunning $25,000 a year (about $500,000 in 1994 money). And yet, mindful of his prospective electorate, he lingered on at Union Street.

A disturbing and, for Rose, prophetic incident occurred in 1901. On September 6, President McKinley, still the idol of the Fitzgerald family, was attending a reception at the Pan American Exposition in Buffalo when an anarchist, Leon Czolgosz, reached forward, seemingly to shake his hand. McKinley was about to respond in kind when Czolgosz fired two bullets into him at point-blank range. For about a week, the president's life hung in the balance. The doctors failed to extract the bullet; they were unable to locate it, because they had failed to use the newfangled X-ray machine that was on display at the exposition. Gangrene set in, and McKinley died.

There is no record of Rose's response to the killing, but there can be no doubt that it horrified her and her whole family. For the Fitzgeralds, the belligerent, noisy Teddy Roosevelt, elevated now from his role as vice-president, was an insufficient substitute. Honey Fitz never warmed to him, even though they had much in common in their emphasis on athletics, loudmouthed optimism and a tough, relentless overcoming of obstacles.

Rose's education badly broken up, she went temporarily to a local school; one of her few breaks was going to see her idol, Sarah Bernhardt, in *La Tosca, Cyrano de Bergerac* and *La Dame aux Camélias* at the Boston Theater in April 1901, an event she would never forget.

At last, in 1903, Fitzgerald cracked before his family's urgent requests and moved them south of Boston to a decent house at 37 Welles Avenue, on top of Jones Hill, in Dorchester. His motive in choosing this particular suburb is clear. It had become the focus for the wealthy Irish whose support he needed far more than that of the illiterate Italian population to satisfy his mayoral ambitions. The contractors and undertakers had moved into Dorchester in full force; of their number, the best known was his friend the financier Harry Nawn, who had made a fortune from building a series of unappetizing structures in and around the metropolis.

The Italians accused Fitz of betrayal, but he had no alternative if he was to receive Irish backing. The house he selected was grand: a wooden neocolonial folly with a circular driveway and a mansard turret that cost him $16,400. He installed a stained-glass window on the second-floor landing with an invented coat of arms adapted from a book of heraldry, his face emerging from a medieval helmet and his name adapted in a scroll, in Gaelic: Shawn O Boo, meaning John the Bold.

Rose became an instrument of his political will when he sent her from the tenth grade at West Concord School to the eleventh grade at Dorchester Grammar (later, High) School, where she could mingle with the children of the Irish New Rich. A schoolmate attracted Rose's attention: Hugh, the handsome son of Harry Nawn. Honey Fitz marked down the boy as Rose's future husband.

Rose emerged once again, moving toward the head of her class. She got A's in algebra, French, Latin and physical education, but only B's in English and physics. Eligible to emerge as a junior belle at the school dance, she had been taking dancing lessons for months. But Honey Fitz, who was building up his preparations for the mayoralty, was fearful of some scandal at her innocent age. He forbade her to attend the end-of-term dance that spring. She was acutely distressed, but her tears and tantrums had no effect on him. It would have been more effective if he had let Hugh Nawn accompany her to the dance, thereby making a social and political point; instead, he came off looking not so much protective as weird.

Rose had a consolation: she was third in a class of 285, and her graduation, close to her birthday in July 1905, was a grand occasion. Her father himself presented her with a diploma and a sterling-silver service; she was the youngest girl to graduate from Dorchester High School (she returned for a postgraduate year).

And then she experienced the thrill of her father's mayoral campaign in the winter of 1905. It began on a sour note: the Italian newspaper *Gazetta di Massachusetts* attacked him savagely, accusing him of shafting the Italians who had supported him for state senate and for Congress, charging that he had failed to obtain a single official post for any of the immigrants. He responded by invading the North End once again, knitting up all of his unraveled relationships.

He dragged the reluctant Josie into his campaign; she stood next to him with Rose, Agnes and the younger children in wind and snow as he addressed excited crowds through his famous megaphone, crying out, as his garish posters did, for a "bigger, better, busier Boston." Photographs of the family were plastered on walls and streetcars; he bought a scarlet Fiat automobile, in which he drove to as many as a dozen locations a day, giving rabble-rousing speeches; he ordered cartloads of soda-water bottles to be dispatched to hospital wards, making sure that arrangements were made for the patients to vote in absentia; he turned up on sales days in stores to harangue shoppers as they besieged the counters; he was heard on streetcars and trains; he moved in an explosion of fireworks to the tune of brass bands.

His was the most garish and spectacular mayoral campaign that staid Boston had ever seen, and $120,000 of good Irish-American money went into it. His rival, City Clerk Ned Donovan, had little chance; nor did the organizational candidate Louis Frothingham, Republican speaker of the Massachusetts House of Representatives. He won hands down; he obtained 44,171 votes, a margin of 8,123. He achieved this remarkable result by whipping up, once again, public hatred of the Bostonian elite, and corralling the usual outcasts, Jews and blacks. One of his ovations took place at Faneuil Hall, when he denounced Theodore Roosevelt for cashiering a black army battalion, charging them with inciting a riot in Texas. Approved by the black newspaper *The Guardian* as being "free from all color prejudice," he secured the black vote almost unanimously.

He succeeded, despite the formidable opposition of political boss Martin M. Lomasney, an erstwhile supporter, and of the ever-annoying Patrick Kennedy. He overcame the enmity of Henry Cabot Lodge, doyen of the Republican Boston establishment and the powerful senator from Massachusetts.

At fifteen, Rose was enchanted with politics. Now came the excitement of her father's inauguration, adding to the existing pleasures of New Year's Day, 1906. She was ecstatic as the chauffeur drove her, her parents and her siblings in the big red car to City Hall through snowbanked, brilliantly sunlit streets at 10:00 A.M. She was mesmerized as, seated in the public gallery of the Common Council chamber under a huge, loudly ticking clock, she gazed down at a chamber packed with over a thousand people, many of them her father's devoted women fans, and saw her father address the crowd. He rushed through his twenty-seven-page speech in twenty-eight minutes, so animated by passion that he never proved boring; the cheers were so frequent he could barely continue.

That night, the family accompanied him to a candlelit banquet; so vast was the crowd when they arrived that he had to be carried over the heads of the people into the hall.

Rose was the toast of Dorchester High School, but soon she would have to answer some awkward questions. Swept up by euphoria, Honey Fitz had no sooner entered City Hall and taken up office than he stumbled badly. In order to win the mayoral race, he had had to make too many promises to his moneyed supporters. He began handing out sinecures like candy.

He fired physicians from the Board of Health and replaced them with saloonkeepers who were more likely to provide the cause of illnesses than their cures; he made a painting contractor Superintendent of Streets, which meant that the man could paint every wall in the city and charge the city for the job. Another businessman friend was handed the job of Superintendent of Sewers, but never descended down a manhole. Another became City Dermatologist, with no knowledge of diseases of the skin; a friend was appointed Watcher of Nightwatchmen; another still was Teapot Warming Supervisor; a third was Good Repairs Quality Checker. Fitz's brothers found jobs in the new administration.

Inevitably, his opponents called for investigations of corruption. Confident that he could overcome any criticism, he set up a finance committee to investigate himself.

Public criticism began to surge toward his office doors. Meantime, the *Gazetta* kept up the onslaught on him, compelling him to appoint a Sicilian to his office.

The summer of 1907 found the family back at Old Orchard Beach, Maine. Honey Fitz moved his wife and children into Old Orchard House, the best hotel in town, with a sweeping view of the Atlantic. While they were there, on August 15, just before dinner, the Emerson Hotel nearby caught fire; in a few minutes, Rose was looking out of her window at an inferno. Honey Fitz ran out to see what he could do to help. As he raced past the Sea Shore House hotel, from which everyone was fleeing, chemicals exploded in a pharmacy and a glass soda container shot inches past his head like a shell.

Rose and her siblings escaped with their mother, spending the night crammed into the local depot; they returned to find Old Orchard House miraculously intact, but so jammed with refugees from the fire that it resembled a displaced persons' camp.

This shattering event made Rose aware of the fact that nothing in life could be relied upon; that terror and danger were frequent alternates to laughter and pleasure. It was the Fitzgeralds' last summer at Old Orchard.

But Rose did carry one good memory from those vacations at the beach. Once again she met the future love of her life, the boy named Joe Kennedy.

Honey Fitz had perhaps hoped to charm, buy, or at least influence the Finance Committee, but its members proved remarkably indifferent to his persuasions. However, as it turned out, he was not without string-pulling ability in extremis, and the committee's reports, though scathing, excused him from the charge of being the chief perpetrator. Instead, the members settled on a scapegoat, thus presenting the Fitzgerald family with a serious crisis of conscience.

The scapegoat was a close friend of the clan: the warm and genial, slightly fuddy-duddy undertaker Michael Mitchell, head of the supply department at City Hall, through whom the favors or spoils rapidly passed from the mayor's office. Mitchell had spent the summer with the family at Old Orchard Beach. His loud voice and sturdy physique, his radiant grins through a thick brown mustache, were a pleasure to Fitzgerald, and to Rose he was the equivalent of a favorite uncle. It was he who was offered up as a sacrificial lamb; it would be reasonable to suspect that the committee had settled on the decision to destroy him in return for the mayor's agreement to turn state's evidence against him.

Shortly after the Fitzgeralds' return from Maine, what became known as the Coal Graft Hearings began at the Old School Committee Building on Mason Street in downtown Boston. They created a sensation; the city was in an uproar, and the crowds outside the gray edifice were overwrought and frantic as they tried to force their way into the limited space of the courtroom. An excited audience, jammed into the cramped wooden seats, gasped before revelation after revelation. Under cross-examination, the unhappy Mitchell fell apart. He was forced to admit that he had given the prominent merchant Maurice Klause an exclusive contract for Boston's entire coal supply in return for a guarantee of votes. Mitchell refused to name Fitzgerald as his instructor in the matter. It seems he had been promised a life income if he would take the rap. It was a promise that his erstwhile friend would not finally keep. Mitchell was held over for trial at a later date.

As accusations of graft continued to swell, Rose was consumed by an ambition to escape. Graduated from Dorchester High, she longed to go to Wellesley, the distinguished women's college situated at Lake Waban, west of Boston. There she could break through the barriers that separated her from the rich and promising children of the Brahmin upper class; there she could experience the ecumenicism of power and money; there she would demonstrate her brilliance in the company of the brightest and the fairest; there she would meet young men from Harvard, go to dances, have a chance to excel at athletics, and in short for the first time enjoy true privilege.

She found no opposition in her father. But an unfortunate incident took place. On one of his weekend walks, Honey Fitz ran into the archbishop of Boston, the imposing William H. O'Connell. O'Connell, who had replaced an eighty-five-year-old prelate and had lately returned from Rome, was determined to clean up local politics in the interests of the Church. He had never approved of Honey Fitz. As they strolled together, he was annoyed to learn that Rose was to be sent to a Protestant college. This was unacceptable and disgraceful and, he made clear, could remove Catholic support for Fitzgerald's administration just when it was needed.

Honey Fitz realized his mistake. He crumbled; he apologized to the archbishop; he saw the ground slipping from under his feet. He may have feared opposition from the Church in his political battle. So colossal a gaffe must be corrected at once.

He called a family gathering at which he delivered a bombshell. Rose, who was packed and ready to leave, would not be going to Wellesley, which had accepted her, because she was "too young," but to the Convent of the Sacred Heart, at 264 Commonwealth Avenue, of which the archbishop was patron. Rose was devastated by the decision. She burst into tears; she screamed in anger at her father's cruelty. She had been made a victim of his political ambition. The decision was the guillotining of all of her hopes. It bothered her for the rest of her life.

Chapter 2

Joe

The Convent of the Sacred Heart, to which Rose was admitted, on September 16, 1907, at a fee of $396 a year, was not a pleasant retreat. Under the charge of Mother Katherine Cantwell, it was a stern, repressive and cheerless institution. Rose entered it with her usual strength of will, but would find that will tested severely in the coming months. She must again guard herself against feelings that were childish, visionary, sensual or exuberant; penance must be accepted; self-renunciation must be the order of the day. Laughter was as forbidden as though it were an expression of lust. Pupils were not allowed to talk except at specified times; they must perform domestic duties; they must attend to needlework, dressmaking, mending, first-aid and nature study, as well as Latin, French, geography and classical history. They had to prostrate themselves before teaching Sisters, on their knees or stretched out on the floor. Students were divided into categories: Lymphatic, Sanguine, Choleric, Nervous, or Melancholic.

We do not know for sure, but "Sanguine" must have been Rose's category. Her cheerful spirit, alive with energy and charm, would always make the best of any situation. But as she continued her grim existence at the institution, she needed all the strength that an unswerving belief in God could give her. The austerity of the ordeal was not unrelieved. On certain days of the week, she was granted dispensation, since the school had no music teacher, to attend classes at the exclusive New England Conservatory on Huntington Avenue. Her imperious teacher, Alfred De Voto, drove her to the point where she became a decent pianist, and she was able to use the excuse of studying music to slip away and attend concerts and operas.

The Christmas holidays brought no succor from knowledge of her father's political troubles. Rumors and hints that penetrated the cloistered seclusion of Sacred Heart broke out in full force around her when she returned home. Day after day her father's cheerfulness and the family's belief in his innocence barely sustained them as newspaper after newspaper headlined more details of his mayoral regime.

Even while she was at school, an incident resulted in garish headlines. Mitchell's clerk, George Koch, collapsed in front of the Finance Committee; his legs gave out from under him, and it was feared he might have suffered a heart attack. Now he was found half gassed to death in his apartment and was rushed to the hospital, where he admitted his implication in graft but somehow managed to protect the embattled mayor.

It was in this atmosphere of tension that the Fitzgeralds had to muster up enthusiasm for Honey Fitz's winter campaign to return to that office. Not surprisingly, he was defeated. With unfortunate timing, a grand jury sat just two days before Christmas on another issue: the matter of improper contracts being handed out for flagstone supplies. Fitzgerald dumped Mitchell; he destroyed him effectively by his testimony. Mitchell was ordered for trial and was held in jail until that trial should take place. The deposed mayor neither protected him nor visited him.

It became obvious even to Honey Fitz that he was in danger of being ruined if Mitchell should change his mind and reveal his role in City Hall graft. The mayor should have learned not to run when charges are in the air. But he was so confident of his popularity, so certain that he would not be made a martyr and so determined to remove Rose from the arena of public calumny that he took off to Europe with her and Agnes in July 1908. He had put her down for entry at the cloistered Academy of the Sacred Heart at Blumenthal, Vaals, near Aachen, in Holland. He hoped that newspapers would not reach that remote and improbable location; that any news of his subsequent disgrace would be filtered and denied; and that Rose would be protected from the anger that resounded through Boston clubs, hotels and committee rooms.

In a dazzle of confetti and streamers, the family sailed on the *Cymric* from Boston Harbor on July 18, 1908. Rose's excitement was so extreme, she was quite unmindful that the voyage had every appearance of a flight from justice. Among those who saw her off were two young men who called on her as her "beaux": Joe Kennedy, the boy she had first met at Old Orchard Beach, and his older rival for her affections, Hugh Nawn.

She celebrated her eighteenth birthday on board by descending, as though from heaven into hell, into steerage, to visit the very poor.

When the ship disembarked at Liverpool, the family took the train to London, where they enjoyed Westminster Abbey, the Houses of Parliament, and the Tower of London with its torture chambers and execution blocks. They saw the family home in Ireland, reminding them of how far they had come; they relished the mountains and lakes of Switzerland; and they walked their feet off through historic sites in Germany and Belgium. As Honey Fitz checked his daughters into the bleak, three-story, gray stone convent at Blumenthal, he received welcome news: his archenemy, Boston prosecutor John Moran, had died that week of tuberculosis.

Blumenthal was one of the most repressive, uninviting and cheerless religious establishments in Europe. When Rose walked into her dormitory cubicle, she found an iron bedstead, a wooden chair, a wardrobe and a small prie-dieu, surmounted by a portrait of the Virgin Mary. The floor was uncarpeted; the walls were bare of pictures or any other form of decoration.

At six o'clock on her first morning, she was awakened by

the loud, clanging bell of the Angelus. As she sat up in bed, a nun appeared, accompanied by an aide who carried a pail of holy water. The nun took a paintbrush, dipped it in the water and flicked several drops over Rose's face and body. Then she continued down the row of partitions to treat each of the pupils similarly.

Silence was called for as Rose and the other girls, hair plaited and ribboned, bathed their faces and hands. Dressed in black, their faces concealed behind black veils, Rose and her companions were marched to chapel, where they knelt in silent prayer. Afterward, they were conducted to breakfast in a hall lined with deal tables. The repast consisted of a few slices of bread and butter; nothing as sinful as jam was allowed, nor as nourishing as cereal, eggs and bacon. One cup of tea per pupil was permitted. Talking was allowed only at a halfway point, and conversation had to be restricted to religious matters. Giggles or light conversation were silenced at once. "Special friendships" were, of course, forbidden; no girl must kiss or embrace another, however innocently.

Every minute of the day was planned, and no deviations were allowed. Lunch and dinner, composed of gruel, meat and more tea, were interrupted by lectures on character, deportment and propriety. Terrified of any hint of lesbianism, Mother Superior ordered the girls, in their infrequent breaks from class, to walk in groups of three.

Each girl's traits, negative or positive, were noted down. Virtues were not mentioned or rewarded. Faults were entered in a ledger. On Sundays, a nun would pick up the ledger and read from it to the school. Every girl had to stand before her fellows and recite, one by one, her sins of pride, desire, hatred, envy or greed. At the end, all present had to promise that they would accept any suffering God should impose upon them. For some, there was self-flagellation with a spiked ring on a leather lash.

Rose was required to make frequent visits to the nuns' graveyard, where she prayed before a crucifix for the souls of the departed. Her letters from home were censored lest they should tempt her with visions of the outside world. The Index Expurgatorius, a list of books proscribed by Rome, was on display in the library, from which all volumes other than religious were banned. Newspapers, domestic or foreign, were forbidden.

Unlike the European pupils, the Americans, of whom Rose was the most impressive, were allowed one privilege: they could wear their own clothes once a month when they went into the village for a haircut. Rose made an effect on these occasions; she managed to be chic in adversity. She was even allowed to put a rug and a photograph of her parents in the cell she shared with Agnes. She was also permitted a trip to Berlin with her sister in December; she saw an opera performance attended by the kaiser and his wife.

On her return, she had to pay the penalty for such pleasure by being shut away in a dark, silent room alone for three days and nights of what was called a "retreat." She was prepared to suffer anything to become a Child of Mary, the highest honor that could be bestowed on a non-novice. She achieved that supreme ambition the following May. But she was beginning to weary of privations; she wanted, by now, to go home. Since she did not have a strong sex drive, chastity and obedience didn't trouble her, but poverty did. However, Honey Fitz didn't dare bring her back immediately.

It is as well she was not informed of what was happening in Boston. Fitzgerald had to appear at a trial of the officials he had himself appointed. He gave the performance of a lifetime: humorous, dodgy, conveniently afflicted by loss of memory, he lied that he remembered little of the events except that Mitchell was responsible for everything. His betrayal was accompanied by a manic humor. Mitchell's career was undertaker. Fitzgerald was asked whether his old friend was in "retail." He replied, to gusts of laughter, that he had never heard of a "wholesale undertaker." He laughed even as he buried the wretched Mitchell for good.

But he faced an ugly moment when Judge Sanderson read the guilty verdict. The jury foreman told Sanderson that "Mitchell was not so deep in this as somebody else who was not charged." It takes no effort of the imagination to determine who that person was. Mitchell went to prison for a year. He received a visit from Fitzgerald's brother Jim, who brought further promises of protection and help when the sentence was completed. He returned with a statement by Mitchell that said, "Fitz is the squarest man I have ever known."

The coast was clear; Fitzgerald could at last bring his daughters home. He whisked them off to Paris, London and Edinburgh; their next stop would be the Isle of Wight to attend the August Cowes Week yacht races, where his good friend, tea tycoon Sir Thomas Lipton, had a famous yacht, the *Erin,* which was among the champion vessels of the hour.

Lipton was a delight to the family; he had a captivating sense of humor. He was one of the dominant figures of Rose's young womanhood. Immensely rich from a grocery-store chain, corners in pork and beef supplies and tea holdings in India and Ceylon, he was a kind of surrogate uncle, occupying the place vacated by the unfortunate Michael Mitchell. His lanky figure, red face and bristling walrus mustache were delightful to Rose. Although middle-aged when he got to know the Fitzgeralds, for years he conducted a harmless flirtation with Rose, joking always that this young woman, so many years his junior, would one day be his bride. Actually, he was the lover of the colorful Parisian star Gaby Deslys, as well as of other glamorous women on both sides of the Atlantic. He didn't believe in marriage; he preferred the thrill of discovery.

He was the friend of royalty, starting with King George V of England, and the kings of Italy and Spain. The guest book of the *Erin* was a cross between *Who's Who* and the *Almanach de Gotha.* King Alfonso of Spain proposed to his future Queen Ena on the boat deck. The doyen of European society, Prince Henry of Battenberg, was his closest friend. Honey Fitz was probably his only parvenu companion. His one unfulfilled ambition—he who could have anyone or anything—was winning the America's Cup yacht races.

To conduct the Fitzgeralds to Southampton, the point of departure for the Cowes races, Lipton commandeered a special train, equipped with a string orchestra. The train housed only Honey Fitz, Rose, her mother and her sister

Agnes in it, along with a traveling group of American athletes and gourmet chefs and staff. However, once they were settled into their hotel, Lipton mysteriously failed to send a motor launch for them to sail to the *Erin*. In order to reach the vessel, where a lunch party was arranged for the great and famous of the world, Fitzgerald would have to commandeer a boat himself.

Every craft was taken. Fitzgerald was unfazed. He strode to the Royal Yacht Club Pier, where the king's launch rode at anchor. With typical chutzpah, he lied to the skipper, "We are guests of the royal family." And then he added, "Please take us to Sir Thomas Lipton's yacht." The captain believed that the obstreperous American had royal authorization to proceed. The Fitzgeralds stepped up the gangway; the launch moved smoothly out to sea. Sir Thomas ushered them aboard with astonished exclamations that the king had lent them his boat.

The launch's master had to return to face a furious King George V, who had just arrived with his consort from London. In later years, the monarch would burst out laughing whenever Lipton brought up the subject.

For years, Rose dined out on the story.

The family returned to Boston on August 20, 1910, where the vindicated Honey Fitz would embark on a new campaign for mayor. His chief backer was another major figure in Rose's life: Boss Martin M. Lomasney. Known as the Boston Mahatma, Lomasney was a ferocious politician; his slogan was "keep it legal," while he constantly infringed on the law. Like Honey Fitz, he was a child of Irish immigrant parents. And like him, he used the poor to promote himself.

Of average height, he was a muscular 180 pounds, with a huge head, a jutting jaw and a full mustache. He always wore a famous, battered straw hat, and carried an umbrella, not only in the rain, but in the sunshine, to keep the sun off his face. His conversation had the constant rat-a-tat of machine-gun bullets. He was obsessed with applesauce and was allegedly the champion applesauce eater of the world, eating more than 270 pounds of it a year.

Apparently asexual, he was never seen with a woman and

refused to marry. He was an obsessed communicant at St. Mary's Church. He would fling off coat, collar and necktie as he gave speeches, drawing affectionate laughter from his adherents and catcalls from his enemies.

Fitz and Lomasney faced a formidable obstacle: the banker and Brahmin society figure James Jackson Storrow, who combined spectacular looks, blue blood and several hundred thousand dollars a year. He was noted for his gifts to the city; among these was the Esplanade, which he had built after draining the stinking mudflats of Boston Harbor. Rallying behind Honey Fitz were not only Lomasney but two powerful Catholic Democrats: his former critic Patrick Kennedy, who was determined that no Protestant would be mayor, and the up-and-coming James Michael Curley, a boisterous young alderman who was already noted as a vote grabber.

Sweeping aside charges of his own corruption, Fitz embarked on his campaign with the slogan MANHOOD VERSUS MONEY. As before, his combination of blarney, poor-versus-rich arguments, high-powered promises and reminders of his own benefits to the city—an aquarium, the zoo— worked against the more sober enticements and grave charges of corruption that Storrow brought to his own campaign. Fitz attacked the wealth and power of the ruling class, who looked out of their exclusive-club windows and sneered at the poor outside. Storrow dragged out the Mitchell affair, corralling the support of almost every newspaper editor in town to insure cartoon after cartoon, editorial after editorial, lampooning Honey Fitz as a vote buyer and a shill.

Returning from vacation after a term at the Academy of the Sacred Heart, 133rd Street, Manhattanville, New York, Rose carried a pile of newspapers into her father's bedroom, sat on the foot of the bed and read out the latest set of accusations while he dismissed them with a wave of the hand.

For years, a popular song, "Sweet Adeline," had been sweeping the country, sung by countless barbershop quartets, men dressed as barbers with handlebar mustaches standing in semicircles on the stages at vaudeville theaters, or by serenaders under nighttime windows. Introduced several years earlier at Hammerstein's Victoria in Manhattan, it enjoyed phenomenal sheet-music sales. Among those who fell in love with the number was Rose, who by 1909 enjoyed playing it on her piano and singing it with great enthusiasm. Her father walked into the parlor one day, heard her and decided to adopt the ditty as his campaign song.

Why not a patriotic anthem instead? The answer is clear: because it called for audience participation and was known by heart by almost every American. As Honey Fitz addressed crowds in assembly halls or beer gardens or on the bandstands in parks on Sunday afternoons, on harbor foreshores or riverbanks, the people would listen in rapture to him as, straw hat perched rakishly on his head, hand pressed to heart, he would bawl out the familiar lyrics. What Josie thought of such inelegance has not been recorded. She must have hated the constant repetition of the number among the potted palms or under the stained-glass windows of her house. Can one doubt that brothers, sisters, cousins, uncles and aunts all joined together in group sings, while Rose banged away at the keyboard in chorus after chorus?

According to an article in *New England* magazine, Honey Fitz sang "Sweet Adeline" an average of thirty-five times to thirty-five gatherings a day—an exaggeration, surely; traveled a total of 2,500 miles around the city, driven by his black chauffeur, Rocket; dictated statements to newspaper reporters while eating breakfast, lunch and dinner; and never ceased to attack the bigwigs, the finance commissions and the reform associations.

Storrow responded to Fitz's critiques of indifference to the poor and cruelty to the oppressed with charges of graft, corruption and deceit. Storrow-influenced newspapers offered cartoons of Fitzgerald, one of which showed the word GRAFTER embossed on his forehead. When Storrow and his team edged their way through the crowded streets of South Boston in their automobiles, Honey Fitz sent a gang of ruffians to batter the cars and crack the windows. Storrow's gentlemanly presence proved impressive, but no one could beat Fitzgerald when he was on a roll.

Rose and the rest of the family were in suspense at the end of the year when the ballot results were so close they seemed almost a tie. Storrow called for a recount, but there was no escaping the final tally: Fitz won with 47,177 votes to Storrow's 45,775.

The New Year celebrations were more exciting for Rose than those which had preceded them. She was flushed with excitement at the inaugural occasion at Faneuil Hall. Her father was not only victorious, but vindicated. And there was icing on the cake: due to recently revised rules of the city charter, Fitzgerald's term would last four years, not one. Could Rose ask for more? The hard-fought campaign and its happy conclusion secured Honey Fitz's name in the popular esteem forever. Once and for all, he had become a celebrity. Magazines from coast to coast interviewed him and published his articles.

By the time Rose graduated from the Academy of the Sacred Heart in the part of New York known as Manhattanville, in June, he was already a name in New York; even the opposing *New York Times* warmed up to him when, along with other Boston representatives at the Hotel Ambassador, he received a standing ovation as he sang "Sweet Adeline."

He was not only rich from the continuing sales of *The Republic* and from his adventures in insurance, real estate, men's clothing and the spoils system, but he was the talk of the northeastern seaboard. It was mentioned that he might one day run for governor. He had sewn up connections in New York's Tammany Hall, insuring his role in anti-labor politics.

Once again, Rose had been used as a pawn in a political game. His selection of New York as her place of education was no accident; her situation there allowed him to explain away his numerous visits to the city.

In her last weeks at Manhattanville and her first weeks as debutante and graduate, Rose began seriously dating young Joe Kennedy. She kept his photograph hidden in her purse at all times. The youth who would one day become the

center of her life was twenty years old and pursuing his
sturdy athletics career at Harvard. He had been born on
September 6, 1888, when his father, Patrick, was state
representative in the 109th District Court of the Commonwealth of Massachusetts. The contrast between his and
Rose's early childhoods was striking. Whereas she had to
endure Avellinean squalor, he was brought up in a pleasant
frame house in East Boston by a father who was not brash,
extroverted and exciting, but cautious, controlled and conservative. A handsome, redheaded child, with a flashy,
heart-stopping, toothy smile, Joe was a heartthrob from the
beginning. He performed odd jobs to augment the family
income, working as errand boy, newspaper salesman and
lamplighter. He was a businessman even before puberty,
when he organized a baseball team with the neighborhood
kids and sold tickets to the games.

Like Honey Fitz, he attended Boston Latin School, where
he mingled with children of the Brahmin families who
would later snub him. He was popular there; he became
colonel of the cadets and starred at both baseball and
football. When he won the Mayor's Cup for his prowess in
the high-school league, it was Fitzgerald who gave him the
coveted honor. This did not lessen Patrick Kennedy's
essential dislike of Rose's father.

Joe had one strange quirk: one thing he was afraid of. He
hated a high, keening wind. It might have been some
ancestral superstition from long-ago Ireland, and it invaded
him; he would become terrified, hiding indoors. He hid that
fear as best he could from his macho, coolly rational
colleagues, but it remained with him for the rest of his life,
and Rose, who loved to walk in the fiercest wind and
heaviest rain, lovingly humored the phobia.

Joe went on to Harvard, much to the annoyance of
Archbishop O'Connell and the Boston Catholic ruling class.
Excluded from the Porcellian, Fly and A.D. clubs, all of
which were restricted to the Protestant elite, he vowed he
would one day obtain revenge.

Once she was released from Manhattanville, Rose saw Joe
as often as she could. They were together when her cousin
Mary Fitzgerald married John Andrew Keane of Salem,

Massachusetts, at the Church of the Assumption in Brookline on June 22, 1910. Rose was maid of honor, making a
dazzling impression in white princess lace over blue liberty
silk and sporting a French sailor hat. Joe was handsome in a
morning coat. Several people noticed that they exchanged
amorous glances during the ceremony.

They walked hand in hand through the Harvard grounds,
past the historical buildings, explored museums and art
galleries, enjoyed standing on bridges looking at small craft
sail by on Sundays, and took in concerts together. Rose
became increasingly captivated not only by Joe's cheeky,
cheerful good looks, lithe, athletic figure and ease of manner, but by the fact that he listened to her when most young
men failed to take her, as a female, seriously. He had the
knack of making her feel the center of the universe.

Her father's opposition to the match stimulated her all
the more.

Her meetings with Joe had to be increasingly surrepti-
tious. There would be clandestine encounters at street
corners; she would find excuses to be in the Harvard
grounds; she enlisted fellow conspirators including her
chauffeur, Target, and her friend, Miriam Finnegan. When
her father asked to see her dance program—on which, in
the tradition of the time, the names of her partners were
inscribed by her—she listed a number of nonexistent men,
whereas in fact Joe was her only partner. Hugh Nawn, who
was approved by Fitz as Rose's future mate, undoubtedly
knew of the trick but gamely played along with it since Joe
was his friend. It is clear that he was as much onto the
deception as Rose herself because he had no interest in
marrying her. He knew the reason for the proposed match:
melding the mayor's interests ever more closely with the
construction business.

Rose had much in common with Joe. They enjoyed the
same songs, the same jokes. The Kennedys were as musical
as the Fitzgeralds. There were unforgettable Sunday suppers
at the Kennedy house when Rose would turn up and she,
Joe and the other young people would relish the oven-baked
bread, Boston baked beans and mince pies that were set out
on the dining table with its snow white damask cloth. After

the delicious dinner cooked by Joe's sister Margaret, there were long evenings in the parlor when, as the Kennedy parents lay back in their basket chairs, Joe led the group singing of Harvard bucks and their girlfriends, bawling away happily as Rose and Joe's other sister, Loretta, took turns playing the piano, and the room was filled with the strains of "Peg o' My Heart," "Danny Boy" or "Molly Malone."

Sometimes they would double-date with ace footballer Bob Fisher, Joe's roommate, who had given up an earlier dream of dating Rose, or with Hugh Nawn, who, much to Honey Fitz's annoyance, had now acquired a girlfriend of his own. Those were innocent days; even a kiss on the mouth was considered daring, and no decent young woman would entertain the idea of fondling—or more.

Rose loved Joe's clean habits; like her father, he neither smoked, drank, took coffee, gambled or told a dirty story. His devotion to athletics excited her. The best days were when she saw him at the freshman games against Yale. She cheered to the echo when he managed two hits out of four and stole two bases. She laughed when, dressed as a girl of ten, he shrilled, "Oh, You Beautiful Doll" to a china baby on the stage of the Hasty Pudding. The capper was that he was—or claimed to be—deeply religious.

Rejected as she was by the Boston clubs, he encouraged her to form her own, which she characteristically called the Ace of Clubs. It was, she was sure, a good deal more fun than the exclusive Vincent Club or the Junior League. She already showed haughty manners. She followed the custom of assuming that everyone had heard of her and refusing to carry cash in her purse. Even as early as Dorchester High, she had told streetcar conductors who she was and had declined to produce the one-cent fare. It was the beginning of a lifetime of stinginess.

One of the highlights of her calendar was the weekly meeting at the Rose Room of the Somerset Hotel, where she learned to make speeches. Soon she became an expert, exciting her audiences with her knowledge of international affairs. Other occasions were the Assemblies, popular balls attended by the cream of the Roman Catholics. Joe Kennedy and (to appease Honey Fitz) Hugh Nawn took it in turns to open these occasions with her as partner, leading the cotillion with striking expertise.

Rose emerged as an actress at the Abbotsford Club, starring in potted versions of Broadway hits in a castellated mansion in the suburb of Roxbury. She was head of the Lenox Club, the Travel Club, and the Public Library Investigating Committee, which prescribed children's books and held classes for Italian children.

It was the best time of her life; never had she looked more radiantly happy. A questionable thrill occurred on September 9, 1910, when she had the ominous experience of seeing her father take off in his first flight in an airplane. An excited crowd of twenty-five thousand watched, along with Rose and her mother, Joe Kennedy and other friends as the mayor, grinning broadly, climbed into the rear cockpit of British air ace Claude Grahame-White's biplane. As the propeller whirled and the fragile craft took off, an observer noted that Rose looked troubled. She glanced at her mother's face to see if it showed alarm, and, although it did not, she couldn't suppress a look of anxiety. The observer noted she seemed to be saying "I don't like this at all. I wish Father would come down!"

She disliked the idea of airplanes after that. And now she was caught up in her father's energetic anti-millinery campaign. In November, she attended a concert with him at Symphony Hall. Seated several rows from the stage, the family was unable to see conductor or orchestra because of enormous feathered hats. Honey Fitz was furious; the next day, he delivered an edict from City Hall forbidding any woman to wear a hat in a public place—a complete reversal of the current rules of fashion. So sensational was his announcement that it made the editorial page of the *New York Times* on November 10. The side effect was that Rose, Josie and Agnes had to go hatless in public—a great mortification.

Boston women's clubs protested, issuing a statement that concerts were for listening, not seeing. But nobody could gainsay the mayor. When he turned up with his family at Symphony Hall that Saturday night, not a hat was to be seen. The Brahmins were unfazed. They continued their timeworn practice of attending only afternoon rehearsals, at which they ostentatiously wore their largest, most extravagant and opulently feathered hats.

That fall, Fitzgerald formed a strong acquaintance, ripening into friendship, with the Republican president, William Howard Taft. His relationship with Taft resembled that which he had developed with William McKinley. Paradoxically, this scourge of the Republicans had never liked the Democrats in the White House. Honey Fitz was a frequent guest of the White House, Rose accompanying him on at least one occasion to dinner.

Rose was busy with classes in piano and voice at the New England Conservatory. At the turn of the new year, 1911, she was faced with the challenge of organizing her debut into Boston society. She and her mother worked tirelessly day and night, all through Christmas, to prepare for it. They ordered hundreds of American Beauty roses brought from hothouses to fill the house from upstairs landings to their drawing room. They hired decorators to convert the veranda into a conservatory, filled with orchids and dwarf palms and alive with multicolored fairy lights, as well as three splashing marble fountains. They bought two dozen giant Christmas trees, which they festooned with ornaments and placed along the front of the house.

Shamrock and Killarney ferns imported from Ireland were strung from the chandeliers and from the bannisters of the staircase, at whose foot Rose placed a Lalique glass swan sitting on a mirror lake. The walls were festooned with mountain laurel. Rose spent hours inscribing more than 500 invitations and annotating in a record book acceptances from 450. On the eve of the party, New Year's night, teams of butlers, waiters and kitchen staff poured in, and fresh cakes, scones and muffins were baked in the ovens so that the guests could enjoy a British-style afternoon tea.

Rose didn't hesitate in her choice of her debutante dress. She selected a white Italian chiffon gown she had bought during a vacation in Paris, and she and her friends, Mollie Welch and Mary O'Connell, made sure that every seam was straight and that the corsage was impeccably in place.

The final touch of celebration was a life-sized clockwork papier-mâché figure of Santa Claus, standing to greet the guests at the center of the hallway, complete with red velvet cap and costume and a white cotton beard, nodding his head sagely at all comers.

On January 2, 1911, as the long procession of automobiles and horse-drawn carriages drew up in a light drizzle at the entrance at 3:00 P.M., Rose stood, her mother beside her, her father nervously pacing about, to meet the 450 guests, including Archbishop O'Connell and the governor of Massachusetts, one by one. For three hours, wearing elbow-length white kidskin gloves, she shook their hands. After tea, Rose discreetly allowed both Hugh Nawn and Joe Kennedy to dance with her. Then the young set went up to Rose's room, where they enjoyed supper and laughter till midnight.

Next morning Rose and her father made a royal visit to the Boston hospitals, to distribute the party flowers to the sick and dying. Interviewed by the *Boston Herald,* Rose said, "I'm sorry I can't do this every day of the year." Neither she nor her father failed to enjoy the wave of publicity that followed her debut.

On Washington's birthday in February she stood smilingly beside Fitz at a press conference and he said, "There are some things Washington did that I would not do, but let bygones be bygones. Washington was hampered by the fact that he and I were not contemporaries. But perhaps it is just as well for Washington's fame that he beat me to it!"

There was a great pleasure that month: her father told her he would be taking her to Palm Beach, the most popular society resort of the age. At first she was excited when he mentioned this at the Somerset Hotel over lunch. But then she realized that she had promised Joe she would go, that very week, to the Harvard Junior Dance as his girl. She said she couldn't possibly make the trip because of the previous engagement. Fitz told her he would not hear of her not coming. She could scarcely control her tears.

On February 25, Rose and her father left by train for Florida. She spent most of the journey hoping for some disaster short of a train wreck that would send her back to Joe, but she soon was consoled. Arriving at Palm Beach was an intoxicating experience, confined largely to the established rich. The Havana Special, the train that came from

New York, chugged into an elegantly appointed depot that was situated in the grounds of the Royal Poinciana Hotel. As it drew up, Rose saw one of the most impressive resorts on the North American continent. The sprawling yellow-painted hotel with its green-and-white-striped window awnings was flanked by palm trees, the Stars and Stripes flying from the roof. Beyond stretched the blue warm Atlantic. As she stepped onto the platform, the hotel orchestra greeted her and the other arrivals with a medley of favorite tunes. Black bellboys in red-and-green uniforms, their shoes and buttons shining, were lined up to take the luggage, in dance step, to the hotel's entrance.

The lobby was alive with the great names of America; the Astors, Vanderbilts and Wideners dominated the scene. Dukes and duchesses, counts and countesses, princes and princesses were everywhere, greeting their friends with exclamations. Even the Otis elevator ride was exciting. The Fitzgeralds' suite was floored with green tatami matting, the furniture of wicker, painted green; the wallpaper was also green. Green and white shutters kept out the sun. The beds were of mahogany, furnished with Irish linen and hand-made Italian damask covers.

A small program on gilt-edged vellum stood by the bed, announcing the events of the day—card parties, dances, performances, yacht trips and golfing, tennis and backgammon events. Journeys to town or to the beach were undertaken by Afromobiles, the contemporary name for bicycle-drawn wicker chairs on wheels operated by blacks. Breakfast, lunch, tea and dinner were accompanied by a palm court orchestra. Dinner was followed by dancing; typically on the menu were bluepoint oysters imported from Maine; roast quail, duck or pheasant; delicate salads; exquisitely fashioned desserts and hotel-ground coffee. White tie and tails for the men and silk or brocade evening gowns for the women were required.

The top of the week was the Thursday-night cakewalk. Blacks in red satin trousers and green frock coats danced to the ecstatic approval of the crowd; the best cakewalk prize was an icing-and-marzipan cake and a bottle of vintage champagne. And at the end of the season came the magnificent George Washington's Birthday Ball.

Rose had at last broken free of the drab existence of Boston. Unrestricted by her city's conventions, she could finally enjoy to the fullest the Protestant children of the rich.

Palm Beach was an ecumenical paradise: money and power were passwords, not birth and upbringing. Browning herself on the sand among the wealthy and beautiful, enjoying swimming-pool races against her father, she was in her element. She much enjoyed the ferry trips each morning across Lake Worth to attend Mass at West Palm Beach; there was no Catholic church at Palm Beach itself.

There was a capper. On June 19, she attended President and Mrs. Taft's twenty-fifth wedding anniversary party at the White House. Congressman James M. Curley, destined to be Honey Fitz's political nemesis and mayor of Boston, acted as her guide in the House of Representatives, and Rose managed to look interested as she sat through a debate on the Canadian reciprocity bill.

Rose began seeing Joe in Boston again, customarily wrapped in a scarf to hide most of her face while they were skating, in a vain attempt to disguise her identity. When she visited Concord, he arranged to be in a tennis match there. Once again she would make up fictitious names to place on her dance cards in case her father should get hold of them, and they sheltered themselves behind potted palms at dances in the hope that no one would see them kissing—a delicious, quite impossible, mildly dangerous masquerade. She came out into the open with her father, watching her hero win his letter at Soldiers Field in the Harvard-Yale football game, unable to resist jumping to her feet and cheering. But even this athletic victory of sturdily handsome Joe Kennedy didn't melt her father's stony heart. As if her calendar were not sufficiently full, Rose learned, in a state of extreme excitement, that her father would take her to Europe on a Boston Chamber of Commerce tour, starting with a second transatlantic crossing, aboard the liner *Franconia*. But once again she would miss Joe.

The departure of the vessel for Europe on June 26, 1911, was an event, one of the most spectacular sailings of any vessel in the history of Boston. At least six thousand people thronged the wharf as Rose fought up the gangway and

made her way to her stateroom. Joe Kennedy and Hugh
Nawn were waiting there to see her off, with champagne and
caviar, both beaux looking more handsome than ever.
American Beauty roses were displayed in enormous wicker
baskets filling almost every foot of floor space. As the family
struggled through well-wishers to the hurricane deck, more
roses arrived, all marked with their name, all piled up along
the corridors and companionways in rich profusion.

The ship sounded horns, whistles and sirens. The band
struck up "The Star Spangled Banner." Honey Fitz waved
the American flag; taking up a megaphone he had brought
with him, he addressed the crowd from the railing, talking
at machine-gun pace about the need for U.S.-European
cooperation. The crowd screamed as the band played
"Sweet Adeline" and Fitzgerald bawled the song across the
wind. Rose and Agnes joined in the chorus as streamers and
confetti swirled around them; the vessel moved slowly out
into the bay.

A shadow was cast over the trip. Rose hoped that Joe
Kennedy might be able to meet her in Europe, but the
demands of his studies were too heavy, and Honey Fitz had
instead cunningly arranged for Hugh Nawn to meet the
party in Ostend. Reporters were along for the voyage,
sending accounts from the wireless room every time Rose
played shuffleboard, military whist or cribbage.

She celebrated Independence Day on board; Fitz was in
charge of everything. Amos Luther of the *Boston Herald*
wrote that the mayor out-talked, out-danced, out-ate and
out-sang everyone else on the ship, and that his Independence Day fireworks, released from the boat deck, almost
set the vessel ablaze. He took over the Sunday service, in the
absence of minister or priest, delivering a sermon that ran
for an hour. He and Rose became known as the Admiral
and the Admiral's daughter.

Rose would shortly celebrate her twenty-first birthday. In
later years, she would portray herself in 1911 as severe,
scholarly, uninterested in social life; she was imposing on
that younger self a figure of straitlaced puritanism equivalent to that of a spinster in a Victorian novel. Photographs
and the day-to-day contemporary accounts by Boston news-

papermen, however, show a young woman who was instead energetic and attractive, with a fierce hold on life. Athletic, she exudes good health; her face, though perhaps not conventionally beautiful, seems contemporary in its appeal. She has a fresh look, with minimal makeup, chiseled cheekbones, eyes sparkling with vitality and humor, mouth parting in smiles over glistening all-American teeth. She could have been a skiing instructress or a swimming coach, with her sturdy figure, not soft and round and plump like most women's at that time, not buxom, full-bosomed and big-hipped. Instead, she is trim, well toned, a touch boyish, her rakish caps, windblown scarves and formfitting dresses augmenting her looks in a way that would not seem amiss half a century later, in a college in the East in the 1960s.

She wasn't cold and hard, as some have portrayed her, but brisk, open and happily in love with the man of her dreams. If she showed a ruthless opposition to her father's enemies, a refusal to believe in his guilts, that was appropriate in a daughter.

The trip to Europe was not a jaunt. The Fitzgeralds met up with the Chamber of Commerce party in London, where they studied social conditions firsthand. Rose was not a camp follower of this expedition, not just a dutiful daughter who helped out with packing and unpacking, dry-cleaning, laundry and tickets.

The tour took the group to France, Germany, Austria and Hungary. Rose made it her business to find out how women were treated in Europe. She was not a suffragette, nor was she a feminist. Staring out of train windows, she was shocked to see that three out of five people scything hay, wheat and rye in the fields were women; and in Hungary she observed with distaste that women used sledgehammers to knock down walls, carried bricks and delivered coal.

She noted female beggars in London; and in Paris, she realized the fact that marriage was a trade, in which a woman, sold by her parents to an eligible man, had no say in the matter. She noted that, after marriage, a European woman ran a household without reference to her husband, attaining a power and influence that would have been unthinkable in America. She found that women in Europe spoke more than one language and were far better educated

than their transatlantic equivalents. When she mingled with
the rich, she saw that they dressed modestly, wore little
jewelry and only a minimum of makeup—a major contrast
with the wealthy women Rose had encountered in Boston.

She took account of the greater emphasis in Europe on
the arts, especially painting. Her conclusion would have
surprised her contemporaries, who suffered from male
indifference and suppression: "Every American woman
should be proud she is an American. There is no place in
Europe where the men are so chivalrous and considerate of
their women as they are here."

One incident marred the trip. Honey Fitz gave a speech in
Hamburg, addressing business leaders on the importance of
commercial and cultural associations. He said, inter alia,
"We hope to make the acquaintance of those two other great
German cities, Vienna and Budapest." His words were
greeted with angry cries; he was reviled in the German and
Boston newspapers.

In Vienna, Hugh Nawn danced with her on the moonlit
deck of a Danube steamer, and she wondered if she loved
him after all—but no, there was only Joe.

The heat left even Honey Fitz exhausted; the family left
the tour in Innsbruck and took train and boat to England to
attend the yacht races at Cowes with Sir Thomas Lipton.
They returned, once more on the *Franconia,* from Queens-
town, Ireland, arriving to a hysterical celebration in Boston
on August 15.

They spent the rest of the summer at the Acorn, their
rented cottage overlooking Vineyard Sound at Falmouth,
on Cape Cod. Situated on a bluff, in the center of the
popular summer resort, the house was filled with the echoes
of Rose and her siblings' running and laughter. Visitors
streamed in by the dozen, throwing themselves into loung-
ing chairs or hammocks while a hard-pressed Josie Fitzgerald ran the staff in serving afternoon teas. Rose and Agnes
frequently invaded the Cottage Club, where they plunged
into *thés dansants* or card parties. They accompanied their
mother to receptions in a succession of Carpenter Gothic
houses; they watched baseball games in the park from their
porch.

Sometimes they enjoyed a flutter at the Casino, or went to balls at the Terrace Gables Hotel. They swam in a boisterous Atlantic and met, on more than one occasion, the Panama Canal's chief construction engineer, Colonel George W. Goethals, who invited an excited Rose to visit the Path Between the Seas before it was completed.

Those were enjoyable days. Rose's cup ran over when Joe Kennedy checked into the Oak Crest Hotel for weekends to risk Honey Fitz's wrath and call on her.

Life in America in 1911 was sweet. The future seemed endlessly bright; nothing disturbed the complacency of a nation that had not been invaded in more than a century and was bursting with prosperity. It was America's Century. In a few months, the sinking of the *Titanic* would create a sense of unease in American society. But not now; not now.

Although Rose talked about becoming her father's secretary, it was only in jest. Instead, she fancied, she might become a concert pianist. She began classes again at the New England Conservatory of Music in Boston under Alfred De Voto, starting on September 14. She was still a devoted pupil, but she would never be more than a party pianist, providing accompaniments to group singalongs.

An odd incident occurred in November. The famous Abbey Players of Ireland were in Boston to perform in J. M. Synge's *The Playboy of the Western World.* The word was out that the play contained dangerous language and criticism of the Mother Church. Honey Fitz forbade Rose to attend it, as well as condemning it generally without having read or seen it. Rose disobeyed him, fled the house and made her way into a cheap balcony seat. The evening was a disaster: the predominantly Irish Catholic audience screamed abuse at the stage, and many had to be thrown out. Rose was appalled by the dialogue; she left disgusted. Her innocence had been breached a fraction, but only a fraction.

It would never, in 104 years, be eliminated completely.

Rose was busy sewing for the poor Italians of North End, organizing Tuesday-afternoon lectures as well at the Ace of Clubs, which still held its meetings at the plush old Somerset Hotel. Every effort she made to join the exclusive Boston Junior League met with rebuffs. So far as the elite was concerned, she, as a Catholic, might just as well have been black or Jewish. The fact that she was the mayor's daughter made not the slightest difference.

She enjoyed a compensation: she was the belle of the ball at the all-women Catholic celebratory party at the Somerset to announce Archbishop O'Connell's elevation to the cardinalate. She accompanied her mother, who, as Mayor's Lady, headed the receiving line. Rose was first usher in white, a scarlet cardinal's ribbon crossing her chest. O'Connell never forgot the honor; Rose had forgiven him for blocking her path to Wellesley.

She took to heart his speech at the party in which he warned the women present that a woman's role was to please, to put her husband and children's welfare ahead of her own. Selfishness, he said, could not exist in a good wife and mother. These were her own mother's words exactly.

That winter, Honey Fitz and Josie suffered from influenza, but they were consoled by a still-deepening friendship with President and Mrs. Taft. Agnes was imprisoned at the Notre Dame Convent School at Elmhurst, Rhode Island. In April, Rose was with her father at a groundbreaking ceremony for a drinking fountain in honor of her grandmother, Rose Fitzgerald; she attended him at an auction of paintings from the estate of the late millionaire James Shepard. She worked tirelessly to raise money for the poor families of the *Titanic* victims.

Honey Fitz's ambition flared. In May 1912, just before the Baltimore Democratic Convention, he had his name put on the ballot in the empty space next to the vice-presidency slot. Hundreds in Massachusetts supported him. At an exhibition of horse jumping in Boston, which earned him much praise, he spoke of his ambition again. He was in Washington on May 28, pulling together New England Democrats for Baltimore, which he and Rose invaded in great spirits at the end of June.

On June 23, Joe Kennedy graduated from Harvard. Only success in business would suffice to shake Honey Fitz's opposition. Rose need not have worried. Joe Kennedy was ambition personified, single-minded in his determination to make good. He left the college with a Bachelor of Arts degree and a fine athletic record. His varsity "H" for the

1911 baseball season, awarded by the Harvard Athletic Association, was the biggest feather in his cap. He had prospered from running a tourist bus concession backed, surprisingly, by Honey Fitz, as well as from a real-estate operation. He wanted a career in banking.

Dominated by J. P. Morgan, the banking world offered unlimited opportunity for a shrewd and forward-looking young man. In 1912, the business was a public scandal. Bankers virtually ran the country, exercising monopolistic practices that would linger on until the 1930s.

James Jackson Storrow, with his sumptuous house, lavish furnishings and membership in the best clubs, provoked Joe's envy as much as he did Honey Fitz's.

Joe's target, Storrow's Lee, Higginson & Company, was an unshakable Boston bastion that a young Irish Catholic couldn't hope to break into. Joe had no alternative but to find a place in a lesser banking institution, The Columbia Trust Company, founded by his father in 1895 to serve the underprivileged. He had to make do with an apprenticeship, as clerk to treasurer Alfred Wellington. He studied to improve his position; he breezed through a civil-service examination in order to become a bank examiner, then threw himself on, of all people, Honey Fitz. Surprisingly, Fitz responded to his pleas and arranged a post for him through the governor, Eugene Foss.

The Fitzgeralds made a splash at the Democratic National Convention of 1912. But at some time during the proceedings Honey Fitz abandoned his plans to be vice-president. The reason was a sudden attack of malaria, from which he had suffered intermittently since the old days at Garden Court. He traveled with Josie and Rose to Falmouth to their summer cottage to recover.

From his sickbed, he seriously discussed the possibility of becoming Massachusetts governor. He was talked out of the idea by District Attorney Pelletier, who warned him that old scandals would be revived if he made so ambitious a move. Soon after, a tiny scandal did erupt: a florist sued him for an unpaid bill of $3,224.63 that included the flowers supplied for Rose's coming-out ceremony.

On November 14, with Sir Thomas Lipton among the guests, Agnes Fitzgerald was given a debut of her own at

Boston's Copley Plaza Hotel. Honey Fitz's warming to Joe Kennedy is indicated by the fact that he included him among the ushers with Hugh Nawn. Reporters asked Lipton to comment on his rumored engagement to a Denver society beauty. He said, "If you want to know who Lady Lipton is going to be, she is right here in this room! Stand up, Rose!" Everyone burst out laughing as Rose said, coyly, "I won't accept you, Sir Thomas. You're much too fickle!" Lipton remarked, "At last, for the first time, I know how it feels to be rejected by a woman!" The story was told for years; Rose was talking about it at least into her eighties.

Chapter 3

A Scandal at Home

The Fitzgeralds were in the news for the next six months. On October 7, they attended the Polo Grounds in New York as guests of Mayor Gaynor for the World Series. Honey Fitz was given the honor of throwing out the first ball. He and Rose cheered ecstatically when the Boston Red Sox won the first game (but later had to grit their teeth when the team's fortunes were reversed). An exhilarated Fitzgerald announced a Boston public holiday as a result.

Even a mayoral ordinance restricting the length of women's hat pins after Fitz sat on one made headlines. So did Rose and Agnes for having their portraits painted by the popular Albert R. Thayer—and even the ceremony of hanging the picture in pride of place over the Dorchester living-room fire.

When Fitz talked of being governor, consul general in London or postmaster general in Washington, reporters flocked to his office. He attacked a production of *Tosca* at the Boston Opera House, succeeding in having it toned down on a threat of depriving the opera company of its license. Every time he attended a party with Rose (insisting on Hugh Nawn as her escort) and Sir Thomas Lipton to organize support for Lipton's America's Cup entry of his yacht *Shamrock II,* the publicity was overwhelming. He banned smoking in office buildings.

Nineteen-thirteen began in shadows. The Finance Committee was busy again, investigating Fitzgerald's granting of locations for sightseeing buses to friends as favors. Joe Kennedy's name was mentioned because of the bus concession Honey Fitz had given him. Fitz stood by his right to make arrangements of the sort since he did not profit personally from them; he supported Joe against charges of corruption. He was weakening in his opposition to Joe's interest in his daughter.

There were other headaches for Rose. Fitzgerald hoped that, with the passage of time and his ever-increasing fame, he would at last be admitted to membership in the more exclusive Boston clubs, and that Rose and Agnes would be able to enter the sacred precincts of the women's clubs. Such hopes were again dashed. He was excluded for feeble reasons. When he was proposed for the Exchange Club, he was rejected on the pretext that he had been seen at his desk at City Hall in his shirtsleeves. Finding that the directors of Boston's Stone & Webster, insurers, belonged to the club's board, he responded with charges that they had failed to use $179 million in annual earnings to build up the city's commerce. He attacked associated money barons who had blocked his plans for launching a steamship line connecting Boston and Galveston.

In April, he accepted an invitation that left the travel-loving Rose in a state of delirium. He agreed to visit, along with the members of the Boston Chamber of Commerce, the uncompleted Panama Canal. Rose gave an account of the trip in the *Boston American* on May 24, 1913.

Traveling in the heavy clothes of the time was onerous on a summer trip. But it was well-nigh unendurable on this visit to the tropics. The voyage was an ordeal, equivalent to sailing in an oven. Yet Rose showed no sign of wear and tear in the photographs taken at various ports of call. More than ever, she had learned the necessity of appearing at her best in adverse conditions.

Sailing aboard the United Fruit Line steamer *Metapan,*

father and daughter arrived in Kingston, Jamaica, on May 1. Rose noted with dismay the sight of women breaking stones in quarries or trudging along dusty roads barefoot, carrying bundles of oranges and lemons. She saw that these Jamaican ladies had a masculine habit: they stopped often to puff away at cheap black cigars. She found that they walked between twenty and forty miles a day to earn between fifty cents and a dollar for a basket of fruit; lodgings cost them two cents a night. At dawn, they would set off in the early heat along dusty roads to start the procedure again.

Rose urged local authorities to raise the child-labor minimum age to fourteen. She talked to women who still washed their clothes in streams, rubbing their dresses with stones to remove the dirt. While other writers drooled about waving palms, snow white beaches and blinding sunsets, she concentrated entirely on social issues.

The *Metapan* sailed on through unruffled waters to Panama. It was an exciting visit, despite a temperature of 100 degrees and humidity so intense that it seemed to be raining indoors. She attended a reception given by the American minister and his wife at the Panama City legation, took a train to Taboga and an excursion to the entrance of the Canal to see the fortifications; she trudged between lines of beds at the American Sanitarium, saw a display of singing and dancing, and, at a ceremony on her return, received from President Porra the freedom of Panama City. She stepped down jungle paths, past spiders, reptiles and snakes, and sailed in a bark canoe, remembering not to trail her hand in piranha-infested waters.

Father and daughter returned to Boston in the best of spirits. Rose's article was accompanied by snapshots; she allowed herself a characteristic touch, noting that during the tours, "the women of our party were swelled with pride over the fact that they are Bostonians and so positively the superior womankind. . . ."

In September, William Randolph Hearst's *Cosmopolitan* displayed its owner's enthusiasm for the Fitzgeralds. A glowing article appeared, in which Fitz, his wife and his daughters were described in purple prose, their photograph dominating the page. The author wrote:

It is ... wholesome discipline that ... has produced
the Fitzgerald girls—young women, sane and comely,
typical specimens of true Americanism. Miss Rose, 22
years old [*sic*], though she looks but 18—comes first in
the galaxy. Brimming with animation and charm and
girlish spirits, she displays strength and depth of mind
rarely found in so young a woman. ... With her dark
hair and vivacious manner she is a foil to her fair-head
sister Agnes ...

This treatment in a popular national magazine set the
seal on Honey Fitz's career.

But already a power had emerged who would unseat him.
The formidable James Michael Curley was determined to
replace him as mayor. A former jailbird (he had served a
sentence for a malfeasance involving a public-service
exam), Curley was a blustering hellion whose massive
shoulders and loud voice made him a terror of the Boston
clubs and political meeting places. He detested Honey Fitz
with all his soul. He found no shortage of men who shared
his view. The mayor had been too successful too long. There
were many who were jealous of his fame; others shuddered
at the thought of one more rendition of "Sweet Adeline."
The defeated opponents of his mayoral campaigns had
never forgiven or forgotten. In the jungle of Boston politics,
he had been marked for imminent demise.

Curley found support in Daniel H. Coakley, who had
risen in the community since he had been lawyer to Honey
Fitz's ill-fated best friend, Michael Mitchell. Coakley was
determined to make Fitz pay for the treachery that had
resulted in Mitchell's destruction. To Coakley, the mayor
was a Judas. Coakley had been no angel himself; he had
betrayed Honey Fitz, from whom he had accepted the
sinecure of Commissioner of Parks, by turning against him
in the Coal Hearings that had almost brought Fitzgerald to
ruin.

Two weeks after the *Cosmopolitan* article appeared and
the telephones in Fitzgerald's office rang with congratulations, a statuesque blonde arrived at Coakley's law offices

and insisted on seeing him. When she stated her business, he had her ushered in. Her name was Elizabeth Ryan, known popularly as Toodles. Toodles was a cigarette girl working at a notorious trysting place, the Ferncroft Inn.

She told Coakley she wanted him to represent her in a breach of promise suit against the Inn's proprietor, Henry Mansfield. She stated that Mansfield had promised to marry her in return for certain favors and had failed to keep that promise.

Coakley agreed to take on her case. But he wasn't prepared for the bombshell that followed. She volunteered a list of men who had shown a sexual interest in her. Coakley could hardly believe his ears when she stated that one of these suitors was none other than John Francis Fitzgerald. Coakley pressed her for more details. She revealed that, horror of horrors, Fitzgerald had actually danced with her at the Inn and had caressed her while doing so; and that he had even presumed to plant a kiss on her lips.

Although she suggested nothing further, that was enough. Here was the pillar of propriety, the scourge of Boston's dance halls, theaters and Opera House, cavorting with a cigarette girl in a questionable public resort! Coakley gleefully showed the young woman out and called Curley. They had the ammunition they needed.

Unaware of impending disaster, Honey Fitz was ironically conducting a morals campaign seldom precedented even in Boston. He invaded dance halls with police, forbidding the newly popular tango because the dancers took suggestive positions; he cleared out anyone identified as under eighteen years of age and sent them home. He issued an ordinance that nobody under the age of consent be allowed to dance at all.

He banned performances of plays if they contained even harmless love scenes. He closed bars and bordellos. He was in the midst of this activity when, in late November, he received a shocking letter. Signed Martin Lomasney, who had promised him support against Curley, it was made up of only one sentence: "That woman you have been going with wants to know when she can see you again."

Fitzgerald stormed into Lomasney's Hendricks Club and

51

demanded to know what the letter meant. Lomasney stared at him icily and said, "I presume you destroyed it. That's enough." He turned his back and walked away.

Another letter arrived at the Fitzgerald residence on December 1. The mayor was out. Since the envelope was marked by a black border, suggesting the death of a friend or relative, Josie opened it immediately. Rose shared its contents. The two women were horrified by what they read.

The anonymous author stated the facts of Honey Fitz's affair with Toodles, and went on to say that, unless Fitzgerald abandoned his plans to be mayor, the facts would be given to the press, and he and his family would be ruined.

Normally, the two women would have dismissed so poisonous a missive with a laugh, seeing it as the ploy of a rival mayoral candidate. But they must have heard of Honey Fitz's dalliance because they accepted it at once as a statement of the truth. Rumors were one thing, a potential public charge was another. Shaken, they sat down to await the mayor's arrival for dinner.

As Fitz walked in, Josie flourished the letter in his face. An ugly scene followed. Mother and daughter talked of shame and disgrace; he of blackmail, lies, and the need to ignore the letter. Josie and Rose refused to accept his explanations. He must withdraw from the race at once.

It is easy to imagine the misery of dinner that night and breakfast in the morning. Fitzgerald told friends that sleep was out of the question. Then, in the early hours of December 3, a telephone call awoke the Dorchester household.

Fitz was told that the Arcadia Hotel, a lodging house that he had condemned as unfit for human habitation, had caught fire. He ran to his car and drove to the corner of Laconia and Washington streets. Firemen led him into the building, where he saw a horrifying sight. Naked men lay dead in doorways, through which they had fought to escape the suffocating smoke. Many, charred almost beyond recognition, were piled on the narrow stairs. As he struggled up to the roof, he saw other corpses. He was told that several had plunged to their deaths as they had tried to leap from building to building.

He called a press conference at Youngs Hotel. He told the

press what he had learned: that spontaneous combustion had exploded a storeroom and that the flames had leapt through the dormitories where men lay naked in three-tiered bunks, their clothes taken charge of by the manager lest they should skip out in the night without paying rent. He attacked the Fire Department for not having ladders high enough to reach the fourth floor. He denounced the owners in Back Bay and on Beacon Hill for neglecting the property, overlooking the fact that the owner was a merchant who was not received in those circles.

Followed by reporters, he spent the morning exploring seven other lodging houses, denouncing their conditions as the pressmen made notes. As the cars, led by his own, plowed along the snowy streets, he was greeted by a spectacle like a scene from Dante's *Inferno*, of dozens of nude men, insecurely wrapped in threadbare blankets, trailing along the sidewalks, looking hopelessly for shelter.

Next day, he was examining the fire escape at Union Lodging House when he had to crawl through a hole to a back staircase. Standing up, he stumbled and fell against an iron bannister. Caught by reporters, he escaped a fatal plunge down a twenty-foot stairwell. He dropped to the floor, almost insensible, groaning in anguish; his secretary, Edward Moore, revived him.

A combination of anxiety over Toodles Ryan, his wife and daughter's newfound contempt for him, the nights without sleep and the fumes of the lodging house had combined to shatter his seemingly indestructible character. Taken home by ambulance, he lay, hardly speaking, in bed for over a week. His long run of confident success had seemingly come to an end.

He managed to rally sufficiently to announce that he was withdrawing from the race on grounds of ill health; the incident at the Union House had saved him from having to answer publicly the charges made against him.

Curley announced that he would give a lecture on famous courtesans of history, from Cleopatra to Toodles Ryan. But as time went on the lecture seemed pointless, and Curley dropped the idea.

Fitzgerald produced a mangy rabbit from his hat. He proposed a stooge candidate: Thomas J. Kenny, president of the City Council, who reproduced in faded colors his master's exaggerated former campaign promises. Rising from his sickbed, Honey Fitz instructed Kenny on Curley's weaknesses, emphasizing his term in jail. The ploy failed to work: Curley clipped Kenny's wings and won the election.

Disillusioned by her father, Rose saw in Joe a bigger hero than ever. While Fitzgerald was engaged in last-minute saber rattling, Joe was involved in an effort to save his father's struggling bank, the Columbia Trust Company, from a takeover.

East Boston's First Ward National Bank was hellbent on absorbing Columbia, its smaller but aggressive rival. Joe got the tough assignment of wrecking the deal. He would have to make a deal with Columbia Trust's shareholders, outmatching First Ward's offer to buy out their shares. He needed a minimum of $100,000, or at least $3 million in 1990s money, and he had less than three weeks in which to raise it.

He fast-talked three of his father's brothers and a sister into investing substantial sums; then he ran into a roadblock. The shareholders insisted on more money. He needed an extra $15,000.

To whom should he turn? He thought of the young and prosperous Henry O'Meara, in whose Old Colony Realty Associates he was an investor. Then he turned to Eugene Thayer, president of Merchants National Bank.

Thayer was no pushover. Joe was tense when he arrived at the bank's headquarters. If Thayer refused to help, he could lose Columbia Trust.

He brought all of his skill and charm to bear on Thayer, pointing out to him the sum he had already raised. Thayer shook Joe's hand; O'Meara came in. An ecstatic Joe had achieved his purpose—his bank was saved.

Glowing from Rose's approval, he was, at twenty-five on January 20, 1914, unanimously voted into office as the youngest bank president in America. Four days later, in one of his last acts as mayor, Honey Fitz appointed him director of the Collateral Loan Company. It would prove to be a decidedly mixed blessing.

Unfortunate events followed. Not content with his triumph over Fitz, Curley subjected him to an ordeal on election day at Tremont Temple. While Fitzgerald sat silent and flushed with anger, the mayor charged him with stripping the city's treasury and repeating his spoils system. No sooner had Curley taken up office than he fired every employee whom the outgoing mayor had hired, including staffs of the Fitz-financed aquarium and zoo.

At this low point, Honey Fitz summoned up the nerve to forge an alliance, which he hoped might result in his future return to office.

The alliance he engineered was with one of his most vociferous critics, Cardinal O'Connell. Why did O'Connell, who must have gotten wind of the Toodles Ryan affair and had always disapproved of Fitz's shenanigans, agree to this accommodation? Because, as much political animal as shrewd churchman, the cardinal clearly saw the benefit of uniting two powerful Catholic families in what he now saw as the approaching match of Rose and Joe.

Cardinal and rogue former mayor met in an opportunistic harmony that resulted in a surprising decision.

While the rumors that flew around Honey Fitz and his defeat in the polls made him uncomfortable about having Rose and Joe wedded in a cathedral, it would be politically desirable to have O'Connell conduct the ceremony himself in the private chapel of his house.

For Rose, it was a consolation prize for losing the gala occasion to which she looked forward. On the first day of summer, June 21, 1914, Rose's engagement to Joe was officially announced.

Simultaneously, Fitz bought the Oak Hall Clothing Company on Washington Street. An advertisement offered a caricature of him embracing the building, followed by an announcement:

Before becoming active in the management of this Old and Famous Clothing Store, it is my desire that all merchandise be sold regardless of its original cost or its cost to me and to this end the (former) management is to be continued. My instructions to them are to sell cheaply and quickly. I want my entrance into the clothing field of Boston to go down in history as the greatest bargain-giving event in the annals of merchandising in all New England. My $12.50 suits go for $6.25 and my $2 trousers for one dollar.

Engagement showers, receptions and gala balls followed. But these cheerful occasions were haunted by threatening events. The United States and Mexico were on the brink of war. On April 21, U.S. Marines seized the port of Veracruz; on June 24, a protocol was signed that ended the conflict and President Victoriano Huerta fled the country. Civil war broke out when Francisco Villa, insurgent lieutenant of the new president, Venustiano Cadranta, caused violent unrest that coincided with the opening of the Panama Canal.

On June 28, Gabrilo Princip, a Bosnian terrorist, shot and killed Archduke Franz Ferdinand at Sarajevo, thus setting off the spark that would result in the conflagration of World War I.

It is typical of Rose's career that the frivolous events preceding her marriage would occur while the outside world became increasingly dangerous. During her stay at the oceanside resort of Hull that summer, an incident occurred that shocked America. On July 11, 1914, it appeared that there was an enemy attack as a series of shells landed on the beach, causing explosions and injuring several people. She must have thought the war had begun. In reality, artillery squads at a Boston fort had been practicing gunfire recklessly and without regard for safety. On August 4, as she was picking out her nuptial gown, Britain declared war on Germany. Could America stay out?

Chapter 4

A Dangerous Motherhood

~❧~

While events overseas were increasingly ominous, those on Rose's home front were not reassuring either. Joe rapidly found that his future father-in-law's placing him on the board of the Collateral Loan Company was not a favor, but rather a trap.

What was the Collateral Loan Company? In effect, it was a glorified pawnbroker, originally created in 1859 as the Pawners' Bank. Those who had neither bonds, land nor houses as collateral would stream into the building from morning until evening carrying with them clothes, jewelry, furniture, anything that would move. Many could not redeem their possessions, and at the end of each year there would be a sad spectacle as lifetime possessions were heaped at the doors and crowds of people fought among them looking for valuables. So widespread was criticism of these ugly events that the bank was finally compelled to give a substantial portion of the proceeds from these jumble sales to charity.

The duplicitous Honey Fitz must have known that he was pitching Joe into a hornet's nest. He no doubt hoped that the young man would both act as a front for the institution's atrocious accounting and clean it up before the government inspectors could move in. Those hopes were rapidly dashed. Instead of hiding the directors' malfeasances, Joe, mindful of his own future and that of his growing family, took the only sensible course, one of complete honesty. He encouraged police and government investigators, accompanying them as they ransacked filing cabinets and turned out desk drawers, uncovering a series of fraudulent activities.

The president of the company was allowed to resign, although a more appropriate treatment would have been to send him to trial. It turned out that, in league with one of the members of the executive board, he had embezzled at least $26,000. The strain of dealing with the matter exhausted even Joe's vigorous constitution; the only relief he had was on weekends, when he could join Rose at dance palaces, where he shared with her the pleasures of the tango her father had publicly condemned, or attend Saturday night concerts at Symphony Hall. There were momentary joys such as a letter from Sir Thomas Lipton, writing aboard the yacht *Erin* at Southampton, England. Received on July 16, it read, "Rose's fiancé is a very lucky chap. He is getting a girl that is one of the best and cleverest that ever breathed. . . ."

War broke out in Europe at the beginning of August. On that date, Joe was busy completing plans to buy a house at 83 Beals Street, in the pleasant, leafy Boston suburb of Brookline. He added to his burden of debt by borrowing $2,000 from his father and taking out the $4,500 mortgage with his own Columbia Trust at three-percent interest.

The neighborhood was very "middle class" at the time; it was by no means an elite neighborhood. Neighbors were lower-level professionals, poorly paid white-collar workers who mingled with higher-level blue collars at the trolley stops or neighborhood meeting places. The house was just two away from a plumber's. At the more fashionable end of the street, there were some large and stately Victorian houses, with eaves and stained-glass windows and proper porches; by the time the Kennedy lot was reached, the size of the homes dwindled and their appearance was notably shabbier.

There were vacant lots to the east side of the house and immediately across the street; these were appealing to Rose, as she wanted her children, as they grew older, to have more than a yard to play in.

Joe Kennedy's was the only house in the neighborhood to have been built, some six years earlier, from a standard model rather than being custom-built for its owners, the latter a surprisingly frequent policy even for the petit bourgeoisie. This humiliating fact must have bitten into Rose's soul. The effect of the house was externally not displeasing, as formal and artificial as a doll's house. But inside, it was, as it remains today, oddly unprepossessing. Too many small rooms were jammed into the limited space. The top floor, or attic, housed the maids. Directly below, the master bedroom was plain and almost square, with twin beds—unusual for those days. Next door was a tiny sewing room. There was only one bathroom, shared by everyone, including the servants. The children's room had illustrated wallpaper, but was otherwise not charming. The dining room on the main floor was cramped, claustrophobic, with just enough space for a dining table seating six and a separate baby table for present or expected arrivals. Customarily, Honey Fitz's wedding gift of a clover-patterned sterling silver service was laid out on the sideboard.

In view of Joe's love of group sings, a piano dominated the living room. Prints of Constable, Rembrandt and Eugène Claude decorated the walls. The kitchen was gloomy; it offered a coal-and-gas-burning Franklin stove, a weird contraption that was used as a toaster, and an ugly soapstone sink. The result was scarcely inspiring. The house was a far cry from the vulgar splendor of the Fitzgerald house on Welles Avenue, and it is doubtful if Rose was ever very happy there.

In her memoirs, Rose summed up that pre-wedding season as one of lazy, prolonged tea parties and leisurely evenings, but clearly time had colored her memories. Struggling to deal with his corrupt and embattled fellow directors, working two jobs, Joe can have had little time for any such indulgences. And the advent of war cast a shadow on the nation. The atmosphere was one of isolationism, a feeling that Americans, whose parents, grandparents or great-grandparents had left Europe to cast aside the conflicts of kings and princes in the freedom and openness of a new land, would not wish to commit themselves to Britain's —and the Continent's—war. Further, millions were of Irish descent, followed the Pope's antiwar statements and had no love of the English. Millions more owed their allegiances to Germany. Why would they want to fight their own cousins? Joe, like most of his fellow Americans from President Wilson down, entirely shared that view.

There was no reason for Rose to differ with it. Like most women, she prayed that her man would not be faced with injury or death on behalf of Great Britain. And indeed it would be hard to believe in the validity of a war that had become at once brutal and pointless, based upon meaningless conflicts in Europe.

A decision had to be made on the circumstances of the couple's marriage. It was not desirable to make of the nuptials a large public event. The controversy centering on Joe's pawnbrokerage as well as the adverse publicity faced by Honey Fitz (worse now because it was claimed that he was overcharging at his clothing store) called for a discreet occasion that would be honored by the highest level of the Roman Catholic Church. Joe and Rose, backed by their separate parents, made an ingenious decision. Cardinal O'Connell, who continued to find Honey Fitz an embarrassment, would be approached to make an extraordinary concession. He would marry the couple in person, not in the Cathedral but in the private chapel of his elaborately furnished mansion at 25 Granby Street. It was a masterpiece of strategy: O'Connell could scarcely refuse.

The wedding took place on October 7, 1914. The only guests apart from immediate family were Kennedy's closest friends, Mr. and Mrs. Joe Donovan. None of Rose's circle was in attendance. Press attendance was limited to those who were known to be supportive. Following the ceremony, the party drove by automobile to the Dorchester House, where there was a quiet wedding breakfast at 10:00 A.M. for seventy-five.

The couple spent the first three nights in their new house. On the fourth morning, they took a train south, with a change in Washington, D.C., to their selected honeymoon resort: the Greenbrier Hotel, at White Sulphur Springs, West Virginia, considered at the time the most desirable of hostelries north of Palm Beach.

The Greenbrier was magnificent both in size and in decor, its public rooms glittering with chandeliers and expensive furniture, a riot of 1914 velvet plush extravagance. It is easy to see why the hotel appealed to the Kennedys. As at Palm Beach, they could mingle with society figures, including the Boston elite, who so definitively snubbed them at home. The Greenbrier, like the Poinciana at Palm Beach, was ecumenical, demanding from its guests only money, position and appearance.

The arrival at White Sulphur Springs depot was appropriately romantic. A stagecoach greeted the Kennedys; trundled along the gravel driveway to the hotel, they were greeted by handsomely uniformed porters, who carried the luggage up to Room 145, situated directly over the north entrance. The chamber was peculiarly chosen; it was the most publicly visible in the hotel, so that in effect they would be conducting their honeymoon in the equivalent of the mezzanine in a popular theater. Given the modest behavior of the time, it is likely they made sure the curtains were drawn every time they kissed.

From their windows, they looked out through a classical façade of fluted columns onto a splendid sight. Manicured lawns flanked by white oak trees turning a brilliant gold in the fall season stretched as far as the eye could see. Horses, their chestnut hides polished and shining, frisked their tails in tethers, ready to be commandeered for daylong rides. Automobiles roared in and out as the wealthy and famous of America arrived and departed in a buzz of excited conversation. The manager, Frederick Sterry, formerly of the Plaza in New York, was a warm and accommodating host. He and his staff did everything to make the honeymoon couple comfortable.

Rose and Joe were inseparable as they lobbed balls across the tennis court, trudged across the eighteen-hole golf course, and rode along scores of miles of trails. In the evening, there were delicious dinners, accompanied by an orchestra playing popular tunes; the couple danced cheek-to-cheek to their hearts' content. And on one balmy night during that unforgettable stay their lovemaking resulted in the conception of their first child.

The biggest event of that week was the spectacular arrival of the multimillionaire steel magnate Charles Schwab, with his wife, maid, valet and chauffeur, who came by private railroad car from New York, and were met by their own special tallyho from the station. While in residence, they used a new-model Rolls-Royce. They took four rooms, 347, 349, 351 and 353, and they caused a hubbub in the hotel, of which they were, for years, frequent guests. Honey Fitz knew Schwab well, and so did many other friends of the Kennedys, and it would be no mere conjecture to state that it was on this occasion, during his honeymoon, that Joe Kennedy formed the basis of what would be a richly profitable professional relationship in the future.

Troubles at the Collateral Loan Company had worsened in Joe's absence. And Rose's beloved uncle George, with whom she had shared many hard times in the North End, was suffering from a paralytic stroke in his early forties. He died at McLean Hospital on October 29.

Settling into the cramped, book-lined Beals Street house was not comfortable for Rose. She couldn't face having the baby in so inadequate a residence. Instead, she returned for the spring and summer of 1915 to Nantasket, hoping that the Boston Harbor garrison would not repeat its lobbing of shells into the residential district. There was the special advantage that Dr. Frederick L. Good, an obstetrician and friend of the family, would be spending his summer vacation there; Rose would trust no other physician to deliver her firstborn.

Since the Nantasket house rented in the summer of 1914 was now in occupancy, Joe instead took the Italianate Villa Napoli at 201 Atlantic Avenue. Overlooking the ocean, it was close to two gambling casinos. Joe spent the weekday evenings at Beals Street and then, on Saturday mornings, drove two hours to Atlantic Avenue to be with Rose until Sunday night.

Honey Fitz, fighting one of his battles with the political leader Martin Lomasney, made a mistake during the stay. Lomasney numbered among his friends Boss John Smith, the roughneck political operator who ran Nantasket as his private domain. Smith owned the Nantasket Ice Company and several other companies, and anyone who spent vacations in the resort had to pay tribute along with the citizens either in the form of invitations to expensive lunches or dinners or making him the guest of honor at parties. In 1911, when a Boston newspaper published a critical article on him, Smith had the reporter's house set on fire.

Honey Fitz attended a Nantasket town meeting and unwisely criticized Smith's political machine. Next day, Rose walked out the front door to find a ditch, five feet wide and seven feet deep, and Joe's attempt to have it filled was refused by local workmen.

On May 7, the *Lusitania* was sunk with a loss of 1,198 lives, including 139 Americans. It was determined, but not made public, that the vessel had been carrying munitions, loaded in New York, in defiance of U.S. neutrality. The news from Europe was bad. Between April 22 and May 25, there was the second battle of Ypres, in which Germans used poisonous gas that caused blindness as well as agonizing death. Then, from June 18, after the second battle of Artois, in which General Petain broke through the German lines and became an international hero, there was a summer lull in the fighting, as the Allies prepared for a great offensive.

Joe and Rose's attitude, that of noninvolvement, did not change. Indeed, Cardinal O'Connell, their mentor, vigorously sustained it. Pope Benedict XV, who had blessed their wedding, made it clear to all American Catholics that the world conflict was unacceptable in the eyes of God and that all must refuse to enter the conflict while he acted as mediator among the warring powers. The couple was deeply influenced by this stance.

At some time in those months, Rose made a remarkable decision. Until the turn of the century, ether or chloroform was customarily used for mothers during childbirth. Ether, in particular, was unpleasant to smell and to inhale; it had caused numerous deaths of mothers and children during the years of its popular use. Because of ether, a baby would be born unconscious; the mother would be unable to help the obstetrician by bearing down during labor. Physicians relied on involuntary muscular contractions, but the child had to be removed by forceps. The doctor would insert this formidable instrument into the passage, and literally drag the insensible infant out, gripping it by the head. One slip and the child could be permanently injured or brain-damaged.

In selecting ether, Rose was being deliberately old-fashioned, working against the overwhelming current trend. By 1915, the prescribed method of treating well-to-do mothers in the United States was known as twilight sleep. The method had been developed at the outset of the war by doctors in Freiburg, Germany; they called it *Dammerschlaf*. An obstetrician's nurse would inject the patient with an equal blend of morphine and scopolamine, which would render her groggy, not entirely insensitive to pain, and capable of assisting in the birth. So popular had twilight sleep become by the time Rose was pregnant that rich Americans traveled to Freiburg at considerable danger to themselves, by train or by automobile, through war-torn France, hundreds of miles with bombs exploding around, and to the accompaniment of machine-gun bullets, to experience the treatment at first hand. American magazines such as *Good Housekeeping* and *Ladies' Home Journal* devoted long and enthusiastic articles to the subject, articles which sent circulation soaring into the stratosphere. Certainly such journals made their way into the well-read Rose's living room at Beals Street.

In Boston, particularly, twilight sleep was the favored treatment, but Dr. Frederick L. Good, Rose's obstetrician, a devout Catholic, and the inventor of the Good forceps, whose wife Lee was a childhood friend of Rose's, and his associate, Dr. Edward O'Brien, did not favor it. Rose evidently could not face even the minimum of pain. And she may not have been entirely wrong in her decision. An unadvertised aspect of twilight sleep was that, in rare cases, there could be an overdose which would cause the birth of a "blue baby," an infant dead of asphyxiation.

There would be no question of the birth taking place at a hospital. Hospitals were considered unsanitary, unreliable and inappropriate if one had money. An obstetrician would install himself in a house with an entire nursing team—midwives had not attended such occasions in the prosperous classes since the turn of the century. Husbands were not admitted to the birth chamber; the custom of the male parent experiencing the joy of seeing his child born did not occur until the 1960s. Childbirth was not thought of as a revelation of life, a sharing of pain and joy by the parents at first hand, but rather as an unpleasant but necessary ordeal, to be overcome as quickly and as painlessly as possible, rather like an operation for appendicitis.

Nor was it likely that a child would come into the world as a result of mutual and uncontrollable desire. Exhaustive surveys of women, released from the restrictions of privacy, indicate that it would be many years after 1915 before the average woman would expect, as part of the marital experience, to enjoy sex. Intercourse was a burden to be endured for the sake of the continuance of a family line. Men did not take into account the need to give their wives pleasure. In fact, popular literature, theater and movies of that age emphasized the fact that women endured their husbands' embraces and remained essentially chaste, while a man would find true pleasure in the arms of a vamp. "Loose" women were supposed to be the only members of the female sex who would actually, and sinfully, relish sexual congress.

Such was the cloud of ignorance under which Rose Fitzgerald Kennedy labored as she awaited the arrival of her firstborn.

The atmosphere of the Villa Napoli was charged on the morning of July 25, 1915, as Joe Kennedy, following the customary tradition, paced outside the bedroom while Dr. Good and his team toiled to drag the child by forceps from the womb. At last, the baby appeared, a boisterous ten pounds, ten ounces, suggesting a potential giant. Losing his customary composure, the doctor announced very loudly, "It's a boy!" Reporters waiting downstairs rushed to the telephone to announce, one by one, the news for which Boston's front pages had already been cleared. Then they ran, some less athletic than others, to the beach to surround

Honey Fitz, who was playing ball with his nine-year-old son Fred. Without hesitation, the irrepressible former mayor announced that the child would be called Joseph, would be entered at once for Harvard, and would in due course become president of the United States.

Rose was reluctant to return to Boston. Apart from the then-recommended policy of having a mother rest for weeks after giving birth, there was danger in the air. Just ten days before Joe, Jr., was born, Heinrich Albert, German agent, accidentally left a briefcase in a Manhattan subway, which was found to contain proof of a spy and sabotage ring operating against American interests. Explosions occurred in Boston, New York and other cities.

It was felt desirable for Rose to remain where she was; Joe returned to Boston, turning up at Nantasket to visit his wife and child weekends.

At last, in mid-September, Joe took Rose and Joe, Jr., home in "the people's car," his brand-new Model T Ford. In the cramped house on Beals Street, Rose did her best to make the living conditions more comfortable. She hired an Irish nurse, Kate Conboy, and a French maid, Alice Michelan, both of whom were accommodated on the top floor; she had a desk put in her sewing room and entered the baby's daily progress on cards instead of in the usual baby book. She put a protective gate on the front porch and an extra fence in the backyard to prevent the child from crawling out of sight. Joe, Jr., proved robust and breezed through every setback of his infancy.

Rose raised her baby on principles drawn from the then sacred pages of Dr. L. Emmett Holt's *The Care and Feeding of Children*. Holt adhered to a policy of disciplined child rearing that appealed to this most strict and orderly of mothers. He forbade fondling the baby, though he did advocate breast-feeding. The feeding was to take place every other hour on the hour. Following Dr. Holt, Rose would bring up her children as though to a metronome, expecting perfection from them as they learned to expect it from her, showing little acknowledgment of any flaws that might exist, because a Kennedy wasn't supposed to be flawed.

Sir Thomas Lipton arrived, with his publicist, Charles

Higham (later, Sir Charles), to see the baby. The house was filled to overflowing with gifts. Meanwhile, Joe continued to be busy. He had surrendered his directorship of the Collateral Loan Company by prior agreement the previous December, but he worked constantly on the affairs of the Columbia Trust.

Nothing could stop his annual winter vacation in Palm Beach, however. On February 29, 1916, he and Rose arrived on the Havana Limited with a large party that included Honey Fitz and Mrs. Fitzgerald, Fitz's brother James, and friends of the family including Milton Duffy, Ben Devine, and the socially prominent Mr. and Mrs. Sanford Petz.

Something happened to spoil the trip. Boston's Mayor Curley, Fitz's political nemesis and still his most persistent enemy, arrived on the same train and throughout the visit the Kennedys and the Fitzgeralds were forced to tolerate his obnoxious presence at the beach festivities, the cakewalk, and at mealtimes.

Back in Brookline, Joe kept the household in a constant state of excitement. Each morning at six, he rose briskly from his bed and plunged into a vigorous series of exercises with Indian clubs, the equivalents of free weights today. Then he strode into Junior's room to see how he was in his cradle and to make sure that Kate Conboy was attending to her duties. He said prayers before breakfast.

After breakfast, Rose went to the sewing room to fill out the baby cards. Joe took off for the bank in the Model T, driving so fast that he was involved in at least one accident—he was far too impatient to take a trolley or a train. He marched through the lobby of the bank building, sat down hard at his desk and roared like a lion for his secretary. He talked a blue streak for hours on end, using a silencer on the telephone in case he should be overheard. His staff were alternately frightened by his yells or melted into submission by his charm. He was generous with loans, but ruthless in collecting when they were not repaid. Not as particular as he should have been about collateral, he repossessed without a tremor.

In addition to putting Joe down for Harvard, he started a savings account for him at Columbia Trust's Savings and Thrift Department, at the age of one month. On the rare evenings when he was home, he and Rose would join their friends Vince and Marie Greene for bridge, followed by a feast of ice cream. Saturday evenings during the season were reserved for Symphony Hall. Rose would sit on the edge of her seat, drinking in the music, while Joe, exhausted after a week of hard work, tended to doze.

Domestic pleasures and strains muffled the terrible news from Europe—of the slaughter in the trenches in the rain and mud of Verdun. On March 24, 1916, the *Sussex* was sunk by a torpedo in the English Channel, and Americans died. The United States was on the brink of war until President Woodrow Wilson's ultimatum forced Germany to suspend, for the time being, unrestricted submarine warfare. But it was only a temporary concession. Losses of the British fleet at the battle of Jutland provoked Charles Schwab and other American steel magnates to infringe the neutrality laws and build ships for England in Canada.

By the summer of 1916, the loss of thousands of gallant young Englishmen changed the temper of American youth. Bored by the restrictions of family and a dull provincial existence, American males saw opportunities for adventure and glory in foreign uniforms. Criticism attached to Joe because he did not share this feeling and did not indicate any desire, then or later, to serve overseas. Yet, for an Irish Catholic, there could be no question of any such commitment. Pope Benedict XV went on issuing pastorals in opposition to the war. On April 24, in response to a military service bill passed by British parliament, the Irish, guided by the Vatican, refused to enlist; the Easter rebellion that followed was rapidly and brutally suppressed.

There can be no doubt where the devout Rose's, and the somewhat less devout Joe's, sympathies in the matter lay. As in World War II, they followed the Vatican and the papal policies more than those laid down in Washington.

In July 1916, three of Joe's Harvard pals, the Protestant athletes Bob Fisher, Tom Campbell and Bob Potter, spent the holiday weekend with him at his parents' house at Winthrop. Independence Day saw the beginning of the British advance on the River Somme, a bloody and desperate battle which would result in the loss of sixty thousand young Englishmen in one day.

Joe's friends applauded the British courage. Joe risked charges of cowardice and violently opposed them. His outburst of pacifistic rage had them driving off in disgust.

Rose found herself pregnant again.

War came to Americans' doorsteps that July. On July 30, just twenty-six days after the confrontation at Winthrop, German saboteurs blew up the naval dock and explosives plant at Black Tom Island in Jersey City, New Jersey.

Rose and Joe remained Roman pacifists.

Honey Fitz agreed with his daughter. Although he later changed his attitude, he felt, with President Wilson, that America could be of the greatest aid to Britain if she were not involved in the conflict, but sent supplies and arms instead. Fitz was convinced that a threat to American neutrality was offered by the fire-breathing Senator Henry Cabot Lodge of Massachusetts. Although Lodge did not favor involvement, but rather increased defenses, Honey Fitz was convinced that Lodge was dangerous. Learning that Lodge would run for reelection in the fall, he decided to oppose him. Though in shaky health, still shadowed by the Toodles affair, and visibly aging, the fifty-three-year-old Fitz was determined to go ahead. With a combination of battered rhetoric and renditions of "Sweet Adeline," he charged through an unopposed campaign for the Democratic primary, polling 64,551 votes. Then, in October, no longer the gutsy Honey Fitz of yesteryear, he panicked before Lodge's political machine. His cries of Lodge's warmongering began to sound like whistling in the wind; he offered to withdraw his candidacy if President Woodrow Wilson would prefer it.

The president did not; he detested Lodge, who, supported by such figures as the navy's Admiral Sims, began accusing Honey Fitz of encouraging cowardice, vacillation and weakness in the military arm. On November 8, Lodge defeated Fitzgerald 267,177 to 234,238, a surprisingly narrow victory. Triumphantly reelected, President Wilson began paradoxically to lean toward Lodge, at least in the matter of building a military machine.

The news was increasingly troublesome. In February, Rose and Joe read that the Germans were seeking a Mexican-Japanese axis that would result in an invasion of

Texas, New Mexico and Arizona. When that plan was revealed by the publication of the infamous Zimmerman note, America was in the grip of hysteria. The lower house of Congress passed, by 403 to 13, a bill to arm all U.S. merchant vessels in the Atlantic. When a filibuster defeated the bill in the Senate, Wilson assumed emergency powers; after German U-boats sank three American warships, America declared war on April 6, 1917.

Honey Fitz changed his tune and not only called for every young American to volunteer, but supported conscription and invaded Washington and the White House demanding that every foreigner, whether intended to be a U.S. citizen or not, must agree to enlistment at once. Joe remained opposed. Although by law he would have to register when conscription became compulsory, Rose prayed he would not be included in the first ballots.

In the last week of May 1917, Rose felt the first contractions that announced the imminent birth of her second child. Dr. Good was summoned, and once again Rose was put under ether. At 3:00 P.M. on May 29, John Fitzgerald Kennedy was born. It is possible the forceps birth affected his spine—a problem that would haunt him for life. Twenty-one days later, a dangerously long interval owing to his weak health, John was baptized by Monsignor John T. Creah at St. Aidan's.

Amid fierce controversy—many Americans associated conscription with dictatorship—the Draft Act, enacted before war broke out, was implemented on June 5, 1917. At a meeting in Washington of political and service leaders on July 20, numbers were drawn from an enormous bowl; the number pulled out by the blindfolded secretary of war, Newton D. Baker, settled the issue of which young man in each town ballot would be chosen for enlistment. He drew number 258; whichever youth pulled that number out of the box would be brought in for medical examination. The enlistees who drew 258 represented over a million men. Surprisingly few were excluded for physical problems.

To Rose's distress, two of her brothers, Thomas and John, Jr., though not numbered in the ballot, chose to enlist: Thomas in the army and John, Jr., in the navy. It is easy to picture her anguish when Thomas was sent to the dangerous and terrifying French front line. From day to day, she was uncertain of his fate. At any time a telegram might announce that he had been killed.

It rubbed salt in the family's wounds when Honey Fitz's political opponent Peter Tague in later years told reporters, who published the story in the Boston newspapers, that Fitz had hidden Thomas deliberately in an obscure corner of Pennsylvania so that he would evade service. When Honey Fitz wrote a letter of denial to the *Boston Post,* which featured this falsehood prominently, Tague had one of his contacts pull a string at the *Post* to have the letter pulled at two o'clock in the morning.

That same month, Rose had only to pick up the paper to read of strikes breaking out all over the country, delaying seriously the delivery of submarines and destroyers. The strike infuriated Joe. On July 2, fifteen thousand employees of the Hoboken and Brooklyn yards walked out; eighteen days later, the unions closed the Staten Island Ship Building Company. On August 30, Seattle longshoremen struck, followed by San Francisco riveters and carpenters. In desperation, the government agreed to pay fifty percent of wage increases, called for by labor's demands, if shipyard owners were found to be making less than ten percent profit in production.

Boston was at the center of similar upheavals, which were provoked by radicals in sympathy with the revolutionary movement in Russia and the provisional government, some members of which wanted to bring the war with Germany to an end.

Twice in June, explosions sent clouds of smoke into the sky as Rose took her boys out with nurse Kate Conboy on their morning walks by baby carriage. It was the start of her own, and Joe's, lifelong fear and hatred of socialism as the greatest of all evils, a threat to their lives and the most important target of criticism from both Pope Benedict XV and Cardinal O'Connell.

Two years before the Great Red Scare of 1919, Boston women feared that socialists would burn their houses and kill their children.

Militant meetings were held by Boston left-wingers, culminating in a full-scale militant parade on Sunday, July 1,

1917. Despite protests by Joe Kennedy and Honey Fitz, Mayor Curley permitted the march to take place, in the interests of free speech. Several thousand joined in it, including members of the Wobblies, the Central Branch of the Socialist Party, and the pro-Lenin Bostonian Jewish Branch.

Following a stormy series of speeches on Boston Common in the heart of the city's business district, the marchers, carrying huge red banners with antiwar slogans, made their way to Tremont Street, where they ran into a thousand furious citizens and three hundred soldiers and sailors. The mob charged them, tore their flags from their hands and beat many to the ground. Women and children, including babies, lay bleeding in the gutter, and a journalist who tried to interview one of the attackers had his glasses broken and was beaten severely. In a matter of minutes, the conflict had exploded into a full-scale riot. Twenty thousand spectators lining the streets joined in battle with the Socialists. Police charged in, beating about them with nightsticks. The mob attacked the pro-Bolshevist headquarters, wrecking it, hurling furniture and the contents of filing cabinets into the street and making a bonfire of them. It was nightfall before the riot settled down.

It was a terrifying time for Rose, with two babies in the house, one of them only a few weeks old. In that painful week, with few Boston citizens sleeping soundly in their beds, it was important to her that Joe should stay as close to home as possible, retaining his positions as head of the Columbia Trust and on the board of Boston Electric. It was with a sinking heart that Rose learned from him that he intended leaving the bank to his father's management; he would move into the most dangerous and inflammatory of businesses of the time, the one commercial enterprise more seriously threatened by socialism than any other: shipbuilding.

He would be up against militant labor; he would be subject to verbal attack, or worse, in his role in management; building battle cruisers and submarines would be a contradiction of his pacifist stance. Because shipyard men were excused from the draft, as their service was considered essential to the war effort, Rose would have to see her husband, more loudly than ever, branded a yellow-bellied draft evader and coward.

Why did Joe want to enter the business? Perhaps to avoid service as a nonpartisan, pacifistic follower of papal precepts; more likely, and paradoxically, to find a way into an enterprise in which war contracts were enriching many.

He heard that Charles Schwab, the dominant presence of his honeymoon week at the Greenbrier Hotel, was looking for a man to act as assistant general manager at the Fore River Shipyard near Boston. Joe was fascinated by Schwab, the idol of millions of young, up-and-coming American businessmen. Schwab's was a classic American success story. Aided by the patronage of Andrew Carnegie, he had risen from stable hand to draftsman and head of Bethlehem Steel in just thirty years. His house, Riverside, on Riverside Drive and West Seventy-second Street in New York, was the largest private residence in the city. While his overweight, miserable wife wandered the mansion's eighty-five rooms and counted her collection of diamonds, terrified a maid might have stolen one, Schwab reveled with a succession of adventuresses and enjoyed the gambling tables of Europe. His vast country estate, his passion for chicken livers and terrapin, his scamming of the government by supplying faulty armor plates for ships, all made headlines.

Charles Schwab was the enemy of organized labor. To join his team was to enlist in a war against the working man. And to defy the government. Schwab was gouging Navy Secretary Josephus Daniels for millions. Not content with the multimillion-dollar support fund paid him for the sale of Liberty Bonds, he was charging excess prices for steel, an annoyance that provoked Daniels to frequent angry comments in his diary.

It was Schwab's policy to hire for his plants across the country clean-cut, bright young college men, athletic and pushy, who might bridge the gap between management and the labor force, to attract confidence in the rank and file. No doubt remembering Joe from the Greenbrier, he dispatched Joe Powell, recently kicked upstairs from general manager of Fore River to Bethlehem Steel vice-president in Pittsburgh, and Powell's successor Sam Wakeman, to look Joe over. They were taken with him at once. Not only did he look bright and did his clothes fit, but they could tell from his successful rehabilitation of Columbia Trust and his expert settlement of the scandal at the Collateral Loan Company that he was expert in accountancy and in book-keeping, creative or otherwise.

He would be paid $15,000 a year as assistant general manager, or about $300,000 a year in present-day terms. This was a very considerable income for those days. But in no time, Joe found there was a catch. He had been dropped into a cauldron. He wasn't told in advance that the Fore River shipyard and its associated Squantum yard, then in the process of being built, were threatened by a strike.

It turned out that Joe Powell had replaced former Chief Navy Instructor Francis T. Bowles, who had been paid $200,000 to quit as manager when he asked too many questions about scamming of the government and fighting the wage scale. Joe and Wakeman received visits from shop stewards almost immediately. By government edict, Schwab would have to pay his men a match of government navy-yard wages, the arrangement beginning on October 15, when Joe began work. But no sooner had this arrangement been entered into than Josephus Daniels announced that, starting November 1, those same navy-yard workers would have to accept a wage cut of one cent a day. Thus, the Fore River workers, all three thousand of them, would have to revert to the wage scale that existed before the increase. Even though the adjustment was tiny, they had had enough. On October 30, Joe drove through a severe thunderstorm to his office, leaving an anxious Rose behind. At a meeting he discovered the machinists, riveters and crane men announcing that they would strike the next day and would not return unless they were granted a continuance of the increased wage they had been promised.

It was useless for Sam Wakeman or anyone else to bring up the subject of patriotism. Most of the workers were indifferent to the war or opposed to it, merely working in a shipyard because it would be a way of avoiding service in the army or navy. A high proportion were Portuguese, and by no means were all workers citizens. Others were Slavs or German-Americans, whose attitudes were, at best, ambiguous. By October 31, Joe looked through the windows of his office at a disturbing sight: the brand-new destroyer that was to have been christened by Mrs. Josephus Daniels the next day, as well as a submarine equipped with the latest torpedoes, lying abandoned on the slipways. Not a soul could be seen; the machinists, crane men, bolters and riveters had gone to their bunkhouses and refused to come out.

When a Jewish worker, Sam Levene, scabbed, workers beat him into a ditch and cut him badly about the eyes. When ministers appealed to the workers on behalf of God and country, they were jeered at and shoved. Charles Schwab didn't help the matter. He refused to abandon a lecture at Wellesley, and when he did turn up received only the crane men, because they didn't belong to a union.

Joe was helpless. Neither he nor Wakeman proved effectual in the crisis. Even when Josephus Daniels announced that the strikers would be included in the draft, they refused to be enlisted. The socialist elements among them made sure of that.

Wakeman closed the canteen. By November 4, the workers, told they would have to quit their bunkhouses, realized the danger of their situation. They began to weaken. The young Franklin D. Roosevelt, assistant secretary of the navy in charge of ship production, sent a patriotic message to the men, which machinist Tom Savage read at a rioters' meeting. It called for a show of patriotic duty: "I urge both sides to sink all minor differences and get together for success in the war at once." The words were greeted by cheers.

Inspired by empty stomachs rather than love of country, the men returned to work on November 6. But just then, the Russian Revolution broke out in full force as revolutionary troops stormed the Winter Palace in St. Petersburg and a sympathetic strike was threatened at Squantum.

Rose learned from Joe that he couldn't overcome the hatred of management that had inspired the first strike and might soon bring about a second. He had to work eighteen hours a day, commuting between Fore River and Squantum, supervising the latter's final building program and the last-minute draining of an evil-smelling swamp bordering the ocean. He tried a sop in the form of the so-called Victory Lunchroom, a canteen servicing Squantum from which, by special arrangement with Wakeman, he would be allowed to profit personally. The men enjoyed the cheap food but otherwise showed no sign of gratitude.

Seldom home, often sleeping on his office couch, soon to acquire a stomach ulcer, Joe, though only twenty-nine, suffered from exhaustion. Meeting the demands of Josephus Daniels and Franklin Roosevelt for more ships, submarines and gun carriages reduced him, on more than one occasion, to helpless tears. It took all of his youth and strength to see him through, as the yards under his control broke records in production despite the frequently recurring go-slow actions of the union members.

To add to Rose's distress, his draft board rejected his January 1918 claim for exemption. He was put in Class 1, despite the fact that normally an exclusion was allowed for a parent with growing children and that his work as a shipbuilder came under the heading of essential services. Amid renewed whispering of cowardice and draft dodging, he begged for reconsideration on February 18, 1918, but was again declared eligible. It was only with the efforts of Joseph Powell, who pulled a string in Washington, that he was excused.

Joe was vindicated on April 20, 1918, when Josephus Daniels visited Squantum and expressed his astonishment at seeing the framework for five destroyers set up in fifty minutes. But he can only have been disillusioned with Schwab, a fellow Roman Catholic, who defied all papal ordinances by praising socialism, of all unlikely things, in those early months of the year. Schwab so provoked the *New York Times* that, in an editorial, it dubbed him a Bolshevist; he was even invited to join the Wobblies. His stance was, however, sheer sophistry on his part: Schwab continued to despise the unions and was only trying to curry favor with them to preclude further strikes.

Rose was pregnant again. She had begun to fret, devout Catholic and devoted wife though she was, against the drab monotony of her existence. And now she had another worry.

Honey Fitz had had uneven health over several months; soon after Rose's first daughter, her third child, Rosemary, was born, on September 13, after chafing at the bit in the political wilderness, he announced that he would be running for Congress again. He would oppose incumbent Peter Tague in the primaries. Preparing his campaign, he would rely on money that Joe would raise, and he would enjoy the support of Martin Lomasney; Lomasney shared his anger at Tague for insisting on Irish conscription.

In addition to Rose's unease about her father embarking on such a strenuous adventure in politics, she had to face other threats. Shortly before Rosemary was born, an influenza epidemic broke out around her. Soon to sweep the world and cause more deaths than World War I, the contagion savaged people of all ages in those dark days some thirty years before antibiotics. Even the young and the fit were stricken—many died, with horrifying symptoms, within forty-eight hours. Fore River and Squantum were decimated; so were the offices of Columbia Trust and Boston Electric. With a newborn baby and two other small children, there was always the terror that some tradesman or delivery boy might carry the virus with him. Rose had to be a prisoner of her own house, and she must have been nervous every day that Joe drove to his workplace, where he would meet with men who could already be stricken.

In his fifties, Honey Fitz would be in crowded halls, in streets packed with enthusiastic citizens, visiting hospitals; he, even more than Joe, could be felled.

Yet, to Rose's relief, neither father nor husband caught so much as a cold in those weeks of sudden death. Honey Fitz proved as irrepressible as ever. He hired voters to place their votes as many as a dozen times. Absentee votes were arranged with dead men's signatures on them; scavengers were hired to comb through hospital wards to have the dying scribble their names on pieces of paper that were carried to the ballot boxes. Ruffians were hired to intercept Tague's campaign officials; his cars were stopped on side streets; stationers in Honey Fitz's pay supplied gumless stickers with Tague's name on them, which fell off walls and windows when attempts were made to affix them. Despite such shenanigans, Tague came very close to beating Honey Fitz. Fitz won by 7,227 votes to 6,998. Tague began plans to expose his opponent as a fraud.

The epidemic gradually subsided, leaving the Boston

graveyards filled to bursting. The war ended in November, to widespread rejoicing, but, for Joe, with the knowledge that demands for ships would decrease, the armistice meant only that he must look for another job.

Then, in May 1919, Rose's worst fears were fulfilled. Peter Tague succeeded in contesting Honey Fitz's election and was promised a full-scale hearing in October. For the next months, he and his team worked day and night, interviewing eyewitnesses, obtaining documents and investigating ballots until a damning case began to build.

As the brave young men, friends of the Kennedys, began to return to the colleges and business world, long delayed in Europe by red tape and military requirements, many began to see the wisdom Joe had expressed in not going to France, which so often had been misunderstood among the Harvard crowd as cowardice.

In their sprightly innocence, these youths had been excited by childish dreams of heroism, war as a romantic experience in the tradition of Lexington and Valley Forge, as proof of manhood, as the glorious expression of youth and muscle against America's enemy. But the reality they had found in France was not glamorous or elevating or thrilling; it was the relentless squalor of rain and mud and lice and rats, and the sweeping doubts that ran through the ranks that youth might be a victim of royalty, corrupt politicians and arrogant careerist generals. They began to feel, as so many of their fellows were slaughtered, that they were wasting their lives in fighting to regain a few hundred yards of earth; they were disillusioned also by the sudden collapse of the German forces before extended combat, rifle to rifle, bayonet to bayonet, could be engaged. They returned to America prematurely aged, embittered, disillusioned.

Popular historians would strive to give the impression that 1919 was a time of joy, of looking forward to the new and jazzy decade of the twenties that lay ahead; but instead it was a time of sadness, reassessment and blame.

For Rose and Joe, who still maintained with the Vatican that the war had been futile and believed that America would have helped Britain far more if she hadn't entered it and imperiled the supply ships, it was a time of self-satisfaction, of misguided optimism and careful planning ahead. For Rose, it was a time of relief, that her man had escaped death in a meaningless conflict disapproved of by her Catholic spiritual leaders—and that he was reasonably healthy and set on his vigorous way to making money and providing a decent future for her children.

With the fall in orders from Bethlehem Steel, Joe began to look for other fields of activity. Numerous legends have grown up about his next venture, most of them surely exaggerated. The truth seems to have been less colorful: he had established a relationship with the portly and genial multimillionaire Brookline resident Galen Stone while they had both served on the board of trustees of Boston Electric. Because they were near neighbors and traveled to New York, they would frequently have met in the parlor car and deepened their already warm acquaintance. Stone was looking for bright young men for his company, Hayden, Stone. That company has been described frequently as a stolid and conservative banking and brokerage firm of the old school.

In fact, it was an empire, a pirate operation that ran container ships and merchant vessels, railroads, sugar, oil, cotton and a variety of metals. It was involved in union busting, attacks on organized labor, fights or deals with foreign governments, extensive interests in France, and the customary degree of larceny and graft.

To conceal the most important reason for the connection, the story was bandied about that Joe invaded Stone's train carriage and fast-talked him into giving him a job. But the truth is that, through her father, Rose already had a stake in Hayden, Stone. She owned stock—some five thousand shares—in the most important company that Hayden, Stone handled: the Atlantic, Gulf and West Indies Shipping Line (known popularly as AGWI), an immensely successful corporation owning container ships that brought Hayden, Stone's Atlantic Gulf Oil Company barrels from Mexico to North America and Europe. Atlantic Gulf Oil was a feisty rival to Edward Doheny's more celebrated outfit and to the Rockefellers' Standard Oil operation south of the Texas border. There can be no question that Rose and Honey Fitz engineered Joe's immediate career elevation.

Hayden, Stone had begun twenty-eight years earlier, in 1892, when Stone, a bustling thirty-year-old financial journalist with a shrewd grasp of economics, hooked up with the tougher, twenty-two-year-old college graduate Charles Hayden to form, on $20,000 each (supplied by indulgent fathers), a tiny company on Milk Street, Boston. They were contrasts: Hayden was a militarily erect, hard-bitten, ruthless climber who talked like a machine gun delivering bullets. His favorite expression was "A man who doesn't know what he thinks doesn't have any business to talk." He seldom let a slow-thinking man finish a sentence ("If I know what is in their minds, why should I wait fifteen minutes for them to get it out?"). Detesting all except the most expert, his creed was "backbone . . . taking a calling down without resenting it . . . always gives a straight answer to a straight question." Hayden later built the Hayden Planetarium in New York City.

By contrast, Stone was calm, bespectacled, a genial tummy rubber with a thin surface of culture. He collected Chinese porcelain, was actually seen reading literary novels, and supported art galleries and libraries.

By 1919, when Joe Kennedy first met the partners, disliking Hayden and liking Stone, Hayden and Stone had built their vast holdings from a base in copper stocks. Through lavish payments they had obtained complete lists of shareholders in several copper companies, offering each individual better conditions of brokerage if he would join them. They raided one company after another in this manner, building up a formidable corner in the metal. Surviving the collapse of the copper market in 1907, they soared rapidly. With numerous bribes to the Mexican government, they fought oil tycoon Edward Doheny and absorbed a great many petroleum wells in and near Tampico, Mexico. Along with J. & W. Seligman and Company of Manhattan, they handled the stocks of the Cuba Sugar Cane Company, the largest sugar enterprise in the world, with a celebrity board of directors. The board included Irénée Du Pont of Du Pont of Delaware, Matthew Chauncey Brush of the Chicago Elevated Railroad, and E. W. Stetson of Coca-Cola, and, for a time, William Harriman. They swallowed up the Minneapolis and St. Paul Railroad and the Chicago,

Rock Island and Pacific Line, and set up Atlantic, Gulf and West Indies.

They owned the Cuba Mail Steamship Company, the international Portland Cement Company, Mallory Steamships and huge interests in China, including oil. In addition to his mansion in Brookline, at which the Kennedys were frequent guests, Galen Stone owned a five-hundred-acre estate, Great Hill, on the shore of Buzzards Bay at Marion, Massachusetts. His wife Carrie was beloved of Rose; they had three attractive daughters, Katharine, Margaret and Barbara, and a handsome son, Robert. Hayden was unmarried, and remained so, expressing a contempt for women's "weakness," and instead devoted his considerable energy to raising thoroughbreds for steeplechases and dabbling in the movie industry in the Mayflower Company Associates. The partners' best friends were the Harrimans, power brokers then and in the future.

For Joe to enter the charmed circle of Hayden, Stone would be a step up in the world, as well as protecting Rose's AGWI interests. Stone liked Joe, who had acted in Stone's interests two years earlier, when he had made every effort to have Schwab build ships for AGWI. When Schwab had refused, Joe's anger had pleased Stone considerably.

In July, to Rose's delight, Joe took over the important job of head of the investment division of Hayden, Stone, in Boston (and New York, a fact that has never been published), commuting frequently to Manhattan with his boss. Hayden had disapproved his appointment at first, but soon came to see the value of this dynamic, young, handsome, athletic stock pusher.

Entering Hayden, Stone's Milk Street offices in Boston was quite an experience for the young executive. No less than eighty clerks toiled away on the main floor at high mahogany desks, perched on stools as they worked in green eyeshades and leather sleeve protectors. Underpaid and overworked, few were at their tasks less than fourteen hours a day.

The executive offices were lavishly upholstered, with marble floors, Indian and Chinese rugs brought back by Galen Stone from his travels in the Orient, T'ang horses, rich tapestry chairs and subdued lamps. The oak-paneled walls glowed with expensive oil paintings. But all of this luxury was threatened from the beginning of Joe's appointment.

No sooner had he settled behind his handsome desk in 1919 than he and Rose were made aware of the Red Menace that was a widely discussed topic. Just two days after he moved in, he found himself unable to get into the office. On July 17, the overhead railroad, trolley car, bus and subway workers struck—inspired, business circles insisted, by Bolshevists. For days and nights, the city was a mass of hopelessly stalled traffic, a bedlam of motor horns and shouts. Everybody, the executive staff of Hayden, Stone included, had to walk many miles to work. The loss of business to the company was substantial. It took the intervention of Massachusetts Governor Calvin Coolidge to send the men back to work with promises of the unthinkable: a forty-hour week and a pay increase of twenty-five cents a day.

In that same week, Rose had more to fear: Boston and New York were roiled by discoveries of Communist cells. At breakfast, after prayers, Rose read in her paper that Carnegie Hall was closed for the summer to all public meetings; that plans were afoot to form a kind of Soviet Union in America with, as its nucleus, disaffected soldiers, sailors and marines; that radicals were causing explosions and fires just about everywhere. The papal pastorals, circulated to all notable Catholic homes such as theirs, contained warnings by Pope Benedict XV of the increasing growth of communism in America and the necessity of flushing it out. There was talk, stimulated by Senator J. E. Watson in Washington, that President Carranza of Mexico was planning a Bolshevist invasion of the United States. Joseph Guffey, Joe Kennedy's associate and president of AGWI and Gulf Oil, took ship to Mexico to try to deal with the situation on behalf of Rose and the other stock- and bondholders. For years, Hayden and Stone had been pouring money into Mexico, contrary to the policies of other oil companies, to appease various Mexican governments.

Joe and Rose received shattering news from Tampico. Guffey had narrowly escaped death. As he set out for the company's oil properties near Tuxpan aboard a motor launch down a local canal, allegedly Bolshevist-backed bandits fired at him and his party from the shore. Guffey boldly ordered his craft to proceed, but the rest of the AGWI group were not as lucky. They were seized, stripped and robbed, then left beaten on the banks of the canal. All attempts to obtain assurances from Carranza that AGWI's oil interests would be protected met with failure.

Soon after a shaken Guffey returned to Milk Street, Rose not only saw her AGWI shares fall, but felt her Beals Street bastion severely threatened. On the night of September 8, Joe discovered that the police who normally patrolled the neighborhood to protect the citizens from possible Red attacks were missing. When he got to the office, police guards used to supplement Hayden, Stone's security staff had also vanished. The impossible had happened. Bolshevist influences had even overcome the cops; they had walked out on strike.

The trouble had begun in August, when Boston Police Commissioner Curtis refused to allow his two thousand men to form a union. They did form it, defiantly, stimulated by the radicals; Curtis was furious when the respectable Boston Central Labor Bureau and Samuel Gompers of the American Federation of Labor gave their blessing. Curtis actually took his own rebellious police shop stewards to court. Just before the trial was to begin, the entire Boston force struck on September 9.

It is easy to imagine Rose's terror when, as a loving and protective parent of young children, she realized that nothing stood between them and mob violence, fire and pillage. Nobody dared go out-of-doors. Shops closed, and so did many offices. Joe defied everyone, got on the phone for hours and summoned up the vigilante battalion known as the Defenders of Public Safety, made up in part of his fellow Harvardians and of present undergraduate and graduate students.

Augmented by these young men, the citizens' committees, army and navy men clashed head-on with the police in a series of battles that resulted in death and injury. Streets of Boston were littered with injured men and splashed with blood. Coolidge again rode to the rescue, and the riot was grimly quelled. Not a single striker was allowed to serve in the police ever again.

At the same time, Joe was involved in a fight with Eugene Grace, Charles Schwab's chief executive, who had promised him continuing profits from the Victory Lunchroom at Fore River after he resigned. Finally, after he protested, he was given a settlement of $12,500; $2,500 less than he should have earned.

To add to Rose's woes, in October Honey Fitz was disgraced. Peter Tague had succeeded through the Committee on Elections of the First Session of the 66th Congress in producing a report, following a prolonged and spirited series of hearings (at one of which Honey Fitz made a voluntary and unsuccessful appearance), which said Fitz was guilty of everything Tague charged him with. The committee found that Fitz had arranged for liquor dealers, bartenders, waiters and porters who worked, but did not live, in the voting areas to place votes for him in those districts as well as their own; that desk clerks of lodging houses whose owners were known to Fitz handed in votes from people who did not live there, if they existed at all. Young men absent on military or naval service were put on the ballots by their fathers; the matter came up again that stickers applied to forms with Peter Tague's name on them in lieu of signatures fell off because the gum suppliers were bribed by Honey Fitz; when attempts were made to arrest fraudulent voters, they were spirited out of the city by Honey Fitz's men.

Although he laughed the whole thing off, her father was in a disgrace that can only have caused Rose agony. And she was to bear her fourth child just four months later.

She now had a problem with Rosemary. The baby could barely move, had to be assisted in everything, seldom cried or laughed, and had to be prodded even to crawl. Rose and Joe fretted over her constantly. The probability that a slip of the forceps at birth had injured her brain—or that the extreme stress Rose was going through might have affected the infant—must have racked them day and night. There was no avoiding the fact that in a family that put a high price on perfection the unthinkable had happened: Rose had given birth to a retarded child.

Rose was wretched; she confessed years later that at twenty-nine she had begun to miss the life of her younger years—the travel, the excitement, the razzle-dazzle of life with Father. Much as she loved her children, Rosemary most of all, they deprived her of a world in which she had flourished; and now, with Honey Fitz's political destruction, that world had disappeared.

Her life had become an endless succession of knitting, sewing, prescribing medications, supervising meals, worrying about everything. And then something happened that triggered the unimaginable. Rose walked out and returned to her parents' home.

Chapter 5

Hollywood

In the spring of 1919, when Joe was talking daily on the train to Galen Stone, Charles Hayden had invested, through the Mayflower company, in a film, *The Miracle Man,* starring the great mime and contortionist Lon Chaney. Chaney's costar was Betty Compson, a heart-stopping honey-blonde of twenty-two, who had been born in Utah, had played the violin in vaudeville as a child, had been briefly married to a Mormon and had started a modest Hollywood career in Al Christie's popular comedies. She was warm, generous, fun-loving, good-natured, impractical with money, and intensely, dizzily romantic.

Later, in 1921, she would become my father's mistress in London.

At her home in Glendale in 1970, sad-eyed as she hung on to photographs Kennedy and my father had given her, she told me her story. Charles Schwab, who loved movies, had been asked to invest in the picture; later, he would make a film about Helen Keller. When Hayden, Stone got involved, they were very tight on budget, but the film turned out to be excellent anyway and made Compson a big name.

She came to New York for promotions ahead of the September 1919 premiere organized by Paramount, with

Joe in the audience. Rose stayed home. Compson fell in love with Joe immediately. She hated the fact that he was married, but he was handsome and young and "brought the most beautiful flowers to the Astor Hotel." He didn't, she recalled, send the flowers with a messenger, but romantically brought them in person.

Her life was complicated by the fact that *The Miracle Man*'s director, George Loane Tucker, was also in love with her, and was also married, with a wife who was on the stage in London.

She lingered on in New York, returning briefly to Hollywood to make another film with Tucker, who was dying of cancer. He set up his room so that he could see her in a series of mirrors but she could not see him and be shocked by the ravages of his illness.

Rose found out about the affair.

In January 1920, Compson was back in Manhattan. Rose moved out of Beals Street in anger and tears over Betty Compson, who in turn grew restless and unhappy at rumors filtering back to her of Joe's infidelities with New York chorus girls. He had become close to the noted theatrical producer Charles Dillingham, who was backed to the hilt by Hayden and Stone. Dillingham, a perennial bachelor, had access to a virtually unlimited supply of pretty young women: he created the elaborate musical shows at the Hippodrome, which called for chorus lines in the scores.

Joe's promiscuity was, Compson said, too much for her, though she admitted that she herself was scarcely a saint. But the fact that he could not, as a Catholic, divorce Rose, and that Compson didn't trust him to be faithful to her anyway, resulted in her breaking off the affair. This time Joe sent her diamonds and furs, but she sent them back; she said she would have preferred it if he had, as before, brought them himself, and not through a messenger. She left Joe for the theatrical and film producer Walter Morosco, who offered to take her to London. At the last minute, she dropped Morosco, left alone, and signed to make a picture there called *Woman to Woman,* of which the young Alfred Hitchcock was assistant director and cowriter.

On her arrival in London, my father gave a luncheon in her honor at the Advertising Club of which he was chairman. She was attracted to him immediately, and was pleasantly surprised when, at the end of the meal, she reached for her purse and found that he had slipped his telephone number into it. She responded by calling him that evening, spent the night with him at his apartment at Savoy Court, and rapidly forgot all about Joe Kennedy. She finally broke off the affair with Father when she realized she would have to give up her career to become Lady Higham.

Rose was no happier back home at Welles Avenue than she had been at Beals Street, even though her beloved sister Agnes was there, along with two of her brothers. For some reason, Honey Fitz did not have domestic staff, and everyone had to pitch in with the duties. Large as the house was, it was overcrowded and claustrophobic, what with her own children, her French maid Alice Michelan and her nurse Kate Conboy as well. There were at least a dozen people in the house at the same time, and she felt she was underfoot. Even an appearance at her annual Ace of Clubs dance when she was far along in her fourth pregnancy failed to help.

Honey Fitz didn't soothe her feelings of fretfulness and restlessness by suggesting in no uncertain manner that she had no business being there and should return to her wifely duties at once. Why was he so emphatic about this? It is clear that he still entertained political ambitions and was nervous of a public scandal concerning Compson (if he knew about her) or other women, a scandal that would be fueled by Rose's flight to his home.

Effectively kicked out, Rose took refuge in a private religious retreat, run under the patronage of Cardinal O'Connell and conducted on the same principles as her Sacred Heart School, where the nuns no doubt reminded her of her marital obligations and urged her to return to her erring husband, if not in a mood of forgiveness, then with prayers that he might improve.

She was scarcely settled back at Beals Street in February when Jack, her second child, took seriously ill at just two and a half. Boston had been swept by an epidemic of scarlet fever that had closed schools, decimated colleges and cut down even the most cloistered convents. Rose was undoubtedly terrified that Alice Michelan, Kate Conboy, or a second Irish nanny, Mary O'Donahue, could be a carrier.

Her much-criticized cloistering of her children was once again fully justified, as the threat of violence was followed now by the threat of infection. Exactly how it occurred is mysterious, unless Rose's fears about Michelan, Conboy or O'Donahue were well founded, but Jack was stricken suddenly with fever, sore throat, vomiting, severe headache, and coated tongue. Dr. Good once again motored to Brookline and made the diagnosis: scarlet fever.

Rose was desperate, as she was only hours away from delivery of her fourth child. As Jack's temperature reached 105 degrees, Dr. Good had to cross the corridor and the sickroom to the natal chamber (most dangerously, in view of the possibility of his own infection) over and over again in those critical hours of February 20. Rose became hysterical, losing her well-known control; she feared Jack might die at the very moment her new child was born.

The household was in an uproar as Joe abandoned work to attend to what was now a critical situation. A blistering rash spread over little Jack's body; his cries of agony mercifully didn't reach Rose as she sank into her ether-induced sleep. Good, who must have been on the edge of total exhaustion, managed to deliver Rose's second daughter, immediately named Kathleen, always nicknamed Kick in later years, without mishap.

Then Joe was faced with an appalling crisis. Brookline's hospital had no facilities for dealing with scarlet fever. Even though Charles Hayden was a director of Massachusetts General, that institution had closed its doors to Brookline residents. Apparently the icy Hayden failed to pull a string; but Joe had some influence through Dr. Good and, after considerable pleading, managed to have Boston City Hospital admit Jack. This was fortunate: it had the best infectious-disease wing in northeastern America outside of New York.

Joe had to wear mask and gloves every time he entered his son's room. Rose was forbidden by Dr. Good to go to the hospital. Her postpartum condition had left her weak, and there was always fear that she might be infected, since she had never suffered from scarlet fever. She was horrified when she learned that all of Jack's skin had peeled off, leaving his flesh raw in the latter stages.

In March, Rose sent Jack to the Mansion House, an expensive hotel in Poland Springs, Maine, where he could take the healing mineral waters. At the same time, Joe yielded to Rose's entreaties to buy a larger house, which would accommodate the several more children they planned. On March 16, he signed the initial papers to purchase, in Rose's name, a large, twelve-room, eaved house at 51 Abbotsford Road, Brookline, not far from Galen and Carrie Stone's. He paid $16,000 for it. For some reason there was a holdup in their taking possession and in the arrangements for Honey Fitz's secretary Eddie Moore to buy the house on Beals Street. The arrangements would not be concluded until August 1920.

During those months, with Jack now fully recovered, Joe became more interested in the motion-picture business. Stimulated by Charles Schwab and by his love affair with Betty Compson, he was fascinated when he learned of the success of such upstarts as South Boston's Louis B. Mayer in obtaining franchises through theater chains or distributing films. Under the Hayden, Stone banner, he snapped up the Maine-Hampshire movie-house chain, and obtained the exclusive right to distribute films made by Harry F. Robertson, a British producer, and an American partner, Rufus Cole, who had just built a studio on Gower Street and Melrose Avenue in Hollywood. Their first major production was *Kismet,* a screen version of Edward Knoblock's international stage success based on the *Arabian Nights* and starring the legendary Otis Skinner. Joe made a killing with his inspired release of the film, and was allowed a percentage of the profits by his bosses, thus establishing the basis of his fortune.

Meanwhile, the problems of companies over whose stocks Joe had control, and in whom Rose was invested so heavily, were more embattled than ever. In particular, AGWI and Atlantic Gulf Oil were embattled—even threatened. On March 30, political riots swept Mexico City and there was an assassination attempt on President Carranza. On April 24, a fight raged over the Hayden, Stone Atlantic Gulf Oil fields. On May 9, Carranza fled; he was killed trying to reach the coast. Rebels entered Mexico City, and a new president, Victoriano Huerta, was proclaimed. All U.S. travelers were forbidden by the new administration to enter the country, and AGWI personnel were evacuated by train on a terrifying, bandit-menaced journey to Texas. AGWI ships had to be moved to Havana.

But worse faced the Kennedys and Hayden, Stone once the ships were moved. The Cuban government, upset by Cuba Sugar Cane's control, along with that of other, lesser companies, set prices exorbitantly high, thus beginning a full-scale sugar war with the U.S. government. This seriously affected Hayden, Stone's interests, and every effort had to be made to protect the American sugarcane growers. In May, sugar rationing began in New York and Boston; several states adopted boycotts; many were tried, fined and even jailed for hoarding. Future president Herbert Hoover set up the Sugar Equalization Board, with President Wilson as majority shareholder, a virtual nationalization of the local industry. Restaurants refused to put sugar on tables; at first, the policy enriched Cuban price gougers, but later it ruined the economy.

Joe and his bosses found a solution. At almost every quarter, they met their increasing debts, both on AGWI and Cuba Sugar Cane, by launching multimillion-dollar bond issues, institutions such as insurance companies snapping them up based on a ten-year prospect, unfazed by current news.

Joe's adept handling of these matters insured his position. Then, one night, he came home to Rose badly cut and bruised and told her a hair-raising story. On September 16, 1920, he was in the midst of discussions with certain of the sugar companies in New York. At noon that day, he was outside the offices of J. Pierpont Morgan, on the corner of Wall and Broad streets, just around the corner from the stock exchange. A clock had begun striking the hour, which was the signal for hundreds of white-collar workers to pour into the street for a quick sandwich and bottled drink in their half-hour break.

Many stopped to stare at a hastily constructed overhead wooden runway built from the Sub-Treasury to the newly constructed Assay Office, across which a procession of uniformed messengers were carrying a total of $1 billion, in the form of gold ingots stuffed into canvas bags.

At the sixth stroke of the clock, an odd sight caught the eye of almost everyone in that crowded thoroughfare. A strange relic or overhang of another age made its way through the throng, provoking a symphony of motor horns as cars were delayed by its pathetically arthritic progress. It was a red-painted wooden wagon, its sides open, its cloth top rippled by the breeze. One of its wheels was dangerously loose. It was drawn by a beaten-up horse that had been lamed in one leg and was about to lose a shoe. The contraption was driven by a man or woman so covered in rags that it was impossible to make out the sex, age or appearance of the mysterious, but undoubtedly poverty-stricken, individual.

Almost everyone stopped to take in this visitor from another America. At that moment, an office safe, insecurely tethered to the body of the wagon, and containing some three hundred window sash bolts, exploded, and horse, driver and cart were blown to pieces. The sash bolts ripped into the crowd, sending a hail of burning steel into the spectators. Joe was flung to the sidewalk. As he stood up, he saw dozens of people lying cut to pieces, bleeding on the sidewalks. Men, women and children lay headless or limb-less in the gutters. Others lay groaning, begging for help. Cars became moving incinerators; a blizzard of broken glass fell from the buildings.

Characteristically, Joe continued to his meeting; to do so, he had to make his way through something resembling a battle zone. Immediately, he, and just about everyone else in America, attributed the explosion to the Bolshevists. And indeed, the circumstantial evidence was overwhelming: the careful timing of the bomb to go off at the noon break; the location between the new resting place of a billion dollars in gold and the citadel of J. P. Morgan; the symbolic character of the old-fashioned wagon, suggesting a decent, rural America, far from the centers of U.S. commerce; the use of a safe, in itself symbolic, as an infernal machine; and an extra touch of cunning detail: the wagon was painted red. Yet the irony was that the bomb, instead of killing J. P.

Morgan or the chief officials of the Assay Office, destroyed the lives of those very simple people that the Bolshevists campaigned for: the bank tellers, janitors, cashiers and others who served the purposes of capitalism without benefiting from it. J. P. Morgan was at a country house in England at the time, and his son sustained only minor cuts.

Years of detective work failed to uncover the perpetrator. Over sixty died, and several hundred were injured, many of them permanently.

The incident exacerbated Joe and Rose's hatred of communism. Here was a case in which Joe's life was actually threatened by the Reds.

In February 1921, Rose and Joe were faced with a problem of a different character: a bear raid on the stock of AGWI. On February 19, a man calling himself Robert Deerfield announced in a statement to the press from a suite at the Palmer House hotel in Chicago that AGWI was broke, that its president and Joe's boss, A. R. Nicol, had shot himself, and that Deerfield was forming a protective committee of shareholders to ask for a receivership in bankruptcy. The result was that AGWI's stock tumbled precipitously, and Rose saw substantial losses in her account.

No sooner had Joe's office prepared a contradictory statement and Nicol announced that he was very much alive than a New York fur merchant and investigator of spiritualism, Aaron Kosofsky, made matters worse. He took an advertisement in every New York newspaper saying that Deerfield's story was unfounded, a sure way of adding fuel to the flames.

He stated that he had heard of Deerfield's "revelations" while at the offices of E. L. Leland and Company, brokers, at Forty-second Street and Broadway. He said he had been tipped off by the Leland partners and trader A. H. Montgomery that the stock was to be forced down. But his statement was quickly questioned. More than one person present in the office supported the Lelands in stating that Kosofsky had received no such information. By now, Rose's stock had dropped from $69.50 a share to $42.50. Joe's stock department came to the conclusion that a group of shareholders in AGWI itself, led by brokers Loring C. Black and W. Bernard Bause, had started the rumors to drive the stock down, then bought more at bottom. Kosofsky called a meeting of shareholders in his séance parlor, presided over by former judge Samuel M. Fleischmann.

It has been claimed that in situations like this, Hayden, Stone, and Joe Kennedy in particular, would go out and buy up more stock for millions of dollars in order to save it. But nothing of the kind took place. AGWI shares continued to fall; the company plunged into heavy losses; it proved impossible for Joe's department to raise money.

Luckily, Rose didn't sell. A. R. Nicol resigned; dividends were paid almost two months late. By June, the investment division was compelled to mortgage the entire tanker fleet; there was talk of selling the Atlantic Gulf Oil Company, and the French side of the business was sold off. This was a devastating blow to Joe Kennedy and his bosses.

The financial crisis in Cuba deepened. When a dividend was passed on Cuba Sugar Cane in June, the stock collapsed. Joe's department was compelled to pass out interest payments and bonds, as no cash was available when the Cuban banks closed that spring. All of Cuba Sugar Cane's assets in the Banco Nacional were frozen. Another burden was heaped on Joe's shoulders when his friend and Honey Fitz's, Boston City Treasury paymaster D. H. Mahoney, killed himself after auditors found a shortage of $40,000 in the books.

Joe tried to find consolation in consorting with more chorus girls, and in July he was frequently in New York, where Charles Dillingham was casting a lavish new musical revue at the Hippodrome starring the ballet dancer Michel Fokine.

Suffering from neuritis, ulcers and other stress-caused conditions, Joe did not make happy company for Rose as she struggled to deal with her heavy losses in AGWI and raise her ever-growing brood. She was worried by the increasingly poor health of her sister Eunice, who was in and out of tuberculosis sanitariums that year. Rosemary was showing more and more of the distressing signs of retardation, her efforts to learn painful to watch. She couldn't manage to handle a sled in winter along with the other children and Rose had to take her for separate walks because she couldn't keep up with her siblings. Although she showed a natural delight in seeing clothes displayed in the lit-up windows of Boston department stores, she was slow in her responses to many other things. If the children went rowing, she was unable to take her part at the oars. She couldn't do anything with her hands. A succession of physicians was unable to offer any suggestions. Backward children were dismissed as morons or near-"mongoloids" in those days, and the attitude toward them was equivalent to that toward witches or hunchbacks in the Middle Ages.

Rose tried to help the child; Rose had governesses and special teachers to supplement her uncomfortable schooling.

The other children were bright. Joe, Jr., was still the star of the family, a combination of physical beauty and strength and sharp intelligence. His chief fault, inherited from his father, was a hair-trigger temper, and Rose had to watch constantly to see that he didn't take it out on the less sturdy Jack. Although they often fought, Jack was remarkably lacking in sibling envy. He held his elder brother in as much awe as the rest of the family did. In turn, Joe was considerate during Jack's seemingly endless procession of childhood illnesses. Joe might bully him in childish games, but would be the first to be attentive when Jack was bedridden.

At first the elder children went to a school within walking distance in Brookline. The Edward Devotion School, situated in a converted private home, was handsomely appointed and well staffed, and the boys proved to be quick studies. Only Rosemary was incapable of keeping up; it may have been unwise to have sent her there. She was not able to perform the various classroom tasks involving handcrafts, making raffia mats or molding plasticine figures, fashioning potholders or even making paper figures. She suffered acutely from her ineptitude, and it is certain that some of the crueler children mocked her for her clumsiness.

Rose has been criticized for her disciplined raising of her children at Abbotsford Road and later. She has even been attacked for dividing her veranda into separate playpen areas with locked gates, as though this were some evidence of her being a kind of prison matron. But she was living in a city that was still, in those early years of the 1920s, plagued by Communist-caused explosions, frequent outbreaks of mob violence, and the prevalence of poorly controlled crime. The Kennedy house was situated on a busy street, haunted by automobiles and trolley cars, into which young children could run and quite easily be killed.

She was typical of moneyed women of her time, and indeed, until very recent times, in carefully regimenting her offspring, teaching them almost from toddler stage that pleasures should be earned, and that politeness, respect of elders and concern for each other were mandatory. Their religious training by the local priests was concomitant.

Indeed, there is no evidence that Rose was singular or vicious in her raising of her brood. Nor do her surviving diaries suggest coldness or lack of tenderness. Hands-on parenthood was not fashionable at that time; nurses, governesses and tutors were the centers of children's existences, and it was quite commonplace for a parent to appear only briefly in the playroom in the morning and evening. Everything we know suggests that Rose broke that particular rule—but she never coddled or snuggled the children.

She followed precepts laid down in parentage books; she passed on the McGuffey's Reader philosophy taught at her mother's knee. And she was even daring in many ways, as well as protective: she took the children to the Brookline shops, walking beside Joe and Jack as they drove a kiddie car along the street; accompanied them to mass at St. Aidan's Church whenever no violence threatened; and even carted them off on one occasion to a Boston banquet.

As for Joe's adultery, which Rose probably suspected, and prolonged absences, these were accepted by women of Rose's class as part of the necessary burdens of wifehood and motherhood. In fact, many women of that time rejoiced in their role of being placed on a pedestal, while the man sowed his wild oats in distant fields. Since sexual intercourse was regarded as somewhat of a burden, chiefly desirable only to provide further children, a husband's disappearances would lessen the ordeal of nightly congress. There could be no threat or question of divorce in the Catholic Church. Only insanity or nonconsummation would justify dissolution.

Rose, so often described as miserable, in fact looks happy and fulfilled in photographs of the time. Her fulfillment was in raising her brood, and not only in that. For all her household responsibilities, she remained the belle of the ball at her own, rebellious Ace of Clubs. She led as much of a social life as was possible, escorted often by her father, brothers or uncles to this or that cotillion.

And above all, despite Joe's nightmarish problems with the Hayden, Stone enterprises, floating bond issues, delaying dividend payments, soothing stockholders, fighting bear raids on AGWI and other companies to protect her interests as well as his own, she knew she had a successful husband who was rapidly growing rich.

Practical to the core, she knew that, with five children now—Eunice, her third daughter, was born in July 1921—and several more expected in the future, money was not only desirable but mandatory. Joe's knowledge of his responsibilities, in no way contradicted by his passion for beautiful women, his desire for sexual novelty, undoubtedly drove Joe on as he began to move toward his first million. He was young, sturdy, handsome, fascinating, with a brilliant, steely mind. If he was explosive and foulmouthed, and if he was ruthless as well, why blame him for it? He would scarcely have survived on Wall Street if he had been a wimp or an angel.

On January 22, 1922, Rose heard grievous news. Her idol, Pope Benedict XV, from whom the Kennedys' opposition to World War I and to the increasing power of Bolshevism had stemmed, died in Rome. Cardinal O'Connell had to leave by ship at once in order to be present at the election of the pontiff's successor; as it turned out, he arrived several hours too late to cast his vote. The Kennedys helped to organize the memorial mass in Boston, and led the family in prayers. Soon, it would be clear that the new Pope, Pius XI, even more firmly than his predecessor, would undertake the cause of religious opposition to the Soviet Union. The Kennedys still shared his horror, expressed in various encyclicals and pastorals over the next thirty-five years, of Russian suppression of the Christian religion. That position would not be changed until death.

In 1922, Joe and Rose had much to plague them. As the trouble in Cuba and Mexico simmered down somewhat, with the Cuban government coming to heel on one side and the Mexican government allowing more license in the running of Atlantic Gulf Oil fields and AGWI ships on the other, the Hayden, Stone railroad interests proved to be a colossal headache. Joe's department's number-one responsibility was the Chicago, Rock Island and Pacific Line, popularly known as the Rock Island Railroad. For years, the belligerent Charles Hayden had waged a war with the railroad unions, joining his fellow barons in refusing to meet the demands of the mechanics, engineers and engine drivers for better wages. That summer, a national railroad strike wrecked Rock Island's business. Passengers were thrown off trains, dumped in remote country areas or swamps so that they had to walk for miles to get help. Mail deliveries were disrupted; mailbags were burned. Strikers pulled spikes, causing crashes; trains were dynamited, freight cars burned, Pullmans stoned; dining-car kitchens exploded. Masked raiders hired by unions terrorized commuters; the list of dead and wounded grew daily.

Charles Hayden, refusing to compromise and calling on the government to ignore labor's demands, was smarting from a humiliation that had taken place that spring when the Minneapolis and St. Paul shareholders had thrown him off the board because of his conflicting interest in Rock Island. Now there was another shock: temporary peace in Mexico was given a bitter flavor when the government announced that Hayden, Stone would have to pay millions in taxes on their oil and shipping earnings all the way back to the beginning of President Carranza's regime, an act of vengeance since Charles Hayden had blatantly bribed Carranza not to subject him to such reduction of income.

Nothing, not even a radical-inspired railroad strike that would compel the family to make a lengthy and crowded journey by automobile, could stop the Kennedys from taking their annual summer vacation together. In July, with the strike continuing in full force, the Kennedys, wearied by the intrusion into their lives of John Smith, ward boss of Nantasket, drove off to spend the first of several summers at Cohasset, a very different kind of Massachusetts summer resort. Instead of the carnival atmosphere of Nantasket, with its garish entertainments, Punch and Judy shows and exuberant fireworks, Cohasset offered expensive, exclusive boredom. It was a sleepy, conservative enclave of the established rich, and the Kennedys should never have even considered it.

Well past its heyday of the 1890s, it still retained much of its disagreeable hauteur. Nouveaux riches, especially Irish Catholic nouveaux riches, were considered quite beyond the pale. Yet apparently Joe Kennedy believed he would find acceptance, perhaps because he had had some business dealings with Cohasset's tin-pot emperor, the wealthy Wall Street financier Clarence W. Barron, whose name is preserved to this day in the business journal *Barron's Weekly*. Barron's house on Coastal Harbor was the focus of formal parties—restricted, despite every effort to invade them, to Protestants with incomes of at least six figures. Barron's elder daughter married the equally snobbish financier Hugh Bancroft, pillar of the local all-Protestant golf club.

In an effort to make a splash, Rose selected one of the more costly summer rentals, a Queen Anne oversized mansion with a portico, known familiarly as a summer cottage, on Atlantic Avenue. It was one of a cluster of similar houses, and was situated spectacularly on the top of a series of high limestone ledges with a rocky path that ran down directly to Sandy Beach.

From April on, Rose and Joe had been using Honey Fitz's real-estate agent friend, Dudley Dean, to try to pry open the obstructive front door to the Cohasset Golf Club. But although Hugh Bancroft and his father-in-law Clarence Barron were not unadmiring of Joe's Manhattan financial shenanigans, there was no way they would break the club's rules to admit Roman Catholics; such an idea would have been as revolutionary as having a Jew or a black allowed on the golf course. In retrospect, Rose and Joe's optimism in the matter seems naive. And her statement later that the reason she left Cohasset finally was because of the exclusion seems baseless. She could never, after the first summer's rejection, have seriously expected the club to change its policy. When she and Joe abandoned Cohasset three years later, it was clearly because they had simply decided to favor another resort.

Joe's response to the railroad strike was to issue more and

more bonds of Rock Island; this proved a temporary shore-up. But when, in November 1922, Galen Stone decided he had had enough and would take his $28 million and retire, Joe knew it was time to move on from the countless headaches that Charles Hayden, who still disliked him, would undoubtedly engender for his future.

While Joe was thinking what to do next, Rose took off on an extended journey to California with her sister Agnes. They returned with a glowing picture of all they had seen, which undoubtedly stimulated Joe to his next professional move. Weary of the prolonged difficulties of the past two years, he decided to firm up his involvement in the motion picture industry.

He still owned thirty-one theaters in his Maine–New Hampshire chain, and, through his continuing relationship with Hayden, Stone, represented the interests of both Robertson, Cole and the Film Booking Office (FBO). It was well known that the controlling interest of the Film Booking Office was held by a consortium in London headed by Lloyds Bank and the Oxford rowing Blue Sir Walter Erskine Crum's Graham Company, of Glasgow and Manchester, which acted as tea merchants, trading mostly with India, a rival to the Lipton interests.

Joe's mother died on May 23, 1923, a severe blow to Rose, who adored her. Soon afterward, the Kennedys left for California. The children were put in the charge of the Eddie Moores.

Joe was still the well-paid advisor to FBO. He hoped, while on the West Coast, to exert his influence on certain of the FBO stars to strengthen his hand in his dealings with the British owners.

One of Joe's purposes in Hollywood was to inveigle into his camp the up-and-coming actor Fred Thomson and Thomson's influential wife, Frances Marion, arguably the leading woman movie writer in Hollywood. If he could get the support of Frances Marion, Joe would obtain great strength in the industry. This talented and beautiful woman had written the successful films *Anne of Green Gables* and *Pollyanna,* one of several vehicles for Mary Pickford, the queen of Hollywood. Marion knew everyone, and could introduce the Kennedys to the top people in the industry. A key to her heart would be to make suggestions that could lead to developing her husband's career. Thomson had all the necessary qualities to be a major star.

In his twenties, he was a blond, strapping six-foot-two Adonis of two hundred pounds of bronzed muscle. His acting ability may have been limited, but his athletic credentials were impeccable. Rose and Joe had followed his career for years, mesmerized by his spectacular performance in winning the 1919 Inter-Allied Games decathlon in Paris. He had won discus-throwing exhibition bouts and equestrian events.

Since it was a foal he had owned a gray outlaw stallion named Silver King, a magnificent animal that could perform an amazing variety of tricks. The horse had already appeared with Thomson insignificantly in pictures. Rose agreed with Joe that Thomson and his horse could rival the great Western star Tom Mix and his own mount, Tony. Not only was Thomson better-looking and younger than Mix, but Silver King could at least match Tony as an animal star. The Kennedys were surprised to find that their genial host and hostess, who were busy supervising the building of an elaborate hacienda that would be known as Enchanted Hill at the top of Angelo Drive in Beverly Hills, insisted they stay not in a hotel but in a just-completed stable designed for Silver King.

When the Kennedys arrived, they were met at the depot in downtown Los Angeles by the Thomsons' chauffeur, who drove them into the thinly settled area known as Beverly Hills. North of Sunset Boulevard, up Benedict Canyon, they passed rich clumps of trees and flowering scrub, until they began climbing up the steep incline of Angelo Drive. The car went up and up, through acres of eucalyptus, sycamore and pine, until a wrought-iron gateway greeted them opening onto a winding drive that continued for over half a mile, snaking up to the top of a hill. Workmen were everywhere, carrying planks, pails of paint, saws and hammers. The noise was deafening. A guest house was being built, its bare boards exposed to a sweeping view of hills with no houses and covered in scrub. To the right was the sprawling stable with dragon-scale red Spanish tiles.

Rose and Joe found themselves sleeping in its loft, in

temporarily borrowed furnishings, with a mahogany floor on which Silver King would soon plant his hooves. It is possible that, for the last time in her life, Rose was compelled, owing to the limited accommodations, to spend the night with her husband in the same bed.

Joe talked the Thomsons into agreeing to start a series of Western dramas in which Thomson would ride Silver King in daring attacks on bandits or Indians, always rescuing a beleaguered heroine just before she suffered a fate worse than death. When Sir Walter Erskine Crum died suddenly in New York in October, Joe had little difficulty in persuading the company bosses to allow Thomson a loan-out to Universal (whose films Joe released in New England) to see how he would handle a serial, *The Eagle's Talons.* It was an immediate success. Joe encouraged Frances Marion to concoct a vehicle for Thomson, *The Mask of Lopez,* produced by Al Rogell, into which Kennedy must have fed many ideas. The story of border raids and abductions, of outlaws and random shootings in the night, mirrored, scene by scene, the AGWI executives' hair-raising experiences during the Carranza regime in Mexico. Al Rogell told me many years later that Joe had everything to do with this first major Thomson Western.

Joe's decision was brilliant; in no time, *The Mask of Lopez* became a huge national hit, and, using another woman as a front, Frances Marion moonlighted from her various top-level bosses in concocting a succession of Thomson vehicles. Within six months, so rapid was his rise, a grateful Thomson was earning $10,000 a week and was on the verge of being in the topmost rank of stars.

Rose and Joe's children loved his films; the boys were delirious when Joe brought them mementoes of their idol, including a spare saddle, spurs and chaps. Soon they would meet Thomson in person.

In September, Jack, age six, began his schooling with his brother Joe at the popular Edward Devotion School.

In the late fall, Joe was in Chicago in connection with the Hayden, Stone interests; Rose joined him there, and they attended a gala concert performance of celebrated bandleader Paul Whiteman and his Leviathan Orchestra. They were enchanted by a young, attractive Irish-American tenor,

Morton Downey, who, in white tie and tails, made a vivid impression on the audience. At a party following, they talked to Downey, and Joe decided to develop the young man's career. Writing of that first meeting years later, Downey said, "Joe had that intangible something about him—radiating knowledge, success, perception and an excitement in living."

With Rose's approval, Joe wrote to his friend, the leading theatrical producer Charles B. Dillingham, recommending that Dillingham should make sure he attended the Palace Theater in New York, where Downey would appear. As a result, Dillingham took up Downey and further developed his burgeoning career. Downey never forgot, and he and the Kennedys became friends for life.

By the winter of 1923, the Kennedy household in Brookline featured numerous film screenings, in which the family rejoiced to the lively images of the great stars of the time. Even though her eldest boy was still only eight, Rose, with great skill, ran her large family, encouraging, along with Joe, much discussion. She put up a bulletin board next to the dining room, on which she pinned various clippings from newspapers, all of which were used as topics of the day. Joe and Jack were asked to proffer their opinions on major events. Even though Rosemary was slow in her responses, she, too, was encouraged to join in. The children who were too young to understand were still present at these lively family discussions.

Rose punished naughtiness, including kicks under the table at meals, racings around the dining room or other mischiefs; for these offenses she had the children perform menial household tasks. Rudeness or physical violence were greeted with spankings, either by hand, or, in more extreme cases, with a coat hanger, a hairbrush or a ruler. This was standard treatment for children at the time.

Rose was in no way out of the ordinary—in fact, quite conventional—in insisting that each child turn up for meals exactly on time or they would miss a meal. An appearance halfway through a course would result in heavy censure, and eating that course would not be permitted.

As soon as a child was old enough, Rose insisted that he or she help her as much as possible. When an offspring reached the age of five, the child was given an allowance of ten cents a week, or about $2.50 in today's money, kept in a tiny bank in the form of a metal safe. The children were urged to save their money until they found something they really wanted at the local five-and-dime or notions store, rather than squandering each dime as it was received on ice cream or candy.

Above all, Rose encouraged them to save for Christmases, so they could afford to give each other and their parents decent gifts. Just before the season, they would invade the store, their bright and shiny faces peeping charmingly over deal countertops, begging for discounts from genial shopowners, who usually proved obliging.

In order to deal with so large a brood, Rose adopted the habit of writing notes to herself regarding the children's meals, medication when ill, snacks of milk and cookies, times of rising and going to bed, and permitted trips to movies or the theater. So numerous were these notes, and so afraid was she of losing them, she stuck them all over her dresses with safety pins, so that she looked like a walking notice board.

She carried with her a reading list for each child. She couldn't help notice that Jack was by far the biggest reader and that he devoured one picture book after another with insatiable desire for learning. He was a complement to Joe, who much preferred running, ragging, and playing neighborhood baseball or football to sitting down with collections of legends or fairy tales. The older boys did well at their studies, much to their parents' delight. Nobles and Greenough School was just a short walk from the house on Abbotsford Road, and it offered an excellent classical education; it was the accepted launching pad for Harvard. Both Joe and Jack learned Latin along with the required curriculum of mathematics, history, geography and athletics. So keen was the school on providing children with a healthy mind and a healthy body that a compulsory requirement was playing track outdoors in winter on boards over the snow.

Joe flourished and grew muscular and sturdy at Nobles and Greenough. Though fiercely keen at everything, Jack still lacked his brother's powerful constitution and was so frequently in and out of school that today the records of his attendance are hopelessly contradictory and incomplete.

For some time, Joe Senior had been wooed by another robber baron, the remarkable Yellow Cab king John Hertz, the idol of bright young businessmen of the time.

The popular version of Joe's encounter with Hertz stems from an inaccurate article in *Fortune* magazine published in 1938. The article stated that, in April 1924, Walter Howey, belligerent editor of the Hearsts' *Boston American,* appealed to Joe in a late-night visit to help him because his shares in the Yellow Cab Company of Chicago and New York were falling rapidly due to a bear raid.

The stocks were falling, certainly, but no evidence of any such bear raid can be found; the story has been confused with AGWI's. The reasons for the stock's problems were far different.

Hertz had been brought to New York from a Tyrolean village at the age of five, and had worked his way up through the classic route of newspaper seller, wagon driver, teenage boxer and reporter on a newspaper. He became an automobile salesman, and by 1913, at the age of thirty-four, he bought his own taxicab. He began building the Yellow Cab Company, choosing that color because he read an article in which it was stated that yellow was the single most eye-catching tint. Within a few years, Yellow Cabs became a staple of every city in America. By 1917, he owned 120,000 of them, and his net worth was approximately $30 million. He managed the bus systems of Chicago and other cities, with the notable exception of New York.

Unadvertised was the fact that he was a crook. Yellow Cabs was a scam operation, breaking every imaginable law. Meters were rigged and, at night, unlighted, so that passengers couldn't read them from the backseat. If there was an argument over the fare, drivers were equipped with a gun, compelling their human cargo to pay up or else. Hertz had the city license commissioners bribed to the hilt. Licenses were issued without any requirements of the driver, including the possession of a driver's license. A criminal record was standard. The worst evils Hertz perpetrated were in New York.

At every major cab rank, most notably those at the New York Harbor Passenger Pier, the Central Park Rank and Yankee Stadium, bribed police kept rival cabdrivers at a great distance, behind barriers, while a long line of Yellow Cabs awaited prospective passengers. When other companies offered money to secure a place on these ranks, they were refused permission; Hertz had to pay only two dollars a year per rank for the privilege.

Joe met Hertz at the old Waldorf-Astoria on the present site of the Empire State Building, soon after setting up his own offices on Milk Street in Boston. He quickly discovered why Yellow Cab shareholders were troubled. In fact, Rose had only to pick up a newspaper to discover it, even if Hertz tried to hide the truth from Joe. Checker Cabs, a tough, upcoming rival of Yellow's, had fought to a standstill Hertz's effort to stop them from using either the color yellow or the eye-catching checker design that caught the attention of passersby. Judge Callahan of the New York Superior Court had decided for Checker; then, shortly before Joe met with Hertz, there was explosive headline news. A grand jury indicted Hertz's president, Morris Markham, and his vice-president, Emil R. Carlson, for bribing Checker Cab drivers to repudiate affidavits in which they had sworn that Hertz and his drivers interfered with their business. Evidence emerged that these executives and others had stood outside Checker Cab's New York garage and threatened, it was alleged with guns, any Checker Cab man who tried to attack Hertz. Joe was in the midst of dealing with this matter, injecting large sums of money into Yellow Cabs by buying authorized blocks of stock and otherwise manipulating the shareholders, when his and Rose's fourth daughter, their sixth child, Patricia, was born, on May 6, 1924. He didn't have time to go home.

That week was charged with stress for Rose, who worried about Joe, since there was a cab strike in New York. When trustees of the Brotherhood of Taxi Chauffeurs pointed out that the strike was caused by unfair wages paid to drivers, they were attacked in Hertz-connected newspapers; because of influence and privilege, Yellow Cab chauffeurs did not join their rivals in other companies. When those same trustees tried to talk to Yellow Cab drivers at the company's

103rd Street headquarters, they were beaten and thrown to the ground. Then, ironically, nine hundred Yellow Cab drivers themselves walked out on May 8. The desire for better wages had proved catching. Finally, even Hertz was compelled to recognize the drivers' union, and the strike ended.

In June, a grateful Hertz made Joe a full partner in a $25 million merger of Yellow Cabs, the Fifth Avenue Coach Company and the Chicago Motor Coach Company, buying out the Rapid Transit Company's fifty-one-percent interest in Fifth Avenue. Joe's involvement in this newly formed conglomerate was reminiscent of his more modest bus operation in Boston financed by Honey Fitz.

Joe moved into Hertz's permanent office suite at the Waldorf, where he expertly handled the joint coach companies' shares. The old single-decker buses were replaced with double-deckers with open tops, pleasant in good weather and intolerable during much of the year. But still, they were immensely popular, especially to courting couples.

With his customary energy, Joe plunged into Hertz's astonishing political shenanigans. He can only have been party to the bold decision Hertz made to involve Mayor Hylan of New York directly in his operation. Not only was Hylan given parcels of shares under the table, but he also allowed the three brothers of his son-in-law to assume executive positions in Yellow Cabs. When reporters besieged City Hall, Hylan exploded with furious denials, but the charges stuck. Michael Donnella, vice-president of the taxi drivers' Mutual Insurance Corporation, stated that Hylan owned thousands of shares in the name of his son-in-law, John F. Sinnot. Again, this was denied; again, ineffectively. In desperation, to save his own neck, Hylan embarked on a full-scale police campaign against Hertz.

In 1924 alone, he arrested 820 drivers, of whom 815 were convicted. He talked to the tax authorities about the fact that $175,000 of stock had gone into the personal account of the police commissioner, who was told to sell them immediately. The tax authorities were also advised that Hertz's revenue in Manhattan alone amounted to over $100 million over three years. Comedians made hay with the matter; a popular exchange to be found on the vaudeville stage was "I don't want to pay this fare." And the answer was "Don't you know? The cab belongs to Mayor Hylan. You'd better pay up or else."

Then, on January 29, 1925, Rose read a shocking announcement concerning Yellow Cabs. One of Hertz's drivers shot and fatally injured Dennis J. Kenny, twenty-year-old nephew of Edward J. Kenny, the honorary deputy chief of the New York Fire Department, outside Kenny's home in Brooklyn, in an argument over the fare. As Kenny lingered between life and death for several days, Hylan, again protecting his embattled reputation, arrested hundreds of drivers. It was discovered that not only the killer but almost the entire Yellow Cab chauffeur force had either been to prison or had paid fines for a variety of criminal activities. Rose's Yellow Cab stock became wildly volatile, especially after February 12, when Dennis Kenny died. The murderer was indicted, pleaded second-degree murder, and was excused the hangman's noose.

Meantime, Hertz had been looking desperately for some evasive tactic to take his shareholders' eyes off the gun sights of the current scandal. With Joe Kennedy, he developed a novelty: the first self-drive automobile agency. Basing his policy on the old tradition in which livery stables rented out horses and buggies, he set up a $1 million corporation known as the Hertz Drive-It-Yourself System, and Joe Kennedy had a spectacular success in floating the shares.

Joe was soon rewarded. Hertz made him a partner in a successful merger, engineered by J. & W. Seligman, of Yellow Cabs, with the Fifth Avenue Coach Company and the Chicago Motor Coach Company on June 26, 1924. At a conference at Hertz's suite at the Waldorf, it was agreed that old single-decker buses would be replaced with double-deckers with open tops, despite the problem presented by New York City's notorious changes of weather.

But a shadow lay over the meeting. It had begun to emerge that, for all of his skill in organizing bond and share issues, Kennedy had not managed to help Yellow Cabs itself into profits. In fact, an August statement showed that the company was down approximately $24,000 from the previous quarter, and the manufacturing company that constructed the cabs had lost about a quarter of a million.

Rose shared Joe's dilemma. How were Hertz and Kennedy, as his chief stock counselor and shareholder, to overcome the problem? How were they to fight an embattled Mayor Hylan and his irritated police commissioner from cleaning up their record by closing in on the company? Serious charges were about to be leveled against Hertz and, by extension, Kennedy that might have resulted in a full-scale inquiry at least on the state level. So Hertz, with the support of Kennedy's department, engineered a skillful changeover: General Motors was offered a deal its directors could not resist. GM would exchange 100,000 shares for 800,000 shares of Yellow Cab common stock. This would effectively give GM controlling interest. At the same time, in a deal to be concluded on September 1, General Motors' truck division would blend with Yellow Cab Manufacturing under one roof; seven directors of GM would serve on Yellow Cab's board; seven directors of Yellow Cab would join GM.

Hylan would not hesitate to take Yellow Cab support; but he would not have dared take on General Motors, several members of whose board were political and business allies who had helped put him into office. Thus, the stock department, with Joe as its chief, trumped the mayor's threatening ace. It seemed the right moment for him to clear out, with profits from his various transactions of somewhere in the region of $2 million, or some $30 million in current terms.

In August 1925, Joe, leaving a six-months-pregnant Rose behind, took a ship to England to try to buy out the shareholders and become sole owner of FBO. He was armed with the substantial sum of $2 million (not $1 million, as was often stated), but the directors held back. Even when chewing-gum tycoon William Wrigley and shoe mogul John Florsheim offered to increase the sum, the partners turned Joe down.

Joe returned just in time to attend the birth of Robert Francis Kennedy, Rose's seventh child and third son, on November 20, 1925.

On February 7, 1926, after much difficult discussion, FBO's owners in London changed their minds and agreed to Joe's purchase of the company. Because of their frequent delays, they had been forced to accept the lower price of $1 million for his controlling interest. He was still backed by Wrigley and Florsheim; other backers were Hayden, Stone; their rival, railroad tycoon Frederick Prince; and several others. Joe put Eddie Moore, John J. Ford, formerly of Bethlehem Steel, and other close associates on the new directorial board, removing all of the late Sir Walter Erskine Crum's associates in the process.

He traveled to Hollywood alone two days later; Rose, with handicapped Rosemary and baby Bobby on her hands, and her older boys at Nobles and Greenough School, was unable to accompany him immediately, but would follow later. Joe stayed with Fred Thomson and Frances Marion. On weekends, the Thomsons drove Kennedy in their Pierce-Arrow automobile to their ten-thousand-acre ranch at Chatsworth in the still-unsettled San Fernando Valley.

At FBO studios that spring, Thomson was completing work on a new Western, *Hands Across the Border,* the exotic Evelyn Brent was appearing as a glamorous spy in *Secret Orders,* and Thomson's best friend, the hefty Western star "Lefty" Flynn, was appearing in *Big Timber.*

According to Viola Dana, Flynn's wife, the beautiful, dark-haired leading lady, Joe had an affair with her, and the result was, she said, that Lefty threatened Joe with a broken jaw. Unable to resist Kennedy, Viola, in her own words, "strayed," and Flynn, unable to get close enough to Joe to beat him up, surrounded as he was by henchmen, stormed out of the studio. Joe immediately signed Viola Dana to a new contract, with better money, and canceled Flynn's. He thus effectively broke up the marriage.

Perhaps getting wind of this situation, Rose came to Hollywood by train in April.

The magnificent Fred Thomson Spanish hacienda known as Enchanted Hill had been completed under the supervision of the architect Wallace Neff. Rose's car bumped over a cobbled courtyard toward a handsome, arched doorway surmounted by a coat of arms invented by the Thomsons. It combined in its four quarters symbols of a horse, a pen, a horseshoe and a camera. On the lawn, a 100-foot pool glittered in the sun, and white sand around it had been tipped out from trucks, carried from ocean beaches. A wrought-iron doorway led to a flagstone hall and then to another arch, and then to a vast sunken living room with thirty-foot ceilings, framed on either side by arches that enclosed a two-way view. The king of Spain could have asked for no better residence; no other movie star could match it. The Thomsons had poured their life savings into it, making it a place of romantic splendor, commemorating their intense love for each other.

One of the Kennedy children's idols was Harold "Red" Grange, the dazzling football star. Joe, Jr., and Jack had begged Joe, Sr., to sign Grange to a contract for movies, and Joe had been at the Los Angeles depot in February when Grange arrived on an FBO contract. Joe had much to do with Grange's first picture, *One Minute to Play,* which was shot in Hollywood that June; he, Rose and Grange formed an intimate friendship, and, in his old age in 1970, Grange reminisced warmly at his Florida retirement home about Joe's influence on his short-lived film career. But one disappointment of that exciting season upset Joe's elder boys. Joe was unable to sign the even more famous Babe Ruth to a contract; he lost him to First National. However, he did satisfy the kids' longing for a circus picture, rashly embarking on *Bigger than Barnum's,* starring, rather daringly, Viola Dana. He plunged into the picture, a story of circus tightrope acrobats, so quickly to satisfy his family's love of the Barnum and Bailey Circus that he forgot to get the rights to use the Barnum name, and had to suffer the humiliation of a major lawsuit, resulting in the picture being withdrawn until all references to the great circus owner were removed.

Joe's and Rose's closest Hollywood friend other than the Thomsons and Red Grange was Joe Schnitzer, Jewish production chief of FBO.

Statements are often made that the Kennedys were anti-Semitic. Yet they frequently attended Schnitzer's strictly non-Aryan Hillcrest Country Club and mingled with Schnitzer's powerful Jewish group of acquaintances at the Pacific Coast Baseball League, of which Schnitzer was treasurer. Additionally, with a touch of humor, Joe put through the picture *Rose of the Tenements,* a direct reference to his wife's origins, starring Viola Dana's pretty sister,

Shirley Mason. It was a pro-Jewish story of an old New York couple, born in Jerusalem, who adopt two orphans in Manhattan; the young boy falls in love with a Protestant girl. There are other Kennedyan themes: two of the characters are Bolshevist agitators, one of whom, Emma Goldstein, based on Emma Goldman, is a radical leader handy with bombs. A ward boss, Gallagan, is one hundred percent Martin Lomasney. Also that summer, Joe supervised *Kosher Kitty Kelly*, based on a play that echoed *Abie's Irish Rose* in its story of the love of an Irish girl and a New York Jewish delicatessen proprietor's son.

More than any Jewish mogul in Hollywood, the upstart gentile Joe Kennedy made picture after picture designed to make the American public aware of the fine qualities of Jewish family life at a time when there were powerful anti-Semitic forces operating at all levels of American society. Indeed, the very presentation of Jewish-Catholic love affairs was almost as daring as portraying a black-white relationship would have been. Later, in the picture *Clancey's Kosher Wedding*, Joe cemented his policy of making such movies, a policy imitated by Carl Laemmle, Jewish head of Universal Studios, in *The Cohens and the Kellys* and its sequels.

Chapter 6

Sic Transit Gloria

Joe and Rose stayed at Enchanted Hill until late May 1926; in a trust for Rose set up at the time, Joe bought the entire stock in Rose's name of Fred Thomson Productions, which, in turn, owned 3,300 shares of Todd Shipyards. Eddie and Mary Moore remained in charge of the children at the Brookline house.

On June 26, Joe, Rose and all other parents with children at the Nobles and Greenough School bought it outright and changed the name to Dexter.

Rose had felt for some time that the family was too disrupted by her long absences from home, and that everyone should get together for the traditional summer vacation. Cohasset was out of the question; the Kennedys had grown tired of the town in the wake of their exclusion from the country club, and had gotten wind of another, far jazzier resort: Hyannis Port.

Situated dramatically on the rocky shore of Cape Cod, Hyannis, as it was popularly known, was much closer to Nantasket than to Cohasset in atmosphere. It had been enjoyed as an unspoiled resort from the 1840s on. By 1873, it was settled as developers moved in, and by 1926 its Craigville Beach was being mentioned as one of the world's best. The Queen's Byway Shopping Center, featuring a windmill and a lighthouse in a touristically conceived "New England" design, and the Hyannis Theater, complete with organ, were both in place by the late 1920s. It was the center of bootlegging activities and a favorite haunt of the Ku Klux Klan. Rose and Joe's favorite bands, Paul Whiteman's and Vincent Lopez's, played there, often featuring their friend Morton Downey (who later bought a summer home on nearby Squaw Island) at the Sun Kist Gardens. The atmosphere was ritzy neocolonial. The town was formalized, whitewashed, sparkling, and swept by bracing sea winds.

On June 10, 1926, the Kennedys started the first of their summer seasons there; Rose and Joe had scouted the area in their Rolls-Royce for two successive years. Honey Fitz had rented from Mrs. Beulah Malcolm the so-called Malcolm Cottage for seasons, and now they took it over from him. It was a big 1903 white clapboard Cape Cod house, with fifteen rooms, an attic, and a wine and fruit cellar, quite similar to their summer home at Nantasket. It had a sweeping view of Nantucket Sound, and a narrow sand path that ran down to the beach—enjoyed by the children but a hazard to adults because of slippage, scrub and tree roots that ran across it.

Joe and Rose fell in love with the house so completely after they had been there a few weeks that they decided to buy it through local real-estate wizard James Woodward, and, on Halloween 1928, they did. Rose was pleased to find she could attend Mass every morning at St. Francis Xavier Church in Hyannis, and she found genial priests to teach the children their catechisms along with her. The house and lawns overflowed with boisterous games and laughter; Rose presided over deafening parties for neighborhood children. Nobody's birthday was forgotten, and tugs-of-war took place which the Kennedy brood were instructed severely to win.

But the Kennedys had not found a perfect paradise. It has been insistently stated that in Hyannis Port the Kennedys found an ecumenical atmosphere, where social doors were opened to all. That is the opposite of the truth. The resort proved to be no more accommodating than Cohasset. Once again, the Kennedys were excluded from the local golf club. This was a particularly severe blow, as the reason for the move must have been that Rose and Joe expected that club to be available to them. How they could have been so deceived may never be made clear.

They did find one loophole, not then but in the immediate future. They learned that the yacht club, which had always been exclusive, had closed its doors many years earlier, due to lack of funding. At Rose's suggestion, Joe put the club on his list of potential investments; by 1932, he would become, very cleverly, a founder member, thus compelling the snobbish individuals involved with it to accept him and Rose as pillars of the revived institution.

As for being accepted by the social bigwigs, and invited to their house parties, that was out of the question. It wasn't so much a matter of the Kennedys being Catholic as that they did not belong to the accepted top level of society either locally or internationally.

Nor were the Boston Brahmins responsible for their exclusion. Oddly, by the mid-1920s, Hyannis Port was no longer a favorite of the elite Boston community. It was actually favored by Pittsburgh money. And the Pittsburgh Protestant ruling families, rich for generations in heavy industry, were unimpressed by an upstart young Wall Street plunger and manipulator who had made scarcely a dent when in the steel industry. It is surprising that the Kennedys didn't pull strings with Charles Schwab, who was still close to them and was, of course, the continuing mogul of Bethlehem Steel, to help them break through the Pittsburghian barriers. But they did not; perhaps pride weighed against the potential move.

When the Moores arrived from Brookline with the brood, the reunion was occasion for great rejoicing. Among the visitors in those first happy days was, to the children's ecstatic approval, Red Grange. Not long after, Fred Thomson followed, with Frances Marion, who had visited the Brookline house separately. Grange, Thomson and Marion loved the Kennedy children, finding them uniformly charming and fun to be with; the two star athletes became the models on whom the Kennedy boys sought to base their lives. Joe, Jr., in particular, worked out hard, and with success, to bring his physique to a level that would be comparable with these American heroes'.

Hyannis Port became the hub of the Kennedys' existence. In order to satisfy his movie-mad clan, which now included Honey Fitz, Rose remodeled the basement, as she had done at Brookline, into a private theater, where the kids could shriek with excitement at the FBO Westerns—Thomson galloping in on Silver King to rescue a beleaguered heroine. The girls could thrill to the romantic stars of the day, Milton Sills, Ramon Novarro and Rudolph Valentino, who died that year.

Another favorite of the children was the work of a new Kennedy discovery: the young and still unknown Walt Disney. Joe had, as Disney later acknowledged, discovered the brilliantly promising pioneer artist in animation. Disney was a former World War I ambulance driver who had made his first career in Kansas City, fashioning cartoon commercials to be shown in movie theaters and humorously known as Laugh-O-Grams. Joe signed him at FBO following his early success with a series, *Alice in Cartoonland.* Under Joe's aegis, Disney developed Mickey Mouse for the first time. His silent cartoons *Plane Crazy* and *Gallopin' Gaucho* were hugely popular. The credits read: "Joseph P. Kennedy presents a Walt Disney Comic."

In the unlikely event there was no film available, Joe would wind up the phonograph and the strains of Rudy Vallee, singing through a megaphone, filled the house. Or there was the jig of such bands as Vincent Lopez's, Fred Waring's, or the sweet tenor voice of Morton Downey.

Since the children played a role in the selection of the family vessel's name, nothing could be a clearer expression of their unity and of their fondness for their strict but loving matriarch than their calling their sloop *The Eight-of-Us.* (Later, when their last children arrived, the Kennedys changed the boat's name to *The Ten-of-Us,* and then *One More.*) When the weather was good, and the choppy waters off Cape Cod were reasonably smooth, Rose, trying to suppress anxiety, and not liking to sail in small craft, saw her husband and children off, day after day, on a series of adventures resembling those in *The Swiss Family Robinson.*

When the sun was shining and the brisk winds blew in from the ocean, Hyannis was an athlete's paradise, and the children grew strong (with the exception of the persistently sickly Jack), brown and sturdy, involved in hilarious activities over which Rose, for all of her inherited love of discipline, could do little to keep control. She tried to maintain some sense of order, but it was virtually futile. On one occasion, when Joe, Jr., proved irritating, she sent him out to the beach to dig for scallops and mussels, an occupation he enjoyed because it gave him a chance to make friends involved in the same occupation.

Rose managed the order of the day to the point that she put electric alarm clocks in every room, which went off shatteringly each morning at 7:00 A.M. Mass came first, then the boys rushed out to the lawn to do their exercises; later, there was a nine-o'clock or ten-o'clock curfew, according to the age of the child concerned. When the weather was bad, the kids joined Rose in charades, board games and Questions-and-Answers. Swimming took up much of the day, full-scale rags involving the boys and races up and down the beach.

A new joy for the Kennedys of living in Hyannis Port was the recently opened restaurant the Toll House, where Wednesday evenings became ritualistic. Situated between the Cape and Boston, the Toll House was owned by Kenneth and Ruth Wakefield, a couple who specialized in delicious cookies, cakes and raspberry turnovers. Every year, the Wakefields mailed boxes to the Kennedy kids with their matchless brownies, and they also could whip up French onion soup au gratin, lobster Newburg, and Boston cream pie.

That fall, Joe was in and out of California several times, the five-day train journeys part of his life. Rose stayed home, rejoicing in Joe, Jr.'s, performance at Dexter School, which, unhappily, was not matched by Jack's. In and out because of his poor health, Jack tended to turn up poor grades and be at the bottom of his class. A brave fighter, he inevitably fell foul of bullying by the stronger boys.

In December 1926, Joe met with a new friend, the shrill, vampire-bat-faced Hoosier film-industry moralist and czar Will Hays. He had first met Hays in 1920, just after Hays had a narrow escape from death: at the last minute, Hays had sent his deputy postmaster general to the Knickerbocker Theater, Washington, D.C., opening of a new movie, *Get-Rich-Quick Wallingford*. The weight of winter snow on the theater roof cracked it open, carrying thousands of tons of concrete down on the audience and killing hundreds, including his deputy.

Disturbed by the event, Hays had become devoutly religious, grateful for his survival. Though, as a Protestant, he directly opposed Kennedy's views, he shared his friend's desire that movies should have a moral purpose. Like Joe, he was conscious of the power of motion pictures to influence the public mind. From his children, Joe had learned how a man like Fred Thomson on the screen could make them want to be heroes, to be decent and virtuous and to oppose wickedness.

In conversations with Hays, Joe confirmed his belief that motion-picture executives shared his and Rose's sense of exclusion from the American elite. They were almost all Jews, confined to their own clubs, despised, laughed at, not least by the very stars whom they had elevated to the heights. It was important to render the individual moguls, and the industry as a whole, not only morally desirable but intellectually acceptable. Rose supported this point of view.

Joe and Hays undertook a bold step: Joe would approach Harvard Business School's Dean Wallace B. Donham to suggest an unprecedented lecture series by film-industry leaders to explain their purposes and to discuss the importance of film. It was a daring idea, particularly in view of the fact that Harvard clubs excluded Jews as completely as they excluded Catholics. Kennedy saw an advantage for himself: he would be able to cross all barriers, which existed because he was a gentile maverick in Hollywood, to the very top of the studios. He was negotiating for a possible deal in which he would sell FBO and himself to Adolph Zukor's Paramount Pictures. It would be a shrewd move to place Zukor at the top of the list of potential lecturers.

After obtaining Wallace B. Donham's approval and fielding attacks from such prominent Harvardians as William Marston Seabury, Joe approached the industry leaders one by one. Overcoming their distaste for Kennedy, whom most of them saw as a Catholic upstart, the tycoons crumbled before his expert flattery. Virtually none had enjoyed the benefit of a college education; several were incapable of sustained reading and had to have synopses or balance sheets read out to them.

As he had planned, Joe went to see Adolph Zukor first; Zukor was negotiating behind his back to steal Fred Thomson from him, but cheerfully accepted the invitation. Marcus Loew, head of Loew's, Inc., which owned M.G.M., was delighted to be selected instead of a much-irritated Louis B. Mayer.

The genial Jesse L. Lasky, also of Paramount, joined the list. He formed a friendship with Joe and Rose as time went on; his colorful background proved irresistible. He had begun as an unsuccessful prospector in the Alaska gold rush; he had conducted a jazz band in Hawaii, played a cornet in vaudeville, and had coproduced the pioneer movie and first large-scale Western, *The Squaw Man.* He was warm, lovable, clever, and Rose found him intensely likable.

It was months before the necessary arrangements could be made for the lecture series, which took place, finally, in the spring of 1927. It was a success; nervous at first, the executives, augmented by Milton Sills and the gentile Cecil B. DeMille, delighted the students, who leapt to their feet, clapping wildly, overjoyed by seeing the elusive movie people in person.

The publisher Shaw, Inc., of New York, brought out *The Story of the Films,* a book containing the lectures, and Joe's knowledgeable introduction, later that year. It was received enthusiastically by the press.

By the summer of 1927, with Rose pregnant for an eighth time, it had become clear that Joe's traveling from Boston to New York, as well as from New York to Los Angeles, would have to be curtailed in view of the increasing pressure of work in Manhattan. For a time he had thought of finding a more convenient house, but Rose, attached to Boston and to her parents, and happy with her children's progress at school, hadn't wanted the disruption. However, by now she realized that if she were to stay in Boston indefinitely, she would lose contact with Joe for long periods of the year. She was forced to accept the move. Joe sent Eddie and Mary

Moore to find a decent rental in New York until they should
be prepared to buy. At the same time, Rose hired a new
nurse, Alice Cahill, known to the family as "Keela."

The Moores located a handsome, thirteen-room house at
5040 Independence Avenue, overlooking the Hudson, in the
Riverdale section of the then-fashionable Bronx.

The village of Riverdale, in Westchester County, had
been annexed to New York City in 1874. It had always been
a wealthy and exclusive neighborhood. From being a tiny
hamlet it had grown into a handsome, growing hamlet,
occupied by such prominent families as the Dodges, the
Van Cortlandts, the Delafields, the Appletons and the
Babcocks. The absence of subway lines through Riverdale
helped it to maintain an exclusive, somewhat rural character. Bus services to the district were not encouraged; zoning
laws restricted commercial buildings. Outsiders were not
particularly welcome; substantial contributions to the political coffers were passports to necessary entree. No doubt a
greasing of the proper palms enabled the Kennedys at least
to not be overtly snubbed, but there is no evidence that they
were made welcome either. Riverdale was bedrock Protestant Republican, and for Rose to go to Mass involved an
excessively long drive; this alone made her feel uncomfortable there.

The house was faced in stucco on brick, with a high roof
featuring four brick chimneys; it was spacious, but not very
warm, in atmosphere. But it did have a splendid garden,
which Rose could see could be developed, and a line of pink
dogwood trees provided a handsome decorative touch. Red
maple saplings ringed the entire one-acre corner lot; they
had been planted shortly beforehand. Depressed though
Rose was, she at least could observe some potential in the
home.

Organized by Rose like a marine squadron, the family
departed from Brookline on September 15 by private
railroad car, which, for all its luxury, offered the usual
unholy mixture of cinder-filled soot blown through the
windows, suffocating heat and cramped conditions for
seven children. Eunice was ill with a stomach disorder. On
arrival, the children fell in love with their new home and
raced around it, exploring every nook and cranny. Soon

boys and girls alike plunged into touch-football games on the lawn: the Kennedy addiction then and later.

The older children were admitted to Riverdale Country School, situated in twelve acres of tree- and flower-filled grounds near the Hudson River.

Rose was unhappily marooned in Riverdale; although she planted a rose bower, which attracted local attention, still, after several weeks, she couldn't warm to the new house and was homesick for Boston. She missed her father and, now that she was pregnant again, dreaded the thought of not having Dr. Good as her obstetrician. She finally decided not to sell the Brookline house, which stood empty, deprived of its furniture. She would move in there again in February, to await the hospital birth of her eighth child.

For Joe, the move was desirable; apart from his film interests, he had a succession of meetings with Will Hays in Manhattan, and was busy planning to extend his interests by obtaining a majority shareholding in the important Pathe Company. In order to spend more time with his family, he eschewed both train and car and made a perilous daily flight by biplane to and from the small airport in Queens. He had recently abolished the stock company of actors at FBO, and had been forced to relinquish Fred Thomson to Zukor at Paramount. Joe replaced him with the former coal miner, sailor, prizefighter and champion weightlifter Tom Tyler, whom he invited to Riverdale as a potential Western star. Rose and the family looked the twenty-three-year-old Tyler over and strongly approved of him. Joe signed him to a contract, with Rose's enthusiastic support, and he soon became a big name among Western fans.

But Joe needed another major star. He was angling for the great cowboy actor Tom Mix, who was under contract to Fox, and word that Mix might be joining him at FBO sent his elder boys into ecstasy.

Now he needed a top female star, and, with characteristic boldness, settled upon obtaining one of the two or three biggest: Gloria Swanson.

Born Gloria Josephine Mae Swenson in 1897, the antic, extravagant, heavily made-up and overdressed thirty-year-old actress had risen rapidly from being an extra in a

Chicago studio to a Keystone Comedy actress; she was
featured as a Bathing Beauty when she couldn't even swim.
Her first husband, actor Wallace Beery, raped her on their
wedding night; the marriage failed after two years. Cecil B.
DeMille starred her in *Don't Change Your Husband* and
Why Change Your Wife?, both of which advocated the
policy Rose and Joe followed diligently: so long as a wife
maintained her position and was well cared for, she would
be wise to tolerate her husband's infidelities; similarly, a
husband should put up with his wife's behavior in order to
maintain the security of a happy home.

By 1925, Swanson had become hugely successful, earning
almost half a million dollars a year. However, she ran
through the money very quickly: $20,000 a year went into
fashion originals, twice as much again in jewelry. She paid
for a personal team of musicians, since she would not
accept those offered by the studio, to play mood music on
the set of her pictures that would get her into the appropriate state of mind to play the scenes; she owned a Pierce
Arrow and a Cadillac; some $12,000 a year went on several
maids, a chauffeur and two secretaries; and she had a staff,
including a personal production manager, an accountant, a
bookkeeper, a lawyer exclusively used for her personal
benefit and, when ill, a twenty-four-hour service of nurses.

She decided to become an independent producer, and,
with no knowledge of French, took off to Paris to make the
film *Madame Sans-Gêne,* a comedy about Napoleon's relationship with a washerwoman. Her interpreter was no less
than the Marquis de la Falaise de la Coudraye, to give him a
shortened title, an impoverished aristocrat who could trace
his lineage back to the twelfth century.

Treating the Marquis (who had been named Henry James
for the American novelist and whose uncle was the Marquess of Queensbury who destroyed Oscar Wilde) with
alternative affection and contempt, Swanson embarked on a
love affair with director Raoul Walsh while making *Sadie
Thompson,* Somerset Maugham's story of the love affair of a
prostitute and a minister. Joe Kennedy had been in the
forefront of moralists attacking the movie before it was
even finished.

Kennedy learned that Swanson was broke by the late fall

of 1927. Owning three houses and a penthouse in New York, she was incapable of controlling her spending and had already begun to off-load her property. Through a contact in Hollywood, he heard that she was on her way to New York, trying to raise money to complete the editing of *Sadie Thompson,* which she had guaranteed the releasing studio she would underwrite herself.

Announcing that she would be staying at the Savoy Plaza, she impetuously changed plans on the train and moved into the Barclay instead.

Rose had been a fan of Swanson for years. With Rose's complete awareness, Joe had lunch with Swanson on November 11. She captivated him at once; she was buoyant, amusing, attractive and no fool except where money was concerned. Kennedy saw her as a good investment: she had an immense following, thousands of fans storming the theaters in which her pictures opened, and her vulnerable financial condition made her an easy mark. Exerting all of the Kennedy charm, he fascinated her, and instantly announced that she could lean on him for all possible financial advice.

To avoid any possible gossip, Rose made a point of contacting Gloria directly, expressing her admiration for her work, and reassuring her that Joe would be expert in taking care of her affairs. Contrary to her published memoirs, *Swanson on Swanson,* Swanson did not return to Hollywood after the meeting, but lingered on at the Barclay until Christmas. During those weeks, Joe was in New York, helping her with the editing of *Sadie Thompson* to reduce the offensive elements that might result in its being prohibited in certain states and in Europe. He liquidated her stocks and extended promissory notes. But whatever money he could raise was swallowed up by the hotel bills, her addiction to buying the latest fashions, and the support allowance she paid to the Marquis.

Rose heard warnings from her parents of an affair between her husband and Swanson, but she ignored them. There is no evidence to suggest that the Kennedy-Swanson relationship was any more than a business merger sealed by unromantic sex, if that.

But Gloria's departure for California at Christmas may

have been engineered by Rose, since it was important that Joe be present at the Christmas celebrations at Riverdale, if only to allay any unfavorable comment in the press. Christmas was a big occasion in the Kennedy household: the children who were old enough had saved from their allowances for most of the year to buy the most expensive gifts they could afford for their parents and siblings; Rose and Joe lavished presents on them, piled in extravagant heaps of silver and gold and scarlet wrappings under the Christmas tree. By contrast with this exhilarating family get-together, Swanson spent a lonely Christmas on the train.

The events of the next few weeks scarcely support the widespread belief that Joe was madly in love with the star. He did not travel to Hollywood, where she was facing a major lawsuit (which she subsequently lost) for having slapped a process server across the face. She moved into a rented house on Angelo Drive in Beverly Hills, just below Enchanted Hill; her own large home on North Crescent Drive had been rented to Norma Talmadge. She barely had room to accommodate her huge wardrobe of clothes, unpacked from seventeen trunks and suitcases, and the personal furnishings she insisted on adding to those already in the house.

She was desperate for money despite Joe's every effort to help her. On January 4, she sent Joe an anguished telegram: Morris Cleary, treasurer of United Artists, had lent her $15,583.62 on a promissory note and she had no money to repay it. Kennedy got an extension for her; but she was so short of cash she couldn't attend the world premiere of *Sadie Thompson* in Washington, D.C., or even the San Francisco opening. The Park Chambers Hotel in New York was demanding payment for rent on her penthouse, unpaid for months even though she had sublet it.

At the same time, Rose made arrangements with Joe's New York staff to reopen the Brookline house, hired two new maids and a chauffeur, and set out plans to have her child in a hospital for the first time. By 1928, births at home had become less fashionable, even among the rich.

By early January, Joe had become the head of the Pathe production-distribution company, running it jointly with a new friend of his and Rose's, John J. Murdock. Rose was very fond of Murdock's charming wife, Ethel, and the couple had visited Riverdale many times.

Murdock had begun his career as an electrician, saving enough to buy a struggling theatrical stock company in Cincinnati in 1900. He made a sensation when he started up Murdock's Roof, a very popular theater in Chicago; by 1906, he had successfully promoted the same city's magnificent Majestic Theater, spreading out into the field of vaudeville, and developing a massive chain that soon linked up with B. F. Keith's and Edward Albee's Keith-Albee circuit.

He lived very largely on goat's milk and honey, which, he claimed, could cure all human ailments. Told he had cancer in 1926, he spent almost a million dollars on a horse serum that, he swore, cured him of the disease (he lived until 1948, when he was ninety). At the time Joe met him, he had become legendary for making the longest long-distance call in history: 350 minutes from New York to San Francisco at a cost of $2,157.80 to avert a musician and stagehand strike in his West Coast theaters.

Joe formed the fledgling Gloria Production Company under his presidency, registered in Hollywood and New York. Not trusting Gloria to handle the stock, he had it issued in the name of the company's vice-president and treasurer, Patrick Scollard, in Manhattan. All of the stock was issued in Scollard's name; Scollard was so nervous about this that he cabled Joe's Hollywood representative, Edward B. Derr, formerly with him at Fore River, IF I DON'T GO TO JAIL OVER THIS DEAL, I NEVER WILL.

Joe left for Palm Beach on January 23, accompanied by the Murdocks and his assistants Edward O'Leary and Eddie Moore, for business meetings, swimming at the beach in the warm Atlantic waters and numerous games of golf. To Joe's delight, his protegé, the up-and-coming young tenor Morton Downey, performed at the Venetian Gardens, the most fashionable local nightclub, the day after Joe and his party arrived. Other friends there were Al Jolson, the producer Sam Harris and the playwright Edgar Selwyn.

While Rose was at Brookline, supervising the arrival of coal, seeing that the water was turned on and interviewing new staff, having left her children at Riverdale, Gloria, with the Marquis, traveled via New Orleans and Jacksonville, arriving in Palm Beach on January 29. Fans and reporters stormed the train.

Gloria later described an improbable scene in which Joe invaded her compartment, kissing her so passionately that he knocked his head on the overhead luggage rack and his glasses fell off. Reporters and fans were crowding the train. In view of the fear of scandal in those days, with both partners married and Gloria's husband only a few steps away on the platform counting the luggage, the story makes little sense.

It has been stated that both Joe and Gloria stayed at the Poinciana Hotel. However, sensibly, Swanson stayed at the Whitehall, the sumptuous converted mansion and estate of the late James Flagler. Had she been under the same roof as Joe, the press would have made something of it.

For years, Swanson relayed a canard that, in the middle of a sunny afternoon, her husband having packed off on a fishing trip, Joe walked into her bedroom in tennis flannels, made love to her and then left. Such an episode would not have been possible in the circumstances. The Whitehall, like all other Palm Beach hotels, was a beehive of gossip; the press bribed maids to report on when a man entered a lady's suite and what sounds emanated from it. Fans threaded through corridors, spying relentlessly on celebrities. Swanson's suite overlooked a courtyard that was haunted day and night by reporters, tourists and fans. Neither Gloria nor Joe could risk exposure, blackmail and possible ruin. Newspapermen were under severe pressure to find a scandal that would make the headlines in any one of half a dozen tabloids. Joe, close as he was to Cardinal O'Connell, having just completed a deal with the morally correct John J. Murdock and cognizant of the need for a clean, scandal-free record as a major figure of Wall Street, had much to lose from any hint of adultery. As for Gloria, had Will Hays gotten wind of any questionable behavior on her part with a man other than her husband, he could have put considerable pressure on United Artists, which distributed her films, and, given the increasingly puritanical climate of the time in Hollywood, in the wake of scandals earlier in the decade, she could have been ruined.

Everything in Swanson's papers indicates that, whatever her misgivings about her husband's uselessness, she was by now changed, and very much in love with him. She had formed an affectionate telephone friendship with Rose. And then, since Joe was in charge of her affairs, she was surely not foolish enough to have risked making herself vulnerable to him by allowing him to make love to her without any preamble, tenderness or consideration.

They appeared frequently, along with the Marquis and several of Joe's aides, at the big parties of the season, of which Mr. and Mrs. Edward Stotesbury's was the most coveted. Although Joe, like Rose, had been excluded from the Palm Beach Social Register, he managed to ride in on Gloria's fame and overcome what would normally be a refusal of admittance to society.

On February 20, 1928, Rose gave birth to a fifth daughter, her eighth child, Jean Ann, at St. Margaret's Hospital in Dorchester, with Joe still in Palm Beach. His absence was criticized, then and later, but, as always, he was following the current custom of not automatically attending a birth or even being present in the same building when it took place. Swanson sent Rose a telegram of congratulations and a large bouquet of red carnations. Fred Thomson cabled: MY ROAD TO FAME IS NOW CLEAR. IN FUTURE YEARS I WILL BE ABLE TO SAY I KNEW JOE AND ROSE WHEN THEY HAD ONLY SEVEN CHILDREN. Rose was captivated by the message; she had forgiven Thomson for deserting her husband for a larger contract at Paramount.

In a complex maneuver in late February, Joe tore up Gloria's contract with Paul Bedard, her devoted secretary and company treasurer, and had her fire him; she acted with starry hauteur in not responding to Bedard's letters complaining of the dismissal. Joe had previously removed her lawyer, Milton Cohen, but Cohen returned to her and remained her attorney for many years. At the end of the month, Joe paid for Swanson's suite at the Plaza in New York; she traveled on to Los Angeles, Joe following, on March 4.

While they were in Los Angeles, Joe hit on a spectacular idea. Still without a property for Swanson, although he had toyed with the notion of casting her as the evangelist Aimee

Semple McPherson, he decided to ask the notorious Erich
von Stroheim to leave Paramount and join him, beginning
with a picture of Stroheim's own devising in which
Swanson would star.

Stroheim was the most discussed director in Hollywood.
He was not a "Von" at all; pretending to be a descendant of
a noble Prussian military family, he was actually the son of
a Jewish men's hatter from Prussian Silesia who had settled
in Vienna. His pictures *Blind Husbands, Foolish Wives,
Greed* and *The Merry Widow* were alternatively reviled and
praised, offending the moralists with their emphases on the
worst aspects of human nature. Stroheim was an underwear
fetishist with a streak of sadism, and his favorite garb on-set
was a military uniform and jackboots. He would never have
been tolerated in Hollywood, since he was insanely extravagant and reckless with schedules, if he had not made a
mountain of money. Seeing a Stroheim picture was like
reading a forbidden book by candlelight under the bedclothes.

Joe encouraged Stroheim to come up with a screen story
that would create an international thunderclap. The director's most recent picture, *The Wedding March,* was due to
be released later that year, and Paramount had so interfered
with it and its parade of sadism, debauchery and masturba-
tory fantasy that Stroheim stormed out of the studio and
was quite prepared for this new adventure.

He whipped up a typical concoction: Swanson would
appear as a convent girl, age seventeen, who would drop her
panties during a country walk with her fellow novices and
would be seen by a lecherous prince, who would whisk her
off to his palace after setting fire to the convent. His wife, a
mad queen, would drive the unfortunate girl headlong into
the street while naked and brandishing a whip. Responding
to a letter from a relative, the girl (who would be named in
the first draft Kitty Kelly, a direct reference to Joe's earlier
film, *Kosher Kitty Kelly*) would go to Africa, where she
would find herself confined in a brothel. Imprisoned there
by a lecherous madam, fat and black in the racist mode of
the time, she would be married off to a decrepit old man,
who would invite the brothel's occupants to watch while he
did his best to consummate the relationship. Reduced to

this abject state, Kitty Kelly would become a helpless drudge, condemned to a lifetime in this tropical hellhole.

Presented with this nonsense, which was designed to offend just about everybody, most notably Will Hays, Joe's mentor Cardinal O'Connell, Rose Kennedy, Pope Pius XI and every straitlaced individual working for or associated with Kennedy, Joe decided to throw caution to the winds to bring off the Stroheim-Swanson coup. He would pay Stroheim $15,000 for the rights to use his ridiculous story; he would pay him $3,000 a week for his services as director. He would release the picture through United Artists. Since United Artists would not contribute any money to the production, Joe had to raise it himself. He had already bailed Swanson out of her substantial debts by raising several hundred thousand dollars on the frail collateral of her name alone from Columbia Trust in Boston, of which he had been president and of which his father, Patrick Kennedy, was now president emeritus. The sum he raised was close to $750,000 for the movie; a lesser sum was extracted from the Bank of America. This was a very bold step on Kennedy's part. It is unlikely Rose learned about it, as she would scarcely have approved it. The total sum of over $1.5 million was a very considerable one in those days. The bank itself remained small, and Joe put it at risk in making the arrangement.

In April, the first official announcement of *The Swamp,* the working title of the film, appeared in the press. Stroheim had added some new touches: there would be the indication of cunnilingus in one scene; the brothel orchestra would play (silent, of course) *Here Comes the Bride* during the wedding scene as an orgy took place; black priests would stand around the wedding bed, watching the consummation of the marriage; in one scene men would dance cheek-to-cheek with each other in a demonstration of homosexuality.

At that time, Rose decided, somewhat against her better judgment, since she would have preferred the Catholic school Canterbury, to put down for Choate Joe, Jr., and Jack, who would begin classes in September 1930. Often portrayed as a stern institution, the exclusive and expensive Choate School, favored by the wealthy and prominent, had been established in Wallingford, Connecticut, in 1896 by

Judge William G. Choate and Headmaster Mark Pitman. Allegedly based on Eton, whose grounds and building it somewhat distantly mirrored, Choate was the opposite in terms of its actual character. At that time, Eton was snobbish, brutal, with an intensely homosexual atmosphere; dressed in their Eton collars and confining, already outdated uniforms, Etonians were raised in an atmosphere of survival of the fittest, buggery and sadism.

At Choate, homosexuality was virtually unknown; a home atmosphere was introduced, in which the teachers took a personal interest in each boy and in which the pupils could come to the headmaster's house at almost any time for personal advice. Many evenings were spent in casual group sings or conversational debates, none of them rigidly organized.

The slightest indication of sickness—and in those days before antibiotics, complications of a cold could turn into pneumonia and even result in death—resulted in a boy being transferred to a well-run infirmary equipped with fully trained nurses and at least one doctor. Religious instruction was deliberately ecumenical so that it was possible for Catholic boys to attend chapel as well as go outside for Mass. The boys formed their own religious society, St. Andrew's.

The emphasis was on a healthy mind and a healthy body, and exercise was given equal weight with study. There was an intense concentration on musical appreciation. Visiting musicians, some of them famous, would turn up regularly for recitals, and the boys were often bused into New Haven to attend concerts. Filmgoing was encouraged, and the whole school would often commandeer a local movie theater. The school enthusiastically supported a local ice-cream parlor, which was the mecca of every boy there. Choate, for all but the most neurotic or unwell, was a paradise of pleasure for kids, and promised to open every social door in the future. Here, unlike their parents, the Kennedy children could truly cross social barriers.

Uniforms were not worn, but the boys were expected to turn up in class in jackets, ties, well-pressed pants and clean shoes. The boys lived in cottages, attractively furnished in Early American style, with only two boys, who were very carefully matched, to each room. There were a fine golf course, eighteen tennis courts, a riding stable, trap and rifle shooting facilities, rowboats and, being built at the time, five ice hockey rinks for winter use. Choate was arguably the most luxurious private school in northeastern America, though not, perhaps, quite as exclusive as Groton.

Rose entered Joe, Jr., enthusiastically. She herself filled in the application form. There was only one flaw in the school's impeccability: a question in the form asked, significantly, whether the proposed pupil was "Hebraic." But anti-Semitism was, after all, the order of the day in 1920s America.

On April 28, 1928, Rose attended the marriage of her younger brother John F. Fitzgerald to Catherine O'Hearn at St. Ambrose's Church in Dorchester. The still inexhaustible Honey Fitz organized an elegant and fashionable postnuptial party.

That same April, much to Rose and her boys' delight, Joe brought off a coup: after months of negotiation, he, at last, succeeded in luring Tom Mix, along with Mix's legendary horse, Tony, from Fox. Joe began by asking Mix, who signed a contract for close to a million dollars, to send Joe, Jr., and Jack a pair of his chaps. They were delirious—especially when the chaps were followed by one of Mix's favorite saddles and a glittering pair of spurs.

Still in Hollywood, Joe packed Mix, who was limping from a recent accident in which he had fallen down stairs in a movie fight scene, off on a nationwide tour to announce the new deal, booking him into the Keith-Albee-Orpheum theaters, of which he was about to obtain a controlling interest. Mix and Tony were mobbed by thousands everywhere, the crowds mostly made up of teenage boys; Jack and Joe, Jr., had their greatest thrill ever when Mix dropped in to the Riverdale house.

In the week of May 14 to May 21, Joe was at the Drake Hotel in Chicago, staying with the Marquis de la Falaise for the FBO annual sales conference. His choice of having the Marquis with him for the occasion lends further support to the conviction that Joe was not romantically involved with Swanson. In those days, for a French aristocrat to be cuckolded was considered damaging to his honor; although the tradition of the duel at dawn had faded out, fisticuffs were still in order when a husband was slighted.

Certainly, the Marquis, often described as a gigolo but deeply in love with Swanson, as his numerous letters in her collection of documents attest, had very strong ideas about a wife's faithfulness, and would never have become intimate with Joe if he had felt for a moment that his wife and Kennedy were sleeping together. The Marquis was with him when Joe passionately addressed his sales force, accompanied at the conference by Joe Schnitzer and his publicist Hyatt Daab, on his plans for movies to be made in the coming season.

On May 19, the *Exhibitors' Herald and Moving Picture World* devoted almost its entire spring gala issue to Joe Kennedy and FBO, establishing him as the coming young major figure of the movie industry. Joe was photographed, looking boyishly handsome in his Harold Lloyd glasses, as a series of lurid illustrations announced his pictures in preparation. Among these was his first part-talkie, *The Perfect Crime: The Red Sword,* which dealt with his favorite subject, the dangers of Russian communism; and a movie on another personal theme, *Lest We Forget,* which would assuage any guilt he may have felt about not serving in World War I as it dealt with the lives of young Americans who had lost their lives on the western front. *Danger Street* would feature "Painted lips—luring! Slitted eyes—watching!" Joe launched the career of the tiny, frantically dancing infant Mickey McGuire—who later became internationally famous as Mickey Rooney—featuring the tot in a series of shorts.

On May 26, the long-delayed conclusion of Joe's Keith-Albee-Orpheum takeover took place. By October, it was known as RKO: Radio-Keith-Orpheum. Backed by the bankers Lehman Brothers, Jeremiah Milbank, Charles Hayden and six other financiers, Joe snapped up a total of $4,500,000 in shares, melding with David Sarnoff's RCA, as well as General Electric and Westinghouse, to secure his interest in talking pictures.

Joe was in New York after Chicago. He entertained Stroheim at the Plaza Hotel; Rose visited at least once.

Meetings continued on the new screenplay and the controversial director gave a series of flamboyant press conferences. What Rose made of Stroheim has not been recorded, but she can scarcely have been left unimpressed by his customary approach to a woman: he would click his heels, bow deeply at the waist and kiss her hand. He had a disconcerting habit of looking a woman up and down, from head to foot, lecherously using a monocle.

By mid-June, plans for *The Swamp* had progressed, although very few liked the title. The original plan was to make the movie in sound and silent versions simultaneously. Swanson, back now in her Crescent Drive house, installed a special projection room equipped for talkies. But the plan was later replaced by one in which the silent version would be shot first and the talkie version second. Joe had to meet an immense bill, covering Stroheim's lavish expenses on the train and in Manhattan. In present-day money, these amounted to as much as $17,000 for ten days.

In July, the Kennedys were at Hyannis Port. Once again, there were the 7:00 A.M. calisthenics on the lawn; the noisy, opinionated breakfasts, with everyone talking at once; and the adventures in boating. There was a hullabaloo when Joe and Jack rescued a young boy from drowning. Rose was less pleased when Joe, Jr., dumped her sister Agnes jokingly off his skiff a hundred yards out to sea, forcing her to swim ashore. She also had to deal with complex feelings when Joe, at thirteen, already into puberty, fell in love for the first time. The girl was fourteen-year-old Eleanor Leavens; Joe had gallantly dived into choppy waters off a pier in an unsuccessful effort to retrieve her Navajo Indian ring. She was so impressed by the gesture that she dropped her overweight date and spent every spare moment with her newfound hero.

Rose was not displeased with this development, nor was Joe, Jr., but Leavens's mother and father were upset. Rich Californians, they were guests of a prominent Boston Brahmin family that was spending the summer at the beach. That family refused to receive the Kennedys and had been responsible for excluding them from the local social clubs. In desperation, the Leavenses whisked their unhappy daughter back to San Francisco, forbidding her to reply when Joe poured out his frustrated feelings in a succession of flowery love letters.

Rose found Joe, Sr., in a furious mood that August. He had been offered and had accepted a crushing addition to his already heavy workload. Though ill, his ulcers flaring up, his weight down by some thirty pounds, his normally robust face drawn and pallid, he had not been able to resist accepting the presidency of the important producing and releasing organization First National. Headlines in many newspapers, and splashy articles in *Variety,* announced this extraordinary appointment, and a meeting was held with its bosses at First National's headquarters in Manhattan. Joe strode into the meeting with his customary athletic confidence, only to find that every one of the agreements reached with the board in previous discussions was reneged on. He had made it clear that he expected total autonomy, and indeed his extraordinary record of success at FBO and Pathe confirmed that he was entitled to make decisions of whatever kind he wanted. RKO was already showing a major profit; Pathe was doing spectacularly; he had moved it from an annual loss of $35 million to a profit of $250,000, and he could point to the rise of Pathe shares from 2 to 7, and 15 to 28 preferred. But the board, stimulated by the aggressive Greek exhibitor Spyros Skouras, flatly denied him the power he sought. He would have to refer to them for every decision.

Joe walked out, angry, and Skouras tore up his contract in front of the other directors. Just days later, without listening to his complaints, they made a deal behind his back with Joe's friend Jack Warner, production head of Warner Bros. in Hollywood, which was booming now with *The Jazz Singer.*

On August 18, 1928, Rose had a post-birthday treat. For years, she had longed for foreign travel, and now the ideal opportunity arose because John J. and Ethel Murdock decided to accompany her and Joe to France and England aboard the luxury liner *Ile de France.* The voyage would present an opportunity to discuss arrangements for the numerous changes Joe and Murdock were planning at Pathe and at Keith-Albee-Orpheum; and at the same time, it would be a pleasant break from raising a family for the two women. If Rose had qualms about leaving her baby Jean, now only five and a half months old, they are not recorded. From royalty on down, it was customary among the ruling classes of the day to follow travel plans regardless of the age of immediate descendants.

The departure on the great ship took place at midnight, in a dramatic rainstorm. There was a commotion at the wharf: the Kennedys and the Murdocks and numerous other wealthy people had invited family and friends, according to tradition, to their suites to see them off with champagne, caviar and laughter. Then, as the distinguished guests made their way down the gangway, they were intercepted by squadrons of Prohibition agents who began, in an unseemly manner, to frisk them to see if they were carrying hip flasks of liquor, smuggled diamonds or drugs.

In view of the fact that many of these visitors were members of ruling families of the country, numbering some four thousand in all, and since some of the officials used the occasion to stroke the women's legs and breasts, there were furious complaints, and the matter became so explosive it made its way into the headlines and even onto some front pages. It is safe to say that the Kennedys and Murdocks made a very loud fuss about this incident.

Suite 264, which Rose and Joe occupied, became their favorite for many years, and they always insisted upon having it thereafter. The bulkheads were covered by the finest African mahogany; the curtains were of French silk; the furnishings were Louis XV antiques. Rose fell in love with the ship immediately. Everywhere, there were classical statues and oil paintings; the decks were spacious and the swimming pool was occupied by the Who's Who of the world. As she came down the grand staircase to the main gray-marble dining saloon, she saw a spectacular sight: from top to bottom of the stairwell there was a vividly colored mural depicting the glories of France. The great room itself was designed in pale gray marble, the ceiling lit by 112 Lalique glass lights which shone on Lalique screens and figures that flanked the dining tables.

They were, as they always would be, at the captain's table,

and enjoyed the chef's brave attempts at haute cuisine. Just before arriving at Cherbourg, there was a grand spectacle; no passenger stayed in his bed that night, in order to be up at dawn to see the ship-to-shore mail plane, introduced on the immediately previous west-to-east Atlantic run, launched from the boat deck. In a choppy sea, the ship's engines were cut off, and, from the bridge, the Kennedys saw the biplane noisily shot off by catapult. The pilot circled the vessel three times, waving a white scarf, and then flew off to deliver hundreds of letters and postcards ahead of the ship's docking.

It was a splendid crossing, which was followed by the excitement for Rose of rediscovering Paris. There was another pleasure in store: the family's favorite Morton Downey opened that week at Les Ambassadeurs; he was a huge success. Then they went on to Deauville, the fashionable coastal resort, to attend his opening there.

They traveled on to London. At the Carlton Hotel in London, the Kennedys met up with the Marquis de la Falaise, who was having a mild flirtation with William Randolph Hearst's mistress, Marion Davies. The only shadow on the trip was the sudden death of Joe's friend and supporter Marcus Loew, from a heart attack. The obituaries in *Variety* and elsewhere followed them to London.

A big event of the London visit was Morton Downey's opening at the Café de Paris. In white tie and tails, seated at a grand piano, singing superbly, he made a sensation. The Kennedys were at ringside. They were often at the Café de Paris, usually with Lord and Lady Castlerosse, to whom they had been introduced by Sir Thomas Lipton; amusing, enormously fat, with goggle eyes, Castlerosse was a popular columnist of the London *Sunday Express*.

A converted basement in Coventry Street, near raffish Leicester Square, based somewhat morbidly on the Grand Saloon of the ill-fated *Lusitania,* the Café de Paris was reached from the Kennedys' limousine through a gauntlet of male and female prostitutes, drug peddlers and thieves. It was oval in shape, on two levels, and it was lavishly furnished. Performers descended a double staircase that framed the orchestra and the oval dance floor. The Kennedys quickly became favorites of the witty and charming Danish headwaiter, Martin Poulsen, who always accorded them the same table.

According to the entertainment historian Charles Graves, Kennedy enjoyed at least a flirtation with the popular showgirl Evelyn Crowell, who starred in *Les Girls,* Sir Francis Towle's popular cabaret at the Dorchester Hotel. It is impossible to corroborate the story.

On September 18, the Kennedys returned with the Murdocks to New York aboard the *Majestic.* On October 31, Rose enjoyed two excitements: Joe bought the Hyannis Port house in her name, and she attended with Joe a brilliant social occasion in Boston—the opening of the $5 million B. F. Keith Memorial Theater.

Decorated with antique statuary and paintings, its lobby furnished with French antiques, the movie house was a masterpiece of kitsch. Ironically, the master of ceremonies was the Fitzgeralds' enemy, the inescapable Mayor Curley, but, by all accounts, Rose and Joe showed no sign of annoyance in dealing with him. Only Honey Fitz's absence from the occasion indicated an unchanged attitude. Following an uproariously funny series of comic vaudeville acts, the feature film *Oh, Kay!* with Colleen Moore proved a hit. Miss Moore recalled the Kennedys vividly: he, a bespectacled version of a movie star, thin but strikingly handsome, and Rose, exquisitely dressed, clinging to his arm as though they had only just fallen in love.

Leaving Rose to stay temporarily with her father, Joe traveled to Long Island, where, at his FBO studios, he watched rehearsals for a new musical, *Stepping High.* Then he left briefly for Hollywood on the fifteenth of November to join Gloria for the first weeks of shooting of *The Swamp,* now retitled *Queen Kelly.*

His lust for sensation and money continued to overcome what must have been increasing qualms at how Will Hays and the army of bluenoses would respond to such flamboyant rubbish. And he had always said he would never make a picture his children could not see.

Neither he nor Rose was able to attend the funeral in Los Angeles on January 2, 1929, of Fred Thomson, who had died at Christmas from tetanus after stepping on a rusty nail. At the height of his career at Paramount, he was only twenty-seven. Rose and Joe could scarcely console the devastated Frances Marion, who went into seclusion for weeks, feeling that the world had come to an end.*

On January 4, 1929, Joe and Rose, with the Murdocks, arrived at Palm Beach and checked into the Poinciana. The city was half empty because of a flu epidemic; the hotel, and several others, had been damaged by a hurricane the previous summer. But they still had a good time; they played cards with the Murdocks, the producer Jim Golden and Rube Goldberg, another close friend. Morton Downey was back for other appearances at the Venetian Gardens, and, with his fiancèe Barbara Bennett, proved to be a charming companion. Rose also had the joy of meeting Florenz Ziegfeld for the first time, with his wife, Billie Burke, and their daughter Patricia. Goldie, Ziegfeld's popular Girl Friday, often spoke of the meeting in later years, impressed by Rose's devotion to Joe and his constant attentiveness to her, dismissing with a laugh Swanson's egregious memoir describing the time. Other friends were the boxer Gene Tunney, and the energetic sportswriter Ring Lardner.

While there, Joe concluded a separation from FBO and Radio-Keith-Orpheum, RKO; but just before he signed the severance papers he agreed to the acquisition of the playwrights Ben Hecht and Charles MacArthur.

Meanwhile, in Hollywood, with Joe absent from the production, which he had visited only briefly the previous November, Stroheim's manic perfectionism was holding up the production of *Queen Kelly*.

In mid-January 1929, disaster struck. An elaborate banquet and coronation scene, in which the captive Kitty Kelly would be made queen of the African brothel, was interrupted when Stroheim had Tully Marshall as Kelly's hus-

---

*Enchanted Hill still stands. Magnificent as ever, though damaged by the 1994 earthquake, it has been unoccupied by its owner for several years. The present caretaker swears that, until at least 1984, Fred Thomson haunted the house, his booted footsteps echoing down the stairs night after night from his small cutting room in the main building to a lower room of which he was fond.

band improvise an action not specified in the script: he told the actor to foam at the mouth and drool tobacco juice onto Swanson's hand as he placed the wedding ring on her finger.

She had just had breakfast and became nauseated as the disgusting fluid ran over her palm. Swanson had had enough. She ran to the telephone and called Joe in Palm Beach. "You'd better get out here fast!" she said. "Our director is a madman!"

Kennedy cut short his Palm Beach vacation with Rose, and, leaving her behind, took the train to Los Angeles. He stopped the picture, fired Stroheim, and told Swanson to take a rest.

Chapter 7

The Day the Market Crashed

With the picture closed down, Rose and Joe saw about $750,000 worth of good Columbia Trust money going rapidly down the drain. Joe asked a recent friend, the colorful, bisexual British-born playwright, novelist, director and songwriter Edmund Goulding to come up with an alternative story that might be picked up and filmed later in the year. While Goulding was working on the matter, Joe and Swanson set up offices in the Pathe headquarters at Culver City, Los Angeles. Built for the late director Thomas Ince, the pretentious building was an exact copy of George Washington's residence, Mount Vernon, down to the inkwells. Cecil B. DeMille had lately vacated it, after separating from Pathe and making arrangements to join Louis B. Mayer at Metro-Goldwyn-Mayer.

There is still no evidence of any serious liaison between Kennedy and Swanson. As usual, Rose had little to worry about. Gloria's stream of telegrams from Mount Vernon or North Crescent Drive to the Marquis in Paris were filled with "loves" and "sweethearts," and his own were replete with plaintive questions about when she would be able to come and see him. It is evident they missed each other painfully, and that, despite the distance between them, there was neither an infringement of their marriage nor any jealousy on the Marquis's part. Nor is there an inkling of gossip to be found about them, even in the most scurrilous newspapers of the time. I do not believe Swanson was so complete a hypocrite as to continue a love correspondence with her husband in view of the circumstances.

On April 28, 1929, Rose's beloved sister Agnes, who had shared so many travel experiences with her, at last married, after a seemingly interminable engagement, the attractive Joseph Francis Gargan, whose family had long ago leased the Kennedys their first summer home in Nantasket. Rose was fond of Joe Gargan and must have wondered why Agnes had taken so long to make up her mind. In pale blue silk, the thirty-eight-year-old Rose, looking at least ten years younger, made a splash at the ceremony, accompanied by her old flame Hugh Nawn and his wife, and the Nawn parents. Joe was unable to make the long trip from Los Angeles.

In California, Joe was extremely busy. Calling Rose whenever he could, he kept her informed of all his activities. It was a pleasure to her to learn that he was proving more helpful than ever to Morton and Barbara Downey.

Joe launched Downey's career in movies, starting with the sentimental musicals *Syncopation* and *Lucky in Love,* in which Downey played a singing Irish stableboy, and *Mother's Boy,* produced by Joe's old friend Robert Kane, about another Irish tenor who flees a Broadway opening to take care of his ailing mother. Barbara Bennett was costarred in *Lucky in Love* and *Syncopation,* and all three pictures involved the participation of Rose and Joe's writer friend Gene Markey, whom Joe introduced to Constance and Barbara's sister Joan, also a prominent actress, and whom Markey would eventually marry.

Barbara and Joan's attractive and wayward movie-star sister Constance was under contract to Joe at Pathe Studios, starring in the picture *Rich People.* The inexhaustible Hyatt Daab cooked up an imaginary conflict between Bennett and Swanson as rival queens of Pathe. Constance formed a crush on Joe, and had an affair with him, despite the fact that she was married to the wealthy, handsome young big-game hunter Philip Plant, with whom Joe had had extensive business dealings in the past, and who was now in New York. That summer, Joe packed Constance off to Paris on a publicity tour, whereupon she left Joe for a liaison with the Marquis de la Falaise. Such bedroom-hopping was typical of Hollywood.

While Joe, with *Queen Kelly* on the shelf, lingered on in Hollywood for several weeks, Rose began making plans to move from Riverdale, and asked Eddie Moore to find her a bigger house. In the meantime, Edmund Goulding was on his mettle to come up with a story for a talkie that would rescue the lost fortune squandered on *Queen Kelly;* the result was *The Trespasser,* a conventional romantic drama that would offer Swanson to her vast army of fans talking for the cameras for the first time. Goulding added to his expertly whipped-up, nonsensical story a song, put together with the actress Elsie Janis, "Love, Your Magic Spell Is Everywhere." Swanson proved to be able to hold a tune, and the result was sensational. Through Pathe and United Artists, Joe was able to set up a recording deal with RCA, which would release a record of the number. At the same time, Joe embarked on a Barbara Stanwyck vehicle, *The Locked Door,* about gangsters and police raids on an off-shore gambling boat on the East River of New York.

Joe returned to Boston for a sad matter: his father, Patrick, had contracted cancer of the liver and was painfully ill at Deaconess Hospital in Boston. Rose and Joe spent many hours at his bedside, along with their children. Sturdy, athletic and outgoing Joe, Jr., was thirteen; the fragile, sickly Jack was eleven; the troubled Rosemary was ten; the very antic Kathleen was nine; the intelligent Eunice was seven; and Patricia, Robert and Jean were five, three and one. Joe and Jack were at Riverdale Country School, Kathleen, Rosemary and Eunice at the Neighborhood School.

At the same time, Rose and Joe had completed plans for the purchase of a house Eddie Moore had found, a twenty-room colonial mansion built on six and a half acres of land in an elegant neighborhood in Bronxville, New York, at 294

Pondfield Road. Built by James Garfield Beman, it was named Crownlands. The house had a handsome classical portico with four Grecian pillars framing the doorway, which was reached up a steep flight of ten brick steps. It was fashioned of Connecticut brick, with louvered windows; two tall chimneys flanked the high-pitched roof. The move was strenuous for Rose, and Joe was able to pay only the briefest of visits to help her. While she dispatched some children to the Bronxville School, arranging for private tuition for the unfortunate Rosemary, Joe was up to his eyes in Hollywood.

Rose handled the moving problems with her customary expertise, and she embarked on plans to install a talkie theater in the basement so that the family could enjoy the latest pictures. It wasn't finished until 1930.

On May 1, 1929, Rose applied for admission for Jack to go to Choate in 1930, following Joe, Jr. Writing to the head teacher from Bronxville, she stated that she hoped that Jack would enter at the beginning of the fourth year in September; he had been inactive since the move from Riverdale, thus creating a hiatus in his education. She cited Frank Hackett, principal of Riverdale, as a good reference, and said she hoped that Joe, Jr., would eventually go to Harvard or Yale.

The entrance examination was due to take place in June; because Jack was weak in Latin, he would work on the language with a special tutor through the summer. Rose was worried about whether he would be able to carry Latin III. Rose wrote, "Jack hates routine work but loves History and English—subjects which fire his imagination." She received a favorable response.

Patrick Kennedy rallied a little in mid-May, and Joe, relieved, returned to Hollywood by train. But no sooner had he arrived than Rose called him to say that his father had died. He made the difficult decision not to return to Winthrop for the funeral, because of the pressing matters connected with preparations for *The Locked Door* and *The Trespasser*. Although he felt guilty about the decision for years afterward, it is doubtful whether he could have reached Boston, in view of the five days it took to cross the country, in time. By family request, the body was not

embalmed, and it would have been malodorous by the time
the mandatory wake took place.

Rose, fighting back tears, attended the last rites with all
except her youngest children at the Church of St. John the
Evangelist in Winthrop on May 21. As so often before and
afterward, Joe, Jr., who was now succeeding strongly at
Choate, took his father's place sturdily as head of the
family. More handsome than ever in his mourning clothes,
he walked beside Rose steadily down the aisle, gently
holding her hand. He sustained her through the protracted
ceremony, and, when she started to cry, put his arm around
her and helped her into the limousine that took her through
the rain to the Kennedy family house on Washington
Avenue for the wake. He never ceased to attend to her
during the ordeal of everyone talking at once over the dead
body in its open coffin, as bootleg liquor flowed freely.

In June, Rose began plans for an August trip to Europe
with Joe, which, she hoped, would be a repetition of the
delightful visit of the previous summer.

By early July, it was clear that *The Trespasser* would be a
great success.

With *The Trespasser* completed, Rose and Joe invited
Swanson to stay with them over a weekend, with her
children, Gloria and Joe, who was adopted, at Hyannis Port
during the summer vacation. With her customary theatrical
flair, Swanson flew in from North Beach, Queens, by Joe's
seaplane on August 6, 1929. The aircraft landed in full view
of the house. Gloria swept up the beach.

Rose was delighted by her presence. Her own and
Gloria's offspring mingled happily; Rose and the rest of the
family fell in love with young Joe Swanson. A grotesque
story appeared later stating that young Jack surprised
Swanson in an intimate situation with his father. There is
no evidence to support this.

When Swanson sailed on August 10, she received a
surprise package: it was thirty inches long and twenty inches
wide, bound in gilt-tasseled blue ribbons and gold cords.
Even in the pile of presents, the exquisitely wrapped candy
boxes, the bouquets of roses and orchids and mountains of
fruit in the suite, the gift stood out. The star, who customarily did not condescend to open presents herself, and whose

maid was busy elsewhere, instructed the cabin steward to open it. He unwrapped it gingerly, revealing inside a laurel wreath, which in turn contained an enormous, musty bottle, and on the label was inscribed, "Bethlehem Rye, guaranteed twenty years old." Who else would have sent it but Joe Kennedy, with its direct reference to his career at Bethlehem Steel?

Excitedly, Swanson ordered the steward to bring soda water, ice and glasses. Everyone stared and nudged each other. After the glasses arrived, Swanson held up the bottle. She was horrified to discover it was empty. What a comment on the fantasy relationship she had cooked up in her own mind! She was furious, but her traveling companion, Virginia Bowker, told a *New York Times* reporter, "That's funny! What a good incident this would make for a comedy film!"

Rose and Joe sailed for Paris on the *Ile de France* on August 20; this time, there were no Prohibition agents to intercept the guests. But a dramatic incident was in store: when the hydroplane with the passengers' mail was catapulted off the boat deck 180 miles off the French coast, it plunged into the sea in heavy fog, and, with the mail badly soaked, was barely able to take off again and struggle into Paris.

The Kennedys stayed at the Ritz. Swanson had arrived in the city two weeks earlier, checking into the Plaza Athenée. A letter addressed to the Marquise de la Falaise was delivered to her in her suite. When she opened it, she was horrified to read a love letter to her husband written by Constance Bennett. It appeared that Miss Bennett, with an insufficient command of French, had accidentally written "Marquise" on the envelope when she meant "Marquis."

Swanson was appalled to discover her husband's infidelity and rushed over to the Ritz to seek Rose and Joe's advice. They had little to give; the matter was equally upsetting to them, since everything indicated the Marquis's devotion to Gloria. In her fury, Swanson decided on a divorce, but there was fear that a scandal might upset the publicity for *The Trespasser,* which was about to open in Paris, Berlin and London. With difficulty, Rose persuaded Gloria to do nothing for the time being. The Marquis later appeared with Gloria publicly.

The best of friends, and certainly not for appearance' sake, Rose and Gloria went to Lucien Lelong's celebrated fashion salon on the Rue Matignon to buy clothes for the Paris, Berlin and London openings of *The Trespasser*. Rose, as she would in the future, had missed the fall showings because of the traditional stay at Hyannis Port, and by arriving in the inappropriate month of August, she had found the fashion house closed until September 1. But she and Swanson, among the first notable figures to arrive at the salon after it reopened, made up for the problem by splurging.

Exactly how Swanson found the cash to buy anything is a mystery, unless Rose and Joe released money from her account. It is not known whether Lelong greeted them in person when they arrived, but it is almost certain that he would have, in view of Swanson's fame. What is certain is that Rose was at a party at his house on September 4, at which Joe, Swanson and the Marquis were also in attendance; the gala event was presided over by Lelong's wife, the ravishing Princess Nathalie Paley, of the Russian royal family, who had been working for him in his perfume shop when he met her.

Although Lelong's styles were a trifle severe for the extravagant and flamboyant Swanson, they ideally suited Rose, with her conservative tastes and slim figure. That July, Lelong had decreed that waistlines would no longer be just above the hips but where they were supposed to be. Influenced by his wife, he favored Russian-style jackets, trimmed with fox furs or sables; skirts were sharply pleated or flared over the hips. He had grown fond of using capes for daytime wear. Only a very thin woman with perfect legs could get away with his styles, and even after bearing eight children, Rose was as slim-hipped as a boy. She looked marvelous in Lelong's creations and remained faithful to him for many years. Later he founded the careers of Balmain and Dior.

She and Joe left for Berlin and the fashionable Adlon Hotel, with the Falaises. They continued to London, where they stayed at the Carlton Hotel; Falaise and Swanson were at Claridges. On September 8, the British premiere of *The Trespasser* at the New Gallery Theater on Regent Street caused a sensation. As Rose arrived with Joe, the Marquis and Gloria by limousine, she could barely make her way through the screaming crowd of five thousand fans jamming Regent Street. The mob broke through the police cordon and swarmed around them hysterically. The party struggled through the lobby to take their seats; the cheering failed to stop even when the curtains opened and the movie began.

When Swanson was first heard speaking, the audience became hysterical and the picture had to be stopped. The management begged everyone to be quiet, but nothing could appease the public except Swanson going to the stage. With her husband, Rose and Joe beside her, she talked to the audience about the movie and asked if she could at least see it. Amid a burst of laughter, she was allowed to return to her place, and, Joe and Rose hugging her excitedly, she began to cry.

When she sang the theme song, "Love, Your Magic Spell Is Everywhere," the audience sprang to its feet and cheered again. At the end of the movie, its delirium knew no bounds. The "four musketeers," as Rose, Joe and the Falaises were known in London, went back to the Carlton for a reception attended by the greatest stars of England. Next night, they attended a gala performance in their honor of Noël Coward's popular musical *Bitter Sweet.*

The Trespasser became an immediate success. Rose and Joe—but not the Marquis—accompanied Swanson aboard the *Ile de France* on September 20 back to New York, where, at the Plaza Hotel, surrounded by Swanson's ten trunks, two toy dogs and a squadron of hangers-on, they sat with her through a protracted press conference on September 28.

There was good news for Rose. Two of the pictures in which Joe was personally involved at RKO, of which he had now officially abandoned control, were hits. *Syncopation,* starring Morton Downey and Barbara Bennett, was the first movie released under the Radio banner. Although Joe had made the mistake of committing the direction to a cinematographer, Bert Glennon, which resulted in a somewhat clumsy production, the movie broke records. It was a pioneer musical, the first ever to use the RCA Photophone system.

Simultaneously, regardless of Rose's feelings, Joe starred his old flame Betty Compson in *Street Girl,* also a musical. Recalling her favorite story of having played a violin on the vaudeville stage, Joe had her act as a violinist in the picture; on an investment of $211,000, it made over $1.1 million that year. It is certain that both movies were featured in the private theater at the Kennedys' Bronxville house.

An important priority on the Kennedys' agenda was contacting Joe, Jr., who had been admitted to Choate on schedule while they were in Europe; and Kathleen and Rosemary, who were at their own schools. Jack entered seventh grade at Riverdale, preparatory to Choate, on September 25, 1929.

Rose shared Joe's pleasure in Joe, Jr.,'s popularity at Choate. Now Joe, Jr., was mingling with the children of the Episcopalian elite; he was crossing the barriers that had prevented his parents from rising to the most exclusive circles in Boston and New York. It seems never to have occurred to the Kennedys that Groton would have been an even better choice, insuring the sort of connections that a young man who might one day be president would find indispensable.

More athlete than scholar, phenomenally untidy, despite his size an early victim of older boys, Joe, Jr., would soon hold his own.

On October 26, Rose made another glamorous appearance at a wedding, the marriage of her brother Frederick Hannon to Rosalind Miller in Boston. Joe was unable to be present; he had gotten wind of storm clouds gathering over Wall Street. Three days after the wedding, the stock market collapsed, ruining countless thousands of small investors who had bought stocks on margin, and, when the call came for cash, didn't have it.

It has been claimed that Joe dumped his movie stocks just before the landslide took place; many of them were held in Rose's name. But the real story is different: true, he had been shedding shares in other companies since the spring, but he held on to his movie shares throughout the Crash and the successive months of a depressed market. This was a shrewd move for him and Rose. He saw that motion-picture companies' stocks, unlike most others, would hold up firmly because of the colossal earnings achieved by talkie pictures. And in addition, since he knew most of the major bankers personally, he determined that they would buy individual shareholders' shares in quantity, holding them for the future when their value would recover.

After Black Monday, the Kennedys' RKO shares plunged from 19¼ to 15¼; their Radio stocks dropped from 40 to 30; and Pathe common fell from 5 to 4. Joe had his banker friends buy up the stocks; within days, they had all recovered, and Radio went as high as 38 within a week. To bolster the stock even further, Kennedy issued new prospectuses, making bullish statements about the future of RKO and Pathe. Although complaining stockholders grumbled then and later, that Kennedy had sold them down the river, it was their own fault (common among inexperienced investors) that they had cashed in the shares as soon as they lost value. Joe protected his experienced friends by advising them not to sell, but rather to purchase, as he did, more as bargains. By January 1930, the wisdom of his policy was proven: RKO and Pathe zoomed, bolstered by the colossal returns on *Rio Rita,* whose purchase from Ziegfeld he had personally engineered.

To show his indifference to the Crash, and to boost the company's shares, Joe, with characteristic élan, continued with plans for one of the most elaborate premieres in recent history. *The Trespasser* opened at the Rialto Theater in New York City just three days after the Crash, on November 1, 1929.

Rose, who hated noise, crowds and razzle-dazzle more than anything, had to face up to yet another excessive display of public enthusiasm as she, Joe, Swanson and Swanson's friend Virginia Bowker fought their way from the Kennedy Rolls-Royce through thousands of fans and a blaze of searchlights. As they arrived, Swanson's voice, augmented by the RCA system, sang "Love, Your Magic Spell Is Everywhere," the lilting melody, destined to be a runaway success on phonograph records, reverberating from the public-address system. Traffic was stopped for blocks; the party Joe threw at the Plaza went on until the small hours.

An exhausted Rose returned to Bronxville, taking care of her younger children, all of whom were doing well, and already making plans for Christmas, while Joe left for Los Angeles to try to salvage *Queen Kelly.* Edmund Goulding, again borrowed from M.G.M., lost patience with Kennedy's obsession with control and walked out on December 3.

Richard Boleslavsky, a hack director who had once been a czarist Lancer and had been brooding over the footage since January, did his best to direct new scenes, but the results were poor and Kennedy decided to shelve the picture for good. Part of the Swanson loan from Columbia Trust was paid off from profits from *The Trespasser,* but for years Swanson unfairly blamed Joe for not releasing her totally from the debt. How could he, he and Rose asked, in the face of his own infuriated shareholders at the bank? She herself had volunteered the financing and he had raised the money on the collateral of her name alone. Wasn't she therefore obliged to repay as best she could?

That Christmas, as proof that Swanson felt no resentment at the time, she sent an expensive gift to the Kennedy children. She had asked her New York secretary to obtain a toy golf course, suitable for use at Bronxville, but this had proved to be unavailable. Instead the secretary had bought a horseracing game, popular on ships at sea, in which "jockeys" moved wooden horses along a numbered linoleum track, the moves dictated by throws of dice; bets were placed on each horse, and the winner received a prize. Jack sent a warm thank-you note to Gloria at the beginning of the new year, 1930, announcing that he and the Boy Scout troop to which he belonged were on their way to West Point for a jamboree.

January found Rose at Palm Beach. Not only had Joe saved her and the family by holding on to his movie shares when the market fell, but he would enrich them even further as the picture business continued to boom. *Variety* stated astutely, as it covered the 1930 Palm Beach season, that most of the "flying high rich" had been wiped out by the Crash and had gone elsewhere, leaving only the "smart elite" to enjoy the resort. The cold, wet, miserable weather kept the family indoors and proved to be cramping, but there was much fun to be had at the dances at the Deauville and Everglades clubs, dodging Prohibition raids at less exclusive nighteries, attending under umbrellas the Biscayne Kennel Club greyhound races, enjoying stone crabs with Tom Mix and the Morton Downeys, and joining the receiving line when Prince Leopold of the Belgians turned up at the Poinciana Hotel with banker Otto Kahn.

There were letters to be enjoyed from Jack, though he complained that his forty-cents-a-week allowance might have been sufficient for ice creams or toy wooden airplanes but was not enough to support his Boy Scout requirements of haversacks, blankets, a flashlight and a poncho; there were sweet, if rather incoherent, notes from Rosemary at the special Devereux School in Berwyn, Pennsylvania, which took care of backward children.

In April Rose traveled with Joe to Hollywood, where he produced a new movie, as yet untitled, with Gloria Swanson. The Kennedys stayed not at Enchanted Hill—the widowed Frances Marion had put it up for sale—but at the Ambassador Hotel. Rose found Frances depressed and lonely in a modest house.

Years later, Miss Marion remembered Rose's amusement at the absurdity of the Pathe headquarters, in the imitation Mount Vernon style, situated in the glum industrial district of Culver City. It made Rose laugh that Joe was ensconced in Washingtonian grandeur in an exact replica of the late president's office.

The unnamed Swanson movie was a concoction made out of bits and pieces of the star's own life; scenes were staged on a replica of the *Ile de France* and in the home of a Paris marquis with the same initials as Henry's (De La Foursbouget). There was a contest for a title for this nonsense, the reward for whose selection was a brand-new Cadillac. At the end of the first run-through, writer Sidney Howard piped up, commenting on Swanson's character of a giddy, romantic woman, "What a widow!" He won the prize; *What a Widow!* actually became the title.

Back in New York on May 5, Rose attended the confirmation of Kathleen and Eunice by the Right Reverend John J. Dunn, auxiliary bishop of New York. Two days later, annoyed by corporate problems, Joe resigned from the presidency of Pathe. He would continue as nominal chairman of the board, production being handed over to the faithful E. B. Derr, of Bethlehem Steel days. Joe was co-chairman, with Elisha Walker, of the Transamerica Corporation. And he still, with Walker and Jeremiah Milbank, controlled seventy-six percent of Pathe stock. When stockholders tried to seize that controlling interest, threatening legal action, he bought them off by allowing a representative committee to nominate three members to the board of directors. The shareholders were still disgruntled: at the annual meeting on June 9, they charged that Pathe hadn't paid a dividend for eight quarters. Kennedy remedied that deficiency.

Then came the summer vacation at Hyannis Port. Rose showed her need to have Jack close to her, with his many health problems, when she wrote to George St. John, principal of Choate (which Jack was supposed to enter that September) asking him if the boy could take his entrance examinations at Hyannis, instead of missing his summer vacation of sand and sunshine.

St. John agreed at once, enclosing three examination papers for entrance to the second form. The consideration shown in the letter was typical of St. John, a booming, balding man with a warm heart ("Tell Jack it won't be too difficult for him to combine examinations with vacation at the shore").

With the exception of the dreaded Latin—the bête noir of schoolboys the world over—Jack did reasonably well in the exams. But Rose had second thoughts. She knew the advantages of Choate in terms of allowing a boy to enter the exalted realm of the Episcopalian elite, and Jack would have Joe to protect him against the bullies. But she was seized by nostalgia for her own Catholic upbringing. And she may have had qualms over the fact that Joe, though he was allowed to attend Mass every Sunday at St. Xavier's at

Wallingford, was also required to attend the Episcopalian services.

It was obvious from reports on Joe that his messy, untidy, typically boyish lack of discipline in terms of clothing and shoes was scarcely being fixed up at Choate. Jack was even sloppier, and would be put in better order at a Catholic school. She decided that Jack would go to Canterbury, a cheerless institution at New Milford, Connecticut, which was prepared to accept his Choate grades and admit him in September. Jack was upset; he had looked forward to being with his elder brother. But Rose was adamant, so he entered in September.

Jack hated the school. He wrote to his mother expressing homesickness; he complained of excessive amounts of religious study, bitter cold and severe discipline. He was irritated by the catechisms and religious talks, as well as, conversely, by irreligious activities, most notably theft. Thieves took his sweatshirt, his five-dollar birthday gift, his stamps, his fountain pens and his pillows. Despite his lack of muscle and his constitutional fragility, he proved to be a normal, agile, quick and spunky schoolboy. He could do a flying tackle on the football field with the best of them; he enjoyed seeing his target writhe in agony on the ground. He could take a whack across the face, a crack on the head or a jump on the neck without tears or anger. If he fainted during Mass, which he did on at least one occasion, he could make his way back to conclude the service without a grumble. He devoured his favorite novel, Sir Walter Scott's *Ivanhoe,* and was able to rattle off passages to anyone who would listen. All of this was a pleasure to Rose.

As disagreeable to her was a problem involving Honey Fitz, an irrepressible sixty-six, who had run for governor of Massachusetts, but had been involved in a series of unseemly brawls and had been charged with shenanigans involving mattress voting. He invented a sickness to avoid those charges, and "on the advice of his physician" had gone home and abandoned the race. The truth was that he wasn't up to the job and his old rah-rah devices had failed to work. Sheltering more in shame than in sickness at the Robert Breck Brigham Hospital in Boston, he lost to former governor Joseph B. Ely. But, amazingly, and perhaps through his own intrigues, he had remained on the ballot, gathering an impressive 84,744 votes.

On October 11, Rose was at yet another wedding, of her brother Thomas to Margaret B. Fitzpatrick at St. Raphael's Church in Boston. Thomas had been in an anguish of grief over his first wife Marion's death five and a half years earlier.

On December 6, Rose read Jack's and Joe, Jr.,'s school report cards on the same day. Neither had been expected to be a dazzling success, but, as it happened, they were both doing well. Jack's grades were particularly impressive: he achieved 86 in English, 95 in mathematics, 72 in science, and 77 in history. Only his Latin was predictably poor: 55. He wrote to Rose that if it were not for Latin he would probably have led the lower school; later, he put on 13 points in Latin, a considerable achievement since he found learning the dead language boring and pointless.

Back in Palm Beach for the 1931 season, Rose and Joe spent much time with Gloria Swanson, who was accompanied by her old friend LeRoy ("Sport") Ward. Swanson had been circulating a rumor that Joe was having an affair with the fiery Paramount star Nancy Carroll, a foolishness she repeated in her memoirs decades later.

Carroll flew in from Havana on January 28, 1931, with friends and moved into the Whitehall; there is not one indication that she could have been seeing Joe on a romantic basis. Actually, despite having a young husband and recent baby, she was enjoying a triangular fling with two handsome German air aces who accompanied her to the Cocoanut Grove nightclub when she appeared as mistress of ceremonies.

Tired of the Poinciana, Joe had taken an apartment for the season while he searched for a house, and Swanson was at Rose's housewarming. As a gag, annoyed by Swanson's rumormongering, Joe introduced Swanson to a newly arrived guest as Nancy Carroll. He laughed heartily over the joke after the party; it is doubtful that Swanson was amused.

In May, Jack developed abdominal pains at Canterbury and had to be rushed to the hospital. It turned out he had an inflamed appendix, which was operated on immediately. Returning to Bronxville for his recovery, he was in considerable postoperative pain, miserable and run-down, and Joe seized the occasion to get his way and have him reentered for Choate. Rose was compelled to agree, although, of course, his illness had nothing to do with his schooling at Canterbury.

Joe wrote to Wardell St. John, assistant headmaster at Choate, on May 14, 1931, suggesting that, preparatory to his admittance, Jack might work with a private tutor. Joe listed the books Jack had studied at Canterbury, saying that he hoped these would be acceptable. Rose, who was vacationing at the Greenbrier Hotel in West Virginia, concurred.

The St. Johns agreed to this arrangement, noting that any change of texts would result now in confusion. Typifying the freedom and openness of Choate, Wardell St. John wrote, "In the final analysis it is the boy and the teacher that count!"

With no reference to Jack's pulling out the previous summer, Wardell went on with a series of warm and urgent advices, all of which would lead to Jack's smooth admission. Once more, the exams would be taken in the summer, and Bruce Belmore, Jack's able Hyannis Port tutor, set to work with him, liking and admiring him as a bright and charming young man.

Latin again became a headache, and on July 3, 1931, Rose wrote, in her characteristic striking hand, to Wardell St. John, discussing the arrangements that were being made at Hyannis Port and saying that although history and English fired his imagination, he was still unsuccessful in Latin. She added that she was delighted by St. John's interest and patience with Jack, but she couldn't resist adding the words "we think" to the statement that Jack had "a very attractive personality." She went on to point out how different he was from Joe.

It was obvious by now that Rose couldn't suppress a degree of disappointment with Jack compared with her paragon oldest son. Joe was not only muscular and athletic, but he was a good mixer, expansive—and clearly, as his grandfather had announced so proudly to anyone who would listen at his birth, destined to be president. Jack was sickly, a hard worker but fragile, with a well-proportioned but thin physique that failed to compensate for his inherited good looks. He was suffering from the effects of the slight spinal curvature at birth. One leg was shorter than the other, probably caused by forceps pulling, which resulted in a destabilization of his back that caused him much pain and called for frequent trips to Boston for therapeutic treatments. Is it possible that Rose blamed herself subconsciously for the fact that a child of hers had been born less than perfect? Did the specter of possible injury caused by forceps birth continue to haunt her? Was she overprotective and nervous over Jack because of this?

It is certain that Rose, who was pregnant again, made the difficult decision to withdraw permanently from the marriage bed; Joe would in future occupy a separate bedroom. In making this decision, as a devout Roman Catholic, she acted in direct defiance of the Church's edicts.

On December 31, 1930, just six months before she made this major move in her life, Pope Pius XI issued the "Casti Connubii," his important encyclical on the subject of Christian marriage, a synopsis of which was automatically read at Mass at every church of consequence in the United States and elsewhere. In that encyclical, the pontiff made it clear that marriage was made by God, not by man, and that a Catholic wife must remain spiritually and sexually one with her husband until death, and no attempt must be made to prevent the birth of a child either by refusal of the obligations of wedlock on the husband's or wife's part, or by contraception or abortion.

What could have provoked Rose to this drastic decision? It is most likely to have been fear. Her refusal to have anyone except Dr. Frederick Good act as her obstetrician, even though the move to Boston might be, and frequently was, extremely inconvenient and involved a separation from her family, indicates that childbearing now made her nervous and she needed to be supported and reassured in the course of it.

She was now almost forty years old, and, to this day, giving birth at forty or older is considered to be risky. The loss of sexual intercourse probably meant nothing to her, since, from secondary sources, it is possible to determine that Joe was not a sensitive and considerate lover. Surprising though it may seem, it is quite possible that, after giving birth to eight children, she was still not sexually awakened. Since all of the evidence we have, including photographs, shows her to have been a cheerful, energetic, healthy and outgoing woman, with a rich enjoyment of friends, travel and the world at large, it is still impossible to show any indication of misery, frustration or sadness in her personality at the time. And she had been married for many years; it would be a rare couple who would still find erotic excitement after so extended a relationship and so many offspring. The truth probably is that there were far more important things in her life than sex, and that people of that time didn't put anything like the emphasis on erotic fulfillment that has effectively marked our own period.

Jack's tutor Bruce Belmore continued to work with him through the summer. He wrote to Choate on July 11, 1931, discussing the advances and retreats of his study with the boy, saying that John was a fine chap and a credit to Choate. More letters arrived on Rose's desk from the St. Johns, confirming their joy in having Jack join them. This correspondence continued through the long, happy weeks of boating and racing around at Hyannis. Then, with Rose back at Bronxville, Jack, to everyone's relief and pleasure, joined his brother at Choate.

Only a few days after his admission, on October 2, the family received grievous news. Sir Thomas Lipton had died in Scotland, leaving a major gap in their lives. They had seen him frequently on his visits to the United States, when he had customarily stayed with Honey Fitz in Boston. They had missed him in London during their fall visits because he had been up and down the New England coast preparing for, and unsuccessfully battling in, the America's Cup yacht races.

In view of the five days' voyage by ship, it was impossible for the Kennedys or the Fitzgeralds to cross the Atlantic in time for the funeral in Glasgow. This was very sad. In addition to getting Jack settled at Choate, Rose had to make

sure her other children were comfortable at school; the thin
and hypersensitive Eunice was admitted to Brantwood Hall,
a private girls' school in Bronxville, and the somewhat
neglected but sweet-natured Jean was at Bronxville School
kindergarten. Sturdy Patricia was also at the kindergarten,
and so was Kathleen. Rosemary, of course, was away in
Pennsylvania at her special school. Indeed, with so much of
her family requiring checking by mail or in person (for she
frequently visited Brantwood Hall and the kindergarten),
Rose sacrificed her annual trip to Europe for the second
year running.

Joe, Jr., had proved to be a model student at Choate. Still
the classic all-rounder, handsome, dashing, a rare mixture
of looks, brawn and brains, he was adored by everyone. But
Jack still lacked the one sure passport to popularity in any
school: a powerful body. Although he made many friends
because of his sheer charm, eagerness and openness of
personality, he was subject to hazings beyond anything his
brother had experienced. And his constant untidiness, the
result, like Joe's, of having maids to pick up for him at
home, proved irritating even to the most considerate teachers. Rose was in despair as she heard he would drop everything on the floor: clothes, books, papers, notepads. He was
neglectful in making his bed in his shared room; he would
be notoriously absentminded and late for classes. And, in
the rough-and-tumble of any school, poor health, along with
lack of muscle, can be a severe handicap, and it proved so in
his case.

Certainly, George St. John and his brother Wardell did
everything to make him happy. Jack, his brother and the
other boys would drop in to Mrs. George St. John at any
time for ice cream and a group sing. Rose was delighted
when she received such news, and gradually overcame her
misgivings at the fact that he was in a Protestant institution.
But she had much to worry about during the chilly, damp
winter months; Jack caught cold, an inconsequential matter
today, but in those days a cause for great distress. The St.
Johns advised Rose that Jack was transferred into the
infirmary, effectively in quarantine since neither his brother
nor his fellow pupils were allowed to see him. As for
parents, they were never welcome in such circumstances,

could be infected, and indeed, even under normal conditions, tended to get in the way.

Rose was pleased to hear that, bookish as ever, Jack took all of his favorite novels to the infirmary with him, so that they were piled high on the bed around him in disordered heaps as he devoured them one by one. She sent him a somewhat dandyish new lavender bathrobe and green-and-lavender pajamas; he reveled in them. Seven months pregnant in December, Rose was at the spectacular all-star opening of the Radio City Music Hall in the party of Roman Catholic politician Al Smith and journalist Walter Lippmann.

In January 1932, Jack came down with another bad cold; he was returned to the infirmary. On Rose's advice, Rose's secretary in Bronxville urged Mrs. George St. John to obtain a bottle of Kepler's malt and cod-liver oil, and to give him a teaspoonful after every meal. Mrs. St. John sent daily bulletins, as the sickness dragged on until January 25. By this time, Rose was back in Boston, expecting her new baby. Perhaps because of worry over Jack, Rose was not well at the time, and was not at her best when, in St. Margaret's Hospital, Dorchester, Dr. Frederick Good delivered her fourth son and ninth and last child on February 22, a plump, jolly boy. An early decision had been to name him George Washington, but fortunately this was abandoned in favor of Edward Moore. The Moores were delirious over this extraordinary compliment.

To celebrate the birth, and to cement his sons' careers at Choate, Joe gave the school an important gift of a Western Electric talkie movie projector which would enable the students to see newly released movies every Saturday night. The first of these would turn out to be *The Vagabond King,* supplied by Joe and indicative of his love of musicals. It was an overwhelming success with the boys and strengthened Jack's popularity even among the belligerent seniors.

But by now he was proving to be more of a problem than ever. For Rose and Joe, who saw him as the future brother of a president, this was especially trying. Jack was getting up to pranks, and on one occasion stole a Mae West placard from a movie theater and was found with it in his bed. A shocked cleaner discovered this and reported it, with predictable results. He was compulsive, had difficulty concentrating, kept losing paper, pencils and books.

Fearful that he was worn out with his studies, Rose asked Mrs. George St. John if he couldn't forget all tutoring and enjoy his Hyannis Port vacation unencumbered. She wanted him to build up his strength at the beach and on their boat; the St. Johns agreed but insisted he attend summer school in August.

Joe was late to Hyannis Port that summer because he was busy working on and helping to finance Franklin D. Roosevelt's presidential campaign. Neither he nor Roosevelt had forgotten their association during the Fore River strike of 1918. They had not been in touch very often in between; but now, with Rose's approval, Joe devoted himself to supporting the candidate. In this, he was supported by Cardinal O'Connell and by Francis Spellman, auxiliary bishop of Boston, who would later play a major role in the Kennedys' lives.

At the Democratic Convention in Chicago, Joe worked hard on the delegates, renewing an earlier association with the Montana politician Burton K. Wheeler. When Montana's Bruce Kremer made a speech at the Congress Hotel seeking the removal of the two-thirds rule for nomination, Joe joined Wheeler in opposition. Joe was certain that this change of the regulations would stop Roosevelt from achieving the nomination because the Southern senators might withdraw from the vote; they had jointly instituted the two-thirds rule. In this way, Joe helped secure the important support of such Southern democrats as senators Bailey, Bankhead and Cummings.

After two years of having Joe largely to herself, except for his sudden departures by his Sikorsky Amphibian airplane to the beach at Queens for his New York visits, Rose had to accept the fact of a lengthy separation as he took off on a nationwide swing on the campaign railroad train with the presidential candidate and his party. He called her whenever possible, or telegraphed her directly from the train itself; he kept her posted on the exciting journey, allowing her to live through it vicariously.

It was a thrilling trip, and included Eleanor Roosevelt's dramatic arrival by plane (a somewhat perilous adventure in those days) to join her husband in Arizona, and a massive rally in Los Angeles, scene of the 1932 Olympic Games, engineered with Hollywood razzle-dazzle by Joe's old friend, Jack Warner, chief honcho at Warner Bros. On the exhausting journey, Joe deepened what would turn out to be a lifelong friendship with James Roosevelt, the president's twenty-four-year-old eldest son. Shrewdly, he had arranged for James to enhance his career as an insurance man in Boston by setting him up with Charles Hayden of Hayden, Stone, and other business associates. Rose had become fond of James's wife, the attractive and charming Betsy Cushing, second daughter of Dr. Harvey Cushing, the Boston surgeon.

After the successful train journey (some 200,000 people greeted Roosevelt in Chicago alone), Joe returned to Rose in October, and they reveled in the celebrations that accompanied Roosevelt's successful election in November. Rose joined Joe for the party the president threw at the Waldorf to celebrate his victory; not the same Waldorf-Astoria where Joe had operated out of the John Hertz office suite (that hotel had been pulled down to accommodate the Empire State Building), but the new and glamorous hostelry on Park Avenue.

The Kennedys, to attend the social events, were in Palm Beach early for the season and were taken off on a pleasure cruise with the president aboard Vincent Astor's yacht *The Nourmahal*.

But the visit, begun so pleasantly, was soon overshadowed. Jack was sick again in February 1933, with yet another severe cold, sinusitis and pain in his knees. Rose fretted over the fact, but was not encouraged to make the long and difficult journey from Florida. In addition to this degree of stress, she and Joe had a frustration: there was no indication yet that Roosevelt would find a place for Joe in his Cabinet. Since Joe had raised at least $100,000 for him through William Randolph Hearst and others, he had expected the normal reward, but no word came week after week, and his disappointment deepened into bitterness.

The cause of this apparent neglect on the newly elected president's part has been attributed to Roosevelt's right-hand man, the hard-edged Louis Howe, who would later become presidential secretary. There is a story that enjoyed wide circulation at the time: a friend brought Joe to see Howe at his office, and Howe was found asleep at his desk. When the friend mentioned that Joe Kennedy had arrived, Howe opened one eye and closed it again; that was the end of the meeting.

Asked if the story was true, as well as the reason for his father's hatred of Kennedy, Hartley Howe, Louis's son, said that he had never heard the tale. He doubted if his father was interested in Joe Kennedy. But he did say that to any New Dealer a Wall Street plunger was anathema; he added that a popular sentence at the time among Roosevelt's inner circle was "Would you want your daughter to marry a banker?" The feeling was strong in those circles that financiers of Joe's character were responsible for the Crash and the Depression and that millions of shareholders were suffering because of short selling and other questionable practices, of which Joe, rightly or wrongly, was considered the leading exemplar.

Hartley Howe points out, it would have created disfavor in the electorate if a prominent financial wizard were included in the government. Louis Howe's objection was not personal, but was guided by common sense. The truth is that there was no place for a Wall Street bull like Joe Kennedy in the delicately furnished china shop of the new administration—yet.

Spring brought Rose no relief from her husband's tantrums at being so summarily rejected; nor did it bring relief from Jack's continuing health problems. Rose was concerned about the pain in his feet, a result of inherited fallen arches, for which she was hoping he would have special exercises and to help which she hoped he would abandon his addiction to wearing loafers instead of proper shoes. And Jack was still having trouble with his back. By contrast, Joe, Jr., at Field Day at the end of May, won the Harvard trophy as the best all-rounder, scholar and athlete at Choate, and graduated with full honors.

Rose, thinking no doubt of delightful trips to England, told Joe she preferred Oxford or Cambridge before the long-planned entry to Harvard. But Joe had fastened on another idea. Certain that his oldest boy would be president one day, he felt that the young man should obtain a sophisticated knowledge of international politics.

Joe reached an astonishing decision. Still an opponent of socialism, never forgetting his and Rose's ordeal during the Red activities in Boston, he would send his son to study at the London School of Economics under Harold Laski, the influential spokesman of the British Labor Party.

Laski was forty years old at the time; he had been raised an orthodox Jew in Manchester, England, and had been educated at New College, Oxford. As a member of the Fabian Society, a convinced socialist, he had opposed the oppression of the Welsh coal miners; in 1919, he had confronted Joe Kennedy directly in an important matter. Lecturing at Harvard, he had fought against Joe's use of Harvard athletes as strikebreakers, fighting against the police who had walked out. When the dean and chancellor refused to attend his demand that the vigilantes be withdrawn, he resigned at once and returned to England. He had been vociferous in criticizing such Kennedy idols as Charles Schwab for their role in crushing labor.

At the London School of Economics, he had continued to support all strikes, and had become anathema to the right wing. At the time Joe decided to send his son to him, Laski was visiting professor at Yale. Although no correspondence survives, nor records of any meeting, it is probable that Joe made the arrangements on American soil.

Rose was horrified by Joe's decision. She fought against it, not least because socialism was condemned by Pope Pius XI as the ally of communism and of Satan. The thought of her favorite son submitting himself to the pernicious teachings of the British left wing was insupportable to her. And she saw that it was only a question of time before Joe, Jr., would be sent, as part of his study course, to the Soviet Union, where he might further be poisoned by an evil ideology.

In taking this position, she was reacting not only as a concerned mother who recalled the Red activities in Boston in 1918 and 1919, but as a devout Roman Catholic. Pius XI had been categorical in his denunciation of Soviet communism in his encyclical, read out at Mass in America, "Ci Commuodono Profondamente." In the eyes of all devout members of the Church, atheist communism was to be rejected and not even an association must take place between Catholics and the socialists. Biographers have tended to regard Joe's position in the matter as being anomalous and contradictory, and that his purpose in sending Joe, Jr., to Laski was to act as an informant on an enemy.

But in fact, Kennedy, fighting his wife's precepts, was acting in accord with Roosevelt's current policy. From the moment he was elected, the president had decided to assist the depressed American economy by expanding the country's economic frontiers, even to the point of including the Soviet Union. In Moscow, Maxim Litvinov, the remarkable Jewish commissar in charge of Soviet foreign affairs, concurred with this proposed future alliance. He was directly linked to Harold Laski through his British wife, the former Ivy Low, a radical writer and niece of a former lord mayor of London, who was a friend of Frida, Laski's wife. Within a year, the U.S. government would agree to extend the Russian debt, incurred when, in 1917, the Aleksander Kerensky provisional socialist government in Moscow had borrowed approximately $10 million through a gold bond issue in America in return for a unilateral agreement to extend trading relations and to allow a free flow of U.S. goods to Russia. A key figure in the negotiations would be William Christian Bullitt, soon to be made ambassador to the U.S.S.R., who had been married to Louise Bryant, celebrated widow of the American communist John Reed.

At Hyannis Port that season, Rose was depressed and angry. Meanwhile, forceful and determined as ever, Joe planned another aspect of the trip to Europe on which Joe, Jr., would be inducted. Knowing that legislation would soon end Prohibition, allowing Americans to drink alcohol legally from the outset of 1934 (he had been accused, without evidence, of bootlegging), he decided to obtain, against much competition, the exclusive rights to distribute the top British liquor products in the United States. These would include Gilbey's gin, Haig & Haig and other popular spirits. He began opening up connections to London, and was endlessly on the telephone, competing with his daughter Kathleen, who spent hours talking to her various boyfriends. Finally, he installed a second telephone in the house.

There was another purpose of the trip. It was Holy Year; American Catholics were up to their eyes in a series of elaborate celebrations. On April 1, thousands of Catholics, along with Jews and Protestants, crowded into Radio City Music Hall for a full-scale ecumenical service. Rabbi Stephen Wise, the prominent Jewish leader in the United States, joined in the goodwill celebrations. Thousands of Italian peasants brought vegetables, fruits and live animals to Rome as a tribute to the Pope; thousands more visited the Holy Shroud, on special display in Turin; crowds of pilgrims knelt before basilicas from Madrid to Rome. Thousands sought cures on Assumption Day later that year when they bathed at Coney Island and the Rockaways, a procedure the Church categorically did not condone. Would this not be the perfect time for the Kennedys to visit Pope Pius XI?

But they were scarcely of sufficient importance to qualify for a private audience on their own. Fortunately, for them, James and Betsy Roosevelt had the same idea. Certainly, the president's eldest son would be welcomed by the pontiff, who had been seeking for some time a full-scale diplomatic relationship with the White House. The Kennedys could go along for the ride.

Rose had found a good reason to make the journey, to compensate for the thought that she was pitching her boy into a socialist situation. In the meantime, that June, after four years of renting a house on Clarke Avenue, Palm Beach, she and Joe concluded the purchase of La Gueroda, a handsome 1923 Addison Mizner American-Spanish, white-walled house with a red-tiled roof that they would enjoy for many years.

Not one of the grander Palm Beach homes, the house was located on two acres of beachfront land at 1095 North Ocean Boulevard, with a sweeping view of the Atlantic, and cost $100,000. The neighboring plot was bought for $15,000. The original owner had been the Philadelphia department store owner Rodman Wanamaker. In ecumenical Florida, the Kennedys had, for some time, belonged to the Everglades, Bath and Tennis and Seminole Golf clubs.

On September 21, Kathleen, age thirteen, entered in the ninth grade the exclusive Convent of the Sacred Heart, Noroton, Connecticut.

Unable to get passage, because of scheduling problems, on the *Ile de France,* Rose and Joe secured a first-class suite on the sleek "Greyhound of the Seas," the North German Lloyd steamer *Europa,* sailing on September 27. A last-ditch effort to have Jack accompany them failed as the St. Johns felt strongly that he should not interrupt his studies. He had not done particularly well in summer school, starting in August.

The Kennedys were overjoyed when the president's mother, Sara Delano Roosevelt, and her granddaughter, Mrs. Curtis Dall, came to see them off as they sailed with Jim and Betsy Roosevelt; a Jewish couple, wealthy in real estate, Mr. and Mrs. Cord Meyer; Betsy's sister, Mary Cushing; Mr. and Mrs. Mason Day; and another friend, Arthur Houghton.

Arrived in London, settled into Claridges Hotel, the Kennedys plunged into a hectic schedule with Ambassador Robert W. Bingham as their host. Bingham behaved with courtly manners that quite contradicted a notorious past. Even when he presented his credentials at the Court of St. James it was generally accepted that he had murdered, through administering morphine, his wife, the exceptionally rich Mary Lilly Flagler (widow of the Palm Beach emperor Henry Flagler, in whose converted mansion Gloria Swanson later dreamed up her erotic encounter with Kennedy). Flagler's convenient and fatal fall downstairs had caused some tongues in high places to wag uncontrollably. But no hint of his dark past disturbed Ambassador Bingham's brow as he entertained the Kennedys.

Joe was busy day and night meeting with the heads of the liquor companies, particularly Sir James Calder of British Distillers; he decided to name his importing company Somerset, a sly reference to the fact that the exclusive Somerset Club of Boston had refused to accept him as a member.

Prime Minister Ramsay MacDonald received the Kennedys and the Roosevelts for dinner at 10 Downing

Street. As was customary in those days, the conversation consisted of generalities and did not include any discussion of politics, on which the Kennedys and the MacDonalds would not have been in agreement in any case. The party was received by Chancellor of the Exchequer Neville Chamberlain and at Winston Churchill's estate in Kent. It is certain that Churchill gave them, as he did all prominent visitors, a signed copy of his newly published life of his illustrious forebear, the first Duke of Marlborough. In London, they were often seen at the Café de Paris, dancing until the small hours with Lord and Lady Ashburton and Lord and Lady Castlerosse.

The decision was made to embark on an extensive motoring tour of Europe, starting in Paris and continuing to Rome. But after a reception by President Albert Lebrun at his official residence on the rue du Faubourg St. Honoré, Joe had to leave Rose and return to London to piece together the final details of his liquor representation deal. He decided to leave for New York on the *Majestic* on October 19 to cement the American end; given his nervous character when concluding deals of any kind, he felt he couldn't wait, and would have to give up the experience of being received by the Pope. This was perhaps just as well, since he had effectively betrayed the papal edicts by having his son played as a wild card in a strictly pragmatic U.S.–Soviet alliance.

Chapter 8

Rome and Moscow

In London and Paris, while James Roosevelt was busy collecting first editions of the autobiographies of political celebrities, Rose was reading, in any hours she could spare from shopping at Harrods or at the salons of Lucien Lelong and Patou, biographical material on Pope Pius XI to prepare her for the audience in Rome. Given her little-known but actual grasp of politics, she was fascinated by what she learned.

Far from being a pro-fascist, as the liberal intellectual press has insisted ever since, Pius XI defied Mussolini from the beginning. Through the Lateran Agreement of 1929, he had separated the Vatican from the Italian fascist state, and in a July 5, 1931, encyclical he condemned the Italian dictator outright. He directed similar attacks on Hitler, but onslaughts on bishops and priests in Germany had compelled him to the unfortunate compromise of the 1933 Concordat that allowed the dissolution of the German centrist Catholic party in return for a promise by Hitler that the German Catholic youth movement would be recognized and the imprisonment and torture of Catholics would cease.

The fact that the Pope was the enemy of fascism in all its forms, despite the fact that Nazi Germany was seen as the opponent of the even more hated communism, was sufficient for Rose in setting the tone of her political attitudes in the future and, despite repeated statements to the contrary in book after book, her husband's as well.

On arrival in Rome, Rose and the other members of the Roosevelts' party were received by U.S. Ambassador Breckinridge Long at the sumptuous Villa Taverna, which Long had persuaded Roosevelt to allow him to lease because the embassy was gloomy and in poor repair. The restored Renaissance villa was a virtual palace. Rose found herself swallowed up in marble and gilt and priceless paintings, pampered by flocks of servants. She discovered in Long a passionate enthusiast for Mussolini; no doubt she kept quiet on the matter, knowing of the pontiff's disapproval.

Later, Long would be disillusioned, warning Roosevelt of the dangers from the dictator and urging him, only half humorously, to equip his diplomatic officials in Europe with gas masks. Actually, Long's support of Mussolini was in part hypocritical, since, like all of Roosevelt's ambassadors, appointed because they were rich and had supported him in his campaign, Long acted as an intelligence source.

The arrangements for the papal audience were concluded. It would take place on October 27, 1933. Rose had to dress in a mantilla and floor-length black dress. The drive to the Vatican was unforgettable. Because it was Holy Year, a crowd of pilgrims filled St. Peter's Square and the surrounding streets as the chauffeured embassy limousine brought Rose and her companions through the cobbled courtyard of St. Damasus to the rear entrance of St. Peter's, where they were greeted by the Swiss guards in ceremonial skirted uniforms. The chauffeur presented the permit issued by the governor of Vatican City and the party could proceed.

With spectacularly clad attendants in scarlet and gold on either side, Rose was joined in the vestibule by Count Enrico Galeazzi, architect of the sacred apostolic palaces at the Vatican, and brother to the chief papal physician. Auxiliary Bishop Spellman had supplied Rose with the necessary note of introduction. Galeazzi welcomed his guests warmly and ushered them into an elevator, which carried them to the third floor. There, Rose found herself in a small, modestly furnished library, with an open fire crackling in the grate, subdued light shining over the leather covers of ancient books. Galeazzi reminded the visitors, as he reminded all arrivals, that politics must not be discussed. After a brief interval, the pontiff appeared, dressed in a simple white cassock.

Galeazzi made the introductions, as Rose and the others genuflected. Looking less than his seventy-six years, the Pope was round-faced, bespectacled, ruddy-cheeked and beaming. He had been up since 6:00 A.M. in an unvarying ritual that included coffee and rolls, followed by hours of official meetings. The appointed time for distinguished Catholic and non-Catholic visitors was now: exactly 1:30 P.M. by the Vatican clock. He would not be taking luncheon until three o'clock.

The Pope asked his visitors about President Roosevelt and sent his good wishes to him. He inquired of Rose about Cardinal O'Connell, who had been a recent visitor. As she left, awed, Galeazzi gave the party a tour of the Consistry and Clementine halls, the Ducal hall, and the Vatican museum. It was conducted with great difficulty because of the enormous numbers of worshipers waiting to be blessed by the pontiff. For Rose, it was the beginning of a lifelong friendship with Galeazzi.

Rose did not accompany James Roosevelt at 5:15 that afternoon when he proceeded to the Palazzo Venezia for a fifteen-minute audience with Mussolini. The dictator suggested that the party examine the new excavations in Rome, Naples and Capri.

Near Naples, Rose trudged through the streets of Pompeii, with dogs and children frozen in lava forever in the movement of their headlong flight from a long-ago volcanic eruption. The women were excluded from the tour of the ancient bordellos with their phallic stone excrescences. The trip to Capri was a joy; Coert du Bois, the American consul general, arranged to borrow a schooner owned by the lawyer Francesco Montefredini to sail Rose and her friends around the island. She found herself lying flat in a small craft, entering the mysterious sapphire depths of the Blue Grotto, the light dancing in perfect reflection in the water. She continued to Ischia and took a donkey ride to the top of Anacapri. On November 1, with the Cord Meyers and

Arthur Houghton, Rose and the Roosevelts sailed from
Naples on the new Italian luxury liner *Rex* for New York.

On disembarking, James Roosevelt raved about the Mussolini regime to reporters gathered on the boat deck. This
cannot have pleased Rose, but such expressions of admiration were accepted in the period. Many, in fact, compared
Mussolini's hands-on regime with Roosevelt's own—the
style of exercising power from the top. When the Kennedys
traveled to Palm Beach for the winter season, the James
Roosevelts accompanied them.

Rose's children had problems that winter. Rosemary
needed constant attention, with her shifts of mood and
constant failure to remember anything; Patricia had developed a delicate system that responded badly to most things,
including drifting plant and flower seeds; Kathleen was
fretting at the strict regimen of Noroton, reminiscent of
Rose's at Sacred Heart on Commonwealth Avenue. All of
the children called for Rose's attention as she constantly
and futilely tried to turn them into the godlike figure Joe,
Jr., was; she missed him badly.

During the stay at Ocean Avenue, Rose received news
from Choate; Jack was stricken with a mysterious illness,
which was later alleged to be agranulycotic angina, a form
of blood destruction occurring in the presence of a severe
infection or exposure to certain toxic chemicals. It caused
spots, ulceration and gangrene of the mouth and larynx and
resulted in fever and prostration, a loss of red corpuscles
and an increase of white. It could recur, and recovery was
very rare.

Rose has been criticized for not attending her son at the
time, for not making the long and difficult train journey
from Palm Beach. But Lee Sylvester, archivist of Choate
Rosemary Hall, says that in those days there was strict
quarantine for such a case, and that no parent would be
allowed near the infirmary, only masked and gloved doctors
and nurses and Mr. and Mrs. George St. John.

Jack recovered slowly, his blood count improving daily,
until at last, in March, he was able to join his family in Palm
Beach. Then Rose had another worry. Joe, Jr., traveled to
Nazi Germany, at a time when even foreign Catholics,
despite the existence of the Concordat, could easily be

harassed by officials. She was upset by the letters he sent home, which reflected the commonplace anti-Semitism of the day, despite the fact that he would soon be joining the Laskis and the Litvinovs in Moscow. Joe, Jr., echoed the familiar Hitler argument that the Jews, running big business in Berlin, had been responsible for Germany's woes, and he said in one letter that if he were a German he would heil Hitler. It has been said that he learned such attitudes at home.

But he had not; Joe and Rose were friendly with the Jewish Adolph Zukor, head of Paramount, and his wife; with Mr. and Mrs. Nicholas Schenck, who owned M.G.M.; with the Joe Schnitzers, Bernard Baruch, Arthur Krock, William Paley of CBS, and the Cord Meyers; and with many prominent bankers, including the heads of Kuhn, Loeb, whom they entertained at Palm Beach or Bronxville.

Apparently, Rose did not take the responses of an intellectually lightweight athlete very seriously. When he got to Moscow, Joe, Jr., seemed as infatuated by communism as he was by Nazism. The day he arrived there, on June 4, as houseguest of U.S. Ambassador William Bullitt, the beginnings of the Russian-American economic alliance were cemented; the U.S.-Soviet Export-Import Bank was set up in Moscow to supply credits toward the importing of American machinery and supplies.

It is doubtful that Rose knew a potential danger lurked for Joe, Jr., in the American embassy. Bullitt was bisexual; the presence of the magnificent-looking youth must have shaken him deeply. But apparently the young man escaped unscathed. He returned to Hyannis Port in July, bursting with praise for socialism. Led by Rose, his family ragged him: would he be prepared to give up his boat for the poor? He had to grin and admit he wouldn't.

That same month, July, after much discussion and preparation, Joe, Sr., at last was rewarded for his financial help to the president during the electoral campaign of 1932. He was made chairman of the newly created Securities and Exchange Commission, designed to regulate stock and bond market practices, which had become increasingly scandalous. This caused an adverse reaction in Republican

Hyannis; Roosevelt was hated by the socialites there, and now they found an actual New Dealer on their doorsteps. One resident told Hyannis Port chronicler Leo Damore, "I've never dreamed a man in Kennedy's position would ever go to *work* for Roosevelt." Disaffected, Rose spent much of that season at a religious retreat some miles away, avoiding the Hyannis crowd completely.

The family was proud of her husband's appointment; the cynics took the view that it was handed out on the basis of "it takes a thief to catch a thief." Certainly, Roosevelt knew that Kennedy was aware of the places where all the bodies were buried. From Kennedy's point of view, there was the chance to clean up his record, even if it meant effectively giving away some of his old associates. Charles Hayden was among those who were furious at the appointment, regarding Kennedy as no better than a fink and a betrayer.

For Rose, despite her pride, the appointment soon became a mixed blessing. She had to face the reality that Joe would be forced to move to Washington, D.C., to maintain his position as the head of an organization with large numbers of employees; he would also have to travel the length and breadth of the country to investigate out-of-state exchanges. He would be conferring frequently with the president at the White House and would be called in to consult on the federal budget, which was a billion dollars in arrears.

Assailed by his enemies, who pointed gleefully to his role in the Libbey-Owens-Ford glass affair, Joe was as cheerful and unruffled as ever as he assumed the post officially on July 2, 1934. He became famous overnight; lengthy interviews with him appeared in the *New York Times* and elsewhere; he was accorded a magnificent residence, Marwood, near the nation's capital; he took off on perilous flights everywhere, through all kinds of weather, forced down again and again in storms.

As his absence from home was extended, Rose thought she might move to Washington, but the idea was impracticable. She would have to pull her children out of their schools; she would have to resettle them yet again in an alien environment. Instead, she devoted her energies to

such important matters as having Joe, Jr., back from
Europe on the S.S. *New York* on July 14, admitted as a
freshman to Harvard on September 24; Kathleen was still at
Noroton; Eunice soon joined her there; Jack was in the sixth
form at Choate. And Joe's alcoholic brother Frederick was
ill at only twenty-eight from cirrhosis and this was a severe
burden.

On her own for once, Rose sailed to France and England
on the *Majestic* to buy haute couture dresses at Lelong and
Molyneux, returning on the same ship on the thirtieth of
September with two new shipboard friends, the actor
Charles Boyer and his wife, Pat Patterson. In her absence,
Rosemary entered Elmhurst, a Sacred Heart Convent at
Providence, Rhode Island.

The family was reunited at Palm Beach at the unusually
early, preseason time of Christmas. From that year on, the
Yuletide ritual never varied. Each of the Kennedys bought a
present for all the others, so that, since there were eleven
members, there were at least 110 gifts in all. But that was
only the beginning; they bought dozens more for other
friends, headed as always by Eddie and Mary Moore, and
for the staff. When the family arrived by specially chartered
Pullman with eleven drawing rooms, they were usually
accompanied by as many as four hundred presents, housed
in the baggage car, which were transferred to the family
Rolls. It took hours to open the beautifully wrapped gifts
piled up around a giant Christmas tree. Unraveling the
yards of silver and gold paper, piled afterward in a giant
heap, was a hilarious event, with everyone more and more
excited. For Rose, this was the top day of the year, one she
had been looking forward to for weeks ahead.

A photograph shows the family glowing with health and
apparent happiness. Rose looks like her daughters' sister
rather than their mother; slim as a girl, despite her nine
children, in an informal print summer dress, she looks
confident, cheerful and full of life. Joe, Jr., tan, handsome as
Robert Taylor or Errol Flynn, is the most formally clad, in a
white Panama suit and dark tie. Joe, Sr., looking worn and
aged, tired by the burdens of office, is next to him; then
Jack, remarkably healthy and good-looking considering his

long struggle with sicknesses; the very attractive Eunice; and pretty Rosemary, showing no sign of her mental condition.

In the next row, beside a smiling, closed-eyed Rose, is the gorgeous Pat (Joe, Jr.,'s rival as the prettiest member of the clan); Jean, with a shock of hair concealing her right eye; and Bobby, already a bombshell. Teddy is chubbily cheerful in a sailor suit. Though posed, the group is clearly not faking its look of togetherness. They are leaning toward each other, protectively, warmly; this family was a championship team.

Throughout the first months of 1935, Rose had to work hard to keep up with her husband's activities. He was giving speeches everywhere, to the Union League Club on regulation of over-the-counter trading, to the New York Produce Exchange as he closed that exchange's securities division, to the American Arbitration Association, and to dozens of other organizations as he campaigned against stock pooling, false prospectuses and the ranks of stock swindlers, of whom, his critics complained, he had been one. In April, he was involved in a role as one of Roosevelt's chief relief advisors; he helped lay the groundwork for welfare—extensive aid to the unemployed. He had proved of great importance in establishing the workability of the Social Security Act, which introduced Social Security to the United States for the first time.

But in July Joe's health was wearing down, and he became aggravated by the House Utilities Bill, with which he disagreed. Rose urged him to retire and take care of his health. As always when overstressed, he lost a great deal of weight, and the endless nagging of his opponents, despite his cool bravado, wore him down.

Rose talked Joe into joining her on a trip to Europe, during which he would investigate economic conditions there.

Yielding to Rose's pressures, Joe resigned from the SEC on September 20. Even John T. Flynn, his most savage assailant in the pages of *The New Republic,* was forced to admit he had done a good job, and indeed it is doubtful if anyone else could have carried it off with equal success.

Later, in an article in the *Saturday Evening Post,* Joe outlined what had been necessary in terms of cleaning up the irregularities of the stock market. Not all of those irregularities had been removed, of course; but he had made a beginning.

On September 25, 1935, the Kennedys sailed on the *Ile de France,* with Jack, who was also to be admitted, to Rose's fury, to Harold Laski's classes at the London School of Economics, and Kathleen. On the rough crossing, Jack spent long periods scribbling letters to LeMoyne Billings, his former roommate at Choate, describing matters of which Rose was fortunately ignorant. He talked of a fat Frenchman luring him into a cabin in an attempt to seduce him; of chasing girls; of getting into other hijinks. Despite his poor health, Jack seemed to be possessed of a normal amount of teenage lust, his tongue as filthy as one would expect.

In London, while Joe, Sr., conferred with various figures of the British government, Jack fell ill almost as soon as he was admitted to the School of Economics with a recurrence of agranulocytosis. The American ambassador to the Court of St. James, Robert W. Bingham, himself suffering from the not-unrelated Hodgkin's disease, was sympathetic, and referred Jack to his own physicians. Rose was painfully distracted as Jack entered the London Clinic, in great distress, again unable to receive family or other visitors. The decision was made to withdraw him after only a few weeks, and bring him back to America.

Meanwhile, surprisingly, Rose admitted Kathleen not to Blumenthal, but to the equally rigorous St. Maux, an austere and forbidding Sacred Heart Convent school in Normandy. Later, she would rebel, and Rose removed her after a few days to another Sacred Heart in the opulent suburb of Neuilly, Paris, where, at least, she could escape and enjoy the city from time to time.

Rose, Joe and Jack returned to New York on the *Berengaria* on October 25, accompanied by Rose's friends Merle Oberon, Charles Boyer and Pat Patterson, and the Chicago millionaire Potter D'Orsay Palmer. Jack would be admitted to Princeton, for which he had been entered along with Harvard; Rose would have preferred the latter choice, since again he would have been joining his older brother. But as it turned out, the choice was not significant; a recurrence of the dreaded disease that struck him twice before forced him to leave that university on December 12.

What was to be done with him? Despite Rose's love of the boy, it is easy to sense, reading between the lines of her letters and her autobiography, an exasperation at his failure ever to get well, to put on a normal amount of weight, to be tidy, responsible and correct. The contrast with his elder brother was always pressing and distracting. Would he ever amount to anything?

After Jack had suffered through a spell at Peter Bent Brigham Hospital in Boston and at Palm Beach, Rose and Joe sent him off to Arizona for sunshine, clean air and horseback riding. He strengthened somewhat, acquired a tan, and Rose felt a little cheered. But Kathleen, at her convent school in Paris, was not confident of his improvement, and Rose had to work hard to reassure her.

Soon, Rose got wind of the fact that Kathleen was beginning to break out of the confines of Sacred Heart training, and Rose sent her money to buy clothes for skiing at Gstaad, Switzerland, where Kathleen spent Christmas flirting—at fifteen—with a handsome American student, Derek Richardson. Later, in Rome, Kathleen was chaperoned by Count Enrico Galeazzi, Rose's host of two years earlier. Rose was uneasy about Kathleen; she feared for her. But Kathleen, with all her love of travel and excitement, was as strictly moral as her mother.

A great pleasure for Rose was spending New Year's Eve with her husband as a guest of the Roosevelts at the White House; it was a good way to see 1936 in, and it was fascinating to her to see how Eleanor had redecorated the executive mansion, which was changed unrecognizably from the days when she had first walked into the East Room, to be greeted by Mr. and Mrs. McKinley, followed by the president's unfortunate compliment to her sister Agnes. It was obvious to the Kennedys that the visit was symbolic: any misgivings Roosevelt may have had about Joe had been swept away at least temporarily by the excellence of his work in running the Securities and Exchange Commission and the cogency of his November report on the

European economy. Would a cabinet post or an ambassadorship be far off?

Nineteen thirty-six would be an election year, and an opportunity for Joe to increase his support, financially and otherwise, for Roosevelt. In the meantime, he had another assignment. He left Palm Beach in January for Hollywood and New York to confer with Adolph Zukor, head of Paramount Pictures, Inc., on questions concerning the studio's financial difficulties. On January 20, Zukor signed him at a six-figure fee to undertake a full-scale examination of the Paramount books and to determine ways of solving its dire and pressing problems.

Joe quickly exposed the extravagance of William Le Baron, who had given him similar problems when he had worked for him at his own studio several years earlier, and of the director Ernst Lubitsch, who had briefly and disastrously been put in charge of production.

Knowing that Joe would be absent on Paramount business and his preparations for the presidential campaign, Rose decided on another trip abroad. She made up her mind to follow Joe, Jr., and visit the Soviet Union. Several of her circle were aghast at her decision, but she was determined to go ahead.

She could scarcely have chosen a worse time. Relations between the United States and Russia had become strained, chiefly because of the belligerent activities of the Communist International in the United States and because of Stalin's fudging over the repayments on the Kerensky gold bond loans, which the U.S. secretary of the treasury could no longer delay demanding. Many thinking people were appalled when Stalin executed commissars over the failure of the cotton crop and even over the loss of reindeer. U.S. Ambassador William Bullitt, who had been married to the famous communist Louise Bryant (Mrs. John Reed), was convinced that he had been mistaken in finding any value in Bolshevism; he was also convinced that Stalin would break the terms of the Litvinov Pact. Just when Rose decided to descend on him, he was preparing to leave Russia for good.

Roosevelt disapproved of Bullitt's new political position; he wanted to maintain relations with the U.S.S.R. and approved the recently concluded Franco-Soviet Pact. Rose could bring to Joe word of Bullitt's disaffections, which could be passed on to the president, and she could also report on conditions in Russia. After all, she had begun as a travel writer for the *Boston American,* and her observations would be valuable. Hating communism, she would be a good gauge of what was going on in Moscow. But unfortunately, Maxim and Ivy Litvinov would be in Geneva at the League of Nations during her visit.

Rose had a double motive in going. Kathleen was homesick at her Paris convent school at Neuilly, and Rose wanted her to have a break by taking her to Moscow. Rose sailed from New York on the *Ile de France* on April 16; she joined Kathleen at the Ritz, and they shopped together at the salons of Lelong and Paquin. Bullitt telegraphed Joe on May 6 that he was looking forward to their arrival—a diplomatic lie, since he wasn't. Their visit couldn't have been more inconvenient for him. They were due on the sixteenth; he was already packing to leave for Berlin, New York and Washington on the eighteenth; many things had been stored, and several rooms of the embassy were dust-sheeted. And there was an enormous amount of paperwork to be prepared for Bullitt's successor, Joseph E. Davies.

Paris was in the grip of a political storm during Rose's stay. It was the week of the national election, held in the face of a threatened general strike. The streets were filled with students waving red flags in honor of the Communist International, sounding off with noisemakers and setting off smoke bombs. By the time Rose and Kathleen left the city, it was clear that the socialist Leon Blum would be victorious—the radical Socialist party won 375 of the 618 seats. This movement to the extreme left was indicative of public approval of the Franco-Soviet Pact, and many of Rose's highly placed friends in Paris were in despair.

Nonetheless, Rose pressed on with her trip. The only way to get to Moscow without spending eternities on trains, as she had at first planned, was by the French national airline to Riga, Latvia, with a change of plane to the Russian capital. It was a terrifying flight; Bullitt had almost lost his life on a similar journey to Poland in 1935. At Riga, Rose was appalled to see the Soviet aircraft tied up with ropes, apparently to prevent it from falling apart. She felt sick as she saw her luggage being carried aboard; worse when she discovered that she and Kathleen were the only passengers, crammed into a tiny cabin behind the pilot and navigator.

The plane skimmed over hills and forests only a few hundred feet up, tossed randomly through turbulence for hours on end. The navigator took his directions from the sun and moon, since the plane was not equipped with a compass. Muttering Hail Marys every few minutes, Rose and Kathleen were exhausted by the time they landed. They were driven by embassy limousine to Spaso House, the ambassadorial residence, in a Moscow suburb, a huge and unattractive former czarist mansion with echoing rooms, high ceilings, and ugly, clumsily made furniture. The dining room was in red marble, like a presidential tomb; the ballroom had a glass dome, ill-fitted so that the wind whistled through its metal framework.

Bullitt did his best to be an accommodating host, but he left forty-eight hours later; his giddy homosexual associate, Carmel Offie, was in charge of Rose and Kathleen's itinerary. What Rose made of Offie is hard to conjecture. Twenty-five years old, not handsome but a charming and witty gossip, Offie knew social figures on both sides of the Atlantic and was a source of much inside information.

Rose was warned that the embassy was bugged and that anything she said on the telephone would be conveyed to Russian Intelligence. This was amusing, but Moscow was not very pleasant; Rose colored the picture in her memoirs. The city was even noisier than election-ridden Paris. The new boulevard known as Lenin Allee was being constructed in the heart of the metropolis, causing clouds of dust amid the ceaseless rattle of pneumatic drills. Ancient buildings, considered to be an obstacle to traffic, were being demolished; the Kremlin was covered in scaffolding, as its walls were being repaired. Men were pulling up trolley-car tracks; buses were grinding through the muddy troughs, foundering frequently and disgorging angry passengers. Holes were being dug in sidewalks for trees to be planted; parking lots were being turned into skating rinks or tennis courts. Not since Baron Haussman had transformed Paris had a city been given so major a facelift and at such a staggering cost.

Famine was epidemic in Moscow, and food was in desperately short supply. Executions were taking place of commissars who had failed to produce fruit or potatoes. As would be commonplace in Russia for the next several decades, overfarming, the corruption of the standardized bureaucracy and wholesale theft of meat and vegetables had left the average Muscovite in a very poor state. Touring the museums and galleries, going to the Bolshoi Ballet, where the audience wore shabby clothes, seeing the new subway, would have been an ordeal for anyone. No matter how warmly (and fictitiously) Rose pictured the city then and later, Moscow presented a vision of hopelessness.

Leaving the city on the same day as Offie, who was going to Berlin on leave, Rose had to rush headlong by plane, via Leningrad and Riga, in severe storms, for France, in order to get to Cherbourg in time for the maiden voyage of the *Queen Mary,* leaving on May 26. Kathleen accompanied her as far as Paris, then left for London, Cambridge—and Derek Richardson.

Prominent people had fought to obtain passage on the magnificent new Cunard vessel, and a giant party was held in London at the Trocadero, which had been dressed up in imitation of the grand saloon, to celebrate the launching. Joe had to pull every string to get his wife and daughter a suite. A crowd was on the wharf when Rose arrived close to midnight; above her loomed the red and black hull topped by three handsome funnels. The vessel was lit from stem to stern, and every craft in the harbor was sounding off guns and sirens. Fireworks exploded from the boat deck; a brass band played patriotic tunes. The passengers had to struggle to get up the gangway, but once they were aboard, everything was superb. A long line of stewards in white, starched jackets with brass buttons and white gloves stood there in welcome, guiding everyone to their staterooms. Several of Rose's friends were aboard, most notably *Time* and *Life* publisher Henry Luce and his enchanting wife, Clare Boothe; Morton Downey's sister-in-law, movie star Joan Bennett; and her husband, writer Gene Markey.

Everyone talked of beating the Atlantic speed record, but that dream was vanquished on the first day out as the *Mary* was slowed down by heavy fog. Rose and the other passengers could only stare glumly through the portholes, or from the decks, into a swirling, dense mass of vapor through which other vessels' lights could barely be seen.

There were other disadvantages of the trip. For all her splendor, the vessel rolled and vibrated in the slightest swell. For Rose, coming down into the enormous dining room was quite an experience. The chandeliers swayed alarmingly; the deck with its garishly patterned carpets moved underfoot; the Art Deco mirrors with their motifs of goddesses and unicorns exploded with shifting light. Expensive crockery and silverware crashed to the floor. It was hard for people to eat at tables that never seemed to be level. And the vibration was so intense that anything that would stay on the table was jiggled up and down.

But for all its delays and discomforts, there was nothing quite like this most delectable of all maiden voyages, with its succession of dazzling parties and its displays at night of the ladies' diamonds, emeralds and rubies. And there were many others aboard whom Rose knew well: Horace Dodge, the automobile millionaire, and his wife, from Palm Beach; Lord Inverclyde, who had played a crucial role in Joe's liquor-distribution negotiations; Louis Gimbel, of the New York department-store fortune; and three new acquaintances, Cecil Beaton and the charming Jules and Doris Stein. It was a riotous, exciting crossing.

The arrival in New York was spectacular. A fleet of ships and small boats accompanied the *Queen* to her berth, sending off salutes; swarms of biplanes flew overhead, ceremonially dipping their wings; a festive crowd with streamers thronged the waterfront, and a taxi line six blocks long—still composed largely of Yellow Cabs—and over a hundred chauffeur-driven limousines awaited. There was a welcome party as ten thousand visitors crowded aboard, the passengers greeting friends with flowers, champagne and caviar.

Joe was unable to greet Rose at the ship, but the Fitzgeralds were at the pier, and there was a joyous reunion. When Rose returned to Bronxville, Joe was completing work there on a book, *I'm For Roosevelt,* designed to show his unqualified support of the president. He was busy with the Paramount Pictures report, and was the recipient of praise for a recapitalization plan he had prepared for his and Rose's friend David Sarnoff's Radio Corporation of America.

Plans were afoot for Jack, following his long sojourn in Arizona, to join his brother Joe at Harvard in September. The plans were concluded by August, when Reynal and Hitchcock published *I'm For Roosevelt,* to excellent reviews.

On September 17, Rose's favorite sister, Agnes, died at the age of forty-three of a chronic heart condition at her home in West Roxbury, Massachusetts. Rose was devastated by the news. She was barely able to restrain her tears at the solemn funeral at St. Joseph's Church. The burial was almost unendurable for her, despite her confidence in the Afterlife. That same day, by coincidence, her vibrant, intelligent twelve-year-old daughter Patricia entered the Convent of the Sacred Heart at Maplehurst.

Agnes left three children, Joe, Jr., aged six; Mary Jo, aged three; and Ann, aged two. Her husband Joe Gargan was unable to take care of them, as he was on secret business in Washington; so Rose took them into her home and raised them along with her own brood.

Rose found them to be astonishingly lacking in discipline. Joe Gargan, Jr., could not use a knife and fork correctly, and it took some time before he was properly trained.

On September 28, Jack entered Harvard as planned, and was set to take economics, history and French as his subjects. Immediately afterward, in his first football game of the semester, Joe, Jr., suffered injuries and had to be admitted to the hospital for an operation. Joe, Sr., broke off a hectic schedule of speech-making and radio broadcasts for the president in order to visit his son at Philips House; Rose was unable to make the trip.

On November 3, in a landslide victory over Alf Landon, Roosevelt was returned to office. Rose and Joe joined in the celebrations, attending parties in New York and dining with friends at popular nightspots. They were at the opening of Clare Boothe Luce's comedy, *The Women,* and the party that followed, at their friend publisher Condé Nast's elegant Fifth Avenue penthouse.

Rose would soon have one of the great experiences of her life. Cardinal Pacelli, who was expected to be the next Pope, made a private visit to the United States, and Joe, as the most socially prominent Catholic in America apart from famed politician Jim Farley, was asked by Cardinal O'Connell to take charge of the arrangements. Joe paid for a private railroad car to take Pacelli and his party (which included the mysterious Sister Pascalina, known internationally as La Popessa, the female pope) from Manhattan to the Roosevelt residence at Hyde Park, New York. The Kennedys accompanied the cardinal on the journey, La Popessa discreetly tucked into another car.

On arrival at the depot, hundreds of well-wishers were standing on the platform, cheering; on the drive to Hyde Park, children waved flags, and Pacelli insisted on stopping the limousine and walking among them, blessing them. The meeting with the president was informal; in Rose and Joe's presence, Roosevelt indicated his desire to establish closer ties with the Vatican. His policy at the time was to strengthen all possible connections to Italy—to separate that country from its increasingly strong alliance with Nazi Germany.

From Hyde Park, the party was driven to Bronxville, where Rose had the rare experience of entertaining a prospective Pope at afternoon tea. The younger children were awestruck, except for Teddy, who, too young to understand the importance of the occasion, hopped on the Cardinal's lap and began playing with his pectoral cross. As Teddy tangled the chain in his fingers, Pacelli laughed; his pinched face and rigid stance melted in the face of this eager, obstreperous child.

There followed a party for eight hundred guests at the palatial Manhasset, Long Island, home of the wealthy Genevieve Brady. As the procession of cars moved up the driveway, they were illuminated by two rows of two thousand candles. Rose had visited the widowed Mrs. Brady in 1933 in Rome, at her opulent Casa del Sol estate on the Janiculum Hill.

The new year of 1937 opened with the Inaugural ceremonies in Washington, which Rose and Joe attended. On March 24, Roosevelt nominated Joe chairman of the United States Maritime Commission, which was responsible for building up the Merchant Marine, not only to enable it to increase its activities in export and import, but to become a naval and military auxiliary in time of war or national emergency. The appointment was confirmed on April 16. Joe would receive a nominal salary of $12,000 a year (about $120,000 in present-day terms).

This was a proud moment for Rose, but also a painful one, since it would involve another long separation. Joe would again have to be headquartered in Washington, D.C., and would have to travel extensively to ports to inspect local conditions. He moved back into Marwood, the twenty-five-room house with gold-plated bathroom fixtures and a sweeping view of the Potomac River in which he had been installed when chairman of the Securities and Exchange Commission. He maintained a lifelong routine of rising every morning at six, working until close to midnight and finding his only leisure in listening to Toscanini's recordings of Beethoven's symphonies on the phonograph.

One problem had to be ironed out in the preceding weeks, a problem that directly involved Rose. For fifteen years, she had remained the possessor of the five thousand shares issued by the Atlantic, Gulf and West Indies Shipping Company that had been the mainstay of the Hayden, Stone organization, and which, in its turn, had owned Atlantic Gulf Oil, the company in Mexico. Atlantic, Gulf and West Indies had been in trouble almost consistently since the bear raids of the early 1920s. Along with a Cuban corporation, the company had been joint owner of the cruise ship *Morro Castle,* which, in September 1934, had burned at sea, killing hundreds. As if this were not bad enough, AGWI had claimed, and collected, a figure in insurance that was in excess of the ship's actual value, and was under investigation by the government at the exact moment Joe took over the commission.

Sealed until now in a secret file of the Roosevelt Memorial Library at Hyde Park, the facts of Rose's investment have been hidden from the public. Had they been released in the anti-Kennedy newspapers they could have created a furor that might have resulted in Joe's being denied his post. He did admit that Rose owned substantial stock in Todd Shipyards through Fred Thomson Productions. He was assisting Thomson's widow, Frances Marion, in the matter. It took a special act of Congress to overcome the conflict of interest.

Joe had his hands full. Not only did he have to work against opposition to build up the Merchant Marine as a defensive instrument for future war (an element of his work for which he has received no credit), but he had to deal with extensive Communist infiltration into the unions. The Australian Harry Bridges, a militant Bolshevist, ran the San Francisco waterfront; Joe Curran of the International Seamen's Union was suspected of similar leanings. Paralyzing strikes kept occurring. In June, Eastern S.S. Line vessels were tied up at the New York wharves. So were two AGWI ships, the S.S. *Oriente* and the S.S. *New York.* Rose worried that Joe would be thought to be favoring her interests in seeking to suppress the union action against the shipping line from which she benefited financially.

A controversy engulfed Rose and Joe in September. Off Montevideo, Uruguay, the crew of the government ship *Algic,* which came directly under Joe's control, exploded in a violent mutiny; the sailors were furious at conditions aboard and charged the captain with the manslaughter of seaman Hank Gill at Victoria, Brazil. Joe acted at once. He telegraphed the vessel's skipper to place the mutineers in irons; the orders were followed, and as a result, the National Maritime Union demanded Joe's dismissal. He went directly to the president, and, following a trial, the mutineers were found guilty. It was the first mutiny on an American vessel in many years.

On October 18, 1937, Rose saw a plunge in the value of her shares as the stock market began to take a fall reminiscent of its collapse in October 1929. Joe had to drop everything at the Maritime Commission when Rose's and his friend Judge William O. Douglas, who was still at the Securities and Exchange Commission, to which Joe had appointed him, called. The SEC's continuing exposure of market malpractice was believed to have caused the correction.

Roosevelt summoned Joe to the White House for a discussion. Kennedy screamed four-letter words at him and everyone who would listen about the exchange's refusal to reorganize. On October 29, Joe met at Douglas's office with exchange representatives and blasted them with his fury. The matter dragged on until finally Richard Whitney, head of the exchange, was found guilty of feathering his own nest, and went bankrupt. Kennedy saw to it that he was convicted and went to prison.

Joe did a good job of improving the Merchant Marine. Rose followed his activities as he cut through miles of red tape; ordered the scrapping of the mothballed fleet that was a hangover from World War I; commissioned 350 new ships; forbade account padding and graft by ship owners; prevented the overpaying of independent companies for carrying mail; improved labor conditions after inspecting thousands of cabins, deck spaces and mess rooms; established minimum wages both on and off shore; and clashed directly with Labor Secretary Frances Perkins in seeking to strip the unions of Communist influence.

In the midst of her busy summer at Hyannis Port, and later at Bronxville, tracking Jack's movements through Europe and his second year of Harvard, enjoying Kathleen's graduation from Noroton and Pat's success at the Convent of the Sacred Heart at Maplehurst, Rose began to hear rumors of an extraordinary probability. Robert W. Bingham, her host in London and companion on more than one sea voyage, was now severely ill from Hodgkin's disease and returned to America in December to die. His vacancy would leave open the most important diplomatic appointment available anywhere. Rose and Joe saw the chance of a lifetime, and Joe began lobbying as early as July, when Rose made a trip to Europe aboard the *Washington* with Joe, Jr., and Kathleen.

Roosevelt initially had mixed feelings about the idea of Joe being ambassador to England; he wasn't certain of Joe's political leanings. But he quickly saw advantages in Joe taking over. Negotiations were proceeding for an alliance of

North and South Ireland that would appeal to many of the president's Catholic supporters. Assets of General Motors, Standard Oil and other major American companies were frozen in Berlin, and, perhaps, Joe could unlock them. American films were threatened with import restrictions under a proposed quota system that would protect the British film industry, and Joe would be well placed to solve that problem. An Anglo-American trade agreement was progressing, which he would support, and he would be helpful in the matter of Britain wishing to postpone the settling of substantial World War I debts. With his experience in the Maritime Commission, he would be ideally placed to conclude a naval treaty that would encourage the British to build up their naval defenses. Roosevelt had in mind Joe's special relationship with Cardinal Pacelli, and the fact that he could continue to advance diplomatic relations with the Vatican.

The president had another purpose. He used his ambassadors as intelligence sources. Each was encouraged to flatter representatives of foreign powers in order to obtain information. Just as Bullitt, even when he had lost confidence in communism, had continued to say good things about Stalin to find out what the Russians were doing, and in Paris had praised the Leon Blum administration to a similar end, so Kennedy could, by associating with German and Italian emissaries to the Court of St. James, give a picture of potential enemies in action. He would also (as emerged at the Japanese War Crime Trials after World War II) associate with the Japanese ambassador to that purpose. Following a meeting with Roosevelt at the White House on December 8, Joe was informed that his appointment to London was confirmed at a nominal salary of $17,500 a year. Robert W. Bingham, who had officially resigned the same day, died ten days later.

Now that the ambassadorship was confirmed, Joe had a problem to face. Since Joe was determined that Joe, Jr., would one day be president, that young man's path would have to be paved in Boston first, where he would run for Congress, and then in Massachusetts, where he would run for the Senate. But if Joe were to show too strong a liking for England in his new role, he would alienate the large Irish-

American population of his native state. Joe must therefore keep his liking for the British (which would, one day, change to hatred) from being too widely publicized, and, should war come, he would have to follow a policy that would undoubtedly be that of the Vatican and Eire: neutrality at all costs.

Several U.S. ambassadors wrote enthusiastically to the president about the new appointment. There were no criticisms from any quarter. John Cudahy, emissary to the Irish Free State, wrote to Roosevelt from Dublin on December 16, 1937, "At this time of the pending trade treaty Kennedy's selection . . . is nothing less than an inspiration." He was referring to the British American Treaty that Kennedy could be relied upon to consolidate.

While Rose began packing up in Bronxville and Palm Beach, in preparation for a lengthy sojourn in England, she managed to snatch weekends in Manhattan with Joe, who traveled each Friday night from his house in Washington. Passionately fond of classical music, the couple was given a treat: their friend David Sarnoff, head of RCA, had signed Arturo Toscanini, who also became a friend, to a long-term contract as conductor of the NBC Symphony Orchestra. Sarnoff included Rose and Joe in the handful attending the rehearsals for Toscanini's Christmas concert. They were captivated; Toscanini became a friend.

The logistics of moving across the Atlantic were considerable. Rose had to have scouts in London search for appropriate British schools for her younger children. Rosemary might present a problem: would she be able to manage the social life of an ambassador's daughter and not embarrass everyone at Buckingham Palace by untoward remarks or behavior? After much cogitation, Rose decided Rosemary should go to London and a place would be found for her in a Montessori School. Joe, Jr., and Jack would continue their schooling at Harvard but would come over for the summer vacation.

The American houses would be kept open for the use of the older boys, with full staffs. Neither Rose nor Joe could bear to be parted from their favorite cars, and even though the embassy would provide a Rolls-Royce or a Daimler, and at least three round-the-clock chauffeurs, they would certainly want to take off on weekends in their own three automobiles, led by their favorite six-wheel 1937 Chrysler sedan. They would leave their own Rolls behind.

They would have to make reservations for at least fourteen staterooms, at immense cost to the American taxpayer, on an oceangoing liner. Further, Joe would have to wind up a number of important tasks at the Maritime Commission even after he had officially resigned. The most significant of these he concluded in January.

General Douglas MacArthur had been pleading for financial help for the shipping lines across the Pacific Ocean, since, as he wrote in his memoirs, "The very life of our military position in the Pacific depended upon keeping open our lines of sea supply." He had been informed that the support would be withdrawn. This was a bad decision, which Joe Kennedy, unacknowledged to this day except in MacArthur's autobiography, decently reversed. In a letter dated February 1, 1938, Kennedy sent a letter of major historical importance to MacArthur, confirming that unlimited help would be given to support the strength of the American Merchant Marine in that critical region.

War was raging between Japan and China, and American properties were being threatened. Kennedy's action in securing American Pacific power cannot be overvalued in the context; it was a lifelong pain to Rose that her husband was never given credit for this effort in the service of his country.

While at Palm Beach on January 24, up to her eyes in packing twelve steamer trunks and sixty-one boxes of household goods to go by the cargo ship *American Trader* on February 6, Rose was stricken with abdominal pains. At first characteristically ignoring the symptoms, she was compelled finally to take medical advice and was told she would have to be operated on for appendicitis. In those days before antibiotics came into general use, there was the dread of peritonitis, which had killed, among other celebrities, Rudolph Valentino.

Because she would not be operated on by anyone other than her trusted Dr. Frederick Good, and because the changes of train would involve at least two days of travel, she had to be flown by special plane, with ice packs pressed against her, to Boston, then rushed by ambulance (because of the heavy traffic) to O'Connell House at Peter Bent Brigham Hospital in Brighton. The operation took place on January 25, 1938. It was a success, and within a few days Rose, showing her usual good spirits, was on her feet, talking to the doctors, enjoying her ever-inexhaustible father, laughing at her own discomfiture.

However, she must have suffered a qualm when she heard from Joe that, flying to Seattle to visit shipyards with Eddie Moore, he had a narrow escape from death in an unadvertised crack-up of his biplane. He had to return, laboriously, by train to join her for her convalescence in Palm Beach, where she had arrived on February 10.

He wanted to linger on until she was fully recovered, but she insisted he must take up his duties in London as America was still without an ambassador there. He thought he would take Kathleen with him to act as temporary hostess for his guests, but, after much discussion, it was decided he would go alone. Sailing on the S.S. *Manhattan* on February 28, he had as traveling companions his and Rose's very wealthy friends Anthony and Katharine Drexel Biddle, ambassador to Poland and his lady. Joe also had an entourage of five, including as junior clerk *New York Times* correspondent Harold B. Hinton, who would help write his speeches, and his friend Arthur Houghton; as personal assistant, he would have an able young woman, Page Huidekoper. In another last-minute decision, Eunice would remain until April at Sacred Heart Convent at Noroton, and Rosemary would remain for the same length of time at Marymount in Tarrytown.

Joe arrived in London on March 2 with his six-wheel Chrysler sedan, exactly a week before Rose departed. Significantly, neither husband nor wife would consider travel on a German or Italian ship, for patriotic reasons as well as reasons of security.

His first meeting was with the Jewish leader Rabbi Stephen Wise, who was troubled by British opposition to resettlement of German Jews in Palestine. Wise wrote to President Roosevelt on March 4, "I think you will find that J.K. is going to be very helpful and that he is keenly understanding, and there is just enough Irish in him to make him sympathetic to those of us who resent the British promise (of help to us) that is in danger of being broken."

On March 11, Joe reported to the State Department that he had visited the French, Spanish and Argentine embassies and learned that Mussolini and Hitler had done very well by their bluffing and wouldn't stop "until someone called their bluff."

Rose and her party embarked on the *Washington* in a dozen staterooms on March 3, 1938. A surviving newsreel film shows Rose on the New York wharf before departure, wearing a rakish flowered hat and an exquisitely fashioned suit. Teddy is supposed to talk to the cameras about his excitement at the prospective trip, but he turns shy for once in his life and Bobby takes over. Amused and delighted, Rose exchanges a loving badinage with him and then, extremely handsome at his young age, and sparkling with life and confidence, Bobby steps forward and rattles off the speech that Teddy was supposed to have made.

In addition to the younger children, Rose brought with her their nanny, Luella Hennessey; the cook, Margaret Ambrose, who would supplement the embassy's chef with down-home American dishes; and the governess, Elizabeth Dunn. A great disappointment was the news that her favorite poodle and Airedale would have to go into six months' quarantine on arrival. Joe had pulled several strings in vain; the rules could not be changed.

Arriving after a rough crossing at Plymouth, Rose expertly fielded a crowd of reporters who boarded the ship from the press launch. Smart in a traveling suit and fox furs, she made a youthful impression, conquering the press at once. The society magazines, *The Tatler, The Sketch, The Bystander,* and *The Queen,* were her fans from then on.

Joe rushed down to greet her; he had just made a hole in one at Stoke Poges Golf Course and was in a happy mood. He hugged Rose unabashedly in front of the reporters.

With the three cars Rose had brought with her as supplements following, the family and its load of luggage took the five-hour train journey to London. A chauffeur driving the embassy limousine picked them up from the station. A flotilla of automobiles drew up outside the ambassadorial residence at 14 Prince's Gate, opposite Kensington Gardens, a legacy to America from J. P. Morgan.

Rose had looked forward to the last word in palatial British buildings, but it was an immediate and sharp disappointment to anyone who saw it. The 1852 structure offered a badly painted and cracked façade of cement stucco finish over Gloucester brick. The balustrades were falling apart. The window boxes were warped and contained dying, unwatered forget-me-nots and daisies; hideous and racist American Indian warrior heads absurdly guarded the windows and the front door. Rose was shown around by sixty-six-year-old housekeeper Alice Garnham and chargé d'affaires Herschel Johnson. It was all very unsettling.

True, the small vestibule and the oval reception hall with its black-and-white Sicilian marble floor were impressive, and there was a grand staircase. But the second- and third-floor bedroom carpets were worn, the basement had damaged linoleum, the Louis XV antiques were in need of repair and the curtains had thinned and shredded with time.

The bathrooms were wretched: little changed in the past several decades, they had no tile floors but instead had wood; the sinks in the kitchen were also made of wood. The chimneys and flues were defective and could cause fires, so that it proved impossible to light any fires in the grates on chilly English nights. There were cracks in the walls, floors and ceilings; pipes were faulty; light-switch plates were loose—a wet hand on a switch could cause an electric shock; builders' rubbish was piled up under sinks; plaster was falling down; toilets were in bad shape; radiators were not working. Paintwork was unfinished, doors were warped, springs and screws loose on cupboards and doors: a disaster of maintenance that occupied no less than sixty-four pages of a memorandum handed to Rose when she arrived.

And both Prince's Gate and the Chancery at 1 Grosvenor Square, which was also in poor repair, were riddled with hidden microphones that relayed everything that was said to MI-5, British Intelligence, in Curzon Street.

There were only eight bedrooms to accommodate the family; how would she squeeze in Eunice and Rosemary,

Joe, Jr., and Jack when they arrived with Eddie Moore, who
would be Joe's secretary? Rose took the creaky Edwardian
cage elevator up to the rabbit warren of the third and fourth
floors, to find there were as many as nineteen rooms for the
servants. She had been granted a staff of twenty-four, only
thirteen of whom, including the butler Frederick, the caretaker Harry and the assistant housekeeper Louisa Whicer,
would live in; she commandeered the remaining six for her
family, but the rooms were shabby and tiny and would have
to be refurnished.

Throughout the house—of which the imposing Louis
XVI ballroom and the Louis XV Pine Room, used for
receptions, were the most attractive features—there were
bare walls, pale in areas where paintings had once hung. Joe
had to call William Randolph Hearst to have pictures
rushed from Hearst's castle in Wales. Rose had already been
warned in a State Department memorandum that there
were no linen or towels; she managed to rustle up a
sufficient number during the next two days. Chargé
d'affaires Herschel Johnson luckily had arranged for two
hundred luncheon and one hundred dinner invitation cards
to be printed up.

The crockery consisted of a set of dreary white American
Lenox china, with its affected coats of arms, standard in
most U.S. embassies. Rose would have to buy better china
out of her husband's pocket if she was going to entertain
properly. She would eventually take the china back to
America for Thanksgivings and Christmases, where it
didn't matter if it was broken.

The condition of the oven was bad; it was an ancient
stove, its flues full of grease, which could cause a fire at any
minute. The garage, which was under the outside servants'
quarters at 14–16 Ennismore Mews nearby, could only
accommodate two of the Kennedys' cars, and the other had
to be housed near Harrods.

Rose summoned her American assistants and her new
British staff, including the general secretary Mrs. Stanley
Wilson and her social secretary Mrs. Darrell Waters, and set
about solving one problem after another with inexhaustible
zeal. She apparently couldn't bring herself to berate Her-

schel Johnson for having slipped up so badly in not taking care of all the necessary comforts.

For the younger children, the house was heaven. While Rose fretted with her aides and Joe took off to Buckingham Palace in a Town Coach to present his credentials to King George VI, the brood, led by a manic Teddy, raced up and down the stairs, slid down the banisters, invaded the elevator, in which Teddy would imprison giggling maids as he drove them up and down the six floors announcing each floor in turn as though he were a department-store elevator operator; he insisted on taking snapshots of everything with Brownie cameras. While Rose and Joe stubbornly played Toscanini conducting Beethoven and Brahms on the drawing-room phonograph, the kids offered deafening Ambrose or Henry Hall swing and jazz.

The house was a bedlam from morning to night; the back garden immediately became not only a touch-football ground but a baseball diamond, with loud thwacking and screams as everyone took turns at pitching or at bat. When the family walked in Hyde Park or Kensington Gardens, sailing toy boats on the Round Pond, or rode in Rotten Row, they were gawked at by everyone from dukes and duchesses to blue-clad nannies, cardiganed housekeepers out for walks and uniformed and becapped schoolchildren.

Rose's first act in London was to abolish the presentation of rich young American women at court; she changed the rule so that only the children of diplomatic or other U.S. government personnel would be presented. She wanted to avoid the burden of dealing with a flood of mail addressed to her on the subject, and Joe agreed. Many wealthy parents were furious with her and did not forgive her.

Rose managed to find time to shop for British-style children's clothes, following her custom of matching boys and girls in specific colors, the boys in maroon caps, blazers and gray flannel shorts and the girls in maroon hats and blue and gray or pink dresses, so that she could find them if she and the nanny should lose them in crowds in Harrods or watching the changing of the guard at Buckingham Palace. She concluded arrangements for schooling, scattering children around London. Teddy she placed at Sloane Street

School for Boys; Pat and Jean at the Sacred Heart school, Rosehampton; and, later, Bobby also at Sloane Street. She booked a permanent stall at the Brompton Oratory for Mass every day. She still kept cards on the children's weight, which she took daily in the bathroom, recording every sniffle or stomach ache.

A threat to shoot the Kennedys, by George Buchanan, came to nothing. But there were other problems. The traffic noise from Prince's Gate was so loud at night, with fashionable partygoers returning at all hours, that Rose had to use earplugs, which caused giggles among the staff. The children had to learn that light switches in England were pressed down to go on instead of up, cotton meant cotton wool, and a rubber was an eraser. She prepared a movie theater in the basement where one of the first films shown was *Snow White and the Seven Dwarfs*.

Many nights Joe and Rose, in love with all things Italian, spent at the Coq d'Or restaurant, run by the genial Henri Sartori from Rome. Later, when Italy entered the war, Joe made sure that Sartori was not interned or sent back to his homeland.

Dinners at home were still antic debating sessions, with the children in pajamas. Subjects like the political situation in Europe were topics for discussion, with children flying out of the room in the middle to find reference books. Even Teddy, with his pet goldfish and postage stamps set aside, would join in.

And now Rose, who was ill prepared due to the rush of departure following her illness and all the problems of resettlement, would have to master all of the intricate etiquette called for from an ambassador's wife. On March 18, she would visit the queen with Joe. She would have to take tea with every ambassador's lady in London, from the most important down to the most obscure. She had to master a curtsey before royalty and learn that royalty must never be touched, nor must conversation with royalty go beyond generalities. She would have to have dresses made, a different one for each ceremonial occasion, and since it would not be possible to fly to Paris every weekend, and she would soon exhaust her French wardrobe, she would have to spend long hours being fitted by Captain Edward Molyneux, the leading London designer. For court presentation, she would have to wear regulatory feathers and a tiara of the finest quality.

In order to meet every requirement that lay ahead of her, Rose needed a good and powerful friend. That friend was the French-born, stately, handsome, distinguished Roberte, Countess Bessborough, daughter of the Baron de Mauflize. Roberte was a fascinating and cultivated companion who knew every detail of court procedure. She explained to Rose such details as that bracelets and watches must be worn *outside* shoulder-length gloves; that the greatest delicacy must be applied in removing the ornaments from the arms before sitting at a dinner table; that the bracelet and watch would have to be replaced so nobody would notice, and the gloves folded neatly on the lap.

Rose discovered who to cultivate at the top of society. The duke and duchess of Norfolk represented the summit of the Roman Catholic hierarchy, and would have to be put on the top of any guest list. But there was no one to match her new friend Nancy, Lady Astor, the most celebrated American woman in England following the departure of the notorious duchess of Windsor for exile in continental Europe (Wallis Windsor's name was not to be mentioned in Rose's presence).

Nancy, who made Rose honorary president of the American Women's Club of Great Britain, became the dominating presence of Rose's life. Born in Virginia in 1879, the attractive, forty-eight-year-old doyenne had dumped a husband when she married Waldorf Astor, the immensely rich scion of the famous family; she had seduced him away from the bedroom of Queen Marie of Romania. In 1938, she queened it over Cliveden, a vast estate near Maidenhead, designed by Sir Charles Barry, architect of the Houses of Parliament. With its thirty live-in servants, including butler, valet, chauffeurs, liveried footmen and fourteen maids, and forty nonresident gardeners, the house had forty-six rooms furnished in antiques, a private theater, a stable, and horses for the use of each guest.

A member of Parliament from 1918, the first woman to sit in the House of Commons, Nancy was aggressive, witty and sparkling. She was a mistress of insults. On one occasion, she said to Winston Churchill, who detested her, "If I were your wife I'd put poison in your coffee." He replied, "If I were your husband, I'd drink it." She got her revenge when he threw a party question at guests to which he vowed no one could reply. It was "How many toes are there in a pig's foot?" Nancy Astor responded with, "Take off your shoes and count."

In visits to Cliveden, Nancy fascinated Rose. She chewed gum while wearing a $75,000 diamond tiara, entertained a range of society figures from Winston Churchill to the German ambassador, and was unjustly dubbed, along with many of her guests, a Nazi sympathizer. The so-called Cliveden Set was an invention of the Communist writer Claude Cockburn, who dubbed it a Nazi enclave. In fact, a weekend at Cliveden would include, along with some Germans, Communists, nonappeasers of the Nazis like Anthony Eden, Americans, Italians and, despite charges that the Astors were anti-Semitic, prominent Jewish figures.

Rose was busy organizing the resettlement in England of refugee nuns who had been driven from Spain in the last stages of the collapse of the loyalist government. She also welcomed the newly arrived Rosemary and Eunice on April 25.

While she was involved in a hectic social life, she found time to write passages of her husband's speeches; by the autumn, this would prove irritating to the State Department and she was asked to stop.

Behind the receptions, glittering weekends, concerts and operas, Rose was aware of distressing changes in the European political scene. Shortly after she arrived, Hitler absorbed Austria with hardly a shot. Czechoslovakia was threatened. Although the aggressive Czechs were unpopular in England and pursued an anti-Semitic policy not dissimilar to Hitler's (the Prague government sent back Jews who had fled the Nazis), and their state was in many ways oppressive, fear of war that might result from defending them prevented strong moves by British Prime Minister

Neville Chamberlain. He knew that Britain was not yet ready for a conflict.

World War I had ended just twenty years before; Rose had not forgotten the many brave young men out of Harvard who had died in the mud and rain of the French trenches. She and Joe sympathized with the British aristocrats who had been deprived of sons, brothers and cousins, fresh out of Oxford and Cambridge, who had been cut down after scarcely reaching manhood. Anything and everything must be done to prevent a recurrence of that slaughter of the innocents.

Hitler was a threat and a nuisance, but people of Rose and Joe's class and generation were besotted by the belief that Hitler could be tamed, bought off, controlled, and that he would never threaten England's or America's safety. It was this wishful thinking, along with the conviction that he provided a block against the Soviets, that played into Hitler's hands during the crises that would darken the next year and a half.

The Kennedys were always in the news. Rose's charm, energy and youthfulness and slimness after nine children were the talk of London. At least one commentator said, "Now I believe in the stork." Joe's $17,500 a year, though approximately ten times that much in current terms, was far from sufficient to entertain, staff and furnish his official residence. Always tight with money, he was compelled to dip into his capital, a common requirement for ambassadors of the United States, who were chosen not only for their support of the president with cash, but because they could supplement their allowance from a well of personal finances. His costs came to at least $250,000 a year. Joe's refusal to wear knee britches (because he thought it effeminate) at state occasions, his putting of his feet on his desk at press conferences, his ample use of four-letter words to which delicate English ears were unaccustomed, his sharply undiplomatic behavior and his clear preference for the conservatives led by his friend Prime Minister Neville Chamberlain over Labor or Liberal leaders, put him constantly in the headlines.

Rose was handled by the magazines like a movie star, and she looked like one; in her magnificent French hats and dress originals, she was easily the equal of a Joan Crawford or a Carole Lombard. The family was photographed everywhere. Reporters gurgled over the boys playing cricket, Teddy's hobbies, the Chancery refurbishing, the trips to the Ascot and Epsom races, and nylons for Rose and the girls that were flown in from Washington by diplomatic pouch.

Even while the political background worsened, Rose's life resembled a fairy tale. Among the best weekends was a trip to the home of another American, Lady Violet Astor, married to Nancy's husband's brother J. J. Astor, owner of the *London Times*. The Astors lived in a medieval castle, Hever, complete with moat, drawbridge and portcullis. Swans floated in the sun-dappled water; liveried servants attended to the visitors' every need; exquisite evenings of champagne and laughter, string music and private theatrical events kept Rose and Joe happy from Friday night until their departure on Monday.

Rose became one of the most successful hostesses in London. Her parties were noted for excellent food, the finest wines—Lady Astor's was a "dry" house, as several of Rose's guests recall today—and a careful juxtaposition of guests.

An especially happy event was the visit to Windsor Castle on the weekend of April 9–11, 1938. The Kennedys drove up at 7:00 P.M., preceded by a valet and a maid who brought the luggage by train, seeing the castle lit from towers to cellar by thousands of glittering lights. As they drove through the main gate, they were received by Brigadier General Sir Hill Child, Master of the Royal Household, who took them to the tower in which they were housed in separate bedrooms. Rose's bed was of red damask; to get into it, she would have to climb on a footstool. At 8:20 P.M., in the Green Reception Room, the king and queen appeared and joined the Kennedys for dinner, along with the Neville Chamberlains. An amusing aspect of the meal was when the king wanted to talk to the queen and couldn't see her because of the flowers massed in vases on the table.

Afterward, there was a disconcerting touch: a bagpipe player, in a tartan kilt, walked through the room, playing with deafening loudness. As the ladies separated from the gentlemen, the queen asked after Rose's children; noticing that Rose was uncomfortable addressing her in the required form of Ma'am, she thenceforth excused her.

In bed that night, Rose lay under the red damask cover listening to the sounds of the changing of the guard and the clock striking eleven, and thought this must all be a beautiful dream.

Chapter 9

The Ambassador's Lady

In April, only a few weeks into his ambassadorship, and undoubtedly with Rose's knowledge, Kennedy was already acting as a supplier of important intelligence to Roosevelt. On the fourteenth, he sent a comprehensive report on the dangerous activities of Germans and Italians in South America, who sought to use the radio industry in that region for propaganda purposes. He revealed that Germany had surpassed any other nation in shortwave broadcasting, thus spreading Nazi doctrine throughout the southern hemisphere. He urged the president to give attention to the matter, and to set up rival radio networks to compete with these anti-American activities of potential danger, and his advice, after a long delay, was acted upon. Such was the early and vital action of an ambassador who, to this day, is charged with Nazi sympathies.

Just five days after this confidential dispatch, Kennedy approvingly forwarded to the president another, of equal importance, from Cardinal Pacelli, his and Rose's friend who visited their home and Hyde Park two years earlier.

The letter from Pacelli was distinctly anti-Hitler, pointing out that the Concordat had been broken repeatedly, and that the German government had failed to show evidence of good faith—that Hitler's activities were against the Divine Law and were illustrative of a new paganism.

In view of Rose's devout approach to Rome, there can be no question that the cardinal's anti-Nazi position, reflecting that of his superior, Pius XI, found a confirming echo in her.

On May 4, the Kennedys witnessed an astonishing scene at Covent Garden opera house. Lotte Lehmann, one of the greatest stars of the period, was appearing as the Marschallin in a performance of Richard Strauss's *Der Rosenkavalier*. Partway through the first act, after the levee scene, she stopped before singing the aria "Als musst's so sein," and told a shocked audience that she was unable to continue. The curtain was rung down. The Kennedys came backstage and offered their help. The star explained that her half-Jewish stepchildren had been imprisoned in Vienna by the Gestapo. The torture of wondering what had become of them had almost broken her spirit. Over the next weeks, Kennedy opened channels to allow Lehmann to make payments to officials in Vienna that resulted in her family being released to her.

In May, according to William Breuer in his book *Hitler's Unknown War,* Joe sought the arrest of a Nazi agent. In New York, Werner Georg Gudenberg had leaked secret information on American aviation plants to the German spy William Lonkowski for transmission to Berlin. Joe wanted Gudenberg arrested and taken off the German ship *Hamburg* at Southampton, but when the vessel arrived the captain told the intelligence officers who boarded it that Gudenberg was too seriously ill to be moved, and he continued uninterrupted on his journey to Germany.

The Kennedys continued their social life at the highest levels of London. On May 5, they attended a luncheon at Nancy Astor's Georgian house at 4 St. James's Square. Bernard Shaw, of all unlikely people, expressed fascist sentiments, Charles and Anne Morrow Lindbergh talked of German air power, and, in an aside, Kennedy discussed the Jewish question with the American aviator.

On May 16, 1938, Joe had lunch with Sir Warren Fisher of the Foreign Office. Fisher told him that Germany was arming as fast as it could, and that the German war plans were based on the supposition that if they declared a state of conflict with Great Britain, Hitler's air force would demolish London completely in one fell swoop. Joe received similar reports from his naval and military attachés, who warned him that the German air force was enormously more powerful than the British and that it would be impossible for England to survive a blitzkrieg at that time. Joe conveyed these intelligences to Washington, but found that, instead of being praised for supplying this privileged information, he was accused of defeatism.

At Rose's parties, she laid out the guest lists and the menus, which were written by a copperplate specialist on tiny cards, set before each guest on a silver rest. The Kennedy parties became more and more popular that spring. To this day, many of the guests, including Lady Glendevon (daughter of Somerset Maugham), recall them with pleasure. Among the members of the nobility, of whom the now Viscount and Viscountess Castlerosse were most frequently present along with the Astors, Rose interspersed sporting figures, including the tennis star Helen Wills Moody; newspaper figures, such as the *New York Times*'s Arthur Hays Sulzburger; and notables of the motion picture world, including Rosalind Russell, the Darryl F. Zanucks and Eddie Cantor.

The Kennedys showed movies to their guests, but Rose stumbled in one selection. She put on a screening of the M.G.M. movie *Test Pilot,* a nonsensical entertainment in which Spencer Tracy and Clark Gable played maverick pilots. Rose's inclusion of Charles and Anne Morrow Lindbergh in the guest list that night was miscalculated; they came close to groaning over the movie's aeronautical absurdities.

Rose became fond of Anne Lindbergh. Joe shared the Lindberghs' view that Britain would have little chance against German might in a future war and that the alternative arrangement, proposed by many, of cementing an alliance with France and Russia would only give strength to the Communists and bring about the end of civilization in Western Europe.

Rose's biggest event of the season was presenting her daughters at court at Buckingham Palace on May 11. The difficulty was that Rosemary might not be equal to the occasion, but such fears were allayed rapidly, as Rosemary, sweetly demure and self-effacing, and busy keeping a London diary, showed no symptoms of oddity or mental retardation.

Rose flew with Kathleen to select the appropriate gowns for her at Paquin; Rose was to be dressed by Edward Molyneux for the occasion. She spent many anxious hours in consultation with Lady Bessborough on the requirements of the evening. She must wear three large feathers known as the Prince of Wales plumes, bought from a shop that had the privilege of the Royal Warrant, and around her head she must fix the plumes in place under a tiara. Stingy, and nervous of possible jewel thieves, she decided not to buy a new diamond tiara, but instead to borrow Lady Bessborough's. She obtained a veil made of tulle, exactly forty-five inches in length, and shoulder-length gloves equipped with twenty-one buttons. The dress was accompanied by a train, no more than forty-five inches in width and two yards long.

Fittings were exhausting and protracted, but Rose, Kathleen and Rosemary were in no state of mind to complain. As for Joe, he still refused to wear the required knee britches, which meant that he would be the only man present in morning clothes other than the lesser waiters.

Rose had been to the palace before, but the occasion was still impressive. Excited, she was able to nibble only a light supper before embarking with her husband and daughters in the embassy Daimler at twilight. The chauffeur had to edge through an immense crowd, which had broken through the police cordons outside the palace gates. In the lingering sunshine of the spring evening, the palace was a blaze of electric lights. As the chauffeur parked the automobile, the Kennedys were conducted to the diplomatic entrance. Separated from Joe, Rose was instructed to walk slowly through the vestibule and up the grand stairway so she would not tread upon the trains of the women ahead.

As Rose mounted the stairs, she saw, to the right and left, the Beefeaters in their time-honored scarlet uniforms. She tried not to be awestruck as she walked through immense salons lined with paintings and gilded mirrors, flanked by liveried footmen. At last she entered the ballroom, which presented a spectacle of hundreds, the women dressed in the height of fashion, King George VI and Queen Elizabeth seated on thrones on a raised, red-carpeted dais at the far end, facing at the other end a dance orchestra that was playing traditional tunes.

Along with the other ambassadors and their families, the Kennedys were seated on gilded chairs to the right of the royal couple. Rose and her daughters curtsied before the king and queen, remembering not to bob their heads in the American style, but rather to keep them raised. At first, Rosemary behaved perfectly; Rose could breathe again. But then Rosemary stumbled, awkwardly, in front of the thrones; she recovered, but there is no describing Rose and Joe's embarrassment. Trained to perfection, the royal couple were expressionless. After the ceremony, everybody danced waltzes and fox-trots.

More parties followed. There was Lady Astor's London ball at 4 St. James's Square, held in a blaze of gold-embossed walls and Baccarat chandeliers, with the royal couple as guests of honor; Anne Morrow Lindbergh was the subject of much whispering because she wasn't wearing a tiara. June 1 was Derby day, followed by another party at Buckingham Palace. Next night, Rose flung a debutante party for Kathleen and Rosemary at Prince's Gate, with the popular Ambrose's band hired for the occasion and a good two-thirds of the eligible bachelors in London present.

Ascot was on June 14; Rose enjoyed lunch in the royal box in the company of the duke and duchess of Kent and the maharajah and maharani of Rajpipla. Rose was fascinated by the procession of royal carriages rolling down the track. She made a sensation by dressing in black when all the other women were in pastel colors.

Amid all this glamour and luxury, there were indications of grim events ahead. Shelters, sandbags and air-raid warning stations appeared all over London. Joe ordered a thousand gas masks and charged them to the State Department; a giggling Teddy posed for photographers in one of them. Rose's beautiful, fragile world began to look as insubstantial as a soap bubble.

On June 13, Joe had a meeting with German Ambassador Herbert Von Dirksen. Joe explained to Dirksen that the Jewish situation in Germany was one of the prime difficulties that blocked relations between America and Germany, and "something should be done about it." Referring back to the matter of the German broadcasting stations in South America, he said that the reason democracies did not want to trade with totalitarian states was that those states were not content to stay in their own countries but were trying to spread throughout South America, exactly what he had written to Roosevelt at an earlier date.

Dirksen admitted that ninety percent of U.S. opinion was against Germany, and that he wanted to correct it. He suggested that Joe come to Germany on the pretext of taking spa waters, to discuss the matter further. Dirksen proceeded to give a different account of the meeting to his superiors in the Berlin Foreign Ministry, stating that Kennedy had expressed strong pro-Nazi and anti-Semitic feelings. Such reports were typical of this ambassador. Dirksen's words have cast a shadow over Kennedy's reputation to this day; no biographer or historian has referred to Kennedy's report of the meeting.

It was painful for Rose to be parted from Joe at any time, but particularly now, with the situation increasingly critical in Europe. One day after having to dinner Rose's friend Clare Boothe Luce, who responded with an exquisite gift to Rose of an expensive evening bag and clip, Joe had to leave on June 15, in order to report to Roosevelt at the White House on his findings on German activities, and to attend Joe, Jr.,'s graduation from Harvard. Rose didn't accompany him because the younger children were only just settled in school. She arranged to import her parents; the timing was ingenious, since Joe continued to have differences with them, and having them at Prince's Gate along with him might have led to difficulties.

Joe's trip on the *Queen Mary* allowed him to meet such anti-Nazi South American diplomats as Raoul Martinez

Vegas, counselor of the Bolivian legation in Paris, and the Venezuelan ambassador to Switzerland, Carraciollo Parra-Perez. He was pleased to find aboard his Bronxville neighbors, Mr. and Mrs. Walker Rey, and the popular actor David Niven.

In the last weeks of June, Rose was busy showing her parents London. Perhaps afraid of her father's tongue, she did not give a party for him, an extraordinary action on her part that must have caused him, though not her ever-reclusive mother Josephine, great annoyance. She did not include them in a dance she gave for Eunice on June 23, at which there was a significant guest: the young, handsome William, marquess of Hartington, heir to the fortune of the duke of Devonshire, who was strongly attracted to Kathleen. Rose did not, at the time, foresee danger ahead as the marquess danced frequently with her daughter. Soon, the developing romance would prove to be a crucifixion for her: Hartington was Protestant; his father was the leading Mason and an anti-Catholic.

Joe returned to Rose after the Fitzgeralds were discreetly packed off to New York at the end of the month. He was in a temper; his reception at the White House had pleased him, and he had supplied valuable information to the president, but soon afterward he had received a shock. He was informed that the Harvard committee that had sat to decide whether he would receive an honorary doctorate had ruled against him, based on the canard that he had upset the stock market before the 1929 crash. He was so piqued that he refused to attend his oldest son's graduation, a decision that Joe, Jr., surprisingly, did not resent. The two Joes—and Jack—returned to London together.

On July 18, Rose attended the annual Buckingham Palace garden party. Kathleen again showed keen interest in the marquess of Hartington. Afterward, to Rose's annoyance, Kathleen was whisked off for the weekend to Hartington's eighteenth-century estate, Chatsworth, with its 150 rooms and 40 servants.

Kathleen lingered on with her father in London, seeing Hartington constantly, while Rose took off to the south of France with the rest of her brood for the summer holidays. She had rented the Villa Madeira at Cap D'Antibes, close to the Hôtel du Cap. These were blissful weeks: the children basked on the sand, swam in the azure sea, ate excessive amounts of rich food and (with the exception of the ever-thin Jack) grew plumper every day.

Rose formed a friendship with Marlene Dietrich, who was there with her daughter, Maria; the younger children liked Maria and joined her in a variety of activities in and out of the hotel. In 1965, Dietrich absurdly boasted to me that she had bedded Joe, Sr., Joe, Jr., and Jack, relieving Jack of his virginity (in fact he lost it in a Harlem brothel).

Another guest at the Hôtel du Cap was the duke of Windsor, who played on the Biat golf course. Although he was supposed to share the same political views, Windsor was anathema to Rose and Joe, and they walked off the course whenever he appeared.

Also at the hotel were the antic British comedienne Beatrice Lillie, the famous decorator Elsie de Wolfe, and the future French Premier Paul Reynaud with his notorious mistress, Helene Des Portes, who was soon to be killed when piled-up luggage in the back of a car fell on her and broke her neck. The presence of Treasury Secretary Henry Morgenthau and his son Henry was scarcely pleasing to the Kennedys. Morgenthau hated Joe, knowing that Joe wanted his job, and the feeling was mutual. Indeed, despite Joe's help to the Jewish cause, in the general manner of the time he often made sharp anti-Semitic remarks, and Morgenthau was a frequent target of his tongue.

Henry Morgenthau, Jr., noted in his diary that Teddy stuck closely to his parents while Joe, Jr., and Jack spent mornings chasing a shapely brunette in and out of the swimming pool. He noted that there was a rumor afoot that Jack had an incurable ailment and had only two years to live.

The European crisis deepened by September, when Rose returned to Paris and London; Hitler was going to add Czechoslovakia to his list of spoils, and neither the British nor American government was capable of controlling him. Joe continued to carry out Roosevelt's foreign policy; there must be no question of America making threats that it was in no military or naval position to carry out, nor must there be an argument with his friend British Prime Minister Neville Chamberlain's position, which was one of appeasement while Britain armed. Had England and America challenged Hitler to the point of saying that they would declare war if he continued trying to annex parts of Europe, they would have been a laughingstock in Germany, since (as both Kennedy and Lindbergh pointed out) Germany was ahead in the arms race. Rose, as always, concurred with her husband in the matter.

Meantime, Joe, with Rose's support (as she would make clear in her memoirs), embarked on plans to assist in the emigration of Jews from Germany. Hitler, who had built his career on the popular basis of anti-Semitism, was anxious to cooperate in that policy; mass extermination was not yet in the cards. The problem Joe faced in tackling the issue was that anti-Semitism was international, intense and unlikely to change. In new meetings with Rabbi Stephen Wise, and in communications with Zionist leader Chaim Weizmann, he had determined that no nation was prepared to accommodate Jews, including Czechoslovakia, Poland, Great Britain and the United States. What was to be done?

Perhaps a resettlement in Palestine, which was plagued by Arab interference, or British Guyana, or the British Colonies in Africa, particularly Kenya and Tanganyika, both of which had received German immigrants? The Germans proved conciliatory, and Kennedy, with Rose lending a sympathetic ear, began arrangements with Rabbi Stephen Wise.

Meanwhile, acting on her husband's advice, Rose went to stay, away from potential bombing, at the Gleneagles Hotel at Auchterarder, near Perth in Scotland, noted for a celebrated golf course, where she played daily and attended the championships. She was isolated there, separated from her younger children, visited only twice by Kathleen. Rose spent much of her visit trudging through rain and cold in Wellington boots.

The political news was more depressing than ever; even a visit to the Perth Racetrack, a trip to the launching of the liner *Queen Elizabeth* by the queen at Clydeside and the spectacular Gathering of the Clans failed to cheer her.

But then, on September 30, Chamberlain returned from a

visit to Hitler; he had managed to buy time for England to arm. The result of the Munich settlement, which guaranteed Hitler power over Central Europe, was greeted by ecstatic crowds outside 10 Downing Street and the wholehearted approval of Rose, Joe and the press. The moral issues were suppressed by the public's hunger for continuing peace and the government's fear of seeing a helpless Britain destroyed.

Back in London for Teddy to have his tonsils out on October 3, Rose joined Joe in the gallery of the House of Commons to witness the Munich debate. They saw Winston Churchill condemn political compromise; they saw Chamberlain receive an ovation as he won on a three-to-one vote. The Kennedys were again jubilant.

Kennedy's appeasement policy, held in keeping with the Vatican's, had its advantages. He was able to maintain unbroken links to Germany and Italy.

Many years later, on March 7, 1950, Ruth Alexander, an award-winning political journalist working on the memoirs of former president Herbert Hoover, wrote to Hoover stating that she had determined that Joe had been involved in much "cloak-and-dagger" work in 1938. In the course of this, General Motors' vice-president James D. Mooney had obtained for the ambassador detailed notes of conversations with Hitler, Goering and Ribbentrop.

That week, David Sarnoff, head of RCA, for whom Joe had prepared the important company report three years earlier, was in London, and joined the Kennedys for dinner. He gave them shocking news: their idol, Arturo Toscanini, was under house arrest in Milan, his passport confiscated by Mussolini because he had dared to criticize publicly the Italian dictator.

Rose was dismayed. Joe acted at once, calling the society hostess Elsa Maxwell, a friend of Mussolini's son-in-law Count Ciano, William Phillips, an old friend and U.S. ambassador to Rome, Cardinal Pacelli and other contacts, all of whom brought pressure to bear on Mussolini. The result was that within forty-eight hours, much to Rose's delight, Toscanini retrieved his passport and flew to France to join a ship for passage to New York just in time for the fall NBC Symphonic Orchestra season. He rewarded Rose and Joe with the precious gift of his favorite baton. While voices screaming "Kennedy is pro-Nazi" were heard, led by Judge Felix Frankfurter (who had accepted the Kennedys' hospitality in London and who was the alleged mentor of Joe, Jr.), Dr. Joseph Goebbels in Berlin put Joe high on his blacklist.

On April 20, former governor of Wisconsin Philip F. La Follette attacked Kennedy at a press conference in the Washington office of Secretary of State Cordell Hull, charging him with pro-Nazism and with supporting undemocratic elements in Britain. Hull said:

> Dr. Goebbels has charged that the Ambassador is a master conspirator in a plot to add the United States to an iron ring around Germany. I certainly don't think there is anything serious about being attacked from a so-called Progressive, Liberal or similar angle one day, and the next . . . being attacked by the opposite angle of reactionaryism. I don't think it is much reflection on our Ambassador. At least, it doesn't make an impression on us, and I doubt if it makes any on the country.

On May 1, Joe sent a report to Cordell Hull on a meeting with Sir Kingsley Wood, of the British government, seeking all possible information, at Wood's request, on shortwave German radio detection of American aircraft. On more than one occasion that summer, Joe reported on meetings with Helmuth Wohlthat, an associate of Goering; these have been commented on adversely, not least by me in other books, but newly declassified documentation shows that, in fact, while floating talk of a gold loan to Germany, Kennedy was sending secret reports to Washington, giving a graphic account of Hitler's ambitions and intentions.

On October 17, Joe went too far in his efforts to pacify Germany to obtain special information. He had worked for ten days on a speech that he would give at the Navy League dinner at the Dorchester Hotel on Trafalgar Day. The issue of naval affairs was a delicate one; unadvertised, he had been working, as a continuance of his work as head of the Maritime Commission, to build the U.S. Merchant Marine both in the Pacific and the Atlantic to enhance his nation's defensive capabilities. He saw the occasion as an opportunity to express his desire to avoid any international conflict while that Merchant Marine was being developed.

In view of the controversy that such statements might evoke, he forwarded, according to his custom, the speech to Washington, for comments by Secretary of State Cordell Hull, and in turn from the president. The speech was returned with minor corrections. Then he showed it to Rose.

Rose was the accepted censor of all he wrote and said. She was concerned about its pacifist tone, even though it reflected Vatican policy. She said, "Have you thought how this would sound back home? You know, dear, our ambassadors are supposed to lose all their powers of resistance when they get to London. You don't want folks to get the idea you're seeing things through English eyes."

She objected to his expression of diplomatic indifference during the Czechoslovakian crisis. He overruled her and retained the statement, "It is unproductive for both democratic and dictator countries to widen the divisions now existing between them by emphasizing their differences— instead, they could advantageously bend their energies toward solving their common problems. . . . After all, we have to live together in the same world. . . ."

Sandwiched between prominent appeasers of the British aristocracy at the luncheon, Rose could only stare straight ahead as her husband delivered his bombshells one by one. The nervous applause indicated he had committed a faux pas. He was not supposed to express such sentiments in public, no matter how they might adhere to official policy at 10 Downing Street. Roosevelt had already moved to a position that indicated that he wanted a moral quarantine established against dictators.

Not for the first time, Joe had stumbled by failing to take Rose's advice. He made it worse by making jocular remarks about her efforts to cut his speech. But she quickly forgave him. She loved him, dangerous opinions and all.

The American press was not as forgiving. With a few exceptions, notably his friend Arthur Krock of the *New York Times,* reporters branded him as endorsing Hitler's aggressions. Nothing could have been farther from the truth; but the charges stuck.

At the same time, the Kennedys had much to absorb in reports that came from William Bullitt and Carmel Offie* in Paris, augmented, with a certain degree of cheerful amateurishness, by Joe, Jr.,'s own comments as he wandered across Europe as his father's information gatherer. Edouard Daladier and his foreign minister Georges Bonnet, supported by Bullitt, broke with the Communist Party in France after it refused to support the Munich Agreement. Soon afterward, the Franco-Soviet pact was ended.

Newspapers and BBC broadcasts preoccupied Rose, who followed everything with complete intensity, and Joe every day. The Poles, later to be glorified as heroes, occupied part of Czechoslovakia by agreement with Hitler. Hungary also received a slice. The Czech alliances with Russia and France collapsed. Kennedy remained silent, following Roosevelt's policy. From the Catholic point of view, which stemmed directly from Pope Pius XI, Stalin was a greater evil than Hitler. The disintegration of the entente that spread from Prague to Paris and had found its cooperation in London, witnessed by Rose at first hand on her trip to Moscow, caused the wreckage of opposition to Hitler, and did more than almost anything else to precipitate World War II.

At the beginning of November, a Polish Jewish youth, Herschel Grynszpan, killed a diplomat attached to the German Embassy in Paris. Hitler used the excuse to launch Kristallnacht, the mass slaughter of Jews on the night of November 9–10, in which Nazis swept through the ghettos of Germany, murdering, raping, and destroying property. This event almost unseated the Munich Agreement, which was continuing between Chamberlain and Hitler, and which would result in Hitler being given a free hand in Continental Europe.

Kennedy, again with Rose's intense interest and approval, continued in his efforts on behalf of the Jews. Rose wrote in her memoirs:

Joe was active, behind the scenes, in helping many Jews escape. . . . Joe proposed the Jews be granted asylum. . . . For months he poured his energies into developing

---

*Who was dubbed by Jack "La Belle Offlet."

this plan, getting the permissions, transportation, facilities, trying to cut through the endless red tape and details, trying to get the vast amount of money needed from governments and philanthropies. . . .

Part of the arrangement was to barter Jews for a new billion-dollar gold loan from the United States to Germany, organized through German economic representative Helmuth Wohlthat.

On November 15, Joe approached Chamberlain at 10 Downing Street, again recommending that the British government offer new homelands in distant colonies, including British Guyana, Tanganyika, Kenya, Northern Rhodesia and Nyasaland, to Jewish immigrants. Field Marshal Goering was put in charge of the arrangements, and on November 17, Chamberlain presented the matter to the House of Commons. Joe, in support of George Rublee, American executive director of the thirty-one-nation Intergovernmental Committee for Refugees, had meetings with Malcolm MacDonald, secretary for colonies and dominions, and Earl Winterton, chairman of the Committee on the German-Jewish Problem, to discuss the issue. Later, he also talked with Labor opposition leader Clement R. Attlee.

There was tacit approval of the matter in London, and some discussion of $100 million being raised. The difficulty was that the Germans laid down punitive conditions: a substantial portion of the wealthy Jewish Germans' assets would be confiscated, the balance put in credit to foreign governments provided that the exiled Jews buy only German goods with the money. Another stumbling block was that still no prominent nation (now only the Dominican Republic) would guarantee Jewish safety and shelter.

The worst problem was that Roosevelt refused to do anything more than protest verbally against Kristallnacht. On November 15, at a press conference in Washington, the president was asked the question "Would you make a suggestion to the British government concerning a place wherein the Jewish refugees would be taken care of?"

In response, Roosevelt said that the U.S. quota system would remain intact and would not be extended to admit any Jews, or anyone else for that matter, to the United

States. This devastating statement closed an iron door in the face of Kennedy's negotiations in London. It is disturbing to note that the leading Jewish financier Bernard Baruch was influential in the president's decision. Kennedy pressed on regardless. Dr. Goebbels triumphantly announced in his newspaper, the *Angriff*, on November 15: "The possibility for Jews to emigrate has greatly diminished. That is not the fault of Germany, but wholly of the countries that on one hand intervened with resounding speeches for the pity of the Jewish people and on the other hand . . . do not think at all to bring in Jews themselves."

There was a concession later that month. Trade concessions were made by the British and Dutch governments allowing for Jewish children to be brought in, while adults were still precluded. The British and French colonies in Africa agreed to accept twenty thousand infants on November 25; again, even though the New York City unions offered to raise funds for children, Roosevelt would not allow them in. Even the unlikely proselytizing of Henry Ford, the last person who would have been expected to take an interest in the matter, could not shake the president.

Working day and night, Kennedy continued with his efforts. Two hundred children went to Liberia; eight hundred entered France; Lord Balfour gave his Scottish home for some of the 196 children who reached England; others were housed in temporary Boy Scout camps. By December, hundreds more were lodged in the Netherlands. Still, Roosevelt would do nothing—even when New York union leaders and their worker followers again offered domestic refuge.

On December 10, 1938, Rose saw Joe off on the *Queen Mary* for New York to confer with Roosevelt on this and other matters and to testify before the House and Senate Joint Military Affairs Committee along with William Bullitt.

Joe sailed to the United States in an atmosphere of harsh criticism. He was accused of being a pawn of Chamberlain, a captive of the Cliveden Set, a sympathizer of Hitler, a prospective president of the United States; it was accused that he was using his relationship with Italy to support Mussolini. Such charges failed to weigh him down.

He was accompanied by the Eddie Moores and U.S. ambassador to Brazil Jefferson Caffery. On the 17th he condemned German treatment of the Jews to the press in Washington. He said, "This persecution . . . is the most terrifying thing I have ever heard of. I doubt whether Germany will cooperate in any acceptable way in assisting Jews to leave the Reich." Asked what he thought of Hitler, he said, "When I'm no longer ambassador, ask me."

Apparently, he felt confident that his family would be safe in central Europe because of the Munich Agreement, since he was happy to have Rose take off with several of her family for a skiing vacation at St. Moritz in Switzerland at approximately the same time. Rose had withdrawn her youngest children from Southern Ireland, to which they had been dispatched from school during the worst period of the October crisis.

At St. Moritz, Rose found herself in the company of members of the British aristocracy, for whom a Swiss winter vacation was the accepted standard of those days. With Joe, Jr., as her escort, she moved into a magnificent suite at the popular Souvretta House Hotel, with six rooms booked for the other children and three for her staff. Photographs in the *Tatler,* the *Bystander* and the *Queen* showed a glowing Rose, bursting with health and happiness, relishing the pleasures of the snow. No inkling of anxiety over the dangerous situation in Europe was reflected on any of the family's faces. Typically, Joe, Jr., took off on wild and dangerous bobsled rides, plunging down steep mountainsides. Rose wasn't surprised when he broke an arm and had to be rushed by sleigh to a neighboring village; he was helped in his recovery by the pretty ice-skating champion of the hour, Megan Taylor. Their romance resulted in more than one extravagant statement in the press that they were engaged to be married.

While in St. Moritz, Rose received an amusing letter from Jack in New York; he had attended the opening night of Cole Porter's new musical, *Leave It to Me,* in which the Kennedys were satirized wittily. The writers, Samuel and Bella Spewack, portrayed the Kennedys as Mr. and Mrs. Alonzo P. Goodhue of Topeka, Kansas, the characters played by Victor Moore and Sophie Tucker. In this version,

Joe is ambassador to Russia; on arriving at the official residence in Moscow, Mrs. Goodhue acts exactly the same as Rose did on arrival at Prince's Gate: she orders all the furniture changed. Like Joe, Goodhue insists on continuing his stockbroker activities, and asks that Moscow introduce a stock exchange.

The Spewacks were clever. A German ambassador tells Goodhue he wants to take over all the U.S. trade in Latin America—exactly Joe's concern in notes to the president and in his meeting with Von Dirksen. Jewish writers both, the Spewacks showed Joe kicking that same German in the stomach; they knew Joe's true sympathies. Perhaps to avoid legal action, the Kennedys were discussed in the production as separate people. At one time, Mrs. Goodhue asks, "Why haven't I got nine children, like the Kennedys (instead of four)?" Goodhue replies, bringing a gale of laughter from the audience, "Because I'm tired!" The final touch of verisimilitude occurs when Goodhue complains that he has to go to dinners with people he doesn't like and "gets indigestion." No comment could be more apt, since Joe always suffered from dyspepsia after rich royal and Foreign Office dinners.

With Joe still absent in Washington, Rose returned to London with her brood. She felt weighted down by the dark, drizzly winter weather, the grimy buildings, the tense atmosphere; assigning Kathleen the role of hostess, giving her instructions on the children's welfare and schooling, she decided to take off after just a fortnight, with her friend Marie Bruce as companion, on a lengthy trip by steamer, train and bus to the Mediterranean countries for six weeks.

On the face of it, bad weather or no bad weather, this seems an odd decision on Rose's part. She would have to miss at least one important reception at Buckingham Palace; she would have to refuse invitations by several Astors to their country homes; she would miss the birthdays of two of her children, Kathleen and Jean, on February 20.

Even allowing for the existence of the Munich Agreement, she would be heading into sensitive areas: to go to fascist Italy was a provocative decision if the international situation should deteriorate. Greece had internal problems, torn between Nazi and anti-Nazi groups. Palestine was in turmoil, principally on the issue of Jewish settlement and Arab opposition that had preoccupied Joe since the previous summer. The only conclusion one can reach is that Rose, like Joe, Jr., who was now in Madrid in the middle of the civil war, and Jack, who had just been granted special leave from Harvard to travel the length and breadth of Europe, was being used as an information source by Joe on changing conditions on the Continent.

Shortly after she left Naples aboard the luxury Italian liner *Conte de Savoia* on January 31 with Marie Bruce, Rose received the sad word from Joe, who had returned from America on the sixth, that Pope Pius XI had died in Rome.

She was in Istanbul on February 15. A car was placed at her disposal for local shopping, and she and Marie Bruce explored the dark labyrinth of the famous bazaar. They were in Beirut, Lebanon, on the twentieth, and visited the remains of Baalbek and Damascus; they continued to the Holy Land. On the twenty-sixth, they arrived at Port Said, Egypt, Rose taking notes every day. Met off the ship, they were taken by train to Cairo, where they were entertained by U.S. Minister Burt Frith, with plans to visit the pyramids and the Sphinx.

On March 6, Rose received a telegram with exciting news. Joe would be representing Roosevelt at the coronation of the new Pope, Pius XII. This was a very unusual decision, since normally William Phillips, the U.S. ambassador to Italy, would have assumed this role. Phillips wrote his passionate approval to the president. Press and radio soon told her of the storm of criticism that followed. The Protestant Church in America condemned Joe's prospective appointment as a violation of propriety, a deliberate joining of Roosevelt with the Catholic hierarchy, and an abrogation of the appropriate separation of church and state.

As Rose knew, the assignment was in fact (and Vatican authority Father Gerald Fogarty now confirms it) a trial balloon to test the American public's reaction to Washington establishing diplomatic relations with Rome. Fogarty also points out that Kennedy was working hard with Cardinal Pacelli to separate Mussolini from Hitler and that Kennedy would be using the Vatican as a listening post.

The Kennedy family, except for Joe, Jr., who was ma-

rooned in Madrid, left London on the eighth, in a Golden
Arrow train private carriage, for Rome. Rose was to fly at
once from Cairo to meet them there. She canceled the rest
of the cruise, and she and Marie flew to the Holy City. She
managed to be at the Rome station to meet her husband and
children when they arrived two days later.

Rose was in the best of moods, excited by Joe's news that
he had been the recipient of an honorary doctorate from
Edinburgh University, a slap in the face for Harvard. She
was also proud of Jack, who would soon be assigned a role
at the U.S. Chancery in Grosvenor Square.

Rose was overjoyed that Cardinal Pacelli had been chosen as Pius XI's successor. Pacelli had drafted his predecessor's 1938 encyclical, "Mit Brennender Sorge," that had
condemned Nazi aggression. When Mussolini banned it,
Pacelli had it printed in Paris and distributed widely. When
Hitler refused to allow it into Germany, the cardinal had it
air-dropped over Catholic cathedrals and churches. Rose
loved the austerity of this new pontiff: his breakfast of black
coffee; his hourlong morning workout in his private gym
that kept him fit and lean in his old age; his grasping of
foreign news through his mastery of eight languages; his
beloved canaries, which fluttered around his head when he
ate his meager dinner of chicken or steamed fish. She had
never forgotten his visit to Bronxville and his tender
treatment of young Teddy as he dandled him on his knee.

Another pleasure of the stay in Rome was having Cardinal O'Connell to dinner at the Grand Hotel. He brought
word of Rose's parents and presumably stifled his opinions,
which were somewhat adverse to Pacelli's.

On the appointed morning of the coronation, March 12,
1939, ten days after the prospective Pope's sixty-third
birthday, Rose was up at dawn. As in 1933, she dressed in
the manner prescribed by the Vatican: a long, shoulder-to-
floor black dress, which austerely hid her figure, and a black
lace mantilla; all women presented to the Pontiff must still
have the appearance and deportment of nuns. Her daughters were similarly dressed for the occasion.

At about 7:30 A.M., the embassy limousines containing
Rose and her family and staff embarked from the Grand

Hotel toward St. Peter's Square. Some 250,000 people were in the streets. For days, armies of workmen had polished and repolished the great church, the fabled Cellini chandeliers brought to a fine finish; the Bernini bronze columns brilliantly glittering; the bronze image of St. Peter dressed in a gold tiara and full canonicals, an emerald ring pressed on the stone forefinger of the right hand. All this Rose saw as she entered, walking slowly, Joe at her left, to the special reserved section for the Diplomatic Corps set up next to the statue of Charlemagne squarely in front of the great altar.

Due to a mix-up, they were placed with their children in the red velvet and gilt seats intended for Mussolini's son-in-law, Count Ciano, his wife, Edda, and their offspring. A furious Ciano arrived just after the Kennedys were seated and exploded in hysteria, quite unassuaged when he was granted another group of seats next to them; he spent much of the ceremony giving the fascist salute and trying to share honors with the Pope.

At exactly 8:30, a fanfare of silver trumpets filled the Scala Regia. Soldiers appeared in sixteenth-century iron armor, carrying swords, spears or pikes; over the armor, they wore black-and-purple tunics, and on their heads instead of helmets were gold-braided peaked caps. An attendant carried the tiara, gleaming with diamonds and rubies on a black velvet cushion; he was followed by others, bearing the sacred miters and the papal crosses. As music resounded through the apse, seven gilded attendants walked forward, carrying tall, flickering votive beeswax candles. They were followed by men with ostrich-plumed, decorative fans and then the Pope, all in white, lean, bespectacled and unsmiling, followed in turn by a procession of patriarchs, cardinals, archbishops, bishops and priests.

A cry broke from the audience of hundreds as incense rose through the air, and the Pope was seated on his throne.

Rose saw Joe walk with the duke of Norfolk, in the latter's role as leading Catholic peer of England, and close to a hundred diplomatic representatives, in the aisle of the Basilica to the full-throated chorus of the Roman colleges, and to further cheers as the dignitaries knelt one by one before the Pope. From the Chapel of the Holy Trinity and of

St. Gregory the Great, Pius XII continued toward the entrance, where he received the obeisances of the cardinals and intoned the Gloria. Fearful of being poisoned during the sacrament, he did not drink the wine himself, but left it to a sacristan.

Enthralled, Rose watched the final procession as the pontiff gave his apostolic blessing, received the traditional white silk purse and twenty-five gold coins from the dean of the chapter, and walked in a blaze of trumpets to the balcony. Rose, Joe and the other Kennedys were rushed out of St. Peter's to a canopied reserved section of the grandstand so they could see the pontiff address the multitude. The piazza was filled with worshipers, who cried again and again as the Pope blessed them. Then, through the public-address system, a priest called for silence, the flags fluttered low on their masts and Rose, her husband and children knelt along with the multitude. There was silence for several minutes as an appointed cardinal placed the tiara on Pacelli's head. Everyone rose; the applause was a tide of thunder. The Pope again blessed the crowd, and as the Kennedys left, the cheers were unending.

The following day, the Pope received the Kennedys in private audience, placing them second only to the German ambassador on his agenda (his initial concern was the state of the Catholic Church in Germany under Hitler). Once again, Rose found herself entering through the special back door that led to the elevator and to the Pope's private library on the second floor. On this occasion, Pacelli was there when they arrived, and he broke all precedent in rising to greet them. Although they had brought boxes full of rosaries, he gave them a rosary each, also a break with tradition.

He spoke warmly of his visit to Bronxville, and he spoke of Teddy playing with his pectoral cross. He dwelled on his happy visit to the Roosevelts at Hyde Park. He blessed them, and was impressed by Teddy's composure. "You are a very smart little fellow," he said.

Not only did he bless each and every one of them, but also the Eddie Moores, and Rose's two favored staff members, Luella Hennessey and Elizabeth Dunn. After the private audience, the Kennedys called on Luigi, Cardinal Maglione, papal secretary of state, who gave them a private tour of the Sistine Chapel.

Joe returned to the library for a personal discussion with the Holy Father, who said, "The tendency of Nazism and fascism is pro-pagan, and as pro-pagan, strikes to the very roots of religion." Joe reported to Sumner Welles at the State Department in Washington, "I am definitely of the opinion that the influence of the Pope could be utilized for the cause of peace in ways under the surface rather than in a big gesture. . . . I intend to keep my contacts close to the Vatican. All with the view of watching the (Italian) moves very carefully. . . ."

That afternoon, Rose and Joe were received for tea at the Pope's private residence, Castel Gandolfo, and that night, at the U.S. Embassy, they were at dinner in honor of Count Ciano. Rose and Joe found Ciano a pompous fool; he kept rushing young women into corners for conversation. Joe wrote to Cordell Hull saying that it would accomplish more to send a dozen chorus girls to Rome rather than "a fleet of airplanes and a flock of diplomats." Among the guests were German ambassador Hans-Georg Vikton von Mackensen and the countess of Perth, wife of the absent British ambassador. The Roman-Catholic Irish tenor John McCormack sang for the guests. Such were the social connections of ambassadors of every political color. Kennedy used the occasion to milk the talkative Edda Ciano of much useful information, which he forwarded on to Roosevelt.

Later, the Pope gave Teddy a personal communion, a very rare privilege for an American child. It was an unforgettable visit.

Rose rushed from Rome to Paris, to assist William Bullitt, now ambassador to France, on an important occasion. On March 25, she acted as his hostess at a dinner dance at his official residence in honor of President and Madame Albert Lebrun. It was an unusual move for one ambassador's wife to help out a colleague in another country; but she and Joe were very fond of Bullitt, and approved of his action against the Soviet Union in breaking the Franco-Russian pact.

One achievement of the Kennedys' visit to Rome was that, in consultation with William Phillips, Joe was able to arrange for a delay of six months in which all foreign Jews must leave Italy. He influenced Ciano to soft-pedal the overall anti-Semitic program. Back in London, Joe continued to work on the Jewish problem. Again involved in the issue of the Jewish settlement in Palestine, he conferred with Rabbi Stephen Wise and Jewish leader Louis Lipsky as well as Neville Chamberlain, to make sure that the British government, which had been wavering between support of Arab and Jewish claims, would give preference to the Jews. He had been disappointed with the results of the Palestinian conference earlier that year, and was upset by the compromised British white paper, which scarcely solved any of the pressing problems that had been raised.

An urgent issue of the time was King George VI and Queen Elizabeth's upcoming visit to the United States. Designed to cement Anglo-American relations in a time of possible war, the visit had been high on Joe's agenda of propositions to Roosevelt from the first days of his ambassadorship. Rose was supportive of the idea, knowing how the naturalness, lack of affectation and down-to-earth charm of the royal couple would impress the average American at a time when the United States was isolationist. An annoyance was that Roosevelt had sought to bypass Kennedy in making the arrangements, but Kennedy had trumped his ace by forming a friendship with the king and queen.

On April 26, the Kennedys, accompanied by James and Betsy Roosevelt, were guests at Windsor Castle, and over the weekend made suggestions concerning the visit, including one that the royal couple must sample hot dogs and hamburgers.

The day after she returned from her visit, Rose entertained at the embassy, giving a party for cabinet ministers and their wives and members of the Diplomatic Corps. The *Tatler* commented, "The house has taken on the jolliest, carefree atmosphere since the Kennedys took up residence in it. . . . There were the loveliest flowers, exquisitely arranged. . . . Mrs. Kennedy looked perfectly charming in . . . navy blue. . . . And there were the two older girls,

Kathleen and Rosemary, chatting unself-consciously. . . ."
The guests included the James Roosevelts.

On the night before the king and queen left for the United
States, Rose faced the challenge of her career. She had been
granted the privilege of the royal couple coming to dinner at
Prince's Gate.

She worked to exhaustion on the preparations. The
dining table would have to be decorated with tiny moth
orchids; she was shocked to find that Constance Spry, the
London florists, was charging an absurd amount for them.
So she had them flown from Paris, where a frantic "La Belle
Offlet" scoured the city to find the appropriate blooms. For
weeks, Rose had tried to get the State Department to spring
the funds to buy a new dining-room rug from W. and J.
Sloane in Washington, D.C.; finally, it arrived, but only just
in time.

From Lady Bessborough and others, Rose took advise-
ment on the correct procedure and etiquette. Joe would
have to walk down the three front steps in person to meet
the royal car. The butler would take the king's coat; Rose's
maid the queen's. The queen and Joe would have to go
upstairs to the dining room first; Rose would follow with the
king. The children would not be at the dining table, but at a
separate table of their own. The royal couple would be
seated facing each other at the center of the table, replacing
the normal placement of host and hostess, who would now
be at either end.

Rose was in suspense as she awaited the arrival of the
orchids and the appropriate foods, which had been flown in
from the United States and were being kept in an ice house
nearby. At last, she saw the van come with the Boston clam
chowder, the shad roe and the strawberries; Margaret
Ambrose hastily whipped up mushroom soup and her
fabled strawberry shortcake. Police drove up to make a
security check of each member of the staff; they were
assuaged by word that all had been former servants at
Buckingham Palace. Two secretaries arrived from the Grosvenor Square Chancery to help Rose prepare the handwrit-
ten menus, which were placed on silver rests in front of each
plate.

At 8:10 P.M., the guests selected by the royal couple arrived ahead of them: William Bullitt; the duke and duchess of Devonshire, whose son William was increasingly interested in Kathleen, much to Rose's displeasure; Viscountess Halifax; Viscount and Viscountess Astor; David and Mrs. Bowes-Lyon; Sir Alexander Hardinge and Lady Hardinge; and the duke and duchess of Beaufort.

Dinner was relaxed and comfortable, with King George and Queen Elizabeth dissolving in laughter at Joe's ready wit. After dinner, Rose took the queen to her bedroom to powder her nose; the queen was fascinated by Rose's face-enlarging mirror.

They talked about their children. Rose said she no longer got up early to see them off to school, but, since she was out almost every night at a social event, slept in late instead. The queen shamed her by saying she would get up half-dressed to see her daughters off and then would go back to bed. Rose vowed to change her habits in the future.

Photographs were taken in the Pine Room; and an uncut version of a new movie, Sam Wood's *Goodbye, Mr. Chips*, was shown. The parting was joyful, with good wishes by all for the monarchs' journey to the United States.

Chapter 10

Bombs over London

The royal American visit was a triumph, and the king and queen were eternally grateful to the Kennedys for having prompted it. Rose decided to experience the tour more closely than she would have been able to through newspapers and the radio in London.

Her extraordinary restlessness is once again illustrated by the fact that, missing the London social season, which was already underway, she now took off across the Atlantic. With her American maid Margaret McKeon, she left the day before Jack's birthday, on May 28, 1939; she occupied a suite aboard the *Normandie* complete with gondola beds, marble baths and suede-lined oval dining room, an Art Deco Paris apartment for the rich and tasteless transposed bodily into a deluxe ocean liner. In a nearby, similar suite were housed her friends of Riviera days, Marlene Dietrich's daughter Maria, and Maria's father, Rudolf Sieber.

The Fitzgeralds were waiting at the pier to whisk Rose off to the New York World's Fair at Flushing Meadows, which she visited on the same afternoon as her arrival.

Rose was especially impressed by the French Pavilion. There, Henri Soulé, a master chef from Paris, prepared delicious dishes in demonstration in front of the tourists.

She was dazzled, and told Joe about him. The result was that Joe financed him later, in starting what turned out to be one of the finest restaurants in America, Le Pavillon. The restaurant became the second home for the Kennedys whenever they were in New York and they heavily invested in it.

Rose took the train that night with her parents to Boston, where she was housed in their suite at the Bellevue Hotel.

She returned to London after four weeks, just in time for Joe to receive an honorary degree at Cambridge. Harvard could stew in its own juice.

The summer of 1939 was the best of Rose's seasons. Admittedly, she suffered from Kathleen's continuing interest in Billy Hartington, but perhaps it would come to nothing. The attractive couple were the center of attention at Eunice's coming-out parties, the first held by Rose at Prince's Gate, the second by Nancy Astor at St. James's Place, and the third at the home of Baroness Ravonsdale. Mrs. John Dewar, heiress to the liquor fortune, whose interests were represented by Joe through Somerset Importers in the United States, gave a smaller party for the couple, and Neville and Anne Chamberlain received the whole family in a private get-together at 10 Downing Street. "Kick" Kennedy, as Kathleen was known, rapidly became the toast of London, popular with all ages.

Rose liked Anne Chamberlain, whose Irish origins she shared. Rose also concurred with Chamberlain's policy, which was to play for time through appeasement with Germany to allow his country to arm. Already, the navy was at full strength, and the air force was starting to build, supplemented by dozens of American planes whose sale to England Kennedy had engineered.

In June, the journalist Walter Lippmann arrived in London. Kennedy harangued him with defeatist sentiments: Britain had no chance against Hitler; Poland and Romania were helpless; the Japanese would attack the West. England knew this was true, and the only sensible course was to give Germany a free hand in Central and Eastern Europe. Democracy was going in England, and now there was the despotism of exchange control.

Statements like this, exploding from Kennedy's mouth,

were never comfortable for Rose and were usually contradictory of his attitudes on other days; he could be British and anti-British, pro-Semitic or anti-Semitic, pro a Russian alliance or anti one, sometimes within an hour. His lack of stability, emotional or intellectual, was a burden to her that she bore as gracefully as she could. In the long run, as she would write in her memoirs, she felt his judgments were correct, but she did not specify which judgments.

On July 4, Rose gave an Independence Day garden party for two hundred Americans of wealth and prominence resident in England and France. That evening at the Dorchester, she was hostess at a dinner for two-thirds of the same guests.

Two weeks later, on July 19, the Kennedys brought Eunice to Buckingham Palace for her presentation.

The month saw Rose entertaining the stiffly formal and dowager Queen Mary at tea. She flung another party for the Harvard boating crew that had won the Grand Challenge Cup at Henley-on-Thames, and for American tennis players, scullers and golfers.

At a Pilgrims' luncheon for departing American consul general Douglas Jenkins, Rose joined in the laughter as Joe said, "I'm not planning to leave London with Doug, although every other day I'm being told my successor is being named!" It was true; the anti-Kennedy rumor mill churned out hints that Roosevelt would remove Joe from his office, but this was wishful thinking. Kennedy's intelligence reports from London were far too valuable for Roosevelt to recall him, despite the president's annoyance at Joe's frequently undiplomatic statements.

On July 28, looking forward to her summer vacation in the south of France, Rose flew to Nice Airport and thence to Cannes, where she was met by her chauffeur and driven to the villa Joe had rented for the summer, the opulent Domaine de Randuin, along the coast at Mougins. The family enjoyed getting together as a unit, tanning themselves away from the pallid sunshine of London, swimming in the ocean, playing golf and fielding a stream of telephone calls from all over the world. Marlene Dietrich was back at the Hotel du Cap at Antibes, along with her daughter, her long-suffering husband and her lover, the novelist Erich Maria Remarque.

The Kennedys spent days at the hotel; Marlene talked to Rose about their children. Jack, who had dated Maria in Paris, resumed a flirtatious interest in her, and Marlene asked Rose whether she should play in a Hollywood Western, *Destry Rides Again*. Rose told her to; so did Joe, and Dietrich went ahead—to one of the triumphs of her career.

Dietrich told me that Joe was so passionately fond of his family, so locked into them, that his obsession was he might lose them in a German bombardment of London; if he had been given a choice between losing all his money, every cent of his $10 million, and losing the brood, "he would have accepted a begging bowl."

Dietrich remembered Rose laughing with the rest as Joe, Jr., the bronzed Apollo of the beach, described how he had been thrown off a similar beach in Spain because he refused to wear a top to swim in ("Everyone was dressed for 1912, the women with pantaloons").

Even in this relaxed atmosphere, Joe was restive and irritable. He sent an extraordinary, long, rambling letter to Roosevelt, personal, not official, on August 9, 1939. He noted, as Rose had done, the ominous degree of anti-Semitism among the golf caddies, waiters and residents of the South of France. He complained of being victimized by "rotten columnists" and wondered if his experience and knowledge were not wasted as ambassador; that he was a "mere errand boy." Used to his *errant* boy, as Roosevelt called him, the president did not respond.

Rose had tensions to deal with. Kathleen begged her mother to give her permission to return to London to attend the coming-of-age party of Billy Hartington at Chartwell, for which a carnival had been hired. Rose refused; she still opposed the match, insisting that Kathleen maintain family unity by not leaving.

Rose had a powerful experience at Antibes. She struck up a conversation with a French woman at the beach. The woman said, with tears in her eyes, that her grandfather had been killed in the 1870 Franco-German War, and that her husband and brother had been slaughtered in the conflict of 1914–1918. She swore she would never let her sons join in any future battle. Rose agreed. Nothing must threaten Joe's and Jack's safety.

The family was back at Prince's Gate on August 22. All were lean and fit now except for Teddy, who had grown to tublike proportions as a result of the French cuisine.

Joe continued his intelligence work. On August 25, he had a meeting with one of his chief informants, Kadri Rizan, Turkish chargé d'affaires in London. Appalled by the newly concluded German-Soviet nonaggression pact, which Joe feared might result in a Communist takeover of Europe, he wanted to know the worst. Rizan told him that the pact contained secret clauses: Poland would be divided between Hitler and Stalin, Russia would be recognized in the Baltic states, Turkey would be granted parts of Bulgaria, Germany would be granted Hungary, Yugoslavia and Greece.

Most startling of all, Russia was to be given a free hand against Japan, even though Japan was supposedly Germany's ally. Joe forwarded the report to Roosevelt, who failed to act upon it. Had this intelligence been forwarded to Tokyo, and leaked to the Japanese government, Japan might have broken contact with Germany, and Pearl Harbor might never have happened.

Kennedy's attitude to Hitler, so often described as sympathetic, is shown in a comment on the document. Hitler had said to Rizan's informant that if he could make a deal over Poland that included the Russians he would guarantee the British Empire against attack for good and would become an artist again. Knowing the Fuhrer's capacity for bluffing, Kennedy added to that quotation, "Hitler is an artist now, but I would not care to say what kind!" He meant, of course, bullshit artist. At the same time, Joe met with the Japanese ambassador, Mamoru Shigemitsu, to discuss the necessity of a permanent alliance between Britain and Japan; unfortunately, he does not appear to have conveyed Rizan's information to Shigemitsu. Rose wrote in her memoirs:

> Joe despised everything about Hitler and Nazism. But, along with all people of sanity and goodwill, he prayed that somehow war could be avoided. Knowing the terrible destructive power of modern weapons, he

realized the widespread death and suffering another world war could bring.

But even when her book came out, those statements were ignored; they remain ignored.

At the end of August, Rose was with Joe at Aberdeen University as he addressed the students. He had been forced by the State Department to eliminate part of his address, a part Rose unquestionably approved. It ran:

> I should have to ask you all if you know of any dispute or controversy existing in the world which is worth the life of a son, or of anyone else's son. Perhaps I am not well informed of the terrifically vital forces underlying all the unrest in the world, but for the life of me I cannot see anything which could remotely be considered worth shedding blood for.

In this respect, neither Rose nor Joe was by any means alone. At least a third of the British public was opposed to any form of conflict with Hitler, preferring to reach a compromise rather than risk their children's lives. The view was shared by the majority of Americans, a view that would be sustained until Pearl Harbor.

Joe was not disloyal to Roosevelt in making such statements, since Roosevelt maintained his popularity in part by promising that no American boy would die in a European conflict.

Pope Pius XII led the Kennedys as always. He worked to break the German-Italian military alliance, sending a peacemaking nuncio to Berlin that August to see Hitler. Following the German-Soviet pact, he issued an allocution, warning all nations that they were rushing headlong into disaster. On August 24, he made a worldwide anti-German broadcast, calling for the use of reason and love ("Empires not founded upon justice are not blessed by God. Nothing is lost through peace. All can be lost through war"). On August 31, he summoned ambassadors for Britain, the U.S., Poland, Germany and France to the Vatican, insisting upon a fifteen-part truce and an international conference.

The situation deteriorated rapidly. At dinners at 10

Downing Street, Rose and Joe felt the anguish of the Chamberlains as they saw all of Hitler's promises become worthless. During the daytime, Joe was back at the same address for further meetings. It became imperative that sufficient shelter be supplied for himself and his family and staff at both Prince's Gate and the Chancery in Grosvenor Square.

Prince's Gate had no air-raid shelter, despite requests for one starting from the first days of Kennedy's ambassadorship. Even Grosvenor Square, with its vital Code Room, had no satisfactory basement in the event of an air raid. Although its shelter could house 150 people, it had no proper escape doors, and, should the upper floors collapse, the floor above the basement would not be able to sustain the weight and would fall in upon the occupants and bury them alive.

The strong room, which contained thousands of bars of silver, was not provided with gasproof screens and doors. It was obvious that arrangements would have to be made for country retreats.

On September 1, Germany invaded Poland and, having broken his guarantees to Austria and Czechoslovakia, a despairing Chamberlain could not avoid declaring war on Hitler. Rose, along with Joe and the rest of the family, was shattered by the news. She was with Joe at 1 Grosvenor Square on September 3, when Chamberlain delivered his radio speech announcing the commencement of hostilities. Three hours later, an air-raid siren wailed over London. Convinced that German bombers were on the way, and in view of the insecurity of the Chancery's cellar, Rose, Joe and the rest of the staff walked across the street to the Edward Molyneux fashion salon where she had spent so many hours in fittings. They walked down the stairs into the Molyneux shelter. It was so overcrowded that many of the Chancery's staff members had to remain in the adjoining corridors.

After the all-clear, announcing that the prospective raid had been a false alarm, Joe's assistant military attaché, Major René R. Studler, under Joe's anxious pressure, scheduled a proper shelter, and soon a reluctant State Department in Washington authorized $10,000 for it. Later, Rose,

Kathleen, Joe, Jr., and Jack sat in the gallery of the House of Commons and heard Chamberlain tell a silent and deeply moved audience of members, "Everything that I have worked for, everything that I have hoped for, everything that I have believed in during my public life has crashed in ruins."

Contrary to Whitehall gossip, which asserted that Joe acted in a cowardly manner, that evening he cabled the State Department that, in view of the fact that the prime minister and the Foreign Office staff had advised him they would remain in London under the bombing, he would not be moving himself. However, he pointed out that "we have nothing here to protect ourselves except our umbrellas, and from all accounts they are not very safe."

As it turned out, the State Department proved annoyingly tardy in supplying the necessary shelters, and Kennedy was forced to make plans to obtain country residences to protect vital records and codes.

He decided that Rose and the children should be evacuated to New York immediately. The Chrysler had already gone aboard the *American Trader* before war was declared. But space on ships was very limited, and they would have to go in installments. The one child who would be kept behind was Rosemary. She was developing increasingly neurotic symptoms, and the Kennedys felt that a hazardous journey by sea or plane to the United States might be too much for her. She would stay at her Montessori School for the time being.

While the embassy staff tried to find a stateroom for Rose, shocking news was announced on the radio. The British Donaldson-Atlantic liner *Athenia,* bound for Montreal, was torpedoed by a German U-boat and sunk 250 miles west of Donegal, Ireland. Many were drowned. Of the 1,400 passengers, 311 were Americans. Tied up at the embassy, Joe was unable to travel to Glasgow, where 152 of the rescued American passengers were brought from Galway by two British destroyers via the port of Greenock. Joe took the bold step of sending the inexperienced Jack to that city to meet with the survivors at the Beresford Hotel.

Although Rose later would describe the meeting as a

success, it was not. The bedraggled, exhausted and furious passengers were maddened by being sent what they described as a "schoolboy," callow and out of his depth, to deal with the matter of their being conveyed safely to their original destination. Ill-equipped to deal with the matter, Jack announced that they would be brought back to New York aboard the American merchant ship *Orizaba*. When asked by the angry crowd what convoy would be supplied, he was obliged to answer that none had been arranged. He added that none would be needed, as America was neutral.

A woman screamed, "We refuse to go without a convoy!" An old man yelled, "There are ninety destroyers being commissioned in the United States. Send one over!" Accustomed to charming everyone in sight, aghast at this harsh encounter with painful reality, Jack fled before an army of bruised, burned and hysterically yelling people. As it turned out, they were forced to leave on the unprotected *Orizaba* anyway, as Jack personally arranged.

The weather in London that week was sunny, oppressive and hot, with thunderclaps causing many to run to shelter, thinking the German bombers had arrived. Prince's Gate and Grosvenor Square were heaped high with sandbags, and the blue sky was filled with fat, floating silver slugs—the barrage balloons. Postboxes were marked with yellow squares, which were supposed to turn green at the impact of gas; Rose, Joe and everyone else in the Kennedy family had to attend gas-mask drills, fitting the smelly rubber masks with their glass snouts over their faces until they looked like figures in futuristic films, and then tucking the unpleasant things in flimsy cardboard boxes slung from the shoulder by straps.

At night, the city was plunged into an emergency blackout, people edging their way through the streets with tiny pocket flashlights or candles in jam jars. Cars hummed along with headlights out; buses buzzed out of London at dawn, with loads of children on their way to country hideouts.

At last, Joe, after pulling every available string, got Rose, Kathleen, Eunice, Bobby and Margaret Ambrose two staterooms on the S.S. *Washington*. Rose took under her wing

Leslie Nast, nine-year-old daughter of the New York publisher Condé Nast, and Robert Cragie, fourteen-year-old
son of the ambassador to Japan.

The group arrived at Southampton on the night of the
departure. They saw an astonishing sight. Next to the
dimmed-out vessel, whose lights from stem to stern glim-
mered as faintly as candles, were no less than sixteen troop
trains, parked in a complex of railroad sidings, heavily
camouflaged, and taking on a seemingly endless stream of
soldiers and marines for shipment across the English Channel to France.

Rose's and her children's luggage was abstracted from
them, since there was no room even for a small suitcase in
the cabins they had been allotted. She would have to
undertake the crossing without a change of clothing.

When she reached her cabin, she was informed that there
would be no maid or room service and she and her family
would have to clean up and make their own beds. She was
lucky to have a cabin at all; and then only because she had
young children, who were accorded hammocks, commandeered from the sailors' quarters and slung from bulkhead
to bulkhead. Two thousand people were squeezed into
accommodations for one thousand. The violinist Fritz
Kreisler and the novelist Thomas Mann had to sleep in a
converted Palm Court lounge with dozens of others in what
Mann would later describe as something resembling a
concentration camp, while their wives slept in a boarded-off
section of the same public room. Movie star Robert Montgomery was given a cot surrounded by dozens of men in the
empty swimming pool and had no facilities for bathing or
shaving; tennis stars Donald Budge and Bill Tilden and
movie star John Lodge were housed in the gymnasium
along with drama critic Richard Watts.

Once at sea, which was remarkably smooth for the
Atlantic, the captain ordered every light turned on with
blazing intensity, never to be turned out at night, which
resulted in few people having any sleep. This was to make it
clear to U-boat captains that the vessel was neutral; British
ships were blacked out. The ship was to zigzag; the band was
instructed to play American anthems at all times, and the
Stars and Stripes fluttered from masts, ropes, bow and

stern. Replicas of the flag were painted on port and starboard sides; radio messages to German U-boats warning them not to strike went out all night and were listened to by many passengers. Bobby Kennedy raced around getting autographs from Robert Montgomery, Don Budge, Bill Tilden and almost every other celebrity on board. Rose found friends at dining-room sittings, including Paolo Marella, an Italian friend of the Pope and Cardinal Spellman; jewelry tycoon Harry Winston; and the impresario Sol Hurok.

A crowd of reporters greeted the passengers at the New York pier. Photographs were taken of Rose and her children. With her customary composure, Rose looked as though she had just stepped out of a fashion show rather than an exhausting and almost sleepless voyage; dressed in an exquisitely tailored Molyneux traveling suit and fox fur, wearing one of her famous rakish, broad-brimmed hats, she looked magnificent, and so did her family, all of whom were impeccably groomed, dressed and shod. They were royalty, after all; the mere absence of laundering, dry-cleaning, maid service or even an iron aboard ship scarcely put a dent in their fashionable, glamorous appearance.

Rose wasted not a minute on arrival. Without spending so much as a night in New York, after depositing Leslie Nast and Robert Cragie at their homes, she took the train with her brood to Boston, checked into the Bellevue Hotel and, scarcely drawing breath, entered Eunice for the Manhattanville College of the Sacred Heart, the same college Rose had attended thirty years before. She attended her parents' fiftieth wedding anniversary, and took care of the American arrangements for Jack's Pan American clipper flight from London and Lisbon to join Joe, Jr., at Harvard. In the midst of all this, she had made sure that a personal letter from Joe, urging Roosevelt on a continuing pacifist course, was delivered to the president at the White House and that her favorite Chrysler six-wheeler, already in New York, was driven to Boston.

Patricia was entered in the eleventh grade of the Convent of the Sacred Heart in Maplehurst, New Jersey; Robert began at St. Paul's School. But Rose decided that there was too much in the St. Paul's curriculum calling for Protestant learning and there were insufficient arrangements for him to attend Mass, so she withdrew him after only two weeks and shipped him off to Portsmouth Priory, a Catholic boarding school at Naragansett. In that decision, she clashed with Joe, who had called from London insisting he go to Riverdale. Within a week, Bobby was in the news, having helped to put out a fire that destroyed the Portsmouth Priory dormitory.

On September 29, 1939, Rose was in Newport News, Virginia, on a patriotic assignment. With great excitement, she broke a bottle of champagne over the bow of a new oil tanker, commandeered for the Maritime Commission at Joe's request and built by the Standard Oil Company under the old family friend William Farish. She named the vessel the *Esso Richmond,* and it was the largest vessel in the Standard Oil fleet. Eunice stood beside Rose as maid of honor, and family investment advisor Harry T. Johnson also officiated. Rose said to Harry as the ship slid down into the water, "Little did I think my tenth christening would be a tanker!"

Rose was increasingly distressed by the difficulty of communicating with her husband in London. Influence had to be brought to bear on British Cable and Wireless, the British telephone company, in order to allow the Kennedys to talk to each other for ten minutes a week on Sundays. They were allowed about seven minutes on the occasion of their twenty-fifth wedding anniversary, October 7. A particularly loving note came from the king and queen of England to Rose at the Bellevue.

With the exception of Rosemary, Rose's other offspring arrived on various vessels in October. Rose worried because Joe was ill in London; he lost fifteen pounds because he was barely able to sleep, and he was suffering from such severe gastritis (and a recurrence of an early gastroenteritis) that he had to send his associate Herschel Johnson in his place to official dinners. This incapacity provoked many cracks at his expense in British Foreign Office memoranda.

From Joe's many letters home to her, Rose learned that he was using his neutral position to insist upon an improvement of British merchant shipping lines and American strength on the oceans. He wanted the British to buy

American ships and fly them under British flags, and he wanted those ships to bring essential wheat from Australia. On November 28, Joe was at Buckingham Palace for lunch.

With his stomach condition, he was unable to eat the main course offered to him by the king: a very British concoction called jugged hare. Breaking all protocol by refusing it, he was offered pheasant instead. The roasted bird was served with a nasty puree of mashed brussels sprouts and potato, which he forced down.

At the luncheon, the queen expressed her disappointment with Charles Lindbergh's defeatist statements, but she agreed that it would be too provocative for the United States to send soldiers to London. Joe agreed. His policy was that America would be of greater use to Britain if it could supply Britain with aid without getting into a war that would result in the sinking of American ships. A neutral vessel could bring armaments and food protected from U-boats.

At the Admiralty that day, Joe saw Winston Churchill. He unfolded to the First Lord his plan for Britain to buy American vessels. Churchill approved the plan. Then Joe flew by Pan American clipper to New York. Rose met him off the plane; she was shocked to find him thin, gaunt, tired, sick and in pain, and whisked him off to the Lahey Clinic in Boston for extensive tests. He was found not to be suffering from gastric cancer, but was warned to take a rest in Palm Beach if he was to be sufficiently well to return to his position in London by the new year.

In his absence, Herschel Johnson obtained, in association with U.S. consul general John G. Erhardt, a secret country evacuation home for the embassy, the American George K. Weeks's Headley Park, near Epsom, Surrey. Just twenty-two miles from London, it had twenty-two reception rooms and bedrooms, six bathrooms, seven servants' and auxiliary rooms, five chauffeurs' rooms and a garage for five cars. It also had its own market garden and cows from which fresh milk could be supplied. Four telephone lines and thirty internal extensions were installed. Work went ahead on the shelter at Grosvenor Square.

At Palm Beach in December, Rose again had her children together, and was joined by her parents. She was happy again, but she knew that she would soon lose Joe, whose duties in London were pressing.

Due to his poor health, Joe lingered on until March, flying to London via Rome on the third. He learned that Von Ribbentrop, Hitler's foreign minister, was about to have an audience with the Pope that might be preparatory to Italy entering the war.

In his absence, Herschel Johnson, counselor and now once again chargé d'affaires at 14 Prince's Gate, received a secret communication dated February 7 from G. M. Liddell of British Secret Intelligence, which stated that the German Secret Service had been receiving from the American embassy, twice a day, reports containing everything from Joe's reports to Roosevelt, including details of his visits to British statesmen. The spy, described as The Doctor, was thought to have been employed in the U.S. embassy in Berlin, but evidence is lacking. To this day, Kennedy has been accused, with no proof, of leaking the reports himself. Quite apart from the fact of his loyalty to U.S. interests, and the contempt for Hitler he expressed to Rose and to the State Department in his letters, he couldn't have managed such treason because Herschel Johnson personally handled all his transmissions and was morally impeccable.

He left Rome for London on March 6, discussing the matter with U.S. undersecretary of state Sumner Welles aboard the Simplon Express. He wrote Rose everything that followed. At Prince's Gate, he despatched Eddie Moore to Rome to learn whatever he could of the Ribbentrop–Pius XII encounter through Count Enrico Galeazzi. Moore proved to be a good spy. Joe flew to Paris on April 1 to meet him. Sick with influenza at the Ritz, Moore brought word of the minutes of the meeting at the Vatican, and also of Ribbentrop's discussions with Mussolini.

It was clear that Britain could not rely on Italian neutrality much longer; Joe took this to indicate danger to Britain, since Italy would join an alliance that already included Russia. On May 15, he cabled Roosevelt that Churchill would be sending a message to the White House saying the chances of the Allies winning was slight if Italy entered the war. This was intended to provoke American aid in the form of thirty or forty mothball destroyers. It worked.

Rose Fitzgerald Kennedy at four (right) with her sister Agnes in 1894. This is the earliest known photo of Rose. [AP Photo]

Rose with her father, John F. Fitzgerald (aka Honey Fitz), the mayor of Boston, leaving on a South American trip. [The Bettmann Archive]

Rose and Joseph P. Kennedy after their 1914 wedding ceremony. [UPI/Bettmann]

Rose with Joe Jr.,
Rosemary, and John.
[AP/Wide World Photos]

Rose with (from left to right) Eunice, Kathleen, Rosemary, John, and Joe Jr. in 1921. [UPI/Bettmann]

Rose and Joe aboard the SS *Aquitania* in September 1928.
[UPI/Bettmann]

Gloria Swanson, movie star extraordinaire.
[AP/Wide World Photos]

The Kennedy clan in the early 1930s.
[Globe Photos/DM]

Rose and her children follow Ambassador Joseph Kennedy to England in 1938.
[AP/Wide World Photos]

Rose with Kathleen, Bobby, and Eunice aboard ship in 1938.
[AP/Wide World Photos]

Rose about to present Eunice to the King and Queen of England in July 1939. [AP/Wide World Photos]

Rose skating with Jean and Teddy in St. Moritz, Switzerland, in 1939.
[AP/Wide World Photos]

Joe, Rose, and the Kennedy children leaving the Vatican after a private audience with Pope Pius XII in 1939.
[AP/Wide World Photos]

From left: Rose, King George VI of England, Queen Elizabeth, and Joe in London in 1939. [AP/Wide World Photos]

Rosemary, Teddy, Rose, Bobby, Eunice, and Jack in Hyannis Port, 1940. [AP/Wide World Photos]

Rose receiving from Admiral Gygax the Navy Cross posthumously awarded in July 1945 to her son Lt. Joseph P. Kennedy, Jr. [UPI/Bettmann]

Standing outside St. Francis Xavier Church in Hyannis Port: Eunice, Joe, Bishop Cassidy, Rose, Jack, Rose's father Honey Fitz, and Teddy in 1946. [AP Photo]

A distinguished Rose in 1954. [AP/Wide World Photos]

Joe and Rose with their daughter-in-law Jacqueline Bouvier Kennedy arriving at St. Joseph's Church in Bronxville, N.Y., for Teddy's marriage to Joan Bennett in November 1958.
[AP Photo]

Campaigning for Jack during the 1960 presidential race. [AP Photo]

Rose and Jackie as President-elect John F. Kennedy
prepares to give his acceptance speech, November 9, 1960.
[UPI/Bettmann]

Whispering to President Kennedy in 1962. [UPI/Bettmann]

Bobby in the mid-1960s.
[UPI/Bettmann]

Adlai Stevenson, Rose, and
President Lyndon B. Johnson.
[UPI Photo]

Rose and the Duchess of
Windsor are a study in
concentration at the
April in Paris Ball at the
Waldorf in 1965.
[UPI Photo]

The tiny Rose needed to use a chair as a platform while campaigning for Bobby in Oregon during the presidential race in 1968. [AP/Wide World Photos]

Walking along the beach in Hyannis Port with her daughters Jean Smith and Patricia Lawford after Joe's death in November 1969. [UPI/Bettmann]

Rose and Jackie leaving St. Edward's Church in Palm Beach in 1973 after attending Mass. Jackie had arrived in Palm Beach aboard the yacht *Christina* with her husband Aristotle, who remained on the craft. [AP Photo]

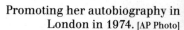

Promoting her autobiography in London in 1974. [AP Photo]

At age 89, stumping for Teddy's presidential campaign in 1980. [UPI/Bettmann]

The Kennedys pose for pictures after Easter services at St. Edward's Church in Palm Beach in 1980. [AP/Wide World Photos]

Celebrating her 92nd birthday in 1982 at the family compound in Hyannis Port.
[AP Photo]

In 1983, commemorating the 20th anniversary of the assassination of President Kennedy, from left: Patricia Kennedy Lawford, Eunice Shriver, Rose, Teddy, and Jean Smith.
[AP/Wide World Photos]

Rose's funeral
at Old St.
Stephen's
Church in
Boston on
January 24,
1995. [All three:
AP Photos]

At the Democratic National Convention in San Francisco in 1960. [© Cornel Capa/Magnum Photos]

Churchill replaced Chamberlain that month as prime minister.

Rose planned to come to England by clipper on May 10. Her purpose was almost certainly to bring Rosemary home. This journey would now take five grueling days, since, due to a changed schedule, the plane would have to travel via Belém, Brazil, and Dakar, West Africa, then proceed to Lisbon. The flight from Lisbon to London would be especially dangerous because it would be by British civilian aircraft, which could be shot down by the Germans at any time.

The British Air Ministry told Kennedy that his wife could not be promised a seat on the crowded experimental Lisbon-London flight, which was being inaugurated on May 23, 1940. This was a great annoyance, and she was compelled to cancel her plans.

Instead, Rosemary flew to America with a nurse and the Eddie Moores on May 26. Hers was a ghastly, sleepless flight. A storm forced an unscheduled landing in Bermuda. British secret agents boarded the plane and seized the mail, nine bags of which emanated from Nazi Germany. Rosemary was shaken by the ordeal, and began to exhibit neurasthenic symptoms which would soon become much worse.

To add to her other stresses, Rose received letters from Joe saying that the bombing of London was terrible, that the situation was critical, that Britain might have to sue for peace with Hitler getting the British navy. Such views were not restricted to him, but were widespread in England. Letters poured into 10 Downing Street and the ministries every day calling for an arrangement with Germany. For the rest of his life, Joe would be attacked for still holding these views; but in fact he obtained them from very high sources. Churchill told Joe, "The chances of the Allies winning is slight."

In his *Modern Times,* the British historian Paul Johnson wrote as recently as 1983, "Churchill . . . knew Britain, even with the Commonwealth, could not beat Germany in the summer of 1940. . . . Whatever he might say in public he did not rule out a tactical deal with Hitler. The Cabinet Minutes record him as saying, 'In terms of the restoration of certain German colonies and the overlordship of Central Europe it would be considered, but it is unlikely Hitler would make any such offer.'"

Churchill was unwilling to send more British troops to France to fight the German invasion because he was convinced that within a month England itself would be vigorously attacked. Joe asked him what the United States could do to help that would not leave America holding the bag for a war in which the Allies expected to be beaten. He offered Churchill all the help possible. But he also knew that the bulk of the American navy was in the Pacific, there were not enough airplanes for America's own use, and its army, hampered by equipment that went back to World War I, was not up to requirements.

Churchill understood this. Newspaper owner Cecil King wrote in his diary in July, "The country is already reconciling itself to the idea of a Nazi conquest."

That summer, Germany occupied the entire coastline of Europe except for Vichy, France, all the way to Spain. By July 1, Churchill was advising his ambassador in Washington that invasion would be imminent. When he made his famous blood, sweat and tears speech, which roused the British public to its highest point of patriotism, he turned from the microphone to Edward R. Murrow and said, according to Kennedy adviser James Fayne, "And if the Germans do come, we shall have to hit them on the heads with beer bottles, because that is all we will have to fight them with." Because Joe became the conveyor of these secret views to the United States, he was crucified, while Churchill remained the public hero of the hour.

At last Joe found a house where he could sleep in an air-raid shelter at night and have some rest on the weekend. That house, owned by U.S. automobile manufacturer Horace Dodge, was named St. Leonard's, and was situated not far from Windsor Castle in the Windsor Great Park. On weekends, Joe visited the royal couple, who traveled to the castle on Friday nights and who sensibly kept their children, the princesses Elizabeth and Margaret Rose, at that location, where there was a well-equipped cellar.

Rose did her best to cheer Joe up by sending him word of

the children. Bobby, she wrote, was losing interest in his favorite hobbies of sailing and collecting stamps, but was busily reading British ambassador to Germany Sir Nevile Henderson's disturbing book, *Failure of a Mission.* She had a taped family recording made, with everybody sending loving wishes.

Rose, sick due to anxiety over her husband, spent May at the Greenbrier Hotel, White Sulphur Springs, where she had been on her honeymoon. In the meantime, Joe, Jr., was a delegate at the Democratic National Convention in Chicago, and Jack was busy writing a book—a development of his Harvard thesis—entitled (at the suggestion of Arthur Krock) *Why England Slept,* an account, based on information supplied in America and Europe, of the basis for England's reluctant involvement in World War II. It echoed Joe Kennedy's continuing emphasis, from the first days of the ambassadorship, on Britain's failure to arm strongly, and made clear the real reasons for the compromise agreement at Munich. A passage reads:

> The policy of appeasement, while it was partly based on a sincere belief that a permanent basis could be built for peace, was also formulated on the realization that Britain's defense program, due to its tardiness in getting started, would not come to harvest until 1939. *Munich was to be the price she paid for this year of grace.* (Italics supplied.)

Jack emphasized slowness in setting up aircraft factories, that five thousand first-class airplanes would have stopped the war, that English opinion was not aroused to protest against the conquest of Austria and Czechoslovakia, and that it was shocking that Canada and Australia had said they would not support England in a world war.

Joe Kennedy showed his true attitude when he wrote to Jack, "One or two of those who have read the book complain that you have gone too far in absolving the leaders of the British national government for responsibility for the state in which England found herself at Munich."

Joe, Sr., persuaded another friend, Henry Luce, to write the introduction. Despite his supposed leanings toward the right, Luce proved to be eager to accept the assignment and was highly congratulatory in executing it. In particular, Luce approved of the sentence, undoubtedly emanating from Joe, Sr., directly, "If God hadn't surrounded us with oceans three and five thousand miles wide, we ourselves might be caving in at some Munich of the western world."

Published in August, the book was well received by the press, which failed to attach any of its theories to its true author in London. This was painful for Rose, who was acutely aware of her husband's influence on the book.

One of the most persistent myths that Rose would have to tolerate in future years was that Colonel William J. Donovan, U.S. Intelligence chief, came to England in July 1940, without Joe's knowledge or approval. This is untrue. On July 12, Cordell Hull advised Joe by cable that Donovan was coming to England to report on British defense and that Hull would appreciate all help Joe could give the colonel. Kennedy arranged the hotel, Claridges, but he regarded the trip, in view of much valuable information, already available, as "the height of nonsense and a definite blow to a good organization." However, he did help as much as he could.

Criticism of Joe continued throughout the summer. It seemed he could do nothing right. Envy of his financial success, enchanting wife, handsome family and rich properties colored article after article, column after column. Charges of anti-Semitism were still distressingly frequent, despite his continuing association with Rabbi Stephen Wise, Chaim Weizmann, Bernard Baruch, Arthur Krock and other leading figures of the Jewish community.

Rose was besieged at Hyannis throughout July with the question "Will JPK resign his post?"

She denied it again and again, pointing out to an Associated Press correspondent on the twenty-third of that month, "Under the circumstances, of course, he will stick to his post where he is so greatly needed." Even the fact that Joe, Sr., arranged to have Jack's English royalties for *Why England Slept* given to the severely bombed city of Coventry never received a word of favorable comment. Rose could not understand this attitude.

By August, Rose had raised a substantial sum through

hardworking charitable-committee members, to pay for the first of a number of American ambulances she would supply for use by the injured in the Blitz. At a ceremony at Windsor, Joe presented the welcome gift to the mayor. On August 20, Joe completed raising £16,000 (the equivalent then of $80,000) from M.G.M., Warner Bros., Paramount, Universal and 20th Century-Fox studios for London voluntary relief organizations helping the bombed-out and homeless.

St. Leonard's, Joe's retreat, was no safer than the heart of London. In efforts to bomb Windsor Castle, the Germans dropped explosives near Joe's house, one of them splitting in half an old beech tree. Another, several days later, destroyed three workmen's cottages. It ironically bore the initials J.P.K. (a Junkers bomber insignium). Far from fleeing the scene of destruction, Joe inspected the craters, walked past what might have been an unexploded bomb, joking cheerfully, and made sure that the homeless workers were housed elsewhere. Another unexploded bomb burst close to Joe's car soon afterward.

Still concentrating on American defense, Kennedy became host to military, naval and air-force figures from Washington in London. On September 5, he presented to the king Rear Admiral Ghormley, assistant chief of U.S. naval operations; Major General Eamons, commanding general, American air-force headquarters; and Brigadier General Strong, assistant chief of U.S. General Staff.

On September 11, Kennedy was on the roof of the Chancery in Grosvenor Square to report to U.S. Secretary of State Cordell Hull what he saw:

> On Sunday night, a high explosive made a direct hit on a house twenty yards from Herschel Johnson's home, killing six people, but he is well and hearty. Today as I came back from the Foreign Office, a delayed time bomb near Bond Street and Piccadilly blew up about fifty yards from my car. Boy, this is the life!

Rose learned of these events painfully, each Sunday, as Joe talked to her across the crackling Atlantic cables. Her heart swelled with pride at Joe's courage even while the scourges kept up their charges of cowardice against him. By now, even Winston Churchill had installed a bombproof bunker under the General Post Office building from which to conduct his operations and a deep shelter for himself and his family at the suburb of Dollis Hill in North London. Like Joe and the royal family, he spent his weekends in comparative safety in the country—at his estate Chequers.

At the same time, Rose learned from Joe and from the newspapers that Kennedy had meetings with Churchill to discuss an exchange of British bases in the Caribbean and Newfoundland on ninety-nine-year leases in return for a supply of American mothball destroyers which could be used to augment the Royal Navy.

Unbeknownst to Joe, the exchange was unfair to Britain. The vessels that would be supplied from the U.S. navy were virtually useless. Churchill told Kennedy at a meeting at 10 Downing Street on August 29, "We have given you a ring of steel, and I beg you not to make public the humiliating terms, as they would have a disastrous effect on British morale." As a result, Joe had to pretend, then and after, that he was not privy to the deal, and he was attacked for that as well.

Joe was appointed by the British government to sell all securities in the United States, and he knew these would be rapidly exhausted; according to John G. Winant, his successor as ambassador, in his book *A Letter from Grosvenor Square* (1947), "the naval and army observers, when asked in 1940 what they thought of the British chance of survival, replied that they had not got a hope."

The criticisms in London were louder than ever. Sir Robert Vansittart, who unofficially was running an intelligence operation for the government, had scribbled on one report that Kennedy was "a very foul specimen of an appeaser." But this libelous operative knew differently: when Vansittart tried to get the Nazi agent Baron Wolfgang von und zu Putlitz into the U.S., Kennedy stopped the move. When it came to a security check, Kennedy was ahead of Vansittart. He did let German movie star Hilde Kruger via London into America, but he contacted J. Edgar Hoover to keep an eye on her, with the result that she was exposed as a Nazi spy and driven into Mexico.

By October, despite encouraging meetings with the king and queen, Joe wrote Rose that he was becoming disillusioned in his post. Suspicions against him emanated from the arrest of U.S. embassy code clerk Tyler Kent, who had been found with Churchill-Roosevelt correspondence in his possession. He had been leaking it via the Italian embassy to Berlin. Though no evidence of Kennedy's guilt was adduced, and he was the first to condemn Kent, the fact that suspicion was entertained at the White House was enough to irritate Joe beyond endurance, especially since he had waived Kent's diplomatic immunity to clear the way for trial and imprisonment, and had condemned Kent to his fate.

Churchill bypassed Joe, and had done so for some time, in sending some secret messages, not by the diplomatic code, which the Germans had effectively broken, but by a special naval code relayed from the Admiralty in London direct to the Department of the Navy in Washington. The instrumental go-between was Rear Admiral Donald J. Mac-Donald, Roosevelt's aide in maritime matters.

Joe was dissatisfied with Churchill's conduct of the war, including a disastrous attempt to oppose the Germans at Narvik, Norway, and a resounding defeat at Dunkirk. He noted Churchill's blunders in the Far East, and that the Germans had succeeded in obtaining Middle Eastern oil supplies.

Like many British and Americans, he was depressed, convinced that England would soon be crushed. Even the resilience and courage of the Londoners, pale but dogged under bombardment, couldn't strengthen a belief in their survival. Emotional, frenetic, given to sudden shifts of feeling, he failed to understand the strength and humor of the British.

The cancer-stricken Neville Chamberlain summoned Joe to his house and told him that he wanted to die. Rose was moved by Joe's reports on the former prime minister's condition; she sent notes to Anne Chamberlain full of prayers for his recovery. But by November he would be dead.

Roosevelt made clear that he wanted Joe to come home. He needed the Catholic vote for the 1940 election, and he knew the extent of Joe's influence. Despite the fact that he was planning a contingency invasion plan of Europe known as Rainbow Five, he still pretended throughout his campaign that no American boy would die in a British-fought war.

It is doubtful if Rose or Joe believed him, but Rose felt that Joe should not turn against the president and support Republican contender Wendell Willkie. She could not countenance betrayal of the Democrats; she knew that Roosevelt was a greater leader than Willkie would ever be.

Rose longed for Joe to return. Worn out by the bombing and missing his family, he ached for Bronxville, Hyannis Port and Palm Beach. It has been said that he used various forms of threat or blackmail to have Roosevelt recall him at the time, but this was an error perpetrated by Arthur Krock. Roosevelt had already decided to bring him home as far too controversial a figure to be representing the United States at its most strategic embassy in time of war.

On October 19, while busy packing, he inspected a parade of the British Home Guard, made up of volunteer citizens in uniform, at St. Leonard's and received a hearty cheer. The following day, he saw the royal couple in private audience; on October 22, 1940, just before he left Joe wrote to Chamberlain that he had in his life met "two men who had dedicated their lives to the good of humanity without thought of themselves: Chamberlain and Pope Pius XII. You are the last good thing before a pall of anarchy falls in the world. . . . For me to have been of any service to you in your struggle is the real worthwhile thing I have done in my career. My job from now on is to tell the world of our hopes. May God watch over you and give you the hope you so richly deserve. . . ."

It was a long journey home. The Dixie Clipper was delayed in Lisbon by engine trouble, so Joe had a brief respite at the port of Covarrubio. He stayed at the Palacio Hotel at Estoril, where Eric Sevareid saw him walking past two German agents, a doctor who had aided in the murder of Rasputin, and Paderewsky, former premier of Poland. Joe continued via Dakar and Belém to the Bahamas and New York, arriving on October 27.

He was exhausted, thin and gaunt as he stepped down the

gangway. Rose was there to greet him with her brood, fighting her way through reporters and photographers. She laughed as she saw a baggage handler carrying a London air-raid siren, which, Joe announced with a grin, he would use to call his children in from swimming.

He refused to say whether he would support Roosevelt. Pressmen noticed the presence of Clare Boothe Luce, who had written agonized letters pleading with him to come home and had invited the Kennedys to stay with her and her husband in New York.

Rose was able to extract Joe from the crowd and get him into a VIP room; Mrs. Luce followed along with other friends. Joe was characteristically testy, barely restraining, in view of his wife's presence, his customary stream of "goddamns" and scabrous four-letter words. He announced that he would vote for Wendell Willkie, that Roosevelt had betrayed him again and again. He railed at his critics; even while he did so, a message came from the White House announcing that he was expected immediately. Even he couldn't refuse an invitation from the president. At 5:00 P.M., Rose walked with him to the Washington plane.

Once aboard, Joe repeated to Rose his determination to support Willkie. Willkie, he said, shared his belief in continuing aid to Britain without America entering the war. He was afraid Roosevelt, in collusion with Churchill, would not adhere to such a principle. His position remained clear-cut: if America were to send armed convoys conducting supply vessels to England, those could be sunk by German U-boats under the provisions of war. But so long as unaccompanied vessels continued on their mission, they would not be torpedoed. By America staying out of the war, she could be of far greater help to Britain; there would be the additional advantage that the American public would not be required to sacrifice its youngest and strongest. Such a point of view reflected that of millions of Americans, who had a nostalgic feeling for England and didn't want to see her go down under bombardment, but also would not send their sons over to fight.

Rose agreed with Joe, but was adamant that he must support Roosevelt. She said, "The president sent you, a Catholic, as ambassador to London, which probably no other president would have done. He sent you as his representative to the Pope's coronation. You would write yourself down as an ingrate in the view of many people if you resigned now." She did not so much mean resign from the ambassadorship as resign from the Democratic Party.

Joe was undecided. An official White House car picked up the couple and drove them to Pennsylvania Avenue. Seated in his wheelchair, hands trembling with tension, eyes snapping behind pince-nez, the president was unusually high-strung. He had double-crossed Joe time and again, and had broken his election promises to keep at arm's length from the war. With his characteristic cunning, he knew that the way to Joe's heart was through Rose. And he knew that she could be rendered vulnerable by flattery of her controversial father.

He began by making falsely complimentary remarks about Honey Fitz. Although she knew she was being verbally seduced, Rose couldn't resist the president's charm. He gained another victory by commenting warmly on Joe, Jr., and Jack. He said to Joe, "For a man as busy as you are, your relationship with your boys is a rare achievement. I, for one, will do all I can to help you if they should wish to run for office." It is doubtful if, as historians have averred, the president indicated that he would help Joe, Jr., run for governor of Massachusetts in 1942. At twenty-seven, Joe would have been absurdly young for such a position.

Two guests arrived along with presidential secretary "Missy" Le Hand: the senator from South Carolina, James F. Byrnes, and his wife, Maude. The Byrneses' inclusion in the party was a shrewd move of Roosevelt's, which Rose recognized at once. Byrnes had supported Joe at the Senate Foreign Relations Committee in the matter of aid to Britain short of war. He had wanted Joe to be chairman of the National Democratic Committee in July. He knew that Joe had fought for the repeal of the neutrality embargo on armaments for Britain and had been the leader in pushing through the legislation on Capitol Hill. More than anyone alive outside of the Kennedy family, Jim and Maude Byrnes knew of Joe's loyalty to the United States and England.

The president had arranged a supper especially for Joe.

Knowing of his gastritis and inability to digest more than the blandest and simplest food, he had ordered scrambled eggs and sausages to be served. Beforehand, Joe gave the president a clear picture of the economic and political situation in England, which fascinated Byrnes particularly. Joe then handed Roosevelt a letter from Neville Chamberlain, urging the continuation of transatlantic noninvolvement.

During the supper, Byrnes urged Joe to make a coast-to-coast CBS broadcast endorsing the president. Joe did not respond. After dinner, the party repaired to the study; Joe suggested he would like to be alone with Roosevelt, but the suggestion was rudely ignored. Finally, his ill-contained temper broke loose. He shouted, "Since it doesn't seem possible to see the president alone, I guess I'll just have to say what I'm going to say in front of everybody!" Accustomed to groveling sycophancy as the benign dictator of America, Roosevelt looked seasick and he shook. Everyone else blanched and shrank back.

Joe stood up, all the frustrations of the past months blazing from him. He railed against Roosevelt, saying he had written him a letter from Cannes offering all manner of things he might do to help the cause of peace, and that he had received no response. He was racked by thoughts of his betrayers: liberals who hated him and feared he might one day be president, led by Harold Ickes, Morgenthau, Frankfurter and Laski. He mentioned Colonel Donovan's spying mission against him; he referred to the infamous cheating swap of American destroyers for the use of British ports at Churchill's expense and how he had scarcely been consulted on the details. He accused the State Department of keeping details of negotiations between Whitehall and themselves from him; he charged lack of confidence and trust, suspicion and vicious backstabbing.

He added that all of these Machiavellian intrigues were conducive to harming his influence in England. Then, at last, with a stream of colorful expletives, he stopped.

Such words had seldom been heard in the confines of the White House since the days of General Grant. Roosevelt lied that he had wanted to tell Kennedy about the Donovan mission, and he made the false promise that he would berate the State Department for not keeping his ambassador informed on everything.

Rose tried to break the tension by saying, "It's difficult to get a perspective on a situation three thousand miles away." Joe was not appeased, nor was the president, who prided himself on having a perspective on everything. In an effort to help, Rose made matters worse. Joe's fierce glance told her not to open her mouth again.

As the evening wore on, Roosevelt at last managed to appease Joe. Supported by Byrnes, he lied that he was committed to keeping America out of the war. He added that a consolidation of the Democratic Party at the top was vital for its survival. He may also have promised to support Joe's plan of continuing aid to Britain short of direct involvement. Whatever he said worked.

During the stay at the White House, Rose heard Joe say that he would go on the air and praise the president. Joe said, "Now I will make that goddamned speech on radio and I will pay for it myself. It will cost twenty-two or twenty-three thousand, but that's all right. I will write the speech myself. You will trust me or you won't get the speech. I will go down the line for you, but that doesn't alter the situation as far as your treatment of me is concerned." Roosevelt trembled and was in shock at such unbridled obstreperousness. Rose cannot have enjoyed that moment. A president was a president, after all. But Joe was a law unto himself, the monarch of everything he surveyed. And one day, always at the back of his mind and Rose's, was the thought that his oldest son would one day be president himself, and a damn sight better than the present one.

Next morning, Joe called the CBS boss, the Jewish, anti-Nazi William Paley, and announced he would buy time, previously accorded to the Democratic National Committee, for a nationwide political broadcast on October 29. He arranged for Rose to follow with a woman's point of view.

The broadcast took place on schedule, its contents ignored to this day. Joe said that he had returned from Europe renewed in the conviction that America must and would stay out of the war. He talked of America rearming, saying that if it rearmed fast enough, the nation would have its guarantee of peace. As in Jack's *Why England Slept,* he pointed out that Munich was but an armistice, an opportunity for the Allies to understand their peril and to arm. He asked, What would have happened to England if the Blitz of the summer of 1940 had occurred in September 1938? That, he indicated, would have resulted in England's destruction, since it was unprepared.

He added another point. If America declared war, it would keep all vital materials from England in favor of the U.S. army and navy. The obligations of the Monroe Doctrine would limit power to give effective aid to England. He mentioned the receipt of a letter which charged that Roosevelt had made a secret commitment to lead the country into war. Such a commitment had been made, of course, but Joe told his audience that there had been no such commitment. He mentioned the sinking of H.M.S. *Empress of Britain* by German bombers. He added, "To suggest . . . that our boys will soon be on transports in this kind of war under these conditions is completely absurd."

He mentioned the bravery of RAF flyers who kept back the German invaders (after Dunkirk). He pointed out that three thousand miles of ocean was not enough protection for the United States. He added that the British fleet was important to America's national existence. He was pleased that Churchill had given assurance on the guarding of the seas. He talked of being hostile to the aggressors, namely Nazi Germany, and (again) of the necessity to prepare. He concluded:

> Already Hitler's conquered nations have made the advances of Napoleon appear puny. It is later than you think. My wife and I have given nine hostages to fortune. Our children, your children, are more important than anything else in the world. I believe Roosevelt should be re-elected President of the United States.

Rose's speech was also eloquent, appealing to millions of American mothers and saying that she trusted that America would not commit its sons to a war. The result was that numerous Catholic voters, certain now that Roosevelt would meet Pope Pius XII's requirements for continuing peace, switched their allegiance from Wendell Willkie to the president and helped to insure his election the following week.

The day after her radio address, Rose appeared with her daughters Kathleen and Eunice at a luncheon and fashion show at the Bandbox Room of Armando's nightclub in New York to benefit King George VI's fund for sailors under the British Allied Relief Fund, with the duke of Kent as president. Then came a disaster.

The *Boston Globe* had been unfriendly to the Fitzgeralds and the Kennedys for decades, and Joe should have refused when its reporter Louis Lyons asked for an interview. On November 8, staying at the Ritz-Carlton Hotel in Boston, he agreed. Unhappily, Rose was in New York or she might have stayed his hand. Ralph Coghlan, head of the *St. Louis Post-Dispatch,* joined in, along with Joe's friend Jim Landis. Much of what he said made sense, but it was deliberately cut and bowdlerized in the press, particularly in Britain.

Joe praised England's queen, discussing her reading habits and the fact that French president Daladier had told him she knew more about French history than almost anyone in that country. He said that, when it came to a question of saving what was left for England, the queen, more than any of the politicians, would do it; that in fact "she had more brains than the Cabinet." Joe noted the fact that she wasn't born into the royal family; her background was "of the people." He meant that she would be the strength of England in its desperate plight. But his remarks were taken to mean that Joe was a potential collaborationist who would make arrangements with Germany for a negotiated peace.

He also commented favorably on Eleanor Roosevelt, saying that she was a wonderful woman and full of sympathy; referring to his years on the Security and Exchange and Maritime commissions, he said, without sarcasm, that she bothered the committees more on getting positions for "poor little nobodies who hadn't any influence" than all of the rest of the people (in Washington) together. That she was always sending him a note to have some little "Suzy Glotz" to tea at the embassy. This warm statement of praise was taken to be anti-Eleanor and anti-Semitic.

He talked of democracy being finished in England and

probably in America. He meant, but unhappily did not explain, that, in Britain, the coalition Conservative-Labor government was imposing dictatorial emergency powers over essential services and food supplies because of the conditions of war. He took this as evidence of excessive communizing and equated the greatly increased degree of socialism in Whitehall as evidence of "national socialism." Even a suggestion of communism would have been more acceptable; but to link the British Labor Party under Clement Attlee to Nazism was misguided and baseless. Unbeknownst to the public, his reasoning was based upon a secret 108-page report that he had prepared in London with his army and navy advisors, dated October 10, 1940, and published in George Seldes's liberal *In Fact* magazine, in which he had disclosed to the president that in wartime conditions, Britain was compelled to introduce a kind of fascist state, which had to match Germany in its speed-up methods, commanding full industrial and military production—that totalitarian methods should be applied; that the Ministry of Food would describe a diet for the masses similar to that issued from Berlin; that there would be a ceiling on wages; and so forth. His reference to the potential death of American democracy was clearly intended as a reflection on Roosevelt's possible dictatorial policies should war come to the U.S.

In view of these sentiments, the *Globe* and *Post-Dispatch* editors felt obliged to read them back to him on the telephone. He did not withdraw them; his travail under bombing, his stress over the separation from his family and the torment of the White House encounter had undermined his already fragile degree of public caution. The articles containing all he had said appeared in nationwide syndication on November 10, 1940. The decent comments he made were omitted by his opponents; his unwise remarks were played up to the limit.

Given her temperate nature, Rose was angry and aghast; she blamed Joe for his lack of control, while saying nothing to anyone except him. She tried to tell him what she felt, but he refused to listen.

The whole family suffered from the calumny that followed. As for Kennedy, his political career was destroyed at a blow, and he was ruined for good in England. Never again would he be considered for high office; as ambassador, he was finished. He tried desperately to state that the interview had been off the record; it had not. He tried to force the newspapers to retract the interview by threatening to withdraw advertising for his liquor company, Somerset Importers, but the newspapers would not bend. All of the good he had done with the CBS broadcast was destroyed. Roosevelt never forgave him.

At a luncheon at Warner Bros. Studios in Hollywood on November 24, guest of his old friend Jack Warner, he addressed an astonished array of Jewish executives, urging them not to make any more anti-Nazi pictures since anti-Semitism was growing in Britain, and Jews—most of the movie-studio chiefs were Jewish—were being blamed for the war. This was a slap at Jack Warner himself, who had made the daring picture *Confessions of a Nazi Spy* in direct defiance of Hitler, exposing as it did the infiltration of the United States by enemy agents. A point Joe made during the address, that such anti-German pictures might provoke Hitler into declaring war on America, was extreme; to insist that pictures like this be discontinued played directly into the hands of his enemies.*

Douglas Fairbanks, Jr., then at the height of his career as a romantic movie star, took it upon himself to send an attack on Kennedy and the Warner Bros. speech directly to Roosevelt. The letter was forwarded by the president to Secretary of State Cordell Hull, who returned it to the White House without comment. Hating Hitler, Hull was nonetheless opposed to such provocations of the Fuhrer. Knowing, as Joe did, that America was not ready to go to war and that such films were not only in breach of neutrality but could cause (they did) reprisals against Jews in the American film industry in Berlin, he evidently concurred with Joe's views, and his memoirs were sympathetic to Joe.

The Kennedys proceeded to Palo Alto, near San Francis-

---

*As it turned out, his attack on Hollywood's policies in the matter bore fruit; in September of the following year, a Senate committee, inspired by such isolationists as Senator Gerald P. Nye, would arraign studio owners on the same controversial issue.

co, to visit Jack, who was studying at Stanford University under the aegis of Joe and Rose's friend former president Herbert Hoover. Jack was spending more time chasing girls and taking them for rides in his blue Buick convertible with red leather seats than attending to his studies. Disappointed with Jack's scholastic performance, Joe and Rose enjoyed lunching with him at the popular students' hangout Restaurant L'Omelette. Rose came to the Pi Phi sorority house to meet Jack's girlfriend Harriet ("Flip") Price, astonishing the well-dressed, well-groomed girls by wearing hair curlers. Such behavior was unheard of. Apparently, the strain of the previous weeks had temporarily derailed her, rendering her uncustomarily eccentric.

She and Joe continued to Wyntoon, their friend William Randolph Hearst's redwoods retreat in the McCloud River Basin, Shasta National Forest. Wyntoon was a hideous imitation Bavarian village complete with a Bear House for the owner and his mistress, Marion Davies. There was a Cinderella House, a structure called The Bend, the River House, and The Gable, where the Kennedys stayed. Joe, Jr., turned up to join Jack in hikes and hunts in the woods. Joe had registered for the draft, and he talked a lot about that. He brought news of Kathleen, who had joined the *Washington Times-Herald* as a reporter. Rose spent much of her time walking through the woods.

At the Waldorf Towers in New York later that month, Joe stayed in a suite adjoining ex-President Hoover's. The Charles Lindberghs were in town, also staying at the Towers. Rose was at the Plaza.

In meetings with ex-President Hoover on November 22 and Charles Lindbergh on November 29, Joe, despite the fact that he had seen the splendid British response to the Germans in the Battle of Britain, and that he had backed Lord Beaverbrook in building the RAF at heroic speed to make that victory possible (details he was to include many years later in an introduction to one of Beaverbrook's books), again expressed despair at Britain's chances in the future. He knew from his own sale of British stocks—still kept a secret—and from his survey of British supplies that the future looked bleak; he talked apocalyptically of death from major epidemics in the British cities, as though he were reliving the fears of the flu epidemic in America in 1919.

But, in the ache for peace, which Rose shared, even peace with Germany, that would save an unprepared America in this dark hour, he overlooked the fact that the character of the British people alone, rationed, almost bankrupt, but stubborn, strong and able to endure, would hold the fortress. Neither he nor Rose could have foreseen the fatal mistake that drove Hitler, instead of invading Britain, to attack Russia, and to declare war on the United States when he did not have to, decisions that set the seal of his ultimate destruction. And the controversial questions can still be asked: Was he not right all along about the danger that England might lose the war? Would England have won it without American military intervention in 1941? Wasn't his only sin that he voiced his opinions when the British government wanted to give the impression of invincibility? And did not his constant emphasis on British weakness provoke a correction of that weakness then and later?

As long as she remained sentient—for the next forty-four years—Rose utterly believed that her embattled husband was right.

Chapter 11

Crash of a Hero

While Rose was at Palm Beach, Joe spent November 1940 in Hollywood, visiting Jack. Years later, Eleanor Roosevelt made up an incident in which Joe came to Hyde Park that month and was blasted by the president for his defeatism and ordered out of the house. There is no documented basis for the story.

On December 1, Rose was with Joe when he sent from Bronxville his resignation to the White House. His fiery wording had been tempered by Jack. Four days later, the *Chicago Daily News* alleged that he had tried to engineer a negotiated peace with Germany via Vichy. Joe denied the charge, and asked for evidence to be produced; it was not.

In the wake of this setback, the Kennedys' enemy and treacherous London houseguest, Secretary of the Interior Harold Ickes, put it on the Washington grapevine that Joe was a traitor. It didn't help when Robert E. Wood, head of the appeasement group America First, offered Joe the job of chairman. He refused, but the offer earned him more adverse publicity.

Rose had to face the agony of picking up the morning papers at breakfast and reading of the hatred that surrounded her husband and emanated directly from the

Supreme Executive. But the family stood firm, and, with them, their distinguished Jewish friends: Arthur Krock, David Sarnoff, Rabbi Stephen Wise, Bernard Baruch.

On December 29, Rose listened to Roosevelt attacking her husband by inference. In a radio broadcast the president declared that the public must be cautious against American appeasers who believed the Axis would win and that the U.S. could preside over a negotiated peace ("Is it a negotiated peace if a gang of outlaws surrounds your community and, on threat of extermination, makes you pay tribute to save your own skins?").

Even worse punishment for Rose was when she opened the friendly Luces' *Life* magazine and saw Joe framed in a chamber-of-horrors gallery of alleged Nazi sympathizers including Lindbergh and Wall Street plunger Ben Smith.

Somehow, in the eye of the hurricane, Rose managed to keep up a Christmas spirit. So distracted had she been that, for the first time in years, she was late arriving and found herself trimming the tree on Christmas Eve.

The new year of 1941 began. Brooding during the past weeks, Joe decided to take a more moderate position; the president was dangling the promise of the ambassadorship to Ireland, suggesting that they should overcome their differences and that Kennedy might be influential with Irish prime minister Eamon De Valera to make harbors available for the use of British ships.

Kennedy was very interested. Cardinal Montini, later Pope Paul VI, was using Dublin as a window into Germany and Japan. But the sly president's motive was to insure that the former ambassador did not unseat his plans for Lend Lease to England by publicly denouncing them on the radio. At a meeting at the White House on January 16, Joe offered to take a moderate position on Lend Lease if the president would swear to him that he would not plunge the country into war. Roosevelt made that false promise.

On January 19, having made his deal with Roosevelt, Joe went to New York with Rose, who sat close to him, approving, proud, as he delivered a historic broadcast on NBC. He attacked the false statements that had been made about him; he talked of the smear campaign that had branded him. He said that just because he had spoken the truth about his fears of British defeat, he had been attacked. He had never thought that it was his function to report pleasant stories that were not true. He praised the morale of the British nation ("It is as fine a display of human courage as was ever witnessed"). Although he mentioned that the German army and people might have an equally strong morale, a statement that seemed almost too audacious in the context, he added that "the prediction now of England's defeat would be a senseless one."

He dismissed as false and malicious the charge that he advocated a deal with the dictators contrary to British desires. This was subtle; he knew only too well that many in England, from the top to the lowliest, wanted peace. He said that the words of the tyrants had been shown to be worthless; but he repeated his wish that America not be included in a world war.

He reasserted his belief that, by not joining the conflict, America would have time to rearm. He added, "This country is certainly committed to acts sufficiently un-neutral to justify a less despotic tyrant than Hitler in declaring war. . . . It is not surprising that we desire Hitler's defeat. The English are defending a society which respects law, which upholds the dignity of the individual. All of us want very much to see destroyed once and for all the attempt at decivilization of the world in the name of Nazi pagan philosophy. . . ."

Rose happily noted his words. He made an astonishing statement: "Frankly, if I could be assured that America, unprepared as she is now, could, by declaring war on Germany, within the space of, say, a year, end the threat of German domination, I should favor declaring war right now." However, he said, America was not ready. He concluded, "Our friends across the water want more than words. Words will not give them armaments. They will not make us strong. Now we must resolve that our lot must be toil and sweat. Then and only then can we hope to spare ourselves and our children from a dismal destiny of blood and tears."

The gist of the speech, for which he has received no credit

by historians, adhered to the doctrines circulated from the Vatican. They exactly matched Rose's own views. The following week, echoing the statement in his radio address that Hitler had slammed the door of peace to all the world, seeking a New Order where no justice could exist, he appeared before the House Committee on Foreign Affairs on the Lend Lease issue. He talked of his love of the British, which has been so often denied, and which Rose shared. He spoke of a little shop near 1 Grosvenor Square, in the front window of which the owner used to hang a sign during the bombing reading BUSINESS AS USUAL. When his shopfront was blown away after an air raid, the owner hung up another sign, reading OPEN NIGHT AND DAY. Joe's story was greeted by the congressmen with appreciative laughter.

Kennedy boldly and un-neutrally called the Nazis "a force which seeks to destroy the rule of conscience and reason, a force that proclaims its hostility to law, to family life, to religion itself—therefore, we ought to arm to the teeth and get as much help as we can to Britain." He talked of the dangers if Britain should be defeated, how to deal with infiltration into Latin America by Nazi agencies. But he emphasized that sending armed destroyers or battleships to accompany supply ships to the United Kingdom could result in a situation in which the Germans would have the right to sink them and Roosevelt would have no alternative but to declare war.

The results of the Lend Lease discussion, much represented since, were not pleasing to the Kennedys. Roosevelt authorized the armed accompaniment of supply ships and continued waging an undeclared war in the Atlantic. Once legislation had gone through, Roosevelt, having used Kennedy to the limit, dumped him once again. The promise of the ambassadorship to Ireland proved to be false.

Faced with this latest setback, Rose, longing for escape as always, took off on a trip with Eunice. On the drizzly midnight of May 9, 1941, at Canal Street in New York City, they boarded the S.S. *Brazil* of the Moore-McCormick-American Republics Line, bound for Bridgetown, Barbados, and Rio de Janeiro. It was a perilous voyage in time of war. German infiltration into Vichy-controlled Martinique had brought U-boats cruising the Caribbean looking for

British vessels. Although the *Brazil* was of American registry, she was vulnerable; more than one neutral vessel had gone down due to errors by German submarine captains. The voyage was nonetheless nostalgic for Rose, harking back to her adventures on the *Matapan* in May 1913.

On May 12, the *Brazil* docked at Bridgetown. Rose visited an Ursuline convent, impressed by the children and describing them as "angels with dark faces." The shipboard life of costume and mad-hatters' parties, bridge tournaments, shuffleboard deck games, elegant captain's-table dinners and long, leisurely days at sea had always attracted her. Now she was far away from the grating controversies surrounding Joe.

On the twenty-first, the vessel steamed into Rio Harbor. There was an unforgettable sight: the Christus figure on the Corcovado peak, Sugarloaf Mountain, the half-moon spread of Copacabana Beach, the white skyscrapers—all presented a magical picture. The *Brazil* was due to sail for Buenos Aires two days later, but Rose had decided to leave the vessel and linger on in the Brazilian capital for a week.

That night, mother and daughter were guests of Ambassador Jefferson Caffery and his wife for dinner at the embassy; Jack flew in to join the party. Among the guests were the wealthy Harry Crockers, socialite friends from Los Angeles and the papal nuncio. Rose was amused to find another set of the Lenox china dinner service used at the embassy in London—she had taken a set home to Hyannis Port—and the ivory menu cards. A last-minute addition to the party, not on the official guest list, was Oswaldo Aranha, Brazilian Foreign Minister, a supporter of Roosevelt, who on March 15 had pledged his country's cooperation with the U.S. in interhemisphere defense. Rose asked Aranha what would happen in the future in terms of Brazilian foreign policy; he pulled her leg by replying, quite in contradiction of his true declared attitude, that Brazil would be influenced by whichever side won the war. Aranha was committed to the American cause and would not have made such a statement seriously.

Rose and Eunice continued by air to Buenos Aires, where Ambassador Norman Armour received them. Douglas Fairbanks, Jr., pursuing the line of antifascism that had inspired his letter to the president regarding Joe, was there as well. Rose and Eunice stayed at the magnificent Carcanos family ranch, Francisco de Vittoria. The family of the absent ambassador to Vichy, Michael Carcanos and his sisters Stella and Anna Carcanos, entertained them in overpowering luxury. Jack enjoyed chasing the girls. There were rides on the thousands of acres of the property, swims in the pool, eagle shoots and long, glorious evenings of local cuisine and entertainment. Rose and Eunice, preceded by Jack, flew to Valparaiso, Chile, to tea with Ambassador Claude Bowers, who commented favorably in his diary, and thence to Peru, Ecuador and Panama, which was little changed in the twenty-eight years since Rose's last visit. The final stage of the journey was Havana, Cuba, where U.S. minister George Messersmith, never a fan of the Kennedys, did his best to be accommodating. Rose was back at Hyannis Port by June 20, telling Joe of all she had seen.

It was the last summer in which the Kennedys would all be together, and she would remember it with painful yearning when she wrote her memoirs thirty years later. She described the sounds that would never be heard the same way again: the sounds of tennis balls lobbed across a court, bronzed young people shouting, Beethoven clashing with hot swing on rival phonographs, boys and girls driving in and out in automobiles from Rolls-Royces to jalopies.

There were changes in everyone's education. Eunice had completed her two years at Manhattanville College of the Sacred Heart; Kathleen had graduated from Finch and had plans to go into journalism, echoing her mother's early achievements; Patricia had graduated from the Convent of the Sacred Heart at Maplehurst.

On June 24, much to Rose's distress, Joe, Jr., contradicting statements he had made against U.S. involvement in the war, enlisted in the U.S. Naval Reserve, class V-5, as seaman second class at Squantum Naval Air Station. This was a nostalgic echo of the past, recalling the fact that his father had been at Squantum in 1918. Joe, Sr., had arranged the voluntary enlistment by pulling strings in Washington; he was fearful that Joe might have been called up as a gob or an army private.

Hitler invaded Russia on June 22, 1941. The Kennedys

were in a dilemma. They should have been pleased, but now the United States embarked on a policy of Lend Lease to the communist empire. Rose and Joe's mentors, Cardinal O'Connell and Archbishop Spellman, found themselves in rare accord in condemning the program. On September 4, 1941, Spellman specifically attacked Lend Lease to the Soviet Union in calls to Roosevelt and in a letter to Pope Pius XII.

The situation confirmed Joe and Rose's opposition to Roosevelt. They had not forgotten the Communist activities in Boston that had threatened their safety. Nor had they forgotten the Communist-inspired unrest in the rank and file of Bethlehem Steel that had disrupted American armament in World War I, or the Wall Street explosion that had almost cost Joe's life. To complicate the matter further, Italy was at war with the United States, and an anti-Italian attitude was mandatory. The Vatican, though officially neutral, was in the heart of Rome. The situation was rendered worse by the fact that Pius XII had issued an encyclical, "Divini Redemptoris," forbidding all Catholics to associate themselves with Russia.

With so much pressing in on her, Rose symbolically built a retreat from the world at Hyannis Port at the time of her official fifty-first birthday, on July 22. She had always treasured silence and solitude above all things; she must often have longed for the peace of her Dutch nunnery, for all of its many privations. There was a still center in herself, a place where she could find a detached calm of being that had carried her through her husband's humiliation and would later carry her through greater travails than she could have imagined. That peaceful place inside her was threatened now; it could easily be blasted apart.

She had carpenters build her a hut on the beach equipped with a desk and chair, a place for her record cards, a cot to sleep on, and a small closet. She adored it; she was delighted when her family dubbed it her Little White House.

She needed that retreat to deal with Jack's enlistment. Pushed by his father, Jack managed to get, despite his back and stomach, to avoid his becoming a private, a desk job in Washington. After signing up as an ensign in the Naval

Reserve, he would join the Office of Naval Intelligence, preparing memoranda for the Daily Information Section. He would edit one weekly and two daily bulletins.

Rose had another burden to bear. Her daughter Rosemary, currently at the Sacred Heart Convent in Washington, but briefly at Hyannis Port for the summer holidays, had been showing disturbing symptoms. She would be seemingly calm, her old, sweet and generous self, when sometimes, without warning, at dinner, on the beach, or at a party, she would explode into an outbreak of temper. She would shout, strike out at strangers, speak of private matters in a harsh and agonized manner, or leave her bedroom at night to wander the streets in search of men.

Rose, who never allowed discussions of sex to be heard in her household, was appalled when Rosemary began to scream out her frustrations. Rose was terrified her daughter would be the victim of a gigolo or money-grubbing male, or that she would be arrested as a vagrant, with a subsequent, scandalous announcement in the sensation-seeking press.

Rose's worst fear was that Rosemary might become pregnant or be kidnapped for a multimillion-dollar ransom. To put her into an insane asylum, as such institutions were known in those days, might not solve anything, since she could easily escape.

Searching for a solution, conferring with doctors in Boston, New York, Washington and Palm Beach, Joe made a harsh decision. He would have Rosemary lobotomized. She would be operated on, an icepick-like spatula drilling into the frontal lobe of her brain; the result would be a calming and deadening of responses, making the patient a passive, quiescent vegetable-person who would live the rest of her life in a placid daydream, mentally disorganized and unpredictable but not likely to explode into violent rages or to become dangerous to others.

Rose would admit to approving this decision in her 1972 memoirs, and then, almost a decade later, deny it to the authorized family biographer, Doris Kearns Goodwin. But given the provisions of the day, both parents would have had to authorize so drastic a procedure.

The operation was performed by doctors Walter Freeman

and James Watts at George Washington University Hospital in the nation's capital.

It was a disaster. Instead of making Rosemary a placid, subdued woman who could be kept at home, it turned her into a mental and emotional wreck, an infantile shadow of her former self. Never again could she function as anything approaching a normal human being. Over thirty years later, she would be found wandering the streets of Chicago.

Rose and Joe sent Rosemary to Craig House, a hospital for the mentally disturbed situated on the outskirts of Beacon, New York, where she remained behind bars for eight years. So complete was Rose's refusal to accept the reality of Rosemary's effective destruction that she swept the matter out of her mind, didn't tell her children where Rosemary was, apparently told Teddy she was dead and didn't visit her unhappy daughter for almost nine years, when Rosemary was transferred to a special convent home, St. Coletta's, in Jefferson, Wisconsin. This self-protection from reality would mark the rest of her life.

On October 16, Joe, Jr., was transferred to Jacksonville, Florida, for advanced flight training in the Naval Reserve. Kathleen was secretary to the editor of the *Washington Times-Herald;* later, she became reporter, columnist and critic. She had inherited Rose's journalistic ability, and she made a strong impression.

That month, Rose learned from Jack that he was hard at work editing and producing his intelligence bulletins in Washington. Though he was careful to keep this from her, and for a time Kathleen kept it from Rose as well, he was also having an affair with the attractive Inga Arvad, a colleague of Kathleen's, who was under suspicion by J. Edgar Hoover of being a German spy. Arvad was married to the much-admired Hungarian film director Paul Fejos, and had been under investigation for some time. No hard evidence against her was produced, but the fact that Jack, working on intelligence reports, refused to break off the relationship under pressure from his father almost resulted in his being cashiered out of the navy. Joe, Sr., had to work hard on contacts to save him.

On December 7, Rose was staying at the Plaza in New York, taking a break from the effort of packing up everything at Bronxville, preparing to sell the house, which had become too burdensome on top of running the household at Palm Beach. At 2:00 P.M., there was a flash news announcement on the radio, which interrupted all broadcasts: the Japanese had bombed the American fleet and shore installations at Pearl Harbor.

This was a tremendous shock; at once Rose was in touch with her family. Joe was at Palm Beach; Joe, Jr., was at Jacksonville, where the entire staff was put on immediate alert; Kathleen was at lunch in Washington with her boyfriend; Jack was returning from a touch-football game in the same city. Bobby was at Portsmouth Priory, where a sudden blackout was ordered and the classrooms were plunged into darkness.

Joe's reaction was immediate: he had known the Japanese attack would happen. From his correspondence with Clare Boothe Luce, it is clear that for years he had been urging the U.S. government not to get into a backdoor conflict with Japan; he detested the way Roosevelt had handled the Japanese. Instead of securing peace with Japan, as Joe had agreed with the Japanese ambassador in London, Roosevelt had provoked Japan by deliberately and swiftly cutting off the oil supplies without which that nation couldn't function, instead of seeking some compromise through sanctions. Mrs. Wellington Koo, widow of the Chinese ambassador to Washington, told me in 1975 that her husband had advised the president that his Chinese Intelligence intercepts (picking up signals from the free Chinese headquarters in Chungking) reported that the Japanese attack on Pearl Harbor was planned and about to be executed. The president waved the matter away. Later, Mrs. Koo told Kennedy about this at Palm Beach. It was, Joe told her, as he had suspected: Churchill and Roosevelt had deliberately pushed the U.S. into the war. But in order not to affect the war effort, Roosevelt had deliberately chosen not to make his views public.

Rose made no bones in her memoirs about hating the war. She detested it; she dreaded the thought that her older boys might die in it. Like Joe's, her hatred of such global conflicts, stemming from her memories of World War I, drove her beyond reason into despair. When Germany declared war on the United States four days later, her depression was complete. Hitler's decision to make that declaration was based on the very matter Joe had opposed. Roosevelt was fighting an undeclared war in the Atlantic in which German vessels were attacked and sunk, and was supplying an unlimited use of armed convoys for supply vessels to England. The secret and unconstitutional Roosevelt Rainbow Five program for the invasion of Europe was conveniently leaked to the isolationist Senator Burton K. Wheeler, published in the *Chicago Tribune* and the *Washington Times-Herald,* and flown directly to Hitler in Berlin. Hitler included the contents of Rainbow Five in his Declaration of War speech; this was omitted in America by all newspapers and radio broadcasts.

Disgruntled as he was, Joe offered his services to Roosevelt, but this was surely a token gesture, which the president sensibly ignored. Roosevelt lied that he had never received the offer when Joe inquired several months later. Rose had to bear in mind that war was against the policies of the Vatican and Eire, which remained neutral throughout the conflict. The Vatican continued to recognize Japan as well as Germany; it could scarcely not have done so, since in its neutral status it recognized the United States and Britain. Caught up in events beyond her control, Rose could do nothing but put on a cheerful face, attend Mass every day, first in New York and later in Palm Beach, and pray for the safety of her boys and an end to humanity's madness.

Joe, always more emotional than logical, and still unswervingly pacifistic, seemed surprised when the president was unable to find a place for him in any aspect of defense. In view of his undiplomatic statements and refusal to behave himself, he would scarcely have made a suitable ambassador to such sensitive areas as Latin America, despite his opposition to Nazi influence there, or in Australia. When, months later, he wrote to Lord Beaverbrook in London improbably seeking a position in Britain, Beaverbrook replied that nothing could be done. Not only was Churchill furious with Kennedy for not having publicly supported America's involvement in the war, but the British public had turned against him, and the idea of his becoming a British citizen was unthinkable.

Rose had on her hands a husband who was, for all his millions, depressed, restless, and emotionally disturbed. He constantly restated his theme that America would be defeated, invaded and crushed, an impossible scenario since neither the Japanese nor the Germans had the facilities to undertake a joint invasion.

Mindful of Jack and Joe, Jr.,'s naval careers, and under pressure from Rose, Joe remained silent on the defeatist issue for the rest of the war.

At Palm Beach for Christmas, Rose concentrated on raising funds through Catholic organizations to send food and other supplies via Archbishop Spellman and Count Galeazzi, who was in New York and Hyannis, from Rome to the beleaguered Vatican City. The arrangements were concluded by a friend, Harold Tittman, who became U.S. chargé d'affaires in Vatican City, on a safe conduct from Mussolini despite the fact that Italy was at war with the United States.

On March 26, 1942, Rose received from the Pope the Pro Pontifice et Ecclesia Cross for her heroic efforts to relieve the suffering of the papal staff in Rome; Archbishop Spellman hung the symbol of her good work around her neck.

Rose was busy organizing servicemen's parties and USO events; Tallulah Bankhead, stage and screen star and daughter of the Speaker of the House, performed at one of these. Joe kept nibbling away at Washington for any kind of a job, but was bitter when all he was offered was the position of head of Todd Shipyards, of which Rose was still a shareholder. He turned it down at once.

In April, Rose flew to San Francisco to join Eunice, who had followed Jack to Stanford and was studying social science. Rose lived on the campus itself, rather oddly attending her daughter's classes as an observer; girls in their late teens or early twenties were astonished to see a fashionably dressed fifty-one-year-old woman in their midst, attending to every word of the lectures and busily making notes.

Rose was too late in returning to Florida to attend a

ceremony at Jacksonville on May 6, when Joe, Jr., received the honor of having his father pin golden wings on his uniform symbolizing his successful graduation. Joe, Jr., then transferred to a steamy and primitive Banana River base in central Florida for further training. He had not told Rose, for fear of upsetting her, that he had drawn up a will at his young age, leaving his savings to his father.

By now Joe, Sr., had found a way to fill his time: through J. Edgar Hoover, he spread out a spy network in which every detail of his children's activities was tracked. He even used a priest, Father Maurice Sheehy, to keep tabs on Joe, Jr. When it turned out that Joe was seeing a Protestant girl, Rose was seriously upset. But the Kennedys were proud when their eldest son, after only three hundred hours in the air and a rather questionable record at training in PB1 Mariner airplanes, became a full-fledged instructor.

With Spellman's indispensable help, Joe poured his volcanic and frustrated energy into real-estate investment. Since he had formed the Securities and Exchange Commission in 1934, he had been out of the stock market, investing in treasury instruments that yielded him several hundred thousand dollars a year. But now, his long-buried greed resurfaced, and he resumed his earlier passion for speculation.

Spellman had at his beck and call a Bronx-Irish real-estate wizard, John J. Reynolds, a raffish, colorful character who enjoyed pretty girls and betting on the races. Joe found in him a kindred spirit. Joe was impressed by Reynolds's deals for Spellman, some of which doubled the New York archdiocese's monies. As a reward, the archbishop had given Reynolds a grace-and-favor house in which he lived free of charge close to the old Kennedy home in Riverdale.

The Kennedys spent much of the summer in New York. Despite wartime conditions, Manhattan was an exciting place. The streets were full of men in uniform, looking handsome, healthy and optimistic. The city glittered with a feverish, electric excitement it seldom had before or since. The Kennedys relished evenings at El Morocco, at the Stork Club and at their friend and protegé Henri Soulé's exquisite Le Pavillon, which richly rewarded their investment. There were dances on the St. Regis's roof, parties at the Waldorf, where Joe stayed, and the Plaza, which Rose preferred. Joe was busy buying apartment buildings; several of them proved to be excellent long-term investments, especially since Kennedy didn't hesitate to double rents, gouging the tenants brutally. The panic of war, with talk of U-boats sailing up the Hudson, resulted in real-estate values crashing. Through Reynolds, Joe was able to make an extraordinary deal in the final sale of the Bronxville house, which was swapped for a large office complex in White Plains, New York, plus land and cash. Joe bought all the property in Rose's name.

Within a year, Joe had snapped up buildings in Albany, New York, previously undeveloped parts of Florida and even as far afield as São Paolo, Brazil. He still owned Columbia Trust Company in Boston, the Maine–New Hampshire theater chain, and the Palm Beach and Hyannis Port houses. Rose was relieved to find him improved by the excitement of this new form of investment. His money doubled and tripled, bringing his fortune to well over $100 million by 1943.

As against this improvement in her husband's spirits, Rose was weighed down by Jack's health problems. A fusion of the right sacroiliac joint caused him excruciating pain and caused him to check into Charleston's Naval Hospital, where it was feared he might have to undergo a major operation. He had been transferred to Charleston because of continuing unease on the part of the authorities over his ongoing relationship with Inga Arvad.

Finally, after numerous X rays, it was found that he could be treated without undergoing surgery. Rose clashed with him at the time because he wanted to conduct an ecumenical Bible class for the staff of the Sixth Naval District; she insisted he stick to the letter of Catholic doctrine and not encourage any Protestant elements in teaching. Shaken in his belief in the precise elements of Roman instruction, he disobeyed her. In July, he was transferred to Abbott Hall, Northwestern University, Chicago, for training in the U.S. Naval Reserve midshipman school.

By contrast, Rose was pleased to hear from Joe, Jr., that, at Banana River, he remained devoted to his religious studies in his spare time, and that he prayed night and morning, sometimes getting on his knees in front of his fellow ensigns. He refused to smoke, drink, use bad language or seek out prostitutes. Luckily, his athletic good looks and immense charm protected him from ribbing or hazing.

Rose did have trouble with Kathleen, who was also beginning to be shaken in her religious beliefs, surrounded as she was by the cynical atmosphere of a newsroom. And Bobby was devout, but he was weak at his studies, lazy at athletics, and generally showed no strength of ambition. In September, Rose pulled him out of Portsmouth Priory with Joe's reluctant approval, and then, with a lack of logic that now equaled her husband's, sent him not to a Catholic school but to the formidably Protestant Milton Academy, where his grades were so disastrous that when he managed to pass a mathematics test his teacher compared it to a victory over the German army in Egypt.

That same month, Rose was in Boston, staying with her parents and backing her father, who, still inexhaustible at seventy-nine, was running for the Democratic nomination for U.S. Senator in the Massachusetts state primary. Honey Fitz was up against Republican congressman Joseph E. Casey and his old enemy Daniel H. Coakley. Joe, who could never accustom himself to Honey Fitz, supplied a mere $1,000 to the old man's campaign; Rose provided more. Fitzgerald stumped with amazing vigor, singing the inescapable "Sweet Adeline" wherever he went. He managed to secure an astonishing 80,456 votes, but Casey defeated him with 108,251, beating him even in his own Suffolk County. But even though he was defeated, Honey Fitz hugely enjoyed the experience, and Rose did too.

That same month, Joe's friend Senator Jim Byrnes offered him a decent job at last: head of the Office of Civilian Supply, which was fighting a prolonged battle through dollar-a-year men to obtain sufficient goods for use in the war effort. Joe made a serious mistake in temperamentally turning down the appointment; if he had made a success of it, he might have defeated the public view that he was a traitor and he could have influenced the president to clear the path for a more important assignment.

Rose would have been happier if he had been granted the

role of ambassador to the Vatican. It would have been the perfect appointment for him, had Roosevelt trusted him. After all, he and Rose had laid the groundwork for diplomatic relations with the Holy See in 1939. Instead, the Kennedys' friend Myron Taylor was accorded the honor; with the usual and surprising safe-conduct pass from the Italian government, Taylor arrived in Rome on September 17, offering Roosevelt's pledge to support the Pope to the limit, a message endorsed by Archbishop Spellman.

On September 23, Rose had Bobby admitted to Milton; on October 1, Jack was at Portsmouth, Rhode Island, where he reported to Motortorpedo Boat Squadron Training Center for PT boat training. He became a lieutenant, junior grade, completing his course on December 3.

The family gathered at Palm Beach for the Yuletide season. Then Jack followed Joe to Jacksonville, sailing his PT vessel from Rhode Island to that base on January 8, 1943. Joe, Jr., was assigned to San Juan, Puerto Rico, on navy airplane duty. Jack wanted to get into active service, so his father pulled a string with Massachusetts Senator David I. Walsh, head of Navy Procurements, and had Jack ordered to the Solomon Islands. Rose hated this decision, but there was nothing she could do. On February 9, Jack set sail aboard the U.S.S. *Rochambeau.*

Joe, Jr., wrote to Rose, describing the tough work of acting as patrol-plane commander off San Juan. He was an arrogant, driving perfectionist, and began to loosen up his moral standards, gambling in the local casinos, dating attractive Puerto Rican women. Fortunately, Joe, Sr., was able to keep such questionable activities from Rose.

In April, Jack was at his Solomons base, training hard, putting up with land crabs, spiders and sweltering heat. He sent Rose pictures, which she fretted over because he seemed thinner than ever; but he looked handsome in his tropical whites. He described to her a life in tents without hot water to shave or bathe in, and sudden dangerous encounters with Japanese. He had found time to read a book, which he recommended to her: Alice L. Moats's *Blind Date with Mars,* a critique of the Soviet Union with which he knew she would agree.

Now Rose was faced with a religious problem on her own

doorstep. Kathleen, who had continued to do well at the *Times-Herald,* had never stopped pining for her beloved Billy Hartington. Against Rose's every objection, she wanted to return to London to be with him. The summer of 1943, Kathleen got wind of Red Cross work being done in Virginia on behalf of Great Britain. She heard that many young American women were working in England in canteens and USO entertainment centers. She decided to join the Red Cross and arranged for a transfer to London immediately.

Kathleen signed up for duty on April 6, and underwent training both in Richmond, Virginia, and as a waitress at the Soldier and Sailor Canteen in Washington. On June 25, she set sail on the *Queen Mary,* which had been converted into a troopship. She wrote her mother during the voyage, saying that she had managed to attend Mass, which was held, of all things, in the synagogue.

Rose had to endure a succession of letters from Kathleen, describing her daily bicycle ride to work at the Hans Crescent Officers' Club in London. Rose got wind of Billy meeting Kathleen secretly at a trysting place, a friend's house in Yorkshire, and of Kathleen's continuing intention to get married.

The duke and duchess of Devonshire were as distressed as Rose; they remained adamantly anti-Catholic, and the duke was still head of the British Freemasons. The religious issues of the prospective match were thrashed out constantly in telephone calls, telegrams and letters. If Kathleen were converted to the High Church of England, she would, according to Rose's beliefs, be condemned to purgatory.

As it happened, Rose was mistaken. Accepting the common fallacy, she had misunderstood the Church's teachings in the matter. In believing that her daughter would be punished in the fires of purgatory, deprived of the bliss of the presence of God, and made to burn until the day of judgment, she followed the misguided common piety that was not based in actual dogma. To state that a Catholic who worshiped in the Protestant faith would be denied salvation was so drastically heretical that she could have been excommunicated for it, a punishment accorded to more than one prominent priest.

The Church never denied salvation to anyone who accepted Christ, even if that person embraced another system of faith. What Rose was right about was that marriage outside the Church would result in excommunication, a denial of the attendance of the Eucharist: the official sacrifice of the Mass.

The Devonshires believed that Billy would be similarly condemned if he converted to Catholicism. If the children were raised as Protestants, Rose was certain they also would suffer the torments of their parents. Their fate would be identical in the eyes of the duke and duchess should they be brought up as Catholics. Joe had long since abandoned adherence to doctrine, and was concerned only with his daughter's happiness. The same was true of Joe, Jr., and even Archbishop Spellman seemed not to take the issue very seriously. Rose was in a state of nerves over the whole matter.

Then something happened that made her feel even more strained. On August 19, 1943, she was listening to the radio at Hyannis Port; Joe was off having a horseback ride at Osterville. The announcer said that Jack had been rescued, after having been thought dead in action, during a PT boat expedition against the Japanese in the Solomons. She sat stunned as the announcer said that he was injured, that his craft had been sunk, cut in half by an enemy destroyer, and that he had rescued men from burning and drowning. She had heard nothing of Jack's danger before this; no word had reached her from the Department of the Navy. In view of her husband's continuing influence with Secretary of the Navy James Forrestal, how could this be?

She was unable to reach Joe at the riding stable. But, minutes later, he called her from a public telephone. He had heard the news while driving home, and had run off the road in his excitement. He said he would tell her more later.

When he reached the house, he astonished her by saying that he had heard several days before that Jack was missing, but he hadn't told her, knowing of her mental state over Kathleen, and not wanting to worry her until he received definite word as to whether Jack was alive or dead. She was relieved, but concerned that Jack had been badly battered by the experience. He had lost even more weight, and was laid up in bad shape for weeks, but he was honored with a Navy Cross, and promotion to full lieutenant, for his heroism.

At the beginning of September, Joe, Jr., was at Hyannis Port, on his way to a post in England, for his father's fifty-fifth birthday celebration. At the party on the evening of September 6, the family friend Judge Joseph F. Timilty, former Boston police commissioner, gave a toast not only to Joe but to "our own hero, Lieutenant John F. Kennedy of the U.S. Navy." Although Joe, Jr., looked pleased at the toast, he was, in fact, angry and upset. He was jealous of his brother because he himself had not yet been in action against the enemy, and, to Timilty's astonishment, he burst into tears in his bedroom that night, exclaiming, "By God, I'll show them!" He flew off to England immediately afterward, to keep an eye on Kathleen and to serve in the First Naval Squadron with the British Coastal Command.

He wrote to Rose frequently, reporting on Kathleen's activities and her dating of Billy Hartington whenever the young man came to London. Much to Rose's annoyance, her old friend Marie Bruce seemed to encourage the relationship; and, to add to her burdens, Joe had a romantic interest in a Protestant married woman, Patricia Wilson, former countess of Jersey. When Billy moved with the Coldstream Guards regiment at Alton Barracks, near London, Rose's anxiety increased. Kathleen made several visits to the Devonshire family estate, Compton Place, near Eastbourne.

A much-needed distraction came that month. A friend of Rose and Joe's, the British playwright Frederick Lonsdale, had written a comedy of manners with which they identified, *Another Love Story,* about a father desperately trying to break off his daughter's romance. Joe decided to back it financially for production in New York. He was able to lure the charming character actor Roland Young from Hollywood to take the starring role, and the popular actress Margaret Lindsay would make her first appearance on the legitimate stage opposite him. The Kennedys spent much time in New York and out of town attending rehearsals and enjoying the company of the Lonsdales. Lonsdale sported a flowing white Aristide Bruand scarf and white kid gloves on most occasions.

On October 12 they were at the first night at the Fulton Theater in New York. The long run of the famous farce *Arsenic and Old Lace* had ended, leaving the beautiful theater vacant. Lonsdale himself directed; Louis Lotito produced.

The Kennedys were shocked by the reviews: one critic said, "Bring a pillow," and another said the performance consisted of actors standing around delivering lines they had apparently heard in a Frederick Lonsdale play. The production, ably acted by the principals, ran a surprising 104 performances, not closing until January 1944, but still losing most of Joe's investment.

In November, the Kathleen-Hartington crisis deepened. Would it be possible to have the marriage sanctioned by both churches? Spellman contacted Count Enrico Galeazzi and Pope Pius XII in Rome. The reply was negative. It was not a good time for such a matter to be considered. United States Air Force bombers were attacking the Holy City, and relations between the Church and the White House were strained past the limits.

Spellman was upset that Roosevelt would not discontinue the air attacks. When the papal summer residence, Castel Gandolfo, was bombed, despite the fact that it was on protected neutral territory, the protests from the Kennedys and from all American Catholics were deafening. Spellman even appeared at Mass at St. Patrick's Cathedral on February 22, 1944, denouncing the president outright on the matter. A joint war waged with the Soviet Union as ally, bombs on the sacred edifices of Rome—this was all Joe and Rose had dreaded might come about.

Bobby was in the Naval Reserve in emulation of his brothers.

One consolation of those early months of 1944 was that Jack came home from the Pacific. An escort aircraft carrier, the U.S.S. *Breton,* brought him from the Solomon Islands via Tahiti and the Society Islands to Honolulu and San Francisco, and he arrived on January 7. Cool as always about arrivals and departures, neither Rose nor Joe, though advised by the navy of his arrival date, flew to greet him.

Nor did he rush to Palm Beach to be with them. Instead, he flew to Los Angeles to be with his old flame Inga Arvad, and then, suddenly, his health fell apart again. He flew to the Mayo Clinic for a prolonged checkup, and thence to Boston for Honey Fitz's eighty-first birthday, which Rose, amazingly, didn't attend. Jack didn't arrive at Palm Beach until the sixteenth.

Playing golf that day, Rose didn't bother to pick him up; Joe was out of town. She was shocked by her son's thinness, and did her best to feed him up, without success. She was far more concerned with Kathleen than with him or any of her other children. On January 23, Marie Bruce wrote to her, annoying her greatly by praising Billy Hartington warmly and mentioning his fine record in the Coldstream Guards. She rashly said that if Rose could only meet the young man and see how well matched he was to Kathleen, she would approve. This well-meaning but naive letter drove Rose almost mad with annoyance. She was furious with Marie for even suggesting that she might come to London, and she blamed her old friend and traveling companion as being part of a wicked conspiracy. She didn't even bother to reply, an unheard-of lapse of courtesy for her.

Then, on March 4, Rose heard from Kathleen directly. The embattled young woman was sad, miserable at her mother's attitude, but unchanged in her romantic feelings. Joe pulled a string and had Joe, Jr., transferred briefly on special leave to London from his billet in the west of England to see Kathleen and try to improve the situation. Joe, Jr., went to see both the prominent author and divine Father d'Arcy and the bishop of London to seek an ecumenical marriage, but the venture was unsuccessful.

Back in Palm Beach, Joe wrote to Kathleen on March 8, overriding his wife and telling his daughter that he was rooting for her. Even Cardinal Spellman, who regarded the matter as less significant than Rose did, took Kathleen's part.

On April 28, Rose suffered another blow. Her beloved mentor and friend of many years, Cardinal O'Connell, died of pneumonia and a cerebral hemorrhage in Boston. She rushed to the funeral and the Requiem Mass, attended by

2,500 grief-stricken worshipers, at Holy Cross Cathedral. O'Connell was buried in a crypt under the same chapel in which Rose and Joe had been married. The cardinal was replaced by Archbishop Richard Cushing, still a close Kennedy family friend.

In a state of acute grief, Rose had scarcely returned from Boston when she received the equivalent of a death blow. On May 1, Kathleen announced her engagement to Billy Hartington.

Rose was heartbroken, horrified. She telegraphed Kathleen insisting that she sacrifice her personal happiness for the grace of God. She clashed with her husband, and also with Joe, Jr., both of whom rejected Rose's old-fashioned dogma.

So desperate was Rose that she returned to Boston and checked in to the New England Baptist Hospital. It seems incredible that, in the circumstances, she should have selected a Protestant institution. In a fever pitch of rage and disappointment, she hid in the hospital, feigning illness to avoid the press, taking no calls except from immediate family, barely able to speak to anyone.

She left the hospital on May 6, then flew to Washington with Joseph Timilty. The same day, Kathleen was married, with Joe, Jr., in attendance, to the Marquess of Hartington in a ten-minute ceremony at the Chelsea Registry Office in London. The Devonshires had relented, reconsidered dogma in the matter, and no longer feared problems. They had warmed to Kathleen, and then provided a lavish reception. Rose was appalled to learn that Marie Bruce was there, and indeed had supplied Kathleen with something borrowed and something blue. Could she forgive Marie?

Kathleen took Rose's hospitalization seriously and wrote to her, in anguish, worrying that she had caused her mother a serious illness. She assured Rose that her children would be raised Roman Catholics, even though the Devonshires had given her no such assurance, and Billy had made clear in a letter to Rose that no such arrangement would be possible. Pressured by her husband into making some meaningless gesture, and threatened by a lashing from the press, Rose pretended she would be shopping for a trousseau (at this late stage) for Kathleen in New York. But there is no record of her doing anything in that direction.

She fretted through the rest of May. She had distractions: on the twenty-second, Honey Fitz, who had made another bold bid at the Democratic nomination for the Senate, finally withdrew; on the twenty-seventh, Bobby graduated from Milton Academy; and on the thirty-first, Jack was admitted to the U.S. Naval Hospital at Chelsea, Massachusetts, with more back and stomach problems.

On June 6, U.S. and British forces invaded German-occupied Europe. The Kennedys were indifferent at best; they remained unregenerately disgusted by the war, just as they had been in 1917 and 1918. It had wrecked Jack's health; it had put Joe at risk in various expeditions by air; it had taken Kathleen to England for the Red Cross.

They were pleased when Jack received both navy and marine-corps medals and a scroll citation in his hospital room at Chelsea on June 12, but neither parent was present for the ceremony nor made more than token remarks of pleasure to the press.

In July, Rose found another distraction: she supported Joe in his efforts to unseat the liberal Henry Wallace for the vice-presidential nomination that would return him to high office; she supported her husband in wanting their friend Judge William O. Douglas to occupy the position. Since the president was ailing and might not live out a fourth term, a prospect that scarcely upset them, Rose and Joe could see a dream fulfilled in having Douglas in the White House. Such an eventuality would clear the path for Joe, Jr.,'s future role as supreme executive.

Leaving Rose at Hyannis Port, Joe was at the Democratic Convention in Chicago on July 19, pushing hard for Douglas. Roosevelt played his usual devious game. Betraying his own vice-president, he excluded Wallace from the official presidential letter in which he named the potential candidates for the vice-presidency. That letter included Harry S Truman and William O. Douglas as being acceptable to him. But then, keeping a finger on the pulse of the delegates, he announced that he had never wanted Douglas, and as a result Truman won. This was a disaster for the Kennedys. Truman regarded Joe as a crook, believing the stories of his stock manipulations in the 1920s, and he was determined that neither he nor his sons would have a chance in this or any future Democratic administration.

Nineteen forty-four could be regarded as the worst year to date of Rose's life, a constant piling up of dust and ashes. She was at Hyannis on Sunday, August 13, just three weeks after a gloomy fifty-fourth birthday. She attended Mass at St. Francis Xavier's as usual that morning, then returned for a light lunch with her husband. As Joe went upstairs for a nap, she picked up a pile of Sunday papers brought in from New York and Boston and began reading them.

At the beach outside, Eunice, who was now studying at Rose's old alma mater of Manhattanville, was playing touch football with Jack, who was just out of the hospital, and Pat, Jean, Bobby and Teddy. Soon, they would take off on their boat for a quick spin up the coast. Their laughter and conversation floated up to the house.

There was a knock on the door. Sunday was the maids' day off, so Rose opened it herself. Two priests were standing there. There was nothing remarkable about that; they often turned up on Sundays, usually in pairs, asking for alms or offering prayers. One of the priests introduced himself as Father Francis O'Leary, an associate of the late Cardinal O'Connell from the Boston diocesan staff. The name of his companion has been lost to history. O'Leary said that he had flown by amphibian to a nearby flying boat base, and that he could only stay a short time, as he was scheduled for duty as ministering priest aboard the U.S.S. *Brooklyn* in the Pacific.

Hesitatingly, with intense sympathy, O'Leary told Rose that Joe, Jr., was dead.

It was what she had dreaded all along. This war in which she had never believed, and in which, she was certain, Roosevelt had improperly pitched her nation and her beloved family, had cost her the life of her most beloved, had destroyed a magnificent athlete and a fine thinker at the height of his youth and physical beauty—the fulfillment of all her dreams as wife and mother, the future president of the United States.

The priest knew few of the details, but managed to

explain that Joe had been blown to pieces while flying on a secret mission to continental Europe. Shattered, but, as always, showing a royal degree of calm and control, Rose walked upstairs to break the news to Joe. She woke him, told him what she knew, and urged him to take hold of himself. Given his nature, so unlike her own, there was no chance of his remaining calm. He exploded with rage, grief and anger. He would never forgive the president, calling him, from then on, "that son-of-a-bitch cripple who killed my son." Forgetting that it was he himself who had engineered Joe's entrance into active service, he was transferring his guilt to Roosevelt, who had known nothing about the appointment at the time.

Still in command of herself, Rose walked out to the beach and told her children. They were in agony, but she advised them to proceed with their boat trip. They were Kennedys; they did.

Jack refused to join them. He took off on a long walk along the beach, alone with the sea breeze, too devastated to speak.

It was not until Father O'Leary and his companion had left and all except Jack among her offspring had sailed off on the boat that Rose finally let go, locked her bedroom door and cried until there were no more tears. That night, and for many nights afterward, she tossed and turned, unable to sleep, seeing her son's body blasted to pieces with nothing left. She would not be able to attend a burial. There was nothing of him to see at a wake, not even a finger to hang on to. He had vanished without a trace.

It would be just over a year before she learned the facts: he and his fellow crewmen had set the fuse on high explosives; they were to bail out at a certain moment. The plane, in essence a guided missile, would find its target, a German rocket base. But someone had miscalculated, and the bombs had burst open too early.

Kathleen, on a special transport plane arranged by Joe, arrived via Boston at Hyannis Port soon afterward. Rose was still so angry with her that even in this extremity of grief she could not embrace or kiss her renegade daughter and refused even to talk to her. She wouldn't look at the touching mementoes of Joe, Jr., that Kathleen had brought:

the photographs and notes from his Protestant girlfriend Pat.

Later, a letter arrived from Joe, Jr., mailed just before his death and saying that his mission offered no special dangers. Rose read the letter in anguish; Joe collapsed in such a torment of grief and fury that he could not be consoled. He locked himself in his room for days, barely eating the meals left outside on a tray, trying to drown his sorrow by playing records of Toscanini conducting his beloved Beethoven symphonies. He would see nothing of the Fitzgeralds, who arrived to give whatever consolation they could.

Finally, Rose relented sufficiently to suggest to Kathleen that she come to Mass. But there was no warmth or tenderness in her voice.

Chapter 12

An Heretical Daughter

On September 13, 1944, Rose and Joe pulled themselves together and decided to have a change of scene. They would travel to New York to try to relax and catch up with the theater. As always, Rose would stay at the Plaza, which was quiet, and where she enjoyed the views of Central Park, while Joe would occupy the neighboring suite to ex-President Herbert Hoover at the noisier Waldorf Towers. As they began to pack for the long drive, a hurricane alert came over the radio. A 140-mile wind was moving northwest from Puerto Rico, headed directly for Cape Cod.

An advance gale announced the impending disaster. The wind swept across Hyannis Port, blowing down telephone poles, whipping trees in the garden and, to Rose's horror, sending her Little White House hurtling out into the sea.

In a matter of hours, all roads, railroads and airports would be rendered useless. There was no time to waste. The family piled into automobiles and drove helter-skelter to Manhattan. By that night, the wind was tearing through the streets outside the Plaza, bringing down power lines and causing the hotel to plunge into darkness.

By midday on the fourteenth, the crackling radio told the hotel guests that thirteen New Yorkers were dead and seventy-nine injured. Outside her window, Rose could see hundreds of Central Park trees completely flattened.

Then, on the sixteenth, with the storm slightly abated, Joe called Rose to tell her that a telegram had arrived at the Waldorf, announcing the news that Billy Hartington had been killed in action during a Guards' attack on a German-occupied farmhouse. Eunice had to make her way through tempest and rain to Bonwit Teller's, where Kathleen was shopping, to tell her the news.

Hating the marriage from the beginning, Rose can only have felt a sense of relief that Kathleen might return to the Mother Church and save her children from purgatory by raising them as Catholics. She told Kathleen that she must defy the Protestant religion, and that it would be appropriate and acceptable for her to attend Mass in New York to pray for Billy's soul.

There is no calculating her response when Kathleen told her she would go to a Protestant church instead. When the storm blew out, Rose was absent from the family dinner at the restaurant Le Boisson; she was not at the airport to see Kathleen off to England for the memorial service; nor did she send flowers. Kathleen inherited nothing of her husband's substantial fortune; British law cut her out of the estate because she was a woman. Knowing how her mother felt, she stayed on in England. Recovering from her grief in November, she resumed her work with the Red Cross.

Back at Hyannis Port, Rose built a new Little White House on a higher elevation; Joe began buying real estate at values depressed by the storm. Damage to the main house was not extensive and was easily fixed.

To add to Rose's travails, Jack spent part of the fall in Chelsea Naval Hospital for more treatments.

Her spirits were not improved when Bobby entered the Navy V-12 unit at Bates College. Fortunately, the studies would keep him ashore and out of wartime action. Bobby was admitted to Harvard as a freshman on November 6, one day before Roosevelt was elected for a fourth term. The same day, Honey Fitz was elected to the Massachusetts Democratic Electoral College.

The family was busy working out its continuing grief in preparing, that fall, a commemorative volume, *As We*

Remember Joe, a tribute to a lost hero contributed to by many friends, who recalled his charm, his vigorous personality, his intelligence. It was a project at once elevating and painful. Jack was the chief compiler. It is possible that Rose could not face the pain of writing about her dead son, because she was absent from the book's pages. Throughout the winter, Jack, though still busy with the editing, was in and out of the Lahey Clinic in Boston with chronic gastritis and colitis, in pain much of the time; he took off to Camelback Inn, Castle Hot Springs, Arizona, for a rest, but he didn't recover strongly.

On February 2, 1945, in agony from a severe attack of rheumatoid arthritis, Honey Fitz was rushed to St. Margaret's Hospital in Boston. He was released after a few days, but he had to face pain for the rest of his life. One piece of good news in March was that the navy, after much lobbying by Joe, commissioned a destroyer to be named the *Joseph P. Kennedy, Jr.* As the ultimate touch of nostalgia, the vessel would be built at Joe's old bailiwick, the Fore River Shipyard.

At that time, Rose formed two friendships that would be the strongest in her life. The first was with the remarkable Mary Lasker. Attractive, strongly determined, and seemingly bland, Mary Lasker looked out at the world from china-doll blue eyes, her pink cheeks shining with health, her optimism persistent and all-conquering. A Wisconsin-born Protestant Radcliffean, formerly married to the New York art dealer Paul Reinhardt, she had wed the advertising sultan Albert Lasker in 1940, queening it over Manhattan society at her luxurious house at 29 Beekman Place.

It is significant that neither she nor her husband accepted the views that Joe and Rose were pro-Nazi appeasers; their circle was almost exclusively Jewish, and they had attacked Hitler, America First and opponents of Lend Lease, at the beginning of the war in Europe. Lasker withdrew his advertising clients from *The Saturday Evening Post* when the magazine published "The Case Against the Jew" in 1942. Mrs. Lasker traveled often with Rose and enlisted Rose's help in supporting the Lasker Medical Foundation. At Lasker's home, Rose and Joe socialized with such prominent Jewish figures as Anna Rosenberg, Andre Meyer

and David Sarnoff at parties in sumptuous rooms decorated
with Renoirs, Van Goghs and Cézannes.

If Mary Lasker was Rose's best friend in Manhattan,
Mary Sanford was her best friend in Palm Beach. Since she
had left her stage and screen career in the early 1930s, the
beautiful former Mary Duncan and her husband, the polo-
playing carpet heir Laddie Sanford, were the unchallenged
king and queen of the resort.

Rose was often at parties at Mary Sanford's Venetian
palace, Las Incas; more than 100 at a time would enjoy the
Sanfords' fabled dinners, served off gold plates to the
sounds of a sixteen-piece orchestra and easily outmatching
Mrs. Marjorie Merriweather Post's square-dance evenings
at Mar-A-Lago. Rose joined Mary at afternoon affairs at
which, around the Olympic-sized pool, the duke and duchess of Windsor (Rose overcame her initial distaste and grew
friendly with the duchess), Fred Astaire and Charlie Chap-
lin browned their limbs. The highlight of the Palm Beach
social season was Mrs. Lasker's annual Polo Ball. Rose
almost never missed it.

For Rose, coming to Las Incas was always an experience;
it would have been a nightmare for a conservationist. She
would walk up the long gravel pathway flanked by bronze
greyhounds; as the butler opened the door, the animal motif
continued. A Bengal tiger-skin rug greeted her, its fangs
bared; stuffed snakes, fish, jungle birds and alligators,
further trophies of the intrepid Mary and Laddie's countless hunting expeditions, stared alarmingly from every
corner. The bar had stuffed elephants feet supporting tables,
and a hammock was a strung leopard skin.

From jungle to ocean; now Rose walked into the Shell
Room. Thousands of seashells decorated the arched en-
trances, the walls, the doors; the chairs were festooned with
coral. The Sanfords entertained there, along with Rose, the
other neighbors, the Robert Youngs and the Wellington
Koos. As Rose did with Joe, Mary ignored the handsome
Laddie's occasional outside affairs with the laughing expression "Boys will be boys."

Mary helped break the taboo against Catholics in Palm
Beach, thus reversing the Sanford tradition: Laddie's father

had banned grocery tycoon James Butler from the New York Athletic Club because he was a "Roman."

Rose found Mary Sanford a warm, loving and informative companion always.

As the war in the Pacific threatened to go on forever, with further losses of American life, Joe began to lobby for a negotiated peace. The Vatican played a crucial role in such negotiations, another reason for his involvement and (we can safely presume) Rose's approval.

Colonel Donovan of the OSS (later CIA) had meetings with Pope Pius XII on the intelligence aspects of this and on the liberation of Rome from 1944; the OSS had had the connection from Pearl Harbor on. It was a relationship that would continue when the CIA was formed, and that would, within a few years, involve Joe himself. Since the Vatican recognized Japan, this gave the OSS a unique link to Tokyo, and the terms of such a negotiated peace, supported by many Catholics as well as Joe, were made clear. Even secret meetings of Emperor Hirohito to discuss the matter were leaked to Washington, obtained from a spy whose code name was Vessel; then it turned out that Vessel was a quadruple agent and most of the information sent to Washington was false. However, the Vatican-Japan-OSS link was genuine, as later events in the Kennedy saga proved.

In the second week of September, Rose and Joe's friend Count Enrico Galeazzi arrived in Washington from Rome, with a safe-conduct pass supplied by Marshal Piero Badoglio. Mussolini had fallen from power. Galeazzi visited the Kennedys at Hyannis Port; they backed him firmly in his pleas to Roosevelt to stop the bombing of Rome. He reported to them in the presence of James Roosevelt that the Germans had a stranglehold on the city, and a great danger was that the Communists might at once remove them and threaten the Vatican's power. Galeazzi was still in America when most of Italy surrendered to the Allies and Germany occupied Rome.

Soon afterward, to Rose's, Joe's and Galeazzi's horror, the Allies bombed part of the Vatican and the Pope's summer residence of Castel Gandolfo. For almost twenty years, Joe fought, with Rose at his side, to obtain reparations for the bombing, corresponding with Galeazzi in Rome during the protracted process.

Two of Rose's children were involved in romances that spring. Joe and Rose vetoed a potential affair between Jean and Paul ("Red") Fay, one of Jack's PT-boat associates, but they could not find fault with Bobby's new interest, the antic, angular Ethel Skakel.

Ethel had been born in 1928, the daughter of a former railroad clerk who had gotten rich in the carbon business. His Great Lakes Coke and Coal Company flourished in the Depression. Ethel was raised Catholic, even though her father was a Protestant. Three of her brothers had been at Canterbury, the school from which Rose had withdrawn Jack, and one of them, George, had been at Portsmouth Priory at the same time as Bobby.

The Skakels were wealthy—almost as wealthy as the Kennedys. From the mid-1930s, they had occupied Rambleside, an imposing house on Lake Avenue in Greenwich, Connecticut, decorated by the celebrated Elsie de Wolfe, who had worked on the Kennedy house at Brookline. The Rambleside garden, which it took scores of gardeners to work on, included a 150-foot ornamental pool, a 75-foot swimming pool, and a fabled collection of sixty thousand irises, Ethel's favorite flower. Like the Kennedys, strangers in a WASP nest, the Skakels were snubbed and excluded from the Social Register.

The dominant presence of the family was not Ethel's hardworking father, but her overpowering mother, known as Big Ann. She was two hundred pounds in weight and almost six feet tall. Her inquisitive eyes peered out from heavy circles of blue makeup; her voice was loud and commanding. A lavish party-giver, she was devout, cramming her seventy-foot library with its black marble fireplace with hundreds of books on every aspect of Catholicism. She partly owned the Guild Book Shop in New York, which supplied religious works to families like the Kennedys.

It took a while for Rose to adjust to Ethel, who, even by Kennedy standards, was hyperactive. In direct contrast to her mother, who ate enormous amounts of food and barely moved, Ethel and her brothers spent much of their time running instead of walking, gabbing instead of talking, and indulging in a variety of madcap activities including swinging from trees, yodeling, chasing a menagerie of fifteen dogs around their house, squirting soda water at each other, firing darts at mahogany panels, driving cars at reckless speeds, wrecking the bathroom and screaming at the tops of their voices.

Ethel was athletically built, flat-chested and overpoweringly spirited. Her clan enjoyed shooting up mailboxes and streetlamps, taking potshots at rabbits or chickens in the family farmyard or tossing glasses at mirrors in expensive hotel bars. Ethel met Bobby through her sister Pat, in whom Bobby was far more interested. When Pat broke with Bobby because he was too young and gauche for her, Ethel took up the slack.

Rose enjoyed her vitality, and the odd contradiction of her devoutness and reckless behavior. The fact that Ethel attended Mass and that her mother had been secretary to the Trappist monk and author Thomas Merton, whose bestseller *The Seven Storey Mountain* was a favorite book of hers, influenced Rose strongly in the young woman's favor.

On March 13, 1945, and simultaneously with Eddie Moore and others involved in Vatican affairs, Joe was given the supreme Catholic honor of being made a Knight of Malta; Rose would later be given the equivalent honor of papal countess. Only ten thousand strong even today, the Sovereign Military Order, composed of wealthy Catholics with strong political, diplomatic and financial ties to the Holy See, founded in the tenth century, constituted the most exclusive private club in the world. Its immensely rich and powerful members, the bane of the left wing everywhere, were protected from arrest by all countries, traveled duty free and on diplomatic passports, and used diplomatic bags free of search or seizure. They could reach any head of state in the non-Communist world merely by reciting the details of their membership; the Pope would come on the telephone at once.

The Knights had very strong intelligence connections: James Jesus Angleton, head of the OSS station in Rome, joined soon after Joe and would play, with Joe, a crucial role in the funding of the Christian Democratic Party in Italy in opposition to Communists and Socialists. When Reinhard Gehlen, former Nazi leader, was enlisted by the CIA against Russia, he too was made a member. The Knights siphoned money to all Latin American anti-Communist states, including El Salvador, Guatemala and Honduras. Its members supported to the hilt the CIA operations in Europe and were a cover for them. Once again, as in 1938 to 1940, while opposing interference with the possessive actions of an enemy power (this time Russia), Joe was, as against Germany, helping to provide intelligence against it.

As We Remember Joe was published in April 1945. Amazingly, Joe, Sr., had suppressed his hatred of Harold Laski to have Jack seek a contribution from the noted socialist, who provided a glowing tribute. An especially sweet article was cowritten by the devoted Eddie and Mary Moore. Joseph Timilty and the ever-loyal Arthur Krock wrote movingly and well of their old friend.

The day the book was published, the marines landed on Okinawa, but it was far from certain even now that America would win the war in the Pacific.

The next day, Franklin D. Roosevelt died at Warm Springs, Georgia, and that same night, another of Joe's enemies, Harry S Truman, was sworn in as president. Truman would often say that he would never drink Scotch whiskey because to do so was putting money in Joe Kennedy's pocket.

Joe, Jr.,'s will went into probate, coincidentally on the same date as his memorial volume appeared. This remains somewhat of a mystery. Although his father had settled $1 million on him when he was still a child, he left only $200,000. In view of Joe, Sr.,'s expert handling of his investments, what did this reduction mean? To avoid taxes, Joe, Jr., had already placed money in the hands of the legatees.

With the war coming to an end in Europe, Jack looked for a new role. His health temporarily improved, and with his mother's and father's approval, he went to work for their old friend William Randolph Hearst. As a reporter for the International News Service, he attended the San Francisco conference held at the Palace Hotel, the basis for the soon-to-be-formed United Nations. Still influenced by Harold Laski, he attacked in one of his pieces the Russian delegate Molotov, who, he had not forgotten, had wrecked the Little Entente against Hitler in the 1930s and had shafted Maxim Litvinov, whose British wife Ivy was best friend of Mrs. Harold Laski.

Jack followed the Hearst line in displaying an uncompromising enmity toward the Soviet Union that reflected the views of Pope Pius XII and the Catholic Church. But he differed from his father in criticizing the compromises of the Yalta Conference. Joe, Sr., pursuing as always his policy of American noninterventionism in foreign affairs, believed during the next years that the Russian ogre would be satiated with its essential control over Poland, Yugoslavia, Czechoslovakia and the Baltic nations. He disapproved of a policy that might lead the United States into World War III.

Rose agreed with him; as always, she followed the dictates of the Vatican in such matters. But she and Joe concurred with Jack in supporting the idea of the United Nations born in San Francisco; they felt that the U.N., not the U.S.A., should bear the burden of foreign conflicts.

The war ended in Europe with Germany's surrender on May 7, 1945. Seven days later, Kennedy signed documents establishing the Joseph P. Kennedy, Jr. Foundation for Needy Children in New York, which endowed homes for the retarded with millions—a conscience salve over Rosemary, whom Rose had not seen since 1941.

Rose rejoiced in her daughter Patricia's graduation from Rosemont College on June 4. Two days later, Jean graduated from Noroton.

Rose was especially fond of Pat, who was athletic, very attractive, an excellent tennis player, and even more expert at golf. She dieted and exercised with fiendish intensity, and as a result had a first-class body. She was fond of pranks and bubbled with insistent good humor. Perhaps the most elegant of Rose's daughters, Pat had the glamour of a motion-picture star. As yet, she had no regular boyfriend; she enjoyed being free, though she had a healthy eye for jocks. Jean, by contrast, was shy and reserved, the most subdued of the Kennedys.

On June 27, at a ceremony at the First Naval District Headquarters in Boston, Rose, in an elegant flowered dress and a rakish hat, was given by Rear Admiral Felix T. Gygax the Navy Cross, posthumously awarded to Joe, Jr. The accompanying citation read, "For extraordinary courage and heroism." Only Jack was missing from the ceremony: he was covering the postwar elections in London that would result in the defeat of Winston Churchill and, much to Joe and Rose's annoyance, the emergence of a Labor government in England.

By the summer of 1945, Rose had mostly recovered from her eldest son's death, certain that he was in heaven and gratified by the posthumous honors showered on him. Her household at Hyannis Port was augmented by her sister Agnes's children, Joey, Mary Jo and Ann Gargan.

Rose still walked around the house like a moving bulletin board with her sweater, blouse or dress covered in safety-pinned instructions so she could keep track of the movements of her clan. She worked ceaselessly, writing out notes to add to the pinned collection on her own and her children's appointments, menus, arrangements for laundry and dry-cleaning, chauffeur pickups from golf and tennis clubs or riding stables, schedules of maids and cooks.

Even more than in previous years, she had to deal with the epic untidiness of the Kennedy offspring, now worse than ever. She had never been able to control the mess, and now it irritated her beyond endurance. The house was constantly strewn with sand from the beach, littered by cast-off shoes, soggy towels flung every which way, socks, T-shirts and tanks, swimming trunks and pants flung in all directions.

One of her prize possessions was her baby grand piano, at which she liked to sit of an evening and tinkle out tunes from long ago. She was appalled when she found a pair of chewed-up sneakers sitting on top of its polished mahogany lid; she charged around the house, insisting on knowing who the culprit was, but everyone she addressed burst out laughing and ran off; by the time she had returned to the piano, another pair of sneakers was sitting on it.

She affixed a note to this second pair, reading, BOBBY, ARE THESE YOURS? She was sure they were. When she returned from the beach, she found that Bobby had scribbled a note reading, NO, THEY'RE JACK'S. She wrote a similar note to Jack. He responded with, THEY'RE TEDDY'S. Teddy, in turn, wrote, THEY'RE PAT'S. Pat blamed Jean, Jean blamed Bobby, and the whole cycle was repeated until finally Rose gave up the struggle.

She was consoled by her new Little White House. She could escape there once more from shrieks, yells and scamperings. Sometimes, she lingered in the main house, watching Joe as he dialed the telephone constantly, talking for hours to bankers, real-estate and stock brokers, newspaper owners and heads of state. Rose would enjoy a light lunch with him; then he would take a nap, and drive off for a game of golf. In the evenings, there would be party games, from Monopoly to charades. When Margaret Ambrose had a day off, everyone pitched in in the kitchen, taking it in turns to prepare favorite dishes. The results ranged from disastrous to desirable, and compliments or insults filled the dining room during the subsequent inquests.

Rose loved the Golf Club dances at Hyannis on Saturday nights, not least because she and Joe had broken the barriers for themselves and their family and were allowed in as Catholics. Always expert on the dance floor, she became the instructress for her children. The girls were skilled, and improved daily; the boys were problems. Bobby was the worst: he pumped his partners' arms and hopped up and down, disastrously ungainly during fox-trots or two-steps. He was out of control when it came to jitterbugging; his date for the evening would wind up in a heap on the floor. The best of the boys was Joey Gargan; Rose dazzled everyone as she waltzed with him, the golf club's Ginger Rogers to his nimble Fred Astaire.

Even Teddy, at thirteen, managed to shape up to Rose's exacting standards.

On July 26, 1945, four days after her fifty-fifth birthday, Rose stood next to Jean, who broke a bottle of French champagne over the bow of the *Joseph P. Kennedy, Jr.* at Fore River. As "The Star-Spangled Banner" rang out across the shipyard, she thought of her magnificent dead son, lost her customary composure and sank into her seat, crying helplessly.

On August 6 and 9, President Truman had the atomic bomb dropped on Hiroshima and Nagasaki. Japan surrendered on the fifteenth.

With the war over, Joe was felt to be a safer bet in politics. Influenced by Senator James Byrnes, a reluctant Truman made Joe chairman of the Government Committee on Commerce. This was a cause of rejoicing; Rose saw Joe, so long tortured by lack of activity, plunge into his assignment with all of his old vitality. Starting on his fifty-seventh birthday, September 6, he made twenty-six speeches in ten days; up at 6:00 A.M., adrenaline flowing, he set up headquarters in New York, starting at his offices in the Grand Central Building on Park Avenue. He managed to drive home nights to be with Rose.

The thrill of this sudden reinstatement stimulated the Kennedys into an extraordinary thought. Would it be possible to launch Jack into politics?

All the dreams of the presidency they had fastened on Joe, Jr., now transferred to Jack, who had returned from his sojourn in Europe. How to begin? Should he be pushed as a potential lieutenant governor of Massachusetts, long since a role they had hoped that Joe, Jr., would fill? The idea didn't appeal to Jack.

Congress was the answer. It would only be logical that Jack would seek election in the 11th District of Boston, which Honey Fitz had represented for the first time at almost exactly Jack's age. The present incumbent was none other than Honey Fitz's old nemesis, the relentless former mayor James M. Curley. Joe began a thorough investigation of Curley's present financial, legal and moral situation, seeking an Achilles heel through which he could shoot that belligerent politician down.

As a special FBI contact since 1943, Joe had no difficulty in bringing up Curley's files in J. Edgar Hoover's office in Washington. They contained little of interest. But a superficial check with other contacts showed that Curley was in desperate trouble. He was guilty of using the mails for purposes of fraud and would soon face trial. He had diabetes, which resulted in kidney trouble, and the treatments, combined with his own extravagant spending, had left him broke. Joe would induce him to abandon his

seat in Congress on the grounds of ill health and run for
mayor again. Joe would pay his medical expenses, hire
defense lawyers for his trial and finance his run for mayor.
Curley could not resist the bargain. He crumbled before his
old enemy's powers of persuasion.

Curley stepped down in November. There would be an
election to select the replacement candidate in the following
summer's primary. Rose resumed her persona of the early
years of the century and became excited by the thought of
grooming her second son for political stardom. She had not
forgotten the thrill of accompanying her father, mother and
brothers through the snows of Boston winters, observing the
public's excitement as her father bawled out "Sweet Adeline" through his megaphone. She would be able to recap-
ture her youth; following the dead years after London, she
would be back in the public arena.

She looked Jack over as objectively as she could. He was
sickly, of course; that would be a handicap. She and Joe
would have to foster him through the ordeal of a protracted
campaign. Luckily, he had kept his tan; that would help.
Though his shoulders were thin and unmuscular, they were
sufficiently wide to inspire confidence. Though he was
spare, his body was athletic and well proportioned. He
tended to speak too fast; he must be taught to slow down.
His nasal twang would have to be modified. He showed
signs of being an intellectual; his sardonic wit and intelligence must be tamed so that he would not seem to be above
the heads of the public. His father would guide him in
dealing with other politicians so that he would not seem too
gauche and juvenile.

Rose knew that the women of Boston, from rich to poor,
would be attracted to her son. The older ones would fret
over his frail physique and would want to feed him up. The
younger women, knowing that he was the heir to hundreds
of millions and seeing his remarkable good looks, would
fantasize marrying him.

Rose would present him at women's clubs, deliberately
avoiding politics and instead telling the audience of her
experiences raising him as a little boy, moving on to being
the guest of the royal family at Buckingham Palace and at
Windsor Castle, giving details that she knew would fasci-

nate women who had seldom traveled overseas. She would emphasize the challenge of acting as hostess for King George VI and Queen Elizabeth in her own home, and she knew she would bring a laugh when she mentioned the shad roe and the strawberry shortcake.

She would introduce Jack, reminding the audience that her son was a naval hero who had dragged a man to safety through fiery waters with his teeth. Jack would walk up to the platform and emphasize his hatred of communism, his need to improve housing and factory conditions in rundown Massachusetts, and his promise to bring easier taxes and better profits to the state. He would skate over the fact that he was essentially a carpetbagger, a political candidate who had not been resident in the Boston area since childhood.

Great care had to be exercised to circumvent charges by other candidates that Joe, Sr., was a coward, an appeaser and a defeatist during World War II. Blaming the father's sins on a son was not uncommon in political campaigns. Rose and Joe tried to take care of the matter. In February 1946, Joe was aboard the *Joseph P. Kennedy, Jr.* to congratulate a uniformed and tanned Bobby on becoming an ensign, just before the vessel sailed off to Guantanamo Bay, Cuba, for maneuvers. That same month, the reliable Arthur Krock had it put in the *New York Times* that during the war Joe had lent a New York mansion he owned to the Friends of Free France, a pro–Charles de Gaulle organization of supporters of the French Resistance. Another article mentioned that Joe would be handing over that same mansion to the United Nations while the Rockefellers cleared the land that would finally be used for the United Nations building.

But Joe's bad reputation stuck.

In severe winter weather, at Hyannis Port, Rose, Joe and the rest of the family plunged into such burning topics as whether Jack would wear a hat during his congressional campaign. Rose felt he would catch cold if he didn't, and that wearing a hat would make him look older. Jack, ahead of his time, refused. Rose tried not to be concerned as Jack drove through snow flurries and icy winds to trudge across dock lands, shake hands with workers, climb stairs to poverty-stricken families, and encounter passersby outside supermarkets, office buildings and garages.

Rose became a general, enlisting every available member of her family to help out. She set up her headquarters with her parents at the Bellevue Hotel, Jack occupying a somewhat dowdy office suite down the same corridor. Joe moved into the Ritz-Carlton. Patricia, Jean, Ethel Skakel, Bobby and even fourteen-year-old Teddy rallied to the colors, Bobby obtaining furlough from the navy following his assignment in Cuba. Only Kathleen was left out, unforgiven by Rose, in England; her persistent Protestantism excluded her from the family circle.

Each district had to be tackled separately. Charlestown, Irish Catholic to its foundations, site of the Fore River dock from which the *Joseph P. Kennedy, Jr.* had been launched, was an easy nut to crack. The North End, where 4 Garden Court, Rose's birthplace, had been pulled down and replaced by a modern apartment building, was a cinch, since Rose could talk to Italian men and women who remembered her from childhood and were devoted to her father. She would be successful with the Irish who had, in the more than half a century since she was born, assumed a majority over the Italians in the district. Since Joe had been raised in East Boston, that area was not difficult to conquer. The toughest obstacle would be Cambridge, where Harvard was situated; despite the attendance at the college by Joe, Jr. (who was a hero there), Jack and Bobby, the populace was captive of the mayor, the attractive and charismatic Mike Neville.

For all districts, Rose needed to enlist the support of her Mother Church. She had several meetings with her old friend, the huge, hearty and backslapping, determinedly cheerful and shrewdly informed Archbishop Richard Cushing. He was a frequent guest of the Kennedys at Hyannis Port for sailing, for lobster dinners and good conversation, and he would fly to Palm Beach winter after winter to be with the family.

Rose and Joe were as hard at work pressing for his cardinalate as they were for Mother Cabrini to be the first American saint, two ambitions they would soon realize. Fortunately, the archbishop loved Jack, and regarded him as the best of his younger friends. By 1946, Cushing was known as "the Kennedys' parish priest," and he at once arranged for Rose and Jack to attend Holy Name breakfasts, and meetings of the Home School Association. Knowing of Joe Kennedy's reputation for being anti-Semitic, and determined to assist Rose in getting the Jewish vote, Cushing, at her request, made sure Jack appeared at every possible Jewish occasion, even bar mitzvahs. Joe, Sr.'s friend Rabbi Stephen Wise was corraled into sending enthusiastic letters to his Boston associates. Since Jack was pro-Jewish, these expediencies were entirely acceptable to him.

It was necessary for Jack to establish an apartment in the city. He found one at 122 Bowdoin Street.

During one of his absences, Rose went there. She was dismayed. The sofa seemed to have been attacked by moths, chairs were broken down, and the coffee table in the living room was broken. She had every stick of furniture removed, only to find to her surprise that the apartment was furnished and that she had no business to take anything from it. So she bought the lot from the landlady at a reduced price and had wall-to-wall carpets and decent store-bought furnishings put in, along with seascapes of Hyannis hung on the walls to remind Jack of home.

In an astonishing succession of Parisian flowered dresses and an equally astonishing variety of flowered hats, fifty-five-year-old Rose enjoyed long hours of campaigning, from soon after dawn until midnight. One of her first triumphs of the spring was standing beside her nervous son as they spoke to the Gold Star Mothers of Boston: women who had lost their boys in the two world wars. When Jack haltingly said, "I know how you ladies feel because my mother is a Gold Star Mother, too," they rushed up and surrounded mother and son, some kissing them on the cheek, many eyes filled with tears.

Rose continued tirelessly, week after week, visiting so many women in all of the districts, holding their babies, coddling their children, talking to them, when needed, in French or Italian, that she wore out several pairs of expensive shoes. She managed to find places to change even in the backs of cars. When she went to a poor district like the one in which she was born, she wriggled out of her clothes, removed her jewelry, set aside her celebrated fox furs and slipped into simple black dresses—though, according to the fashion of the time, she was never seen without gloves.

She and Jack became a team, her chief irritations his perpetual lateness and habit of losing his watches. She was also annoyed by his rich boy's refusal to carry money in either clip or wallet, or even loosely in his pocket. On one occasion, when they were due to address a particular women's club, he arrived half an hour late, smilingly unaware of his unpunctuality. When she glared at him, he thought it was because he wasn't wearing a hat. She corrected him sharply, and several women in the audience clapped nervously. In a taxi one day, she asked the driver who he would vote for. He answered, "A young war hero named Jack Kennedy. His grandfather was a pal of mine; he came from the North Side." "I'm glad to hear it," Rose said. "I'm Jack Kennedy's mother." "Great," the driver went on. "You can pay me the dollar-eighty-five fare he owes me from last Wednesday!"

Rose hit on an idea that would prove efficacious in the future. In the 1920s, Sir Thomas Lipton had launched the Lipton tea-drinking campaigns in America in defiance of the coffee tycoons; the idea had come from my father. Providing what came to be known as "the Boston Tea Party in reverse," Lipton staged elaborate tea festivals, chiefly in Boston, gathering hundreds of women who drank tea while he lectured them on its numerous benefits. Rose adopted the idea for an occasion that was scheduled to take place at the Commodore Hotel in Cambridge on June 15, 1946. Rose and her daughters worked like stevedores, toiling day and night personally writing names on as many as two thousand engraved invitation cards edged in gilt. Over fifteen hundred responded that they would come.

Harvard Square became a bedlam of automobile horns and frustrated cries as the army of women discovered that there weren't enough parking spaces and that Rose had failed to supply attendants. Many took fines at fire hydrants and bus stops. The crowd, talking excitedly, delirious at the thought of meeting one of America's most famous mothers and a handsome young war hero and up-and-coming politician, jammed the Commodore's ballroom and lobby. Rose, very well dressed as always, walked up to the podium and to general cheers and applause described with much wit and charm her visits to Buckingham Palace and Windsor Castle, talked affectionately about Jack's naughty-boy childhood, and left the audience in a state of rapture.

Jack followed, staying away from hard-core politics and asking, with an assumed degree of humility, for support. Thereafter, the Kennedy daughters passed through the crowd with cards on which women were to inscribe the names of others who might be voters. There was a standing ovation, and Rose and Jack stood for two and a half hours to shake hands with everyone.

The next day, Jack marched through the Boston streets with the Veterans of the American Legion in the Bunker Hill Day parade. Carried above his head was a handsome embroidered banner with his name on it; thousands flanked the procession, cheering lustily.

The other candidates for nomination didn't stand a chance. Jack won by a landslide, taking 40.5 percent of the vote. Rose joined her exhilarated husband, sons and daughters at a celebration at which Honey Fitz, without much prompting, groaned out the familiar lyrics of "Sweet Adeline." All except Rose and Joe drank champagne.

Neither parent doubted that Jack would win at the November election. In the best of moods, eleven days later, Rose dedicated a Kennedy altar at St. Francis Xavier's Church at Hyannis Port in memory of her late eldest son. Then, on August 12, she was present with Joe at Archbishop Cushing's house in Boston to hand a check for $600,000 to the Franciscan Missionaries of Mary for a poor persons' convalescent home.

That fall brought a new figure into the Kennedy orbit, the first since Ethel Skakel to be given recognition at the court of which Rose was queen. Sargent Shriver, from Maryland, was showing a romantic interest in Eunice, whom he had met at a party. Sarge was tall, strong, dependable, a perfect match for any society daughter, even though he was not rich. Rose described him with characteristic succinctness as "blue blood; no money."

While the Kennedys were eking out a living on an Irish farm, the Shrivers had been on the North American continent for two centuries. David Shriver had been a signator of the Bill of Rights; General T. Herbert Shriver had been adjutant general of Maryland. Sarge's father had converted to Catholicism to please his mother. Head of the Baltimore Trust, he had gone broke in the Depression and had died in 1942.

In many ways, Shriver was a Kennedy before he even became one. Like Joe, Jr., he had emerged as a college athlete; like Rose, Bobby, Jack and Kathleen, he had been a journalist, editing and contributing to the Yale campus's *Daily News.* Like Rose and Joe, he was a critic of communism and had advocated staying out of the war in 1940 so America could arm. He had formed the isolationist America First chapter at Yale at the same time as Joe, Jr., had performed a similar function at Harvard. He had enlisted in the navy and had trained aboard ship; he had obtained a law degree and had seen action at Guadalcanal.

After the war, he joined a Wall Street law firm and he also worked as an assistant editor at *Newsweek.* After he met and fell in love with Eunice, Joe, Sr., showed him Joe, Jr.'s diaries and asked if they could be published. Shriver had the nerve to say no. Impressed with his courage, Joe hired Shriver as an associate.

Rose looked him over and was impressed. His manners and subdued masculinity were exactly what she looked for in a man. He was attentive, even subservient to Eunice's wishes. He attended Mass every morning. She couldn't find fault with such a paragon.

With her oldest son a certainty for Congress, and Bobby and Eunice in line for decent marriages, Rose had to settle the endlessly difficult question of Kathleen. She sailed on the *Queen Mary* on September 6 and checked into Claridges in London. Kathleen invited her to a welcoming dinner party, to which that rebellious daughter had also asked the duke and duchess of Devonshire.

Rose needed to be assured that, with the Devonshires' approval, Kathleen had reverted to the Roman Catholic

Church, had confessed her sin of marrying a Protestant, and, should she marry again, would only consider a Catholic.

Rose arrived, looking chic, at Kathleen's town house on Smith Square. The dinner went fairly well. Afterward, according to tradition, the gentlemen repaired to the library to smoke cigars and enjoy glasses of brandy, while the ladies went to the drawing room for coffee and polite conversation.

Instead of settling down to generalities about rationing, taxes, troublesome children and schools, Rose, with terrifying sharpness, confronted Kathleen in front of the others. She snapped at her daughter, "What are you doing for our Church? What are you doing for our charities?" In England, such questions were reserved for private conversation between parent and offspring, never aired before friends or strangers. The ladies fell silent, shocked beyond words.

Desperate, since she was doing nothing for Catholic causes, Kathleen replied, "I go to the Central Office once a week." She was calculating that Rose wouldn't know what that office was; it was in fact the headquarters of the Conservative Party. Thinking it must be a London Catholic diocese, Rose expressed her pleasure; she left for Paris buoyed on a cloud of illusion, for her usual stay at the Ritz, attendance at Balmain and Dior, and visits with her old friend from Rio de Janeiro, U.S. ambassador to France Jefferson Caffery.

She returned to America by air in October. The next month, Jack was elected to Congress.

Rose thought it was time for Eunice to have a job in government. In December, Joe wrote to Attorney General Tom Clark, asking him if he could find a place for Eunice. Interested in young people's problems, Eunice had become fascinated by the issue of postwar juvenile delinquency.

Clark replied on Christmas Eve. He had decided to set up a division of the Department of Justice that would deal with the delinquency issue, and would be happy to offer Eunice a job as executive secretary. There would be no money for a salary, but she would be given travel and per-diem expenses, an office and a secretary. She would be in contact with the Children's Bureau and other national organizations.

Rose and Eunice were delighted. On the twenty-seventh, Joe called Clark's assistant, Colonel Timothy A. McInerny, accepting. Eunice would begin work in a few days. Joe offered to foot the department staff bills and running costs. Thus he became financier of the Juvenile Delinquency Division.

Eunice and Jack shared a house in Washington. Among their guests were Richard Nixon and Joe McCarthy.

Jack was sworn into Congress, a touching and fraily youthful figure as contrasted with so many older, bulkier and more confident political figures. Mistaken for a page, he pressed for page uniforms, which then became standard. He sat on the District of Columbia Education and Labor Committee with such Brahmin enemies as Senators Leverett Saltonstall and Henry Cabot Lodge.

On January 19, to Rose's delight, Jack was named one of the ten outstanding young men of the year by the U.S. Junior Chamber of Commerce. His success was matched by Eunice, who, with a stretched budget and a skeleton staff, did a very good job of her own.

There was talk of Joe becoming secretary of the navy, an appointment that he would have filled with distinction, but, with characteristic rashness, he attacked President Truman's administration of his office in *Life* magazine and was automatically crossed off the list. He soon opposed Truman's promise of economic aid to countries threatened by communism such as Greece and Turkey, convinced that all possible monies should be kept at home and that communism should be allowed to run rampant in Eastern Europe and the Middle East provided that American defenses insured protection against the enemy at home.

On July 16, he was accorded a position he could usefully fill. He joined the so-called Herbert Hoover Commission, run by the ex-president, and designed to study and report on the operations of the Washington executive departments. Soon he would expose wasteful spending, particularly abroad.

On August 31, Rose saw Jack off to Europe, where he would examine Communist activities in the labor unions, the enemies of his parents since the 1919 Boston police strike and the radical-inspired unrest that dogged his childhood. He was walking in his father's footsteps. He shared his father's view that communism sought to undermine the principles of organized labor and that, in the United States, there was already an enemy within.

Rose decided to follow him. She would be accompanied by Patricia, now her favorite traveling companion and a most charming, pretty and athletic embellishment of any ocean voyage. Mother and daughter sailed on the U.S.S. *America* on the seventeenth, proceeding from London to Ireland and the Devonshires' ancestral home, Lismore Castle, on the Blackwater River in County Waterford.

Rose was overwhelmed. Once the home of Sir Walter Raleigh, the castle was a romantic picture-book edifice, evoking the age of chivalry. Creepers and dark green moss covered the ancient walls. The interior was furnished with romantic opulence, mirroring centuries of the family's history.

Among the other guests were Pamela, Mrs. Randolph Churchill; Anthony Eden; and the Irish novelist Shane Leslie. Kathleen looked radiant. Rose didn't suspect the reason: Kathleen was in love again.

She had become involved with the scion of yet another anti-Catholic Protestant noble family. Peter Milton, Lord Fitzwilliam, was immensely rich, with properties in both Britain and Ireland, and a string of racehorses. He was married. His wife was scarred permanently when, shortly before their wedding, excited about their marital prospects, she had run into a plate-glass door. The couple, who had a daughter, had been separated for years. Fitzwilliam was an ardent womanizer, with several mistresses. Nobody at Lismore dared tell Rose of Kathleen's affair.

Buoyed by illusion, protected from the truth as so often in her life, Rose enjoyed her visit. She was disappointed that Jack had missed her by two days, traveling to London and checking in at Claridges. She decided to catch up with him there, but on arrival was told he had been transferred to the London Clinic.

She was shocked to learn that he had collapsed; the doctor Sir Daniel Davis had told him he was suffering from Addison's disease, a failure of the adrenal glands believed to be caused by incipient tuberculosis. The symptoms were chronic exhaustion, weight loss, poor appetite, low blood pressure, brown pigmentation of the skin, dizzy spells, vomiting, chills and stomach pains. Rose learned that her son might not live a year. His white-blood-cell count indicated that he might have a form of leukemia; in any case, Addison's disease was fatal. After all her efforts to have Jack replace Joe, Jr., on a path to the presidency, he, too, might die.

She found Jack in very bad shape, pale, weak and barely able to speak. He lingered on in his private ward until Rose had him brought home aboard the *Queen Mary* for admission to the Lahey Clinic in Boston. There, Sir Daniel Davis's diagnosis was confirmed. But Jack decided he would continue his political career; he pulled himself together, got out of the hospital and, in November, was back in Congress. Rose and Joe had to face the fact that he might not live out another session; by the spring he might be gone.

In January 1948, Count Enrico Galeazzi spoke to Joe about America financing the Christian Democrats in the coming Italian elections, thus defeating the Communists. Joe raised a private contribution, perhaps as much as a million dollars—the CIA supplied far more. Money was released through the Vatican via Cardinal Spellman. The Christian Democrats won the election.

Rose fastened her hopes on Bobby. Graduating from Harvard in March, in the family tradition, he became a correspondent, writing for the *Boston Post*. Armed with a letter of introduction to Church leaders from Rose's friend Cardinal Spellman, Bobby sailed from New York to Europe on the fifteenth on a fact-finding trip aboard the *Queen Mary*.

Rose corresponded with him throughout the trip. Following her 1939 itinerary, he was in Cairo and Tel Aviv; Rose wrote to him at Beirut, Lebanon, on March 31, advising him on correct etiquette. Bobby's letters to her were pro-Semitic, reflecting both his father's and brother Jack's efforts on behalf of the Jewish state. He attacked the British in the *Post* for their anti-Jewish policies in Palestine. He called for the U.S. to bring peace to the Holy Land. He continued, again in Rose's footsteps, to Istanbul, Athens and Rome, showing, at twenty-two years of age, a degree of articulateness that Rose greatly admired and appreciated.

Late in March, Rose received one of the most exciting invitations of her life. She had formed a friendship with Anita Young, sister of the painter Georgia O'Keeffe and a Palm Beach neighbor married to the multimillionaire railroad tycoon Robert R. Young. Like Joe, Young had been branded a Nazi sympathizer and appeaser at the outbreak of World War II. Young's friendship with the duke and duchess of Windsor had not improved that image. He was given to remarks like "If Hitler had been differently handled, World War II might have been avoided." At the time the Kennedys got to know him, he was pushing for a through railroad from New York to Los Angeles and San Francisco that would avoid the traditional change of train in Chicago; he published widely the slogan that made him famous, referring to through freight trains, "A hog can cross the country without changing trains, why can't a passenger?" By 1946, he was locked in an effort to seize control of the New York Central Railroad.

Young had bought the Kennedys' honeymoon hotel, the Greenbrier at White Sulphur Springs, West Virginia, which Rose had visited several times over the years. It had been occupied by interned German diplomats during the war. Anita, in conference with Rose, had been put in charge of converting the hotel from its battered prewar elegance to a sumptuous hostelry for the rich. She had hired Dorothy Draper, the popular interior decorator of the 1940s, to redo the hotel in her inimitable style.

The Youngs set about giving what Cleveland Amory would describe as the premier resort party of the twentieth century. Rose and Joe were high on the guest list, which included the names of every prominent figure of wealth and position. Young supplied a private train to bring the Kennedys and other guests to the Springs. A limousine greeted Rose, Pat, Eunice, Bobby, Jean and Kathleen (who had flown in from England and had been staying with the Kennedys for several weeks). Jack, followed by Joe, would fly in later by private plane.

As Rose walked into the lobby, she saw the spectacular results of Dorothy Draper's work. Using "romance and rhododendrons" as her theme, the decorator had transformed the fabled hostelry into a palace of vivid colors. She had supplied thirty miles of richly luxurious carpeting, forty-five thousand yards of fabrics, fifteen thousand rolls of pink, green and blue wallpaper. She had replaced the lobby's worn parquet floor with black-and-white checkerboard marble. Chandeliers glittered from the ceilings; there were splashes of bright tints everywhere—a riot of Technicolor vividness that made people expect to see Betty Grable emerge at any minute to sing and dance.

Placed in a suite above her more modest honeymoon accommodations, Rose found herself mingling with such friends as Mr. and Mrs. Anthony Drexel Biddle, accompanied by their beloved dog Monkey, lawyer Clark Clifford, Henry and Clare Boothe Luce, Elsa Maxwell, banker Winthrop Aldrich, British film tycoon J. Arthur Rank, hostess Perle Mesta and polo player Winston Guest. John Jacob Astor and William Randolph Hearst, Jr., arrived soon after.

Next day, following a screening of his film *The Emperor Waltz,* Bing Crosby introduced the ladies' amateur golf tournament, which Pat won. A stir was caused when the duke and duchess of Windsor arrived with 120 pieces of luggage and an entourage of servants, occupying one-third of an entire floor. Rose, who had insisted the Windsors' name never be mentioned in her presence in London, had finally succumbed to their charm and mingled with them happily; later, they would become friends.

Dinner that night was a feast. Following a screening of *Mr. Blandings Builds His Dream House,* the Colonnades Dining Room offered beluga caviar, green turtle soup Greenbrier, English pheasant Smitane, Virginia ham and mushrooms, all accompanied by pink champagne. The lights were turned out and waiters in white tuxedoes marched in carrying dishes of Bombe Alaska, lit with candles and aflame with brandy, blazing in the dark. Everyone clapped.

Dancing began in the ballroom. Bing Crosby sang "The Whiffenpoof Song," "Now Is the Time" and "White Christmas." The audience was ecstatic when the duke of Windsor joined Meyer Davis's band, playing the drums to a rendition of "How Are Things in Glocca Morra" from *Finian's*

Rainbow, at Kathleen Kennedy's request; it was her favorite song. There followed the auction of a gold-and-diamond Tiffany cigarette case supplied by the duchess of Windsor. Joe bought it for Rose.

It was a glorious evening, and Rose and Joe were in the best of moods as they returned to their suite with the rest of the family.

Then something appalling happened. Pale and nervous, her hands clenched, her brothers and sisters unable to stop her, Kathleen wheeled on Rose. High on champagne, she burst out the truth about her prolonged affair with Lord Fitzwilliam, and announced that she would be married to him in the Protestant Church and that her children would be raised Protestant. It was an atrocious moment for her to have made the announcement; she could have broken the news to her mother gently and in private at any time before the society weekend.

Rose started back in horror. Since the family didn't share her surprise, she realized she had been deceived by them, probably for years. Kathleen, for a second time, was betraying both her religion and her mother. Kathleen was defiant, inexcusable, certain to go to purgatory. Her children would be equally condemned.

First Rose stared in disbelief, and then she exploded in hysterical anger, screaming at Kathleen in front of everyone. She told her that she would be excommunicated, and for good. She would be cut off without a penny. And if Joe should take her side, Rose would part from him forever, would never speak to him again and would seek a dispensation from the Pope for dissolution of her marriage. The irony was appalling: in the same hotel in which she had begun her marriage, it might now come to an end.

Everyone was ordered out, and Rose, beside herself, went to bed.

Supportive of Kathleen, and much distressed by the conflict, Joe took off for England on the *Queen Mary* to investigate aspects of the Marshall Plan in Europe on April 20. No sooner was he on the New York wharf to prepare for sailing than he was arrested and carried off to a room where he was held for hours, almost missing the ship. He had been dodging subpoenas in Hyannis Port and Palm Beach to appear as a witness at a trial in which the Dollar Line, which he had taken over under the Maritime Commission in 1938, was suing the government to enable it to return to the Dollar family's private hands. Despite a call to the White House, where an unsympathetic President Truman refused to help, he was forbidden access to the vessel until he had dictated and signed a deposition. The Dollar Line lost the case.

Breaking her promise never to speak to Kathleen again, and still in a frenzy of rage, Rose decided to go to England and try to argue her daughter out of the marriage. She overcame her normal dislike of flying to rush for a week's stay in London on April 30. She invaded Kathleen's house, haranguing her on the danger to her soul that would result from her appalling action. But Kathleen proved intransigent, and Rose was forced to retreat, returning to New York by air.

Suffering from physical and mental stress, she sought refuge by taking the waters at Hot Springs, Arkansas, staying at the Arlington Hotel.

On May 13, Eunice called her from Washington with shocking news. Kathleen and Lord Fitzwilliam had been killed in a plane crash near Lyons, France. They had been on their way to a romantic weekend at Nice. Despite thunderstorm warnings, they had insisted on continuing, and the plane had lost altitude and plunged into a mountainside. According to Nancy Astor's biographer, Christopher Sykes, "Nancy believed and vehemently insisted that the accident had been engineered by Vatican agents because Lady Hartington . . . had married in a registry office without the Church's blessing."

Rose flew to Hyannis Port for the Mass on May 18. She told Judge William O. Douglas the crash was God's punishment. She said to others, "God pointed his finger at Kathleen and said no." Joe arranged for his daughter to have a memorial service in London, attended by many of the leading figures of England. The unhappy young woman was buried in Edensor Churchyard, near Chatsworth, the Devonshires' traditional residence. They put on her tomb,

JOY SHE GAVE AND JOY SHE HAS FOUND. It was an ironically misstated inscription with which Rose profoundly disagreed; she sent Mass cards out to Catholic and other friends with Kathleen's photograph, asking them to fill the cards with prayers that Kathleen might be released from purgatory. Many, disgusted, returned the cards; Kathleen— "Kick"—was adored in England.

Chapter 13

Jackie

⁓⋟⋞⁓

For Rose, the early months of 1949 were happily devoid of dramatic incident. Her father celebrated his eighty-sixth birthday at the Bellevue Hotel in Boston on February 11, and on March 1 the first Hoover Commission concluded its business, its job well done, with much overspending in government exposed.

Once again Joe was without an assignment, and Rose saw him fretting for more work. On June 7, Jean, still the most reserved and subdued of Rose's children, graduated with a B.A. from Manhattanville, a joyous occasion, which Rose attended.

Then, on July 1, after many years at Craig House, Rosemary was transferred by Joe, with the assistance of Archbishop Cushing, to St. Coletta's School for Exceptional Children at Jefferson, Wisconsin. Joe had endowed the corresponding school near Boston through Cushing's good offices, and now Rosemary would have her own small house, chauffeur and maid. The decision to send her out of state may have been occasioned by fear that Boston reporters would invade the Massachusetts institution, question the nuns, and find out about the years that Rosemary had been neglected. This could have proved damaging to Jack's political career.

Rose had never been to Craig House. Now, perhaps seized by conscience because she had not seen her daughter for almost a decade, she summoned up her courage and journeyed to Jefferson. She was warned that despite the fact that a lobotomy was supposed to remove stress, anger and misery, Rosemary was subject to fits in which she would burst out in rage. She was considered potentially dangerous and had to be watched at all times.

When Rose walked into Rosemary's room, her daughter looked at her blankly, not able to recognize her. When Rose explained who she was, Rosemary turned her back on her and refused to speak to her.

Rose left in anguish. Whenever she returned in subsequent years, the situation did not improve. Apparently, Rosemary blamed her mother for her abandonment, and nothing could heal the wound.

An incident then occurred that may have occasioned a change of heart in Rose concerning her dead daughter Kathleen. Father Leonard Feeney, Jesuit head of St. Benedict's Center in Cambridge, Massachusetts, had been supportive of the Kennedys during Jack's congressional campaign. He had spoken on Rose's behalf and had shared her views on the importance of having a Roman Catholic in Congress.

But now he suffered a fall. He had taken the position, which Rose followed, that any Catholic who abandoned his faith would be denied salvation and condemned to purgatory. He attacked his fellow Jesuits, the Paulists, and even Cushing, for taking a benign attitude to those who, while retaining their worship of God, refused to be Catholics. On July 27, 1949, in a direct criticism of Feeney, the Congregation of the Holy Office in Rome stated categorically:

> That one may obtain eternal salvation, it is not always required that he may be incorporated into the Church *actually* as a member, but it is necessary that he at least be united to Her by *desire* and *longing*. . . .

Rejecting the dogma, Father Feeney was excommunicated on October 28, 1949. Coincidentally or not, Rose's comments on Kathleen's punishment in purgatory ceased thenceforth.

The summer brought an annoyance. The State Department published German diplomatic records, one of which contained Ambassador Von Dirksen's report on his meeting with Joe Kennedy on June 13, 1938. The document showed Joe making pro-Nazi and anti-Semitic remarks. It is unfortunate that Joe, since he was hard at work on his memoirs at the time in collaboration with Jim Landis, did not retrieve his own report of the meeting, which contradicted that of the German emissary. Instead, he made a statement to the press, raging that the document was "pure poppycock"; the matter would resurface later when Jack was running for the Senate.

In January 1950, much to Rose's delight, Bobby and Ethel decided they would get married in the summer. Joe wanted Bobby to complete his law course at the University of Virginia, feeling that he should be earning an income before he made the commitment. But Rose was anxious for grandchildren. Unlike so many women of her age, fifty-nine, she had no fear of seeming to be an old woman by reaching grandmother status; on the contrary, she wanted to see the continuance of the Kennedy family line.

Eunice showed no signs of accepting Sargent Shriver's hand; Jack seemed to be bent on having affairs with women in whom he had no emotional interest; and neither Pat nor Jean had found a sustained relationship.

On February 1, 1950, Rose cabled Jack at the House of Representatives from Palm Beach, asking him to draw up a list of names for Bobby and Ethel's wedding before she rushed off for a quick trip to Europe. He came up with a star roster, prepared by his secretary Francis X. Morris, that included Judge William O. Douglas, the William Randolph Hearst, Jrs., and Archbishop Spellman.

Rose had to postpone her trip. She traveled to Greenwich, Connecticut, facing up to Big Ann Skakel to go over the details. The women didn't warm to each other, but they clung to a common purpose; it was decided that the nuptials would be spectacular, the most elaborate in recent Connecticut history. Both women, given the moral standards of the day, rejoiced in the fact that Bobby, more correct and controlled than his brother Jack, had never suggested to Ethel that their relationship should go beyond the limits of chastity.

The loving pair left for Sun Valley, Idaho. In the wake of their departure, Rose had welcome news from Jack. The miracle drug cortisone was coming into use, and Jack had persuaded his doctors to allow him to experiment with it. Implanted in pellet form under his skin, it proved effective in controlling the ravages of Addison's disease, and for the first time in years he was taken off the danger list and was expected to enjoy at least several more years of life.

That spring saw the publication of Joe Kennedy and Jim Landis's book, *The Surrender of King Leopold,* in which they sought to exonerate the Belgian monarch, a friend of theirs from Palm Beach days, of treasonably handing over his forces to the Germans in 1940. Apparently they had not seen the records of Nazi leader Ernst Kaltenbrunner, which showed that Leopold was maintained by Himmler in luxury for the duration of the war in a castle in South Germany, instead of taking decent exile in London. The book was a mistake (though today its argument has its supporters), because it drew attention to ancient controversies and started people talking again, in the wake of the Von Dirksen document, about Joe's activities as an alleged defeatist and appeaser.

On June 10, Rose threw a pre-wedding party at the Hyannis Port Golf Club for Bobby and Ethel, to which scores of friends were invited. It was a double celebration. The day before, Teddy had graduated from Milton Academy, in the presence of Rose and Joe, Joe reading the commencement address. There followed a big party at the Kennedys' house, complete with dance band.

To Rose's annoyance, when the engaged couple were called for at midnight, to give speeches, they were missing (they had flown to New York by private plane, accepting an invitation from the Stork Club's proprietor Sherman Billingsley, who flung a lavish party in their honor).

It was an ominous week. Communist forces, heavily

augmented by the Soviets, were threatening invasion of South Korea. But it is doubtful if many of the guests for the wedding thought about the crisis as they swarmed into Greenwich, causing gridlocks in the narrow streets. Since Big Ann had refused to have the Kennedys stay in her house, Rose was forced to get up at dawn to drive from Hyannis Port, while Joe came from New York with his sister Loretta.

The wedding took place at St. Mary's Church at 11:00 A.M. Jean, Eunice and Pat were bridesmaids; Pat had been dating Ethel's brother Jim. The service was presided over by Reverend Terrence L. Connelly.

An unfortunate incident occurred. As the organist played "The Wedding March," Ethel's brother George flung pennies down in the aisle. He told Jack's college friend Lem Billings, whom he thought to be homosexual, and longed to humiliate, to retrieve the pennies. When Lem bent over to pick them up, George Skakel kicked him in the buttocks. Lem sprawled to the floor before the bride and her father. There was nervous laughter and applause.

The couple honeymooned in Hawaii. Ethel wrote to Rose, describing her happiness.

Then, on June 25, the Korean War began. As Truman authorized military support for South Korea, Joe opposed intervention, true as ever to his pacifistic/Vatican precepts, stating in interviews that the U.S. had no business being involved and that the result might be war with Russia.

On September 7, just before leaving for her delayed visit to France, Rose presented a check for $2.5 million to a home for neglected children in the Bronx. She had visited Honey Fitz in Boston, finding him seriously ill; but, in the family tradition, she decided not to make a change in her arrangements and proceeded on course as usual.

On October 3, she received word at the Ritz in Paris that her father had died of a coronary thrombosis. With the detachment that would increasingly mark her life, Rose didn't return home for the wake, the procession in which the old Bostonian was carried through the streets to the strains of "Sweet Adeline" or the High Requiem Mass that was sung at the Cathedral of the Holy Cross, Archbishop Cushing presiding.

Two Brahmins whose families had kept the Fitzgeralds out of Boston clubs ironically acted as pallbearers: Senator Henry Cabot Lodge and Leverett Saltonstall. They were accompanied by James M. Curley, who had spent most of his term as mayor in prison. Other pallbearers were Eddie Moore; Speaker of the House Joseph W. McCormack; and one of Jack's most outspoken critics, the crusty Thomas P. ("Tip") O'Neill. The body was buried at St. Joseph's Cemetery.

Almost as though he had foreseen that Rose would not attend his funeral, Honey Fitz left her no legacy in his will. He gave her the task of executor, stating that the reason he had not bequeathed her anything was "for reasons best known to herself." Had there been a falling-out between them? He left only $76,000, divided between his wife and Rose's brothers John, Jr., and Tom. After taxes, there would be little left. Rose and Joe sustained her mother for the rest of her life.

On November 7, 1950, Jack was reelected for a third term in Congress. He was restive, longing to become senator, and Joe and Rose began to think about that possibility. It was important that Joe stay out of the public eye and suppress his inflammatory nature, but he couldn't resist trumpeting the futility of the Korean War at every opportunity. On December 1, he made a strong criticism of the conflict in which young Americans were dying, addressing the University of Virginia senior law class with an embarrassed Bobby as host. He shocked the students, many of whom were girding their loins for active service. Fortunately for her peace of mind, Rose was not present to see the young men's reaction to her husband's latest outburst.

It didn't please Joe that Jack insisted on increased U.S. military involvement against the Communist threat worldwide.

Rose had compensations. Returned from an audience with the Pope in Rome, and with the Senate more clearly in mind, Jack spent much time in Boston throughout March and April, addressing, with Rose at his side, women's clubs and organizations on the Irishman's creed, love of family, love of country and love of God. Rose was with him when he addressed Jewish groups and when he talked to Italian clubs about the necessity of building up Italy with Vatican assistance against Communist aggression in Southern Europe. Jack continued his association with Joe McCarthy.

Rose was in a good humor as summer approached, finding Jack more devout than he had been hitherto. But she was not to be allowed peace of mind. Teddy would be the next disaster on Rose's list.

Teddy had been struggling with language courses at Harvard, devoting too much of his time to the athletic field. Impressive at football, at six foot two and two hundred pounds, he was the biggest and most powerful member of his family. But his Spanish was weak, and, knowing his father was banking on his passing his exams, he resorted to a desperate measure. His classmate and friend Warren O'Donnell offered to sit in for him, using his name, during the Spanish exam, and he foolishly agreed. The exam proctor didn't know him or O'Donnell, and the ruse might have succeeded; but at the last minute, another proctor substituted who knew O'Donnell very well. When he saw O'Donnell present the paper with Teddy's name on it, he was furious and immediately reported the matter to the dean. As a result, to Rose's and Joe's horror, Teddy was expelled on June 11.

This was the worst possible disgrace for the Kennedys. No Kennedy had been thrown out of a college; no Kennedy was supposed to lose in any field. Joe's motto, expressed to such unlikely individuals as San Francisco Communist dockland leader Harry Bridges, was "Never be found out."

Teddy was found out. When he arrived in Hyannis Port, the house became a war zone.

If Jack's brother was named a liar and a cheat it could damage his political future. Rose and Joe dared not make a fuss in case the press should get onto the matter. They managed to suppress the scandal; even the most venomous columnists made no mention of it. But worse took place. In desperation, anxious to escape from the tension at Hyannis Port and from his parents' wrath—anxious also to express Jack's militaristic anti-Communist policies through personal action—the guilt-ridden young man, still only nineteen, enlisted as a private in the army.

Joe was beside himself. He who had forced his elder sons into officer rank in 1941 to avoid their being drafted as privates in a future war he dreaded had to face his youngest son's enlistment in the ranks as a common soldier! And Teddy might be sent to Korea, the very war that Joe publicly condemned at every possible opportunity.

When Teddy broke the news to his parents that he had joined up at Fort Devins, Massachusetts, Joe screamed, "Don't you ever look at what you're signing?" He couldn't seem to accept the fact that Teddy had made the move voluntarily. On July 5, 1951, Teddy reported for basic training in the 39th Infantry of the 9th Infantry Division at Fort Dix.

One day before he began, deeply troubled by the matter, Rose had a consolation: she became a grandmother for the first time. Bobby and Ethel's firstborn—on the Fourth of July, how perfect for a Kennedy!—was a daughter. Now that Rose had forgiven Kathleen, she made no demur when the child was christened Kathleen Hartington. Eighteen days later, Rose turned sixty-one.

At the time, a remarkable figure turned up at the Kennedy house at Hyannis Port: future president Ngo Dinh Diem from Indochina. The forceful, fiftyish Diem, a monastic celibate, was introduced to the Kennedys by Cardinal Spellman, who, with the support of Pope Pius XII, decided to invest both time and money in the Roman Catholic hierarchy in Indochina. Rose and Joe joined Spellman as Diem's sponsors, as he took up residence at the Maryknoll Seminary at Ossining, New York, and later at Lakewood, New Jersey. The Kennedys backed Diem personally and had him as a friend because he represented a spearhead against communism in the region. Their support, and Jack's, of Diem's regime against the French government, a support which was fully sanctioned in the Vatican, proved provoking to the Kennedys' friends in Paris. It would eventually cause not only a rift with General de Gaulle; it would backfire and result in Diem's destruction, sowing the seeds for the Vietnam War.

In October, Jack, using his own money, and accompanied by Bobby and Pat, set out on a personal fact-finding mission to Europe. Rose heard from him constantly, as he flew to

Paris to meet with General Eisenhower, discussed American military defenses in West Germany, flew to Teheran, Iran, for a similar purpose, and in India saw Prime Minister Nehru. In Pakistan, he conferred with Premier Liaquat Ali Khan just hours before Liaquat was assassinated. He proceeded to Saigon, Singapore and Tokyo, where his Addison's disease and bad back flared up and he was forced to come home.

Two days after Jack's return, Teddy joined the Counterintelligence Corps in Fort Holabird, Maryland. On November 21, Rose was delighted when Bobby, who had graduated with honors from the University of Virginia Law School, was admitted to the Massachusetts bar.

But her greatest joy came on December 13. She and Pat were on a visit to the Home for Underprivileged Children in the Bronx, touring the wards, noting how beautifully the children were taken care of, when a nun asked them to come to a particular public room. As they walked in, Rose was amazed to see a crowd of friends and well-wishers applauding her vigorously, almost as if it were a surprise birthday party.

She was more astounded when a beaming Cardinal Spellman brought her up to a platform and told her that the Pope had bestowed upon her the title of papal countess. Rose was overcome, on the verge of tears, as he went on, describing the reason she was being granted the honor: "for her exemplary life and for her many charities in this country and all parts of the world." He read out a message from Pope Pius XII that reminded her of the many years of Pius's admiration for her.

It was the supreme moment of her life to date; the fulfillment of her dreams. But as so often in her life, a great moment was not unshadowed. Three days later, her favorite uncle, John, brother of Josie, fell to his death from a mast while doing repairs on a ship at West Concord Harbor, Massachusetts, at seventy-four years of age.

Nineteen fifty-two began with the family's decision that Jack would run for the Senate. Rose had qualms, fearful that the all-powerful incumbent, Henry Cabot Lodge, whose grandfather had been Honey Fitz's nemesis and whose Republican influence in Massachusetts was profound at every level, would allow no opponent to take his place. But Joe was adamant: Jack must succeed in this latest step up the political ladder; he must lay the groundwork for an assault on the White House.

Another family honor followed. On February 13, Jack was awarded the Star of Solidarity, First Order, the highest civilian award of the Italian government, which followed his obtaining of U.S. government aid for the Christian Democratic Party and his push, welcomed by the Pope, toward Italian armament against Soviet influence. Jack was the first member of Congress to receive the award.

On February 28, Rose was thrilled when Bobby was assigned to be special assistant to the attorney general in the criminal division of the Department of Justice, his first entry into government and a definite advance in his career.

In February, the Kennedy machine geared up for Jack's campaign. Rose decided to enlist the family except for Teddy, who was serving as a military policeman, successively in Georgia and New Jersey. Three months pregnant with her second child, despite a baby in tow, the irrepressible Ethel would pitch in. Rose enlisted Jean, Eunice, who had been working at the charitable House of the Good Shepherd in Chicago, and Pat, who was in Hollywood.

On April 24, Jack officially announced his candidacy. After a brief rest at the Greenbrier Hotel, Rose arrived in Boston for preparations. One of the criticisms she and her husband had faced in the 1946 campaign was that they lived apart. Now that the Senate was the target, and beyond that the presidency, Rose and Joe had to give the appearance of solidarity in their marriage. They took an apartment on Beacon Street, not far from Josie Fitzgerald at the Bellevue. Jack took an apartment on Bowdoin Street, where he would have a masseur and a big, old-fashioned bath he could soak in at night.

Rose developed her 1946 tea-drinking nomination parties to the fullest. Her niece, Polly Fitzgerald, carried out her instructions. She would launch at least three hundred teas, at which the women of Massachusetts would meet her and her oldest son. In a fit of nostalgia, she favored the use of Lipton tea bags for the campaign.

She and her daughters sent out thousands of invitations, engraved on white-and-gold cards; fingering her rosary under the hair-dryer at her favored salon, she mustered up more support. Even Republican women changed sides when they found that the sharp-voiced, tiny lady sitting next to them was the famous Rose Fitzgerald Kennedy.

The first big event of Rose's campaign was held at the Hotel Sheraton in Worcester in April. Once more, Rose talked of her experiences of raising Peck's Bad Boy and of enjoying the fashion salons of Europe while acting as ambassador's lady. To cheers, she was joined by Jack, who was on crutches. He was disheveled, as he had been five years earlier, his shock of hair resisting the efforts of brush or comb, his suit unpressed, his feet shod in bedroom slippers. But he looked better: the cortisone treatments were working, and he had filled out considerably. His looks were enhanced by his increased weight, and he was well tanned from a mobile sunlamp that went with him everywhere.

As in his run for Congress, acting on the advice of his parents and associates, Jack avoided politics in the addresses to women; instead, he simply called for support, asking those who attended to form separate committees of fifty or more. The members were asked to supply flat silver and Irish lace tablecloths for further afternoon teas.

As Jack got underway, Joe told him, at a summit meeting at the Beacon Street apartment, and in front of Rose, "Beating Lodge will be tough. But you will do it. If it happens, you will be president. I will work out the plans. You will need to get twenty men to get you the nomination. I will find them."

With amazing energy for a woman approaching sixty-two, Rose, hating flying, never forgetting that two of her children had died in plane crashes, flew to every part of the state to save time, discovering unconquered areas where she could fast-talk potential voters into succumbing to her charm. She never bothered with casual conversation between engagements. She alienated several appointed drivers or fellow automobile passengers who tried to milk her for family gossip when she cut them off completely, announcing that she needed to rest her voice and taking catnaps in backseats. As in 1946, she endlessly wriggled out of clothes in the backs of cars, changing from designer models to inexpensive off-the-rack dresses according to the income level of the area she was to appear in. She would change from the expensive Kennedy three strands of pearls to modest seed pearls when she thought it desirable.

July 4 fell on a Friday. Celebrating Kathleen Kennedy's first birthday, the family retreated to Hyannis Port to give their biggest tea party to date.

On Saturday evening, Jack brought a newcomer to the circle, a rather awkward but pretty young woman named Jacqueline Bouvier, in whom he had a romantic interest.

This was an unusual step on his part. Normally, his girlfriends, even movie stars like Gene Tierney or Grace Kelly, were not, by general agreement, brought to the family home. It was understood that unless a woman was a candidate for marriage, she would not be introduced to Jack's parents. Jackie had made a brief visit to Palm Beach the previous winter, but this was the first time Rose had met her.

She was a doe in a tiger cage. Tall, towering over Rose, she had wide shoulders, a long waist, coltish long legs and large feet. She spoke oddly; she picked her way through words with a nervous, slow drawl, as though she had just learned English, phonetically. She had gentle manners; she was subdued, shy and ill at ease. She had dressed up for the occasion, not having been briefed by Jack that nobody, not even Rose, followed the fading custom among the rich of dressing for dinner. When Joe looked her up and down, saying, rudely, "Where do you think you're going?" Rose butted in protectively with, "Oh, don't be mean to her, dear; she looks lovely."

At that moment, Joe stood up and produced a sheet of paper, a cross between butcher paper and the Magna Carta, and read out a list of rules for visiting the Kennedys. He stated that Jackie must prepare herself by reading the *Congressional Record, U.S. News and World Report, Time* magazine, *Newsweek, Fortune, The Nation, How to Play Sneaky Tennis,* and *The Democratic Digest.*

She must memorize at least three good jokes. She must anticipate that each Kennedy would ask her what she thought of another Kennedy's dress, hairdo, backhand and latest public achievement. She must be sure to answer, "Terrific."

If she didn't play touch football, she would be fed in the kitchen and nobody would speak to her. (She did play.) She must be careful, because even pregnant girls would make her look silly. She was not to suggest any plays, as the Kennedys had the signal-calling department sewed up, and all of them had A-pluses in leadership. If any Kennedy made a mistake, she was to say nothing.

She must run madly on every play, and make a lot of noise. She must not appear to be having too much fun or she would run the risk of being accused of not taking the game seriously. She must never criticize the rival team. It would be full of Kennedys, and they didn't like that. If she wanted to be popular she must show raw guts. To show raw guts, she must fall on her face now and then. She must smash into the house once in a while, going after a pass. If a hole was torn in her best suit, or if she twisted an ankle, she must laugh off the mishap.

The recitation over, Jackie was stunned. It was early for dinner; this sheltered young gentlewoman was plunged into activities that left her exhausted. She was dragged into beach jogging, rigging up family sailboats, wrestling and ragging. After dinner, she was subjected to Monopoly, Scrabble and charades.

The madness continued. As Rose appeared with her blouse covered in pinned notices, everyone threw their clothes around, there was sand on the floor, and scattered shoes, towels and shorts everywhere.

By weekend's end, Jackie hit it off well with Joe, calling his bluff by refusing to be browbeaten. To her, he was a dear, gruff grizzly bear. Jackie wrote later, "When I first met him, I did not realize that I was supposed to be scared of him—so I wasn't. That may have been *lèse-majesté*—but it was a wonderful way to start."

By contrast, Rose didn't feel strongly for Jackie, nor Jackie for her. Rose found Jackie's chain-smoking as grating as Jack's constant macho chewing on Havana cigars; Jackie was irritated by Rose's high-pitched voice and constant corrections.

Then, and in the weeks that followed, Rose began to

understand Jackie a little better. The young woman came
from a broken home. Her father, the notorious Black Jack
Bouvier, had divorced her elegant, snobbish and impeccable mother Janet; Janet had married the Washington stockbroker Hugh D. Auchincloss, cousin of the celebrated
society novelist Louis Auchincloss.

Jackie was her mother's artifact, elegant and as near to
perfect as possible. Her family trees on both sides were as
much an invention of Mrs. Auchincloss as Yggdrasil, the
tree of fate in Norse mythology. Janet would say that she
was descended from the family of the Confederate general
Robert E. Lee, and she even spoke on the subject at social
events when she was in the South. She put together a
genealogy to prove her point, a genealogy that no member
of her family appears to have preserved, but that several
members admit was inaccurate.

Her grandfather, the formidable real-estate tycoon and
banker James T. Lee, who detested Joe Kennedy because
Joe had beaten him to the punch in the purchase of the
Merchandise Mart, pretended to be the son of a high-
ranking Confederate officer in the Civil War and to have
been born in New York City. Neither statement was true.
He was almost certainly part Jewish, a Levy—hence the
fantastic lengths he and his daughter went to in order to
hide his origins.

Black Jack's chief claim to fame was that he had allegedly
been the lover of Cole Porter. The Bouviers were supposed
to have been aristocrats, but were, in fact, artisans.

Told by her mother that she was a blend of American
Southern gentlefolk and French nobility, Jackie played the
part better than the genuine articles. Raised in a sheltered
atmosphere from childhood, she was overwhelmingly absorbed in the world of horses. Janet, whose greatest boast
was that she had bested the wealthy Liz Whitney at a
foxhunting event, put Jackie through the rituals of exhibition horse jumping, but also, to support the fantasy of a
French aristocratic background, encouraged her to learn
that language, and to appreciate fine arts and music. She
taught Jackie how to entertain properly, how to sit, stand
and cross her legs. Jackie had to learn to talk as a gentle-

woman was supposed to talk; whereas Janet talked very fast, running her words together, she made Jackie speak very slowly, in that soft, measured, mechanically correct form of speech.

Jackie was trained in the most ladylike way possible: at Miss Porter's School, Vassar and, of course, the Sorbonne. She learned to conceal the toughness and determination inherited from the Lees and the extravagance and self-indulgence inherited from the Bouviers. Exquisitely tactful and restrained, she succeeded in assuming a mask of total innocence. She learned the technique of asking questions of everyone she met instead of supplying information herself. It was a method of disguising her thoughts, which she hesitated to share with anyone.

Her stepbrother, Janet's stepson Jamie Auchincloss, feels that, inside, she had a single-minded strength and ambition. His brother Hugh D. feels that her job as reporter for the *Washington Times-Herald* was obtained, in part, because she could use the technique of questioning strangers as a mask for herself.

The idea that Jackie was setting her cap for Jack Kennedy displeased Janet Auchincloss, not only because her father detested the Kennedys, but because they made no bones about their origins, and completely lacked the pretentiousness she carried like an umbrella. In her fantasy, she had presumably matched Jackie to a French nobleman, or, at the very least, a Vanderbilt or a Rockefeller.

Rose researched Jackie, noting that she was a cousin of Mother Katherine Drexel of Philadelphia, who had founded the Order of the Blessed Sacrament in Torresdale, Pennsylvania. Against this pleasing fact could be placed certain disadvantages: Jack was allergic to horsehair, scarcely the basis for a promising relationship with an equestrienne. She had set fire to a car at the age of four. She had a disconcerting habit of making direct and unflattering remarks in her soft-voiced, seemingly innocent manner; when her sister Lee had told a young man he looked handsome, Jackie had contradicted her by saying he resembled a weasel.

She had a habit of writing verses for people's birthdays,

and she wrote children's stories, including one entitled
"The Adventures of George Woofty, Esq.," about the affair
of a terrier and a schnauzer.

There is no record of Rose being impressed by these
accomplishments, or by Jackie's habit of caricaturing people she met in somewhat unflattering sketches, or her
Grandma Moses paintings. Soon, Rose would have to put
up with Jackie's imitation of her voice, Jackie's habit of
sleeping late and not coming down to breakfast with the
family, her amused critique of Rose's doll collection, and
her general disregard of time. The unpunctual were always
on the top of Rose's hit list.

In sum, despite truces and mutual appreciations, these
two remarkable women, Rose and Jackie, never became
close friends; they never found a common ground. Rose's
correctness, precision, and perfectionism clashed with
Jackie's casual tastefulness, relaxed ecumenicism, and imp-
ish sense of intellectual humor. For Rose, religion was
everything; Jackie was a liberal woman whose attitude to
the Church was that it was good for rituals. To Rose, the
most important things in life were not aesthetic: they were
adhering to dogma, running a family by the rule book,
holding the family together around her own firm center.
Jackie was a modern woman, open, capable of change,
letting things drift, going with the flow of life.

Rose wasn't even *interested* in her husband's affairs: if
when he was younger he brought young women to a family
screening room and caressed them, or slept with a variety of
staff or casual acquaintances (probably far fewer than has
been claimed; the appearance of a conquest was more
important to him than its actuality, and soon he would lose
his prostate and his sexual power would be gone anyway),
Jackie was contemporary in resenting Jack's compulsive
satyr's longing for sexual novelty, his only release from
pressure and physical pain.

Rose's and Jackie's strengths were not compatible, but
they were not less to be admired because of it.

Jackie agreed to join Rose and her daughters in supporting Jack in his run for the Senate. She turned up at Fall
River and Concord that summer, to express, shyly but
effectively, her admiration for the candidate.

After the July 4 weekend, Joe dispatched Pat and Eunice to Chicago to report as spies on the events of the Republican National Convention. They supplied a helpful fact. Henry Cabot Lodge had abandoned presidential candidate Robert A. Taft, thus causing dissension and losing Taftian support for his campaign.

Nothing could stop Rose from going to Paris for the previews of the fall fashions in late July; she couldn't make her usual visit in September because the primary ballot results would be in by then.

While at the Ritz, she visited with Teddy, who was in the lowly position of honor guard, standing outside the U.S. SHAPE military headquarters, an embarrassing fact that had to be buried for purposes of the senatorial campaign. Rose rushed back with trunks full of dresses in time to show off a red crêpe Dior creation at the New Bedford Hotel on August 28. The ladies were entranced as she modeled the new fashions, talking of the emphasis on tighter, longer skirts.

Joe set her up on a local television show, "Coffee With the Kennedys," the format inspired by criticism from coffee manufacturers like Folgers that she was giving too much attention to the tea industry. Callers could use a toll-free line to ask questions.

Joe corrected Rose when fantasy took over from fact in her discussions of Jack's childhood. She mentioned picking blueberries with him in Maine. Joe called up saying, "The blueberries are out."

Jack suffered a setback that month. Showing off at a fire station in Springfield, he slid down the pole and injured his back. He had to spend much of the rest of the campaign on crutches. But he was more than compensated by the results of the primary; on the sixteenth, he obtained 394,138 votes. Now there was the challenge of defeating Lodge. Because of Massachusetts rules, he had less than two months to do it in.

Joe left his offices on Park Avenue in New York to muster up every last ounce of support. Such stalwarts as Jim Landis and John J. Ford (from the old Bethlehem Steel days) were enlisted. Money changed hands in newspaper publishers' offices: when the *Boston Post* proved threatening, Joe greased the necessary palms with half a million dollars, and overnight the editorial policy changed in Jack's favor. Other newspapers proved equally amenable.

Meanwhile, Rose intensified, if that was possible, her tea campaign.

She was distracted in the midst of her efforts by Ethel's spending. She felt that Ethel was draining Bobby's allowance excessively now that he was working without income as Jack's campaign manager. Rose broke off her state tour to rush to Greenwich to confront Big Ann Skakel in her lair; in an attempt to trump Rose's ace, Mrs. Skakel, instead of having a private meeting with her, invited her to lunch with several society women.

Annoyed that she would not have the opportunity for an intimate discussion, never fazed by the idea of talking in front of others, Rose burst out in rage in the middle of the meal. She declared that Ethel was spending far too much money. While the guests sat astonished, Ann said, equally tastelessly, "The Kennedys can well afford it." Forgetting the million dollars Joe had settled on Bobby, Rose said that Bobby could not. She got up and stormed around the room, with such dramatic emphasis she might have been Bette Davis or Joan Crawford at the height of a movie melodrama. Receiving no response from Big Ann, she slammed out and ran to her car. Mocking laughter followed her. She remained furious.

Rose plunged back into the campaign. Her daughters' earrings carried Jack's initials; their skirts featured his face superimposed over the Capitol dome. Joe spent scores of thousands on advertisements, which flared in buses, subways, and steam trains and on bumpers of automobiles. He snapped up space in newspapers and splurged on radio and television commercials. Lodge was handicapped, in part by losing the Taftians, in part by the fact that he was out of state campaigning for Eisenhower for several weeks, and he was far too cavalier about Jack's chances. On one occasion, his limousine was caught next to Jack's in a traffic jam. He leaned out of the window and said to Jack, "Isn't this one hell of a way to make a living?" Jack laughed.

Rose worked gallantly, using her shaky Italian, on the

appropriate districts. Lodge produced his brother John Davis's Italian wife, the glamorous Francesca Braggiotti, who had been with Rose on the September 1939 sailing of the S.S. *Washington*. Speaking the language fluently, Francesca impressed the voters even in Rose's birthplace.

There were details of Francesca's past that Rose certainly knew about. Rose was in Rome in 1939, when the city was covered in enormous and vulgar placards announcing the fact that Francesca Braggiotti was the star of *The Defeat of Hannibal*, the most expensive film ever made in Italy, financed, produced and allegedly written by Mussolini and his son Vittorio, and mirroring, in its account of the Roman Scipio's conquest of Carthage, Mussolini's triumphant destruction of Ethiopia. She could have mentioned the fact to Jack, who would have remembered it also, but she did not; nor, apparently, did anybody in Mrs. Lodge's audiences recall that the movie was seen in New York that same year.

As in 1946, Rose worked hard on the Jewish vote; whenever the question came up of Joe's alleged anti-Semitism, Jack was ready. He mentioned his father's friends Arthur Krock, Bernard Baruch, Rabbi Stephen Wise and Herbert Bayard Swope.

Rabbits were pulled out of the Kennedy hat. The Japanese commander of the destroyer that had rammed the PT-109 was induced to issue a statement, which Joe made sure was circulated in the press, stating that Jack, in forgiveness of the episode, was contributing to the promotion of friendship between Japan and the U.S. The commander overlooked Jack's opposition to Japanese textile imports, which were threatening the industry in Massachusetts. Eleanor Roosevelt was corralled into an endorsement on October 20, saying that Jack was a tower of strength in opposing the oppression of minorities throughout the world. To seal the Catholic vote, Enrico Galeazzi in Rome engineered that city's Iupa Romana Award for Jack on October 27, 1953.

The campaign tensions increased. Dwight D. Eisenhower would certainly be president; if Jack were to succeed, he would be overturning an Eisenhower stronghold in Massachusetts. But his television appearances, even in the gray and washed-out images of the time, were irresistible.

On November 4, the family gathered at Jack's apartment

for the results. Jack was so nervous that he paced the floor, roaming from room to room, one minute certain he was a loser, the next certain he had won. He was so jittery that, having removed his coat to try to relax, he put it on inside out. Joe lost his temper and told him to calm down. Rose said nothing.

By nightfall, he was ahead, but not by as large a margin as he would have wished. The final count, relayed over the radio, was 1,211,984 for Kennedy, 1,141,217 for Lodge. Lodge ceded wryly, making the remark, when asked how he felt, "I have been drowned in an ocean of tea." The ocean had a strong current; in the end, it would help in sweeping Rose's eldest son to the White House.

Joe told Jack it was only a question of time before he became president. Rose's daughters jumped for joy as Rose crowed, remembering her father's humiliations, "We have beaten the Lodges at last!" Years later she told Doris Kearns Goodwin that, as the family rejoiced, she thought about her father as a little boy, shivering with cold in the servants' quarters of Lodge's great-grandfather's house as he sheltered from his newspaper run ("In his wildest dreams that night could he ever have imagined how far both he and his family would come?").

In victory's wake, Rose could take pride in the fact that during his career in the Senate, Jack would seek to fulfill, in a manner uncommon among politicians, his campaign promises. He would never cease to emphasize protectionism for Massachusetts industry and the necessity to oppose communism, even if that meant supporting Joe McCarthy.

With the presidency in mind, he knew he must set the seal on his success by marrying well. He told staff member Ruth McMillan, "People will say I'm queer if I don't get married."

That wasn't a likely slur, but his image as a womanizing bachelor had to be suppressed. Rose considered the religious aspects. Jackie was all right when it came to upbringing, since her father was a Catholic. But there was no getting over the fact that Jackie's stepfather was a Presbyterian and a Mason, a reminder for Rose of the dread situation involving Kathleen. There was another disadvantage in the match: Black Jack Bouvier and Hugh D. Auchincloss shared George Skakel's dislike for Joe because he had damaged their stockbroking careers via the Securities and Exchange Commission in the 1930s and had sent their friend Richard Whitney, chairman of the Stock Exchange, to jail.

There were no other contenders. Attractive, healthy, Jackie would be a suitable mother for Jack's children. Although she was not romantically in love with him, she was fond of him, amused by him, and enjoyed mothering him. She discouraged his habit of leaving his hair uncombed, his suits unpressed, his feet shod in shoes of different colors, and his ankles encased in white woollen socks.

In January, when Jack accompanied Jackie to Eisenhower's Inaugural ball, the die was cast. That same month, after seven years of effort, Sargent Shriver persuaded Eunice to be his bride. Rose rushed off to Paris to buy dresses, returning just in time.

Eunice's wedding took place at St. Patrick's Cathedral in New York on May 23, 1953, Eunice in a Dior gown for which Rose had arranged. The guest list included Mr. and Mrs. William O. Douglas, Mr. and Mrs. James F. Byrnes, former postmaster general James A. Farley, the Robert Youngs of Palm Beach and Newport, Margaret Truman (defying her father's hatred of Joe Kennedy), Bernard Baruch and Thomas J. Watson of IBM. Notable by her absence was Jackie Bouvier, who left the day before (showing her independence—she could have waited twenty-four hours) for London to cover Princess Elizabeth's coronation on June 2.

Rose supervised the event with her customary skill. The apse was darkened, lit only by candles; Morton Downey sang "Ave Maria" as the organ pealed. Bride, groom and guests made their way through an enthusiastic crowd to the Waldorf-Astoria, one half of whose Starlight Roof Joe had commandeered for the reception.

Jack telegraphed Jackie in London, proposing to her. Stimulated by the fact that her sister Lee had married the handsome Britisher Michael Canfield in April, she accepted.

Rose, barely recovered from the hard work of preparing Eunice's wedding, would have to make preparations for Jack's. It would be a short engagement; neither Rose nor Joe could trust Jack not to change his mind.

According to custom, Black Jack Bouvier and Janet and Hugh D. Auchincloss would have to be talked to in the matter of the wedding arrangements. Joe targeted Black Jack. Womanizers both, fond of discussing their bedding of many women, they hit it off immediately, and Black Jack forgave Joe his role with the SEC. Rose was delegated the unenviable task of facing up to the formidable Janet. Neither Joe nor Rose could bear the thought of spending much time with Hugh D., since he had stated openly that he regarded them as "low-class Irish micks."

When Jackie returned from London, a meeting was arranged at Newport. Rose stayed with the Robert Youngs at their magnificent imitation Tudor house, Fairholme, on Ruggles Avenue, before making her way to the humdrum Auchincloss fortress, Hammersmith Farm.

Arriving on a warm July afternoon, Rose drove up a long driveway that led through acres of grounds overlooking Narragansett Bay. On one side were the famous flower gardens, on the other rolling pasture grass where Argyle cattle grazed.

Built in 1887, the farmhouse was a sprawling Victorian folly with a bristle of chimneys and eaves. A maid answered the door. Rose walked through a red-carpeted hall. Hugh D. Auchincloss's Williamsburg-blue study was to her left. The Deck Room was furnished without distinction, chintz-covered chairs and brown couches scattered with multicolored cushions. A stuffed pelican dangled from the ceiling, moving slowly in the breeze, exhibited as proudly as though it were an Alexander Calder.

Janet Auchincloss appeared: stiff, correct, guarded, dressed in subdued colors. She hadn't deigned to have Rose for lunch, but announced that Rose was invited to Bailey's Beach Club instead. Jack walked in wearing a T-shirt, shorts and bedroom slippers. Jackie Bouvier followed.

All four drove to Bailey's. Rose sat in the front with Janet; Jack and Jackie sat in the back. Jack ran into the water for a swim. Rose shouted at him as though he were a six-year-old boy, ordering him out of the water and insisting he towel down before the meal. Mrs. Auchincloss, unused to loud and peremptory behavior, was not amused.

The luncheon was tense. It was obvious that Janet shared her husband's disdain for Rose. Rose was eager, bubbling and talkative; Janet was still, cold and distant. Rose said she wanted a full-scale society wedding, with a press contingent and a galaxy of celebrated guests; Janet had no interest in any such proposal. She wanted a family occasion, with only close friends in attendance, almost no press, and certainly no party, dance band or singers.

For once in her life, Rose was forced to beat a retreat. There was only one thing to do. Joe flew up to Newport to charm the haughty bird off its tree. He did—but Hugh D. proved tougher. If Joe wanted a circus, he would have to pay for it. The father of the groom, not the father of the bride, would pay for the wedding.

On July 7, 1953, Rose was shopping in Hyannis. Turning the corner of Chase and Harvard, she drove her car through a stop sign at forty miles an hour, colliding with an automobile driven by county treasurer's clerk Laura M. Burge, with her seventeen-year-old daughter Marlowe as passenger. Both Burges were injured; the mother suffered a lump on her forehead, a bleeding right eye, a bump on the back of her left ankle, soreness in her chest and a minor concussion. Marlowe Burge hurt the middle finger of her left hand and was sore from head to foot and in a dazed condition. Both lost time from work. They sued Rose for $12,000. After a Superior Court hearing and lengthy depositions, the court made an irritable Rose pay just $1 damages. The family reached a separate verdict: she must engage a chauffeur.

Jack couldn't resist a last fling as bachelor. He took off on July 20 on a Mediterranean cruise, women loaded up to the gunwales of a chartered yacht, using as a public excuse the fact that he would be conferring with French government officials in Paris on the Diem situation in Indochina. He returned on August 7.

On the sixteenth, Rose heard the sad news that Eddie Moore had died in Boston. She attended the funeral, no doubt recalling happy times in America and in England.

On September 10, Hugh D. Auchincloss gave a bachelor dinner at Newport's Clambake Club. He watched helplessly as Bobby and Jack tossed the fabled Auchincloss crystal glasses into the fireplace.

At a subsequent family affair at the same location, Rose laughed uproariously when Jack said he was marrying Jackie to remove her from the Fourth Estate. Jackie responded with "He only once sent me a love letter—from Bermuda; it read, 'Wish you were here.'"

The ceremony took place at 11:00 A.M. on September 12 at St. Mary's Church, Newport, with Archbishop Cushing presiding. Rose and Joe's chauffeur edged slowly through the narrow streets, a crowd of eight thousand struggling against cordons as reporters scribbled and cameras popped. Screams greeted the arrival of Marion Davies; few recognized General David Sarnoff, Joe's old colleague of the 1930s, Senator and Mrs. Estes Kefauver, Lee and Michael Canfield or Rose's mother Josie, who was by now very infirm. Black Jack Bouvier was absent. Drunk, he had been locked in his room at the Viking Hotel by the Auchincloss clan. "Grandy" James T. Lee did not go to the wedding, because Janet Auchincloss had refused to countenance the presence there of his sisters Florence, Genevieve, Madeline, Amy and Eliza, and because he had never forgiven Joe for outwitting him in the purchase of the Merchandise Mart.

Jackie showed no sign of her annoyance as she arrived with her stepfather. She was elegant in a wedding dress made by black designer Ann Lowe.

The Pope's benediction was read. As Jackie, smiling happily, walked up the aisle, family friend John White startled her by waving a dollar bill in her face. He had bet her the money she would not marry Jack. Bobby as best man reached for the wedding ring. He couldn't find it. Rose turned to stone. He searched and searched and at last he found it. Everyone breathed again.

The reception followed at Hammersmith Farm. The

terrace had been covered to create a dance floor; Meyer
Davis's fifteen-piece society orchestra played as dancing
began. Joe looked ecstatic as he waltzed with Jackie; Rose,
smiling bravely, danced with the dreaded Hugh D.
Auchincloss. As everyone changed partners, the atmosphere
was joyous; Ethel, Eunice and Pat, energetic as always, ran
in their bridesmaids' gowns across the lawn, clowning
furiously for the press while Janet Auchincloss tried to
conceal her offended propriety.

After dancing, the society guests, 750 in all, repaired to a
blue-and-white-striped tent built over the lawn. Lunch was
served. By mistake, the Moët et Chandon champagne was
delivered to a tent occupied by the limousine drivers and
other help, while the cheap California wine was delivered to
the guests. Morton Downey sang, and a violin trio sere-
naded the tables, each of which was crowded with flowers
from the Auchincloss gardens.

In a shower of rice, the couple drove off to Manhattan for
a wedding night at the Waldorf Towers. They flew to
Acapulco, Mexico, where Joe had arranged for his friend
President Miguel Aleman to loan them his pink oceanfront
villa. Jackie, following an old tradition, wrote to Rose
throughout the honeymoon, describing Jack's struggles with
Spanish and his hooking a sailfish after a three-hour strug-
gle in which she splashed water over him to keep him cool.
They flew to Los Angeles, where they stayed at Marion
Davies's beach house, then traveled north to see friends in
San Francisco.

In October, Jackie (temporarily) removed Rose's reservations. She sent Rose a Stephen Vincent Benét–like doggerel
poem, evoking Jack as a lover of the sea and of his New
England political heritage. It was a campaign press release
in rhyme.

Rose was in a good humor in the aftermath of the
wedding, which seemed to be symbolic of a new era of
optimism in America. The Korean War had ended in July,
its beginning and termination framed between the marriages of Bobby and Jack; Bobby was busy in Washington,
pursuing the issue of extensive American aid to Red China,
and, as always, the matter of communism in the United

States. Teddy was back at Harvard in September, forgiven for his sins. The country was enjoying great prosperity. The baby-boomer generation seemed to have unlimited prospects for the future.

Rose planned her most elaborate foreign trip to date: as a reward for missing her customary journey to Paris that fall, she would go with Pat on a journey that would circle the world. Mother and daughter would fly to Honolulu on January 14, 1954; they would continue to Tokyo, sailing from the port of Yokohama on the S.S. *President Wilson* on the twenty-eighth for Hong Kong and Manila, fly to Bangkok, Calcutta, Benares, New Delhi, Agra to see the Taj Mahal, then to Bombay, Madras, Bangalore, and Colombo, Ceylon. They would pick up the S.S. *Independence,* sailing to Aden in the Red Sea, Suez, and thence fly to Cairo, which Rose had not visited since March 1939. They would return home via Paris and London. Suffering from a calcium deficiency not uncommon at her age, sixty-three, Rose had to be assured of milk supplies at each station of the journey.

In December, Deputy Undersecretary of State Robert Murphy, whose gifted actress daughter, Rosemary, was a friend of the Kennedys, began writing letters of introduction to such figures as Admiral F. B. Stump, commander in chief of the U.S. Pacific Fleet, and numerous ambassadors and consuls general. He wrote on behalf of "Misses Rose and Patricia Kennedy," not Rose and her daughter. This was doubly embarrassing in view of a possible confusion with Rosemary, who was still at St. Coletta's. When Joe and Rose received copies of the letters, they were upset; Murphy had to send corrected notes to all concerned. Joe wrote to Murphy, "It is bad enough for me to pass as Rose's father without you establishing the precedent on this trip!"

While preparations for the journey advanced, Rose's relationship with Jackie deteriorated again. On a visit to Hyannis Port just before the Kennedys took off to Palm Beach for the winter season, Jackie complained of the cold in the house; Rose was stingy when it came to expensive heating bills and other matters. Instead of turning up the heat, Rose suggested that Jackie should come down to the basement, which was warmer, and see a movie. It was colder there; Jackie was upset.

Tolerant at first of Jackie's disinterest in playing touch football, Rose became annoyed when her daughter-in-law continued to abstain from the sport. "The exercise will do you good," she said. Jackie replied sharply, "It's about time everyone around here exercised his mind instead of his muscles." Rose was furious at the slight.

Jackie tended to linger in bed, sometimes not even wanting to get up for lunch. When Rose sent a secretary to waken Jackie, Jackie refused to come, giving a sharp and cruel imitation of Rose's high-pitched voice. Then she went back to sleep.

Despite her annoyance at Jackie, Rose couldn't help but notice that Jack's appearance was improving under his wife's careful guidance. He began wearing well-cut suits, monogrammed shirts (though he did sometimes pull out the tail to wipe his glasses), and he actually polished both shoes, not one, as before. When at the office, he stopped loosening or removing his tie and kept it firmly in place and well knotted, and he expected his staff to do the same. Before Jackie's advent, he addressed his employees by their Christian names. Now, he spoke to them by their surnames, and expected them to do the same where he was concerned.

But, like Rose, Jack was unable to improve his driving habits, as he became guilty of moving violations, ignoring traffic signals and refusing to carry a driver's license. Stopped by police on several occasions, he expected them to recognize him and was irritable when they did not. When Ted Sorensen or another of his aides explained who he was, he was let off with a caution. This encouraged him to continue driving as dangerously as before.

Excited by her world travel plans, Rose found them rudely interrupted. The indirect cause was Peter Lawford. After only a handful of meetings, Pat fell in love with the weak and feckless thirty-year-old movie actor, whose musical *Good News,* shown in the Hyannis Port basement several years earlier, had dazzled the whole family. Lawford had first met the Kennedys in 1940, when, as an almost penniless British immigrant, the son of retired English general Sir Sydney Lawford, he was working as a car-park attendant at Palm Beach and took care of the Kennedy Chrysler. Joe overtipped him a quarter.

He had met Pat at the Republican National Convention in Chicago in 1952, and she and her sisters were overcome by the presence of a movie star.

Pat became fascinated by Lawford at a bad time in his career. M.G.M. had dropped his contract, and he had been forced to retreat to the second-grade studio Columbia, to make *It Should Happen to You*. His prospects seemed dim.

Rose was concerned that he might be a fortune hunter, so Joe invited him to Palm Beach in December. They looked him over. Tall and tanned, nicely built, he was even better-looking in person than on the screen; he had dressed carefully for the occasion, in just the right degree of elegant casualness. Only his ghastly red cotton socks were disconcerting. Joe read the Magna Carta of family rules to him; unlike Jackie, he didn't blanch. Athletic—despite a British accent, he had played an American college football hero in *Good News*—he joined vigorously in the touch-football game and was bright enough to score well at Monopoly and Scrabble. He fitted in fairly well; but neither Joe nor Rose felt he was marital material. An actor whose career was slipping who had once parked their cars scarcely seemed suitable for marriage to their most attractive daughter. They had in mind instead Pat's long-term suitor Frank Conniff, an attractive and promising International News Service journalist, whom Rose planned to meet with Pat in Japan.

By January, it was obvious that Pat and Peter were deeply interested in each other. Rose canceled her elaborately planned world trip in order to bring off a particular scheme. She would send Pat on her own to Tokyo to tell Frank Conniff she was ready to marry him.

Everything went according to plan. But once Pat arrived in the Japanese capital, she received a phone call from Peter with a definite proposal. An engagement ring would be waiting for her on her return. She was unable to resist. Much to Rose and Joe's disappointment, she flew back immediately and made it clear that she would marry Peter in the summer.

The Kennedys had strict rules in such matters. Peter would have to see them in order to present his case to them before they would consent to the match. They were in New York hotels—Rose as usual at the Plaza, Joe at the

Waldorf—when Lawford arrived for the interviews. He succeeded in charming Joe so that Joe gave a tacit approval, but then he ran a check on the young man. As a continuing Special Service agent of the FBI, and a friend of J. Edgar Hoover, Joe was able to bring up the Lawford file in a matter of days. He was gratified to find that there were no references to Lawford's rumored homosexuality in the dossier, only to his attendance at Lee Francis's bordello in Hollywood. A further check with Louis B. Mayer confirmed that there was no evidence that Lawford had had relation-ships with men.

Though she couldn't deny Lawford's attractiveness and ease of manner, Rose was opposed to the match. She hated the fact that Lawford was a lapsed Episcopalian, and probably an agnostic. He was actually a hedonist, far too casual, self-indulgent and superficial to have any serious interest in religion of any kind. She made it clear to him that he must at least take instruction from Catholic digni-taries and that his children must be raised as Catholics. She would expect him eventually to convert. When he agreed, she weakened.

Joe checked Lawford's finances. He had heard that the actor was broke, but was surprised to learn that he had managed to save $100,000, the equivalent of half a million in 1990s money. Rose stopped fighting the inevitable and, on February 12, the engagement was announced.

Rose had not foreseen another obstacle. She may have heard rumors about Lady May Lawford, Peter's mother, but she couldn't have imagined what she would be up against in this alarming woman. At least Big Ann Skakel, for all her vulgarity—she had recently installed a toilet in her Green-wich home in the shape of a red-velvet throne—had money and power; at least Janet Auchincloss had a degree of cultivation and proper manners. But May Lawford, though the highest-born of the three women, was also the most monstrous. Her posthumously published memoirs were, with a degree of honesty, entitled *Bitch*.

The daughter of a well-to-do army man, raised partly in Ceylon, May Bunny (her unfortunate maiden name) mar-ried another army officer, Captain Henry Ashley Cooper, in 1902. Disgusted by sex, she fled the bedroom on her wedding night; three years later, still unable to arouse her, her husband unwisely shot himself.

May married another military figure, Captain Ernest Aylen, in 1906; as frustrated as his predecessor by her indifference to her marital obligations, he tried to poison her with oleander leaves ground into pills. Disposing of him in the divorce court, she married the well-to-do Sir Sydney Lawford, who had reached an age at which he required her sexual attentions only once a month. Unfortunately for her social reputation, Peter was born, Sir Sydney's son, before her divorce from Aylen was finalized.

Peter Lawford, who remained his mother's only child, was dragged by his parents all over the world during the 1930s. Their money sequestered in England under wartime regulations, the couple wound up in Palm Beach in 1940. On a brief visit to Hollywood, Peter had appeared in a minor part in a Mickey Rooney film vehicle, *Lord Jeff.*

Back in Los Angeles, the young man obtained a name under contract to M.G.M., but never reached the top of stardom. A mediocre actor, his success depended on his charm and flashing smile, which made him the idol of more than a few bobby-soxers.

At the time Rose and Joe faced up to Lady Lawford, she herself had appeared in films, first in the comedy *Mr. Peabody and the Mermaid,* from which her part was cut, second in *Hong Kong,* starring Ronald Reagan, in which she played, rather well, the haughty society wife of British nobleman Nigel Bruce.

Joe took her to lunch at the Plaza, Rose to dinner. Furious at the typical Kennedy questionnaire, she stormed out of both meals in a fury. She made no secret of her hatred of the Kennedys, calling them "barefoot Irish micks." Anti-Catholic and anti-American, snobbish and foolish in equal degree, she embarrassed Rose as she publicly denounced her without restraint.

There could be no marriage at St. Patrick's Cathedral, nor would it be possible for Spellman or O'Connell to preside; the fact that Lawford was not a Catholic would rule out any such possibility. Instead, the nuptials took place on April 25, 1954, at the Roman Catholic Church of St. Thomas More in Manhattan, the ceremony performed by the Reverend John J. Cavanaugh, who had been the recipient of Kennedy endowments when he had been president of Notre Dame University, and was now president emeritus.

At the pre-wedding party at the Plaza, Lady Lawford was noisily drunk and was pushed off from the family table into a corner, imprisoned there by Cavanaugh to make sure she did not insult her host and hostess. To make matters worse, she arrived at the wedding with a Nazi agent, her best friend, a woman Rose detested. Hitler's associate Princess Stephanie Hohenlohe had been imprisoned as a Nazi spy in 1941, one day after Pearl Harbor, and had spent most of World War II in a Texas jail.

The ceremony was simple compared with those of Bobby, Eunice and Jack. Pat had only one bridal attendant, her sister Jean. Lawford's friend J. Robert Neal, Jr., of Houston, Texas, was best man. Jack, Bobby and Teddy were among the ushers.

There was a party afterward, again at the Plaza, in the Terrace Room. The couple left for an extended honeymoon in Hawaii.

Four days later, Eunice and Sargent Shriver's first baby, Robert Sargent III, was born.

On May 11, Cardinal Spellman conferred on Rose the Catholic Youth Organization's Club of Champions Award.

Throughout the summer, Jack felt a recurrence of back pain, hampering his continuing and impassioned campaign against communism expressed in speeches all over the state. He sought increased funds for military defense, but was defeated in the Senate. On August 17, much to Rose and Joe's distress, he announced that he would have to undergo special surgery following Congress's adjournment, and he was back on crutches every day.

At the beginning of September, Rose and Joe were in Paris. It was there, at the French Foreign Ministry on September 20, that they attended a ceremony at which Air Secretary Diomede Catroux presented them with the *Légion d'Honneur* and the *Croix de Guerre*, awarded posthumously to Joe, Jr. The honors, long delayed, moved Rose deeply.

She traveled with her husband to the South of France,

where, high above the sea in the medieval village of Eze, they rented the Villa Les Fal Eze, on the Moyen Corniche not far from their old favorite, the Hotel du Cap. The hotel gave them pool privileges at Eden Roc; they could swim, just as they had done in the late 1930s, in the landlocked saltwater pool. It was a happy, nostalgic time.

But there was bad news from America. There was no reversing Jack's decision to have an operation, and on October 11, while they were still in the South of France, he was admitted to Cornell Medical Center at 321 East Forty-second Street in Manhattan. After an X ray and a series of tests, it was clear that there was a ruptured disk in his spine and that he would have to be given a double fusion to repair the problem. Rose and Joe flew back at once.

On October 21, 1954, Jack underwent hours of major spinal surgery. Dr. Philip Wilson, leading specialist in such operations, did a magnificent job, but Jack's immune system was weakened, and he suffered from an infection that spread from the urinary tract. Rose and Joe came to the hospital twice, and on the second visit, at which Jackie was also present, Dr. Wilson advised them that he might not live. Cardinal Spellman arrived to give extreme unction. Rose was as strong as ever, but seeing his son's promise threatened with extinction, all hopes of a Kennedy becoming president once again swept away, Joe burst into tears when he mentioned his son to friends.

Then Jack rallied. Rose was quite impressed by Jackie's devotion as he fought for his life through two grueling weeks. Whenever he was conscious, Jackie told him funny stories, waved comic toys in front of his nose, made jokes about the picture of Marilyn Monroe above his bed.

Rose prayed day and night, attending Mass at all hours, fingering her rosary wherever she went. At last, her prayers were answered. Dr. Wilson told her Jack would live.

That season, Rose and Joe discovered that the Palm Beach Country Club, just down the road from them, and to which they had belonged since the 1940s, was, after much neglect and even a partial closure, being reopened by a group of Jewish businessmen in defiance, since they were precluded from membership of certain strictly gentile clubs. It was a similar situation to that which had confronted Rose in Hollywood in the 1920s when she and Joe were given honorary membership at the Hillcrest Country Club, courtesy of Joe Schnitzer of FBO. Had they been anti-Semitic—the charge, of course, still stuck strongly to Joe—they would certainly have resigned at that moment, and even more certainly the Jewish owners would have explained that the club was restricted and asked them politely to leave.

But they stayed on, as established in records by historian Larry Youngs. It is disturbing to reflect that no columnist remarked that they were the only gentile members. They were instantly welcomed and accepted and formed many new Jewish friendships.

On December 2, the Senate voted 67 to 22 to condemn Joe McCarthy for abuses that stemmed from his inquiry into communism in government offices. Jack abstained from the vote, a fact for which he was condemned by many, led by an angry and unforgiving Eleanor Roosevelt. But aide Ted Sorensen made clear in a subsequent memoir that Jack left any such action to him; Sorensen decided that an absentee vote would not be appropriate.

Jack was discharged from the hospital on December 21 and flown to Palm Beach. Rose was pleased to note that Jackie's care of him never ceased. Jack dismissed the nurse, and Jackie, fighting her natural squeamishness, every day dressed and redressed the gaping wound in his back.

During his period of recovery, in pain much of the time, Jack devoted himself to putting together a book, later to be entitled *Profiles in Courage*. He called on the assistance of researchers and writers, including Ted Sorensen and Arthur Krock. The book reads like an extended defense of his father by inference. He began with John Quincy Adams, his long-ago predecessor as Massachusetts junior senator, and his father's predecessor as minister for the United States in Britain. Adams had been head of a movement for negotiated peace with England, a parallel here with Joe's alleged role as peace negotiator with Germany. Jack described Adams as "narrow, unbending and intractable," words applied frequently to his father.

In portraying Daniel Webster, in the matter of Webster's presenting the secession of the South in 1850, Jack defended the politician from the charges of appeaser that Joe had had to face. In repeating the gist of Webster's famous March 7, 1850, speech against the separation of North and South, Jack could have been writing of Joe's radio address some ninety-one years later on the issue of England's plight ("Necessity compels me to speak true rather than pleasing things . . .").

Thomas Hart Benton was, like Joe, "assailed as a coward and a traitor"; he was capable of "stinging sarcasm . . . bitterly heated debate . . . bulldog persistence . . . ferocious egotism." He was branded appeaser; he was "ignominiously dismissed from service and called home," a significant parallel with Roosevelt's recall of Joe in 1940.

Sam Houston was called "appeaser" and "traitor." He was charged with "immorality and cowardice" when he became governor of Texas, in 1859. Edmund Ross, one of seven Republican senators who gave a not-guilty verdict at the impeachment trial of President Andrew Johnson, was branded a traitor. Lucius Lamar of Mississippi, appeaser of the quarrel between North and South, was charged with making "such haste to join the ranks of the enemy that he went stumbling over the graves of his fallen comrades." George Norris was "emotional in his deliberations, vituperative in his denunciations, and prone to engage in bitter and exaggerated personal attack instead of concentrating his fire on the merits of an issue."

What could be a better description of Joe Kennedy?

The last chapter was the most daring. Jack went all out in approving of Joe's friend and idol Robert A. Taft, in particular Taft's disapproval of the Nuremberg Trials, in which the senator, who had died in 1953, was supported by Kennedy friend Judge William O. Douglas. Taft had been criticized for stating that a trial of vanquished by victors could not be impartial, that the spirit of vengeance was seldom justice, and that Nuremberg, based on the ex post facto statute of crimes against humanity, was a blot on American Constitutional history: Joe's view exactly. For Jack to defend Taft in the matter was daring in the extreme, drawing attention to his father's desire to secure a German alliance at the beginning of the war.

Profiles in Courage would earn for its author excellent reviews and a Pulitzer Prize.

As Jack strengthened, Rose felt sufficiently confident to embark on her long-delayed journey around the world. She took with her, starting on March 27, her niece, Mary Jo Gargan. She stopped off in Santa Monica, California, to visit Pat, who gave birth on the twenty-ninth to her first child, Christopher, at St. John's Hospital. Rose turned nursemaid, taking care of mother and son at the Lawfords' beach house. She annoyed Lawford and his mother by taking over the whole household, issuing instructions in every direction. They were relieved when she took off with Mary Jo at the end of the month.

As always with the Kennedys, Rose's was not merely a vacation, but a fact-finding trip as well. Asia was in turmoil in April 1955. There were riots in Saigon, where she met her friend Diem, and disruptions in Cambodia.

Communist influences infiltrated everywhere. At the time Rose was in New Delhi, for an audience with Prime Minister Nehru, he was preparing for a visit to Moscow, to begin on June 7, in which an agreement would be signed for Soviet economic and technical assistance to India; by November, Premier Nikita Khrushchev and Marshal Nikolai Bulganin would be in New Delhi.

Ignoring such matters as heat, contagious diseases, hotels without air-conditioning and grueling flight schedules, Rose arrived, looking attractive and fit, in Paris in mid-May, having learned in detail of USSR infiltration in Asia. She met with Jean at the Ritz, for shopping in the fashion salons. Jean told her that she felt a strong romantic interest in Stephen Smith, an attractive and well-educated young man descended from penniless Irish immigrants, who was working for his family's successful transportation company. Rose liked the fact that he was a good Catholic and that his grandfather had twice been a congressman in Honey Fitz's day. Not knowing at the time that he was a heavy drinker, she approved of Jean's desire to marry Smith.

She returned to Hyannis to see Bobby admitted to practice law before the Supreme Court on June 6. On the tenth, she helped Joe host a party for four hundred prominent legislators, congressmen and state officials; the purpose was to build a closer relationship between state and federal authorities for the benefit of Massachusetts—a move toward Jack eventually running for president.

Five days later, Ethel's fourth child, David Anthony, was born, and on June 23, Joe ended the second term of the Hoover Commission, again a job well done.

Chapter 14

The CIA–Vatican Connection

Restless as ever, after only two months back at Hyannis Port, Rose was off again, this time with Joe, to their villa at Eze near Antibes. This nostalgic sojourn would be repeated each summer, for six years.

In August, Count Enrico Galeazzi stayed with them, enjoying the long, lazy summer days and the jasmine-scented evenings under a sky glittering with stars. During the visit, he discussed various plans with them. They were committed to restoring the crumbling Church of St. Anastasia at the foot of the Palatine Hill in Rome and the Arch of Constantine in the same city. These proposed improvements would prove to be an ideal cover for an extraordinary cloak-and-dagger operation involving the Kennedys, Pope Pius XII, Galeazzi, Cardinal Spellman, Clare Boothe Luce (who was now ambassador to Italy), CIA chief Allen Dulles and Jack Kennedy.

All were concerned about Communist advances in the Christian Democrat government of Italy, the government that the CIA and Joe had backed secretly with large sums of

349

money via Galeazzi in April 1948 and that was supposed to provide a bulwark against the Soviets.

It was a time when France, Belgium and Germany were falling under the Russian spell, a fact that, owing to the discrediting of Joe McCarthy, tended to be ignored by many liberal-minded Americans. On June 26, 1955, Antonio Segni had become Italian premier and there was a fear that he would set up a stronger relationship with the USSR.

To combat this threat, the CIA increased its operations in Rome to the tune of $25 million a year. The financial arrangement was authorized by President Eisenhower. It was run by Allen Dulles in association with such figures as Cord Meyer, Jr. (son of Rose Kennedy's old friends of the Italian visit of 1933), acting as liaison with Washington, local chief William Colby and Ambassador Clare Boothe Luce. The operation was designed to flush out Communist cells in the labor unions, arrange tax audits on suspected evaders who might have Communist connections and eliminate dangerous elements that had caused outbreaks of violence in several cities that year. The CIA headquarters, located in the heart of Rome, was in constant danger of bugging and exposure. Therefore, Galeazzi had decided to enlist the Kennedys' aid in setting up a CIA listening post in the heart of the Vatican. CIA chief Gerald Miller was involved in this operation; Colby was not.

In order to facilitate the arrangement, money would have to be paid to Pope Pius XII and his treasurers, money whose origins and purpose would not be suspected by KGB agents. At least a million would be needed. To this end, Joe Kennedy suggested reviving his and Rose's idea, first presented in 1948, of making reparations for the U.S. Army Air Force's bomb damage to the Pope's summer residence at Castel Gandolfo in 1944. The bill would be introduced in the House and the Senate by Italian-supported Massachusetts politicians, including John W. McCormack, Democratic majority leader.

Joe traveled with Galeazzi to Rome on August 29. He decided to leave Rose behind, perhaps because he feared that her safety might be endangered, or, more probably, because he wanted no distractions during the complex negotiations. But he kept her fully informed. After a meeting with Pope Pius the same day, he appeared at the Don Orione Rest Home at Monte Mario, where Alberto Folchi, undersecretary of state, presented him with the Star of Solidarity of the First Class of the Italian Republic in recognition of his and Rose's work for the equivalent institution in Boston. Rose was disappointed that she was excluded from this public recognition of her acts of charity.

Following a meeting with Clare Boothe Luce to get the arrangements started, Joe picked up Rose and flew back to New York. On September 5, Galeazzi officially provided Allen Dulles with the necessary cover: a memorandum detailing the Vatican's claims for restoration of the Castel. Two days later, in a secret document, Galeazzi wrote to Joe at Hyannis Port, emphasizing the importance of a close alliance between the Vatican and the CIA, stating the "need for communion of effort to keep communism back."

Jack Kennedy flew to Rome to continue the arrangements at Castel Gandolfo on September 19. He had a prolonged meeting with the Pope; the official topic of discussion was Poland. Meanwhile, Joe met with John W. McCormack, who agreed to introduce the bill.

As arrangements proceeded, Bobby and William O. Douglas, granted permission by the Russian government, conducted an on-the-spot investigation into Russian handling of its dependent countries, while Jack and Jacqueline proceeded to Poland.

The Kennedy intelligence-gathering machine was working overtime when, on October 3, Rose and Joe received dramatic news at Hyannis Port.

For years, Ethel Kennedy's parents, George and Big Ann Skakel, had been using a converted B-26 bomber, arguably the most uncomfortable method of transportation available (and a successor of the aircraft in which Joe, Jr., had died), as a fast means of transportation to get them from place to place; they were too impatient to use commercial aircraft. Those foolish enough to accept an invitation to join them on their trips often found themselves housed in a cramped and uncomfortable bomb bay.

Taking off from Tulsa, Oklahoma, en route from Connecticut to California, they had, stubbornly as ever, failed to take note of weather warnings and apparently pressed their pilot to fly through a severe electrical storm. The plane exploded in midair; they were killed instantly.

By early November, there was talk of Jack pursuing the role of vice-president at the 1956 Democratic Convention. Rose was opposed to the idea; she was disturbed to think that Jack might wind up as running mate to presidential contender Adlai E. Stevenson. Joe was certain Stevenson would lose the election, because he was too intellectual; he lacked the common touch, military background and powerful sense of leadership of Eisenhower. If Jack went down with him, he would be blamed for the failure because he was Catholic. The Kennedys were haunted by Catholic candidate Al Smith's repeated defeats decades earlier.

Joe was also uneasy about Stevenson's attitude to Russia. He was afraid that Stevenson would take a soft line on communism, that this formerly conservative governor of Illinois was turning slowly but surely to the left.

Jack was his own man. He didn't listen to his parents; he conferred with Stevenson into the winter of 1955. Irritable over the matter, Joe continued his efforts on behalf of the Vatican-CIA connection.

In December, Cardinal Spellman called Joe at Palm Beach and, reminding him of their joint sponsorship of the Vatican-backed Ngo Dinh Diem in 1951, urged Joe to assist in having President Eisenhower support the Diem regime in South Vietnam. Eisenhower had grown dubious about the regime's effectiveness as a Catholic bulwark against communism, but Spellman and Joe were determined to adhere to the Vatican's wishes in the matter, and Kennedy's CIA/Eisenhower/Rome link became invaluable. On Spellman's advice, and in the interests of Pius XII and Count Galeazzi, Kennedy arranged for Joseph Buttinger, of the International Rescue Committee, who was acting on Diem's interests, to meet with Senator Mike Mansfield and with Ted Sorensen in Washington. Joe and Spellman arranged for Buttinger to meet editors of all leading American newspapers, and for him to write an article in the *Catholic Reporter* in support of Diem.

Spellman flew to Saigon, where, significantly, in 1958, the Catholic William Colby, Joe and Clare Boothe Luce's contact and chief of the CIA operation in Rome, would be transferred to further the secret war against communism. The result of Joe Kennedy's and Spellman's efforts was the birth of the Vietnam lobby, unattributed in most media to the Vatican connection.

Joe made arrangements with Eisenhower to be appointed to the Board of Consultants on Foreign Intelligence on January 13, 1956. He was to report to the president and to concentrate on the intelligence situation in the South of France and in Rome, as well as seal up the Vatican link. According to the requirements of the office, Joe's friend J. Edgar Hoover, though bearing in mind that Joe was still an FBI contact, conducted an investigation into Joe's political background, and certain old files were dug up. Examining these today, it is easy to see that charges of bootlegging during Prohibition and espionage on behalf of the Nazis had no basis in documented fact.

While the Vatican matter proceeded, *Profiles in Courage* was published to favorable reviews. The Kennedys were proud of their son, but they were not pleased when, on March 8, Jack pledged his support to Stevenson, thus insuring the candidate the state of Massachusetts.

Eight days later, Rose attended a ground-breaking ceremony of the Manhattanville College of the Sacred Heart at Purchase, New York, for a dormitory and physical-education building to which she had given a check for $300,000 in February. In a two-thousand-word speech, all past blame of her daughter buried for good, she spoke of the fact that the two buildings were in honor of her dead daughter Kathleen ("It is . . . fitting to have her memorial in the form of a sports center because, as a little girl, she was . . . fond of athletics").

On May 4, Jean Kennedy, still the quietest and least-publicized of Rose's daughters, was officially engaged to Stephen Smith, and on the nineteenth they were married at St. Patrick's in New York. The nuptial Mass, performed by

Cardinal Spellman, was accompanied by the customary blessing from the pontiff. Eunice was matron of honor and the only attendant; Smith's brother Philip was best man, and among the ushers were Jack, Bobby and Teddy. The least spectacular of the Kennedy weddings, it was followed by a reception for family members and friends at the Baroque Suite and Crystal Room of the Plaza.

The month following the wedding, Rose was concerned about the lingering illness of the Kennedys' beloved friend Ambassador to Italy Clare Boothe Luce, who had been in and out of hospitals in America for weeks. The truth of her condition was complex. In January 1955, she had complained of feeling ill. She suffered from nausea, cramps and headaches that were not helped by the heavy Italian cuisine at her dinner parties and those at which she was a guest. She became paranoically convinced that the Communists were poisoning her food.

It emerged that a fine film of dust in her ceiling, loaded with arsenic from seventeenth-century painted cherubs, was descending on her, dislodged by the vibrations of a newly installed washing machine. Because of her weakened condition from infected gums, toxic dust had an especially adverse effect on her. Her social secretary, Letitia Baldrige, had a higher arsenic count in her blood, but was healthy, because she was energetic and athletic whereas Mrs. Luce lingered behind closed windows indoors.

In November, a virus had invaded Mrs. Luce's system through her gums and laid her low; now she was suffering from anemia. Rose was worried about her friend's condition; letters and phone calls flowed between them constantly. Henry Luce, not wishing to draw attention to his wife's unglamorous dental condition, which she was extraordinarily lax in attending to, had his *Time* magazine staff prepare a story in which the ceiling was solely responsible. The public fell for it.

Mrs. Luce's illness delayed Joe's work in implementing plans for the CIA-Vatican connection.

That these plans were still in progress is clear from correspondence between Mrs. Luce, Joe and Rose in the summer of 1956. Rose flew to Paris in the second week of June; Joe followed on the twenty-fifth aboard the U.S.S. *United States*. En route to the dock, he dictated a note to Clare, who was now in Washington, setting out his plans for himself and Rose for the rest of the season and inviting her to stay with them at Eze. He reserved any reports or comments until he met with Clare there.

On June 1, while Rose and Joe were at Eze, with the retired Gloria Swanson at the Chateau Barlow as their neighbor, Clare wrote Joe from Rome, preparing him for his arrival in Rome nine days later, where he would confer with CIA chief William Colby. She gave an account of the necessary elements of espionage against the Russians. This letter, mysteriously, was not classified.

Luce wrote that effective intelligence was not so much a matter of evaluating the facts as evaluating their handling by the enemy. It was important to know the mental state of Russian operatives; to determine the Russian response to Britain's determination to fight for its oil against Russian influences in the Middle East; to know what went on in the hearts of Khrushchev, Nasser (Egypt) and Nehru (India). She added that a student of human nature, history, cultures, symbols and, perhaps, geography and climate, could turn a better score in the intelligence field than the most brilliant economist, scientist, politician or military man. Clare Luce referred back to 1940 in evoking a conversation aboard the *Queen Mary* between Joe and Henry Luce, in which Luce had said that England's war was America's war. Joe had said, "Do you want to go into a war with FDR? Do you trust him to make peace?" She mentioned the Yalta Conference, in which much of Europe had been handed over to Stalin; she said that the present situation in Europe resulted from facts about Russia being sifted through Roosevelt's mind and evaluated by Harry Hopkins and Alger Hiss; the matter would, she said, certainly be discussed at Eze.

After conferring with the CIA in Paris on June 10, Joe flew to Rome. He was furious when William Colby refused to give him the names of key agents in Italy. Colby called Mrs. Luce in New York, and told him to give Joe all the information he needed. Joe investigated the $25-million-a-year CIA operation in Rome. He felt that there was much overspending; but in general he approved the CIA operation, which was infiltrating the Communist and Socialist parties, undermining them wherever possible and strengthening the Christian Democrats against Soviet penetration. It was clear to him that the Vatican-CIA connecting operation was not run by William Colby (who today states that he knew nothing about it) but by Gerald Miller, head of CIA operations in Western Europe, whose flirtatious letters to Mrs. Luce, using a childlike, absurd code, make extraordinary reading today.

Joe met with his fellow Knights of Malta and close Vatican associates including Cardinal Tardini, Vatican secretary of state, and the Pope's nephew, Prince Marcantonio Pacelli, as well as the Vatican's intelligence chief, Cardinal Montini, later Pope Paul VI.

On June 26, Gerald Miller wrote to his friend Mrs. Luce commenting on Joe's visit. He said that Joe had been gentled by his friends at the Vatican who had confirmed to him that the CIA activities in Italy met with their support. In a direct reference to Joe's role, Miller said in the letter that Joe was, despite differences, a "constructive friend of the Secret Assemblage of Silent Sam." This was a commonly used code meaning the CIA; Sam, of course, was Uncle Sam.

Mrs. Luce wrote to Joe referring to the shaken state of "my boys in Rome, who were trembling in every nerve and shaking in every joint" after his visit. She pointed out that Colby had benefited from the "blood transfusion" from "a red-headed Irishman." She confirmed in a letter dated July 3 that she would be "transacting some business" with the Kennedys in the first week of August at Eze.

Rose wrote an affectionate note to her saying that she was delighted by the news; that Clare would not need her own maid, as Rose's would be available; and that Clare could wear a bathing suit all day if she wanted, both at Eze and at Eden Roc. And she invited her to a Friday gala at Monte Carlo.

Clare and Henry were welcomed by Rose at Eze on August 12; they had been sailing for weeks aboard the Greek shipping tycoon Stavros Niarchos's yacht the *Creole,* starting with embarkation in Lisbon. Although Niarchos had a fine house near the Kennedys' on the Moyen Corniche, the Luces preferred to stay with Joe and Rose. Others who were at the house that week were Rose's friends Father Cavanaugh of Notre Dame and Lord Beaverbrook, who was involved in the secret war against communism.

During the charged days and nights at Eze, as Clare discussed arrangements with the CIA in Rome and her connections to Gerald Miller, Joe was in a terrible temper. He suffered from day-and-night constant pressure to urinate, but when he did so, only a dribble would come out. Sleep was almost impossible. His condition was due to an enlarged and diseased prostate, very common in men of his age (sixty-seven), and he would need rapid attention, but he refused to go to a hospital.

Distracted by his illness and by the problems attaching to last-minute arrangements with the Vatican, neither Joe nor Rose was able to be in America during the Democratic National Convention in Chicago in mid-August. The day of the Luces' visit to Eze, the movement to secure the vice-presidential nomination for Jack strengthened as delegates from across the country pledged their support. The race for the party's second slot was led by Kennedy, Estes Kefauver, Albert Gore and the popular Hubert Humphrey.

On August 16, Bobby called to say that Stevenson had won the Democratic Party's nomination for president on the first ballot; he had defeated governor Averell Harriman of New York and senators Lyndon Johnson of Texas and Stuart Symington of Missouri. Jack delivered Stevenson's nomination speech. To the disappointment of many, Stevenson fudged the task of naming his running mate, preferring to throw the choice on the convention floor. When Bobby advised his father by telephone, the sleepless, miserable and exhausted Joe exploded in hysterical rage, screaming in four-letter words that Jack shouldn't have been seeking the nomination anyway. He was cut off when a thunderstorm brought down the telephone line.

The next day, Rose and Joe had better news. Bobby called

to advise that, on the second ballot, Albert Gore had withdrawn from the race in favor of Kefauver, thus giving the latter the necessary votes, which defeated Kennedy for the nomination. Joe was delighted; soon, he and Rose would learn that Jack's defeat was, paradoxically, a victory.

Millions had watched the convention on television, fascinated by Jack's looks, charm, figure and impeccable deportment. The grace with which Jack, worn-out though he was, yielded to Kefauver earned him countless fans. The visual medium had done something for him that neither radio nor the printed word could have done. It had made him a star—an idol not only of women but of men as well.

It was an age in which the clean-cut, the athletic, the open-faced public figure was insured of acceptance. Jack symbolized an era of imagined American innocence, commercial success and unlimited future. Jack was a product of postwar prosperity; he was St. George, fighting the Communist dragon.

A flawed St. George. Jackie was nine months pregnant at the convention's end, her nerves frayed and her health threatened by the frenzied atmosphere of high-level politics that she hated. She needed Jack with her at that moment, to attend to her lovingly when her child came. But instead of staying with her, instead of taking her to the hospital when her labor pains began, Jack left her, flying off with Teddy and Senator George Smathers, to join Rose and Joe at Eze.

He arrived on August 22. Rose wrote to Clare Boothe Luce, who had returned to Rome, and said she was impressed by his healthy appearance and deep tan, but noted that he was "pooped" from loss of sleep. Never sympathetic to Jackie, she did not upbraid Jack for leaving his wife at this moment. Scooping up starlets, Jack set sail on a chartered yacht for Genoa. No sooner had he left than Bobby called Rose to say that Jackie was ill, the baby had miscarried, and Jackie was home with her parents at Newport.

Rose added a footnote to her letter to Clare, announcing without any show of emotion, "Jackie lost her babe!" And she added, equally unemotionally, "heartbroken, I'm sure." She would try to reach Jack aboard his yacht; it has been claimed that she was unable to do so. But this is unlikely.

French maritime law required all vessels, small or large, to carry a ship-to-shore radio and telephone system. A more likely version of the truth is that Jack received the message but was insufficiently interested to dock the boat and fly home. When the yacht tied up in Genoa Harbor, Senator Smathers advised him to return at once. He did.

By September, Joe was so sick that it was obvious to Rose he would have to be gotten to a hospital. He refused help until, on September 2, four days before his sixty-eighth birthday, he agreed to fly with her to Paris for a checkup at the American Hospital at Neuilly. He would stay, as always, at the Hotel Raphael; Rose would stay at the Ritz. The diagnosis was clear: his prostate was enlarged and there were early signs of cancer. An operation would have to be performed. The surgeon would cut through the abdomen; recovery would be painful and protracted, lasting as long as three or four months, and would involve a catheter inserted into the penis, an excruciatingly uncomfortable procedure. Sexual impotence would be a probable result. Such was the fate of many virile males in their sixties and over. For a man who fancied himself a Casanova, it was a humiliation.

With her customary detachment, even indifference, as unemotional now as she was when reporting Jackie's loss of her baby, Rose did not fly with her husband to Boston. Joe was operated on at New England Baptist Hospital on September 13. She kept in touch with him by long-distance telephone, through the nurses and through Bobby. Jackie filled the role that Rose might have been expected to take by tending lovingly to him, whom she thought of as her "grizzly" and "dear grandpa."

As he struggled with the catheter and postoperative pain at Hyannis, Rose had another burden to bear. Jack and Bobby embarked on a coast-to-coast campaign for Stevenson, often in rickety single-engine aircraft, flying through electrical storms, risking their lives for a presidential candidate who was changeable and ungrateful and slowly but surely lost their respect.

Busy at the Paris salons, Rose learned that Jack had bought, for about $45,000, an attractive seven-room white clapboard cottage next door to her at Palm Beach, the gardens connecting. Bobby also bought a house, thus creating what became known as the Kennedy Compound—a term Rose hated.

Following Stevenson's defeat by Eisenhower in November, and knowing that Eisenhower would not be allowed to run for a third term, Joe was convinced that Jack would have a chance for the presidency in 1960.

Rose's movements in the next weeks suggest that her decision to stay on in Europe may not have been entirely motivated by coolness about her husband's medical condition, but may have involved her wanting to continue his contacts in the CIA-Vatican matter.

In Zurich on September 18, she stayed at the Dolder Grand Hotel. Zurich was one of the headquarters of Allen Dulles's European operations. Before she left Switzerland, she wrote Clare some odd questions, illustrating the fact that she had not been in Rome since 1939. Would she be able to get her favorite Sanka at the Villa? Would she need a hat if she went out to lunch? Should she bring a pink embroidered evening dress? Should she bring a copy of the French magazine *L'Officiel* (which had an article on Clare)? Clare saw to it that Rose was housed at her official residence: the 1569 Villa Taverna was restored and far more luxurious under Mrs. Luce's care than it had been during Rose's previous visits, in 1933 and 1939. Clare had carefully tended the cypress and ilex trees with a swarm of gardeners, two of whom were borrowed from the Pope. Water splashed in the exquisite stone fountain of the baroque garden; boxwood hedges alternating with orange trees were retrimmed after years of neglect.

Walking through the tall glass doors, Rose found herself in a creamy-white hall, flanked by antique columns, mirrors and a marble Venetian table. She walked across the ceramic-tiled floor to the living room, which was alive with tropical plants flourishing in priceless T'ang Chinese jardinieres. The walls of the salons were covered in silk damask, while the Luces added a dazzling collection of works by Delacroix, Manet, Matisse, Degas, Renoir and Rouault to the walls. Ming- and T'ang-dynasty horses and camels led a splendid, priceless porcelain parade of Chinese art.

Clare arranged parties for Rose's arrival. On October 3, in the magnificent dining room with blue-and-gold chairs,

Rose was at a dinner in honor of Princess Aspasia of Greece, with the German, Belgian, Greek, Indian, and Brazilian ambassadors also present. On October 4, Clare gave another luncheon for her, at which Count Galeazzi, Prince and Princess Pacelli, her old friends from Rio and Paris and several Atlantic crossings the Jefferson Cafferys, and Monsignor W. A. Hemmick of the Sovereign Order of Malta, were prominent.

She cabled Joe from Rome on October 3 that she was having a wonderful time; she told him she would be seeing Count Galeazzi at a meeting later that week. A scrap of paper left behind in her room at the embassy survives in Mrs. Luce's papers to this day: it contains a characteristic shopping list, including dolls for her international collection, (lantern) slides, mats, and mantillas (she had assembled many of these since those she had worn at the papal audiences in 1933 and 1939; Clare had supplemented the collection by mail to Eze). Rose returned to Palm Beach in November.

Transferred by her to the house there for the winter, Joe turned censor, mirroring Honey Fitz's earlier campaigns as he banned Elia Kazan's controversial motion picture *Baby Doll* from the theaters he still owned in Maine and New Hampshire.

Joe proved as feisty as ever in fighting with the New York City administration over the property he owned on Columbus Avenue in Manhattan. Marked as the site of Lincoln Center, the land was owned by his and Rose's children. He argued with the Rockefeller family, which sought to make arrangements for the buildings; he fought savagely over the price, charging far more per acre in the final negotiations than any other property owner.

Jackie was at Palm Beach at Christmas, recovered from her miscarriage, grating on Rose once more, just as Rose grated on her. When asked, in a family discussion, where the 1960 National Democratic Convention should be held, she exasperated everyone by saying "Acapulco." Matters were not helped when she described Rose as "a dinosaur without a brain." Her spoiled-rich-girl's love of buying vast amounts of clothes and shoes maddened Rose, the pot calling the kettle black; Jack complained constantly about

the bills. The family began to wonder what kind of a First
Lady Jackie would make—would her delicate manners,
fondness for highbrow reading (Proust, Malraux) and addiction to fine arts irritate a public that was accustomed to
housewives like Bess Truman and Mamie Eisenhower?

In the midst of these tensions, Gloria Swanson wrote to
Rose, enclosing details of a fringe-medicine cancer cure for
Joe. Rose did not reply from Chicago, where she was staying
with the Shrivers. Joe got out of bed at Palm Beach and
became mobile on January 7, 1957.

Good news was that Bobby was making a name exposing
racketeering in the labor unions on a Washington committee; better still, Jack was awarded the Pulitzer Prize for
Profiles in Courage on May 6. In June both the House and
Senate approved close to one million dollars in reparations
to Castel Gandolfo, and the CIA's arrangements with the
Vatican could continue. On June 28, 1957, Jean and Stephen Smith had their first child, Stephen Edward, Jr.

After three months at Eze, Rose and Joe returned to
Hyannis in October to begin a campaign for Jack as
president that would last for three and a half years. Rose
attended the dedication of the Kennedy buildings at
Manhattanville College of the Sacred Heart, Purchase, New
York.

Soon afterward, a Sacred Heart student, Joan Bennett,
namesake of Morton Downey's movie-star sister-in-law,
had two dates with Teddy, which developed into a strong
romantic interest. Tall and attractive, daughter of a
Bronxville-based New York advertising executive, Joan
appealed strongly to Rose.

Rose was then off to London, without Joe, who was
persona non grata there, and then to Paris, returning for the
birth on November 27 by cesarean section of Jack's daughter Caroline, named (such was Jackie's independence from,
even indifference to, Kennedy family requirements) for a
distant ancestor.

Rose attended the December 13 baptism at St. Patrick's,
held near the altar the Bouviers had long since dedicated.
The Auchinclosses, Jackie and Church authorities led by
Cardinal Spellman were infuriated by the reporters and

cameramen who crowded the church during the ceremony, but the Kennedys were delighted.

That week was stormy even by Kennedy standards. On December 9, Joe and Rose were watching the Mike Wallace interview on ABC television when columnist Drew Pearson announced that *Profiles in Courage* was ghostwritten, alleging that the future presidential candidate had obtained the Pulitzer Prize by false pretenses.

Joe let out a scream and called his Washington attorney Clark Clifford, announcing that he would sue ABC, Pearson and Wallace in Jack's name for $50 million. Clifford suggested mediation; Joe shouted his refusal.

The day before Caroline's baptism, Joe and Clifford met with ABC boss Leonard Goldensen in New York. Meanwhile, Kennedy aide Ted Sorensen produced evidence that Jack, while calling on Sorensen for much advice, had created the book himself; other contributions had been substantial, but Jack was the true author. Evan Thomas, Jack's editor at Harper's, confirmed that he had seen Jack writing the book painfully on boards while bedridden at Palm Beach and in the hospital.

The evening following the baptism, Oliver Trayz, vice president of ABC, read a retraction at the beginning of the Mike Wallace show; Joe was sufficiently appeased to drop the case.

The Kennedys' stresses continued. Black Jack Bouvier died of cancer. Out of an advance on her inheritance Jackie bought a white Jaguar as a Christmas present for Jack. He returned it to the dealer and used the cash to buy a Buick, keeping thousands in change. She was badly upset; she came to Palm Beach for the season in a mood of deep depression. Rose was again unimpressed.

Nineteen fifty-eight promised calm seas ahead: there was every indication that Jack would be unopposed at the primary that summer when he sought the nomination to return to the Senate following the expiration of the mandatory six-year period in which he had been in office. But in January, yet another tragedy hit Rose.

She had continued her friendship with Robert Young and his wife Anita; since Jack's wedding, she had visited them more than once at Fairholme, at Newport, and had returned to their Greenbrier Hotel whenever she could. The Youngs were neighbors at Palm Beach, as were the Charles Wrightsmans and Mary Sanford.

One January morning, Anita called to say that her husband was dead. Worn out by business problems, exhausted by his struggle to fight the railroad tycoons on their own turf, he had locked himself in his study, placed a shotgun between his legs, and blown his brains out.

Back from Paris at the end of May, Rose found Teddy very serious about Joan Bennett. She considered the matter carefully. Joan's father, Harry Wiggin, who was now with the Joseph Katz advertising agency in New York, was a Protestant, a dread thought indeed. Fortunately, though, his wife Virginia was a devout Catholic, and, of course, Joan had the inestimable advantage of having been a student at Rose's old alma mater, now called Manhattanville College of the Sacred Heart at Purchase, New York.

As always, Joe ran a check on the entire family; the FBI files showed nothing. Rose called Mother Elizabeth O'Byrne at Purchase and was pleased with the response. Joan had been a devout pupil, was a Child of Mary like herself, and had been selected to impersonate the Blessed Virgin in a recent pageant.

Harry and Virginia Bennett announced their daughter's engagement to Teddy.

Nominated unopposed, Jack made preparations for his senatorial campaign against thirty-four-year-old Boston Republican lawyer Vincente J. Celeste.

Rose appeared in a campaign film, *At Home with the Kennedys,* filmed at Hyannis Port in October and shown on television. She looked as awkward as she had ever looked, providing a lopsided, insincere smile that made it seem she had had a bad facelift. Rose introduced Jackie, without any warmth, as a "new addition to the family" since the last campaign movie in 1952. She asked Jackie, with a notable lack of enthusiasm, to give an account of her experiences during the campaign.

Jackie addressed Rose as "Mrs. Kennedy." She talked of visiting 184 communities with Teddy, who was on leave from the University of Virginia, as campaign manager. Rose congratulated her coolly. Then Jackie let her have it: "Jack has been so ungallant as to suggest that you have been campaigning for sixty-five years." This was absurd: Jack could never have said that his sixty-eight-year-old mother had been stumping from the age of three. It was a stab, delivered with considerable sweetness. Rose replied, with an equally deadly smile, "That is not quite true, because in those days women didn't have the vote, so we didn't go to rallies."

As we know, she had accompanied her parents to rallies from the age of six.

After an easier exchange with her daughters, Rose talked about the need to educate children in history and introduced home movies of her grandchildren. Toll-free questions were taken, sifted carefully to make sure none was controversial or difficult.

Jack was returned to the Senate on November 4, with a record-breaking 1,362,926 votes against Celeste's 488,318. The same day, Rose found herself with another grandchild, Pat and Peter Lawford's third, Victoria. So far, not one of Rose's offspring had named a child after her. Six days later, Jack, anticipating Alaska's statehood, and wanting to put it in his pocket when he ran for president, flew there in severe weather conditions.

On October 8, 1958, Pope Pius XII died in Rome, which meant that it would be difficult, in view of the election of his successor, for Cushing or Spellman to preside over Teddy's wedding. Both would be appointed cardinals by newly elected Pope John XXIII in December. However, Spellman, in view of his fondness for Rose, agreed to officiate.

The wedding took place on November 29, at St. Joseph's Church in Bronxville. Rose and Joe flew in the night before and stayed at the Gramatan Hotel. A storm swept the city, knocking down power lines, splintering trees, breaking windows. As Rose left for the church in a chauffeur-driven limousine, she saw streets strewn with broken glass and rubbish. As the chauffeur took her past her old home on Pondfield Road, it was almost invisible in the driving rain. She and Joe were greeted at St. Joseph's by a crestfallen Jack, who had failed to bring correct clothes and was dressed in a morning suit that barely met across his chest;

the trousers came above his ankles. Rose was appalled and insisted he make a quick change with a male friend who was two sizes larger than he was. Jack ended up looking like a scarecrow.

The party afterward was held at the country club that had excluded the Kennedys as Catholics decades before. Attractive in mauve velvet, at first Rose looked pleased, but then she became irritated: where were Bobby and Teddy? Instead of helping to entertain the guests, they were in the Grill Room, watching the Army-Navy game on television. Joe summoned them back.

Teddy and Joan flew off for a honeymoon at Lord Beaverbrook's estate in the Bahamas.

Nineteen fifty-nine was a uniquely uneventful year. Bobby continued with his bulldog tactics in the Rackets Committee hearings. Mindful of his future run for the presidency, Jack joined Bobby in attacking Jimmy Hoffa, denouncing Hoffa on the Jack Paar show. Teddy graduated from the University of Virginia Law School; in October, he was admitted to the Massachusetts bar. In September, Jack bought a twin-engine Convair, christening it the *Caroline,* which he would use as his presidential campaign aircraft.

On the brink of that campaign a potentially inconvenient letter arrived at Palm Beach from the changeable Gloria Swanson. Misspelled, overemotional, it was full of random and unsubstantiated charges of Joe's mishandling her affairs some thirty years before. ("Last night I had a dream about you—not a pretty one, though you had a charming smile all the time—it still was diabolicle [sic].") She wrote that "God's spotlight" was turned on the matter of her long-ago finances, that "God, you and I" know the truth of *Queen Kelly,* and "does one really set oneself free from one's own conscience?" by confession? She predicted that his reaction would be one of indignation and self-righteousness, which "knows no bound."

The letter went, understandably, unanswered.

At Palm Beach, over Christmas and New Year's, the Kennedys convened, making plans for the 1960 primary. The formidable list of opponents included Hubert Humphrey of Minnesota, Adlai Stevenson of Illinois and, of all people, the family's friend George Smathers of Florida, whom Joe had backed against Claude Pepper several years before.

It was agreed that Rose would make visits to supporters in difficult states; Bobby would break off his career as scourge of the racketeers by resuming his role as campaign manager; Ted Sorensen would be the strong hand behind the writing of the speeches; Teddy would handle the Western states; Steve Smith would run the financial end; Sargent Shriver would come in from Chicago as another stalwart; and Pat, Peter Lawford, Ethel, Eunice and Jean would all pitch in.

At the time, Rose formed a new and firm friendship, quite against Joe's advice or approval, with the wealthy Charles and Jayne Wrightsman. For years, Charles Wrightsman, the tyrannical and terrifying Oklahoma oil multimillionaire, had refused to receive the Kennedys at his house adjoining their estate at Palm Beach. A Republican of the fire-breathing school, he called Joe an "Irish crook." In turn, Joe called him an "upstart Okie." The situation was complicated by the fact that Wrightsman's younger daughter Charlene was married to the prominent Hearst newspaper columnist Igor Cassini, who was a friend of Joe's and a warm acquaintance of Rose, Jack and Jackie. Wrightsman had been furious when Charlene, before her marriage to Cassini, had had an affair with Jack at the time he was a congressman.

Now that it looked as though Jack had a good chance for the presidency, Wrightsman saw the advantage of being close to the center of power, both for his own sake and in hope of protections for the oil industry, in which Joe had a major hand. He began to invite the Kennedys to his parties; only Joe refused to go. Jayne, Wrightsman's second wife—a beautiful and cool former perfume saleswoman who had risen to become an authority on antique furniture and painting, investing her husband's millions in profitable transactions at Sotheby's auctions—became a friend of Jackie's and Rose's.

Rose was fascinated by Jayne, and enjoyed numerous visits to her house at 513 North Country Road. They had in common a friendship with Stephane Boudin, the noted French interior designer, through the duke and duchess of Windsor, whose Paris house Boudin had redecorated. The Windsors joined Rose at the Wrightsmans' parties; the Wrightsmans flew them in from France first-class. When Rose was at the Ritz in Paris in a modest room, the Wrightsmans rented the entire second floor.

The Wrightsmans hired no less than Francis Watson, the queen of England's personal art advisor and curator of the Wallace Collection, as their personal consultant and cataloguer, beginning with a fabled collection of Meissen birds and graduating to Joubert Louis XV desks. Their collection grew mightily. When Rose visited their homes at Palm Beach and New York she saw porcelain elephants, eighteenth-century ivory Indian chairs, marble-topped consoles, Chinese wallpaper on the walls, ormolu-encrusted commodes, Renoirs, Vermeers, Kaenfler ceramic birds. Charles Wrightsman (who voted for and supported Richard Nixon) began contributing, through various sources, an aggregate of over $100,000 to Jack's campaign.

Rose saw Jack on television declaring his candidacy in the caucus room of the Senate office building in Washington, D.C., on the second day of 1960. Jack glowed with confidence in the future. He talked of bringing "new life to society," making it clear that he intended to revitalize a nation that had grown tired and weak under the Eisenhower administration. He could point then and later to the nation's decline from its fat and sassy postwar years: Russia had the lead in space, Castro had overthrown the Batista regime in Cuba without American intervention, the school-integration issue was more severe than ever, unemployment was growing, and there was danger of Communist influence in South America.

Against Jack were his youth, his wealth, his father's troubled reputation, and, above all, his Catholicism. There were whispers about his private life, his list of adulteries that, if exposed, could have wrecked Rose's chaste and self-protective fantasies and his political future at the same time.

But as he spoke of fulfilling a noble and historic role as the defender of freedom in a time of peril, and of his love of the American people for their confidence, courage and perseverance, there was no denying that he stirred millions of hearts. His inspirational approach was exactly what many rank-and-file Democrats, especially those under thirty, wanted to hear. Those were less cynical times, and few were interested in examining the finer points of detail of what he had in mind. As it turned out, his policy of aid to Europe and Asia short of war against the Soviets echoed his father's attitude toward Germany in 1938–1940. It was not a parallel he would have been wise to have drawn.

Older Democrats were concerned about his lack of experience. Protestants were concerned that he would be under Vatican influence to the point that he would be taking his instruction more from the Pope than from the American people.

To kick off the campaign for the primary, Joe, through the areas of influence he had established since his time at Bethlehem Steel and Hayden, Stone, helped to settle the steel-industry disputes that had handicapped the country for months. His first targets would be New Hampshire, Wisconsin and West Virginia—all three states were anti-Catholic strongholds in which Hubert Humphrey would be expected to prevail.

Bobby decided that Rose would precede Jack into the first and second of these states, but not the third. This seemed strange to her; after all, she had spent her honeymoon in West Virginia, a topic of discussion when addressing women's groups. But Bobby pointed out that her position as papal countess would grate on the Protestant citizens of the state; West Virginia was a desperately poor area, with mass poverty and unemployment, in which the Greenbrier Hotel resembled the Palace of Versailles at the time of the French Revolution.

There is another reason she was not encouraged to go to West Virginia. According to members of the family of Sam Giancana, the well-known gangster, Bobby invited a Las Vegas mobster to the state, where he was authorized to use criminal tactics in insuring votes. Although, as the daughter of Honey Fitz, Rose would not be unfamiliar with such methods, she must be protected from knowing this at all costs.

Rose flew into New Hampshire for two days in late February, in freezing weather conditions, and she met with housewives and Democratic campaign leaders. After a rest at Hyannis Port, she set out on a demanding eight days in Wisconsin, a long-term stronghold of Hubert Humphrey as the neighboring state of his own Minnesota. She had planned to speak to German-American groups in their own language, learned long ago at the convent in Blumenthal, but Bobby dissuaded her; such a gesture might reawaken old charges of Nazi sympathy lodged against Joe.

Rose arrived in Milwaukee on March 16, 1960, dressed in an ermine hat she was careful to describe as rabbit, a bright red coat, and a simple black dress, white kid gloves and modest pearls. In order to appease the coffee-company campaign backers, she took coffee, not tea, with her first hostess, Mrs. Val Phillips, at 1633 Brown Street, with several Milwaukee aldermen's wives and Democratic National Committee members present.

Asked whether Jack was not too young to be president, Rose replied that he was old in wisdom; asked for her age, she lied that she was seventy; she was still only sixty-nine. She said that Jack was only slightly younger than Richard Nixon, and that he had been in the Soviet Union as an observer from his teens. Asked about religion as an issue, she said, dodging the question, "It's wonderful for children." Asked to comment on whether Jack would drag the country into war, she replied, "His older brother died in World War II. He knows the sorrow, the grief, the tears and the heartbreaking loneliness that come when a mother has lost her eldest son."

Rose held to that line throughout her tour. She gave teas, met with Mother's Club presidents, attended Jewish gatherings, but carefully avoided Holy Name breakfasts. Bobby arranged her days to conserve her energy. She never had to rise before 8:30 A.M. or retire later than 10:30 P.M.; her appointments were spaced out. Time was arranged for daily visits to the beauty parlor; limousines and private planes were always at her disposal. It was made clear to her escorts that she would want to sleep between engagements, thus allowing her to take catnaps in cars, and precluding her from the necessity of indulging in small talk with strangers.

She was in Hyannis Port in June to help the family take stock and weigh the prospects of the Democratic National Convention, which was to be staged, boldly, in Los Angeles, in Nixon's native state of California.

Defeated in West Virginia, Hubert Humphrey had withdrawn from the race. When Harry Truman, charging vote buying, and Eleanor Roosevelt both condemned Jack, it gave the family some qualms, and when Lyndon B. Johnson announced his certain entry for the nomination they were uneasy. But when they flew into Los Angeles on July 6, they were in an optimistic mood.

Rose stayed with Joe at Marion Davies's house on North Beverly Drive in Beverly Hills; ill from cancer of the jaw, their friend moved out in order to make them more comfortable. The Lawfords took a suite at the Beverly Hilton; Bobby's campaign headquarters were located at the Biltmore Hotel downtown. Jack took movie actor Jack Haley's apartment on North Rossmore Avenue. Adulterously involved with more than one woman, Kennedy used it as a hideaway from the press. Jackie, pregnant again, did not come to Los Angeles.

The convention was held at the Los Angeles Sports Arena. It was preceded by an all-star gala party at the Beverly Hilton Hotel presided over by Frank Sinatra. Among the luminaries Rose met there were Judy Garland, Tony Curtis, Janet Leigh, Milton Berle, Sammy Davis, Jr., and Angie Dickinson.

On the morning of the convention, Rose was negotiating some steps at the Biltmore with her old friend Joe Timilty when she twisted her ankle. Showing no sign of pain, she stood in agony for two hours in the receiving line, shaking supporters' hands. Then, still refusing to have medical treatment, resplendent in a red silk Courreges dress, Rose attended the manic events that followed at the Arena, joining the family in cheers as Jack won on the first ballot.

She sat next to him as he gave his acceptance speech at the

Coliseum. She smiled approvingly as he said, "We stand today on the edge of a New Frontier, a frontier of unknown opportunities and perils, a frontier of unfulfilled hopes and threats." He talked of "not what I intend to offer the American people, but what I intend to ask of them."

Knowing there would be demands on her energy during the electoral campaign, Rose decided on a long summer vacation. She flew with Ann Gargan to New York, joined Joe there, and continued with him to Paris and the South of France. The villa at Eze was no longer available, so Joe rented, for the equivalent of $1,000 a month, the Villa Bella Vista, conveniently close to Eden Roc, where he again leased Cabana 511 for the season.

Each morning, the couple rose at eight o'clock; Rose went to Mass at the Church of La Garoupe, while Joe took off for the golf course, where he had an attractive caddy, Françoise, the source of much baseless gossip. Rose shopped and wrote letters. In the afternoon, following her siesta, the Kennedys swam at Eden Roc; they would bring their wet bathing suits home. Tourists and other passersby were amazed to see, hung over the five-foot fence that surrounded the Villa Bella Vista's garden, the swimsuits hung out to dry.

Rose returned to Hyannis Port on September 3; in consultation with Bobby, she worked out a nerve-racking schedule. She would be flying to some forty-six cities in fourteen states, and would be taking tea or coffee with an estimated thousand people. Although Bobby arranged her schedule as before to conserve her energy and provide her with sufficient sleep, the tour was a major challenge for a seventy-year-old woman—a challenge to which she rose strongly.

As feisty and demanding as ever, a Kennedy PT-109 badge pinned firmly to whatever she was wearing, Rose took off aboard a succession of private and commercial aircraft through all kinds of weather, frequently braving severe thunderstorms.

Now that she was campaigning, she tirelessly addressed limousine or taxi drivers, manicurists, hairdressers, companions under the dryer, porters and waiters wherever she went. She would only reveal who she was at the end of the conversation, often insuring a vote as her addressee dissolved in appreciative laughter.

Now that the presidency was at stake, she could no longer restrict her speeches and interview statements to mere trivia; she had to come right out, face-to-face with her interlocutor, on the subject of Jack's Catholicism and adherence to the papal doctrines that were her daily bread. She pointed out repeatedly, and often with a note of sharpness, that Catholics in Congress did not vote as a bloc, and thus the Catholic issue in the matter of the presidency was nonsense. She was not asked the one question that might have resulted in an explanation of how Jack's foreign policy would or would not mesh with that of the Vatican. She sidestepped, as Jack did, the fact that his neutralist, peaceful-coexistence view toward the Soviet Union, a contrast with that of his opponent Richard Nixon, reflected that of the newly elected Pope John XXIII rather than that of the inflexibly hostile Pius XII. Pope John was even encouraging the rebellion of certain elements in the Communist-controlled world provided that they rejected Marxist doctrine.

Above all, Rose had to make it clear to her attentive audiences that her son would not take direct orders from the Vatican, while she knew full well that as a secular president he would be mindful, through her influence, of the Pope's revisionist teachings. Indeed, his later support of the aborted Bay of Pigs invasion of Cuba, initiated by the CIA under the Eisenhower regime, would not meet with the disapproval of the pontiff.

Jack's speech on September 12, before the Greater Houston Ministerial Association at the Rice Hotel in Houston, when he talked of his desire to preserve the division of church and state, was regarded by Rose with a degree of ironic amusement.

On September 26, after weeks of touring, Rose was at her old haunt, the Arlington Hotel in Hot Springs, Arkansas, to see the first television debate between a smoothly confident Jack and a haggard, sickly Richard Nixon. The debate occurred on the same day that Fidel Castro provoked the Kennedy family by saying at the United Nations General

Assembly that Jack was "an illiterate and ignorant millionaire," and Castro was cut off in midspeech.

Fingering her rosary, praying, Rose watched on TV, with
some sixty million other people across the country, her son
breeze expertly through the debate with all flags flying. She
recorded her conflicting feelings; though she noticed how
Jack left Nixon at the starting gate, she missed the old, thin
look he had that she thought of as Lincolnian. She worried
that he spoke too fast and in too high-pitched a Harvard
accent. She can only have recalled her husband in 1938 as
Jack referred to American weakness and the country's need
to build up its strength.

Rose called Jack in Chicago after the telecast, following
his outright victory, to point out what she saw as his
deficiencies. He listened patiently.

For the second debate, on October 7, she was stranded in
a storm in Jacksonville, Florida. It was her wedding anniversary, and, as she always did, she managed to call Joe,
minutes before the debate came on. Again, Jack echoed his
embattled father in 1938–1940, as he declared an appeasement policy. He said that the U.S. should not be dragged
into war with Communist China over the issue of the
Formosa Straits islands of Quemoy and Matsu, which both
Republican and Nationalist China claimed as their own;
only a few caught echoes of Joe vis-à-vis Poland, Czechoslovakia and Eastern Europe after World War II. Nixon
suggested the islands should be defended at all costs. He
was again defeated.

Rose was in Chicago to watch the third debate, on
October 21. Once more, Jack triumphed, appealing to the
millions of Americans who dreaded the thought of nuclear
war, who feared Nixon might commit to it and were
prepared to tolerate coexistence with the Communist world
if need be. This, rather than the much-advertised comparative lack of charisma shown by the Republican candidate,
influenced the public's leaning toward Kennedy for president.

Near the end of her campaign, Rose was asked by
reporters about Joe's political background, and this time
she dodged the issue. She would have been capable of giving

the reasons why he had been misunderstood before Pearl Harbor and had been effectively rendered silent ever since, but she sensibly did not sound a defensive note, perhaps since to have done so would have involved more complicated explanations than either a TV interview or an organized Democratic Party tea audience could have absorbed. Rose said that Joe was sure Jack would make it; that she was an old-fashioned wife who believed what her husband believed, and he had "so often been right." Asked again about Jack's youth, she said that he had been in politics for ten years, and that her belief that he would succeed had grown only gradually ("I'm used to the idea now"). She occasionally broke into a note of humor ("If Jack is elected, I look forward to baby-sitting in the White House").

Her nerves began to snap at last; at a public gathering in Chicago, asked a needling question about Jack's affairs, she snarled, "I don't answer that kind of question!" She refused invitations to private lunches and dinners even from strong supporters. She proved testy when hecklers suggested that Joe had greased Chicago mayor Richard Daley's ever-open palm. Even a hint of discussion of Illinois machine politics had her waving a dismissive hand.

The campaign reached a pitch of intensity in the first days of November. While Rose was in Detroit, Jack made a brilliant stroke by calling Coretta King to sympathize with her over the arrest of her husband, the Reverend Martin Luther King, Jr., and Bobby pulled a string to have him freed on October 27. Nixon's failure to act in the matter handicapped him severely. Black voters rallied to the Kennedy flag.

Jack's choice of Lyndon B. Johnson, his chief opponent at the primary, as running mate for vice-president further strengthened the Southern vote, and Joe's pocketbook continued to improve matters in Illinois and West Virginia. When Jack announced a Peace Corps as an alternative to three years' selective service, he was echoing his father's position at Fore River in World War I, as well as providing a rallying call to American youth.

Rose was at Hyannis Port with the family for election day on November 8, 1960. On the evening of the seventh,

Bobby had tables set up with telephones on the sun porch of his compound cottage. Thirty tables were set up to be manned by volunteers, headed by Jack's secretary Evelyn Lincoln. Jack would be able to receive word from every electoral district in the country. He augmented the living-room TV with others situated in the master bedroom and in his children's playroom. Dolls and mechanical toys went with the children to Joe and Rose's house.

The family slept well. Rose was up at sunrise, driving off to Mass. She returned in time to enjoy a breakfast from which only the late-sleeping Jackie was annoyingly absent. By midmorning, Rose saw Jack sitting on his cottage veranda, wrapped up and trying to relax.

Later, Jack joined Bobby, Teddy, Sargent Shriver, Steve Smith and Peter Lawford in the game of touch football which, even on this day of days, was a sacred and inescapable ritual. At noon, according to Bobby's instructions, the television crews began to set up cameras and lights in the adjoining yards. Reporters drove in; soon they were shouting down the telephones. Teletype machines chattered; TVs were at full blast. Rose, restless, saying her rosary, making her Hail Marys, dodged trailing cables as she walked in the brilliant sunshine and keening wind from house to house, climbing the stairs to Bobby's playroom command post, returning to her house to see how Joe and the younger children were doing, then going to Jack's to check on Jackie, unable to watch the televisions for more than a few moments at a time, nervous as she kept saying to herself, repeatedly, "Jack will win."

By late afternoon, the wind off the sea had turned sharp, clouds scudded in the sky, and the sunlight had grown pale and fragile. Rose wrapped up in a heavy overcoat; she kept on praying and pacing. The news changed minute by minute: Maine appeared to be lost, then Tennessee, then Kentucky; but were they? Alabama was won—but was it? Vermont seemed to be a disaster; so did Indiana, Mississippi and South Carolina. Rose grew silent and somber. She walked silently, frowning.

As it grew dark, there was a ray of hope: Kentucky, at least in Campbell County, showed Jack ahead. He remained calm; so, even, did Bobby. Democratic strongholds were still to be counted. But by close to seven, even the coolest showed stress.

Nobody was in a mood to sit down to dinner. Morton Downey, the old reliable, walked around serving sandwiches. At 7:15, Associated Press had made a count: Nixon had 203,626 votes to Kennedy's 166,693. CBS declared that IBM, on which it based its computerized findings, was predicting that Nixon would beat Kennedy 100 to 1.

Jack urged everyone to keep calm; he said the machinery was crazy. When everything looked dark, there was a change: Republican citadels in Connecticut, including Greenwich, were for Kennedy. Bobby ran down from the control room yelling for joy, and Peter Lawford, following him down the same stairs, gripped Rose's hand and told her the news, all enmity forgotten. Crittenden County, Vermont; Burlington in that same state; Fountain Hill, Pennsylvania: all were for Kennedy.

At 8:00 P.M., IBM gave Jack a one-percent majority, and Rose joined in celebrating. Everyone fell silent as President Eisenhower, aging but bulldoggy, turned up on TV to urge his party workers to keep up their efforts. But the old man was unimpressive. Chicago, bought or not, came out for Kennedy as Mayor Daley had promised; Daley called Bobby with the news.

At 10:30 P.M., the electoral wind turned sour: bad word flowed in from Michigan, Ohio and Wisconsin, despite sterling efforts in those states.

But at midnight, everyone was jubilant: Jack was two million votes ahead, and there were sounds of crumbling even in Nixon's California. The pregnant Jackie, although she felt sick, got excited then, but Jack had to caution her that the game was far from being won.

Still pacing, praying and fingering her rosary, Rose, weaving her way through the cables and cameras and lights on the compound lawns, was unable to sit still. By the time she yielded to exhaustion and took to her bed at 3:00 A.M., the situation looked far from certain.

Rose was a champ; she slept well and arose at six. Jack reported that Nixon had appeared on television shortly after she retired, and he had refused to concede. After Mass, she took off with family members for a 7:30 A.M. walk along the beach. Photographer Jacques Lowe ran ahead, taking pictures. Rose looked comfortable in sunglasses, jumpsuit and sensible shoes. Pat and Eunice flanked her, Steve and Jean ahead. Teddy, Bobby, Joan and Sarge were behind.

She returned to find Jack barely 100,000 votes ahead, and eleven short of the 269 electoral votes required from the states. Everything hinged on Illinois and Minnesota.

Then, just before lunch, at 12:33 P.M., with everyone in Bobby's living room gazing tensely at the TV set, the two contested states came in for Jack. The game was won!

But it was a very narrow victory, the narrowest in many decades; and it was to be heavily shadowed by charges of vote buying in Illinois, where Joe Kennedy was accused of corralling Chicago's Mayor Daley into a questionable alliance with mob contacts, and of vote enforcement in West Virginia, a perpetual bellyache of Richard Nixon. Nixon would be on the edge of calling for a recount, pressing with hobnailed boots the wine of sour grapes, but decided against it because, he claimed, the country would be in turmoil for months during an investigation. Kennedy supporters maintained that Nixon couldn't have made the charges stick and that he knew it.

Rose did not fail to note that so fragile a mandate, even if confirmed by the antiquated processes of the Electoral College, would result in a centrist presidency, if not an actually conservative one; and with her own politics, that gave her satisfaction. But she made no comment, and there was always the family's carefully cultivated liberal image to be considered.

The Kennedys went to the Hyannis Armory, where their supporters had waited out the long, nerve-racking night. The line of limousines was ready, the cameramen and reporters poised to strike the moment the family emerged. Rose dressed quickly; then Jacques Lowe burst into her room, insisting she sit down with the others for a formal victory photograph. She groaned and so did Joe; nobody else was happy either. Lowe would not be put off; this would be a picture for the ages. He corraled the Kennedys into the library, but Jackie, to Rose's annoyance, as usual could not be found. At this supreme moment, when she was supposed to be getting ready for the armory, she had taken off for a walk on the beach.

Was she a Kennedy at all?

Jack ran out to fetch her back. She changed into a red dress. Rose complained when she saw her that the color was too close to her own and there was no way they could be seen side by side in the photograph. For once, she was overridden; any further delay in getting to the Armory would be unthinkable.

Lowe went ahead. His efforts were worthwhile: Rose was seated, looking relaxed, wearing two strands of pearls, elegantly groomed as though she had just come from a beauty parlor, looking not a day over fifty. Joe perched on the arm of her chair, flashing his irresistible smile. Jackie sat pertly upright, her pregnancy concealed by Teddy's right arm. Jack stood at the group's center, giving no hint of the fact that he had barely enjoyed four hours' sleep. Everyone looked fresh, bright and rested.

With the exception of Joe, the family walked toward the cars. While Jackie got into the first, Jack leaned against a fence and was covered in paint. Someone rushed for lighter fluid to clean it. "Don't use any matches," Ann Gargan said. Dave Degnin, for years the Kennedys' devoted chauffeur, was in the driver's seat when Secret Service operatives appeared and ordered him out. They had their own driver. Jack was furious, but could do nothing. Suddenly, he had an idea. He ran back into the house, grabbed Joe and insisted he come along. Joe reluctantly agreed; Dave became his driver.

The armory reception was overwhelming.

Days were spent trying to settle down afterward. Rose kept up her golf, playing nine holes a day, sometimes sneaking, as was her wont, onto the course to avoid paying fees. In the evenings, she enjoyed such films as *Cimarron, Fanny,* and *The Sundowners:* Joe had organized Cinema-Scope equipment, and the screenings took place outside the house, under the stars.

Rose prepared for Thanksgiving. She pulled out the American Lenox china she had souvenired from the embassy in London in 1939; the advantage of using it was that if anyone broke a dish, she wouldn't be sad. As always, she supervised the table: four Victorian sterling-silver candlesticks down the middle, the mahogany brought to a fine polish, crystal glasses for milk, apple cider, water or wine. The cook, Mathilda Heldal, worked overtime on the Boston clam chowder; two 22-pound stuffed turkeys garnished with parsley; apple pie and ice cream. Rose abhorred pumpkin pie, but she reluctantly added it to the menu because Jackie liked it.

Rose had further conflicts with Jackie. Rose announced that Caroline must go to a Sacred Heart school when she was of age. Jackie snapped, "You want Caroline to be just like you. I want her to be like me!" Jackie's attitude, despite her required appearances at Mass, was that the Roman Catholic Church was only good for funerals and was not much more than an excuse for busy little men in black to run about. Rose sensed this, and another rift formed between them.

Jackie's sickness cast a shadow. She flew back to Washington on November 24, and the next day went into labor. She had not been expecting her baby until the following month. Jackie suffered greatly.

The child, a boy, was delivered by cesarean section. John Fitzgerald Kennedy, Jr., later dubbed John-John, had a lung problem and had to be placed in an incubator for nine days.

Right after this crisis, there was another. Security guards noticed a prowler, seventy-three-year-old Richard Pavlick, haunting the Kennedy house in his car. Arrested, he admitted he had hoped to kill Jack, Jackie, Joe, Rose and other family members by driving his automobile, loaded with explosives, into theirs when they were all together. He was deflected from his purpose by seeing a picture of Jackie and Caroline in a magazine; he had been touched by the vision it gave him of a happy mother and daughter.

On December 4, a sour note was struck when registered nurse Gladys Ghiz filed suit in Boston seeking $10,430 from Rose for unpaid wages earned while Mrs. Ghiz took care of the ninety-five-year-old Josie Fitzgerald. The case was settled out of court.

Christmas was the family's biggest ever. Rose resurrected

a mechanical Santa Claus, reminiscent of South Boston days, that rang a bell when wound up; it stood two feet tall at the front door. A clockwork dog that kept saying "I'm tired" ran around the living-room floor. Assisted by Ann Gargan, Rose trimmed the tree and lined the mantels with silver and green angels, holly and ivy. Rose placed Santa drawing a reindeer sled in the middle of the dining-room table.

Three-year-old Caroline was the center of attention as she rushed about, examining Rose's decorations approvingly and fingering the mesh stockings that hung over the fireplace. When Caroline woke on Christmas morning, feeling the delicious pressure of piled-up gifts on her feet, Rose and the rest of the family were there to share her joy.

For the first time ever, Jack replaced Joe at the head of the table, and everyone addressed him solemnly as "Mr. President." He led the laughter, but Rose could never be induced to call him by any other name than Jack.

On one matter everyone agreed: Bobby must be attorney general. When Clark Clifford had the temerity to question Joe's decision in the matter, on the ground that an attorney general should perhaps have had a period practicing law, Joe heard him out and then said, "Goddammit, he wants to be it and he will be. I want him to be, and that's that."

Rose was busy all through late December, with a number of leading political figures arriving to stay at the house. Jack felt it would be a bad image for the Kennedys if their visitors were to be lodged in a hotel. Rose would hide with Ann Gargan in her bedroom, watching the press close in on every new arrival. There was a major problem of space; the house had a limited number of bedrooms.

There were several mix-ups. Lyndon B. Johnson was accommodated in the room normally accorded to Caroline's British nanny Maude Shaw, and Miss Shaw had to move out with John, Jr. When Rose suggested that Caroline be housed with her brother, Jackie refused. Then Lady Bird Johnson arrived, adding further to the confusion. Finally, Jackie was forced to have her two children moved in with Nurse Shaw. When Senator Mike Mansfield arrived, he was put in with the help. On his way to the bathroom in the dark, he accidentally walked into the bedroom of Jackie's Swedish masseuse, who cried out, thinking she was about to be raped.

By January 4, the house was bedlam; Rose could find no refuge. Oleg Cassini, the fashion designer, arrived to dress Jackie, who refused to emulate Rose's addiction to Paris originals because as First Lady she wanted to support American couturiers. Richard Avedon bustled in to take photographs. Hairdressers Kenneth and Jean-Louis fought over which one would do the women's hair. Rose settled on Kenneth, thus annoying her Palm Beach hairdresser, but Kenneth's carefully arranged waves came apart when she played golf in the wind.

Rose was endlessly active, driving Jackie to irritation as she fussed over whether John, Jr., would catch cold; complaining that Miss Shaw was rocking the baby too vigorously; grumbling because the Secret Service men were forever locking doors inside and out and she had to search for the keys. Insisting she be given an unguarded exit and entrance, she was told that was impossible; finally they settled on a route through the kitchen.

Rose took off on January 18 to Washington for the Inauguration. She flew into a snowstorm. She was driven not to Jack's town house, where she might not have been welcome, but to the more modest home owned by Jean and Steve Smith. That night, she glittered in a Givenchy sheath at the Smiths' party for 130 show-business guests, including Frank Sinatra, Leonard Bernstein, Ethel Merman, Ella Fitzgerald, Nat King Cole and Sidney Poitier.

In a chauffeur-driven limousine Rose made her way to the Inaugural gala at the Armory, with most of the show-business figures performing. The snow fought the windshield wipers as the driver struggled to break through at less than ten miles an hour. An extra man sat in front in the passenger seat, armed with a shovel; he jumped out every few yards, scraping up the snow so the chauffeur could proceed. Arriving at the Armory, Rose was dismayed to find the concert reduced to a shambles by the weather. Performers were delayed for hours, and the program was a jumble. She left for home at midnight, long before the conclusion, insisting that Joe and Jack get some rest, but they stayed on till the end, then partied at a local restaurant until 4:00 A.M.

Even on this day of days, Rose was determined to attend church. For some reason, the White House staff had not arranged for an early-morning Mass for the family, though the East Room would have been perfect for it. Not to be thwarted, she set out on foot to the nearest place of worship, Holy Trinity Church in Georgetown. She hadn't arranged a car, nor did she wake anyone to obtain one. Instead, she walked out of the door into an icy morning wind and tried to hail a cab.

The streets had been cleared of traffic at that early hour in view of the day's events and she had to walk. She had to dodge snowbanks piled up along the pavements, and instead she had to negotiate Pennsylvania Avenue itself. At last she reached the church. She made her way to a front pew; almost nobody was in the building, and Low Mass had been canceled. As she got up from her kneeling position, she was amazed and delighted to see Jack, who walked right past her down the aisle and knelt to pray. He didn't look at her closely; she was just an old woman in an overcoat and a scarf, who might have been anybody.

She didn't join him; she didn't want to interrupt his prayers. Instead, she started to leave. A security man looked her over suspiciously; he didn't believe her when she told him who she was. When she asked him, in a whisper, if he would arrange to have her driven back to the White House, he looked at her as though she were either eccentric or insane. As a result, she was compelled to make the return journey on foot. She felt better for making the effort, and the walk in the snow did her good.

Rose was in a fine temper the next morning, but when she arrived at the Capitol Plaza for the Inauguration ceremonies she was furious. Somebody in charge of the seating arrangement had placed her far off to the side, in protocol order below the nephew of Kathleen's father-in-law, the duke of Devonshire. She sat, looking artificially composed, as the venerable poet Robert Frost struggled to read some verses and was compelled to give up, concluding with another poem. Cardinal Cushing was reading the invocation when a wiring difficulty sent smoke rising up around his lectern, suggesting a complaint from the Nether Regions.

Rose was galvanized by Jack's speech, which announced a new era of youth and vigor, and as she listened, favorite phrases ran through her head: St. Luke's "Of those to whom much has been given, much will be required," and Cardinal Newman's "He will do good; he will do God's work."

Chapter 15

Rose at the White House

With little time to spare, the moment the Inauguration ceremony was over, Rose had her driver rush her to the Mayflower Hotel, where there was a late lunch buffet for family members before the afternoon parade. The buffet was a chaotic affair, with some sixty people present, and was quite unnecessary since, within two and a half hours, there would be a late-afternoon family reception at the White House.

Rose and Joe were visibly restive, not recognizing many of the people present, and they spoke to almost nobody. The president and First Lady were at the traditional luncheon at the Old Supreme Court Chamber. The Bouviers, the Lees and the Auchinclosses kept to themselves; so did the Kennedys and the Fitzgeralds. As they were ranged on either side of the room, one of the Auchinclosses was heard to say, "We're the enemy, and that's all there is to it."

Rose returned with Joe to the reviewing stand outside the White House, where she sat in the president's section for

the brassy and protracted march-and-drive-past. The cold
had now become intense; even the rugged marine guards
shivered. She wrapped her tight black coat around her;
perhaps she didn't consider furs dignified for such an
occasion. Seeing Jack without a topcoat worried her; apparently she didn't know he was wearing thermal underwear.
She thought of him as a little boy in thin trousers and no
sweater, setting out from Bronxville on equally chilly days,
responding to her demand that he put on a heavy coat and
scarf with a wave, a smile and a promise he would take care
of it. She had always known with amused despair that he
would not do what she asked.

She didn't see the parade to its conclusion. She had to
make her way to the White House for the reception. She and
Joe were appalled when they walked into the room. It had
been bad enough at lunchtime, with so many people invited, but this new collection of guests was beyond the pale.
They appeared to be numbered in the hundreds. She looked
across the sea of faces and could barely pick out a dozen
that were familiar to her. Joe was furious. He turned to
White House Social Secretary Letitia Baldrige and said,
"Who are all these goddamned freeloaders?" He didn't
quite dare say "crashers." Miss Baldrige was equal to the
occasion. Smiling sweetly, she replied, "They're members
of your family, Mr. Kennedy." "Not *my* goddamned family!" he exclaimed. "Just freeloaders! Goddamned freeloaders, that's what they are!" Several of the crowd looked
aghast at his words. Letitia stood her ground. "Just pick out
some of them and ask them who they are, Mr. Kennedy,"
she said.

He answered the challenge. As Rose stood wordless, he
walked up to two women who were enjoying the punch.
"Who are you?" he snapped. Coolly, they replied, "We're
Jackie's cousins." They explained further their relationship
to the First Lady. Now it dawned on him that numerous
members of the Auchinclosses and the Lees, quite beyond
his personal acquaintance, had been added to the original
party list. Letitia had drawn up the list, assuming that he
would want everyone to be present, and certainly wanting
to be sure that the new First Lady would not be caught
snubbing even the most distant relative.

Joe went back to Miss Baldrige and apologized. He grinned broadly, and took her hand, admitting his mistake. From that moment on, she was somewhat in love with him. She realized, as Jackie had done, that when you called the old grizzly's bluff, he could become an angel.

But Rose remained subdued and flustered during the party. She was irritated that Jackie had not condescended to come down and help out with the introductions. She and Joe were officially hostess and host. But since they couldn't recognize everybody present, they were unable to make those introductions. As a result, Janet Auchincloss took over; she became the hostess at Rose's party, usurping Rose's normal role when Joe was footing the bill.

As a result, Rose walked around with a tight, crooked smile she reserved for circumstances in which she felt a queenly displeasure. Awkward moments followed. Several archconservatives in the room were alarmed to find that the caviar they had been enjoying, heaped in a giant bowl, was a gift of Nikita Khrushchev. Jackie's author cousin, John H. Davis, went up to Joe, looked him straight in the eye, and asked him if he had a vision for America's future that John F. Kennedy could realize. Joe laughed at him.

The diminutive Edie Beals, on the poor side of the First Lady's family, stood firmly in front of Joe, looking up from her five feet boldly into his eyes, and delivered the faux pas of the evening: "I was engaged to Joe, Jr., remember? If he hadn't been killed, he would be president today, and I would be First Lady." Joe was thunderstruck; resisting a sharp response, he simply walked away. Someone asked him where Jackie was. "She's resting, goddammit!" he snapped.

Rose grew more and more restive at the First Lady's absence. Janet Auchincloss invaded Jackie's bedroom and insisted she come down. Jackie refused. She not only wanted to avoid most members of her family, as well as the Kennedys and the Fitzgeralds, but, still a little weak after her cesarean operation, she was saving her energy for the evening.

At last, Rose and Joe were able to escape the family zoo and changed for the ball at the Armory, one of five such occasions being staged that night. Joe managed to squeeze into the morning suit he had worn for his presentation to

King George VI in 1938. Rose wore the same Molyneux gown in which she had been presented at court in 1938. They arrived at the Armory and were taken to the president's flag-draped box. Neither made forays onto the dance floor.

It was so crowded that it was almost impossible to move around, and Meyer Davis's band could barely be heard above the screaming chatter. The First Lady left early; Rose was gone by midnight.

Joe was housed in a normal guest bedroom; Rose, as befitted her Kennedy rank, was accommodated in the queen's bedroom. She didn't like it, because of the dreary view of Pennsylvania Avenue, and it was decided that on future visits her accommodation would be the gloomily imposing Lincoln bedroom.

Excited but exhausted, she returned to Palm Beach. Because the weather continued to be severe, the First Lady had reluctantly decided to leave her children under the care of British nanny Maude Shaw at the house for the season.

Rose found herself in charge of Caroline and John-John. She adored both of them; Caroline was sharp and bright, and, with her own lifelong love of dolls, Rose appreciated the child's obsessive love of her Raggedy Ann. But Rose was distracted by the menagerie that accompanied the children. She was overrun with puppies, dogs, kittens and cats; parrots screeching; falcons that flapped alarmingly over the roof; hamsters that managed to escape their cages; and white mice racing across the floor and causing maids to jump onto chairs. By early February, it was obvious she was living in an aviary, zoo and kennel combined. Ethel and Bobby's brood of seven arrived, followed by Steve and Jean's and Peter and Pat's offspring.

She treated the children as a strict and loving McKinley-era grandma, so that all but the most undisciplined practically tiptoed in her presence. When she was out at Mass or playing golf, they ran headlong around the house, raced up and down stairs, slid on the banisters, played games of touch football in and out of the house, in imitation of their parents. But when she came home they tended to behave with comic formality, as correct as tiny cadets.

Rose worked hard with John, Jr.,'s special nurse, Elsie Phillips, and with the old retainer Luella Hennessey, making sure that the baby had six milk-feedings a day.

In March the Office of Heraldry in Dublin sent for Rose's and the rest of the family's inspection a coat of arms, a conceit equivalent to Honey Fitz's Shawn O Boo. With considerable ingenuity, the officers had adapted the escutcheon of wealthy O'Kennedy landowners of the tenth century; fortunately, no direct descendants of that group existed to complain. The heralds mingled the O'Kennedy insignia with an ancient Fitzgerald coat of arms in a concoction as fantastic as the monkey-puzzle family trees of the Lees and the Bouviers and the shield set up by Fred and Frances Marion Thomson above their Beverly Hills front door. One of the figures was an eagle holding a quiver full of arrows, a nice image in view of the president's current position.

Visiting the White House in March, Rose found herself in the promised Lincoln bedroom. Its somber historical importance was not matched by a degree of comfort. The enormous bed had a mattress that was some three feet off the floor, and the headboard was nine feet high. In order to get into the bed, Rose, at barely five feet, had to climb onto a footstool and vault up between the sheets. She complained again, but on this occasion was asked, quite firmly, to stay where she was. She made her way past the wardrobe with its mirrored doors and the original Lincoln armchairs to the desk where she would write her correspondence. She found it occupied by the Gettysburg Address in the original handwriting in a glass case, which left little room for inscribing even a picture postcard. There was a compensation, given her customary tightness with money. She would receive free franking privileges for her mail. She wrote letters all day.

She was soon back at Hyannis Port.

The new president made it clear he would fight against segregation in the South. Hyannis was still a Republican stronghold; blacks were seldom, if ever, seen there, even as servants. They were excluded from almost all hotels, clubs and even restaurants, except as help. A vicious group of segregationists in the South decided on a practical joke. They advertised widely in the newspapers and on bulletin boards that Hyannis, in view of the fact that the president was a long-term resident there, had changed its policies, and that it would be employing black people extensively. Many blacks who had supported Kennedy because of his friendly gestures toward the Martin Luther Kings and other leaders, and needing work desperately, decided to travel to Cape Cod. The prosegregationists, through dummy contacts, arranged for their transportation. As a result, Hyannis was overrun; households were besieged. Conservative ladies were forced to confront angry arrivals when they announced they knew nothing of the advertisements.

Rose had been sympathetic to black people, all the way back to her trip to the Caribbean in 1913. But she had a full staff, led efficiently by housekeeper Evelyn Jones and cook Mathilda Heldal, and she needed no more. One afternoon, she opened her front door and saw standing there a heavy black lady who said that she was advised that Rose wanted a maid. Rose was astonished and shocked, seldom able to deal with unexpected situations, and she summoned staff members. She explained to the woman that there was no work for her. The woman refused to budge. When everyone said that the household was full, the visitor burst into tears, talking of her children. Rose insisted she be given money and taken to the bus; still the woman wouldn't move. Finally, in desperation, Rose sent for a costly topcoat and presented it to the woman as a gift. That did it; the lady left. The coat was at least seven sizes too small.

April brought Rose ominous news from the Caribbean— news that directly involved Joe, though the public did not know it. Just before Jack's Inauguration, General Anastasio Somoza, the brother of Nicaragua's president, had flown to New York for a secret meeting with Joe at Joe's office in the Pan American Building above Grand Central Terminal. At that meeting, Joe, still liaising between the government and the CIA, had laid the groundwork for an Eisenhower invasion plan against Cuba, the result of which would be the overthrow of President Fidel Castro. Other prongs of the invasion would come from Florida, Louisiana and Guatemala. The attack would be financed partly by the CIA and partly by wealthy Roman Catholic Cubans who had been deprived of their properties. The Vatican was privy to the plot. Somoza flew directly from the New York meeting with Joe to Washington to talk with Allen Dulles. Now Jack Kennedy arranged to carry out the plan.

Simultaneously, a papally approved scheme was launched to bring Catholic children out of Cuba—since Pope John XXIII was strongly ecumenical, Protestant children as well. Under the aegis of Catholic priests, the children were settled in Miami, adopted by exiled families. Questions began to be asked in Congress by pro-Castroites, stimulated by the Friends of Cuba Committee. Castro began to turn Cuba into an armed camp, ready for any invasion; by March 29, almost every sugar and tobacco worker who was fit and over eighteen was in uniform. Twenty thousand Cuban refugees fled to Florida.

At the same time, Joe, undoubtedly with Rose's knowledge, became involved in an intelligence plot as highly charged as the CIA-Vatican intrigue and connected to it.

Rose continued to be friendly with Charles and Jayne Wrightsman, their daughter Charlene, and Charlene's husband, Hearst columnist Igor Cassini. Jayne became a favorite of Jackie, her chief advisor on antiques and paintings at the White House and her chief shopper at auctions. Jayne arranged for Stephane Boudin to come from Paris to remodel the White House. Igor's brother Oleg was Jackie's chief clothing designer, using the classic and timeless lines that had helped to make his former wife and Jack's former lover, Gene Tierney, an elegant motion-picture icon.

White Russian by birth, Igor Cassini was a long-term and passionate opponent of communism, much disliked by the liberal press for his Hearst-backed hard line during the McCarthy era.

Early in January, Allen Dulles, formerly the Wrightsmans' lawyer, now head of the CIA, came to Palm Beach to stay with the Wrightsmans. He visited Rose and Joe, and they played golf together at the country club. Dulles indicated to Joe, while playing nine holes, that there was fear, engineered by CIA spies, that Generalissimo Trujillo's regime in the Dominican Republic was getting out of hand, and that a communist coup was about to take place, backed by Fidel Castro and the Soviets. Perhaps a coup might instead be engineered by the CIA itself, replacing Trujillo with a more moderate figure. In either case, there would be problems. Both Joe and Igor Cassini were friendly with Trujillo's son-in-law, the playboy Porfirio Rubirosa, and they believed that Trujillo presented an effective opposition to communism. If Trujillo were deposed by authorization of Jack Kennedy, and Rubirosa consequently ruined, Joe could also be adversely affected: from the old Hayden, Stone days, Joe had retained his sugar connections in Cuba, and was friendly with the exiled Cuban sugar baron Julio Lobo and his wife, the former Nazi agent Hilde Kruger.

Joe felt that a coup d'état was out of the question. He suggested that Igor Cassini, who had made the connections that had allowed Trujillo to be represented by a public-relations firm in New York, should go to the Dominican Republic, to the capital of Ciudad Trujillo, and talk to the generalissimo in the company of the family's old friend, former deputy undersecretary of state Robert Murphy. With wholehearted presidential approval, this top-secret mission would, it was hoped, result in an amelioration of Trujillo's regime, a reestablishment of diplomatic relations between the two countries, and Trujillo's acceptance as a member of the Organization of American States.

Trujillo proved amenable at the meeting, and there was some discussion of Joe meeting him aboard his yacht at sea. But the liberal wing of the CIA was determined to continue with the proposed coup and talked Allen Dulles into it.

The plan, devastating for the Wrightsmans and to Rose and Joe, threatened the future of both Igor Cassini, who might be exposed and ruined as an alleged Trujillo associate, and the neurotic Charlene, whose chief joy in life was being the glamorous toast of society as the wife of a popular columnist.

Oleg Cassini could also suffer from the coup; he was co-owner of Martial and Company, the PR firm that was indirectly associated with Trujillo's PR man. As Jackie's designer, he would be in an awkward position. As her advisor on art, Jayne Wrightsman could see her position with the First Family equally imperiled. Indeed, at the very outset of the new presidency, Joe found himself in conflict not only with Allen Dulles, whose association he valued highly, but with the president as well.

Another of Rose and Joe's friendships that disintegrated during the presidency was the long-term, affectionate relationship with the Jewish conservative *New York Times* Washington correspondent Arthur Krock. Krock had remained loyal to the Kennedys through thick and thin; his strong defense of Joe through the bitter years of controversy on the issue of Joe's defeatism had earned him much calumny, in part because it was stated that he was a reluctant Jew, an agnostic, and not a man who was committed to Jewish causes. But he never wavered in his loyalty, and the rewards for him were rich, not least in Rose and Joe's friendship, but also in Joe's sage advice on stock-market investments and in the supply of much inside information on Washington politics.

The seeds of trouble had been sown as early as 1940, when Joe returned from London, because Martha Blair, Krock's wife, a haughty Episcopalian from Chicago society, called the Kennedys "shanty Irish," and never approved of them. Although, in the years since, she was prepared to entertain them and to accept their hospitality at Palm Beach (her son William by a previous marriage spent his 1952 honeymoon there), she never grew to like the Kennedys. The alliance became increasingly more political (and politic) than social.

When Krock began to criticize Jack's domestic policies, the president was unforgiving and cut him out of the White House, even disconnecting him from vital news sources. Rose was compelled to see her old friend banished from the Camelot court.

On March 31, just before the Good Friday Mass, an anonymous note reached Rose at Palm Beach, stating that Caroline, who was there for the Easter holiday, would be kidnapped at any moment and held hostage against any future attack on Cuba. Joe sent word to Jack, who was playing golf with Bing Crosby at the country club. Four Miami Cubans caught hanging around the house were held for questioning, but nothing could be proved against them, and the note's originator was not found.

The security guard around the house was doubled as Caroline and John-John were flown to Washington under tight protection and kept under lock and key at the White House. The invasion plan of Cuba known as Operation Zapata continued.

The cloak of secrecy was torn apart by the newspapers every day. On April 6, *The New York Times* published that between five and six thousand Cuban exiles had been trained for an attack for the past nine months; this was front-page news and not presented as a Castro allegation. The breach of security should have resulted in a postponement or abandonment of the plan, but day after day, further details were in the papers, and Adlai E. Stevenson, who had been appointed ambassador to the United Nations, was compelled to issue a denial to the General Assembly.

The situation was charged when Rose arrived in Washington in mid-April for a week's stay in the Lincoln bedroom.

On April 16, unbeknownst to her, the president launched the attack on the Bay of Pigs. But he made a fatal mistake. Adlai Stevenson had discovered, after his denial to the United Nations General Assembly that any such invasion was afoot, that indeed it would take place. At a meeting at the White House between the president and cabinet members Dean Rusk, Chester Bowles and William Pawley, Stevenson begged Kennedy not to embarrass him before the UN. If American B-26 planes were launched from carriers as a cover for the invasion, and any of them were downed, America's direct involvement, which he had been continually denying, would be exposed, and both his and the president's reputations would be ruined. Kennedy yielded, and thus doomed the expedition to failure.

On the day of the invasion, April 16, an irrelevant event took place at the White House. Rose had to smile through a state luncheon for visiting Greek premier Constantine Karamanlis. After lunch, news of the invasion's failure emerged. Next morning, Rose read of the disaster in the newspapers. She tried to call her son, to console him in his anguish, but she could not reach him.

When she telephoned Joe at Hyannis Port, he told her that Jack had been on the phone to him for hours, almost crying with despair. He was blaming Allen Dulles and the CIA for getting him into the mess. Joe made it clear to him that, as president, he must shoulder the blame; any attempt to attach the failure to others would indicate to the public that he was less than presidential.

It illustrates the degree of Jack's dependence on his father, and the extraordinary role Joe played in both the presidential campaign and its successful conclusion, that Jack would turn to him first in this time of stress.

The same evening, there was a dinner at the Greek embassy, a return of hospitality by Karamanlis. Rose, the president and First Lady struggled through the event in a state of agonized uncertainty and boredom, waiting for more news from Cuba. The instant they returned to the White House, Jack snapped and ran headlong to his office.

The First Lady, sympathetic toward Rose for once, turned to her and told her of the whole horrifying afternoon in which he had been racked with anguish, complaining bitterly, again and again, about Allen Dulles. Although, by general consent, he would act on Joe's advice and take the blame publicly on television and to newspaper reporters, he marked down Dulles for dismissal. He replaced him with John McCone as soon as he could conveniently do so. He was wise enough not to point out that not only had the CIA given him bad advice, but Stevenson's influence had proved disastrous and the American press's inability to keep a secret had further wrecked the expedition.

The Bay of Pigs was not only a severe blow to the presidency, but to the continuing secret war of Catholicism versus communism, in which Joe, Jack and Rose Kennedy were so deeply involved.

In an effort stemming from the Vatican to pacify the Soviets, when the sum of $2,925,000 was paid in reparations as well as Caterpillar tractors and other supplies, Cardinal Cushing put up a million from diocesan funds, sure proof of the Rome connection. He asked Joe for a contribution; Joe angrily refused.

In view of these events, Rose took off to Paris for the spring, leaving on May 10. So precipitous was her departure that she missed a Mother's Day Mass in her honor at St. Andrew's Church in Palm Beach, five days later. The president presided over the occasion, stating that, in addition to Rose, the Mass was dedicated to Catholic anti-Castro Cuban mothers in exile.

Rose was back at the Ritz. After using various rooms (she was too stingy to take suites), she settled on the modest Room 94, on the fourth floor, overlooking a small courtyard. The management did the room over in her honor entirely in rose: carpets, wallpapers, furniture and bedspread, all in the same color. It cost her just $30 a night.

Knowing that the president would soon be in Paris for a summit meeting with General Charles de Gaulle, she took a taxi from Mass each morning to a French-language teacher, trying to iron out her persistent American twang, which, a wag had said, made her sound as though her French were "fried in bacon grease." Looking for an appropriate gown for the state occasion, she swept through the salons of Balenciaga, Dior and Chanel, finally settling on Givenchy. Too late, she found out that he would also be designing Jackie's dress.

The Wrightsmans were in Paris too. Rose spent many pleasant days and evenings with Jayne, who was shopping for furniture for the White House and had brought with her a handsome gift for de Gaulle: a letter signed by Lafayette. Rose met with the duke and duchess of Windsor's decorator, Stephane Boudin, who was working with Jayne in the White House. Because of their political notoriety the Windsor connection to the White House was hidden.

Then, on the last day of May, with the president due to arrive at any minute, Rose read dire news in the papers. President Trujillo had been ambushed and killed in the long-planned CIA-engineered coup d'état of which Joe had disapproved. Supporters of the murdered dictator invaded and wrecked the Dominican consulate in New York and seized thirty-one hostages. Rose knew that this would mean the end of Igor Cassini's newspaper career and disaster for Charlene Wrightsman.

Either then or later, Charles Wrightsman made clear he would do nothing to help; he dissociated himself cruelly from the situation. Soon, he and Jayne would leave for London to bid at Sotheby's for Goya's legendary small portrait of the duke of Wellington. They got it, but to their annoyance had to return it at cost when the British government complained.

That same morning, May 31, a limousine driver picked Rose up at the Ritz and drove her to Orly Airport to meet the president and First Lady off Air Force One. Rose was greeted by the de Gaulles in the VIP reception room, and she startled the haughty and austere French president by asking him whether, if she sent him a photograph, he would autograph it. He said with a grimace that he would.

As she talked with Madame de Gaulle about children, she saw through the plate-glass windows the orange-nosed plane dipping down from a cloudless blue sky. Looking handsome, her son and daughter-in-law stood for photographs on the ramp.

An embarrassing moment followed: after shaking hands with de Gaulle, the president began to walk straight ahead. De Gaulle grabbed him by the arm and rapped out a quick instruction that he must stand still and take the Color Guard salute.

After the introductions, Rose was conducted to the shiny black Citroën limousine that would take her to a succession of official occasions, starting with luncheon at the Hôtel de Ville and the reception at the Quai d'Orsay. There had been a heated discussion of where to place her in the order of protocol; she wound up in the car with the wives of the U.S. ambassador to France and the French ambassador to the United States.

That afternoon, she left a party at the Elysée Palace to change at the Ritz for the banquet at the Palace of Versailles. General Louis Norstad, head of SHAPE, and his wife accompanied her there. It was one of the most brilliant occasions she had ever attended.

The legendary palace of the French kings was illuminated by thousands of candles, and many treasures had been taken out of storage to embellish it. The Hall of Mirrors, in which the post-World War I Versailles Treaty had been signed, was exquisitely prepared. The immense table, running the length of the salon, was glowing with Baccarat crystal, Sèvres china rimmed in gold, and gold knives, forks and spoons. Outside the tall windows, illuminated fountains splashed in a light drizzle. After dinner, there was a son et lumière demonstration of the palace's history, followed by a performance of the Ballet Rendezvous in the gilded Louis XV theater. Rose had no chance against Jackie's glamour and expert French, which so captivated de Gaulle that he sometimes forgot to talk to the president. Gamely praising her daughter-in-law's beauty and deportment in her memoirs, Rose could not resist a small stab; she said that Jackie's had been, that dazzling day in Paris, a succès fou.

Despite the cheering crowds that greeted every appearance of Jackie and her husband, Jack's meetings with de Gaulle dissolved in an atmosphere of mutual disappointment. De Gaulle was not prepared to be less than independent in his relations with the United States. Above all, he advised against Kennedy's proposed military interference in Indochina, which, he correctly saw, would lead inexorably to disaster.

He may not have been aware of the nature of Rose and Joe's connection to the matter. Their protégé and friend of 1951, Ngo Dinh Diem, whom they had helped through the papal connection, had become Catholic dictator in South Vietnam and would prove to be as inconvenient in terms of anti-communism as Trujillo in his own nation. De Gaulle knew, as he made clear in his memoirs, that the more Kennedy became involved in the war against communism, the more Communists would trumpet themselves as champions of national independence.

Knowing that Jack would continue to Vienna for a summit meeting with Soviet Premier Nikita Khrushchev, Rose asked him if she could hitch a ride on Air Force One. He could scarcely deny her request, although it provoked a nightmare of protocol. She had not been invited to Austria; President Adolf Scharf had to be advised immediately. Vienna was crowded; a hotel room somehow had to be found. She had to be fitted in at the last minute to the Hotel Imperial and the State banquet at Schönbrunn Palace. As she was driven past the Danube, Rose indulged in a nostalgic reverie: she remembered her romantic waltz with Hugh Nawn on the deck of a river steamer decades before.

At the reception before the dinner, there was a surrealist scene, typical of international diplomacy, as the supreme heads of the United States and the USSR chatted like old friends. Rose, typically, was a strong royal card in the game, talking, as if to a new member of a contract bridge club, to Mrs. Khrushchev, a homebody who was a good deal cleverer than she looked, a teacher and a mistress of several languages, even better informed than Rose on international matters, her dowdiness a perfect image to satisfy the Russian people.

With her sudden decision to go to Vienna, Rose had not done any research on her interlocutor, but Mrs. Khrushchev, with less than forty-eight hours to prepare, had evidently gotten hold of TASS, the Russian wire service, and pulled up a dossier on Rose. She had even found, and read carefully, an article in the supercapitalist *McCall's* magazine, scarcely the customary reading of Russian housewives, in which Rose had answered questions on her life. She talked to Rose about her children and grandchildren with amazing knowledge, while Rose didn't know what to ask her in turn. Cleverly, Rose drew her out on the subject of her family, which somewhat eased the imbalance of the situation. At least in one respect, Rose was ahead of her: when they went to the powder room, Mrs. Khrushchev gazed with envy as Rose touched up her lipstick and powdered her nose. She had never worn makeup.

The banquet was elaborate, but largely useless as an amelioration of strong enmities. As Rose learned afterward, Khrushchev drubbed Kennedy, seeking out the flaws in his political knowledge. Insufficiently briefed, overconfident, the U.S. president showed a complete lack of understanding of the nature of Marxism, to which Khrushchev brutally

pointed. He also insisted on raising the issue that states
behind the Iron Curtain might be encouraged toward independent governments. Jack's insistence on the status quo
being maintained in European countries showed a degree of
naiveté that the Russian leader couldn't resist mentioning
in his memoirs, written several years later. As in his
meetings with de Gaulle, Kennedy was out of his depth on
Southeast Asia and Cuba. The superficial images on television, showing the Khrushchevs and the Kennedys smiling
in evening clothes, contradicted the actuality of a disastrous
mission for America.

As her son and daughter-in-law left, somewhat battered,
for a more congenial visit to London, Rose showed no signs
of embarrassment. She set out for days of shopping in
Vienna, enjoying visits to the opera, to art galleries and
museums. She traveled on to Cap d'Antibes, where Joe
joined her at their villa, rented for a second summer.

There, she cemented an earlier acquaintance with her
fellow Irish-American Princess Grace of Monaco, and
agreed to augment the guest list for the princess's International Red Cross Ball by pressing some celebrated family
friends to come.

Of several of these Rose did not approve, and indeed she
tended to ignore their very existence. These included
Sammy Davis, Jr., who became the host of the occasion,
and Frank Sinatra. She invited Tony Curtis and Janet Leigh,
for whom she had a soft spot; but the couple had quarreled,
and only Janet Leigh agreed to come. Leigh arrived at the
same time as Peter and Pat Lawford; Leigh stayed at the
Racquet Club, the Lawfords at the Kennedy villa.

The evening in Monaco was a success, and Rose was at
her most impressive—dressed by Givenchy, mingling with
the stars. A stickler for social deportment as always, she was
dismayed when Janet Leigh, without warning and in a flood
of tears, fled the dinner table and made her way to the
powder room. Rose found out that she had a reason. Joe
called Tony Curtis in New York and discovered that Leigh's
father had, loaded with debts, killed himself; the moment
he died was the moment of her outbreak of grief. This
telepathic response was extraordinary. Rose was sympathetic and did her best to console the young woman; but, as a

Catholic, she of course regarded suicide as a mortal sin and
there was little she could say in consolation.

On September 6, Rose flew to Copenhagen to attend the
wedding of an old friend, William McCormick Blair,
ambassador to Denmark, to Katherine Gerlach of Chicago
at Fredriksburg Castle in the presence of the king and
queen. She attended a tea party at the castle given for her by
the monarchs and a bridal dinner at the Belle Terrace
restaurant of the Tivoli Gardens. It was a gala occasion.
Rose liked the city, explored historical sites with her customary energy, and lingered on far beyond her invitation,
picking up some dolls for her collection.

Back at Antibes two weeks later, Rose heard troubling
news from Hyannis Port: a hurricane had swept down,
battering the house and forcing Jackie to take refuge with
her own, Pat's and Teddy's children, at nearby Otis Air
Force Base.

On October 2, Rose was at the Grand Hotel in Rome. She
went to the Vatican for a private audience with Pope John
XXIII, in the same library in which she had been received
by previous pontiffs. The rosily smiling Pope was the
opposite of the austere Pius XII, but he was no less
enthusiastic in welcoming one of the Church's leading
benefactors. It is safe to say that a Catholic U.S. president's
war against communism, the Central Intelligence Agency's
activities through the Vatican and Rose's social connection
to such operations were not on the list of topics for
discussion in the twenty minutes she was there. As always
on such occasions, the conversation was surely generalized
and friendly, referring largely to Rose's donations and
works. She proceeded from the Vatican to meetings with
Count Galeazzi, which may have been of a more political
character.

In Rome Rose snapped up a new wardrobe and numerous
new dolls, acquiring so much on the fashionable Via
Condotti that her purchases had to be packed in a series of
old-fashioned steamer trunks and flown by stages to Hyannis Port. They preceded her arrival on November 11, filling
much of the entrance hall and dismaying the staff. Tight as
ever when it came to wages or other household expenses,

Rose was, in terms of her personal purchases, unceasingly extravagant.

On November 13, Rose was at the White House for a dinner in honor of Governor Muñoz Marin of Puerto Rico, which featured a memorable concert starring the cellist Pablo Casals, who, with Alexander Schneider and Mieczyslaw Horzowsky, joined in a peerless trio for a distinguished audience. Always a lover of classical music, Rose was in her element. Despite her frequent misgivings about Jackie Kennedy, she appreciated the fact that her daughter-in-law had arranged such an occasion, overcoming, with her husband, the Spanish Casals's objection to the U.S. government's recognition of General Franco. Casals had agreed to play on the condition that it was understood that he had not varied from his condemnation of the Spanish dictator.

Back at Hyannis Port, Rose, perhaps because she was now recognized as America's Queen Mother, had become remarkably imperial in her behavior and would remain so for the rest of her life. When she found that her recently appointed chauffeur, Francis (Frank) Saunders, a former navy man, was driving the staff to go shopping and on other errands on her behalf, she told him sharply, "You are my chauffeur, not theirs." Not content with the reprimand, she called a staff meeting and announced that Saunders was for her, and nobody else's, use, and to stop any such nonsense in the future. To cement the matter even more, she sent a circular to her entire family making her feelings clear.

When she went out shopping, usually driven by Saunders, she instructed him that, as he helped her carry her purchases, he must address her not as Mrs. Kennedy but as someone else. He was aghast. Not a soul in Hyannis would fail to recognize her—how did she imagine that the use of a pseudonym, overheard by passersby, would make any difference? And if he called her by a pseudonym in front of store clerks, it would be pointless, since she would have to charge up her buys in her own name. She grumblingly conceded the point, and ordered him to address her as "Madame." It was to be pronounced in the English manner, as "Moddom." The rest of the help was so instructed.

She made it clear to her housekeeper and maids that, after a meal at which other than family were present, the spring water poured into the glasses was to be put back into a carafe and not drunk by any member of the staff. She checked it carefully. She counted the strawberries left over in dessert dishes later, after they were put back in the refrigerator.

She was equally strict in other matters. The nightly screenings of movies in her basement were projected by Saunders, whose duties as chauffeur she expanded to milk the utmost drop from him—he even had to do the laundry at various times. He was instructed to begin projecting at exactly 9:00 P.M., and she checked him with her watch. If anyone, family member or not, was late, they would have to miss the opening scene, as she would not have the reel rerun.

The staff began giggling behind her back, as her seeming eccentricities increased. Not only did she continue pinning notices to her dresses with a variety of safety pins, she began using tapes ("Frownies") on her facial wrinkles, so many at times that she began to look like a refugee from *The Mummy's Curse*.

She would suddenly be seized by the idea of revisiting the past. The occupants of her house would be kept awake at night by banging around as she rummaged through her *Citizen Kane* attic, pulling out steamer-trunk drawers, disemboweling ancient chests, resurrecting menus, hotel bills, letters and telegrams from long ago, aiming a flashlight on the yellowed pages of abandoned scrapbooks and photo albums in an orgy of nostalgia.

On one occasion, she called for Saunders to help her drag out an enormous brown paper package stuffed with some object she could not determine. When he stripped off the paper, he expressed amazement at finding it full of lace curtains. At first, she refused to recognize the curtains, but finally she told him they came from her old home on Beals Street, now scheduled to become a national monument. As she fingered the drapes, she said to her chauffeur, "We were lace-curtain Irish, weren't we?"

Most of all, she brooded over her doll collection, housed

in a basement room next to the movie theater. The maids chuckled behind their hands as they saw her fondling the two-foot cardinal and priest dolls she had picked up in Rome, the Japanese geisha doll souvenired from her trip around the world with Mary Jo Gargan, the Spanish and Portuguese dolls she had picked up and the Caribbean and Brazilian dolls from 1940. She didn't notice. She loved her dolls as additional children.

Not surprisingly in view of her activities in the attic, Rose developed pain from a hernia. She was aware that she needed attention, but neglected the symptoms despite the potential danger.

After Thanksgiving, at which the family was present, Rose stayed on at Palm Beach. Joe was working hard on real-estate deals in New York, and in Chicago on matters connected to the Merchandise Mart. He returned, visibly exhausted, causing his family some worry, on December 10, 1961.

A checkup showed his blood pressure very high; his doctors had warned him for months to try to relax his manic intensity, to take medication to avoid a possible stroke, to reduce the salt in his diet and to walk fast, as much as possible, but, hating to be inconvenienced and childishly stubborn as ever, he proved inflexible and resistant to advice. Rose had long since given up trying to make him do anything he didn't want to do. He had dizzy spells and even fell from his horse, but he still failed to act on medical advice. The best he would do was a few laps in his pool and nine holes of golf at the country club.

On the evening of December 18, after hours of dictating to his secretary Diane Winter, Joe joined Rose at dinner at the president's borrowed house, lent by the Wrightsmans. Jack went off to Washington the following morning; he was busy preparing notes for the Bermuda summit meeting with British prime minister Harold Macmillan a few days later. Rose went to Mass and then shopping as Joe saw the president off.

Rose went to the country club to play a few holes, taking the back course because the front was too crowded. Suddenly, there was a commotion. She looked up. She could hardly believe her eyes when she saw Frank Saunders, driving at maximum possible speed in a golf cart, riding past hole after hole, screaming at golfers to get out of the way; they scattered angrily.

As he drew up to her at the tee, he told her that Joe had had a stroke. Rose was certain he was exaggerating; it must be a minor heart attack. She was annoyed at this interruption of her favorite game, and furious that Saunders had made a spectacle of himself in front of the golfers.

Even if the news he brought was correct, she would not fall apart, especially in front of others. As always, she would keep calm.

Saunders insisted she come home. Finally, shrugging irritably, she said she would. He drove her back to the house. A distraught Ann Gargan told her that Joe had collapsed earlier that day while on the back golf course at the eighteenth hole. Rose wondered why nobody at the country club had mentioned it. She asked, calmly, if he had been able to walk into the house; Ann said that he had. She looked into his room, where he seemed to be resting fairly comfortably, still in his golfing outfit. It must be just another of his spells . . . after all, he was seventy-three years old. There was nothing to be alarmed about; she calmed Ann down and reassured her staff.

But it soon became clear that Joe was in bad shape; he was showing symptoms of vagueness and weakness. She told Saunders to send for the paramedics. She was sure he would receive emergency treatment at St. Mary's Hospital, which the family had endowed with a Joseph P. Kennedy, Jr., floor. She drove herself, to keep her nerves steady, back to the country club, to finish her game.

When she returned, Saunders told her that papers would have to be signed by her, authorizing an immediate operation. She dismissed the idea out of hand; she would not go to the hospital. She acted with the same detachment she had shown when she had not flown with Joe from Paris to Boston when he was suffering from severe prostate problems. While Saunders looked astonished, she swam in the pool, several laps, very slowly, still telling herself she mustn't weaken before the family and must keep exercising. She even took a long shower while Saunders paced about, increasingly nervous and upset. By the time she finally agreed that he should drive her to St. Mary's, it was already nightfall.

She met a frantic Ann Gargan and doctors Newburn, Johanssen and Colley; Teddy arrived with cardiac specialist Dr. William T. Foley. As it turned out, no operation would be necessary, since Joe had suffered a stroke that could not be relieved by surgery. The left side of his brain was affected, in what was known as a cerebral occlusion; his right side—and he was right-handed—was completely paralyzed. This most aggressively talkative of men was rendered speechless.

Rose went to the St. Mary's Hospital chapel to pray. She called Cardinal Spellman, but he was on his way to Germany and could not be reached. She was also unable to get hold of Cardinal Cushing, who was ill. Shortly before 8:00 P.M., the president arrived; the hospital chaplain, Reverend Eugene Seraphin, administered extreme unction to be on the safe side.

Rose wasted no time in applying the rationalizing salve that this whole experience was an extra test, a cross for her to bear in the wake of the loss of a son and a daughter. She perked up quickly, driving the hospital hard with her numerous requirements.

Royal families, self-appointed or not, did not ordinarily change arrangements because of near-fatal illnesses. In 1936, the doctors killed King George V of England by needle ahead of schedule to make the morning edition of the *London Times*. With his father on the danger list, the president flew to Hamilton, Bermuda, to meet with Harold Macmillan, who, though he shared the British establishment's contempt for Joe Kennedy, expressed sympathies.

By December 21, Rose had flown in long-term family nurse Luella Hennessey to help out with the patient. Warm notes came from the Pope, Clare Boothe Luce, the Wrightsmans (who visited the hospital), Mary Lasker and other friends. Even Rose, composed and impervious, cannot have failed to feel stress as she saw Joe's agony. He struggled to communicate by smiles, frowns or guttural sounds. He was able to scream the word "No," but could not speak otherwise. All efforts to train him to use his left hand to write notes failed. Medication and nourishment had to be pumped intravenously through his hand, since he could not swallow. He began to strangle on Christmas Eve, and pneumonia set in, forcing his doctors to perform a tracheotomy, opening his windpipe. Although Rose insisted on trimming the tree as usual, the Yuletide season lay under a heavy pall. Jackie, who still adored her grandpa, took his illness the hardest.

Rose faced up to the new year and the necessity for extra staff. After interviewing several applicants, hiring them and summarily firing them for not meeting her expectations, she settled, soon after Joe returned home at the beginning of January, on the Irish-American Bostonian Rita Dallas.

Rose found in that excellent Catholic duty nurse a woman made of tungsten. Nothing shook her—not the unhappy patient's constant screams, not the struggle to carry him to and from the toilet, not his impatience and bad temper; not Rose's strict demands nor Ann Gargan's tender but often overreactive behavior.

Dallas's hiring was odd. Apparently, and quite uncharacteristically, Rose had forgotten the 2:00 P.M. appointment to see her, and had taken to her bed for her siesta at the time. The determined nurse, after ringing every doorbell in vain, had to squeeze through an aperture in the yard wall, push open a living-room door and roam through the house before she finally found Luella Hennessey. Even then, Rose did not see her immediately, but finally interviewed her from her car window on the way to the golf course, leaving Mrs. Dallas standing awkwardly on the drive.

From the beginning, Rose had to referee a constant, day-to-day fight between Rita Dallas and Ann Gargan, neither of whom would yield their control over the patient. Dallas believed in a professional, cool approach, never pampering Joe in order that he would not become totally dependent. She wanted him to type with his left hand or be trained to write with it; Ann did not. Ann, who loved her uncle deeply, spoiled him all too sweetly.

Joe probably enjoyed the contest. Years of banked-up hostility to Rose, concealed and buried in their relationship, burst out horrifyingly. For years, he had been irritated by her perfectionism, her cheerfulness and her composure in the face of life's setbacks. Now that he was partly paralyzed, none of the prior respect he had for her strength, her acumen and her sharp intelligence emerged. When she came into his room, he screamed a long, drawn-out "No!" She left disheveled, tearful, angry at his rejection.

Rose expected her nurses to wear starched, white, well-pressed uniforms at all times. It had increasingly become the custom for domestic nursing staff in wealthy households to be dressed in street clothes, but Rose wanted a full-scale hospital atmosphere.

There was one awkward occasion. Mrs. Dallas said it would be good for Joe to come to breakfast one morning; it would make him feel part of things, that he wouldn't always be confined to his room. Rose was annoyed by the idea; she said that Joe couldn't stand the thought of drooling in front of the family and that he wouldn't consider such a suggestion. Dallas said he would. As it turned out, he agreed with Dallas, and did come to the table.

The meal progressed fairly comfortably. Then, according to Rita Dallas, without warning, Ann Gargan got on all fours on the floor, crawled up to Joe, poked her face between his legs and did an imitation of Rose; she would indulge in such antics to cheer Joe up. Rose chose to ignore the exhibition and concentrated on reading her morning newspaper. Joe began to laugh. Then he had an inexplicable attack of hysteria, and laughed on and on, screaming, finally, with such terrifying intensity that Ann burst into tears. He began flailing about, banged his fist on the table and sent glassware and dishes crashing to the floor. The maids ran in; Mrs. Dallas, Ann Gargan and Luella Hennessey combined were unable to control him.

Rose fled the room. From behind her, she could hear Joe sobbing.

Rose wandered distractedly about the house, then ran into Rita Dallas's room, saying that such a thing must never happen again. But, by evening, Joe indicated in sign language he would be happy to attend breakfast calmly in future. He did.

There were moments of relief. Bobby returned from a tour of the Orient that included visits with President Diem, then went to Rome for an audience with the Pope, with rosaries obtained for all the Kennedys.

There was some discussion in the house of an incident when Mrs. Dallas, asked by Rose to bring towels to her sons, found them naked in the sauna. Since childhood, the Kennedy males had formed a nudist colony, sunbathing naked on the roof as well. When Dallas walked into the hot room, shocked by the Kennedy maleness in full force, Teddy introduced her laughingly to his friends as though she were at an elegant cocktail party.

In March, Rose's stomach pains became severe, and she suffered from vomiting spells and dizziness. She conceded at last that she did in fact have a hernia. Avoiding the press, she swore Rita Dallas to secrecy, told staff members she was going to a religious retreat, and instead of going to St. Mary's, which was handier and at which, in view of family endowments, she would get a special rate, she flew all the way to Boston, checking into St. Elizabeth's Hospital on the fifteenth. Eunice had had her appendix out there the year before.

So uninformed was her family that they first heard about her subsequent operation in the newspapers. Characteristically, she wanted none of them to be bothered or to see her in her hospital shift, and she would allow no press or visitors before or after surgery. On the day of the operation, she insisted on making some half-dozen social calls, including one to her elderly mother, Josie.

Three days afterward, when most people would have been exhausted, she was up and about and ready to return home. Despite the fact that her hernia was, almost certainly, caused by her addiction to shifting furniture, she began to move it again within the week.

The operation gave her an excuse to take off to Paris, where she settled comfortably at the Ritz. While there, she learned that Dr. Howard Rusk of the New York Institute of

Rehabilitation, which had had a great success with stroke patients, had invited Joe to his new model facility, a kind of miniature house attached to his headquarters in Manhattan.

Rose flew back on April 30, barely in time to join other family members accompanying Joe to New York aboard the *Caroline*. Getting Joe up the gangway in his wheelchair was an ordeal. Panicking that he might be thrown out as an attendant tilted the chair to squeeze it through the cabin door, and shocked, illogically, by the presence of cameramen and reporters, Joe screamed at Rose and the others with wordless, hysterical anger. Finally, Dr. Rusk talked him into making a more or less dignified entrance.

Rose was dismayed when she saw the cramped facility in which Joe would be housed for at least several weeks. She couldn't seem to grasp the fact that the house was deliberately built on a small scale, so that the patient could be supervised closely, and so every device for the handicapped would be at his disposal. She railed at the tiny, doll's-house living room, with its modest furnishings, minuscule bathroom (with a narrow shower with steel railings on which the occupant could support himself), and the kitchen, more restrictive than even her own in her birthplace at Garden Court. Rose fretted over the plumbing. An astonished Bobby, the attorney general, presented an alarming sight as Rose turned him into a plumber, forcing him to bend over the toilet and flush down bits of paper repeatedly until she was sure it worked.

The facility, pretentiously called Horizon House, began to resemble the overcrowded cabin in the Marx Brothers' comedy *A Night at the Opera*. Day after day, Dr. Rusk and his team, Bobby, Ethel, Sargent and Eunice Shriver, Steve and Jean Smith, Ann Gargan, Mathilda Heldal, Rita Dallas and Dora, the French maid who doubled as waitress, as well as Rose, Joe and half a dozen more, crammed into the small living room. Mathilda was in a state of shock at the sight of the kitchen. Dora also complained about it. How could there be anything approaching cuisine in such an environment? They told Rose they couldn't function; they could barely squeeze around each other between the oven and the refrigerator.

Rose was not fazed. When they refused to prepare dinner, she called one of her favorite restaurants, La Caravelle, and arranged with the owners, Robert Meyzen and Fred Decré, to have the evening meal delivered every night, along with table, perfectly pressed cloth, candles in silver holders and specific waiters, as well as the appropriate dishes and glassware, until further notice.

Rose had dinner served precisely at eight. She dressed each night in an evening gown; Joe was in an elegant Sulka robe and pajamas. He was impressed; he no longer screamed, no longer ordered her out of the room. He would sit still while she relayed the latest social or political news.

On May 19, she enjoyed a much-needed break from Horizon House when she attended a JFK birthday party for 17,500 people at Madison Square Garden, to raise $1 million for the New York State Committee for the Democratic Party. Rose joined Bobby and Jack in the Presidential Box.

She was busy at the time preparing for Teddy's run for nomination for the Senate at the September primary. Especially fond of her youngest son, since Joe Jr.'s death perhaps her favorite, she wanted to do everything she could to ensure his success.

She made Father's Day, in June, a special occasion. She had the president, Bobby, Teddy and others dress up in an absurd dramatic sketch that Eunice concocted, the room filled with stuffed animals Joe had always liked, and decorated with motto pillows, embroidered with risqué squibs that made him laugh.

Everything began well that evening until Joe realized that Ann Gargan was missing from the party. He managed to convey his annoyance.

Rose had been competing with Ann in the handling of the patient, and had dismissed her to her sister in Detroit.

Ann called from that city to wish him well, crying helplessly on the line that she had been exiled. His response as he spoke to her was to cry out in anger. Rose asked the doctors if Ann should be brought back; they refused. But finally she felt that restoring Ann to the circle would be the only way to appease Joe. When she announced this, he went into a reversal and cried out in rage again. There seemed no way to satisfy him; his frustration and misery expressed themselves in total perversity.

Rose took off to Hyannis in despair to open the house for the summer season.

Chapter 16

A Death in Dallas

❦

Much improved, Joe returned to Hyannis Port for the July 4 weekend, and was even able to sail with Jack, Teddy, Joan and Ann Gargan aboard the *Marlin* for a cruise around Sanford Island, and later to Lewis Bay. Rose, disliking small boats, did not join them.

Over the weekend, the president asked Rose to stand in for the First Lady at a banquet later that month in honor of President Carlos Julio Arosemena of Ecuador. Once again, as in Rome, Rose was being used as a royal card in the international political game. The banquet was a delicate assignment that Jackie had decided to dodge, going instead to Greece for a cruise with her sister, Lee, and brother-in-law Prince Radziwill, a voyage during which Jackie met Aristotle Onassis.

Arosemena had an unsavory political history. The previous November, he had ousted President Jose Velasco Ibarra's government by sending Air Force planes to bomb Quito, the Ecuadorian capital, killing at least thirty-five and injuring hundreds, and forcing the army and government to accept him as leader.

He simultaneously declared an alliance with Russia and

Cuba. Under pressure from the White House and the CIA, he had broken those ties in April, thus facing a threatened revolt from pro-Castro military forces. His visit to Washington was designed to whitewash him; Rose was chosen to act as his hostess because he was devoted to his own mother, was an allegedly devout Catholic and had a young son whom he was training to assume the presidency in the future, and in whom he placed his greatest confidence.

Rose visibly rejoiced in her role, ignoring, assuming she had read of it, her guest's lamentable record. She broke diplomatic protocol in the middle of the luncheon by correcting Arosemena sharply when he expressed doubts about his son's future as a military cadet. She spoke of the proper training for leadership from which her own sons had benefited, conveniently forgetting that she had been opposed to their entering the armed services.

Almost exactly a year after the banquet, Arosemena was finished; overthrown by a military junta and driven into exile. His son never became president.

Rose campaigned for Teddy's run for the Senate nomination for three weeks, again blending affectionate reminiscence with political know-how. Then she took off for the South of France to visit Princess Grace, and to renew other acquaintances. Pointedly, she did not fly to Naples and Capri to visit with Jackie, who was staying there with her sister, Lee, Princess Radziwill. Nor, apparently, did Jackie invite her.

Rose returned to see Teddy win the television debates against a feisty Edward J. McCormack, whose venomous attacks on him backfired. Teddy won the primary by 559,251 votes to 247,366.

Rose devoted the fall to Teddy's fight with Republican candidate George Lodge, son of Jack's old political opponent, who was now, for reasons of expediency, a presidential appointee as U.S. ambassador to South Vietnam. She traveled restlessly, all over the state, with Frank Saunders at the wheel. Squeezing a rubber ball in her palm to help the arthritis in her hands, napping in her black sleeping mask, enjoying a frugal diet composed mostly of steamed chicken, milk and frosted angel-food cake, she was as tireless as always. In order to enhance her populist image, she ordered

Saunders to abandon his customary uniform and wear a modest, off-the-rack suit while driving her, a device meant to suggest that her family was just like ordinary folk—whereas in fact a tiny percent of the population would even imagine having a chauffeur.

Her emphasis on posing as a common person led her into a bizarre situation. In Milton, Massachusetts, the time had come for her to change from an elegant Paris suit into a humble dress. Every hotel room in the city turned out to be booked. Saunders knew of a striptease joint named Soto's Lounge. He suggested that she might use the dressing room, without telling her the nature of the place. In her usual state of tunnel vision, she walked briskly down a corridor, ignoring the fact that the women who passed her were clad only in G-strings. When she got into the room, she realized where she was, but chose to ignore her surroundings. The strippers stood aghast as the president's mother changed, nodding to them and talking to them as though they were novices in a convent.

She liked to read the newspapers when she was being driven on the highways, but she disliked having them litter up the car. As a result, once she had finished reading a page, she pulled it out and flung it from the window, often to the danger of other drivers, who would find the flapping pages blinding their vision on their windshields.

Rose spent much of the campaign with Teddy's wife, Joan, for whom she continued to have affection and admiration. She had Joan accompany her as she gave a series of "lantern slide lectures." When the lights went down, she would say, to general amusement, as a slide came on showing Teddy as a little boy, that she had wanted him to be a priest, graduating to bishop, but her hopes had been dashed when he had met a beautiful blonde one night. At that moment, she shone a flashlight on Joan, who was in the audience, and everybody laughed.

On September 25, Rose broke off her tour to attend at the National Theater in Washington the opening night of *Mr. President,* Irving Berlin's last musical. The president himself had bought out the theater for the occasion. Rose was there, along with Bobby, the First Lady, Clare Boothe and Henry Luce, Lady Bird Johnson and William Paley.

Because of the First Lady's paternal origins, the emphasis was heavily French; the French ambassador was present with an entourage. Since the situation with Cuba was deteriorating, and a possible nuclear world war was being discussed, the theater was packed with security guards.

It was an evening that Rose, Jackie and most other people present would have preferred to forget.

First, the plans for the orchestra to play "Hail to the Chief" before the overture had to be canceled because the Chief was still at the White House. When the patriotic overture, a satire on the national anthem, began, the audience, with the notable exception of Rose, stood up, thinking it was "The Star-Spangled Banner." When the producer told the audience the characters in the play were not based on the Kennedys, there were groans from the rich who had looked for titillations.

When the president, played by Robert Ryan, and the First Lady, played by Nanette Fabray, turned out to be physically attractive, many felt a sense of relief. Just as everyone relaxed, there was a disaster. Robert Ryan as president said that his wife "must not underestimate de Gaulle; he has a mind like a steel trap." The French ambassador, and the First Lady next to him, looked frozen and tense. And when the reply came, "Yes, and it snapped shut years ago," the ambassador turned to Jackie in fury. There were groans and boos, calls for the curtain to be rung down.

The play continued. The president turned up at intermission, but the evening did not recover; the musical was written off as a catastrophe and an embarrassing ending to Berlin's grand career.

Rose was on the road in Massachusetts in October when the Cuban missile crisis took place and the world came to the brink of nuclear war. Typically, she refused to interrupt her tour during the crisis, not even seeking to find out where the president might have provided a family bomb shelter. Nor did she loudly rejoice when Teddy beat George Lodge by a large majority. It was the least she would expect of her youngest, now her favorite, son.

Eleanor Roosevelt's death on November 7 apparently left her indifferent; on the twenty-first, as if to celebrate the temporary truce with Russia (always her desire, under papal influence, despite her adverse view of communism), Rose joined Teddy in entertaining twenty-five members of the Bolshoi Ballet at his Squaw Island house near the Hyannis compound on the thirty-seventh birthday of the great Bolshoi star Marya Plissetskaya.

The next month came an event Rose had dreaded: the professional demise of her good friend Igor Cassini. The press had taken a savage position against Cassini. It was inaccurately charged that his firm, Martial and Company, jointly owned with Jackie's designer Oleg, represented Trujillo in public relations. The truth was that they had simply recommended their associate Paul Englander to handle Trujillo, but now Bobby Kennedy branded Igor an unregistered agent of a foreign power. When, in 1962, Senator Fulbright began to look into Washington pressure groups hoping to retrieve their Cuban sugar interests, Bobby became anxious.

He feared that the matter might lead to his father's front door—that investigations might go back to the Hayden, Stone years, that Joe might be charged with backing dictatorships set up against Castro in view of his seized Cuban sugar interests. It was not to be forgotten that Joe had played a crucial role in engineering the involvement of President Somoza of Nicaragua in the Bay of Pigs fiasco.

Cassini had to be made the scapegoat to save Joe from public revelations that might kill him. By destroying Igor Cassini, Bobby could get his whole family off the hook. He and Jack decided on a way out: they would persuade the unwitting Cassini to plead nolo contendere, an effective admission of guilt designed to prevent a court trial. Oleg Cassini, concerned with his position at the White House, and only anxious to help his brother, did not understand the meaning of nolo contendere and urged Igor to go ahead. Unwisely, Cassini agreed. It is unfortunate that his attorney, Louis Nizer, did not advise him against any such procedure. The reason may have been that the cost of a trial would have been beyond Cassini's means; today, Cassini confirms this. Cassini suspected he was also unseated by the fact that his former wife was now married to William Randolph Hearst, the head of the newspaper chain of which he was senior columnist. He was forced to resign, and his newspaper career came to an end.

During the missile crisis, Rose was notably silent; indeed, she would make no comment on it on her campaign tour. The reason is clear: as a Catholic, she could not have approved her son's involvement in the confrontation. As in World War II, as in the Bay of Pigs situation, the Vatican's position was determinedly neutral; and so was Russia's toward the Vatican (when Pope John XXIII died the following year, the Soviet ships' flags hung at half-mast). The policy as always was to maintain peace and avoid a destructive war from which nobody would ultimately benefit. At the same time, both sides sought to infiltrate and undermine the other through secret intelligence networks: a game of chess instead of a game of war. The dangerous potion made up of corruption, naiveté and belligerence that marked the Kennedy presidency allowed for no such compromises.

As she supported Teddy in his run for the Senate, Rose avoided not only the matter of the crisis but the issue of Jack's increasingly secular presidency. And the results of the crisis, announced by the president as a triumph, were in fact merely a triumph of public relations. Cuba remained a thorn in America's side, and it still is; there is little evidence that the missile bases were removed, and Khrushchev knew they wouldn't be.

Rose was in London as the guest of U.S. ambassador David Bruce, when, on April 10, she heard that Igor Cassini's beautiful wife Charlene, of whom she had always been fond, had locked herself in a room of her Fifth Avenue apartment, and had taken a fatal overdose of barbiturates. Only thirty-eight years old, she left two sons, aged fourteen and eight. Her mother, Charles Wrightsman's first wife, had killed herself a few months before.

Charles Wrightsman did not attend his daughter's funeral.

It had been years since Rose spent that length of time in the British capital. Although many remembered Joe's defeatism and condemned her for her cruel attitude to Kathleen (who is still beloved by her generation in London society), Mrs. Bruce was able to muster up society figures for lunches and dinners in her honor.

She returned to Palm Beach on April 14 for Easter Mass, the first ever held in the house. It took place in the living room, with Tom Wicker of the *New York Times* present. Teddy became altar boy for the occasion. The president and First Lady drove over from the borrowed mansion of C. M. Paul. Caroline was perched on the president's lap; all the children were beautifully dressed in white. Jackie was pregnant with her third child, due in August.

One of the friendships that meant the most to Rose during that time was Herbert Hoover's. Over the years, a stream of affectionate notes had passed between them; the fact that the aged ex-president had been unable to attend the Inauguration because weather conditions had forced his plane back to New York was a great disappointment to her. Whenever she was in Manhattan, she made a point of visiting him at his home at the Waldorf Towers. Their rapport was intense and abiding; apart from Joseph Timilty, he was the closest of her male friends.

He always sent his published and unpublished writings to her, and in April forwarded her his book, *Fishing for Fun*. Her letter of thanks, dated April 27, 1963, is revealing, getting to the essence of her soul. She wrote to him expressing her profoundest yearning—which was for quiet and solitude above all things.

It was the longing that had animated her desire for peace through several decades and had driven her for refuge to her Little White House (now long since lost), time and again. It was the impulse that sent her walking alone on the beaches of Massachusetts and Florida when something critical happened in her life.

She recalled in her letter an episode in Switzerland in 1956, after Joe had returned to Boston for prostate surgery and she was on her way to see Clare Boothe Luce in Rome. She recalled she had taken a funicular railroad car to a high point in the Jungfrau, wanting to spend a few hours of blessed isolation, when she found the place rattling with pneumatic drills as a new winter sports palace was being built. Almost seven years later, the experience still grated on her.

She did not write of the contradiction in her nature that also made her love parties, dances and lecture tours.

Preparing at this early date for Jack's 1964 run for president, she embarked, in May, on an extended journey, emphasizing, in a new series of lantern-slide talks for charity, his many good qualities. She talked of his being made Father of the Year, of his achievements in launching men into space.

The Luces' *Time* magazine was as supportive as ever, announcing in its May 31 issue that her "An Evening With Rose Kennedy" was "the liveliest show on the Massachusetts lecture circuit" and that the president's mother "packs 'em in and sends 'em away delighted."

She showed photographs of Windsor Castle, praising the Queen Mother and giving a history of the royal family; she pointed at a slide of Neville Chamberlain and, in describing his attempts to keep England out of war until the country was fully armed, proved loyal to her and Joe's old friend. Mentioning Chamberlain's famous umbrella, she advised, to general amusement, her audience to carry one when they traveled to the United Kingdom, but she warned them not to take too much heavy clothing, which would weigh down their luggage, in going to Ireland or Switzerland, where reports of severe cold in winter were exaggerated. This not-very-sage advice was probably ignored.

She showed Joe with the Pope in Rome during the Coronation of 1939, and described Teddy's first communion at the hands of Pope Pius XII. She discussed wearing her tiara at her presentation at court, saying that this form of decoration wasn't all it was cracked up to be; it could be very heavy on one's head. She surprised listeners with praise for Mrs. Khrushchev ("She speaks English well, shows a lot of initiative and fulfills her position skillfully").

She brought the biggest response when she told one particular story. At the meeting with Khrushchev in Vienna, she had asked him for his autograph. He had suggested she send him a picture, to which he would then add his signature. She forwarded one to Moscow, and received it in the mail at Hyannis Port with the Russian leader's autograph scrawled across the base. Jack got wind of this, and said, jocularly, that before contacting heads of state Rose might consider talking to him or to Dean Rusk, secretary of state. She had replied, "I'm glad you mentioned it. I was just about to send a photograph of Castro." She brought the house down.

On June 3, while still on tour, Rose heard of the death of Pope John XXIII. She was able to attend more than one Mass in his honor. Cardinal Montini, Joe's contact in Rome, who had played a crucial role in the secret war against communism as the Vatican's head of intelligence, would now become Pope Paul VI.

In July, Rose heard of the downfall of a friend who was even closer to the family than the ill-fated Igor and Charlene Cassini. James Landis, former dean of the Harvard Law School, coauthor of Joe's memoirs (never published because they were too inflammatory), had arranged both Bobby's and Teddy's admission to the University of Virginia. He was a frequent guest at Hyannis Port and at Palm Beach, and he was allowed the use of the Kennedy office suite in the Pan American Building on Park Avenue in New York. Rose had made him a trustee for her children and grandchildren, and Jack had accorded him the role of special assistant to the White House, liaising with, and at the same time checking on, the CIA and the FBI.

It was determined that Landis was five years behind on his income tax. He had been through a messy divorce, his children had health problems and he had become an alcoholic. Just before the stroke, Joe had managed to bail him out temporarily, but now the Internal Revenue Service had passed the matter on to the Department of Justice, and, in his role of attorney general, Bobby was forced to prosecute.

It was an agony for the whole family, but Bobby dared not refuse. Landis, ill and depressed, was put on trial, admitted guilt and was sent to an institution for the insane in lieu of jail, a harsh and uncommon sentence when such a plea usually resulted in a moderate fine and community service. The following year, Landis overdosed and drowned himself in his swimming pool, the second suicide on Kennedy hands in a short time.

Rose's lecture tour concluded in August. Always looking for new excitement, she decided to go, in the wake of the president's recent visit, to Germany and visit the Berlin Wall. It was a symbolic trip, because, following the Cuban missile crisis, the tensions in the Berlin capital had eased, and soon half a million West Berliners would be allowed to cross the Wall to visit their relatives in the eastern sector. Rose was the guest of Mayor Willy Brandt, who much admired her. Just as Joe had backed the Social Democrats in Italy, so did Jack support the German Social Democrats, of whom Brandt would become the leader.

Rose was on a tight schedule. She had to fly back after only three days in the German capital to make Joe's seventy-fifth birthday on September 6. It was unusual for her to go out of her way for such an occasion. The party was geared more to the children than to the adults; there were large servings of ice cream and rich cake, and, in the afternoon, the family performed for Joe and Rose an antic vaudeville piece Ethel had written. As gusts of wind blew rain against the windows, Joan pounded away at the piano, followed by Rose, who nostalgically tinkled away at "Sweet Adeline" while her sons formed a barbershop trio and vigorously shouted the lyrics. Even Joe laughed at the end of the concert, and everyone joined in with "Happy Birthday."

On the last day of September, Jackie left between a morning reception and a dinner in honor of Emperor Haile Selassie of Ethiopia in order to attend a Mediterranean cruise on Aristotle Onassis's yacht. Rose was delighted to be hostess at the dinner, enjoying the company of the short and bearded emperor, whose regime was scarcely preferable to Arosemena's.

Once again, the president was dealing Rose's royal card in the Cold War poker game. Selassie had signed a secret agreement with Washington, not made public until 1970, to obtain U.S. military instructors and personnel against the Russian-backed Somalis in Ethiopia. He ran his country as a malign dictatorship, which the American government was happy to support. U.S. backing was given him for his brutal suppression of the Somalis; hundreds were dead and wounded in the fight.

During the evening, Rose mentioned to the emperor that she and he had the same birthday, July 22(!), and were the same age. He was too gallant to tell her that his birthday fell on July 23 and that she was two years older.

The fall brought painful news to Rose of the downfall and destruction of still a third friend whose usefulness had expired. Like Trujillo, the celibate Catholic President Diem of South Vietnam had proved to be averse to the purposes of the Kennedy administration, using dictatorial methods which had attracted bad publicity. Although he had rescued thousands of Catholics in flight from North Vietnam, and had wholeheartedly supported the Vatican/CIA cause in the region, the decision was made that he must go.

Ambassador Henry Cabot Lodge, on the president's orders, set in motion the groundwork for a coup d'état, a move that CIA chief in Saigon William Colby to this day angrily deplores. Lodge was derelict, and so was Jack Kennedy, in failing to invoke the support of Pope Paul VI in summoning Diem to Rome or sending Cardinal Spellman to Saigon to discipline the unruly leader. Instead, the coup d'état resulted, as Colby confirms today, in a disaster that was to affect America's future in the region and lay the basis for the Vietnam War. Diem was ambushed and murdered. The strength of Catholicism was destroyed in Southeast Asia, just as Trujillo's demise had wrecked Vatican influence in the Caribbean.

Rose could only remain silent. When Diem's sister-in-law, who was in San Francisco and later in New York and Paris, demanded hysterically and unsuccessfully a response from the White House on why Diem had been fed to the wolves, she received no response. Only two and a half years before, Vice-President Lyndon Johnson, returning from Saigon, had called Diem "the Winston Churchill of Asia." Now the official (and cynical) American position was that he was a Hitler.

Rose remained active at social events. She was at the April in Paris Ball at the Plaza Hotel in New York on October 25, accompanied by Joseph Timilty.

It was a joyous moment for her when the president signed on October 31 the first bill authorizing help for mental retardation through building communities and health centers and setting up research facilities. She gave an interview to Edith Asbury of the *New York Times,* saying that retarded children should no longer be shunted away, unmentioned. She mentioned Rosemary, and her visits to her, and she spoke of Jean Kennedy's work in fund-raising.

On November 17, following a dinner at the Albert Laskers', Rose attended a charity occasion for the retarded, a screening at New York's Warner Cinerama Theater of Stanley Kramer's noisy comedy *It's a Mad, Mad, Mad, Mad World.* She sat gamely through the film, returning to Hyannis Port to prepare for Thanksgiving.

November 22, 1963, dawned dark and threatening. As Rose got out of bed, shortly after 6:00 A.M., a foghorn bellowed off Nantucket Sound, waves were black and tossed, yachts swayed at anchor. Rose dressed and buzzed Frank Saunders. He normally did not drive her to Mass at St. Francis Xavier's Church, but this morning she needed him. As she walked through the entrance hall to meet him at the front door in the white Chrysler, Rose saw Ann Gargan's suitcases, already packed for a trip to Detroit for the Thanksgiving holiday, standing there.

Saunders helped Rose into the back of the car. She fretted, as they went down the drive, at the chilly day, the dampness, always the curse of the old, and she clutched and clutched again at her rubber ball. She told Saunders how she hated the sight of elderly people with their hands twisted and gnarled into claws and hoped the exercise with the ball would help her arthritis. He asked her what her plans were for the weekend. She said that Henry Cabot Lodge would be arriving in the wake of the Diem assassination, and reminded him that both Caroline's and John-John's birthdays were imminent.

Saunders parked the car at the church and walked her inside. She attended the Stations of the Cross, genuflected at the altar and took the communion wafer and wine from the Right Reverend Leonard J. Daley as celebrant. After the Low Mass, she did not wait for the second at 8:00 A.M., but returned to the house for a frugal breakfast. She found Joe watching the television news, which showed the president at Fort Worth, Texas.

In midmorning, with Saunders at the wheel, Rose went

with Joe for a drive to cheer him up. The fog and murky skies cleared, the sun shone brilliantly from a clear blue sky. It was a perfect day, and the golden fall leaves, the white clapboard houses, the well-tended lawns, the turquoise sea were enchanting. Yachts were already out in the Sound, white sails tossing and gleaming.

After lunch, Rita Dallas took Joe to his room to rest, and Rose lay down on her bed for her customary siesta. The time of peace, silence and sleep was important to her at seventy-three, since, like most people her age, she slept fitfully during the night.

To her annoyance, she was awakened by the sound of yelling and a radio, or perhaps a television, from down the corridor—Ann Gargan's room—blaring loudly. She got up, threw on her robe and opened the door, her hair tousled from the pillow. She was astonished to see Dora, the maid, slumped on the staircase in a flood of tears. Frank Saunders, Rita Dallas and Ann Gargan were huddled in consultation outside Ann's room, talking loudly.

She asked them what was going on, said that they had upset her with the din and said that Mr. Kennedy would be disturbed. She could now hear the radio from the kitchen, as well as Ann's TV going full blast. There was something about a shooting; she couldn't make out the details. As she insisted the sets be turned off, Ann Gargan broke into tears.

Saunders and Rita Dallas blurted out that Jack had been shot and wounded. Rose said, "Don't worry. He'll be all right. You'll see." She went back to her room and began pacing. She told herself the whole thing must be a false alarm, a sensational news story without substance. Even if it were true, she reminded herself that Jack had been through many other crises, his near-death from scarlet fever in infancy, the cutting in half of the PT-109, his narrow scrape with death after his back surgery.

The phone rang; it was Bobby. He told her that Jack had indeed been shot, and there was very little hope for his recovery. She began fingering her rosary, praying, saying Hail Marys. Then she pulled herself together. Whatever happened, Joe must not be told the news. She went out into the corridor. She saw Ann walking into Joe's room. She called Rita to stop her before she could blurt out anything.

Joe fretted because the TVs were not on, allowing him to see, as he always did, the 1:00 P.M. news. Rose, Ann and the staff entered into a loving conspiracy. Saunders was told to pretend that Joe's set was not working, and to unplug it from the wall. All other sets were to be played at such low volume he would not be able to hear them. As he demanded a TV repairman, Rose decided Joe must be distracted by being taken in the handicapped elevator to the basement theater to see a movie. Doubling as a projectionist as usual, Saunders put on Elvis Presley's movie *Kid Galahad,* but Joe disliked it and after fifteen minutes he was back upstairs. By now, Bobby had called again, and the news was that Jack was dead.

No longer able to endure the house and its confines, Rose took off for a long walk on her own along the beach. The weather had turned sour again, the clouds a silvery black, the sea leaden and threatening. She tried to concentrate her thoughts, praying for Jack's immortal soul, asking God, *Why?*

She knew that if she collapsed, the whole family would fall apart. She must be strong and resolute whatever happened.

She returned to get a heavier coat at 4:00 P.M. Suddenly overcome, she sank on the doorstep and hung her head down. Then she stood up and walked indoors. Calls had come in from cardinals Spellman and Cushing, Henry and Clare Boothe Luce, the Wrightsmans and Mary Lasker, among others. As she entered the house, the Johnsons were on the line. They gave her what comfort they could. Although she never warmed to Lyndon Johnson, she was fond of Lady Bird and was touched by her condolences.

Joey Gargan arrived from Boston and accompanied her back to the beach. Teddy and Eunice, who had flown in from Washington, joined them. They walked, wrapped up against the cold, to Teddy's house across the Squaw Island Causeway, as Rose kept saying pointless things to keep her nerves steady. She told Gargan to read the works of Lord Marlborough, Charles James Fox and Thomas Burke, that he needed to read more, like Jack.

They discussed the funeral arrangements, deciding to leave everything to Jackie. They returned to the house to find Joe furious. Though unable to speak, he made it clear that he had wanted to see Jack's arrival in Dallas and was angry that no TV repairman had arrived. They managed to persuade him that no man was available; Teddy crawled on the floor behind Joe's TV set and, pretending to try to fix it, disconnected the wires.

The decision was that Joe would be told the news in the morning, when he had had a chance to rest. Rose took to her bed for a fitful sleep; she kept her bedside lamp burning throughout the night.

Early on Saturday morning—some say late the night before—Teddy and Eunice went into Joe's bedroom and told him what had happened. He must have suspected it, because he didn't break down but sat silent and numb, calmly absorbing what they told him, tears trickling down his cheeks.

Rose attended both services at St. Francis Xavier's, at 7:00 and 8:00 A.M. Reporters swarmed around, wanting comments, but the picture of Rose with her bowed head, in the black mantilla she had used for papal audiences, silenced even the boldest and they drew back from her as she walked to her car.

The First Lady had decided that there would be Lincolnian elements in the ritual of death. She sent her staff with flashlights into the darkened Library of Congress and the National Archive to obtain books and articles dealing with the arrangements in 1865. They revealed that after his assassination, Lincoln's body had been placed in the East Room of the White House and had thence been taken to the rotunda of the capitol dome to lie in state.

No other imitation would be possible. She did not copy the procedure of allowing the public to come in from the White House lawn to see the body on its bier; she would have only family and friends attending within the building.

She gave no Lincolnian order to have every church bell in Washington, Georgetown and Alexandria sound in farewell; the guns did not discharge, as they had done in 1865, from surrounding batteries. And young men, fit and strong, not army veterans, would guard the body, and the handicapped would not be given special access.

The arrangements, of which Rose was advised, were

imitative, fond and picturesque, but, except for the touch of a riderless horse in the subsequent procession, lacked the somber theatrical majesty of the original. There would be no funeral train. The president would be taken to Arlington National Cemetery, a peculiar irony because Arlington was the confiscated property of General Robert E. Lee, to whom Janet Auchincloss falsely declared Jackie's family allegiance.

Rose got through the day. She followed the TV coverage, seeing the lying-in of the president in that same East Room in which, as a child, she had been introduced to President McKinley, who was soon to suffer an identical fate.

On the afternoon of Sunday, November 24, Jack Ruby's shooting of Lee Harvey Oswald was announced. As she saw the pictures on television, Rose lost her composure for the first time and cried out in horror.

She attended the funeral. She flew with Eunice and Teddy on the *Caroline* to Washington, arriving at 6:40 on Sunday evening. Bobby had moved out of the Lincoln bedroom for her. Shaken by the flight, still struggling against grief, she walked into the dark room, with all of its dark associations of presidential assassination.

Sargent Shriver was there. In charge of the post-death and funeral arrangements, he told her what the program for burial the next day would be. As he spoke, she fell in helpless tears into his arms. He embraced her; she poured out a litany of despair, talking of Joe, Jr.'s and Kathleen's deaths when so young and so fair, of Rosemary's tragic life, and now this. Why did this have to happen? Why?

She sent for her daughters one by one, and gave them the black veils she had used in Rome, one of them for Jackie, and several pairs of black stockings.

Then something odd happened. Instead of having supper with the immediate family, she was joined by, of all people, the First Lady's brother-in-law Prince Radziwill, whom she did not know well. It is possible the others were too busy conferring on the burial arrangements to eat with her.

Afterward, Rose attended a family meeting presided over by Jackie, to decide which passages would be read over the grave following the burial at Arlington National Cemetery. When neither Rose nor her daughters said they felt up to it, the First Lady decided that Bobby and Ted would read. As it turned out, they did not.

Shortly after 10:00 P.M., Rose arrived at the Capitol rotunda where the president's body lay in its coffin on a catafalque. The rotunda was supposed to have been closed at 9:00 P.M., but of the quarter of a million mourners who had waited since before noon, many were still in line, and they were allowed to see the president lying in state.

Rose walked with Eunice and Ted through the south entrance, saw the guards standing at the four corners of the catafalque and kissed the coffin, draped in the American flag.

She returned, exhausted, to the Lincoln bedroom. Waking on Monday morning in the vast bed of an assassinated president with its twelve-foot canopy, feeling ill, Rose felt that she was in some kind of a tomb herself.

She told Sargent Shriver, who was in charge of the execution of the funeral arrangements, that she could not face the walk from the White House to St. Patrick's Cathedral, in which the rest of the family (save only the younger children, who would go by car) would take part. Shriver arranged for Ann Gargan and a cousin, Robert Fitzgerald, to accompany her in a limousine.

Following the private Mass in the East Room, at which she took communion, she breakfasted lightly and made her way to the waiting Cadillac. The chauffeur drove slowly past long lines of silent mourners on either side of the street, while the sun shone with ironic brilliance from a blue sky.

As she arrived at St. Patrick's and walked unsteadily into the apse, Cardinal Cushing's immense form suddenly loomed over her, and he bent down to embrace her. She loosened herself from his grasp and rejected his indication that he should conduct her to the front pew. She made it clear that she would wait with her companions until the rest of the family arrived.

The military bearers carried in the coffin at 12:15 P.M. Only now did she walk to her seat, taking her place between the First Lady and Caroline. She sat, very still, visibly dazed and tired, as Cushing intoned the Kyrie Eleison, the 129th Psalm and a part of St. Paul's letter to the Thessalonians, followed by the Dies Irae.

When Bobby motioned to Rose to accompany him to the altar to receive the sacrament, she shook her head gently; she would not receive the eucharist twice in one day.

Next to her, the First Lady began to cry, so loudly that the congregation could hear her despite the swelling organ music. Auxiliary Bishop Philip P. Hannan read passages the First Lady had chosen from the Scriptures, part of Jack's Inaugural address, and the Lord's Prayer. Cushing scattered incense on the coffin and, in a break with Catholic tradition, which dictated that only Latin should be spoken at such a service, delivered a prayer in English over the casket.

Now Rose had to face the ordeal of the burial ceremony. She was driven over Memorial Bridge across the Potomac River, to the sound of muffled drums; the chauffeur stopped beyond Memorial Gate on Sheridan Drive, which sloped up to the grave site. An official appeared, asking him, as he had asked the drivers ahead of Rose, to wait before he released his passengers until the ritual jet fly-past accompanied by Air Force One should be completed. The planes roared above, in formation and on schedule. Rose got out, aided by a cemetery attendant, and began walking, with Ann and Bobby flanking her, up the gravel above the old Lee mansion, while crows wheeled and cawed over her.

The Marine Band struck up the national anthem, and the air-force pipers marched past, playing the strains of "The Mist-Covered Mountain." Rose stood to the west of the trench that would receive her son, closing her eyes at the sight of it, praying, holding her rosary, as the casket was carried from its vehicle caisson.

Cardinal Cushing spoke the benediction, interminably and fulsomely in his grating voice, and the references to "Jack" and not to "the president" were gratingly personal for the occasion, even though Cushing was a close friend.

Bobby turned to Rose, offering her a taper with which to touch the eternal flame. She did not see him; her eyes were still closed tight. He passed the taper to Teddy instead.

She walked, as best she could, back to the limousine, Ann supporting her arm. The day wasn't over yet. She would have to steel herself to attend the reception for the world leaders at the White House.

Shriver had accorded her the West Sitting Room in which to compose herself, and, after a brief rest in the Lincoln bedroom, she walked there. The two people Shriver designated to keep her company were not on her list of favorites. Of Peter Lawford she still did not warmly approve, and she was not close to Evelyn Lincoln, the presidential secretary.

She was more at ease when the door opened and in walked Charles de Gaulle, who reminisced with her about her visit to Paris in 1961. Then came Emperor Haile Selassie, who talked to her of their recent companionship at the banquet in his honor; he renewed an earlier invitation that she should visit him in his capital of Addis Ababa.

The venerable, almost blind Irish premier Eamon De Valera followed, talking to her of Jack's visit to Dublin and to the family village. Prince Philip of England greeted her warmly; she had never forgotten how his parents-in-law, King George and Queen Elizabeth, had been kind to her and Joe.

There was talk of Rose attending John-John's imminent birthday party, but she had had enough and, that evening, she flew home on a specially commissioned air-force jet after a brief appearance at the reception, at which she greeted Kathleen's parents-in-law the duke and duchess of Devonshire.

Somehow, she must pull herself together to prepare for Thanksgiving Day. This was Monday; Thanksgiving would, of course, be on Thursday.

The former First Lady arrived at Hyannis on Wednesday evening. She ran into the entrance hall, carrying with her the American flag, folded in quarters, which had been taken from her husband's coffin before it was interred. She told Rose she would give it to Joe, and would tell him of the details of the assassination and burial of which he might not have been aware. Horrified, Rose tried to stop her; the sight of the flag and the worrisome details would surely upset Joe. But there was no thwarting Jackie, who gently pushed Rose and her objections aside and ran up the stairs. She emerged from Joe's room several minutes later, telling Rose she would be back the following day for the family luncheon.

Rose went to bed early. At 2:00 A.M. on Thanksgiving morning, a heartrending scream woke her from her sleep. It was Joe's voice. Rose ran to his room; Rita Dallas was at her side. What Rose saw froze her heart.

Joe was sitting up in bed, shrieking in horror. The coffin flag covered him except for his face; his left hand clutched at it, trying to pull it off. It was as though he were being buried himself, as though he were sharing his son's death. Rose and Mrs. Dallas pulled the flag off him, furious, wondering who was responsible. Ann Gargan appeared, admitting, ruefully, that she was the loving culprit.

Rose went in a daze through the day's family rituals. On Friday, she faced yet another ordeal. Cushing arrived, booming that he was there to repeat the graveside benediction to Joe. Rose heard his voice from upstairs and fled to her room, telling Mrs. Dallas to inform the cardinal that she was ill and could not receive him. Cushing strode into Joe's room; Rose learned later that as the cardinal went on and on with the interminable blessing, Joe threw his eyes up to the ceiling in dismay and irritation, and, at the end, burst out with a strange, gargling laugh. The absurd solemnity of the address had caused him to break through grief into mockery. The humorless Cushing, determined not to be offended, had responded with the words "Laughter is good for the soul."

The house no longer had a Secret Service guard. Such a guard was available only to presidents in office and to their families.

Of course, Bobby could have arranged for one. It is clear that Bobby was certain there was no danger; he was fixed on the idea that Lee Harvey Oswald was a lone and demented assassin, with no significant accomplices, and that he was not the active figure in a conspiracy. Therefore, no police or FBI guardianship for Hyannis Port would be supplied.

Bobby had told the press he would not be present at Hyannis for Thanksgiving; instead, he would be at Hobe Sound, Florida, where he arranged for no special protection. Florida was a center of Mafia activities; he apparently feared no danger from that quarter, even though, more than his brother, Bobby had pursued the Mob and sought to suppress it.

Florida was the home of most Cubans in exile from Castro. He clearly expected no problem from them; they were Catholics, Jack had arranged for their children's rescue and he had dedicated many religious services to them. Had Bobby believed that Castro might take revenge for CIA-engineered attempts on his life, he would surely have arranged maximum security for his parents and siblings. And why should he fear J. Edgar Hoover as the culprit behind the assassination—Hoover was close to his father. And the CIA? The CIA owed its huge, multimillion-dollar budget and full support to the Kennedys.

Rose was napping after lunch one day when Rita Dallas walked into her room and told her of something that had happened: Mrs. Dallas was downstairs when she saw a man running into the house. She cornered him in the kitchen, and he told her that he was a TV repairman. She didn't know of any sets that needed fixing. She told him to wait, saying that she would see which of the sets needed attention. She left him there, then ran outside to find the one detective the family had in attendance; he was sitting in his car eating his lunch.

When they returned to the kitchen, the man was gone. Arrested while standing unthreateningly near the fuse box, he said he was from—Dallas. There was no evidence he intended bodily harm to anyone.

In the wake of Jack's death, Rose devoted herself to the cause of mental retardation; she appeared continually in public places, giving awards and making speeches. She spent as much time as she could with Bobby, who remained devastated with grief.

An uncomfortable incident occurred on February 27, 1964. President Johnson came to Palm Beach with Lady Bird. Rose was never fond of Johnson; the family had not forgotten his cruel remarks about Jack's face and slight physique in earlier years. Rose did her best to make the couple feel at home, but when she took them in to see Joe, he greeted them in his robe and slippers and virtually ignored them, looking at the ceiling while the new president droned on. In her diary, Lady Bird remembered "the poignancy of the special hour we spent at Palm Beach." Like Rose, the new First Lady knew how to avoid realities.

As for her predecessor, Jim Bishop reported in his book *The Day Kennedy Was Shot* that in March 1964 Rose told him, "I haven't heard from *Mrs. Kennedy* since the funeral."

The emphasis was deliberate; Rose always thought of *herself* as Mrs. Kennedy.

In March, Rose accepted an invitation from André Malraux, author and French minister of cultural affairs, to appear at a ceremony renaming the Quai de Passy, on the Right Bank, the Avenue du President John F. Kennedy. In an icy wind on the sixteenth, Rose made the dedication, then left to visit with Loel and Gloria Guinness, friends from Palm Beach, at their house in Normandy. Then she spent time with the duke and duchess of Windsor at their converted mill near Paris.

She returned to America in early April. Joe was transferred to Philadelphia on the twentieth of that month for treatments at the Institute for the Achievement of Human Potential. After almost a month there, he went back to Hyannis Port.

Rose spent much of the summer arranging for wealthy people with large estates to make their homes, from which they would be absent in certain seasons, available to handicapped children. She dedicated cottages at the Joseph P. Kennedy, Jr. Home for Neglected Children in the Bronx.

On June 4, she had horrible news. Her oldest friend, Mary Moore, widow of Eddie Moore, was caught, at the age of eighty-one, in a fire at the Centerville, Massachusetts, nursing home and severely burned. Brought to Cape Cod Hospital in a state of shock, she died on June 30.

On the morning of June 20, Rose heard that Teddy had been involved in a plane crash. It took all of her strength not to collapse; Teddy, her youngest, her favorite. Would he die, too? Like Joe, Jr., Kathleen, Billy Hartington and the Skakels?

Teddy had left Washington after voting in support of the historic Civil Rights Bill that his brothers had worked hard to forge. He was flying in conditions of poor visibility in a private twin-engine aircraft to the Massachusetts Democratic State Convention at West Springfield. With him were Senator Birch Bayh of Indiana and Bayh's wife, and Edward Moss, Teddy's administrative aide. Due to foggy conditions, the plane had crashed into an apple orchard.

One of the staff had been killed; Bayh had climbed out through a broken window and dragged Teddy free. Teddy was taken to Northampton Hospital with fractures of the second, third and fourth vertebrae of the lower back, and second, third and fourth transverses of the spine. He had broken ribs, and was badly cut on his legs and hands.

Rose was advised not to fly to him at once; Pat, Joan and Eunice kept her in touch on the details. After three blood transfusions, Teddy began to recover. He was in an oxygen tent until June 21, and then had to be hung in a canvas frame from rope rigging and moved almost constantly to relieve pressure.

At Teddy's request, instead of spending periods at his bedside, Rose went out substituting for him in his campaign for the Senate. She gave a speech in Philadelphia in his place; in every way she proved valuable as she talked of him glowingly in several locations.

Bobby had committed to visit Poland and West Germany. In Warsaw on June 29, he said, in his only public statement of the time, that Lee Harvey Oswald had committed a single act of a person protesting against society—that although Oswald was a professed Communist, the Communists in Russia and Cuba had nothing to do with him. This was, and remained, the family's unchanging view.

Rose resumed her lantern-slide lectures, this time for Flame of Hope perfumes, scents prepared by the handicapped, asking people to bring lit candles to confirm that they would contribute to the campaign against mental retardation.

She began working sporadically on her memoirs, which would occupy her, on and off, for the next nine years.

On September 3, Bobby resigned as attorney general. He was endorsed for Democratic nominee for the New York

Senate, withdrawing as Massachusetts delegate. He would prove victorious after a campaign to which Rose significantly contributed.

On August 8, Josie Fitzgerald died at the age of ninety-eight. Now almost completely unaware, she had not been told of her grandson's assassination, nor of Teddy's accident.

Rose was at Mt. Burgenstock in Switzerland when she heard the news. Just as she had failed to attend her father's funeral, so she did not attend her mother's. Her nephew, Reverend John F. Fitzgerald, of St. Jude's Church, presided at St. Brendon's in Dorchester.

Rose continued to Paris, saying nothing to reporters about her mother. Josie, who left a modest $30,000, had made sure there was no legacy for Rose, not even a simple memento from the past.

Joe experienced chest congestion in September, but Rose was not present to assist him. She was in Canada, touring for Flame of Hope, and from there proceeded to Montreal to promote the John F. Kennedy Foundation for Retarded Children as the guest of industrialist Joseph Timmins.

She was back in Europe in late November, after penning a tribute to her husband for a book that Teddy worked on during his convalescence, *The Fruitful Bough,* a collection of essays on his father.

She was in Paris, at the Palais de Chaillot, on November 27, to open an exhibition illustrating Jack's past, and to which she had given items from her attics in Hyannis and Palm Beach. In the presence of a large crowd, she pointed to such objects as the rocking chair Jack used for his bad back, his favorite desk, under which John-John used to hide, drafts of the nuclear test treaty, papers relating to the Cuban missile crisis and other significant objects. She had set herself the task of accompanying the exhibit through Europe, and, on December 9, she opened it, in the company of Queen Ingrid of Denmark, at Copenhagen Town Hall.

As he was leaving the hospital on December 15, Teddy wrote to Gloria Swanson asking her for a contribution to *The Fruitful Bough.* He sent her previous essays by friends as illustrations; he went on to wish her a happy Christmas and New Year. She did not supply a contribution. Later, she published her own memoir, including an account of the relationship with Joe that her daughter, Gloria Daly, dismisses today as "completely invented; my mother was ashamed of the book and disowned it to me."

Rose was in Athens in February 1965 for the next opening. She returned to New York for the dedication ceremony at the Jewish Yeshiva University's Rose Fitzgerald Kennedy Center for Research in Maternal and Child Health and Human Development, for which she had raised $1.45 million.

Through much of the year, Joe's health was very poor; he often became weakened and nauseated, partly through the amounts of medication he was taking.

Then Rose herself had a scare; in July she found a swelling on her neck and rushed to Dr. John Converse of the Manhattan Eye, Ear and Throat Hospital for a checkup. After a biopsy, Dr. Converse advised her that the tumor was benign. The operation was simple, and she recovered with her customary speed.

She was in Paris when, at the end of that month, Joe was admitted to New England Baptist Hospital with throat and chest congestion.

On September 18, she attended a fund-raising dinner for the retarded in Toronto, where Prime Minister Lester B. Pearson gave her a painting of the John F. Kennedy, a 13,880-foot Canadian mountain peak, which Bobby, though acrophobic, had recently and perilously climbed.

Nineteen sixty-six began on a sour note, with Pat Kennedy's civil divorce—the first Rose had had to endure in her family—from an increasingly drunken, drug-ridden and shockingly aged Peter Lawford, who, no longer the lazy charmer of motion pictures, had inherited his mother's disgusting private and public behavior. Pat was granted custody of her four children, Christopher, Sydney, Victoria and Robin. An ominous note was struck when the Archdiocese of New York, in answer to questions from the press, announced that she would "only lose her standing with the Church if she remarries."

It was not a pleasant time for Rose, who still regarded the

marital state, whether or not the partners were compatible or faithful, as permanent.

She bore another burden: Jean was the first of her daughters to commit herself to a romantic relationship outside of marriage. As her companion, she chose the gifted but neurotic lyricist Alan J. Lerner, who had written *Camelot*. Luckily for Rose, Jean's interest in Lerner didn't last, or there might have been another family divorce that year.

These were ominous indications, in the mid-1960s, that the center of the world Rose had known since childhood would not hold in the last decades of the century.

Her husband's infidelities of long ago had never troubled her. She had turned a blind eye to Jack's own alleged affairs, particularly his supposed relationship with Marilyn Monroe. Such were the transgressions of men the world over, which women must endure in order to secure their homes and their children's welfare. These matters were simply not discussed by her; much less did she want them dragged into the public eye, in the divorce courts or out.

Divorce and female adultery were simply not in Rose's vocabulary. Other people indulged in such shenanigans, not her own. And the advent of rock and roll during the previous years, the increasing lack of discipline of the younger members of her family—all distracted her and irritated her, though she did her best to contain her annoyance.

She did make one concession to the modern world. Just as she had asked Frank Saunders to wear plain clothes while driving her, she now had Rita Dallas change from starched white uniform into slacks. But the moment Rita put on a rose sack suit, Rose grumbled because she felt it was her color, and Mrs. Dallas had to change again.

When Joe had a dental problem, instead of bringing any one of the family's dentists to the house, all of whom advertised their skills whenever a Kennedy opened his mouth, she had the ancient practitioner who had taken care of herself and Joe during the early days of their marriage flown in from Boston.

Joe screamed when he saw the old man hobble in, and the dentist was furious. Suspecting Luella Hennessey and Rita Dallas of laughing at him behind his back, the dentist thrust them into a clothes closet and locked them in. Joe bit the dentist on the ear; the old man fled.

Rose insisted that lights be turned off every time a staff member left a room. One light seemed forever to be on, though, in one of the linen closets. One day Rose managed to hide her five-foot frame under a closet shelf and waited to catch the culprit. She saw Mrs. Dallas walk into the room. As the nurse left, the light remained on. Rose jumped out and grabbed her, accusing her of being responsible for sending up the electric bills. Mrs. Dallas had to explain to her that the light came on automatically when the door was opened, and had she closed it a minute later, it would have gone off. Marveling at the modern invention, Rose apologized.

Her tightness with money hadn't changed. When she found that Frank Saunders was getting free coffee, a normal expectation of the staff, she compelled him to put a dime in a kitchen saucer every time the cook gave him a cupful.

Yet she still spent enormously on her clothes. She made a splash in a Givenchy original at the April in Paris Ball at the Waldorf-Astoria in October. She walked through an avenue of vegetables representing the Les Halles market and found herself staring at a replica of the Arc de Triomphe that had been erected over the bandstand. When Chairman of Decorations Mrs. Alfred S. Levitt shook her hand, Rose saw that Mrs. Levitt had her fingernails painted in red, white and blue.

There were commotions: thieves made off with Mrs. Levitt's handbag and Mrs. Arthur Karoff's earrings. At the end of the evening, Rose was handed a boxful of gifts. Fortunately, she didn't lift it, or she might have been in the hospital with another hernia. It weighed twenty pounds.

The next month, she was at Truman Capote's famous masked ball at the Plaza in honor of Katherine Graham. Dressed in Givenchy, Rose outdazzled the other guests by wearing a cat's-eye mask with feathers sprouting vertically from her forehead. At first the conversation consisted largely of how much each of the wealthy guests had spent on their masks; they vied with each other in declared cheapness. Capote announced he had bought his in a dime store for thirty-nine cents, only to be upstaged by the ancient Alice Roosevelt Longworth, who said she had paid thirty-five cents for hers.

Many leaders of international society declined to come. The duke and duchess of Windsor and Jackie Kennedy were notable by their absence. Lee Radziwill was there, and so were Frank Sinatra and his wife Mia Farrow, Cecil Beaton and Mrs. Henry Ford II.

Rose danced to the music of Peter Duchin and his orchestra. She left before the party came to an end at 3:30 A.M.

The Venice masked ball, which Rose attended on September 9, 1967, was more impressive. Given in aid of the victims of the Italian floods, it had Clare Boothe Luce as organizer.

Rose left the Hotel Danieli in an excited mood shortly after 8:00 P.M., and headed in a motorboat for the seventeenth-century Palazzo Rezzonico. She was again dressed by Givenchy and wore an exquisitely designed copy of an eighteenth-century Venetian mask. As her craft made its way down the Grand Canal, a downfall of rain came close to drenching her; she was barely able to find shelter under a flimsy awning. The boat rocked as it sped through a churning canal full of refuse—the open sewer of Venice.

There was a noise ahead of her; a launch had crashed into Mrs. Luce's, and the former ambassadress was covered in slivers of glass from a shattered windshield, narrowly escaping being cut.

When Rose's boat reached the palace's open courtyard, the water was so deep on the cobbles she had to remove her shoes and wade in her stockings to the door. The hard-pressed footmen, dressed in livery, could barely protect her; they had only six umbrellas for hundreds of hatless guests. Rose exploded in a temper, losing her public composure for the first time in her life, as she struggled, damp and shivering, into the vestibule.

Mrs. Luce expressed her annoyance to Gore Vidal and composer Gian Carlo Menotti when they arrived without masks. The Viscomtesse Jacqueline des Ribes criticized Douglas Fairbanks, Jr., for wearing a face that was a copy of

Cyrano de Bergerac's and insisted he break off the very phallic nose. He refused. Princess Grace of Monaco was in a state because her mask had not arrived in time.

Elizabeth Taylor, asked to bring only Richard Burton, dragged along Richard Burton, her brother, sister, couturier and hairdresser. And she didn't bother to wear a mask.

Chapter 17

Nightmare Train

A grotesque incident occurred on Halloween. In an effort to cheer Joe up, Frank Saunders put on a blond woman's wig and a dress, covered his face in rouge, smeared lipstick on his lips and danced with fake effeminacy, holding his hands on his hips, into Joe's room. The old man screamed in horror at this display, and suffered a minor heart attack which caused him to pass out. Saunders, with his painted lips, applied mouth-to-mouth resuscitation. Fortunately, Rose was absent at the time.

Rose was at 83 Beals Street, Brookline, which had been expertly restored (in part with nostalgic items she had discovered in her attics at Hyannis and Palm Beach) and which was about to be turned into a historic monument. Showing great charm, radiantly cheerful, she chatted, about her children's upbringing, on network television with a respectful Harry Reasoner.

She showed a typical touch of humor, as she referred to her early efforts to keep track of her children by using catalogue cards as a symptom, not so much of efficiency, as of "despair." She laughed as she told Reasoner of her efforts to forbid Jack food when he was late for meals; he could always talk the cook into providing him treats. She spoke of

Bobby as the opposite, a stern self-disciplinarian. Teddy, she said, had authentic joie de vivre. It was a marvelous interview, showing Rose at the top of her considerable form.

On December 2, Cardinal Spellman, still one of the most influential figures in Rose's life, key instigator in the Vatican/CIA connection, mutual friend of Clare Boothe Luce, spiritual leader of American Catholics, died of a stroke at the age of seventy-eight. For some inexplicable reason, Rose did not attend the Mass as he was buried under the high altar of St. Patrick's Cathedral, New York. Six cardinals, including Cushing, attended, with Bobby and Mrs. Luce.

In March 1968, after discussions at Palm Beach, despite Rose's understandable fears for his future safety, Bobby, as consumed as ever with ambition, decided to try for the presidency. He was helped when, on the thirty-first of that month, President Johnson announced he would not run for a second term.

Rose, sharing her husband's views of peaceful coexistence with the heathen Soviets, supported Bobby's opposition to the Vietnam War, which her elder son had unwittingly helped to precipitate.

Rose was a good campaigner, traveling extensively for Bobby through Indiana, Nebraska and Oregon. She repeated the entertaining vaudeville shtick of her appearances with him during the New York State election. Introducing him from the stage, she praised him with good humor, then mentioned, to general laughter and applause, that she had spanked him with a ruler when he had been naughty as a little boy. Sitting down, she yielded the microphone, but then, irrepressible as always, she got to her feet and interjected something witty. He responded, with mock ruefulness, that he had little chance against such a star performer and that perhaps Rose should run for president in his place.

At almost seventy-eight, she showed no signs of fatigue in her travels, only stumbling when she gave an ill-advised interview to *Women's Wear Daily* that echoed in its indiscretion Joe's 1940 interview to the *Boston Globe*. Asked about spending family money to win her sons' political campaigns, she snapped back, "It's our money and we're free to spend it any way we please. It's part of this campaign business. If you have money, you spend it to win. And the more you can afford, the more you'll spend."

On April 4, 1968, Martin Luther King was murdered, and Bobby became the chief remaining hope of American blacks. Bobby spoke of King's death with feeling, urging no reprisals; only the most ardent Republicans accused Bobby privately of cynicism. Bobby walked, his face marked with grief, behind King's coffin on the way to the interment in Atlanta. Rose sent a note of sympathy to Mrs. King.

Rose worked harder than ever on the campaign trail, but there was much to worry her even as American youth embraced Bobby as their idol. On April 11, when he was due to arrive in Lansing, Michigan, a sniper had to be strong-armed by police off a roof directly over his motorcade.

Eugene McCarthy, though scarcely a populist figure, was making inroads and winning states. A problem of the campaign was that the two men had difficulty in finding arguments against each other's positions on such pressing matters as Vietnam and civil rights.

California became a crucial state. Before leaving for the West Coast, the family gathered at Hyannis Port. Jackie turned up and said to all, "Won't it be wonderful when we get back in the White House?" Ethel turned to her. "What do you mean, 'we'?" she asked.

Bobby told his father, "Dad, I'm going to do it just the way you wanted me to. I'm going to win." Joe laughed. Bobby hugged Rose and said, "How will you feel, being the mother of two presidents? That makes you quite a girl, doesn't it?"

Rose felt a twinge of fear; her face went dark.

Rose made an impression in Los Angeles. Dazzling in Dior creations that showed off her still-good legs and trim waist, her trademark cartwheel hats perched rakishly on her head, she had a young woman's vitality and sparkle as she addressed crowds of excited women. She emphasized (daringly, in view of rumors that the Mafia had been involved in Jack's death) Bobby's attacks on organized crime.

On the morning of June 5, in a good mood because of Bobby's victory in California, Rose woke up and turned on her television set to see the early-morning news. She was horrified.

She saw a confused scene at the Ambassador Hotel in Los Angeles; flashbulbs were popping and people were screaming, swarming around Bobby, who lay on the floor. Then, out of sequence, the newscast showed Bobby giving the V for Victory sign before a crowd of supporters, standing, cockily self-assured, grinning, waving, talking to Ethel affectionately, walking through a back door behind the platform—then a further commotion, with men gesticulating at the camera and pushing people aside.

It was a replay of something that had happened earlier that morning, shortly after midnight West Coast time. The commentator was saying that Bobby had been shot at point-blank range and the gunman, a young man, had been apprehended. Bobby had been taken to a hospital, severely wounded, but still alive.

Rose ran into the corridor crying, "It's Bobby! It's Bobby! He's been shot!" Ann Gargan greeted her, explaining to her that a call had come in sometime after 3:00 A.M., telling her of the incident, but that she had not wanted to awaken Rose and Joe. The phone rang and Teddy was on the line, saying that Bobby had indeed been shot in the head, but was still living.

Rose decided it would be pointless flying to Los Angeles. She steeled herself not to become overwrought, put on her black coat and mantilla and had Saunders drive her to St. Francis Xavier's, arriving just before 7:00 A.M. She sat silent through most of the drive, twisting her handkerchief, fighting back the tears. When she got to the church, the reporters showed none of the restraint of the press in 1963 when Jack was killed. No sooner had she got out of the car than they surrounded her, cameras flashing, faces and microphones pushing at her. Someone screamed right in her ear, "Do you feel as badly as when the president was shot?" Another yelled, "Have you talked to Bobby?" A third screeched, "Do you think he'll live? Are you going to L.A.?"

Saunders glared at the journalists; he felt like striking at them with his fists. Rose maintained her dignity. She said nothing and walked with amazing steadiness into the church. Even the press didn't invade her privacy as she prayed, but the moment she left, they swooped down on her again.

Exhausted, she returned to the house, as Joe, weeping, received the news. Teddy and others called her, making clear there was no hope, and at 1:44 A.M. the following day, Bobby died.

Rose arranged a small Mass at the house, and attended another at the church. Cardinal Cushing arrived, and she told him, with remarkable firmness, that Bobby's death was God's will, that God did not give humans crosses too heavy for them to bear.

Cushing noted later, "She has more courage than anybody I have ever met; she has more confidence in Almighty God than any priest . . . she is taking everything in stride and leaving it to the Lord."

Rose wound up comforting Cushing, then called Eunice, whose husband Sarge was ambassador to France, but Eunice had already left Paris for New York, where the funeral would take place at St. Patrick's.

The emphasis in the ritual in 1968 was on the Resurrection rather than on mortal death.

Rose flew by Northwest Airlines from Hyannis to Boston, changing planes for New York. Gertrude Ball, her Manhattan secretary, picked her up in a limousine and took her to the family apartment at 24 Central Park West.

By 4:00 P.M., Rose was at Bergdorf Goodman buying a new black funeral outfit; she was attacked by columnists for going on a shopping spree immediately after her son's death.

That evening, she went to St. Patrick's to pray; because Fifth Avenue had been cleared of traffic, she had to go there in a police car. She passed a crowd standing silent in front of windows decorated with black sashes and black-bordered pictures of Bobby, behind the police barriers in suffocating heat.

She had to crawl under a barrier to get into the cathedral. Archbishop Cooke gave a small prayer service. She left for the second family apartment at the United Nations Plaza.

The details of the memorial Mass were laid out for her. It would be the most ecumenical service ever conducted at St. Patrick's. Ethel and Jackie were its essential proponents. It would, they decided, in keeping with Bobby's love of entertainment, be an Occasion.

Instead of the gloom and grim intonings of Jack's Mass, it would be alive with nonecclesiastical music. Jackie had persuaded the religious authorities to allow women singers in the choir for the first time in history; she had arranged for an appropriate choral group of nuns from Sacred Heart, Manhattanville. She asked Leonard Bernstein to conduct the string section of the New York Philharmonic in the *andantino*, the meditative slow movement of Mahler's Fifth Symphony, with its emphasis on peace, reflectiveness and an escape from the world's stresses.

Very late that night, Rose went back to the cathedral to pray again. Teddy, who would remain, keeping vigil, until daylight, was there ahead of her.

Next morning, she rose early. She was admitted after 5:00 A.M.; thousands had been filing past the casket to pay homage.

The Mass began at 9:55 A.M. Archbishop Cooke and his four assisting priests wore purple; evidently, a white Mass was considered, at the last minute, too controversial. After the *andantino* of Mahler, there was an extraordinary moment: Andy Williams, not approved by Bernstein, sang "The Battle Hymn of the Republic" a cappella from the choir loft. The single voice proved moving and effective.

Teddy's eulogy, his voice breaking on certain words, was simple and deeply affecting.

As Rose left the cathedral, reporters jumped on the pews to harass her; the dreaded cameras flashed. Milton Berle glared angrily at the intruders, waving his fists; Jackie Cooper struck at one, holding a Mass card in his hand.

A silent and grief-stricken multitude watched Rose and her family make their way through the traffic-cleared streets to Pennsylvania Station. Rose walked, a little unsteadily, to Track 11.

The funeral train that would take Bobby's remains to Washington, in imitation of the Lincoln train that had gone from Washington to Springfield, Illinois, was unimpressive. It had been cobbled together from unused cars, and none of the cars matched. An observation car had been commandeered to take the casket, but no one had foreseen that it would be impossible to carry the casket over the back platform.

As Rose arrived, the scratched and dirty observation-car windows were removed and the coffin passed by thirteen official pallbearers to an equivalent number of railroad personnel, who placed it on a small, foot-high wooden platform.

The effort to set the casket in place delayed the departure and depressed and upset everybody. Rose had to climb into an observation car that had not been properly swept, and which still had the stale, toxic stench of old cigarettes. At least it was air-conditioned, but it was not cool enough, and the day became intolerably sweltering and airless.

Rose took her place. This was a far cry from the elegant steam trains of her youth. The windows, once sealed, could not be opened again, so that the train, with its twenty-eight sterile cars, resembled an elongated coffin. Two engines, coupled together, were required to pull it along. As it rattled out of the station, a crowd, almost entirely black, swarmed across the tracks, trying to see the casket, but it was below their sight lines. At Jackie's suggestion, the bearers propped the casket up on four parlor-car chairs; but as the train gathered speed, it jolted and jogged appallingly. Family and other friends were forced to hold it in place for the rest of the day.

Rose needed all of her strength to deal with what followed: a nightmarish journey that lasted, instead of the normal three hours and fifty minutes, just over ten. Neither a distraught Ethel, nor Rose, nor Jackie, nor anybody else in the family or its advisors had had sufficient foresight. Whereas in Lincoln's day the crowds had been controlled and all other trains canceled, on this occasion they were not. As Rose sat still, occasionally looking out of the window or praying, the train swayed and rattled out of Elizabeth, New

Jersey. She and everyone in the observation car heard screams outside; something terrible was going on.

The northbound Chicago–to–New York Admiral Express cut into the crowd that spread across the tracks to see the casket, or who laid down coins or medals to be pressed by the funeral-train wheels for souvenirs. A woman and two men were killed, their limbs scattered about. A child, not more than three years old, was caught in a wheel and spun around, but lived.

The funeral train stopped; police boarded it to talk to witnesses; ambulances screamed in over a bridge.

After an hour, the train squeaked and groaned and started to move, and once again the casket shifted on its chair rests. Aide Jerry Bruno called Washington and, after a furious argument, succeeded in having all northbound trains stopped on the threat that if they were not, this southbound train would be.

Irish-Americans in the parlor car started a boisterous wake; congressmen, supplementing a minimal and hard-pressed staff, went up and down serving sandwiches from carts. Orthodox Jews wailed in anguish. Rose could hear the sounds of bellowed Irish songs and unconstrained crying down the corridors.

Ethel and her ten children—she was pregnant with another—made their way through the coaches to thank everyone for coming. Rose had several of the children go to the windows and wave at the spectators, joining them as they did so. At Princeton, the air-conditioning failed; then struggled on again; then went off. At Trenton, a young male spectator, perched on a boxcar, touched an 11,000-volt wire and was severely burned.

Reporters banged on the observation car's sliding door, but were kept out. Andy Williams joined Rose to give her what comfort he could. Art Buchwald was commandeered to help balance the coffin. Lauren Bacall, Shirley MacLaine, George McGovern and John Kenneth Galbraith mingled with friends in an effort to keep up their spirits. Teddy and Jackie went out on the back platform for a breath of air; Lord Harlech, former British ambassador to Washington, played hopscotch and heads-or-tails with the younger children.

As the train drew up at the platform of Baltimore Depot, a black crowd sang "The Battle Hymn of the Republic." As it grew dark, the air-conditioning failed again and the train ran out of food, drink, ice, coffee and cigarettes. The lights failed; the passengers stopped their group sings and conversation, turned off their transistor radios and sat exhausted, silent and sweating.

At last, the journey ended, and Rose walked out onto the platform.

The bearers, brushing aside the proffered help of a navy guard, carried the casket over a red carpet to the white-velvet-lined hearse. The Johnsons, who had flown from New York after attending the Mass, greeted the family, and Lady Bird affectionately took Rose's hand. As the navy band played "Eternal Father, Strong to Save," Rose was assisted into her limousine. It was 9:30 at night.

Police and troops lined Constitution Avenue in a drizzle, with thunder about. The funeral procession stopped at the Department of Justice Building, and again stopped at the Lincoln Memorial, where the Marine Band played and a choir sang "The Battle Hymn of the Republic." A multitude of blacks took up the strains, many of them from Resurrection City, the model shantytown that had been built symbolically under the Civil Rights program for which Bobby had fought so hard.

It was dark at Arlington. Teddy's request for flaring torches, another Lincolnian touch, had proved impossible to accommodate, and instead the people carried candles, or burning, rolled newspapers, many singeing their fingers in the process. Rose saw a line of flickering lights across the rise of the driveway. She walked to the grave site. Ahead of her, the pallbearers, confused by their directions, walked farther up the hill, and had to be guided back to the correct place.

Cardinal Cushing was notable by his absence; he had been taken, ill, off the train. Archbishop Cooke and Cardinal O'Boyle officiated. After the mercifully brief dedication, astronaut Colonel John Glenn folded the flag and gave it to Bobby's son, Joe, Jr., who in turn handed it to his mother. Jackie took sprigs from the grave and laid them on her husband's burial place.

Rose, holding a funerary candle, stood, head bowed in prayer, as the Harvard University Band played "America, the Beautiful." Her feet puzzled in the moist grass, Rose slipped a little as she walked back to the driveway, but recovered herself quickly, and, not crying, made her way to the car.

Even now there was no relief. Back at Hyannis, she had difficulty in consoling Teddy, who brooded for days and nights, sometimes trying to find consolation in the wind and the sea, sailing alone from dusk till dawn. He drove to Washington to see his staff to discuss the future, but turned around before entering the building, unable to face them.

On June 19, a letter arrived at Rose's house, postmarked Orange, New Jersey. It was signed by F. Merilli, of the Merilli Association, claiming that that association was "left-wing" and received bids from the Cosa Nostra, as well as the longshoremen's and teamsters' unions. A certain Boston financial corporation, the letter said, had offered Merilli half a million dollars to liquidate Teddy, who was expected to run for president. Protection was required in the form of a million dollars, to be packed in a briefcase and placed in a designated spot behind a telephone booth on Pleasant Hill Road, Orange, New Jersey, as soon as possible.

Teddy put the letter in the hands of J. Edgar Hoover (evidence that he affixed no part of the blame for Jack's or Bobby's deaths on Hoover and the FBI). No firm or person named Merilli could be found. On June 29, Merilli sent another letter, reminding the family of the needed blackmail money and saying that if Teddy ran he would be killed. The same day, Adlai Stevenson, who had become a friend of Rose's, was told that if the money wasn't paid, and if he did not help to arrange the payment, he would have Kennedy blood on his hands.

No money, in marked or unmarked bills, was delivered to Pleasant Hill Road; the source of the letters was never traced. The FBI files show that an exhaustive effort was made by the Bureau. The threats ceased.

Meanwhile, Jackie proceeded with plans to marry Aristotle Onassis, whom she had been seeing for some time.

Many felt she was tasteless in making wedding plans so shortly after her brother-in-law's death.

As the plans went ahead, with a premarital agreement that was extraordinarily detailed and expertly worked out by Jackie's attorneys, Rose left for Paris in August. Just before her departure, Rose experienced chest pains. It was feared she might be having a heart attack, but the fears were dispersed, and she summoned the energy, the night before her departure, to fly to Boston to see her brother Tom, who was in Massachusetts General Hospital. By the time she was on the plane to France, she was completely recovered.

Jackie's wedding date was set for October 17. Rose was pleased. She had always liked Onassis, who had been at Hyannis briefly the previous summer. Money and power fascinated her; Jackie's half-brother Jamie Auchincloss recalls that the Greek tycoon had been flattering to Rose at seventy-eight, making her feel like a woman again. His charm was irresistible; many forgot his lack of looks and short physical stature when they were in his presence.

But Rose's chief reason for not discouraging the match was monetary. Quite apart from the fact that having Jackie out of the country for much of the year would be no hardship for Rose, Jackie's extravagance at the family's expense infuriated her. Rose traveled coach class on airplanes, at what would later be called Apex fares. Why shouldn't Jackie, who not only traveled first class, but who took the seats around her so as to avoid talking to strangers? Herself prone to running up substantial bills in Paris dress salons, Rose was outclassed by Jackie, who spent tens of thousands of dollars a year on originals. Rose had abandoned her beloved Ritz because the Plaza Athénée in Paris offered better rates, and, by virtue of being situated opposite her favorite Dior salon, saved her the cab fare.

Joe was going through one of his periodic relapses, and Rose called Hyannis every night to ask Rita Dallas how he was doing.

Rose returned to find him in poor shape, and had to decline the invitation to the Onassis wedding on Skorpios, Onassis's private island off the coast of Greece. Pat Lawford, Jean Smith, Hugh D. and Janet Auchincloss,

Caroline and John-John attended the Greek Orthodox ceremony.

The religious elements of the marriage gave the family trouble. The Vatican made clear that Jackie would now be considered "a public sinner" for marrying outside the Church, that she would be in danger of excommunication and would not be allowed to receive communion.

Rose found in Cardinal Cushing a strong opponent to Pope Paul VI's judgment in the matter; Cushing actually told the press that any Catholic woman should be free to marry whomever she chose.

The reversal of dogma infuriated Cushing to such an extent that he said he would resign his prelacy if the Pope did not soften, but Paul VI remained unyielding. This, to Rose and the rest of the Kennedys, was more disturbing than the press's condemnation of Jackie for marrying beneath her.

It is doubtful if Jackie was affected personally by all this. She had taken advice from Cushing before her marriage, but her devotion to the Church was not profound, and, despite her magnificent handling of Jack's and Bobby's funerals, she was apt to make slighting remarks about Vatican policy.

The early months of 1969 provided a prolonged torment for Rose. Every time she picked up a newspaper, it was filled with the details of her sons' assassinations, recalled in seemingly endless discussions of conspiracy theories. On the first day of the new year, a book entitled *Farewell, America,* of mysterious origin and never published in the United States, though written in English, got some attention in the *New York Times*. It randomly accused the American power structure of being responsible for Jack's murder, asserting that he was condemned by a committee of Texas and Louisiana notables, and that the Texas police supported the execution tribunal.

The trial in New Orleans of C. L. Shaw on charges of conspiring to kill the late president filled the newspapers, followed by his acquittal on March 1. Desperate efforts by the later discredited New Orleans district attorney Jim

Garrison to prove a conspiracy did not cease with the verdict. Rose continued, along with the rest of her family, to dismiss such proceedings as a waste of public money, preserving her view that two demented individuals were responsible for the assassinations, and that each had acted alone.

Rose had to endure the prolonged trial of Sirhan Sirhan. She only had to turn a page to read of Sirhan's statement that he had been furious when he saw the late senator on television helping the Israelis to celebrate their independence, and that he had written in his notebook that Kennedy must die.* Sirhan was convicted of first-degree murder on April 17, and sentenced to death in the gas chamber on the twenty-fourth. Teddy later pleaded for clemency. In the end, the abolition of the California death penalty saved Sirhan's life.

Meanwhile, a disturbing event took place. According to Frank Saunders, at the outset of the year, driving back to the Palm Beach house one night, Teddy, drunk, took a wrong turn off North Ocean Avenue and piled up in a sandbank, narrowly missing a seawall. He banged on Frank Saunders's cottage door and sought Saunders's help retrieving the car. The matter was never discovered by the newspapers.

In April, while the Sirhan trial was on, Rose joined Onassis and Jackie on a two-week Caribbean cruise that included Nassau and the Virgin Islands. Rose had visited the 1,800-ton yacht *Christina* before, at a party in Monte Carlo when Onassis had been there several years earlier.

The vessel had been refurbished from stem to stern. The nine staterooms, including Rose's, were absurdities of pink satins and silks, all monogrammed with the owner's initials —but the swimming pool, with its Greek mosaic tiling, was a sapphire allure, and at night the base was hydraulically raised to be level with the deck and form a dance floor under multicolored fairy lights.

The bulkheads of the master cabin and office were decorated with paintings by El Greco, Pissarro and Gauguin, a

---

*It is doubtful if it occurred to Rose that there was a certain irony here: her husband had been accused for years of being anti-Semitic, and here was her son being killed because he was pro-Semitic.

reckless display since the yacht rolled badly in heavy weather, seawater splashed in, and they could be damaged. Rose disliked small craft, and the *Christina,* top-heavy with gilded trappings, yawed sickeningly in the swell. It is doubtful whether she enjoyed the fine vintage champagne and four-star cuisine along the way.

On her return, Rose had one of her very rare encounters with contemporary literature; now her reading was usually confined to Proust, Flaubert or Colette in the original French. She was at the pool one day when she saw a young male member of her household staff reading, with considerable enthusiasm, Philip Roth's recently published novel *Portnoy's Complaint.* She asked the young man what Portnoy was complaining about. The young man didn't have the nerve to tell her, nor could he pluck up the courage to show her the book.

Annoyed, she invaded the Hyannis public library and checked it out. She didn't get much further than the flyleaf. When she read that Portnoy suffered from "a disorder in which strongly felt ethical and altruistic impulses are perpetually warring with extreme sexual longings, often of a perverse nature," she gave up. Luckily, given her steel-plated innocence, she didn't go on to read a book the chief subject of which was masturbation. She had raised four sons and five daughters, and the subject was still alien to her.

On July 19, 1969, three days before her seventy-ninth birthday, Rose was in a good mood. Always happy to be solitary, it did not distress her particularly that most of her family was scattered all over the world. Teddy was the closest geographically; he was running one of the family boats in the Edgartown Regatta, a sparkling annual event that Joe had entered years before and that Rose had often attended.

Rose planned to go that afternoon to a charity church bazaar at St. Francis Xavier's, at which she would auction autographed copies of *The Fruitful Bough* and other family publications.

She was dressing to leave after lunch when the telephone rang. Teddy was on the line. Usually his greeting was boisterous, cheerful, joking; he always cheered her up when he called. But now he sounded tortured and anxious; he was breathless, his words slurred; he said that something terrible had happened. He was coming home at once to explain.

When she told him she was planning to go to the bazaar, he told her not to, to cancel it at once, or she would be besieged by the press. Then he hung up.

Rose placed a call to the bazaar organizers and told them she wasn't well enough to come. Then, with her customary strength, she waited as patiently as she could for Teddy's arrival.

Later that afternoon, he walked into the house. She was shocked by his appearance. Instead of the robust, loudly extroverted charmer she knew, Rose saw a bedraggled, nervous wreck, miserable, barely able to speak. He said nothing to her, but, still in many ways a nervous little boy trying to prove himself to his dad, he invaded Joe's room and blurted out, in the presence of Rita Dallas, that there had been an accident, that a young woman he had been driving to a ferry late at night had been drowned, and he had dived in to try to save her and had swum to get help, but she was dead, and that it was an accident.

Joe sighed deeply, faced with this new agony, but, still speechless and semiparalyzed, could give no more comfort than a squeeze of the hand. Teddy did not communicate with Rose. As the day turned to night, and as Teddy paced restlessly about, she had to pick up pieces of information. Rose was shocked to find that the young girl who had died was a friend of hers, one of Bobby's most devoted campaign secretaries, the devout Catholic Mary Jo Kopechne. Rose was told that Teddy had been enjoying a party with Mary Jo and several of Bobby's campaign secretaries in a small cottage on Chappaquiddick Island following the regatta, that he had driven Mary Jo to the ferry so she could return to her motel by midnight, but instead had taken the wrong road and his car had plunged off a narrow, wall-less bridge that looked more like a causeway or breakwater on its wooden posts.

Within hours, several of Teddy's entourage turned up, among them Joe Gargan and Ted Sorensen. Teddy called all of his family to Hyannis. Pat flew in from California, Eunice and Sargent Shriver from Paris, Joan from Majorca.

Ethel also arrived. Jackie turned up from Greece and accommodated Teddy's committee, which soon included Arthur Schlesinger, Jr., Robert McNamara, Richard Goodwin and Peter Markham, in her house. Reporters arrived, swooping on Rose when she went to Mass, invading the compound, asking endless questions, as photographers in helicopters took pictures from the air and television teams strove to get into the house. Teddy spent hours in conference with his team at Jackie's cottage.

Rose never faltered in her belief in his innocence. She was annoyed with Joey Gargan and the other men at Chappaquiddick for not accompanying Teddy on his drive to the ferry. It was an old tradition in politics that a man unaccompanied by his wife would always have another man present if he had a girl in his car. This was intended to remove any suspicion of a romantic affair; Joe had always made such an arrangement. Why couldn't one of Teddy's friends have thus protected him from potential scandal?

More details, not favorable to Teddy, emerged. There was evidence that he had been seen in his automobile after midnight. He knew the area well, so why had he driven in a direction diametrically opposite to the ferry wharf? Even if he had made such an unlikely mistake, why had he not made a U-turn and gone back? Why was a handbag belonging to another campaign secretary, Rosemary Keough, found on the passenger seat and not Mary Jo Kopechne's? Since the car plunged into shallow water, so shallow that the wheels were visible as it turned upside down, why had he not been able to drag Miss Kopechne free? Why, after finding her apparently dead or trapped alive, did Teddy not go to any one of the houses on the road leading to the bridge, wake up the occupants and have them assist him in an attempted rescue? The questions went on and on.

It is safe to say that Rose asked none of them, nor sought an answer when she heard them asked.

There was the question of an autopsy. It required (or so it was said) the permission of Mary Jo Kopechne's parents. They refused. Why? Years later, in an interview in *New Times* magazine, they gave the reason. An anonymous caller had advised them that they wouldn't want an autopsy; that

Mary Jo was four months pregnant, the caller didn't say by whom. As devout Catholics and pillars of their community in the Pennsylvania coal belt, they would surely wish to avoid so extreme a scandal.

Rose's sympathy went out to the parents, who refused to accept payment for the funeral. Aggrieved, they put on a show of not being angry at the Kennedys.

It was ironic that the day of the funeral, July 22, was Rose's official birthday. Teddy left by private DC-3 for Wilkes-Barre, Pennsylvania, and was driven to the coal-mining town of Plymouth for the low Requiem Mass.

Rose did not accompany him; she could not leave Joe, whose health showed an almost instant decline as a result of the situation. His insistence on watching everything on television and on reading the newspapers scarcely helped.

There was a surreal moment at the buffet lunch following the burial when Mary Jo's father introduced his nephew to Teddy as "a good Democrat," and Teddy replied, "You're really something, Mr. Kopechne."

On his return, Teddy didn't go to his house on Squaw Island but insisted on nesting at home, seeking his parents' support with anguished, childlike dependence, as he had done all his life, especially following the cheating scandal at Harvard.

He had tortured conversations with Rose near the flag-pole on the lawn that sported the Stars and Stripes. The content of the conversations has never been revealed, but reading between the lines of Rose's memoirs and diary notes, it would be a reasonable guess that she advised him to make a clean breast of everything, to prove himself presidential material by not faltering in admitting his negligence.

Rose had to endure word of the inquest, the court hearing, Teddy's admission that he had left the scene of the accident and his two months' suspended sentence that followed.

Teddy had to make a statement on television. The original decision was to have him talk on CBS from his own house. But when the TV truck with its heavy equipment drove in, it proved to be too wide for the causeway to Squaw

Island and the production team went ahead in the living room of the main house. Rose, Steve, Jean and Pat watched from the adjoining library as Teddy took his seat. When Joan offered to join her husband during the telecast, he asked her to leave the room.

His statement, co-drafted with Sorensen, was measured and controlled, but satisfied few. But the Massachusetts Democrats, and the bulk of his fans among the electorate, rallied to the Kennedy colors and confirmed that they would support him to the limit. At the end of July, Teddy had his Boston office announce that he would resume his duties as senator and assistant majority leader as soon as possible, and that he would run for reelection when the time came.

Even as charges of voluntary or involuntary manslaughter began to be heard, Rose took off to Paris in extremis. Showing no trace of anxiety, she unhesitatingly confirmed her belief in her troubled son. She gave interviews to the French press at the Plaza Athénée and to the *New York Times,* insisting that the accident was just that, that it had been turned into "a political issue" by Teddy's right-wing enemies. Oddly, the Russian papers, *Pravda* and *Izvestia,* took exactly the same position.

According to Rita Dallas, Rose called Hyannis Port every night while she was in France, wanting to get reports on Joe's condition, which became serious enough for her to return in October. She cheered the old man somewhat by sitting with him, holding his hand, in the evenings, listening to his new favorite Edith Piaf and his old Toscanini Beethoven recordings. Rose and Joe loved the *Perry Mason* television series. He was attentive and appreciative, closer to Rose than he had been for many years, but his heart was broken. After losing one son as president and another as a prospect for the White House, he was all too painfully aware that his third son would never become the national leader.

By November 16, his condition was so serious that he didn't recognize Rose, Teddy or anyone else. Joan, who had miscarried after Chappaquiddick; Ethel, who had relinquished her frenetic activities and was sick and disturbed; and Joe's favorite doctor, Russell Boles from Boston, could bring no response. Jackie flew in from Greece, saddened by Joe's condition and trying to bring what comfort she could to the family and to the man she still called her beloved grandpa.

Joe began to sink. Rose, exhausted by the long hours of vigil, was taking a rest in her room when she was told he was slipping away. She walked into his room, knelt by the bed, and rested her head on his hand. She lost control and sobbed on and on. She motioned that she wanted a rosary. Jackie found one, but oddly, instead of giving it to her, handed it to Rita, who pressed it between Rose's fingers. Rose prayed to the Virgin and placed the cross against Joe's mouth. But there was no hint of breath. He was gone.

Each of the family took up the words of the Lord's Prayer, verse by verse, until Rose finished it with the words, "forever and ever, amen." There was a profound silence in the room.

Rose decided on a white funeral at St. Xavier's, unencumbered by heavy ritual. Following the simple service, the body was taken by hearse to the family plot in the Holyhood Cemetery in Brookline. The procession of cars drove through increasing rain to the grave site. Rose sat stiffly upright, refusing to show intense grief in public, one part of her life brought firmly to an end. The obituaries were decently cautious, but the old charges of anti-Semitism and pro-Nazism surfaced again.

The will had been craftily put together. Most of Joe's hundreds of millions had been disposed of to avoid taxes, with at least $10 million going to Rose directly. Officially, she received only $500,000 and the Standard Building in Albany, New York. His offspring had all received large sums in advance. His sisters were named as receiving $25,000 each. Rose was not left the houses, but, by arrangement, would live in them without charges for the rest of her life.

She had never paid a domestic bill from the beginning; every invoice was sent to the office on Park Avenue in New York.

Nevertheless, with her customary tightness, and in a move that seems ruthless in the circumstances, Rose disposed of her staff in one go. Rita Dallas recalls that she spent two days tidying up, then left. For years, Rose had warned Frank Saunders that she could no longer afford him when Joe died. Now, within less than twenty-four hours, she fired him. The devoted housekeeper Evelyn and the maid Dora were given severance pay and released; Mathilda, the reliable cook, returned to Norway.

Letting these excellent people leave her service was one of the worst mistakes of Rose's life, and several of those dismissed, especially Saunders, who would later return briefly (she wouldn't recognize him), were embittered.

She hired very little help after that. She let the Palm Beach house decline. Already run-down, it became a pathetic echo of the days of Mizener glory. Tiles, knocked off the roof by wind, lay shattered and unswept on the patio; coconuts ripped from the garden palms splintered the party tables; bougainvillea and rhododendrons grew rank, and the louver blinds on the windows hung from their rusted hinges. The fight against rust in any oceanside dwelling was given up; locks and window catches proved unmovable. The paint peeled from the walls both inside and out.

Despite her age, seventy-nine, Rose refused to have banister rails put on the old stone staircase, and she frequently slipped, narrowly escaping a dangerous or even fatal plunge into the hallway.

Hyannis was better kept up, but it still had an uncared-for look.

While Rose neglected her homes, she seemed to obtain a new lease on life. She traveled more restlessly than ever, and spent more time in New York than she had for years. She worked hard on Flame of Hope, the collection of perfumes prepared by the handicapped.

When she arrived at B. Altman's store in Manhattan on May 4, 1970, she was besieged by the public. She gave a ninth-floor press conference, then invaded the perfume counter and, wearing a purple Givenchy minidress and huge white straw hat, with a thousand women standing in line, she shook hands with everyone and gave away samples of New Flame and Espere. She was her old self when photographers came in for a close-up; she told them, smiling but sharp-tongued, to make long-distance shots only, and they obeyed. She brought laughter as she said, "These perfumes are very alluring. If everybody bought them, it might help the pollution problem!"

Within days, she was off to Switzerland. Then she flew to Athens to join the *Christina* at the island of Skorpios. She arrived at her destination shaken and bruised; the flight had been turbulent; cavalier as ever in the face of possible danger, she had failed to fasten her seat belt.

She found a strained atmosphere on the yacht; Onassis's first wife, Tina, had been found dead in mysterious circumstances, Onassis had suffered business losses, and, increasingly annoyed by Jackie's extravagances, he had renewed his old affair with Maria Callas. The house he was using temporarily while he built a mansion on Skorpios was not impressive, but the view of the ocean from the patio was appealing, and Rose enjoyed the late-night walks in the full moon to the pier below, where the *Christina* was moored.

She was pleased to find herself on the most-admired-American-women lists, along with Golda Meir and Mamie Eisenhower.

On July 20, accepting the earlier invitation from Ethiopia's Emperor Haile Selassie, she flew to Addis Ababa to spend her eightieth birthday with him. Jean, who had been on safari in Kenya with her two young sons, joined her. There they attended the opening of the John F. Kennedy Library, which the family had donated. Rose found herself comfortably accommodated in an elegant guest house near the Imperial Palace, surrounded by a beautifully planted garden. Her only problem was that the air at the 8,500-foot altitude was very thin and made her almost constantly tired.

Rose's extraordinary capacity for self-containment—for seeing life through glasses that matched her name in hue—can be seen in the fact that nowhere in her published notes on her visit, or in her recollections of it shortly thereafter, is there any reference to the fact that Ethiopia was a dangerous and unpleasant place to be visiting that year. The anti-American feeling was bitter; Peace Corps volunteers came back to America beaten and often badly injured. The Moslem Liberation Front kidnapped the U.S. consul general in Asmara and the *National Geographic* team.

Rose sailed through every district as though nothing untoward was going on; she, her daughter, and her two grandsons could easily have been kidnapped and killed.

Rose enjoyed an extensive tour of the surrounding countryside with Jean and her boys. The birthday party in her honor took place on the twenty-second, Haile Selassie's on the twenty-third. She made the unfortunate discovery, just before she left for the banquet on the first of the two dates, that she was not the same age as the emperor, but two years older.

Her party was the opposite of festive. According to Ethiopian tradition, nobody was allowed to speak above a whisper in the Imperial presence, so there were no speeches or toasts in her honor; she might as well have been attending a funeral.

After six weeks of local travel, carefully scheduled by the authorities so that she would see nothing of the people's oppression and suffering, Rose returned to Hyannis in August.

She settled down to an almost solitary existence; she sat at the head of an empty table for a spare regime of Sanka with gelatin, French bread and an occasional egg for breakfast; her customary steamed chicken sandwich for lunch; and chicken or fish for dinner. She played few holes of golf now, but still swam and took a weekly massage. She listened to her favorite French novels on record, read everything she could get her hands on that was neither obscene nor filled with violence, and sat at her desk, decorated with photographs of her nearest and dearest both living and dead, writing, in her still excellent, well-rounded hand, in black notebooks with recipes, household tips and moral maxims.

She could always make a stir. In the July 21, 1970, *New York Daily News* journalist Fred Sparks described a typical scene at La Caravelle in New York. At one table sat the duchess of Windsor, at another Truman Capote and Mrs. William Paley; then:

Bam! There mesmerizes at the entrance a *grande dame* whose dynamic presence makes all heads turn as if they were at a tennis match and she were the ball. As the *grande dame* advances, she acknowledges the attention by waving to one and all, a discreet wave, just from the wrist; A Queen Mother's wave . . . she is none other than Rose Kennedy, surely the world's best known Mother and Grandmother.

She remained imperious on all occasions; when she walked into Maxim's in Paris to join Jackie and Aristotle Onassis, she had the table flowers changed to smaller ones so she could see clearly across them. Whenever she arrived anywhere the hotel had to have her clothes ironed and hung up, even if it was 3:00 A.M. "I should care," one Paris tailor told Sparks after telling him she had gotten him out of bed at 11:00 P.M. to press her wardrobe. "Mrs. Kennedy is a gracious lady—and she tips like one of those Saudi Arabian princes."

She still spent lavishly on clothes—several thousand a year at the age of eighty. One journalist wrote, "If all the skins in her wardrobe came suddenly back to life, Hyannis Port would be a veritable zoo." Cartier that year estimated her jewelry collection at $3 million.

She could slap down even the most famous. When Frank Sinatra came to her table one day, she looked at him blankly. He introduced himself and reminded her how he had supported her sons. She said, "Oh, I remember you now. You're the senator from Montana."

She returned from a trip to Paris to attend Cardinal Cushing's funeral at the Cathedral of the Holy Cross in Boston on November 7, 1970. Sometimes maddened by his sententiousness, booming voice and long-jawed, medieval face, she would never forget his loyalty to and his love of the family over so many years. Jackie, Teddy and Ethel, with Ethel's handsome son, Joe, Jr., joined her in the pew in the presence of no less than eight cardinals. He was buried at the Massachusetts branch of St. Coletta's home for the retarded at Hanover. He had made the instructions for the crypt eighteen years earlier; it faced a playground for the handicapped. He had wanted in death to watch over the children closest to his heart, and whom he had so lavishly and lovingly assisted.

The following month, following declassification, British

documents of World War II were published. They were negative as to Joe, indicating the detestation so many British political figures had for his defeatism and his refusal to take the position, before Pearl Harbor, that America should plunge into war with Germany. The family ignored such prejudiced assertions with its customary indifference.

Teddy had been reelected to his third term in November; it was a time now for building monuments and burying the less fortunate aspects of the past.

On May 28, 1971, Rose was at the gala preview of the John F. Kennedy Center for the Performing Arts in Washington. Nan Robertson of the *New York Times* described Rose, with agreeable exaggeration, as looking "stunningly youthful" in a white satin Yves St. Laurent coat trimmed with white marabou, and a pink-and-white Givenchy gown. Rose hobnobbed with Andy Williams, Pierre Salinger, Christina Ford, Mamie Eisenhower, Herman Wouk and Bill Blass. She renewed a happy acquaintance with theatrical producer Frederick Brisson and her friends Mary Lasker and the Angier Biddle Dukes. Meyer Davis, the old reliable, conducted his society orchestra as ably as he had at the Greenbrier and Jackie's wedding. At 11:30, Rose clapped like a child as fireworks exploded from Theodore Roosevelt Island on the Potomac River.

On June 29, she gave a television interview to David Frost. He asked her directly about her sons' assassinations, and she responded, without emotion, that the killers were on their own and didn't know what they were doing. Referring to Bobby, she told Frost that she didn't believe anybody would deliberately destroy the life of a man with eleven children. She said she had never read the Warren Report and had no intention of doing so.

Asked if she saw Teddy as a future president, she said he had assured her he was in no hurry for the office, but should he decide to go ahead, she would campaign for him, even if she was ninety.

On September 8, Rose attended as guest of honor the premiere of Leonard Bernstein's *Mass* at the Kennedy Center. Jackie was absent from yet another official occasion, despite the fact that she had requested the work. Rose shared the presidential box with Teddy and Aaron Copland.

She smiled, and many eyes turned toward her, as Center chairman Roger Stevens spoke from the stage of Jack Kennedy's achievement in lending dignity to the role of the arts in America.

At the end of the performance, which was some 100 minutes long, Bernstein hugged Rose joyfully; she had been supportive of him from the beginning. Rose gave a press conference—at eighty-one her energy was unabated—where she said, "The work is stupendous. Jack would have loved it . . . he was interested in culture, art, joy, and pleasure in the arts."

Despite a savage review in the *New York Times* by Harold Schonberg, the *Mass* remained one of Rose's favorite compositions. She shared Bernstein's aching desire for peace expressed in it. Although the *Mass* was ecumenical and composed by a Jew, it matched the views of the Vatican that she held sacred. Her opinion of it has not been widely shared.

Rose kept in touch as much as she could with her grandchildren, especially Bobby's eldest child, Kathleen, whose second name, Hartington, always evoked painful memories. It was strenuous for a woman in her late seventies to keep track of Bobby's ten other children: Joe, Robert, David (although she had an affinity for him), Mary Courtney, Michael, Mary Kerry, Christopher, Matthew, Douglas and Rory, not to mention the children of her other offspring. It was good to know that Kathleen was at Radcliffe; Rose endlessly grilled her on every aspect of her studies, in a voice that had grown more querulous with time.

Rose saw everything in the blacks and whites of the McKinley era; everything was sewn up into a proper pattern laid down by God. Kathleen was typical of her generation: no certainties, no definite answers, no final trust in God's power to control human destiny in a disintegrating America she was too young to see as decadent. The rift between them was clear; so was the guarded affection. Rose dreaded the rock music Kathleen and her other grandchildren found as an opiate, an etherizing of the spirit as powerful as Rose's youthful waltzes and schottisches.

Luckily, Rose learned nothing of the ghastly antics of some of her descendants—from hanging a cook by her arms from a tree branch to pulling knives, stealing gifts and firing BB guns through church windows.

On November 18, Rose's sister-in-law, the charming Loretta, died, aged eighty; her death must have evoked fond memories of the group sings at Loretta's when Joe was courting Rose, so many years ago.

Rose had been working for years on her memoirs, but still did not have a satisfactory draft. On November 30, 1971, Ted Sorensen, acting as her agent, made a publishing deal for her. Outbidding W. W. Norton's Evan W. Thomas, Doubleday's Stewart Richardson secured her with an offer of $1,525,000, the payment to be made to the Joseph P. Kennedy, Jr., Foundation for the mentally retarded. Richardson selected one of the Luces' favorite *Life* magazine journalists, the able Robert Coughlin, as ghostwriter.

Named third-most-admired woman in the world in the early months of 1972, Rose worked hard with Coughlin, talking from 10:00 A.M. till 12:00 noon each day, into his tape recorder, breaking off to join him for swims or light lunches. She avoided most unpleasant subjects, which was unfortunate. She was ideally placed to dismiss, once and for all, the legend of Joe's prolonged affair with Gloria Swanson, the charges of pro-Nazism leveled against him, the accusations that he had helped evoke the Wall Street crash by selling short, and the story that he had been involved in a stock raid on Yellow Cabs. Instead, she provided what amounted to the autobiography of a saint, filled with an excessive number of flattering comments by friends and family and broken up far too often into excerpts from her diaries. The result was a superficial, though entertaining, potpourri, which became further affected by family interjection, censorship and control. The book was named *Times to Remember*. When it was published two years later, in 1974, it was accorded respectful reviews and became a best-seller, not least because the public knew that proceeds from its sales would go to charity.

Chapter 18

Twilight and Evening Star

❦

The early 1970s brought no easing of Rose's continually strained relationship with Jackie Kennedy Onassis.

The two women had managed to deal with each other more or less comfortably on Rose's several voyages aboard the *Christina* in different parts of the world, but in many ways Rose was more sympathetic to Jackie's husband than to her, and Rose was annoyed that the press kept picking up ugly stories of her daughter-in-law's quarrels with him. She always warmed notably when she saw Onassis; even when she was eighty-two, he looked her over appreciatively and still made her feel she was a woman. His rugged virility and strength fascinated her.

Matters with Jackie reached a head in the early winter of 1972, when the Onassises arrived on their yacht and docked at Palm Beach. They elected, probably on Jackie's decision, to stay aboard rather than with Rose in a house that was increasingly dilapidated and even letting in rain.

Jackie and Onassis came to dinner; the atmosphere was very strained. Then that night, suddenly and without warning, Jackie, after a particularly ferocious quarrel with her husband, walked off the *Christina* and took refuge with Charles and Jayne Wrightsman.

Then she, with equal impetuosity, decided to forgive Onassis and return to the yacht. But the Wrightsmans' chauffeur was busy, and Jacqueline would not consider a lowly taxi.

She arrived at Rose's house and walked through the open front door unannounced. She summoned Frank Saunders's replacement as chauffeur, Jim Connor, and told him imperiously that she expected to be driven to the pier, where she could pick up the motor launch. He had to tell her he couldn't help, that Rose needed the car to go shopping on Worth Avenue. Would she like him to call a taxi? "OK, you're fired!" she snapped.

Rose walked in, furious. "Jim is working for *me*," she said. "How *dare* you fire him? He isn't working for you!" Connor called an angry Mrs. Onassis a cab; it was some time before the two women spoke to each other again.

Christmas 1972 was unexciting. Rose showed little interest in it and even less when she heard that the dreaded Lady Lawford died in January. Rose was left cold by the news that the crazed old bird of prey had left a memoir, condemning the Kennedys out of hand—and that she also left a note, charging them with being responsible for her death.

The seventies were a decade Rose could readily have done without. She hated the fact that several of her grandchildren were charged with speeding, and were on drugs; she obtained little compensation from the news that Sargent Shriver ran for the presidency in 1976 and lost; that the Vietnam War she despised and that her son Jack had unwittingly provoked had ended. It is doubtful if she was impressed by the pious statements of President Nixon and others, and the Watergate affair provoked no comment from her.

She witnessed a nation's moral and spiritual disintegration along with that of her younger family. The Kennedy image was dented as frequently as the handsome boys' fenders. She saw the contrast in them between physical

beauty and personal confusion and misery that marked the
wealthy young in that decade.

There is no indication that she, behind the seawall she
had built up around herself against life's storms and disap-
pointments, let it bother her.

She was preoccupied with plans for the John F. Kennedy
Library, designed by architect I. M. Pei, which was kicked
out of Cambridge when the city leaders decided that the
town would be swamped by tourists. The library would be
built in Dorchester instead—a nicely nostalgic touch.

Rose was notable by her absence from Ann Gargan's
belated marriage, to Thomas G. Logan of BOAC, in
Norwell, Massachusetts, on July 15, 1973. Her eighty-third
birthday a week later was lonely; only Ethel and Eunice
were at Hyannis for the traditional clambake. Teddy was on
his way to India on the Pakistan-refugee issue.

September brought the release of Bobby Kennedy, Jr.,
and Sargent Shriver, Jr., from a thirteen-month probation-
ary period at Barnstable, near Hyannis, following charges of
possessing marijuana. Rose showed no reaction to the news.

Instead, Rose gave a lengthy interview to three Irish
priests for a television program in their country, in which
she held the battered family image together as firmly as she
could. She was happy with the results, but not with Rita
Dallas's vivid and well-written memoir of her years with
Rose. A complaint to the American Nurses' Association,
brought by the ever-defensive family, that Mrs. Dallas had
acted in breach of professional etiquette, was a waste of
time, although the association did publicly reprimand the
author. There was no libel suit; the book was accurate and
compassionate. And there was no invasion-of-privacy suit
either; how could a Kennedy charge invasion at this stage?
Rose said nothing. She didn't read the memoir.

At 2:30 P.M. on August 14, 1973, Joe Kennedy III was
involved in a serious driving mishap, the worst family
scandal since Chappaquiddick. The handsome, charismatic
youth, clad in swim trunks after a day at the beach, was
driving a jeep with his brother David, three miles east of
Nantucket, when he lost control and it overturned. He was
thrown clear, and so was David, but the girls in the back
were crushed. One attractive young woman, Pamela Kelly,

nineteen, had a fractured spine and was paralyzed. The Kennedys settled with her parents. Joe, charged with negligent driving, was fined only $100. There were the usual expressions of contrition all round. Rose made no statement to the press.

There was even worse news in November, when Teddy called her to say that his twelve-year-old son Teddy, Jr.— another flawed athlete in the family's long list—had bone cancer in his lower right leg, which would have to be amputated. The date chosen was November 17, the same day planned for Kathleen, Jr.,'s marriage to David Lee Townsend in Georgetown. It was typical of the Kennedys that they didn't postpone the wedding until the operation was concluded, and that Rose had to attend both the hospital and the church in Washington on the same day.

She flew in on the sixteenth; Teddy's aide Richard Burke picked her up from the airport. Rose spent the journey to Georgetown University Hospital saying her rosary and repeating Hail Marys for her grandson's recovery. As she walked into the hospital corridor, waving from the wrist to the fascinated nurses, a woman on a gurney, being wheeled out of a room, seized her hand, gripped it and said that she loved John and Bobby and prayed for Rose now. Rose said gently that she would pray for the woman in turn.

Rose went to Teddy, Jr.,'s room. The boy was made of Kennedy steel and despite the fact that he was about to lose not only a limb but his athletic future, he proved as brave and resilient as she would have wished. She fed her strength into him. Though she was some seventy-one years older, she was as strong as he was at this moment.

Without drawing breath, Rose went straight from the hospital room to the pre-wedding dinner at Ethel's house at Hickory Hill, in McLean, Virginia. Now showing no signs of concern over the operation that would affect the young boy's life, she chatted gaily with Angie Dickinson, Andy Williams and Art Buchwald. Dressed to the teeth, she was the star of the wedding, held at Holy Trinity, the same church she had attended on the morning of Jack's Inauguration. She was seen smiling at the attractive bride and groom, who was a Loyola graduate and student at Harvard.

Rose visited Teddy, Jr., as often as she could as the boy struggled with exhausting months of chemotherapy.

On November 22, dressed in white, she attended a memorial Mass for Jack, on the tenth anniversary of the assassination, at St. Edward's Church, Palm Beach.

Rose spent the Christmas almost alone. She was so despondent that when she saw the Christmas tree trimmed, she had the chauffeur Jim Connor give it away to the poor. With Joe gone, the season had little appeal for her, and anyway she wasn't feeling well. She was suffering from severe and persistent headaches and by February they were worse. She didn't have the energy to fly to Boston to her favorite hospital, New England Baptist, but instead checked into St. Mary's at Palm Beach on February 19, 1974. Teddy postponed his planned tour to Eastern Europe and Russia to be with her, and Pat came with him.

Tests at the hospital conducted by Dr. Saul Rotter showed that Rose had a ruptured blood vessel in the brain, causing a minor cardiovascular accident, or slight stroke. She recovered with her customary swiftness and was home resting by the twenty-third.

Through the early months of 1974, Rose saw Teddy follow his father and brothers' policy in seeking peace with the Communist world. On April 21, he addressed students and faculty at Moscow State University in terms that echoed Joe's in 1946.

On June 13, she saw Kathleen, Jr., graduate with honors from Harvard with a bachelor's degree in American history and literature, and on the twenty-fifth of July, Joe, Jr., was posthumously awarded the Second Air Medal—an oddly late date for such an honor.

Rose, in her last years, had gradually stripped her households down to the barest essentials. Although her investments earned her several hundred thousand a year, she managed with one cook, maid and cleaner, and successive and combined caretakers, guards and chauffeurs.

She refused to pay for a security guard, and indeed, from her son's assassinations on, had gone willingly almost unprotected.

She may have questioned the wisdom of this when, on her beach walks at Hyannis Port, a disturbed woman heckled her. Teddy had the woman committed to an institution. When a powerfully built, six-foot-three-inch man suddenly materialized in her entrance hall, she quietly asked him to leave, and confronted by all the power inside this five-foot woman, he very meekly did.

Rose went through a long line of social secretaries, including such patient and resolute stalwarts as Diane Winter and Denise Smith, and now, when Denise announced she would get married, Rose decided she needed a new one. She interviewed the bright young Barbara Gibson, who combined looks with brains, without realizing that Miss Gibson was a shrewd observer and not a fan of the Kennedys.

Rose interviewed her one summer morning at Hyannis at the odd hour of 8:00 A.M.; most rich women past a certain age would only interview, or be interviewed, after 4:00 P.M., when the light was kinder, they had had an afternoon nap, and had spent several hours at a beauty parlor and deciding what to wear. Rose told Barbara to be seated on the Bronxville couch once used by Pope Pius XII and asked her a pertinent question, which Miss Gibson answered with dispatch. Asked for a sample of her typing, the super-cool applicant, instead of producing one, had the nerve to do the unthinkable: she walked to Rose's desk, plucked out unasked a sheet of Rose's Cartier engraved stationery, set it in Rose's portable typewriter and began tapping away at lightning speed. Then, without further ado, she gave Rose, who was quite put out, a flawless fait accompli. Rose had no choice but to hire her.

It seemed that Rose had almost met her match, her most courageous employee since Rita Dallas. But Rose was not to be outdone: she showed Miss Gibson out the back door, just so the secretary would know there was only one boss in a Kennedy house. And the surprised amanuensis was told she was to use the same door in the future; she was only a servant, after all.

Very soon, Miss Gibson, emulating Rita Dallas and Frank Saunders, began keeping a record of all that happened. It was a wise decision; she had a flair. But Rose made sure she became not so much cicerone as lady-in-waiting, required to walk several paces behind Rose on shopping trips and to occupy a pew at the back of St. Francis Xavier's while Rose sat at the front. Gibson noted a number of pertinent details as she continued her days of work, among which was that Rose required everyone in the family to stand whenever she appeared, thus forcing people, including some of her grandchildren, to take awkwardly to their feet, even in the swimming pool.

Rose sent back her empty nail-varnish bottles for refunds, sold old clothes to thrift stores rather than give them to the poor. She traveled to Europe by coach class, packing her own sandwiches and spending the entire trip in a sleep mask.

Rose spent much of her time at Hyannis in her pink and green bedroom, writing away at endless letters at her desk, and looking at Joe, Jr.'s, Jack's, Bobby's and Kathleen's Mass cards pinned in front of her for inspiration. She had some awkward exchanges with Barbara. When Miss Gibson told her she looked thirty-eight years old in one dress, she snapped, "Don't you mean twenty-eight?" And matters were not helped when Miss Gibson saw Rose looking at a picture of the London court presentation in 1938 and said to her, "You were beautiful then."

Nor was Rose pleased when Gibson looked dismayed when Rose returned her Christmas gifts for credit, including a Cartier frame from Barbara Walters and Porthault bedsheets from Jackie. Rose counted the chicken pieces and eggs, and had the spring-water delivery men drain off the last drop into a carafe before they took the bottle away.

Despite her hatred of drugs, Rose became a kind of addict herself, taking so many at night to sleep, or when she traveled, that Gibson often had to flush several pills down the toilet; Rose fixed her by hiding others in a locked suitcase.

A painful matter was bringing Rosemary to Hyannis in July 1974, and to Palm Beach that winter, a habit Rose would maintain for years. Partly paralyzed on her right side in a strange echo of Joe's condition, Rosemary was awkward and unresponsive when Rose talked to her nicely, played and sang "Sweet Adeline" for her on the piano or tried to cheer her in other ways.

Rock-and-roll records of bongo drums had to be placed out of Rose's hearing in the compound, no easy task.

She walked in rain and wind without a tremor; more than once she had to be rescued by Barbara as she sank, soaked and exhausted, on the porches of strangers' houses. Sometimes she would forget to straighten her corset, which made her look odd, or put her false eyelashes on at an angle, and they would fall off. She had a unique idea of what constituted a gift; she gave Gibson a worn-out brassiere. When Rose handed Gibson a bottle of vintage champagne from her cellar, not bought outside, she asked the secretary to estimate how much it was worth now.

Rose became a traffic cop, helping people to drive out of the compound by walking into the street dressed in Courreges and diverting the traffic. She would not tip anyone, handing waiters or parking attendants autographed Mass cards instead, or postcards of her two famous dead sons with an accompanying passage from the Inaugural address, telling the unhappy recipient that the "tip" would be worth something one day. She began spying on her neighbors through binoculars; she sent notes to her nieces and nephews and anyone else she favored with instructions on diet and religious observation. She listened to Proust's entire *Remembrance of Things Past* in French while she was being massaged, and she sang duets with the cook or with author Doris Kearns and husband Richard Goodwin in an Irish inn. And she suddenly decided to cut the allowance to the remaining Fitzgerald family from $20,000 a year each to $500 despite all pleas.

Onassis's death and Jackie's widowhood in 1975 left her unaffected as she concentrated more and more on her errant grandchildren. She wrote to the younger ones throughout the decade, urging them not to drink Coca-Cola or Pepsi-Cola but milk instead, to protect the image of the Kennedy teeth, still a dentist's dream. She was furious with Bobby Shriver when he borrowed her typewriter; she fretted at several of her youngster descendants using her Lincoln Continental. She was annoyed when Maria Shriver turned

up in a halter-top dress; she was upset when Christopher
Lawford proved to be a late sleeper. But she approved every
grandchild's success at school in warm personal notes, a
long-outmoded habit in America; correcting the grammar
and spelling in the letters her grandchildren sent her, she
replied in the immaculate prose of another era.

She was impressed by Bobby, Jr.'s television wildlife
programs and Courtney Kennedy's career at Stanford.
Caroline and John Kennedy, Jr., fascinated her with their
good looks and charm.

She did not forgive spreading waistlines, food dropped on
her rugs or noisy dogs anywhere. Bad language was instantly
punished. Unsuspecting kids of a drug generation found
themselves being required to learn "The Midnight Ride of
Paul Revere" or the Declaration of Independence, which
they were expected to recite to her. A desperate few succeeded.

In October 1975, after attending Mass at St. Peter's
Catholic Church in Chicago, where she was Eunice's guest,
Rosemary wandered off from the vestibule. Eunice was
frantic; she ran out and hailed a police car, telling the cop
that her sister had disappeared. Then she called her family;
Rose was distraught, all her old fears of rape and kidnap at
that moment resurfacing. Five hours later, a reporter for
WBBM-TV found that Rosemary had gone shopping near
the Chicago Art Institute. Rose could breathe again.

In summer 1976, at almost eighty-six, Rose took off again
for the campaign trail, to help Teddy in his effort to defeat
three challengers for the Massachusetts primary in September. She brought laughs wherever she went with her still
antic humor and uncrushable charm, especially when she
spoke the line "It's all right to be campaigning when you are
sixty-six, or even seventy-six, but when you are eighty-six,
it's a little too much. Don't let your children do it to you!"

There was much discussion of an alleged assassination
plot against Teddy, led by Robert White, David King and
Sandra Rondeau, who were charged with conspiracy to
murder in Springfield, Massachusetts. The alleged plan was
for Miss Rondeau to have breakfast with Teddy at the Oaks
Inn and then for White to shoot him while he was eating.
The charges were dropped.

Next month, Rose was at the Sheraton Hotel in Boston on the campaign trail. She was supposed to attend a reception that night. She arrived with Barbara Gibson, perfectly dressed, then suddenly announced to all and sundry in her suite that she would take a bath. She took the bath, then, with several campaign women present, climbed into bed in front of them. Teddy and Joan arrived. Seeing her between covers, they were understandably dismayed; she must get up at once and prepare for the reception. She was unwilling. Miss Gibson chased her round the room. At last, she grumblingly put on her best costume and descended in the elevator. But she was unhappy; she trembled during the receiving line, gave a strained speech ("If I hadn't had nine sons I wouldn't have one now"), fled to her car in the parking lot and lay down in the back. She wasn't senile, she was ill and in great pain; adhesions from her old operations were closing her bowels and she could have died.

She was rushed to New England Baptist Hospital, treated for three days, and released without another operation—incredible at her age. And Teddy was, to her great joy, reelected.

But there were signs, by 1977, at eighty-seven, that she was starting to decline. When she attended the ground-breaking ceremony for the Kennedy Library on June 12, she was sick and confused as she picked up her silver spade and Teddy had, tenderly and affectionately, to take over. She was stronger when she was given an honorary doctorate of humanities at Georgetown University on October 1.

She stumbled next month at Hyannis and hurt her knee. She went to New England Baptist for a week but was out in time to dance up a storm at the April in Paris Ball in New York.

She picked up considerably when campaigning for Teddy again in 1978; she outwalked most of her family at the beach.

A link with her childhood snapped on March 28, 1979, when her brother John died in Boston, aged eighty-one.

Now she was bent on having Teddy as president; he must run against Jimmy Carter for the Democratic nomination in 1980. The thought buoyed her, but her life was becoming burdensome in many ways. She had to fight against stomach trouble and arthritis to give a series of interviews to women's magazines denying that, at almost ninety, she was in less than perfect health.

The struggle to be superhuman was starting to wear her down, and in September she had another operation—a loop of a bowel had strangled as a result of adhesions from an earlier operation for a hernia, and had she not had immediate treatment at New England Baptist she might have become gangrenous and died.

After enduring tubes in the nose and intravenous feeding she was operated on successfully; she wanted to attend the final opening of the JFK Memorial Library, but Eunice told her if she did she would not live. She watched the ceremony on television. She was impressed by the embattled Joe II's speech, recalling his father Bobby's human-rights activities. A few days later, Rose became a great-grandmother with the birth of Maeve Fahey to Kathleen and David Townsend.

On November 7, 1979, Teddy officially announced his candidacy for the presidential nomination. Rose was present at Faneuil Hall, with its host of memories of Honey Fitz, on November 7, to hear the announcement and give public support to Joan, who unfortunately didn't hesitate to talk to journalists about her drinking and troubled private life. Rose was always against such confessional frankness.

On January 4, 1980, the House Select Committee on Assassinations opened old wounds again by agreeing to requests for a new investigation, which would prove inconclusive. Now Rose went out on the campaign trail, in Iowa and Florida, undoubtedly the world's oldest parent in support of a son as a head of state. She was as brisk and bright as ever, brushing off a myriad of awkward press questions about Teddy and Joan with effortless expertise.

Teddy's opponent, Jimmy Carter, was not far removed from Teddy in terms of his concerns with the ecology, civil rights and peace abroad, but he had the advantage of an impeccable reputation. He won, to Rose's great disappointment, in New Hampshire; Vermont; Florida, where Rose's efforts proved fruitless; Alabama; and, of course, Georgia. He conquered Illinois and Puerto Rico; Teddy won Connecticut, New York and Pennsylvania; Carter was at home in

Kansas, Wisconsin, Louisiana and Texas. The battle went on; Teddy did quite well; but by August it was obvious to Rose it was a hopeless fight.

On the eleventh, Teddy dropped out of the race; and by November Ronald Reagan was elected and the Republicans were back in power—a bad blow.

It was followed, for Rose, just one day later, by another: Teddy and Joan announced they would divorce. It was an unthinkable event for her.

On July 20, 1980, Rose led a parade, smiling and waving, through the streets of Hyannis to raise funds for the Special Olympics for Retarded Children. Six Massachusetts cities held rose parades to celebrate her ninetieth birthday. On September 25, she went back under the surgeon's knife for the second time in a year to relieve the obstruction of her bowel; she was out within a week.

On August 24, 1981, Boston College awarded Rose an honorary doctorate of humane letters. But, back in the hospital with a recurrence of her bowel problem, which was entering a vicious circle, she could not attend. She was surrounded with graduations and marriages, and more and more births. Not strong now, she had a struggle to keep up with everything. Victoria Lawford had graduated with a B.A. from Mount Vernon; Bobby's son Michael married Victoria Gifford; Robert Sargent Shriver graduated with a law degree from Yale. Rose was proud of them all.

In 1982, Rose took pleasure in Bobby Kennedy, Jr.'s law degree at the University of Virginia, and his swearing-in as Manhattan assistant district attorney. In November, Teddy was elected to his fifth term in the Senate. On June 6, 1983, John Kennedy, Jr., much the best-looking of a handsome family, graduated from Brown University with a B.A. in history.

Rose was beginning to fail. The last spark she showed was at Thanksgiving 1982, when she said to a large family gathering at the toast, "You are not just Kennedys. You are Fitzgeralds too." She played and sang "Sweet Adeline" but she seemed more aware of events thirty years before than now, a common symptom of old age. She managed to attend the wedding of Sydney Lawford and James Peter

McKelvey at Our Lady of Victory Church, Centerville, Massachusetts, on September 17, 1983, but she was confused and had a severe struggle getting up the steps, even with Ted and Pat supporting her. Jackie was as mischievous as ever, annoying Pat by switching the place cards at the reception at Hyannis Port so that she could sit next to the deteriorated Peter Lawford. Rose appeared only briefly.

To celebrate Rose's ninety-third birthday, the family gave $1 million to St. Coletta's at Jefferson, Wisconsin, where Rosemary was still an inmate. And then, on December 13, for the first time, a Kennedy baby was named Rose: Rose Katherine, daughter of Katherine Kennedy and David Townsend.

Sadly, this decent, belated gesture came barely in time for Rose, who was fast slipping downhill.

At Palm Beach in April 1984, as Easter approached, she was troubled when her daughters argued as to who should take full care of her. When somebody tried to have her walk or move her limbs in the swimming pool, she showed she wasn't up to it. She seemed unable to distinguish between fact and fiction, and sometimes her speech wandered incomprehensibly. There was fear that she might not survive another closing off of her bowel and another operation.

Then, on Good Friday, she seemed to be looking forward to Mass when she collapsed. David Kennedy, drugged and miserable, came to see her with his brother Douglas and was shocked at her shrunken, shriveled form and face. Soon afterward, he was found dead with 1.3 grams of cocaine in his wallet in his apartment at the Brazilian Court Hotel. He had overdosed on that drug and on Demerol and Mellaril; two bellboys were held in connection with his death and released.

Rose knew nothing of this. A second stroke now left her without awareness and in a semiparalyzed condition. She entered a twilight world; it is uncertain whether she had more than a vague awareness of life after that. Hers was a more merciful state than Joe's, but it was agony for the family to see her so helpless. She was flown to Hyannis Port.

For years Teddy and her other children and her grandchildren came to see her; she was never without careful nursing care day and night. Whenever she was shown, in better days, on TV, Teddy called to let her know; but, at last, he stopped calling.

She was spared knowing the family's strain when Teddy made a great show of the hundredth birthday, from which Jackie was conspicuously absent. He told the press the unlikely story that Rose made a quip just before the party: "I'm like old wine, they don't bring me out very often, but I'm well preserved."

She made an appearance, in a large straw hat, slumped in a wheelchair, for the cameras, but it is doubtful if she knew what was going on. She was placed in her room, at the window, like a beloved statue, as Maureen McGovern sang "My Wild Irish Rose" and "The Rose of Tralee."

Some fancied they saw a flicker of recognition in Rose's time-dulled eyes.

When a hurricane struck Hyannis in August 1991, wailing the banshee wail that Joe so hated, she didn't show any response; she was moved to a safe place in the house. Nor did she display a twinge of fear when Teddy, bold as ever in defying the fates, sailed into the storm in the teeth of the wind.

She was not aware—indeed, she was kept from the TV the way Joe was—of the events at Palm Beach when William Kennedy Smith was put on trial for rape. And she was also spared the misery of seeing *JFK,* Oliver Stone's extended fantasy of the assassination, or Teddy's 1992 second marriage to Victoria Anne Reggie.

Jackie's funeral she did watch, probably uncomprehending, on television.

It seemed cruel that she was alive all those years, instead of being, if her lifelong and passionate beliefs were well founded, released to Paradise, where, she had always been confident, she would find Joe, and Joe, Jr., and Kathleen and Jack and Bobby. It was clear that, with so many in the family lost in death or personal ruin, none of the Kennedys, when it came right down to it, could bear to let their astonishing and overwhelming matriarch slip away into her final and well-deserved rest.

The family kept showing her a video film, on a VCR, of her life, with all the deaths and agonies removed, over and over again, in an act of reassurance. It was a version of her life, unstained, sweet, perfectly happy. It was her family's last-ditch and most loving effort in the campaign that had gone on for decades: to protect Rose, who had never been comfortable with harsh reality, from the truth, just as they tried still to protect her from the final reality.

And then, at last, they could not protect her. She died on January 22, 1995—precisely six months to the day before her official birthday, and, oddly, on the same day of the month as Jack died in November 1963.

The wise decision was made to have the funeral at the same St. Stephen's Church in which Rose was baptized. Cardinal Bernard Law presided; eight hundred people crowded the unostentatious church, situated in a North End that had changed beyond recognition. A large crowd stood quietly and respectfully outside.

John F. Kennedy, Jr., whom Rose had adored since childhood, quoted from one of Rose's favorite passages from the Gospel according to St. Paul: "I have fought the good fight. I have finished my course. I have kept the faith."

Teddy called her "a rare and wondrous person, a shining example of faith that sustained her through even the hardest sorrow. She had an inner strength that radiated from her life. She was a symbol of family in this country and around the world. She was the most beautiful rose of all." He added that everything the family had done began and ended with Rose and Joe Kennedy.

The Pope and President Clinton sent messages. Clinton sent several members of his cabinet and Mrs. Albert Gore, wife of the vice-president.

Jean Kennedy Smith, ambassador to Ireland, spoke of Rose knowing many poems by heart and of the family discussions of politics. There was much warm comment on Rose's role in helping the mental-retardation cause.

Teddy, Jr., remembered Rose saying that the most important element in human life was faith: "If God were to take away all his blessings, health, physical fitness, wealth, intelligence, and leave me but one gift, I would ask only for faith."

Representative Joe, Jr., remembered how Rose appreciated all the simple delights of the earth. William Kennedy Smith spoke of his grandmother's patriotism.

Teddy brought laughter when he told a story that the summer Rose turned 101 he showed her his tennis racket. She said, "Are you sure that's your racket, Teddy? I've been looking all over the house for mine!" It was a loving, improbable tale.

The hearse and motorcade drove slowly to the Holyhood Cemetery in Brookline. Rose was buried next to her stormy, unpredictable husband, as she had wished.

At last, she was reunited with all of her lost loved ones, in the final peace that passeth all understanding.

Acknowledgments

My chief debt is to Jeffrey Hearn, who tirelessly conducted the immense job of obtaining (and in some cases declassifying) thousands of relevant documents in Washington, D.C., including ships' passenger lists; Victoria Shellin, who typed the book; Christopher, Edward and all the Palafoxes and Nicole Moyer, who undertook the formidable task of filing some forty thousand pages of documents. Mark Dupee handled the Los Angeles end of the research; thanks to Marc Wanamaker and Ned Comstock, Los Angeles archivists, and to Dr. Michael Stefan, medical supremo, who answered sundry medical questions. There is no calculating my debt to Christopher Ely and Lesley Davidson, who researched the unindexed Hearst files at UC Berkeley and did sterling work in Boston, Concord and Old Orchard Beach; Father Gerald Fogarty, Jesuit and scholar, who answered countless questions and supplied information from the elusive diaries of Cardinal Spellman; Stephen Pockross, who did extensive work in Connecticut; Sara Clark, who researched the Gloria Swanson papers at Austin, Texas; David Bafumo, who handled the Roosevelt research; William Colby, former CIA chief, who gave generously of his time; Marshall Bullitt Watkins, who sent me a shoal of vital documents; Igor and Oleg Cassini, brothers of great fame and greater charm; Rita Dallas, family nurse; Lois Geraghty, book detective; Randy Soule of the Truman Library; Sioban Shirley, who handled the British research. My agent, Dan Strone, and my editor and friend, Tom Miller, kept up my enthusiasm and were supportive always.

The staffs of the University of Glasgow and the University of Birmingham were of great assistance to my researchers through the Sir Thomas Lipton and Neville Chamberlain papers; Rosemary Murphy, actress, talked about her father, Robert Murphy, whose papers, housed at the Hoover Institute of Peace and War at Stanford, Palo Alto, California, were very useful; the Hot Springs, Arkansas, Public Library staff and Dr. Robert Conte of the Greenbrier Hotel were most helpful on Rose's visits; Hugh D. and the enchanting Jamie Auchincloss, Frank d'Olier and Mimi Cecil were valuable on Jackie Kennedy; William Blair, nephew of Arthur Krock, was indispensable (Arthur Krock's papers at Princeton and his oral history at Columbia were rich addenda to his published memoirs); also Henry S. Lodge; Lance Emetz, curator of the Charles Schwab archives, Hugh Moore Historical Park and Museum, Easton, Pennsylvania, and Chris Barker, Hagley Museum, were strong sources. I am grateful to Charles Hayden executive Henry Spreckelson; the staff of the Baker Library of the Harvard Business School was courteous and tireless; Cari Beauchamp took time off from a crowded schedule to conduct me to Enchanted Hill and fill me in on details supplied to me by the late Frances Marion; Kay Stammers, tennis star (Mrs. Thomas W. Bullitt) and Mrs. Barbara Bullitt were rich sources; Miles Kreuger and his Institute of the American Musical and Gerald Turbow, counselor and friend, were very wise sources; Letitia Baldrige was vivid and amusing on Rose and Clare Boothe Luce in Rome, Paris and the White House; Susan Duncan of the Palm Beach Historical Society and Alex Taylor were tireless in their help; so, too, Kenneth Rose in London. Pierre Sauvage proved informative and cautionary on the Jewish aspects; the staff of the Hebrew University of Los Angeles was always helpful.

Selective List of Interviewees

(Some were spoken to before the book was planned; those deceased are in italics.)

John Henry Cutler; Marsha Moss; Miles Kreuger; Rita Dallas; Jack Beatty; Dr. Robert Conte; Edward Shorter; Dr. Gerald Turbow; Mrs. Frederick Good, Jr.; *Viola Dana; Shirley Mason; Betty Compson; Lady Ruth Higham* (later Ruth Nelligan-Deacon); François du Sardou; *Frances Marion;* Cari Beauchamp; *Al and Sid Rogell;* Marc Wanamaker; *"Red" Grange;* Mrs. Wildred Daly; *Raoul Walsh;* Mrs. Mathilda Clough; James D'Arc; *Princess Nathalie Paley; Howard Strickling; Don Prince; Nancy Carroll; Joan Bennett;* Lee Sylvester; Kenneth Rose; *James Roosevelt; Elliott Roosevelt; Franklin D. Roosevelt, Jr.;* Robert Parkes; Mrs. Barbara Bullitt Christian; Kay Stemmers Bullitt; Marshall Bullitt Watkins; Benjamin (son of Sumner) Welles; *Jules and Doris Stein;* Father Gerald Fogarty; Fleur Cowles; *Lotte Lehmann;* Lady Glendevon; Mrs. Harold Phillips; Lady Anne Wake-Walker; Sir Nigel Strutt; *Marlene Dietrich; Ruth Alexander;* John Costello; George F. Kennan; Rupert Allason MP (Nigel West); *Henri Soulé; Eric Sevareid; Mrs. Norman Armour;* Mrs. Wellington Koo; Jerry Oppenheimer; *Mary Sanford;* William Colby; Lily Lodge; Francesca Braggiotti Lodge; Henry S. Lodge; Jamie Auchincloss; Hugh D. Auchincloss; Frank d'Olier; Mimi Cecil; Letitia Baldrige; Julio Vera; Thomas DeLong; *Morton Downey, Sr.;* Morton Downey, Jr.; Clark Clifford; Eddie Brandt; Heidi Brandt;

487

Donovan Brandt; Jacques Lowe; Hubert de Givenchy; Igor Cassini; Oleg Cassini; William Blair (nephew of Arthur Krock); Janet Leigh; *Francis (Frank) Saunders; Miguel Aleman; Merle Oberon; Peter Lawford;* Rosemary Murphy (daughter of Robert Murphy); Tamar Cooper; Shelley L. Davis; Mortimer M. Caplin; Gerald Clarke; *Aleksander Kerensky,* and Sergei Khruschev; and others who preferred not to be quoted by name.

What follows is, in essence, a guide to the Charles Higham collection of papers at Occidental College, Eagle Rock, California, so that the scholar may readily obtain the sources of the information contained in these pages. In view of the immense volume of State Department documents, line-by-line attributions would have called for a separate volume.

Source Notes

Chapter 1

BIRTHDATE: Birth certificate supplied by Registry Division, City of Boston; baptismal certificate, St. Stephen's Church, North Boston; BIRTHPLACE: Sanborn Insurance Maps, Library of Congress; 1890 tax records, Boston Archives, Hyde Park, Massachusetts; Census destroyed; WILL: Boston Probate Court files; HARVARD: Harvard archives; HONEY FITZ: Memoirs, Boston *Globe*, 1914, *passim;* John F. Fitzgerald scrapbooks, Holy Cross College, Worcester, Massachusetts (from now on: JFFS); ITALIAN NORTH END: Anna Maria Martellone: *Una Little Italy nell' Afene d'America* (Note: a rich and untapped source; translation available in Charles Higham papers; UCLA Research Library); William De Marco: *Ethics and Enclaves: Boston's Italian North End;* Sanborn Insurance Maps; RISE OF HONEY FITZ: JFFS; James M. Curley papers, Holy Cross; McKINLEY: JFFS; CONCORD PERIOD: Marsha Moss, West Concord Public Library; JFFS; Sanborn Insurance Maps; McGUFFEY READERS: Then on West Concord school curriculum and on all New England curricula, source: Massachusetts Historical Society; Boston Public Library; OLD ORCHARD BEACH: Old Orchard Beach Historical Society; ROSE AS CHILD: JFFS; Rose Kennedy: *Times to Remember;* BOARD OF STRATEGY: John H. Cutler: *Honey Fitz;* JFFS; 8 UNITY STREET: 1900 Boston city census; Sanborn Insurance Maps (address not mentioned in any standard source); WAR IN ITALY: *Una Little*

Italy; PHILIPPINES/MEAT: JFFS; ADVERTISEMENTS: JFFS; SARAH BERNHARDT: *Times to Remember;* Programs courtesy Christopher Ely; HOUSE IN DORCHESTER: Cutler; JFFS; Sanborn Insurance Maps; Grantor-Grantee books, Boston archives; SHAWN O'BOO: Cutler; DORCHESTER SCHOOL: Dorchester Library; ITALIANS: *Gazetta di Massachusetts;* CAMPAIGN/INAUGURATION: JFFS; All Boston newspapers (from now on, when all papers are searched, the general reference will be BN); FIRE: Old Orchard Beach *Mirror;* MITCHELL: Cutler; COAL GRAFT HEARINGS: Boston *Post* and *Herald.*

Chapter 2

SACRED HEART: The Sacred Heart Review, 1907–1913 (Library of Congress); Margaret Williams: *The Society of the Sacred Heart,* etc.; GEORGE KOCH: BN; SINECURES: BN; Note Boston *Post* in particular; BLUMENTHAL: Gunther Gerr, Bischofliches Diozenarchiv, Aachen; Diocesan archives, Holland, Aachen; Mary Colum: *Life and the Dream;* Lawrence Leamer: *The Kennedy Women;* TRIAL: BN; LIPTON: Lipton scrapbooks, University of Glasgow, Scotland; SWEET ADELINE: Interview, Miles Kreuger; Sheet music courtesy Institute of the American Musical; MAYORALTY: J. F. Fitzgerald: *The Duties of a Modern Mayor: New England Magazine,* June, 1906; AIRFLIGHT: *New York Times;* JFFS; DATING JOE KENNEDY: Drawn from a multiplicity of sources including Doris Kearns Goodwin: *The Fitzgeralds and the Kennedys; Times to Remember;* JFFS; David E. Koskoff, *Joseph P. Kennedy;* etc., etc.; FEAR OF WIND: Interview, Rita Dallas; ROSE LECTURES: BN; PALM BEACH: *Palm Beach Entertains, Then and Now* (Junior League of Palm Beaches); Palm Beach Life; Palm Beach Historical Society files; JOE AGAIN: BN; FRANCONIA: Amos Luther series in Boston *Herald;* EUROPEAN TRIP: Boston Chamber of Commerce News, Library of Congress; STEAMBOAT RENDEZVOUS: *Times to Remember;* FALMOUTH: Falmouth Historical Society.

Chapter 3

TOSCA: JFFS; LIPTON: Lipton scrapbooks; PANAMA:
Boston *American;* FAMILY: *Cosmopolitan,* September,
1913; CURLEY: Cutler; Beatty, Jack: *The Rascal King;*
Interview, Jack Beatty, telephone, 1994; COAKLEY/
TOODLES: Interview, Jack Beatty; BN; FIRE: Boston
Herald; other BN; Cutler; JFFS; THE BANK: JFFS;
O'CONNELL: Cutler; OAK HALL: JFFS; EXPLOSION:
New York Times.

Chapter 4

COLLATERAL LOAN: Boston City Archives; BN; LIP-
TON LETTER: Lipton scrapbooks; BROOKLINE HOUSE:
Brookline Historical Society; Brookline Chronicle (also
December 1, 1966); DESCRIPTION OF HOUSE: Christo-
pher Ely and Lesley Davidson; Author visit to house, 1978;
Parks authority guidebook and staff help; Photographs;
WEDDING: BN; GREENBRIER: Interview, Dr. Robert
Conte, hotel historian; Guest books; Hotel official history;
HOUSE AGAIN: National Parks Service, "Interview with
Rose F. Kennedy" on film; NANTASKET: Nantasket His-
torical Society records; Sanborn Insurance Maps; SMITH:
William M. Bergan: *Old Nantasket;* ETHER/TWILIGHT
SLEEP: *Good Housekeeping; Ladies Home Journal; Cosmo-
politan* magazine; for dates see Readers' Guide to Periodi-
cals 1914–1918; Interviews: Dr. Michael Stefan, Mrs. Fred-
erick Good (daughter-in-law; widow), telephone;
CHILDBIRTH; WOMEN'S SEXUAL ATTITUDES: Ex-
haustive documentation assembled by Edward Shorter for
A History of Women's Bodies; BIRTH: BN; JFFS; *Times to
Remember;* STAFF: Boston census records; LIPTON: Lip-
ton scrapbooks; CHARLES HIGHAM: Source is author's
stepmother, *Lady Ruth Higham, later Mrs. Nelligan-
Deacon;* HAVANA LIMITED: Palm Beach *Life,* various
issues; JOE AT OFFICE: Contributions by staff member to
Edward M. Kennedy (editor): *The Fruitful Bough;* VINCE
AND MARIE GREENE: *The Fruitful Bough;* THREE
HARVARD PALS: Doris Kearns Goodwin; FITZ/WAR/

LODGE: *New York Times;* Cutler; JFFS; MEXICO: *New York Times;* BAPTISM: St. Aidan's Church; BALLOT: *New York Times;* BROTHERS AT WAR: Contested Election Case: Peter F. Tague vs. John F. Fitzgerald, 10th Congressional District of Massachusetts, December 26, 1918; STEEL PROBLEMS: *Survey,* November 23, 1918; *The New Republic,* August 10, 1918; *Shipping Board Operations: Hearing before Select Committee on US Shipping Board Operations, 66th Congress, Third Session, 1921;* Williams: *The Wilson Administration and the Ship Building Crisis; American Magazine,* February, 1916; *New York Times;* RIOTS: BN; SCHWAB: *American Magazine,* February, 1916; Robert Hessen: *Steel Titan; Current Opinion,* April 1917; Schwab archives, Hagley Museum, Wilmington, Delaware; Also at Hugh Moore Historical Park and Museum, Easton, Pennsylvania; LEVENE: *New York Times;* FDR VISIT: FDR Memorial Library, Hyde Park, NY; *Fore River* papers, journal; JOSEPHUS DANIELS VISIT: *New York Times;* TAGUE: *Tague vs. Fitzgerald,* op. cit.; GALEN STONE: Hayden, Stone ledgers at Barker Library, Harvard Business School; *New York Times; Wall Street Journal; American Encyclopedia of Biography;* STRIKE: BN; MEXICO/AGWI: *New York Times;* GUFFEY: *New York Times;* BOSTON POLICE STRIKE: BN; TAGUE: *Tague vs. Fitzgerald,* op. cit.; ROSEMARY: *Times to Remember;* Doris Kearns Goodwin; MORTON DOWNEY: *The Fruitful Bough;* Author's conversations with Morton Downey, New York, 1961, and Morton Downey, Jr., Chicago, 1981; ROSE RUNNING FAMILY: Doris Kearns Goodwin; *Times to Remember;* HERTZ: *New York Times; Fortune* article is to be ignored in its entirety; JOE TO ENGLAND: *Variety;* VIOLA DANA: Author conversations with Viola Dana, Hollywood, 1971; ENCHANTED HILL: Author conversations with *Frances Marion,* West Hollywood, 1971; Author conversations with Cari Beauchamp, Marion's biographer, Beverly Hills, California, 1994; Author's visit to Enchanted Hill, 1994; *Off with their Heads* and *Spiders in a Bottle* (Marion's published and unpublished memoirs); Edgar M. Wyatt, *More Than a Cowboy;* Interview with Edgar M. Wyatt, telephone, 1994; "RED" GRANGE: Author's conversations with "Red" Grange, Naples, Florida, 1970;

OTHER MOVIES: *Variety;* ROSE OF THE TENEMENTS: *Variety;* JEWISH FILMS: *Variety.*

Chapter 5

COMPSON: Author's interviews and conversations with *Betty Compson; Mrs. Ruth Nelligan-Deacon; Viola Dana,* London, Hollywood, 1970; UNHAPPY AT WELLES AVE-NUE: Doris Kearns Goodwin; STAFF: 1920 Census; ILL-NESS: *Times to Remember;* BROOKLINE HOUSE: See earlier references; POLAND SPRINGS, MAINE: Poland Springs Library (family made many visits from 1910 on); KISMET: Files of USC Doheny Library; AFTERWARDS: USCDH; SUGAR: *New York Times; Wall Street Journal;* EXPLOSION: 47 sources including all New York, Boston and Washington papers; Best account in Frederick Lewis Allen: *Only Yesterday;* AGWI: *New York Times; Wall Street Journal;* Note: no contemporary references discovered on so-called bear raid on Yellow Cabs; ROSEMARY: *Times to Remember;* Lectures by Rose F. Kennedy, *various;* Laurence Leamer: *The Kennedy Women;* ROSE ATTITUDES: Leamer; Doris Kearns Goodwin; *Times to Remember;* O'CONNELL: Archdiocese of Boston; BN; STRIKE: *New York Times;* Hayden-Stone papers, Harvard; COHASSET: Cohasset Historical Society files; MOVIES: *Variety, passim* (searched: 1919–1938; copies in Charles Higham papers; no index); USDCH: THOMSON/MARION: Interviews with Frances Marion; Frances Marion: *Off with Their Heads,* published, *Spiders in a Bottle,* unpublished; Interview with Al and Sid Rogell, Hollywood, 1970; Conversations with Cari Beauchamp; Edgar M. Wyatt; Wyatt: *More Than a Cowboy,* etc. (Note: Rose F. Kennedy's stays in Hollywood omitted by all biographers.)

Chapter 6

ROSE'S SHARES: File available at Roosevelt Memorial Library, Hyde Park, care of Robert Parkes (sealed until after death of Joseph P. Kennedy) obtained by David Bafumo; HYANNIS: Confidential information obtained by Christopher Ely and Lesley Davidson at Hyannis Port;

MARION/GRANGE visits: Interview with "Red" Grange;
Frances Marion; DISNEY: Author conversations with Walt
Disney, Burbank, California, 1963; Walt Disney contribu-
tion to *The Fruitful Bough;* SCREENINGS AT HOUSE:
Frances Marion; BOATS: *Times to Remember;* THE TOLL
HOUSE: Contribution of owners to *The Fruitful Bough;*
HAYS: Hays papers, UCLA; HARVARD: Harvard Archives;
RIVERDALE: Bronx Historical Society files; Sanborn In-
surance Maps; DECISION TO KEEP HOUSE: Gloria
Swanson papers, Austin, Texas (copies of Swanson papers
are hand copied in Charles Higham collection, courtesy
Sarah Clark); TOM TYLER: *Variety;* SWANSON: Papers at
Austin; Ignore *Swanson on Swanson,* disowned by her as
fictitious; Interview with Mrs. Wilfred Daly (daughter)
confirms this; BROOKLINE REOPENING: Swanson papers; MURDOCK: *Variety* obituary; IF I DON'T GO TO
JAIL: Letter in Swanson papers; WHITEHALL HOTEL:
Author visits to Flagler mansion, numerous; Flagler Mansion *Illustrated Guide;* Palm Beach Historical Society files;
numerous documents in Swanson files; contract's accepted
version in Swanson memoirs; CHOATE: Numerous letters
from and to Rose F. Kennedy, various teachers including
Mr. and Mrs. St. John, documents supplied by Lee Sylvester; TOM MIX: *Exhibitors' Herald and Motion Picture
World* (USC; courtesy Ned Comstock); Academy of Motion
Picture Arts and Sciences; DRAKE HOTEL: Magazine
cited; ATHLETICS: Doris Kearns Goodwin; FIRST NA-
TIONAL: EHMPW; *Variety;* USC files; ILE DE FRANCE:
Author knowledge; On board ship for several sailings; *New
York Times.*

Chapter 7

GOULDING: Edmund Goulding Papers, American Film
Institute, Los Angeles; MOUNT VERNON: Cecil B.
DeMille papers, consulted in 1973, Laughlin Park, Los
Angeles (now at University of Wyoming); SWANSON:
Swanson papers; AGNES: Marriage in BN; DOWNEY/
BENNETT: Author's conversations with *Joan Bennett,*
Scarsdale, NY, 1971; RIVERDALE MOVE: Swanson

papers; PATRICK KENNEDY: BN; CROWLANDS: New York Historical Society; CHOATE: Choate Rosemary Hall archives; Interview: Lee Sylvester, telephone, 1994; PATRICK KENNEDY FUNERAL: BN; WEEKEND AT HYANNIS PORT: Swanson papers; SURPRISE PACKAGE: *New York Times;* ILE DE FRANCE: *New York Times;* DE LA FALAISE LETTER: Doris Kearns Goodwin; Swanson papers; THE TRESPASSER: *Variety;* LUCIEN LELONG: Paris *Soir; Vogue;* Author's knowledge of Princess Nathalie Paley, friend of *Sir Charles Higham;* BRITISH PREMIERE: London newspapers; PRESS CONFERENCE AT PLAZA: Swanson papers; *New York Times;* EARLY MUSICALS: *Variety;* CHOATE: Choate Rosemary Hall archives; HANNON WEDDING: BN; CRASH: *Variety* supplied all FBO and Radio Pictures holdings; values before and afterward; conversations with *Howard Strickling,* Hollywood (1971); Don Prince, Beverly Hills (1968); Other industry figures; TRESPASSER OPENING: *Variety;* SWANSON GIFTS: Swanson papers; PALM BEACH: *Variety;* JACK'S LETTER: Swanson papers; AMBASSADOR HOTEL: Frances Marion; Cari Beauchamp; CONFIRMATIONS: BN; *Variety;* CHOATE: Choate Rosemary Hall; FITZGERALD: BN; THOMAS WEDDING: BN; NANCY CARROLL: Author conversations with Nancy Carroll, New York City, 1963; *Variety;* APPENDIX: Choate Rosemary Hall; TUTOR, same; ROSE/JACK: Letters from Rose to Choate; WITHDRAWAL FROM MARRIAGE BED: Doris Kearns Goodwin; Nigel Hamilton: *JFK, Reckless Youth;* LIPTON DEATH: *London Times;* CHILDREN: Doris Kearns Goodwin; CHOATE: Choate Rosemary Hall; Doris Kearns Goodwin; Nigel Hamilton; BIRTH OF EDWARD: Choate Rosemary Hall; PROJECTOR, same; PRANKS, Same; JOE/ROOSEVELT: Michael Bechloss: *Kennedy and Roosevelt;* TRAIN: *New York Times;* ASTOR YACHT: *New York Times;* LOUIS HOWE: Author interview with Hartley Howe, 1994; FEET: Choate Rosemary Hall; LASKI: Krannick and Shockman: *Harold Laski, A Life on the Left;* ALLIANCE WITH RUSSIA: *New York Times; Washington Post;* State Department records; Author's conversations with Alexander Kerensky, Berkeley,

California, 1961; ALCOHOL IMPORTS: BN; Higham family knowledge; HOLY YEAR: *New York Times;* HOUSE AT PALM BEACH: Grantor/Grantee records; Palm Beach Historical Society files; EUROPA: Passenger lists; SEE OFF: *New York Times;* MURDER: Interview: Marshall Bullitt Watkins, telephone, 1994; CALDER/MacDONALD: *London Times;* CHURCHILL: London *Daily Express;* MAJESTIC: Passenger lists; Author's conversations with James Roosevelt (Newport Beach, California), 1971–1973.

Chapter 8

ROSE IN LONDON/RESEARCH: James Roosevelt; ARRIVAL IN ROME: James Roosevelt; DETAILS OF RITUAL: Thomas G. Morgan: *A Reporter at the Papal Court;* Breckinridge Long papers; State Department papers, consular and ambassadorial; Herschel Johnson papers; ROOSEVELT/MUSSOLINI: State Department papers; JACK'S ILLNESS: Interview, Lee Sylvester, Choate; numerous letters to and from Rose Kennedy, Choate archives; JOE JR. IN EUROPE: Choate archives; Hank Searls: *The Lost Prince;* BULLITT: Interviews: Barbara Bullitt; Marshall Bullitt Watkins; Orville Bullitt; Bullitt letters; State Department files (the Moscow files appear to be missing); SEC: SEC records, National Archive, Suitland, Maryland; MAJESTIC: Passenger lists; CHRISTMAS: *Times to Remember;* Photograph: Harvey Rachlin: *The Kennedys;* SEC/Social Security: *New York Times; The New Republic;* LETTERS TO LEMOYNE BILLINGS: Nigel Hamilton; LONDON: Doris Kearns Goodwin; ST. MAUX: Lawrence Leamer; BERENGARIA: Passenger lists; FRIEND OF BOYER: Conversations with Charles Boyer, Phoenix, Arizona, 1963; JACK'S ILLNESS: Nigel Hamilton; DEREK RICHARDSON: Leamer; NEW YEARS EVE: *New York Times;* HOLLYWOOD VISIT: *Variety;* RISE TO RUSSIA: *Times to Remember;* Interviews with Barbara Bullitt, Marshall Bullitt Watkins; *For the President; Private and Personal;* Nora Bullitt: *Three Weeks in Russia;* CONDITION OF MOSCOW: *New York Times;* State Department Files; PARIS POLITICAL STORM: *New York Times;* MAIDEN VOY-

AGE OF QUEEN MARY: *London Times; New York Times;* Conversations with *Joan Bennett,* 1970; *Doris Stein,* 1983; *Cecil Beaton* diary; Passenger lists: National Archives; DEATH OF AGNES: BN; HARVARD: Harvard archives; PACELLI: All biographies, especial reference to: Joseph F. Dineen: *Pius XII: Pope of Peace;* TEDDY/LAP: Doris Kearns Goodwin; CONFLICT OF FINANCIAL INTEREST: Roosevelt Memorial Library, closed file: Joseph P. Kennedy, courtesy Robert Parkes; *New York Times;* MORRO CASTLE: *New York Times;* LOBBYING FOR AMBASSADORSHIP: Koskoff; Whalen; ALGIC: State Department files; KENNEDY SCREAMED: Simon: *Independent Journey;* MERCHANT MARINE: *New York Times;* Maritime Commission files, National Archives; BINGHAM: Koskoff; Whalen; Doris Kearns Goodwin; VARIOUS PURPOSES OF KENNEDY TRIP: State Department files; Also some 37 sources read including BN; TOSCANINI: *The Fruitful Bough;* Contribution by David Sarnoff; ARRANGEMENTS FOR TRIP TO ENGLAND: Joseph P. Kennedy State Department file (from now on SD); Declassified for Charles Higham; LETTER TO MacARTHUR: MacArthur memoirs; ROSE TRUNKS: 123 SD; ILLNESS: SD; NARROW ESCAPE: Joseph P. Kennedy letter to Franklin D. Roosevelt (at Hyde Park); ENTOURAGE: SD; WISE: Letter in FDR files, Hyde Park; BLUFFS: SD; QUARANTINE OF DOGS: SD; PLYMOUTH: Magazines cited in text; HOUSE: SD file at Suitland, Maryland; STAFF NAMES: SD; Numbers of files cited Intelligence on Radio Stations: OF 3093: TS: SD; FAMILY EXCITEMENT: *The Tatler; The Queen; The Bystander; Woman's Day,* etc.; ROSE SHOPPING; EARPLUGS: *The Queen;* Higham family knowledge; MOLYNEUX/FEATHERS: Journals cited; CORRECT WEAR: Author conversation with Kenneth Rose, friend of Countess Bessborough; NANCY ASTOR: Higham family knowledge of Lady Astor; Virginia Cowles, *The Astors;* Anthony Masters: *Nancy Astor;* CLIVEDEN: Hon. Gavin Astor in *London Times;* KENNEDYS IN LONDON: All London newspapers; magazines cited; interviews with Lady Glendevon, 1994; VIOLET ASTOR: Virginia Cowles; *London Times;* correspon-

dence, Hon. Waldorf Astor; WINDSOR: Doris Kearns
Goodwin; Chamberlain papers, University of Birmingham,
England.

Chapter 9

KENNEDY REPORTS: 123 Kennedy, Joseph P. State
Department files (hereafter, 123 JPK); PACELLI: 123 JPK;
LOTTE LEHMANN: Author conversation with Lotte Leh-
mann (Santa Barbara, 1965); Conversations with Margue-
rite Wilbur, patroness of the arts (Santa Barbara, 1971);
BREUER: Book cited; FISHER: 123 JPK; PARTIES/
SOCIAL LIFE: Interviews with Lady Glendevon (daughter
of W. Somerset Maugham), Mrs. Harold Phillips, Lady
Anne Wake-Walker, Sir Nigel Strutt, all guests at Prince's
Gate (Note: in 1938, the apostrophe was omitted); LIND-
BERGHS: Anne Morrow Lindbergh diaries (*The Flower
and the Nettle*); REQUIREMENTS FOR PRESENTA-
TION: Higham family knowledge based on their own
presentations; Details confirmed by Kenneth Rose, Lady
Bessborough, Sir Dudley Forwood (New Forest, England,
1986); ASTOR PART: *The Flower and the Nettle;* GAS
MASKS: Numerous letters in 123 JPK; also SD files
740/445; DIRKSEN: Kennedy version: 740/445; Dirksen
version: Documents on German Foreign Policy; LUCE:
Luce correspondence, letter from Rose F. Kennedy, Clare
Boothe Luce papers, Library of Congress; QUEEN MARY:
Passenger lists; EXCLUSION OF PARENTS: Not on de-
tailed guest list in *London Times;* HARTINGTON: Lynn
McTaggart: *Kathleen Kennedy;* Interview, Lady Glendevon;
CAP D'ANTIBES: Author conversations with Marlene
Dietrich, Sydney, Australia, 1965; HARLEM BROTHEL:
Marlene Dietrich later admitted this (1966); GUESTS AT
HOTEL: Henry Morgenthau, Jr.: *Mostly Morgenthau: A
Family History;* FOREIGN POLICY: JEWISH EMIGRA-
TION: 123 JPK includes letters from Rabbi Stephen Wise;
Further evidence of JPK cooperation; *Times to Remember*
confirms from firsthand knowledge of RPK; Also see Chaim
Weismann papers, Hebrew University, Los Angeles; Docu-
ments missing from Rabbi Wise papers; All material
Charles Higham collection, Eagle Rock; GLENEAGLES

HOTEL: Information at Perth Public Library; MUNICH: 123 JPK; Chamberlain papers (extreme caution should be used concerning Nigel Hamilton's *JFK: Restless Youth,* part one of a discontinued trilogy; numerous documents that illustrate Joseph P. Kennedy's grasp of events and sympathy to the Jewish cause are omitted); DEBATE: Hansard; RUTH ALEXANDER LETTER: Copy in Herbert Hoover archives; TOSCANINI: David Sarnoff contribution to *The Fruitful Bough;* confirmed in State Department documents; Also in *RSVP:* Memoirs of Elsa Maxwell (omission of the story in Hamilton op. cit. and other adverse biographies is to be noted); BATON: Frank Saunders found the baton in the attic at Hyannis Port, as recorded in *Torn Lace Curtain;* LA FOLLETTE/HULL: 123 JPK; WOHLTHAT: My own *Trading with the Enemy* and *American Swastika* gave an adverse account of the matter, echoed in Nigel Hamilton op. cit.; Further research shows true purpose of Wohlthat meetings, which also took place with prominent figures in Whitehall that summer; Also see James D. Mooney papers, Georgetown University; Final result of nee research: Wohlthat had no real power; Proved useful as intelligence source; SPEECH: Letters between JPK and State Department, 123 JPK, etc.; BULLITT: 123 JPK; Interviews with Marshall Bullitt Watkins; Conversations with Benjamin Welles; KENNEDY/JEWS: *Times to Remember,* 123 JPK; PRESS CONFERENCE: Transcript at FDR Memorial Library, Hyde Park; UPI; DR. GOEBBELS: *Angriff;* Copy in Charles Higham papers; PERSECUTION OF JEWS; COMMENT BY JPK: *New York Times* (omitted by Hamilton, along with all subsequent JPK anti-Hitler broadcasts); ST. MORITZ: *The Tatler; The Queen; The Bystander* (files at Colindale, London); LEAVE IT TO ME: play script courtesy Miles Kreuger, Los Angeles; ITALIAN TRIP: Name of ship (missing in all biographies) and itinerary in Herschel Johnson papers; NEW POPE: TRIAL BALLOON: Father Gerald Fogarty: *The Vatican and the American Hierarchy,* supplemented by interviews, numerous, with Father Fogarty; PIUS XII CORONATION: Drawn from 56 sources including contemporary Italian newspapers; RC newspapers in England and the United States; 123 JPK; U.S. Embassy and Consular files; Author conversation with Edda

Mussolini Ciano, Rome (1988); PRIVATE AUDIENCE: Confidential Vatican source on 1939 protocol; Files closed; TEXT OF JPK MEETING WITH POPE: 123 JPK; Letter to State Department; ROSE AS HOSTESS IN PARIS: *New York Times;* ROYAL VISIT TO USA: 123 JPK; Foreign Office Records, Kew, near London; DINNER FOR ROYAL COUPLE: *Times to Remember;* 123 JPK; *London Times;* CARPET: 123 JPK.

Chapter 10

NORMANDIE: Passenger lists; conversation with Marlene Dietrich, 1965; HENRI SOULE˙: Interview, Oleg Cassini, Atlanta, Georgia, 1994; Author knowledge of Le Pavillon (frequently there; family knew Soule˙); HARTINGTON/ KATHLEEN: Lynn McTaggart: *Kathleen Kennedy;* Confirmed in interview with Lady Glendevon, Jersey, Channel Islands, 1994; CHAMBERLAIN: Chamberlain papers, University of Birmingham (unindexed: research: Victoria Connerty); LIPPMANN: Walter Lippmann; PARTY: *London Times;* PILGRIM'S LUNCHEON: Much correspondence in 123 JPK; LETTER FROM SOUTH OF FRANCE: Copy at FDR Memorial Library; KATHLEEN BEGGED: McTaggart; ANTIBES: *Times to Remember;* RIZAN: 123 JPK; SHIGEMITSU: Japanese War Crimes Trials; PIUS XII PEACE PROPOSALS: *London Times;* AIR RAID SHELTER: State Department files 124, 411; MOLYNEUX: Same source; COMMONS: Hansard; CHRYSLER: 123 JPK; ATHENIA: 123 JPK; WEATHER: Author memories; Confirmed in Molly Panter-Downes's dispatches in *The New Yorker; London Times;* CROSSING: Interviews with Lady Lesley Bonham Carter, London; Lily Lodge, New York, telephone, 1994; Thomas Mann diaries; Courtesy Dr. Gerald Turbow; END OF VOYAGE: Newsreels; Photograph in *New York Times;* ROSE'S MOVEMENTS: 123 JPK; ESSO RICHMOND CHRISTENING: *New York Times;* IN TOUCH WITH JOE: *Times to Remember;* HEADLEY PARK: 123 JPK; JPK AS SUSPECT: For adverse views see John Vostello: *Mask of Treachery;* Nigel Hamilton; my own *American Swastika;* SD JPK corrects these views; ROSE TRIP TO ENGLAND: British Foreign Office Files, Kew;

For complete list see FO indexes, numerous documents removed; ROSEMARY TO NEW YORK: *New York Times* (note error that she traveled by ship in standard sources); MOORES: Leamer; CHANCES SLIGHT: Kennedy to Cordell Hull, FDR Memorial Library; Cecil King diaries; references in *The Fruitful Bough;* 123 JPK, etc., etc.; WHY ENGLAND SLEPT: reference to text; CORDELL HULL CABLE: 123 JPK; INTERVIEW WITH ROSE: *New York Times;* AMBULANCES: *New York Times; London Times;* BOMBS: 123 JPK; EXCHANGES: 123 JPK; 10 DOWNING STREET: 123 JPK; Chamberlain papers; VANSITTART: Scribbled note, British Foreign Office files, Kew; TYLER KENT: Complete transcript of Tyler Kent trial in author's possession; CODED MESSAGES VIA MacDONALD: MacDonald oral history at Truman Library; CHAMBERLAIN: Chamberlain papers; RAINBOW FIVE: See my *American Swastika;* interviews with General Albert C. Wedemeyer, Miami, Florida, 1984, others; JPK LETTER TO CHAMBERLAIN: Chamberlain papers; RETURN HOME: Eric Sevareid memoirs; 123 JPK; Clare Boothe Luce papers; *Times to Remember;* Roosevelt papers, Hyde Park; WHITE HOUSE MEETING: James F. Byrnes memoirs; best account in Eugene Gressman papers, Bentley Historical Library; Account by RFK inadequate; treat Arthur Krock account with caution.

Chapter 11

BROADCAST: Date cited; AMBASSADORSHIP TO IRELAND: Roosevelt Memorial Library; KENNEDY BROADCAST: Date cited; TRIP TO SOUTH AMERICA: Ship not identified in *Times to Remember,* but determined from *New York Times* shipping lists; BRIDGETOWN: *Times to Remember;* also RIO; JEFFERSON CAFFERY: Jefferson Caffery papers; GUEST LIST: Caffery papers; ARANHA: Not mentioned on guest list; *Times to Remember;* NORMAN ARMOUR: State Department files; DOUGLAS FAIRBANKS: National Archives, document filed in Room 13 E, courtesy Kathy Nicastro; Also in Charles Higham papers; ARGENTINA: Nigel Hamilton; CHILE: Claude

Bowers papers; NOSTALGIA FOR SUMMER DAYS: *Times to Remember;* ENLISTMENT: Standard JFK biographies; SPELLMAN: Spellman diaries, cited by Father Gerald Fogarty; LITTLE WHITE HOUSE: *Times to Remember;* Conversations with Frank Saunders; LOBOTOMY: Doris Kearns Goodwin; *Times to Remember;* DETAILS/CRAIG HOUSE: Lawrence Leamer; JACK IN WASHINGTON: Naval Intelligence Division: National Archives; Nigel Hamilton; PEARL HARBOR: *New York Times;* HATING THE WAR: *Times to Remember;* MRS. KOO: Conversation with Mrs. Koo, 1975, courtesy Cynthia Lindsay, Malibu, California (the Wellington Koos lived for many years at Palm Beach); OFFERED SERVICES: Letter in Roosevelt Memorial Library; LETTER TO BEAVER-BROOK: Beaverbrook Papers, London; PALM BEACH/ROSE HELP TO VATICAN: Citations for various awards, Vatican; CONNECTIONS TO VATICAN: Father Gerald Fogarty; ROSE ON CAMPUS: Doris Kearns Goodwin; JOE IS TRAINING: Standard JFK biographies; CHANGES OF SCHOOLS: Rachlin: *The Kennedys;* FITZGERALDS: Same source; Also BN; KATHLEEN: Lynn McTaggart: *Kathleen Kennedy;* Doris Kearns Goodwin; HEARING ABOUT JOE JR.: Lynn McTaggart; TIMILTY: Hank Searls: *The Lost Prince;* LONSDALE: *New York Times;* Higham family knowledge of Frederick Lonsdale; Conversation, Miles Kreuger (friend of Louis Letito); CASTEL GANDOLFO: Father Gerald Fogarty; JACK'S JOURNEY HOME: Nigel Hamilton; KATHLEEN: Lynn McTaggart: *Kathleen Kennedy; As We Remember Joe;* O'CONNELL DEATH: BN; *New York Times;* KATHLEEN/CRISIS: Lynn McTaggart; WILLIAM O. DOUGLAS: Douglas papers; ROOSEVELT AS BETRAYER: *New York Times;* PRIESTS: Searls: *The Lost Prince;* Names thereof: Confidential informant, Boston Diocese.

Chapter 12

HURRICANE: *New York Times;* Only possible route to New York by highway; All airplanes, trains suspended; DEATH OF HARRINGTON: Nigel Hamilton; CLASH WITH KATHLEEN: Doris Kearns Goodwin; FITZ ILL-

NESS: Rachlin; DESTROYER: *New York Times;* MARY LASKER: *New York Times,* various, also obituary, 1994; Gail Cameron, *Rose;* ETHEL: Jerry Oppenheimer: *The Other Mrs. Kennedy;* Conversations with Jerry Oppenheimer; MARY SANFORD: Author conversations with Mary Sanford, Palm Beach, 1985; Descriptive matter, history supplied by Palm Beach Historical Society; KNIGHTS OF MALTA: Records of Knights of Malta; History obtained by Jeffrey Hearn, Washington, D.C.; WILL: Probate files; *New York Times;* SAN FRANCISCO CONFERENCE: *New York Times;* San Francisco, *Examiner, Chronicle;* NEEDY CHILDREN: Rachlin; CITATION: Rachlin; MESS IN HOUSE: *Times to Remember;* Diaries at JFK Library, Boston; GOLF CLUB DANCES: *Times to Remember;* CHRISTENING OF SHIP: BN; JOE WORKING: *New York Times;* ELECTION: Standard JFK biographies; ROSE EXCITEMENT: *Times to Remember;* ROSE INTRODUCTIONS ETC.: Doris Kearns Goodwin; JOE KENNEDY ACTIVITIES: *New York Times;* DISCUSSIONS: Doris Kearns Goodwin; BN; CUSHING/ROSE: Biographies of Cushing; APARTMENT: *The Fruitful Bough;* CAMPAIGN ANNOYANCES: Cameron: *Rose;* Doris Kearns Goodwin; BN; KATHLEEN IN LONDON: Interview, Lady Glendevon; McTaggart; PARIS: Jefferson Caffery papers; LETTERS TO AND FROM TOM CLARK: Charles Higham collection; Tom Clark papers at Truman Library; JACK'S ACTIVITIES: Nigel Hamilton; HOOVER COMMISSION: Hoover Commission staffing and reports, Hoover Library, West Branch, Iowa. TRIP TO IRELAND: *Times to Remember;* Author knowledge of Shane Leslie (*not* Sean Leslie, as in all sources); Much correspondence in Charles Higham collection; SD papers (Ireland); McTaggart; Doris Kearns Goodwin; JACK'S ILLNESS: Interview, Kay Stammers Bullitt, Lexington, Kentucky, 1994; GALEAZZI LINKS: Interview with William Colby, former CIA chief, Rome and Saigon, Washington, D.C., 1994; ANITA AND ROBERT YOUNG: Charles Higham: *The Duchess of Windsor: The Secret Life;* GREENBRIER: Dr. Robert Conte, Greenbrier Hotel; SCENE AFTER THE BALL: McTaggart; JOE'S ARREST: Truman papers, Truman Memorial Library; DOLLAR LINES: *New York Times;*

ROSE TO WILLIAM O. DOUGLAS: William O. Douglas papers.

Chapter 13

ROSEMARY'S TRANSFER: Lawrence Leamer; FEENEY AFFAIR: Father Gerald Fogarty; VON DIRKSEN: Documents on German Foreign Policy; BOBBY/ETHEL: Cable in National Archives (obtained by Jeffrey Hearn); Copy in Charles Higham collection; MEETING WITH MRS. SKAKEL: Oppenheimer; CORTISONE: Interview, Kay Stammers Bullitt; Doris Kearns Goodwin; LEOPOLD: Copy of book at Library of Congress; PARTY FOR BOBBY/ETHEL: Oppenheimer; WEDDING: BN; Oppenheimer; ETHEL WROTE TO ROSE: Oppenheimer; ROSE NOT AT FUNERAL: *New York Times;* NO LEGACY: Rachlin; SPEECH AT UNIVERSITY OF VIRGINIA: *New York Times;* ROSE/JACK: BN; TEDDY'S EXPULSION; AFTERMATH: Burton Hersh; DIEM: Trevor Barnes: *The Secret Cold War* in *The Historical Journal* (UK), v. 23. n. 3, 1984; Interview with William Colby; BOBBY'S AND TEDDY'S MOVEMENTS: Rachlin; ROSE AS PAPAL COUNTESS: *New York Times;* UNCLE JOHN'S DEATH: Rachlin, BN; CABOT LODGE: Interview, Henry S. Lodge, courtesy Lily Lodge, 1994; STAR OF SOLIDARITY: Rachlin; Father Gerald Fogarty; ROSE CAMPAIGNS: BN; Ted Sorensen; Numerous television documentaries; *New York Times;* JACQUELINE BOUVIER: Interviews, Jamie Auchincloss (stepbrother); Hugh D. Auchincloss (half brother); Mimi Cecil (cousin); Frank d'Otier (uncle); DEAR GRUFF GRIZZLY BEAR: *The Fruitful Bough* (contribution by Jacqueline Kennedy); FAMILY BACKGROUND: Research done by genealogist Julio Vera; Robert E. Lee genealogy shows no trace of James T. Lee or his father; Frank d'Otier, Mimi Cecil and Jamie Auchincloss confirm Janet Auchincloss, Jackie's mother, invented the family trees; Bouvier genealogy equally inaccurate; ROSE IN PARIS: Burton Hersh; *BOSTON POST* BRIBE: Whalen; VISIT TO MRS. SKAKEL: Oppenheimer; CAMPAIGN: Interview, Henry S. Lodge; BRAGGIOTTI: Conversations with

Thomas de Long, biographer of John Davis Lodge; *The Motion Picture Guide;* Author meeting with Francesca Lodge, 1975; Westport, Connecticut; CAMPAIGN TRICKS: BN; RECEPTION: Network television coverage; MISTAKE IN DELIVERY OF CHAMPAGNE: John H. Davis: *The Kennedys;* ALEMAN: Conversations with Miguel Aleman (when Minister of Tourism), Mexico City, 1980; POEM: *Times to Remember;* PLANS FOR WORLD TRIP: Letters of introduction, Robert Murphy papers, Hoover Institute, Stanford, California; CONFLICTS BE-TWEEN ROSE AND JACKIE: Heymann; Jamie Auchin-closs interviews; PETER LAWFORD: James Spada; PETER LAWFORD FLIGHT TO JAPAN: Spada; LADY LAWFORD: *Bitch;* PARIS; CROIX DE GUERRE: Rachlin; SURGERY: Standard biographies; PROFILES IN COUR-AGE: Author's interpretation; ROSE IN CALIFORNIA: Spada; WORLD TRIP: Murphy files, Hoover Institute, Stanford; OCEAN OF TEA: Interview, Henry S. Lodge, son of Henry Cabot Lodge; SHIVERING WITH COLD: Doris Kearns Goodwin; RUTH McMILLAN: Interview on CBS-TV with Ruth McMillan, 1990; DISLIKE OF JOE: Inter-view, Jamie Auchincloss; Frank d'Otier; WEDDING: *New York Times;* Oppenheimer; Conversations with *Morton Downey, Sr.,* and Jr.; FAIRHOLME: Newport Historical Society; HAMMERSMITH FARM: Material supplied by Hammersmith Farm Museum; Interviews, Jamie Auchincloss; Mimi Cecil; BIRD OFF TREE: *The Fruitful Bough;* CRASH: Burge vs. Kennedy, case file; Barnstaple Superior Court; BROKE GLASSES; WISH YOU WERE HERE: C. David Heymann: *A Woman Named Jackie.*

Chapter 14

Galeazzi: *The Fruitful Bough* (contribution by Count Enrico Galeazzi); CIA/ROME: Clare Boothe Luce papers, Library of Congress; Interview, William Colby, former CIA chief in Rome; Interviews and documents from Spellman diaries: Father Gerald Fogarty; SKAKEL DEATH: Oppenheimer; Declassified files on Joe Kennedy, FBI; GROUND BREAK-ING: *New York Times;* JEAN'S WEDDING; CIA/

VATICAN: Clare Boothe Luce papers; FURIOUS WITH COLBY: Colby memoirs; Interview with William Colby; CLARE AT EZE: Luce papers; REPAIRS: Fogarty; TELEPHONE FROM BOBBY TO EZE: Luce papers; JOE'S ILLNESS: Rachlin; COMPOUND: *Times to Remember;* ZURICH TRIP: Luce papers; Conversations with Joan Bennett; Burton Hersh; PROFILES IN COURAGE AFFAIR: Clark Clifford Memoirs; YOUNG SUICIDE: For more details see Higham: *The Duchess of Windsor;* CAMPAIGN FILM: Courtesy Eddie Brandt Video, Hollywood; WRIGHTSMANS: Material supplied by Palm Beach Historical Society; BOBBY/WEST VIRGINIA: *Times to Remember;* MILWAUKEE: Milwaukee newspapers; TOUR: *Times to Remember;* CALIFORNIA: Los Angeles newspapers; Leamer; EDEN ROC: BN: ROSE/DEBATES: *Times to Remember;* SCHEDULE OF SEEING THEM: Rachlin; ELECTION DAY: Jacques Lowe; *Times to Remember;* All newspapers and standard biographies; Theodore H. White: *The Making of a President* (No single source gave sequence of events; some 75 separate sources consulted); THANKSGIVING: Updated unsourced clippings in Harvard Kennedy papers, Harvard; PAVLICK: CHRISTMAS: *New York Times.* ATTORNEY GENERAL: Clifford memoirs; MIXUP: Conversations with James Roosevelt, 1971; MASS STORY: *Times to Remember;* INAUGURATION: White; All newspaper sources; RAN THROUGH HER HEAD: *Times to Remember.*

Chapter 15

BUFFET: John H. Davis; INTERVIEWS: Jamie and Hugh D. Auchincloss; Mimi Cecil; Frank d'Otier, telephone, 1994; ROSE'S FEELINGS: *Times to Remember;* BALDRIGE: Interview, Letitia Baldrige, telephone, 1994; WE'RE JACKIE'S COUSINS: Baldrige; ROSE'S BEHAVIOR: John H. Davis; EDIE BEALS: John H. Davis; HERALDRY: *New York Times;* LINCOLN BEDROOM: Letitia Baldrige; BLACKS IN HYANNIS PORT: Frank Saunders: *Torn Lace Curtain;* MEETING OF SOMOZA: Ana Stasco; Somoza: *Nicaragua Betrayed;* CASSINI MATTERS: Interviews, Igor Cassini, Oleg Cassini, 1994; Igor Cassini: *I'd Do It All Over Again;* KIDNAP NOTE: FBI files; KROCK: Interview with Krock nephew, William Blair; KARAMAN-LIS: *Times to Remember;* BAY OF PIGS: Somoza memoirs; Interview, Don Carlos Rodriguez, Somoza associate and publisher, Los Angeles, 1992; STEVENSON: Lewis L. Strauss report, Hoover Library, West Branch, Iowa; APARTMENT IN PARIS: Gail Cameron; WRIGHTS-MANS: *New York Times;* ROSE AT AIRPORT: *Times to Remember;* HALL OF MIRRORS: de Gaulle memoirs; DIEM: de Gaulle memoirs; VIENNA: Nikita Khrushchev memoirs; Interviews, Sergei Khrushchev (son), Serge Tukovsky, Boston and Moscow, telephone, 1994; *Times to Remember;* RED CROSS HALL: Janet Leigh: *There Really Was a Hollywood;* DENMARK: *New York Times;* HURRI-CANE: *New York Times;* AUDIENCE: *New York Times;* DOLLS: Frank Saunders; CASALS: Casals memoirs; IMPERIAL BEHAVIOR: Saunders; RUMMAGING IN ATTIC: Saunders; DOLL COLLECTION: Saunders; STROKE: Saunders; HIRING RITA DALLAS: Book by Rita Dallas; Interviews, Rita Dallas; EPISODE IN HOUSE: Dallas.

Chapter 16

AROSEMENA: *New York Times,* also his political history; telephone call to Quito Library; ROSE TOURS; DRESS-ING ROOM SCENE: *Torn Lace Curtain;* MR. PRESI-DENT: Lawrence Bergreen biography of Irving Berlin; play script courtesy Miles Kreuger; CASSINI: Interviews, Oleg Cassini; CUBA, ETC.: Conversations with exiled Cubans including Julio Vera, 1994; EASTER MASS: *New York Times;* HOOVER LETTER: Hoover papers, West Branch, Iowa; TOURS: *Time* magazine; LANDIS AFFAIR: Shelley L. Davis; Oral history with Mortimer M. Caplin, IRS Commissioner, courtesy Shelley L. Davis; ROSE AT BER-LIN WALL: *New York Times;* BIRTHDAY: *New York Times;* Rita Dallas; HAILE SELASSIE: *New York Times;* DIEM DOWNFALL/MURDER: Interview, William Colby; APRIL IN PARIS BALL: *New York Times;* CHARI-

TY SHOW: *New York Times;* Frank Saunders; DEATH OF
JACK: Interview with Rita Dallas; Frank Saunders; William
Manchester: *The Death of a President;* Jim Bishop: *The Day
the President Was Shot;* DETAILS OF FUNERAL: B. C.
Mossman and M. W. Stark: *The Last Salute* (official Army
record); PLANE CRASH: *New York Times;* All biographies
of Edward M. Kennedy; ROSE ON TOUR: Frank Saunders;
DEATH OF JOSIE: Frank Saunders; Interview with Rita
Dallas; EXHIBITION: *New York Times;* ILLNESS/NECK:
New York Times; PAT/JEAN: Laurence Leamer;
DALLAS/SLACKS: Rita Dallas; CLOSET LIGHT: Rita
Dallas; PARTY: *New York Times;* MASKED BALL: Gerald
Clarke: *Truman Capote;* All New York newspapers; VEN-
ICE BALL: *New York Times;* Luce papers.

Chapter 17

SAUNDERS: *Torn Lace Curtain;* CBS INTERVIEW: CBS
taping; SPELLMAN DEATH: BN; *New York Times;* BOB-
BY FOR PRESIDENCY: Rachlin; All sources; ROSE
CAMPAIGN: TV news footage: CBS, NBC, ABC; Author's
collection; WOMEN'S WEAR DAILY: As cited;
BOBBY/KING: Newsreels; SNIPER: *New York Times;*
JACKIE AT HYANNIS: John H. Davis: *The Kennedys*
(eyewitness); ROSE IN LOS ANGELES: All Los Angeles
newspapers; TV news; BOBBY DEATH: *Torn Lace Curtain;*
TV news for sequence on television; SERVICE: *Torn Lace
Curtain;* ROSE SCHEDULE: *Torn Lace Curtain;* Kennedy
Library; FUNERAL AND AFTERMATH: George Plimp-
ton and Jean Stein: *American Journey;* Also see standard
Bernstein biographies; TRAIN/BURIAL: Based on numer-
ous interviews conducted with passengers by George
Plimpton and Jean Stein; Author reading of New Jersey,
Delaware and Washington, D.C., newspapers for additional
details; BURIAL: Carl Sandburg: *Abraham Lincoln* pro-
vides a salutary and unflattering comparison; MERILLI
AFFAIR: FBI files; Declassified for author, 1992; CHEST
PAINS: BN; *Torn Lace Curtain;* ONASSIS: Interview,
Jamie Auchincloss, 1994; ROSE'S ATTITUDE TO
JACKIE: Same source; ROSE IN PARIS: Interview, Rita

Dallas, 1994; ROSE/CUSHING/MARRIAGE: Cushing biographies; ASSASSINATION NEWS: All media; C. L. SHAW: All Media; DID NOT READ WARREN REPORT: Interview, Rita Dallas, 1994; SIRHAN: All media; TEDDY DRUNK: *Torn Lace Curtain;* CRUISE: *Nassau Guardian;* Biographies of Onassis; PHILIP ROTH: *Torn Lace Curtain;* CHAPPAQUIDDICK: All biographies of Edward M. Kennedy; *Torn Lace Curtain; Times to Remember;* Interview, Rita Dallas, 1994; Leamer; Doris Kearns Goodwin; *New Times;* ROSE IN PARIS: *New York Times;* Interview, Rita Dallas, telephone, 1994; DEATH OF JOE: Rita Dallas; WILL: Probate files; DISPOSAL OF STAFF: *Torn Lace Curtain;* Interview, Rita Dallas, 1994.

Chapter 18

ONASSIS VISIT: David Heymann; LADY LAWFORD: *Bitch;* KICKED OUT OF CAMBRIDGE: BN; PROBATION: BN; *New York Times;* IRISH PRIEST: *Irish Times; Variety;* DALLAS: *The Kennedy Case;* REPRIMAND: *New York Times;* DRIVING MISHAP: *New York Times;* TEDDY, JR.: Rachlin; VISIT TO HOSPITAL: Richard E. Burke: *The Senator; My 10 Years with Ted Kennedy;* WOMAN ABUSED HER: *New York Times;* BARBARA GIBSON: Barbara Gibson memoirs; NAIL VARNISH, OTHER CHEAPNESS: Gibson; DRUGS: Gibson; DISLIKE OF MODERN LIFE: Gibson; TRAFFIC COP: Gibson; RELATIONSHIP WITH FAMILY: Gibson; ROSEMARY DISAPPEARANCE: *New York Times;* Chicago papers; TEDDY CAMPAIGN: Rachlin; Leamer; WHITE, KING: *New York Times;* SHERATON INCIDENT: Burke; SICK AND CONFUSED: *New York Times;* DOCTORATE: *New York Times;* HURT KNEE/BALL: *New York Times;* JOHN DEATH: BN; HEALTH SETBACKS: Gibson; ILLNESS/OPERATION: *New York Times;* Gibson; JOAN/DRINKING: Leamer; CAMPAIGN: Leamer; *New York Times;* DIVORCE: *New York Times;* ROSE PARADE: *New York Times;* FAMILY SUCCESSES: Rachlin; THANKSGIVING: Leamer, based on family interviews; SWITCH OF PLACE CARDS: Leamer; 100th: Leamer; HURRI-

CANE: Leamer; COLLAPSE, STROKE: Leamer; DEATH: All media: January 22, 1995, exactly six months from her official 105th birthday and, like Jack's assassination, on the 22nd of the month. She was buried at the church in which she was baptized—St. Stephen's, North End, thus bringing the incredible wheel of her life full circle, as she would have wished.

Bibliography

Manuscript Collections Consulted

Astor, Nancy and Waldorf, Papers, University of Reading, Reading, England.

Baruch, Bernard, Papers, Seeley G. Mudd Manuscript Library, Princeton University, Princeton, NJ.

Bernhard, Harry F., Papers, American Heritage Center, University of Wyoming, Laramire, WY.

Bowers, Claude, Papers, Lilly Library, Indiana University, Bloomington, IN.

Bumgardner, Eleanor, Papers, Bentley Historical Library, University of Michigan, Ann Arbor, MI.

Caffery, Jefferson, Papers, Archives/Special Collections, Edith Garland Dupré Library, University of Southwestern Louisiana, Lafayette, LA.

Chamberlain, Neville, Papers, University of Birmingham, Birmingham, England.

DeMille, Cecil B., Papers, American Heritage Center, University of Wyoming, Laramie, WY.

Douglas, William O., Papers, Manuscript Division, Library of Congress, Washington, D.C.

Eisenhower, Dwight D., Papers, Dwight D. Eisenhower Library, Abilene, KS.

Fire insurance maps of the Sanborn Map Company, Geography and Map Reading Room, Library of Congress, Washington, D.C.

Fitzgerald, John F., Scrapbooks, Holy Trinity College, Worcester, MA.

Foreign Office Papers, (British) Public Record Office, Kew, England.

Goldstein, Alvin, Papers, American Heritage Center, University of Wyoming, Laramie, WY.

Gray, David, Papers, American Heritage Center, University of Wyoming, Laramie, WY.

Greenbrier Hotel Papers, White Sulphur Springs, WV.

Gressman, Eugene, Papers, Bentley Historical Library, University of Michigan, Ann Arbor, MI.

Harriman, Averell, Papers, Manuscript Division, Library of Congress, Washington, D.C.

Hayden, Stone and Co. Records, Special Collections Department, Baker Library, Graduate School of Business Administration, Harvard University, Cambridge, MA.

Hays, Will, Papers, Indianapolis Public Library, Indianapolis, IN, and UCLA Research Library, Los Angeles, CA.

Hearst, William Randolph, Papers, University of California, Berkeley, CA.

Hoover, Herbert, Papers, Herbert Hoover Library, West Branch, IA.

Ickes, Harold L., Papers, Manuscript Division, Library of Congress, Washington, D.C.

Johnson, Herschel V., Papers, Harry S Truman Presidential Library, Independence, MO, and Southern Historical Library, University of North Carolina Library, Chapel Hill, NC.

Johnson, Louis A., Papers, Special Collections/Manuscripts, Alderman Library, University of Virginia, Charlottesville, VA.

Kennedy, John F., Papers, John F. Kennedy Library, Columbia Point, Boston, MA.

Kennedy, Joseph P., Jr., and John F. Kennedy, Records, Choate-Rosemary Hall Papers, Choate School, Choate, CT.

Kennedy, Joseph P., Jr., and John F. Kennedy, Records, Harvard Archives, Harvard University, Cambridge, MA.

Krock, Arthur, Papers, Seeley G. Mudd Manuscript Library, Princeton University, Princeton, NJ.

Landis, James M., Papers, Manuscript Division, Library of Congress, Washington, D.C.

Lipton, Sir Thomas, Scrapbooks, University of Glasgow, Glasgow, Scotland.

Long, Breckinridge, Papers, Manuscript Division, Library of Congress, Washington, D.C.

Luce, Clare Boothe, Papers, Manuscript Division, Library of Congress, Washington, D.C.

McKinley, William, Papers, Manuscript Division, Library of Congress, Washington, D.C.

Messersmith, George, Papers, Special Collections Department, University of Delaware Library, Newark, DE.

Mooney, James D., Papers, Georgetown University, Washington, D.C.

Murphy, Frank, Papers, Bentley Historical Library, University of Michigan, Ann Arbor, MI.

Murphy, George, Papers, Bentley Historical Library, University of Michigan, Ann Arbor, MI.

Murphy, Robert, Papers, Hoover Institute of Peace and War, Stanford University, Palo Alto, CA.

Pegler, Westbrook, Papers, Herbert Hoover Library, West Branch, IA.

Pollack, James Kerr/Hoover Commission, Papers, Bentley Historical Library, University of Michigan, Ann Arbor, MI.

Record Group 38, Records of the Office of the Chief of Naval Operations Office of Naval Intelligence, National Archives, Washington, D.C.

Record Group 59, Records of the Department of State, Decimal File. National Archives, Washington, D.C.

Record Group 84, Foreign Service Posts of the Department of State, Consulate Records London, National Archives, Washington, D.C.

Record Group 84, Foreign Service Posts of the Department of State, Embassy Records London, 1938–40, including household records, Rome, Vatican, Moscow, Rio de Janeiro, Buenos Aires, Santiago, Cairo. National Archives, Washington, D.C.

Record Group 85, Records of the Immigration and Naturalization Service T715: Passenger and Crew Lists of Vessels Arriving at New York, NY, 1897–1957. National Archives, Washington, D.C.

Record Group 178, Records of the U.S. Maritime Commission, National Archives, Washington, D.C.

Record Group 266, Records of the Securities and Exchange Commission, National Archives, Washington, D.C.

Roosevelt, Franklin D., Papers, Franklin D. Roosevelt Library, Hyde Park, NY.

Roosevelt, Theodore, Papers, Manuscript Division, Library of Congress, Washington, D.C.

Scanlon, Martin F., Papers, American Heritage Center, University of Wyoming, Laramie, WY.

Schwab, Charles, Papers, Hugh Moore Historical Park and Museum, Easton, PA, and Hagley Museum, Wilmington, DE.

Stevenson, Adlai E., Jr., Papers, Seeley G. Mudd Manuscript Library, Princeton University, Princeton, NJ.

Strauss, Lewis L., Papers, Herbert Hoover Library, West Branch, IA.

Swanson, Gloria, Papers, Hoblitzelle Theatre Arts Library, University of Texas, Austin, TX.

Taft, William Howard, Papers, Manuscript Division, Library of Congress, Washington, D.C.

Trohan, Walter, Papers, Herbert Hoover Library, West Branch, IA.

Truman, Harry S, Papers, Harry S Truman Library, Independence, MO.

Weizmann, Chaim, Papers, Hebrew University, Los Angeles, CA.

Wilson, Hugh R., Papers, Herbert Hoover Library, West Branch, IA.

Wilson, Woodrow, Papers, Manuscript Division, Library of Congress, Washington, D.C.

Wood, Robert E., Papers, Herbert Hoover Library, West Branch, IA.

Published Works Consulted

Abraham, Richard, *Alexander Kerensky: The First Love of the Revolution.* New York: Columbia University Press, 1987.

Ainley, Leslie G., *Boston Mahatma: A Biography of Martin Lomasney.* Boston: Rendible, 1949.

Allen, Frederick Lewis, *Only Yesterday: An Informal History of the Nineteen-twenties.* New York: Harper and Brothers, 1931.

Associated Press, *Triumph and Tragedy: The Story of the Kennedys.* New York: William Morrow, 1968.

Baldrige, Letitia, *Of Diamonds and Diplomats.* Boston: Houghton Mifflin, 1968.

———, *Roman Candle.* Boston: Houghton Mifflin, 1956.

Baruch, Bernard M., *Baruch.* 2 vol. New York: Holt, 1957–60.

Beatty, Jack, *The Rascal King: The Life and Times of James Michael Curley.* Reading, MA: Addison-Wesley, 1992.

Beaverbrook, William M. A., *The Three Keys to Success.* New York: Duell, Sloan and Pearce, 1956.

Bechloss, Michael R., *Kennedy and Roosevelt: The Uneasy Alliance.* New York: Norton, 1980.

Bergan, William M., *Old Nantasket,* Rev. ed. North Quincy, MA: Christopher Publishing House, 1972.

Bergreen, Laurence, *As Thousands Cheer: The Life of Irving Berlin.* New York: Viking, 1990.

Birmingham, Stephen, *Jacqueline Bouvier Kennedy Onassis.* New York: Grosset and Dunlap, 1978.

Bishop, Jim, *The Day Kennedy Was Shot.* New York: Funk and Wagnalls, 1968.

Bjerk, Roger, "Kennedy at the Court of St. James," Ph.D. dissertation, Washington State University, Pullman, Washington, 1971.

Blair, Joan and Clay, Jr., *The Search for JFK.* New York: Berkley, 1976.

Bradlee, Ben, *Conversations with Kennedy.* New York: Norton, 1975.

Brody, David, *Labor in Crisis: The Steel Strike of 1919.* Philadelphia: Lippincott, 1965.

Brown, Thomas, *JFK: History of an Image.* Bloomington: Indiana University Press, 1988.

Buck, Pearl S., *The Kennedy Women: A Personal Appraisal.* New York: Cowles Book Co., 1970.

Bullitt, Nora Iasigi, *Three Weeks in Russia.* Louisville, KY: Privately printed, ca. 1936.

Bullitt, Orville H., Ed., *For the President, Personal and Secret: Correspondence Between Franklin D. Roosevelt and William C. Bullitt.* Boston: Houghton Mifflin, 1972.

Burns, James MacGregor, *Edward Kennedy and the Camelot Legacy*. New York: Norton, 1976.

———, *John Kennedy: A Political Profile*. New York: Harcourt, 1960.

Burton, Humphrey, *Leonard Bernstein*. New York: Doubleday, 1994.

Burton, Katherine, *Witness of the Light: The Life of Pope Pius XII*. New York: Longman, Green, 1958.

Byrnes, James F., *All in One Lifetime*. New York: Harper, 1958.

Callan, Louise, *The Society of the Sacred Heart in North America*. London, NY: Longman, Green, 1937.

Cameron, Gail, *Rose: A Biography of Rose Fitzgerald Kennedy*. New York: Putnam, 1971.

Carr, William H. A., *Those Fabulous Kennedy Women*. New York: Wisdom, 1961.

Casals, Pablo, *Conversations with Casals*. New York: Dutton, 1957.

Casals, Pablo, as told to Albert E. Kahn, *Joys and Sorrows: Reflections*. London: Macdonald, 1970.

Cassini, Igor, *I'd Do It All Over Again*. New York: Putnam, 1977.

Cassini, Oleg, *In My Own Fashion: An Autobiography*. New York: Simon and Schuster, 1987.

Chellis, Marcia, *The Joan Kennedy Story: Living with the Kennedys*. New York: Simon and Schuster, 1985.

Cianfarra, Camille M., *The Vatican and the War*. New York: Literary Classics, 1944.

Clarke, Gerald, *Capote: A Biography*. New York: Simon and Schuster, 1988.

Clifford, Clark, *Counsel to the President: A Memoir*. New York: Random House, 1991.

Clinch, Nancy Gager, *The Kennedy Neurosis*. New York: Grosset and Dunlap, 1973.

Coit, Margaret L., *Mr. Baruch*. Boston: Houghton Mifflin, 1957.

Cole, Wayne S., *Charles A. Lindbergh and the Battle Against American Intervention in World War II*. New York: Harcourt Brace Jovanovich, 1974.

Collier, Peter, and David Horowitz, *The Kennedys: An American Drama*. New York: Summit, 1984.

Collis, Maurice, *Nancy Astor: An Informal Biography.* New York: Dutton, 1960.

Colum, Mary, *Life and the Dream.* Garden City, NY: Doubleday, 1947.

Cooney, John, *The American Pope: The Life and Times of Francis Cardinal Spellman.* New York: Times Books, 1984.

Costello, John, *Mask of Treachery.* New York: William Morrow, 1988.

Cowles, Virginia, *The Astors.* New York: Knopf, 1979.

Curley, James M., *I'd Do It Again: A Record of All My Uproarious Years.* Englewood Cliffs, NJ: Prentice-Hall, 1957.

Curran, Robert, *The Kennedy Women: Their Triumphs and Tragedies.* New York: Lancer, 1964.

Cutler, John H., *"Honey Fitz": Three Steps to the White House: The Life and Times of John F. Fitzgerald.* Indianapolis: Bobbs-Merrill, 1962.

Dallas, Rita, and Jeanira Ratcliffe, *The Kennedy Case.* New York: Putnam, 1973.

Damore, Leo, *The Cape Cod Years of John Fitzgerald Kennedy.* Englewood Cliffs, N.J.: Prentice-Hall, 1967.

David, Lester, *Ethel: The Story of Mrs. Robert F. Kennedy.* New York: World, 1971.

———, *Good Ted, Bad Ted: The Two Faces of Edward M. Kennedy.* Secaucus, NJ: Carol, 1993.

Davis, John H., *The Kennedys: Dynasty and Disaster, 1848–1983.* New York: McGraw-Hill, 1984.

de Bedts, Ralph F., *Ambassador Joseph Kennedy 1938–1940: An Anatomy of Appeasement.* New York: Peter Lang, 1985.

———, *The New Deal's SEC: The Formative Years.* New York: Columbia University Press, 1964.

De Holguin, Beatrice, *Tales of Palm Beach.* New York: Vantage, 1968.

DeMarco, William M., *Ethnics and Enclaves: Boston's Italian North End.* Ann Arbor, MI: UMI Research Press, 1981.

Dinneen, Joseph F., *The Kennedy Family.* Boston: Little, Brown, 1960.

———, *Pius XII: Pope of Peace.* New York: McBride, 1939.

_____, *The Purple Shamrock: the Hon. James Michael Curley of Boston.* New York: Norton, 1949.

Documents on German Foreign Policy, 1919–1939. Series D (1937–45). Washington, D.C.: G.P.O.

Donaldson, Frances, *Freddy.* Philadelphia: Lippincott, 1957.

Donovan, Robert J., *PT 109: John F. Kennedy in World War II.* New York: McGraw-Hill, 1961.

Douglas, William O., *The Court Years, 1939–1975.* New York: Random House, 1980.

_____, *Go East, Young Man: The Early Years.* New York: Random House, 1974.

Duncliffe, William J., *The Life and Times of Joseph P. Kennedy.* New York: Macfadden-Bartell, 1965.

Elwell, Edward H., *Portland and Vicinity: An Illustrated Souvenir and All-the-Year-Round Guide to the City of Portland, with Sketches of Old Orchard Beach.* 3rd ed. Portland, ME: Loring, Short & Harmon, 1888?.

Fogarty, Gerald P., *The Vatican and the American Hierarchy: From 1870 to 1965.* Stuttgart, Germany: Hiersemann, 1982; and Collegeville, MN: Liturgical Press, 1985.

Fuchs, Lawrence, *John F. Kennedy and American Catholicism.* New York: Meredith, 1967.

Gates, John D., *The Astor Family.* Garden City, NY: Doubleday, 1981.

Gaulle, Charles de, *Memoirs of Hope: Renewal and Endeavor.* New York: Simon and Schuster, 1971.

Gibson, Barbara, with Caroline Latham, *Life with Rose Kennedy.* New York: Warner, 1986.

Gill, Brendan, *Lindbergh Alone.* New York: Harcourt Brace Jovanovich, 1977.

Glass, Beaumont, *Lotte Lehmann: A Life in Opera and Song.* Santa Barbara, CA: Capra, 1988.

Gonella, Guido, *The Papacy and World Peace: A Study of the Christmas Messages of Pope Pius XII.* London: Hollis and Carter, 1945.

Goodwin, Doris Kearns, *The Fitzgeralds and the Kennedys: An American Saga.* New York: Simon and Schuster, 1987.

Grafton, David, *The Sisters: Babe Mortimer Paley, Betsey*

Roosevelt Whitney, Minnie Astor Fosburgh: The Life and Times of the Fabulous Cushing Sisters. New York: Villard, 1992.

Grant, James, *Bernard M. Baruch: The Adventures of a Wall Street Legend.* New York: Simon and Schuster, 1983.

Graves, Charles, *Champagne and Chandeliers: The Story of the Cafe de Paris.* London: Odhams, 1958.

Grigg, John, *Nancy Astor: A Lady Unashamed.* Boston: Little, Brown, 1980.

Hamilton, Nigel, *JFK: Reckless Youth.* New York: Random House, 1992.

Hardy, Stephen, *How Boston Played: Sport, Recreation, and Community, 1865–1915.* Boston, MA: Northeastern University Press, 1982.

Harrison, Rosina, *Rose: My Life in Service.* New York: Viking, 1975.

Hatch, Alden, and Seamus Walshe, *Crown of Glory.* New York: Hawthorn, 1957.

Herrmann, Dorothy, *Anne Morrow Lindbergh: A Gift for Life.* New York: Ticknor and Fields, 1992.

Hersh, Burton, *The Education of Edward Kennedy: A Family Biography.* New York: William Morrow, 1972.

———, *The Old Boys: The American Elite and the Origins of the CIA.* New York: Scribners, 1992.

Hessen, Robert, *Steel Titan: The Life of Charles M. Schwab.* New York: Oxford University Press, 1975.

Heymann, C. David, *Poor Little Rich Girl: The Life and Legend of Barbara Hutton.* Secaucus, NJ: Lyle Stuart, 1984.

———, *A Woman Named Jackie.* New York: Lyle Stuart, 1989.

Hickey, John J., *The Life and Times of the Late Sir Thomas J. Lipton: From the Cradle to the Grave, International Sportsman and Dean of the Yachting World.* New York: Hickey, 1932.

Higham, Charles, *The Duchess of Windsor: The Secret Life.* New York: McGraw-Hill, 1988.

Holt, L. Emmett, *The Care and Feeding of Children: A Catechism for the Use of Mothers and Children's Nurses.* New York: D. Appleton, 1894 numerous subsequent editions.

Ickes, Harold L., *The Secret Diary of Harold L. Ickes*. 3 vols. New York: Simon and Schuster, 1953–54.

International Military Tribunal for the Far East, *The Tokyo War Crimes Trial*. 22 vols. New York: Garland, 1981.

Johnson, Paul, *Modern Times: The World from the Twenties to the Nineties*. New York: Harper & Row, 1983.

Junior League of the Palm Beaches, *Palm Beach Entertains: Then and Now*. New York: Coward, McCann and Geoghegan, 1976.

Kaiser, Robert Blair, *"R.F.K. Must Die."* New York: Dutton, 1970.

Kane, Paula M., *Separatism and Subculture: Boston Catholicism, 1900–1920*. Chapel Hill: University of North Carolina Press, 1994.

Kavaler, Lucy, *The Astors: An American Legend*. New York: Dodd, Mead, 1968.

Kennedy, Edward M., Ed., *The Fruitful Bough: A Tribute to Joseph P. Kennedy*. Privately published, 1965.

Kennedy, John F., Ed., *As We Remember Joe*. Cambridge, MA: Privately printed at the University Press, 1945.

Kennedy, John F., *Profiles in Courage*. New York: Harper, 1956.

Kennedy, Rose F., *Times to Remember*. Garden City, NY: Doubleday, 1974.

Koskoff, David E., *Joseph P. Kennedy: A Life and Times*. Englewood Cliffs, NJ: Prentice-Hall, 1974.

Kramnick, Isaac, and Barry Sheerman, *Harold Laski: A Life on the Left*. New York: Allen Lane/Penguin, 1993.

Landis, James M., *In the Matter of Harry R. Bridges: Findings and Conclusions of the Trial Examiner*. Washington, D.C.: G.P.O., 1939.

Langhorne, Elizabeth C., *Nancy Astor and Her Friends*. New York: Praeger, 1974.

Larrowe, Charles P., *Harry Bridges: The Rise and Fall of Radical Labor in the United States*. New York: L. Hill, 1972.

Lasky, Victor, *J.F.K.: The Man and the Myth*. New York: Macmillan, 1963.

Lavelle, Elise, *The Man Who Was Chosen: The Story of Pope Pius XII*. New York: Whittlesey House, 1957.

Lawford, Lady May, with Buddy Galon, *"Bitch!": The*

Autobiography of Lady Lawford. Brookline Village, MA: Branden, 1986.

Lawford, Patricia S., *The Peter Lawford Story: Life with the Kennedys, Monroe, and the Rat Pack.* New York: Carroll and Graf, 1988.

Leamer, Laurence, *The Kennedy Women: The Saga of an American Family.* New York: Villard, 1994.

Lehmann, Lotte, *My Many Lives.* New York: Boosey and Hawkes, 1948.

———, *Wings of Song.* London: K. Paul, Trench, Trubner, 1938.

Leigh, Janet, *There Really Was a Hollywood.* Garden City, NY: Doubleday, 1984.

Lerner, Max, *Ted and the Kennedy Legend: A Study in Character and Destiny.* New York: St. Martin's Press, 1980.

Lincoln, Evelyn, *My Twelve Years with John F. Kennedy.* New York: David McKay, 1965.

Lindbergh, Anne Morrow, *The Flower and the Nettle: Diaries and Letters of Anne Morrow Lindbergh, 1936–1939.* New York: Harcourt Brace Jovanovich, 1976.

Lindbergh, Charles A., *Autobiography of Values.* New York: Harcourt Brace Jovanovich, 1978.

———, *The Wartime Journals of Charles A. Lindbergh.* New York: Harcourt Brace Jovanovich, 1970.

Liston, Robert A., *Sargent Shriver: A Candid Portrait.* New York: Farrar Straus, 1964.

Lochner, Louis, *Fritz Kreisler.* New York: Macmillan, 1950.

Longford, Lord, *Kennedy.* London: Weidenfeld and Nicholson, 1976.

MacArthur, Douglas, *Reminiscences.* New York: McGraw-Hill, 1964.

Madsen, Axel, *Gloria & Joe.* New York: Arbor House/William Morrow, 1988.

Manchester, William R., *The Death of a President: November 20–November 25, 1963.* New York: Harper and Row, 1967.

———, *Portrait of a President: John F. Kennedy in Profile.* Boston: Little, Brown, 1962.

Mann, Thomas, *Diaries, 1918–1939.* New York: H. N. Abrams, 1982.

Marion, Frances, *Off with Their Heads: A Serio-Comic Tale of Hollywood*. New York: Macmillan, 1972.

Martellone, Anna Maria, *Una Little Italy nell'Afene d'America: La Comunita Italiana di Boston dai 1800 al 1920*. Napoli, Italy: Guida, 1973.

Martin, Ralph G., *Henry and Clare: An Intimate Portrait of the Luces*. New York: Putnam's, 1991.

Masters, Anthony, *Nancy Astor: A Biography*. New York: McGraw-Hill, 1981.

Maxwell, Elsa, *R.S.V.P.: Elsa Maxwell's Own Story*. Boston: Little, Brown, 1954.

McCarthy, Joe, *The Remarkable Kennedys*. New York: Dial Press, 1960.

McDermott, Thomas, *Keeper of the Keys: A Life of Pope Pius XII*. Milwaukee: Bruce, 1946.

McTaggart, Lynne, *Kathleen Kennedy: Her Life and Times*. Garden City, NY: Dial Press, 1983.

Messer, Robert L., *The End of an Alliance: James F. Byrnes, Roosevelt, Truman, and the Origins of the Cold War*. Chapel Hill: University of North Carolina Press, 1982.

Meyers, Joan, Ed., *John Fitzgerald Kennedy: As We Remember Him*. New York: Atheneum, 1965.

Milton, Joyce, *Loss of Eden: A Biography of Charles and Anne Morrow Lindbergh*. New York: HarperCollins, 1993.

Morgan, Thomas B., *A Reporter at the Papal Court: A Narrative of the Reign of Pope Pius XI*. New York: Longman, Green, 1937.

Morgenthau, Henry, III, *Mostly Morgenthau: A Family History*. New York: Ticknor and Fields, 1991.

Mosley, Leonard, *Lindbergh: A Biography*. Garden City, NY: Doubleday, 1976.

Mossman, B. C., and M. W. Stark, *The Last Salute: Civil and Military Funerals, 1921–1969*. Washington, D.C.: Department of the Army, G.P.O., 1972.

Murray, Robert K., *Red Scare: A Study in National Hysteria, 1919–1920*. Minneapolis: University of Minnesota Press, 1955.

Nash, Jay Robert, and Stanley Ralph Ross, *Motion Picture Guide*. Chicago: Cinebooks, 1987.

Newfield, Jack, *Robert Kennedy: A Memoir*. New York: Dutton, 1969.

O'Connell, Cardinal William H., *A Memorable Voyage*. Brighton, MA: n. p., 1939.

O'Donnell, Kenneth P., and David F. Powers, *"Johnny, We Hardly Knew Ye": Memories of John Fitzgerald Kennedy*. Boston: Little, Brown, 1972.

O'Leary, Mary F. M., *Education with a Tradition*. New York: Longman, Green, 1936.

Oppenheimer, Jerry, *The Other Mrs. Kennedy: Ethel Skakel Kennedy, An American Drama of Power, Privilege, and Politics*. New York: St. Martin's Press, 1994.

O'Toole, James M., *Militant and Triumphant: William Henry O'Connell and The Catholic Church in Boston, 1859–1944*. Notre Dame, IN: University of Notre Dame Press, 1992.

Oudendijk, Petrus J., *Pope Pius XII and the Nazi War Against the Catholic Church*. Brisbane: M. W. Kennedy, 1944.

Panter-Downes, Mollie, *Letter from England*. Boston: Little, Brown, 1940.

———, *London War Notes, 1939–1945*. Edited by William Shawn. New York: Farrar, Straus and Giroux, 1971.

Parmet, Herbert S., *Jack: The Struggles of John F. Kennedy*. New York: Dial, 1980.

———, *J.F.K.: The Presidency of John F. Kennedy*. New York: Dial, 1983.

Rachlin, Harvey, *The Kennedys: A Chronological History, 1823–Present*. New York: Pharos/World Almanac, 1986.

Reeves, Thomas C., *A Question of Character: A Life of John F. Kennedy*. New York: Macmillan, 1991.

Robertson, David, *Sly and Able: A Political Biography of James F. Byrnes*. New York: Norton, 1994.

Rogers, Warren, *When I Think of Bobby: A Personal Memoir of the Kennedy Years*. New York: HarperCollins, 1993.

Rollins, Alfred B., *Roosevelt and Howe*. New York: Knopf, 1962.

Roosevelt, Felicia Warburg, *Doers and Dowagers*. Garden City, NY: Doubleday, 1975.

Ross, Walter S., *The Last Hero: Charles A. Lindbergh*. Rev. ed. New York: Harper and Row, 1976.

Ryan, Dennis P., *Beyond the Ballot Box: A Social History of the Boston Irish, 1845–1917*. 1983, reprint; Amherst: University of Massachusetts Press, 1989.

Ryan, James H., *The Peace Points of Pope Pius XII: An Interpretation of the Holy Father's Peace Points, with Interpolated Discussion Outlines and Lists of Related Readings*. Washington, D.C.: National Catholic Welfare Conference, 1943.

Salinger, Pierre, *With Kennedy*. New York: Doubleday, 1966.

Sandburg, Carl, *Abraham Lincoln*. Reprint; New York: Harcourt Brace, 1954.

Saunders, Frank, with James Southwood, *Torn Lace Curtain*. New York: Holt, Rinehart, and Winston, 1982.

Schewe, Donald B., Ed., *Franklin D. Roosevelt and Foreign Affairs, January 1937–August 1939*. 10 vols. New York: Garland, 1979–83 contains numerous documents relevant to Joseph P. Kennedy.

Schlesinger, Arthur M., Jr., *The Age of Roosevelt*. 3 vols. Boston: Houghton Mifflin, 1957–60.

————, *Robert Kennedy and His Times*. Boston: Houghton Mifflin, 1978.

————, *A Thousand Days*. Boston: Houghton Mifflin, 1965.

Schoor, Jean, *Young John Kennedy*. New York: Harcourt, Brace and World, 1963.

Schwarz, Jordan, *The Speculator: Bernard M. Baruch in Washington, 1917–1965*. Chapel Hill: University of North Carolina Press, 1981.

Searls, Hank, *The Lost Prince: Young Joe, The Forgotten Kennedy, The Story of the Oldest Brother*. New York: World, 1969.

Secrest, Meryle, *Leonard Bernstein: A Life*. New York: Knopf, 1994.

Sevareid, Eric, *Not So Wild a Dream*. New York: Knopf, 1946.

Shadegg, Stephen C., *Clare Boothe Luce: A Biography*. New York: Simon and Schuster, 1970.

Shannon, William V., *The Heir Apparent: Robert Kennedy and the Struggle for Power*. New York: Macmillan, 1967.

Shaw, Maud, *White House Nannie: My Years with Caroline*

and John Kennedy, Jr. New York: New American Library, 1966.

Sheed, Wilfrid, *Clare Boothe Luce.* New York: Dutton, 1982.

Shorter, Edward, *A History of Women's Bodies.* New York: Basic, 1982.

Simon, James F., *Independent Journey: The Life of William O. Douglas.* New York: Harper and Row, 1980.

Sinclair, David, *Dynasty: The Astors and Their Times.* New York: Beaufort, 1984.

Sire, H. J. A., *The Knights of Malta.* New Haven: Yale University Press, 1994.

Smit, Jan O., *Angelic Shepherd: The Life of Pope Pius XII.* New York: Dodd, Mead, 1950.

Somoza, Anastasio, as told to Jack Cox, *Nicaragua Betrayed.* Belmont, MA: Western Islands, 1980.

Sorensen, Theodore, *Kennedy.* New York: Harper and Row, 1965.

―――, *The Kennedy Legacy.* New York: Macmillan, 1969.

Sovereign Military Order of the Knights of St. John of Jerusalem and Malta, *The Official General Roll of the Grand Magistery, 1949.* Milan, Italy: Ciarrocca Edition, 1949.

Spada, James, *Peter Lawford: The Man Who Kept the Secrets.* New York: Bantam, 1991.

Stein, Jean, *American Journey: The Times of Robert Kennedy.* George Plimpton, Ed. Harcourt Brace Jovanovich, 1970.

Stiles, Lela, *The Man Behind Roosevelt: The Story of Louis McHenry Howe.* Cleveland: World, 1954.

Stuart, Janet E., *The Education of Catholic Girls.* Reprint; Westminster, MD: Newman Press, 1964.

Swanson, Gloria, *Swanson on Swanson.* New York: Random House, 1980.

Sykes, Christopher, *Nancy: The Life of Lady Astor.* New York: Harper and Row, 1972.

Thompson, Robert E., and Hortense Myers, *Robert F. Kennedy: The Brother Within.* New York: Macmillan, 1962.

Todisco, Paula J., *Boston's First Neighborhood: The North End.* Boston: Boston Public Library, 1976.

U.S. Congress, House of Representatives, Committee on Elections No. 2. *Contested-Election Case of Peter F. Tague v. John F. Fitzgerald, from the Tenth Congressional District of Massachusetts.* 66th Congress, 1st session. Washington, D.C.: G.P.O., 1919.

U.S. Congress, House of Representatives, Committee on Elections No. 2. *Contested-Election Case of Tague v. Fitzgerald: Hearings.* 66th Congress, 1st session. Washington, D.C.: G.P.O., 1919.

U.S. Congress, House of Representatives, Committee on Foreign Affairs. *Hearings on H.R. 1776 (Lend-Lease).* 77th Congress, 1st Session, 1941. Washington, D.C.: G.P.O., 1941.

U.S. Congress, House of Representatives, Select Committee on U.S. Shipping Board Operations, *Shipping Board Operations: Hearings.* 66th Congress, 3rd Session. Washington, D.C.: G.P.O., 1921.

Vieth, Jane Caroline, "Joseph P. Kennedy: Ambassador to the Court of St. James, 1938–1940," Ph.D. dissertation, Ohio State University, Columbus, Ohio, 1975.

Warner, Sam B., Jr., *Streetcar Suburbs: The Process of Growth in Boston, 1870–1900.* Cambridge, MA: Harvard University Press, 1962.

Waugh, Alex, *The Lipton Story: A Centennial Biography.* Garden City, NY: Doubleday, 1950.

Wayman, Dorothy, *Cardinal O'Connell of Boston.* New York: Farrar, Straus and Young, 1955.

Wechsberg, Joseph, *Dining at the Pavilion.* Boston: Little, Brown, 1962.

Weiss, Murray, *Palm Beach Babylon: Sins, Scams and Scandals.* New York: Carol, 1992.

Whalen, Richard J., *The Founding Father: The Story of Joseph P. Kennedy.* New York: New American Library, 1964.

White, Theodore H., *The Making of the President, 1960.* New York: Atheneum, 1961.

Whitehall, Walter M., *Boston in the Age of John Fitzgerald Kennedy.* Norman: University of Oklahoma Press, 1966.

Wicker, Tom, *Kennedy Without Tears.* New York: William Morrow, 1964.

Williams, Margaret A., *The Society of the Sacred Heart:*

History of a Spirit 1800–1975. London: Darton Longman and Todd, 1978.

Williams, William J., *The Wilson Administration and the Shipbuilding Crisis of 1917: Steel Ships and Wooden Steamers.* Lewiston, NY: E. Mellen, 1992.

Wills, Garry, *The Kennedy Imprisonment: A Meditation on Power.* Boston: Little, Brown, 1981.

Wilson, Derek A., *The Astors, 1763–1992: Landscape with Millionaires.* New York: St. Martin's Press, 1993.

Woods, Robert A., Ed., *Americans in Process.* Boston: Houghton Mifflin, 1902.

Wyatt, Edgar M., *More Than a Cowboy: The Life and Films of Fred Thomson and Silver King.* Raleigh, NC: Wyatt Classics, 1988.